Edmund Waterton

The Pietas Mariana Britannica

a history of English devotion to the most blessed Virgin Mary Mother of God

I0592351

Edmund Waterton

The Pietas Mariana Britannica
a history of English devotion to the most blessed Virgin Mary Mother of God

ISBN/EAN: 9783742860217

Manufactured in Europe, USA, Canada, Australia, Japa

Cover: Foto ©Lupo / pixelio.de

Manufactured and distributed by brebook publishing software
(www.brebook.com)

Edmund Waterton

The Pietas Mariana Britannica

IVORY STATUE OF ENGLISH WORK, DATE ABOUT 1280.

Formerly in possession of the Nuns of Sion House.

(*Height, 9.5 inches.*)

PIETAS MARIANA BRITANNICA.

A HISTORY OF·ENGLISH DEVOTION TO THE MOST BLESSED
· VIRGIN MARYE MOTHER OF GOD,

WITH A

CATALOGUE OF SHRINES, SANCTUARIES, OFFERINGS,
BEQUESTS, AND OTHER MEMORIALS OF THE PIETY
OF OUR FOREFATHERS.

BY

EDMUND WATERTON F S A.

Knight of the Order of Christ, of Rome.

LONDON:

ST. JOSEPH'S CATHOLIC LIBRARY,
48, SOUTH STREET, GROSVENOR SQUARE.

1879.

INSCRIBED

MOST AFFECTIONATELY TO

FATHER FRANCIS CLOUGH, FORMERLY RECTOR,

FATHER EDWARD IGNATIUS PURBRICK, RECTOR,

AND

THE COMMUNITY OF

STONYHURST COLLEGE,

BY THEIR GRATEFUL AND DEVOTED FRIEND

AND BEDESMAN.

PREFACE

IN my childhood the idea of popular devotion to our Blessed Ladye was brought vividly before my mind in a tour through Germany and Flanders, and a residence of nearly two years in Rome. The Fathers at the Gesù, to whom I often said, "We have none of these nice customs in England," told me that those very observances, which so pleased me in Rome, had been practised in England in Catholic times, and that the day would dawn when England would again love and venerate, as in bygone times, the Blessed Mother of God.

My education at Stonyhurst was well suited to strengthen these early impressions. In 1846 I chanced to read Mr. Kenelm Digby's noble work, the *Ages of Faith*. It seemed as if those glorious pages gave me an insight into the practices of Catholic devotion, and had power to impart something of the spirit which animated our forefathers. I resolved to do my little best to increase devotion to our Blessed Ladye in England.

In 1852 I formed the definite idea of writing a book on popular devotion to our Ladye; and the plan which I then sketched out, and which is now before me, has been followed very faithfully in the First Book of the present work. In the original design it had been intended that England should receive special but

not exclusive attention; and for many years I continued
to collect materials to illustrate the popular devotion
of all Christian nations. It was only in 1870, at the
suggestion of the learned Bollandist, Father Victor
de Buck, whose loss we so much deplore, that I
determined to set apart for a separate volume my
notes on England and English Sanctuaries; and from
him I accepted the title as it now stands. The Catalogue
of Shrines, which forms the Second Book is reprinted
from the *Month and Catholic Review*, the managers of
which have also taken on themselves the separate
printing of the First Book and the publication of the
whole work. Every word in this work has been transcribed at least twice by my own hand. I have made
no quotations at second hand — perhaps with half a
dozen exceptions of books with which I could not
meet; and these I have taken on the authority of
Mgr. Malou, and my old friend Canon Rock, whose
names are sufficient attestation of accuracy. I have felt
it due to myself to say this much, lest it might be
inferred that I had largely availed myself of the labours
of my friend, Father Bridgett. The only use, which I
have allowed myself to make of his interesting work,
has been to take occasion from reading it to curtail
or omit much of what I found that he had given.
I sincerely hope that those who may see the *Pietas
Mariana Britannica*, and have not yet read Father
Bridgett's book, will not fail to do so.

I have now the pleasing duty of acknowledging
various acts of kindness which I have received in the
course of many years.

I beg to offer to the Fathers of the London Oratory
my hearty thanks for free access to their rich and

valuable library; a favour which I appreciate the more
as I was a stranger to all save one of them. I also
gratefully acknowledge a similar privilege accorded to
me by an old friend, now no more, Father Perrone, S.J.,
in regard of the Library of the *Collegio Romano*, and
by the Fathers of the Society of Jesus and the Redemp-
torist Fathers, at Boulogne-sur-mer. I have received
much courtesy from the accomplished librarian of the
Bibliothèque de la Ville, at Boulogne-sur-mer, Monsieur
Cougnacq, to whom my warm thanks are offered.

I am under deep obligations, which I gladly record,
to my friend Edward A. Bond, Esq., the Principal
Librarian of the British Museum. I have often had
to consult him; and on one occasion he had the
kindness to collate some proofs himself, which I had
enclosed to him for collation by a reader. To
Monsignor Consitt, Provost of Hexham and Newcastle, I am indebted for the impression of the figure
of our Ladye taken from the coffin of St. Cuthberht.

My very cordial thanks are also offered to the dear
and most valued friend of my boyhood and of after
years, Father Francis Clough, S.J., formerly Rector of
Stonyhurst, for allowing me free access at all times to
the College Library, whensoever I paid a visit to our
dear old Alma Mater; a privilege which has also been
continued to me in the kindest manner by the present
Rector, Father Purbrick, who has proved his friendship
in many ways, and to whom I am indebted for the
loan of several precious books, which have been of very
great assistance to me. I beg him to accept the expression of my heartiest thanks. I am also much
indebted to Father Kingdon, S.J., Prefect of Studies
at Stonyhurst.

My deepest gratitude is due to the Bollandist
Fathers, who not only most kindly gave me the ex-
ceptional privilege of access at all times to their
magnificent library, but, in their generosity, mag-
nified a trivial act of service which it had been in
my power to render them, and presented me with
a key of the Library, and of the case which contains
the most precious of their MSS. I can never cease
to be grateful for that act of courtesy. If ever I
forget the Bollandist Fathers, *oblivioni detur dextera
mea.* During a period of over four years, there was
seldom a day, except during some brief absence from
Brussels, of which I did not spend some portion in
their Library and enjoy the privilege of their conversation. Yet those sunny memories are not unclouded
with some selfish sorrow. Two of the good Fathers,
whose friendship I so highly valued and from whom
I received unbounded kindness — Father Victor de
Buck, and the accomplished scholar who knew thirty
languages, Father Henry Matagne—have gone to their
reward, and are now enjoying the Beatific Vision
with those Saints, whose glories they so strenuously
celebrated on earth. I cannot omit to record my
obligations to the obliging and good old Bollandist
Lay-brother, Brother Nicolai.

My hearty thanks are also due to another old
friend, Father Aloys De Backer, the learned biblio-
graphist, and librarian of the College of the Society
of Jesus at Louvain, through whose kindness I was
enabled to consult several rare books which were not
in the Bollandist Library.

I have to express my cordial acknowledgments to
Messrs. Macmillan and Co., for electrotypes of the Eton

seal and foundation deed, furnished in the most obliging manner; to Messrs. Parker and Co., of Oxford, for courteously permitting me to have electrotypes taken of such of their blocks as I required; and to the Council of the Royal Archæological Institute of Great Britain and Ireland for a similar permission.

To Father J. S. Walford, S.J., are due the admirable translations of the *Votum* of Erasmus, and the anthem *Nesciens Mater.*

To Father A. G. Knight, S.J., who kindly submitted to the labour of the final revision of my work, my warmest thanks are given.

I humbly submit what I have written to the Infallible Judgment of the One Holy Catholic and Apostolic Church, protesting before God, and the Chivalry of Heaven, that what She may approve I approve, and that what She may condemn, I, by anticipation, condemn. *Loquatur Petrus, Petrum sequor.* I also make the usual protest, in accordance with the Decree dated the 13th of March, 1625, of Urban the Eighth.

And in laying this most feeble tribute of love, gratitude, and duty, at the feet of the Most Glorious and Blissful Queen of Heaven, the Immaculately-conceived Maiden Mother of God, our Dear Ladye Saint Marye, whose Dower England is, I, as her hereditary liegeman of that Dower, do with all humility pray, as my forefathers of twenty-eight generations have prayed before me, that she would vouchsafe to be my Mediatrix with her Divine Son, my Judge, and to intercede for me with Him, so that He be merciful to me at the dread hour of death, *propter amorem Matris suæ.*

Que si vostre grâce plustot que mon mérite me permet d'attendre quelque loïer d'un seruice à vous deub, que ce soit donc celuy O Roine débonnaire qu'auez promis aux plus affectionez de vos humbles cliens qui elucideroient la Gloire de vostre nom, loïer incomparable de la vie éternelle.

EDMUND WATERTON,

Knight of Christ.

Athenæum Club,
Pall Mall.

CONTENTS.

PART THE THIRD.

THE ICONOGRAPHY OF OUR BLESSED LADYE IN ENGLAND.

BOOK THE SECOND.

BOOK THE FIRST.

History of English Devotion to our Ladye.

INTRODUCTION.

Da mihi, O Diva, quam præsentem animo contemplor, quod pie sancteque institui rite et feliciter exsequi, Nomini et cultui tuo propagando, pietati et sanctimoniæ augendæ; quos duos profiteor huic scriptioni esse fines.

Justus Lipsius.[1]

SOME years ago the Faith of our Fathers did not burn with its usual English brilliancy in certain quarters. The Litany of our Blessed Ladye began to be distasteful; endeavours were made to introduce a modified form of it on the plea that it would be "more acceptable to converts;"[2] and in one church the image of our Ladye, which had been erected over her altar, was removed to satisfy the "prejudices" of divers weak members of the congregation.[3] This proceeding was a disgrace to all concerned; I fear our common "Profession of Faith" must have grown somewhat out of use in those parts. Some, only in name Catholics, not satisfied with recording their protest against the introduction into England of Italian terms of endearment in addressing our Ladye, seem really to have believed that Italians went quite too far in the love itself which prompted such expressions. They complained that the "Italian form of devotion to the Virgin" was far too pronounced for us—a sort of exotic not suited to our northern clime, and only kept alive by the care of a few well-meaning but inexperienced neophytes; that it was not adapted to the spirit of the age, and that it was widely different from the old English practice of that devotion. If it was widely different, the following pages, I think, will show that at least it was not more fervent or outspoken. In heartiness of affection and emphasis of speech the devotion to

---

[1] D. Virgo Hallensis. Antv. 1616, p. 3.

[2] See *Essays on Various Subjects.* By his Eminence Cardinal Wiseman. London, 1853, vol. i. pp. 377—430.

[3] *Life of Mother Margaret Mary Hallahan.* London, 1870, pp. 157, 159.

our Blessed Ladye, as practised by our Anglo-Saxon forefathers, and by the descendants of those who accompanied William the Norman into England is second to none in the world. The Italian will call our Ladye *mamma mia* as a term of the greatest endearment; but the Englishman, who does not quite appreciate the language, prefers, after his blunt fashion, to address her as "Holy Marye, Mother of God, and my Mother." St. Alphonsus Liguori was especially blamed for extravagance of language in his book entitled the *Glories of Mary*, but that grand work is, in reality, only a collection of the sayings and sentiments of the Fathers of the Church of all ages, blended together in a sweet harmony; nor is any portion of this tribute of praise offered by a great Saint in the eighteenth century more "pronounced" in its tone than "a good orison to our Ladye" made for Englishmen of the twelfth or thirteenth century, which singly might suffice to show that enthusiastic worship of Marye is not a plant matured under more sunny skies, and little suited to our temperate zone.

> Christ's meek Mother, Saint Marye !
> My life's light, my beloved Ladye !
> To thee I bow and my knee I bend,
> And all my heart's blood to thee I offer.
> Thou art my soul's light, and my heart's bliss !
> My life and my hope, my safety therewith indeed.
> I ought to honour thee with all my might,
> And sing the song of praise by day and night,
> For thou hast holpen me in many ways,
> And brought me out of hell into Paradise.
> I thank thee for it, my beloved Ladye,
> And will thank thee while I live.[4]

The fine old English love of our Ladye, which prompted this "English Lay," has left, in spite of desecrated churches, and plundered shrines, and mutilated images, indelible traces all around which it will be my pleasant task to try to enumerate. It is written in letters which he who runs may read, that the Blessed Mother of God was once the Ladye of the land; and still her gentle influence may be felt within the confines of her ancient Dower, though it is sadly true that she is not loved as

---

[4] *Old English Homilies of the Twelfth and Thirteenth Centuries.* Series I. Early Eng. Text Soc. vol. xxxiv. p. 120, n. 190. The orison is given at full length by Father Bridgett in the *Dowry of our Ladye*, pp. 143, seq. London, 1875.

her liegemen loved her in other days. Even those who have been taught that it is wicked to name her name in prayer, yet call their children by that sacred name by force of habit or unrecognized tradition, and many a grace her holy hands bestow on those who, not in malice but in ignorance, try to please her Son without seeking aid from her.

Perhaps the simplest and the clearest proof that our Blessed Ladye still deigns to show her power in England may be found in the unreasoning enmity manifested by the dignitaries of the Church as by law established. Her image as Mother of God exerts a strange influence over them, seeming to cause instinctive dread. In a place of worship, as an object of veneration it cannot be tolerated; but mark the inconsistency! A picture by Cimabue, Giotto, Beato Angelico of Fiesole, or Raphael, which represents the Blessed Virgin Marye as the Mother of God, is by an Anglican lover of the fine arts able to gratify his taste, eagerly purchased at any price, and regarded as a faithful exposition of true Gospel history. He does not consider the subject mythological, or the treatment savouring of idolatry. This only he never doubts, that a picture of the Mother of God is quite out of place in a temple dedicated to her Son. With many Anglican divines it seems to be a point to lose no opportunity of waging war, like Nestorius, against the Mother of God. They take as addressed to themselves, we must suppose, the celebrated words in Genesis which were uttered to the father of sin: *Inimicitias ponam inter te et mulierem.*[5] According to some of them the Mother of God is not a "Scriptural character;" therefore her image is removed from the north door—which is peculiarly her door—of a cathedral, as at Bristol.[6] It is utterly incomprehensible how any one who recites the Apostles' Creed or the *Magnificat*, both of which are included in the Protestant Liturgy as set forth in

[5] Gen. iii. 15.

[6] S. pp. 223, 224. In the following pages a capital S in the references refers to the second portion of this work containing the *Series* or Catalogue of the Sanctuaries, &c. I have recently seen a photograph of this image of our Blessed Ladye, which the Dean declared to be of an "unscriptural character" (see S. p. 224). The group which was considered to be so objectionable represents in reality the adoration of the Three Kings! Our Ladye seated with her Divine Son on her knee forms the centre, two of the Magi are on their knees presenting their offerings to our Lord, the third is standing behind, waiting to come with his gifts, and St. Joseph is standing on the other side,

the Book of Common Prayer, could hold such an opinion. But
Bristol enjoys an unhappy notoriety. In 1851, during the
excitement caused by the anti-Papal agitation, it was proposed
to drag the image of our Blessed Ladye through the streets
in derision, and flog it![7]   At the church of St. Marye, Abbot's
Kensington,[8] it was intended by the restorers of the edifice to
represent our Ladye with her Divine Son on her knee, according
to the ancient seal, and a beautiful image was carved in stone;
but the authorities insisted that our Lord must be removed
from His Mother's knee, and the Bible substituted for Him.
Our Ladye thus represented is now placed above the east
window, on the outside of the church, and below are the words,
Ecce ancilla Domini.   It is not, perhaps, surprising that the
parishioners should mistake this extraordinary representation
of our Ladye for Queen Elizabeth!   Catholics, on the other
hand, raise their hats as they pass by, and salute our Ladye,
thus deprived of her Son.

   The words of Ward vividly recur—

> O horrible ! What work they made ;
> There you might see an impious clown
> Breaking our Saviour's image down.
>
>   .   .   .   .   .
>
> Here you might see another stand,
> Hacking with axe in cruel hand
> The Infant in our Ladye's lap.[9]

   The armorial bearings of the old Catholic sees of Salisbury
and Lincoln have our Blessed Ladye with her Divine Son in
her arms, and are yet borne, as a matter of course, by the Anglican dignitaries who occupy those sees; but in 1846 the Bishop
of Exeter withdrew his name from the Archæological Society
of Cambridge on the plea that the seal of that Society bore the
image of our Ladye, crowned, with her Divine Son in her arms,
and two other saints unknown to his calendar.   This the Bishop
considered as a gratuitous insult to the feelings of Protestants,
and therefore he believed it to be his duty to make a protest

---

   [7] *Life of Mother Hallahan*, p. 325.
   [8] This is the correct designation of the Church, which in the Vestry and other
notices is usually given as St. Mary Abbots.   Kensington belonged to the Abbot of
Reading; hence the appellation. See Faulkner, *Hist. and Antiq. of Kensington.*
Lond. 1820, pp. 60, 61.
   [9] *England's Reformation.*   London, 1719, canto i. p. 96.

by withdrawing from the Society, which, nevertheless, has continued to flourish. Yet they profess to read the Bible. Some there are who have eyes, yet see not; others read, and understand not that which they read, because they have no rule of faith, and "sit in darkness and the shadow of death."[10] *Practically*, it would seem, few Protestants admit the Blessed Virgin to be the Mother of God. Yet to deny her this title is to fall into the heresy of Nestorius, who was not a Christian because he refused to believe that Jesus, the Son of Mary, was God. It is logically impossible to accept the New Testament and to refuse to honour the Mother of God; and it is equally impossible to refuse to honour the Blessed Virgin Marye without denying the truth of the Incarnation.

But I by no means wish to be understood as maintaining that all Anglicans approve of these acts, or share in these opinions, of many members of their communion. Many reverence the Blessed Virgin in sincerity of heart, and give her the title of Blessed. I once went to see the Protestant church of St. Alban's, in Baldwin Gardens, and there, on the right of the chancel-arch, I beheld a picture of our Blessed Ladye with her Divine Son in her arms, and two candlesticks with wax tapers before it. It is very gratifying to see our Ladye's light on a bracket in a Protestant church. And one very remarkable Protestant prayer-book, entitled *Oratory Worship*, by "Brother Cecil, S.S.J."—these cabalistic letters appear to mean "of the Society of St. Joseph"—contains the "Rosary of the Blessed Virgin Marye;" the *Angelus*, and *Regina Cœli; the Salve Regina;* the *Memorare;* two "Litanies of the Incarnation," one of which is a "Litany of our Ladye;" and a "Litany of Reparation to Jesus for want of devotion to His Blessed Mother," and sundry hymns to our Ladye and St. Joseph.[11] Mr. Lyne, who has dubbed himself "Brother Ignatius, O.S.B.," strenuously inculcates the recital of the Hail Marye.[12]

[10] St. Luke i. 79.

[11] *Oratory Worship;* containing Benediction of the Blessed Sacrament, and other devotions, minutely rubricated. Edited by Brother Cecil, S.S.J. (permissu superiorum). London, The Church Press Company, 13, Burleigh Street, Strand. 1869, pp. 50—57, 59, 60, 61, 63, 66.

[12] *Llanthony Tales*, vol. ii. pp. 101, 216. London, Bentley, 1871. In vol. ii. p. 101 of the *Llanthony Tales*, entitled, "Leonard Morris, or the Benedictine Novice, by the Rev. Father Ignatius," is given the following paragraph, which I

In truth, the limits of the devotion due to the Blessed Virgin
are very carefully laid down by Holy Church. To God, and
to God alone, is due Divine honour, or *latria*. The Saints
receive an inferior honour, distinguished as *dulia*, which honour
in a superior degree, designated as *hyperdulia*, is given to our
Ladye, and to her alone. The whole doctrine is fully set forth in
the Catechism, which every school-child is taught, as soon as
he can learn; nevertheless it seems to perplex the majority of
Protestants. Hence *Mariolatry*, a word which is evidently used
to denote Divine honour paid to Marye, and with which they
seem to be so familiar, since they have no other idea of
devotion to our Ladye, does not, and cannot, and could not
exist in the Church. The Collyridian heretics attempted
to introduce *Mariolatry*, but the folly began and ended with
them. From the writings of the English Fathers, Bede the
Venerable, Alcwine, St. Anselm, St. Edmund, Archbishop
Baldwin, and many others, it is easy to see how grateful and
pleasing to our forefathers were the praises of our Ladye. Thus
it was that her love burnt so brightly in England; and like
the mystic cloud, it covered the land, and pervaded everywhere.
Her image graced the royal Crown of England; our kings
invoked her in their hour of danger; the warrior wore her
image on his surcoat, or engraved on his keen-edged falchion;
the earl constituted her the lady of his lands, and himself her
vassal; fields were held by the service of reciting so many *Aves*
yearly; alms given in her love were called our Ladye's meat,
and our Ladye's loaf; the shopman painted her on his sign-

---

presume describes the practices of Mr. Lyne's Anglican Community. "The abbot
felt that there was something seriously important, and gave orders that the monks
should at midnight go barefoot in procession to the shrine of the Blessed Virgin in
the wood, in the ravine under the abbey, reciting the fifty-first Psalm, as they walked
through the deep snow. When they reached the shrine they were to repeat one
hundred 'Our Fathers' and one hundred 'Hail Mary's' for the conversion of Captain
Scott." Another curious passage, and expressed in still more objectionable language,
occurs at p. 216 : "''The devil seems checkmated for once somehow,' whispered our
old friend Brother Oswald to his companion Brother Pancras. ' I have a queer feeling
that something out of the ordinary way has happened. I fancy that hundred Hail
Mary's last night at Matins are taking effect, if they have not already done so.'''
"Our friend Brother Oswald's piety had not become any more sentimental than when
he used to talk of 'bothering the Blessed Virgin' with Hail Mary's for Brother
Placidus. Indeed, the young novice still said, he never should make what he called
a 'pious saint!'" I spare my readers any further infliction of extracts so offensive
to Catholic ears.

board; prosperous merchants built churches and bedehouses in her honour; the sailor named his ship after her, and when tossed on the raging billow, invoked the Bright Star of the Sea.

Now what was the practical result of this truly national and popular devotion to our Blessed Ladye? Simply this. It made men love God. It spoke to the unlettered by signs. It constantly reminded every one of the Incarnation. It softened stubborn nature, for no one could refuse a favour when asked in our Ladye's name. It represented everywhere the Blessed and Immaculate Mother of God with her Divine Son in her arms, in the homeliest and most domestic of types, *Mother and Child.* This it was that humanized, so to say, rough nature.[18] Men learned to respect the female sex, for our Ladye's love. Wife-kicking and wife-beating, which now, unfortunately, are of such common occurrence, were crimes unknown in the days when England was Catholic. Did a man feel angry with his wife, his passion was calmed by the sight of the little image of the Immaculate Mother of God with her Divine Child in her arms over the chimney-piece; for who, that said the Hail Marye, could ever strike his wife! No better illustration of the spirit of this devotion need be sought than in the hymn of the Church to our Ladye—

> *Virgo singularis,*
> *Inter omnes* mitis,
> Nos, *culpis solutos*
> Mites *fac, et castos.*

[18] Cf. Haxthausen, *Transcaucasia,* c. x. pp. 344, 345, quoted by Marshall, *Christian Missions,* vol. ii. pp. 581—583.

DIGNARE ME LAUDARE TE, VIRGO SACRATA,
DA MIHI VIRTUTEM CONTRA HOSTES TUOS.

PART THE FIRST.

Our Ladye and her Liegemen.

CHAPTER THE FIRST.

England the Dower of Marye.

Dos tua, Virgo pia hæc est; quare rege Maria
Words attributed to Richard the Second, King of England.

MANY nations, in addition to their usual nomenclature, have other titles in hagiology, either on account of some particular act of consecration by their sovereigns to our Blessed Ladye, or from some other special reason, or *consensu gentium*. Thus Ireland, whose hierarchy represents an unbroken line from St. Patrick, and whose national religion is still the faith of Christ our Lord which the Saint taught, and not the creed of the Thirty-Nine Articles, has long been known, *consensu gentium*, as the Island of Saints. But the

> dear realm
> of Engle-land,

the home of St. Cuthbert and Bede the Venerable, of St. Eadward and other saints of our Anglo-Saxon Church; of St. Thomas of Canterbury the "blissful martyr," the glorious St. Edmund of Abingdon, and St. Simon Stock of the Anglo-Norman Church; and other men and women, saints of God, down to Sir Thomas More, once Lord High Chancellor of England, and Cardinal Fisher—both of them glorious martyrs, England, I say, which has produced this galaxy of devout clients of our "precious Ladye,"[1] alone rejoices in the grand title of DOS MARIÆ, the Dower of Blessed Marye the

[1] So called in the Ancren Riwle, p. 77, Camden Soc.

Virgin Mother of God and Queen of Heaven. And this beautiful title still remains the inheritance and possession of our sea-girt isle. Would that we were as worthy of it as our fathers before us.

In different ages many nations and kingdoms have been solemnly consecrated to our Blessed Ladye. Emperors and kings were proud to be the vassals of her who is the Mother of the King of kings by Whom kings reign, and, as our Anglo-Saxon forefathers called her, the Queen of the whole world.[1]

It is greatly to be regretted that hitherto no record has been discovered either of the occasion or the circumstances under which England was consecrated to the glorious Mother of God and given to her for her dower. *Dos* implies an act of dotation and endowment; and Ducange particularly mentions that, in English practice, *dos* signifies the gift with which the husband endows his wife in the marriage contract. Equally, *dos* is applied to the dower of a church; thus Berhtuulf, King of Mercia, having endowed Croyland with some lands, says in his charter, dated Friday, March 27, A.D. 851 : *Hæc est hæreditas Domini, dos ecclesiæ Christi, solum Sanctæ Mariæ.*[3]

A legend relates that on one occasion our Blessed Ladye appeared to St. Simon Stock, and told him that she took England for her dower;[4] but I have searched, and hitherto in

---

[1] Aelfric's *Homilies.* Edit. Thorpe, vol. i. p. 439. The Irish invoked her as "Lady or Mistress of the Tribes ;" see the Leabhar Mor, now called Leabhar breac, f. 121, in the Library of the Royal Irish Academy. O'Curry, MSS. of Irish Hist. p. 380; and Append. p. 615, n. cxxiii. Hungary is called the *Familia Mariana* (*Act. SS.* t. 45, p. 772); Mexico, the *Natio Mariana* (*Pareri de' Vescovi sulla difinisione dell' Immacolato Concepimento della B. V. M.* Roma, 1851-4, vol. iii. p. 175); France is the *Regnum Mariæ ;* and Flanders the Patrimony of the Blessed Virgin (*Le S. Pèlèrinage de N. D. de la Paix à Ennetières-en-Wappes,* par le R. P. Possoz de la Comp. de Jesus. Tournai, 1859, p. 7). For other interesting particulars of nations consecrated to our Ladye cf. Bonfinius, *Rerum Ungaric.* decad. ii. lib. i. p. 179. Francofurti, 1581 ; also Goldonowski, *Diva Claramontana.* Cracoviæ, 1642 ; also Guéranger, *Liturgical Year.* Dublin, 1867. Advent, p. 402, but the date mentioned is incorrect (cf. Zurita, *Annales de Arragon.* Saragoça, 1610, lib. x. p. 414); also Gravois, *de ortu et progressu cultus ac festi Imm. Concept. B. Dei Genitr. V. M.* Lucæ, 1764, Summar. p. 32; also *Pareri de' Vescovi,* vol. i. p. 262 ; vol. ix. p. 129; also Marracci, *Cæsares Mariani,* cap. v. § vi.; also *Libellus de Sodalitate B. V. M.* auct. R. P. Fran. Costero è S.J. Antv. 1607 in præfat.

[3] Cod. Dipl. Aevi Sax. vol. ii. p. 41, ch. cclxv.

[4] Quoted as a legend (1) in the *Little Gradual.* By Ambrose Lisle Phillipps. London, 1847, p. 94; and by Northcote, *Celebrated Sanctuaries of the Madonna.* London, 1868, p. 286, note.

vain, for any solid authority for this alleged vision. The Benedictine, Bucelin, says that Eadgar the Peaceful consecrated England to our Ladye, but in the *Series*, under the head of Glastonbury, I have shown his misconception.[5]

The historian, F. Alford, *alias* Griffiths, S.J., says that in all ages Britain devoutly venerated the Blessed Virgin Marye, and, that in consequence of the pre-eminent devotion of the British the Anglo-Saxons, and the Anglo-Normans to her, England deserved to be named *Dos Mariæ*. He also adds that in his time there existed in the English College at Rome an ancient painting of a King and Queen, who, on their knees, are making an offering of England to our Blessed Ladye for her dower through the hands of St. John, with this inscription : *Dos tua Virgo pia hæc est, quare rege, Maria.*[6]

Now these were the portraits of Richard the Second, King of England, and his Queen, daughter of the Emperor Charles IV.; and the attitude in which they are represented would certainly seem to commemorate some act of consecration or donation, on their part, of England, to our Blessed Ladye for her dower. I have been unable to trace the history of this picture, or to ascertain any details about it ; but it was not in the English College when the first students were sent out from England to take repossession of it in the year 1818. Neither have I found England described as being the dower of our Ladye earlier than the reign of Richard the Second, but it is then spoken of as an acknowledged fact.

Father Adrian Van Lyere, or as his name is Latinized, Lyræus, S.J., asserts that one of the Edwards gave England to our Ladye, for her dower, but quotes no authority, adding, that this donation was afterwards confirmed by Richard the Second, as is to be seen in a very ancient picture in the English College in Rome, together with the inscription which I have already cited.[7]

This evidence tends to show that at some period England was solemnly consecrated to our Blessed Ladye as her dower.

A precious document of the last year of Richard the Second,

---

[5] S. p. 46.
[6] *Fides Regia Anglica.* Leodii, 1663, tom. i. p. 57.
[7] *Trisagium Marianum.* Antv. 1648, p. 324.

1399,[8] describes England as the *Dos Mariæ* "in common parlance," so that this title was then well known. At the special desire of the King—whose name is not mentioned—Thomas Arundel, Archbishop of Canterbury, issued a mandate, dated at Lambeth, the 10th of February, 1399, in which these words occur :

"The contemplation of the great mystery of the Incarnation has brought all Christian nations to venerate her from whom came the beginnings of redemption. But we, as the humble servants of her own inheritance, and liegemen of her especial dower, as we are approved by common parlance—*nos quidem veluti propriæ suæ hæreditatis servuli, ac peculiaris Dotis adscriptitii, ut communi comprobamur eloquio*—ought to excel all others in the fervour of our praises and devotions to her."[9]

Dom Thomas of Elmham, a Benedictine monk of St. Augustine's, Canterbury, wrote a metrical life of Henry the Fifth,[10] and most probably during the lifetime of the King, who reigned from March 21, 1415, till August 31, 1422. In this work, which is divided into regnal years, England is several times called the *Dos Mariæ*. Thus in the third year, when the King enters Normandy.

> *Dextra Dei regem regit mediante Mariá*
> *Cui Dos Anglia stat.*[11]

Then in the description of the battle of Azincourt—

> *. . . sacerdotes a tergo vociferantur*
> *Cum gemitu, Nostri nunc miserere Deus !*
> *Nunc miserere Deus !   Anglorum parce coronæ,*
> *Regia jura fave ; pro pietate tua*
> *Virgo Maria fave, propria pro Dote. . . .*[12]

In the fifth year, when asserting that the crown of France had belonged to England from the time of Edward the Second, *jure uxoris*, Thomas of Elmham thus terminates the chapter—

---

[8] The reign of Richard the Second ceased on the day of his abdication, the 29th September ; and it is proved by the Rolls of Parliament that Henry the Fourth became King on the 30th of the same month (Harris Nicolas, *Chronology of History*. London, 1833, p. 302).

[9] Wilkins, *Concilia*, tom. iii. p. 246.

[10] *Liber Metricus de Henrico V.* printed in the Memorials of Henry the Fifth. Rolls Edit.

[11] P. 106, lines 247, 248.

[12] P. 121, lines 525, seq.

Rex Judeorum Jesus est, ut origine Matris,
Sic Rex Anglorum lilia Franca legit.
Anglia Dos tua fit Mater pia, Virgo Maria
Henrico Rege, tu tua jura rege.[13]

He concludes his poem with a "hymn to be sung by the English people in the praise of Marye the Mother of God, for the favourable expedition of King Henry the Fifth, and for the assistance she afforded the Kingdom of England, her dower, and who, by her prayers, has destroyed all heresies, together with the heresiarch, John Oldcastel." This hymn is what is called a *Te Deum Mariale*, or an adaptation or paraphrase of the *Te Deum* in honour of the Blessed Mother of God, and it is shorter than the well-known one usually attributed to St. Bonaventure.[14] I shall give only two verses—

Te ergo quæsumus Angligenis subveni quos pro Dote Propriâ defendisti.

Salvum fac populum tuum, Domina, et a mortis peste Dotem tuam libera.[15]

The MS. concludes with a prayer to our Blessed Ladye, in the form of an acrostic, giving the name and profession of the writer, THOMAS ELMHAM, MONACHUS: it is a prayer in which all our Ladye's liegemen may join—

Te Matrem Christi prece laudamus jubilantes;
Hostes depelle, floreat Alma Fides.
Obsta schismaticis, hereses prece destrue cunctas,
Monstra te Matrem, libera stet tua Dos.[16]

Thus from a mandate of the Archbishop of Canterbury, issued at the close of the fourteenth century, there is positive evidence that England was then well known as our Ladye's dower, and Englishmen as the "liegemen of her especial dower,

[13] P. 154, lines 1180, seq.

[14] Forms of the *Te Deum Mariale* were common. Another was composed by John Bracey, Abbot of Michelney, in Somerset, A.D. 1470—1489, and is given in the preface to the Memorials of King Henry the Fifth. Rolls Edit. p. lxi. Another quite different from the three already named is inserted in the *Viage Literario a las Iglesias de España*, vol. i. p. 108, where it is described as being copied from a MS. of the fourteenth century in the Library of the Cathedral of Valencia. I have also two others, one in the *Hortulus Animæ*, Mogunt. 1511; the other in the *Septem Hore Canonice*, composed by Albert de Bonstetten, chaplain to the Court of Frederic the Third, Emperor of the Romans, in 1493. The book consists of twenty-eight leaves, without either place, date, or name of printer.

[15] P. 164.

[16] P. 166.

as they were approved in common parlance." And Thomas of
Elmham corroborates it in the early part of the next century.

England has never lost the glorious title of our Ladye's
dower. It is quite true that England fell away from the unity
of the faith of Christ, and that the sweet name of the Blessed
Mother of God was blasphemed and reviled in her dower, but
although our Ladye lost for a while the full possession, so to
say, of her ancient dower, England never lost the name of
dower of our Ladye, which through all the dark ages of apostacy and of persecution remained unchallenged and unques-
tioned, because it is *territorial*, and belongs to the soil of
England hallowed with the blood of martyrs, not to the people,
who were, as I have shown, the " liegemen " of that dower.
Consequently England is as truly the dower of our Ladye as
England is England. But even if, according to the *Te Deum
Mariale* just quoted, the title had more properly belonged to
the English than to England, it would still be retained, as I
proceed to show.

In the fourteenth century peerages by Letters Patent, and
limited to heirs male, were unknown. A title by writ, once
created, becomes extinct only when every descendant or heir
general of the body of the grantee, has died out. I will, therefore, consider our ancestors in the reign of Richard the Second
as a body of men in whom was vested the title of *Dos Mariæ*.
Now no one, even of alien sympathies, would venture to assert
that the Catholic faith was ever wholly extinct in England.
The Penal Laws prove the contrary. Many ancient Catholic
houses which have outlived those laws, and have, by God's grace
and our Ladye's help, preserved the faith of their fathers as a
precious inheritance, at a heavy temporal sacrifice, and at the
cost of many a broad acre, still exist in male line, forming the
connecting links in the chain of faith which unites the old with
the revived English Church. Like the early Christians of the
Church in the catacombs, the English Catholics of the days of
the penal laws and the " Church in the hiding-places " have given
a glorious period to our national history, and one which
neophytes do not always seem either to appreciate or to realize.
As a recent writer most appropriately remarks : " Much as we
owe to the martyrs and confessors for the faith whose lot it has
been to bear witness to our Lord before tribunals, or in prisons,

great as are our obligations to the missionary priests, who went about from place to place to administer the sacraments and to preach the Word of God, during those troublesome times, we must never forget our debt of gratitude to the great body of the faithful, who had to suffer and bear witness in their turn from time to time, as occasion required, while the ordinary tenure of their lives consisted in the quiet practice of Christian virtues in their own homes, and the bringing up of their children in the holy discipline of the Catholic Church. It is from this great body that the martyrs and missionaries came forth."[17] Now the members of these privileged English families which sent forth martyrs and missionaries, and which themselves suffered a civil martyrdom, are all hereditary liegemen of our Ladye's dower, and descendants of the liegemen spoken of by the Archbishop of Canterbury in the reign of Richard the Second. How then can England be said to have lost the title of our Ladye's dower?

Such an idea was never thought of during the last two centuries and a half. An author writing in the year 1685 says: "England is by an immemorable privilege the proper dowry of holy Mary the Mother of Jesus; it having ever been the hereditary endeavour of the Catholic Kings and Queens of the British Empire to propagate the glory and veneration of the Mother of Jesus, through their rich and potent kingdoms."[18]

In the rare little book entitled, *An Abridgement of the Rules of the Sodality of our Blessed Ladye under the charge of the Society of Jesus at St. Omer's*, printed there in the year 1726, it is stated that the object of this sodality is to promote true devotion towards the Most Sovereign Queen of Heaven, so that "she may have, once again, a full and quiet possession of her *ancient dowry.*" This fully bears out my argument. Our Blessed Ladye had lost for a while the "full and quiet possession of her ancient dowry," but, on the other hand, England has never lost the title of dower of our Ladye.

---

[17] *Month*, Third Series, vol. viii. (xxvii.) pp. 407, 408.
[18] *Contemplations on the Life and Glory of Holy Mary the Mother of Jesus.* By J. C., D.D. Paris, 1685. Epist. dedicatory.

CHAPTER THE SECOND.

Our Blessed Ladye's Name.

Cum nomen audio Mariæ Virginis,
Vel sacris lectito scriptum in paginis.
Sonus vel litera sacri vocaminis
Pastu me recreat miræ dulcedinis.[1]

FROM the earliest days of Christianity the name of our Blessed Ladye has been held in the highest reverence; although curiously enough, this veneration has differed widely in its expression in different ages. At one time the name of Marye was refused even to queens; at another, it was to be found in almost every family.

"Although it is not sufficiently certain," says Benedict the Fourteenth, "whether the name of Marye was announced by the Angel, and ordered by God to be conferred, as the name of Jesus was, and that of His precursor, St. John; nevertheless the Church always had a great veneration for it, so much, indeed, that women, although of royal birth, were not allowed to bear it, as if the dignity of this holy name would be compromised by being conferred upon women, even though they were queens."[2]

Many centuries elapsed before the name of Marye was habitually conferred or borne, and this out of reverence for our Ladye. Nevertheless, a few early instances are mentioned by Baronius in his edition of the Martyrologium.

To omit mention in detail of Poland,[3] Castile,[4] and other

[1] Latin Poems, commonly attributed to Walter Map or Mapes, edited by T. Wright, M.A., p. 196, Camden Soc. In the Magna Vita S. Hugonis his name is given as Map, p. 280. Rolls Edit. As given by Wright the line runs *Cum numquam audeo*, &c. From the context it evidently should be *Cum nomen audio*.

[2] De Festis B.V.M. c. x.

[3] Our Ladye was proclaimed "Queen of Poland" by a decree of the Diet in 1655 under John Casimir; from which time the Poles have continued to invoke her in the Litany as *Regina cæli et Poloniæ*; to which in Lithuania they add, "Duchess of Lithuania" (Montalembert, *Œuvres*, t. iv. p. 245, Paris, 1860). Cf. also Marracci, *Reges Mariani*, c. iii. § viii. and c. xvii. § iv.: also Theop. Raynaud, S.J., *Diptych. Marian.* Opp. t. vii. punc. 2, n. 12.

[4] Lyræus, *Trisagium Marianum*, p. 395. Also Benedict XIV. l.c.

countries,[5] in their mode of honouring the name of Marye; it
may be noticed that the Council of Buda, in Hungary, A.D. 1279,
prescribes that all whenever they hear *Ave Maria* during Divine
Office shall reverently bow on bended knee.[6] The Ancren
Riwle, written in low West-Saxon about the year 1260 anti-
cipates this rubric.[7]

At what period the name of Marye began to be habitually
conferred in England, I will not venture to say; but I do not
remember to have found an instance of it in the Saxon
Chronicle, or the Codex. Stowe, however, mentions that
St. Marye Overies, now St. Saviour's, in Southwark, was
originally founded as a house of sisters by a maiden named
Mary in Anglo-Saxon times.[8]

Our Anglo-Saxon forefathers were wont to call the Blessed
Virgin, ure Lavedi, ure Lafti, our Ladye Saint Marye; and this
form was continued by the Normans, and perpetuated to our
day, although endeavours have not been wanting on the part
of some with Italian sympathies to supplant this thoroughly
English name, a precious inheritance from our Catholic forefathers, by *Madonna.* "Our Ladye" is applied to the Blessed
Virgin alone; *Madonna* is not.

It would be difficult to mention a nation, except Ireland,
which has not adopted this pleasing form of addressing our
Ladye. That solitary exception has its reason in the facility
afforded by a beautiful language for the use of terms which
to other nations would be impossible without the sacrifice of
elegance and euphony. The Fathers of the Greek and Latin
Church used the title "Our Ladye" constantly and continually
from the earliest ages.[9]

[5] Mabillon, *Acta SS. O.S.B.* sæc. vi. pt. i. p. 692; *Acta SS.* t. 40, p. 527.

[6] Labbé, *Concilia*, t. xi. col. 1077, Paris, 1672.

[7] P. 19.

[8] S. p. 140.

[9] Δέσποινα ἡμῶν, *Domina nostra*. So too we find *Notre Dame, Nostra Donna,
Nuestra Señora*, and in Old Catalan, *ma dona Santa Maria*. In Germany and
the Low Countries our Ladye is called *unser liebe Frau, onze Lieve Vrouw*,
i.e. our dear Ladye. Madonna was not applied exclusively to our Ladye,
thus Polo Capello calls Lucrezia Borgia Madonna Lucrezia, and the *Fioretti*
of St. Francis speaks of Madonna Giacoma or Iacoma. Mone gives a hymn
of the fourteenth century in the Venetian dialect, in which our Ladye is
called *Madona de le done*. Cf. Fioretti di S. Francesco, Venice, 1585, ff. 72, 97 b.,
99 b.; also Italian *Relation of England*, p. 23, Camden Soc. 1847; also *Polo*

The Irish carried their reverence for the holy name of Marye to a very remarkable degree. Influenced in early ages by profound feelings of humility and respect, they never assumed the names of the Blessed Virgin or of the Saints, reserving them exclusively for those holy persons who had borne them, and adopted the prefix of *Mael* or *Maol*, so common in Irish names, which signifies servant.[10] Thus Maclisa means servant of Jesus; Maelmuire, servant of Marye; Maelphatraig or Maelpadraic,[11] servant of Patrick. Maelmuire was borne both by men and women.

To quote at random from the many instances given by the Four Masters:

A.D. 893. Maelmuire, son of Flannagan, Lord of Feara-Li died.

A.D. 964. Maelmuire. daughter of Nial, son of Aedh, died.

The chronicle of Hy records the death of Maelmuire, daughter of Cinaedha mic Ailpin in 913. She was Queen of Fiunliath, monarch of Ireland from 863 to 879, and was mother of Niall Glundubh, King of Ireland.[12]

Capello, Relazioni, &c., serie 2, v. iii. p. 14, Firenze, 1846; also Mone, *Hymni Latini Medii Ævi,* v. ii. p. 168, Friburgi Brisgov. 1853; also Montargut, *Hist. de N. Dame du Mont-Serrat,* p. 241, Paris, 1697; also *Teutsch Romisch Brevier,* translated from the Latin for the use of Nuns, p. 491, Augspurg, 1535; also S. p. 202. In Spain children often receive the name of one of the feasts of our Ladye, such as Concebida, Annunciata, Dolores, Rosaria, Assunta, and the like. At Cremona, in Andalusia, there is a celebrated sanctuary of Our Ladye of Grace, and nearly every woman there is called Gracias. Cf. Martorelli, *Teatro Istorico della S. Casa Nazarena,* v. ii. p. 406; also *Essays on Various Subjects,* by Card. Wiseman, v. i. p. 451, Lond. 1853. To this day nearly all the women inhabiting the broken remnants of the old Reductions in Paraguay bear the name of Marye, together with some one or other of our Ladye's titles by which latter denomination they are familiarly called, as Loreto, Asuncion, Dolores, Parto, Rosario, Immacolata, and the like. *Month,* new series, vol. i. (xii.) p. 519, note. Mrs. Jameson was greatly mistaken when she said that the "title of 'our Lady' came first into general use in the days of chivalry, for she was the 'Lady of all hearts,' whose colours all were proud to wear" (*Legends of the Madonna,* introd. p. xxvi. Edit. 1872).

[10] *Memoir introductory to the early history of Primacy of Armagh,* p. 87. By Robert King, M.A. (privately printed). Armagh, 1854.

[11] A.D. 923. Maelpadraic mac Morain princeps de Druimcliabh et de Airdsratha mortuus est. *Chron. Hyense.* p. 391. Rolls Edit.

[12] *Ibid.* p. 392. P. Goffinet, S.J., who accompanied the Abyssinian expedition in 1868, mentions that on the 28th of May he met a good priest called Ghebra Miriam, or servant of Marye—*Précis Historiques,* v. xxvi. (2 ser. v. vi.) p. 515. Cf. also Il Gran Nome di Maria, &c., opera del P. Domenico Antonio Moscati della Comp. di Gesu, Napoli, 1749.

No translation can give the full beauty of this unique and happy combination; and few would guess that the real name of the celebrated monk of Ratisbon, known under the Latinized form of Marianus Scotus, was, in reality, Maelmuire.

Giolla or Gilla, a servant, whence the term, gilly, gillie, is also used as a prefix; thus in the Four Masters:

A.D. 1018. Gillamuire, son of Ceinneidigh, was killed.

A.D. 1159. Gillamuire, Ankoret of Ard-macha, died.

The *Eulogium Historiarum* says that King Arthur, after going to Ireland, took King Gillamurius prisoner.[13]

These combinations yet survive in the family surnames of Gilchrist and Gilmurray, meaning servant of Christ and servant of Marye.

One curious fact is mentioned in the life of St. Godric, by Reginald of Durham his contemporary. A maiden, Juliana, had been miraculously cured at the tomb of the saint, and changed her name into that of Marye.[14] This would seem as if, having been chosen by God as an object for the manifestation of His Divine power, she was now considered as worthy of bearing the sweet name of the Mother of God.

Many villages and hamlets in the United Kingdom yet bear the names which they received in the ages of faith. We find Ottery St. Mary, St. Mary Tavy, and St. Mary Clist, in Devonshire; St. Marychurch and St. Mary Hill, in Glamorgan; St. Mary Bourne, in Hants; St. Mary's Bridge, in Derbyshire; St. Mary's Cray and St. Mary, in Kent; St. Mary's, in Huntingdon, Norfolk, and Morayshire; Maryculter and Marykirk, in Kincardine; Maryburgh, in the shires of Ross, Kinross, and Inverness: Maryhill, in Lanark; Marypark, in Banff; Maryton and Marywell, in Forfarshire; Maryport, in Cumberland; Maryston, in Devon; and Marylebone (Marie la bonne) near Wigan, and in London; Ladybank, in Fife; Lady's Bridge, in Banff; Ladyburn, in Renfrewshire; Ladyhall, in Cumberland; Ladykirk, in Orkney, and in Berwick; Ladylands, Stirling; and Ladywell, in Kent,[15] and in Wales the ever recurring Llanvair (Church of Mary).

[13] Eulogium historiarium, &c., a quodam monacho Malmesburiensi exaratum, vol. ii. p. 319. Rolls Edit.

[14] *Libellus de vita S. Godrici*, p. 435. Surtees Society.

[15] *Railway and Commercial Gazetteer of England, Scotland, and Wales.* London, 1869.

CHAPTER THE THIRD.

First Fruits.

§ I.—CHILDHOOD AND BOYHOOD.

Maxima debetur puero reverentia.

BRITISH children were carefully trained up in the love of our Ladye. Great St. Dunstan, whilst yet a boy, was sent by his parents to Glastonbury to devote himself to the service of God, and of Blessed Marye Mother of God.[1] St. Margaret of Scotland instructed her children, amongst other things, to give a sovereign honour and absolute adoration to the Most Blessed Trinity; and to have a particular respect and devotion to the Most Blessed Virgin the Mother of God.[2] This is what is related of the early youth of St. Thomas of Canterbury in the Icelandic *Saga* of the "Blissful Martyr."

"The blessed Thomas grew up in London, obedient to father and to mother, pleasing and gentle towards every man, bright and blithe of visage, and of a turn of countenance, as it seemed to wise men, that the sweetness of God's grace was clearly seen in him. And now since this is the first season of learning in the growing up of man, that a good and loving mother talketh Christian words to him, maketh known unto him the fear of God, and teacheth him holy lore, so young Thomas hath even such a school to begin with, for his mother Maild was both wise and willing to give counsels to him. Concerning these counsels there is this, amongst other matters, to be read, that she taught him to adore and reverence the Blessed Maiden, God's Mother Mary, beyond all other saints, and to select her as the wisest guide of his life and of all his ways; and without doubt the blessed Thomas took this good counsel readily to his heart, to love our Lady, for in her he had, next indeed to Christ Himself, all his trust and faith, and in return therefore the Virgin Mary set such a loving heart on him, that already when he was still in the years of youth she

[1] *Act. SS.* t. iv. Maii. p. 348.   [2] *The Idea of a Perfect Princess,* p. 35. Paris, 1661.

herself chose him to be the highest among teachers, which resembleth after a fashion what is read of the holy David that the Lord chose him to be king over Israel, and anointed him by the hands of Samuel, even in his childhood, already when he was but a little swain a-shepherding. That this comparison is not set forth in heedless words will appear clearly from the events themselves and the things which hereinafter follow."[3]

In the Instructions for Parish Priests, composed by John Myrc about the year 1450, god-parents are to teach their god-children the *Pater, Ave*, and *Creed*.[4] The font at Bradley in Lincolnshire has this inscription :

Pater Noster, Abe Maria, and Creed, leren pe chyld pt es nede,[5]

thus bearing out the lesson inculcated by Myrc. In the unique copy of the Manuale of Sarum use of 1506, printed by Pinson, the following instruction is given in the *Mundatio fontis* : "God-faders and godmod's of this chylde we charge you that ye charge the fader and the moder to kepe it from fyer and wat[r], and other perels to the age of vii. yere, and that ye lerne or se it be lerned the Pr. Nr., Ave, and Crede," &c.[6]

Hence after God, children were taught to love our Blessed Ladye, and they ever loved her as their Sweet Mother, their Ladye, and their Mediatrix and Advocate with her Divine Son. Children having been taught the *Hail Marye*, the next lesson for them to learn was that of courtesy, in which " alle vertues arne closide ;" so the Lytylle Childrenes Lytil Boke, dating about the year 1480, says :

> Lytylle childrene, here ye may lere
> Moche curtesy that is wretyne here ;
> For clerkis that the vii. artez cunne,
> Seyn that curtesy from hevyn come,
> When Gabryelle oure lady grette
> And Elizabeth with Mary mette.
> All vertues arne closide yn curtesye
> And alle vices yn vylonye ;[7]

---

[3] *Thomas Saga Erkibyskups; or, the Story of Archbishop Thomas*, translated and edited by Eiríkr Magnússon, M.A., Sub-Librarian of University Library, Cambridge, c. iv. pp. 17—19. Rolls Edit.

[4] Early Eng. Text Soc., vol. i. 1868, p. 5.

[5] *Ibid.* p. 73, note.

[6] In the Stonyhurst Library. This is fully described in the printed catalogue of the black-letter books, privately printed.

[7] *Babees Book*, Early Eng. Text Soc., 1868, p. 16.

thus it brings home to the children's mind the Annunciation, and the Angelical Salutation, and the great mystery of the Incarnation. And these precepts of courtesy were not without fruit. In the *Hye Way to the Spytell Hous*, the wealthy London tradesman thus addresses the door-keeper of the God's house:

> " Porter," sayd I, " God's blyssyng and our lady
> Haue ye for spekyng so curteysly
> To those poore folke ; and god his soule pardon
> That for their sake made this foundacyon."[8]

This was in the days when England was Merrye England, and when workhouses and the race of Bumbles were unknown.

In Catholic Ireland, at the present day, the usual salutation given by those who speak the native language is "Dia's Muire duit "—God and Marye save you ; and the reply, " God and Marye and Patrick."[9]

Almost contemporary with the Lytylle Childrenes Lytil Boke was the Boke of Curtesay, printed by Caxton about 1477 —78. Lytyl John is told to take hede and listen to what is said to him :

> In the morenynge whan ye vp rise,
> To worshipe gode have in memorie
> With crystes crosse loke ye blesse you thrise,
> Your pater noster saye in deuoute wyse,
> Ave Maria with the holy crede
> Thenne alle the day the better shal ye spede.[10]

Moreover it appears that the Office of our Blessed Ladye was a favourite daily devotion with English children almost as soon as they could read. Lytyl John is admonished—

> While that ye be aboute honestly
> To dresse your self and do on your arraye
> With your felawe wel and tretably
> Our lady matyns loke that ye saye
> And this obseruaunce vse ye every daye
> With prime and ouris withouten drede
> The blessed lady wil quyte you your mede.[11]

It is evident that Chaucer, although he places the scene of

---

[8] Ames' *Typographical Antiquities*, vol. iii. p. 124. Edit. Herbert, Lond. 1785.
[9] Moran's *Essays on the Early Irish Church*. Dublin, 1864, pp. 239.
[10] Caxton's *Boke of Curtesay*, Early English Text Society, 1868. Extra Series, vol. iii. p. 5.
[11] *Ibid.* p. 9.

the Prioresse's tale in a great cite in Asia, has left us the beautiful picture of an English school of his time :

> Amongst these childrē was a wedows son
> A litel clergion, that vii. yere was of age
> That day by day to schole was his won
> And also eke, where he sey the image
> Of Christes mother, had he in vsage
> As him was taught, to knele adoun and say
> An Ave maria, as he goth by the way.
>
> Thus hath this wedow, her litel child itauȝt
> Our blissed lady, Christes mother dere
> To worship aye, and he foryate it naught.
> .   .   .   .   .   .
> This litel child his litel boke lerning
> As he sate in schole at his primere
> He Alma Redemptoris Mater herd sing
> As children lered her antiphonere
> And as he durst, he drew aye nere and nere,
> And herkened to the wordes and the note
> Till he the first verse couth all by rote.

He did not understand the Latin, and he asked his companion,

> Full oft time, vpon his knees bare,

to expound this song, and tell him why it was in usage.

> His felow which that elder was than he
> Answerd him thus, this song I haue herd say
> Was made of our blessed lady fre
> Her to salew, and eke her to prey
> To ben our helpe and succour when we dey.
> I can no more expound in this mater
> I lerne song, I can but small grammer.

Then the dear innocent child, on being told that it is sung
in reverence of our Ladye, determines to learn it, at the sacrifice
of his primer, and in the consequent certainty of being beaten
thrice within an hour ; but the love of our Ladye absorbed
his fear of a thrashing. Truly is she the *Raptrix cordium ;*
truly was the lad worthy of being an Ængle !

> And is this song imade in reuerence
> Of Christes mother, said this innocent ?
> Now certes I woll done my diligence
> To conne it all er Christenmasse be went
> Though that I for my primer shall be shent
> And should be beten thrise in an houre
> I woll it conne, our lady to honoure.[11]

[11] *Works.* London, 1602, f. 68, b.

Readers of *Tom Brown* will remember the sensation caused at Rugby when Tom took the part of his young *protégé*, George Arthur, who had caused no little surprise by kneeling down at his bedside to say his night prayers, as his mother had taught him to do at home.[13] To a Catholic, whose morning and night prayers form a part of his very existence, this appears incomprehensible. Dean Stanley, however, records—

"That at the period when Dr. Arnold was elected head-master of Rugby (*i.e.* in 1827) the absence of systematic attempts to give a more directly Christian character to what constituted the education of the whole (non-Catholic) English gentry was becoming more and more a scandal in the eyes of religious men, who at the close of the last century and the beginning of this—Wilberforce, for example, and Bowdler—had lifted up their voices against it. A complete reformation, or a complete destruction of the whole system, seemed to many persons sooner or later inevitable. The difficulty, however, of making the first step, where the alleged objection to alteration was its impracticability, was not easily surmounted. The mere resistance to change, which clings to old institutions, was in itself a considerable obstacle, and in the case of some of the public schools, from the nature of their constitution, in the first instance almost insuperable ; and whether amongst those who were engaged in the existing system, or those who were most vehemently opposed to it, for opposite but obvious reasons, it must have been extremely difficult to find a man who would attempt, or if he attempted, carry through, any extensive improvement.

" It was at this juncture that Dr. Arnold was elected head-master of a school which, whilst it presented a fair average specimen of the public schools at that time, yet by its constitution imposed fewer shackles on its head, and offered a more open field for alteration than was the case at least with Eton or Winchester."[14]

The great object which Dr. Arnold had was "the hope of making the school a place of really Christian education."[15]

---

[13] Part ii. ch. i.

[14] *Life and Correspondence of Thomas Arnold, D.D.*, late Head-master of Rugby School, &c. By Arthur Penrhyn Stanley, M.A. London, 1846. Ch. iii. p. 77. This chapter is of " School Life at Rugby."

[15] *Ibid.* p. 48.

The conclusion therefore from these words is that as Rugby presented a "fair average specimen of the public (Protestant) schools" in 1827, the religious element was at a very low ebb indeed. The words of the Prophet-King, *Initium sapientiæ timor Domini*,[16] seem to have been forgotten. So much for the results of the "Reformation." The author, however, records the good effects produced by young Arthur, and concludes with remarking, "that before either Tom Brown or Arthur left the school-house, there was no room in which it had not become the regular custom. I trust," continues the author, "it is so still, and that the old heathen state of things has gone out for ever."[17] In that wish every Christian parent will join. But a question naturally presents itself : "By whom was this 'heathen state of things' introduced, or how, under proper care, could it ever have existed ?"

---

[16] Psalm cx. 10.

[17] My copy of *Tom Brown* contains a letter to the author from an old friend, who signs himself "F. D." Its object is to draw attention to the bullying, and whilst admitting that the author has denounced this cowardly practice, F. D. observes, "You hardly suggest that such things should be stopped, and do not suggest any means of putting an end to them." After saying very much, *ad rem*, he concludes : "I believe there is only one complete remedy. It is not in magisterial supervision, nor in telling tales, nor in raising the tone of public opinion among schoolboys, but in the *separation of boys of different ages into different schools.* There should be at least three different classes of schools : the first for boys from nine to twelve ; the second for boys from twelve to fifteen ; the third for those above fifteen. And these schools should be in different localities. There ought to be a certain amount of supervision by the master at those times when there are special occasions for bullying, *e.g.*, in the long winter evenings, and when the boys are congregated together in the bedrooms. Surely it cannot be an impossibility to keep order and protect the weak at such times. Whatever evils might arise from supervision, they could hardly be greater than those produced by a system which divides the boys into despots and slaves." If the writer of this excellent letter were to pay a visit to Stonyhurst, or any other College of the Society of Jesus, and study the working of the Constitutions of St. Ignatius of Loyola, he would be pleased to see that what he here recommends and suggests has long ago been carried into practice. At Stonyhurst boys on their first arrival must be under the age of fourteen ; any above that age, like the late Roger Tichborne, can only be received as "Gentlemen Philosophers," and they have no intercourse with the boys. At Hodder Place, which is within a mile of Stonyhurst, about sixty or seventy of the younger lads are placed, whilst at Stonyhurst there is a complete separation between the higher and lower classes, or Rhetoric, Poetry, and Syntax, and the four lower schools, which have their respective recreation rooms and playgrounds. The strict martial order, decorum, and silence observed in the dormitories would delight such an observer ; and so careful are the provisions for insuring perfect tranquillity of repose, that if any young gentleman has the evil habit of snoring, he is at once removed to a separate dormitory reserved for such offenders, where they may snore in chorus to their hearts' content.

It is evident, from the words of Dean Stanley, which I have just quoted, that Eton and Winchester had fallen into an irreligious state, and that they were so bound by shackles as not to offer a very open field for alteration. Eton is, so to say, the daughter of Winchester. Eton, founded in honour of our Blessed Ladye, and King's College, Cambridge, were both modelled upon the plan of Winchester, and the statutes of William of Wykeham were transcribed without any material alteration. The royal founder of these two colleges took the greatest personal interest in his pious work. He did not employ commissioners to report to him on the organization and working of Wykeham's College; he judged and acted for himself. During the building of the colleges, Henry the Sixth went to Winchester five times, that, in the words of the Protestant historian, "he might more nearly inspect, and personally examine, the laws, the spirit, the success, and good effects, of an institution which he proposed to himself for a model." From hence it appears that his imitation of Wykeham's plan is not to be imputed to a casual thought of his own, or a partial recommendation from another, or an approbation founded only on a common report or popular opinion, but that it was the result of deliberate inquiry, of knowledge, and experience.[18]

Henry the Sixth was careful to obtain the ratification by Parliament of his various grants made from time to time by letters patent. One of the most extensive confirmations of property and privileges was made in 1445-6, and the College caused it to be transcribed with great care, and paid the sum of £1 6s. 8d. to a certain William Abell for adorning it with an illumination. It is a most interesting example of English art. The King is represented within the initial letter of his name, on his knees at a *prie-dieu*, offering his charter to our Blessed Ladye, who is figured in her Assumption, being borne up by five angels and crowned by the Most Holy Trinity. Over the King is a label bearing " *Henricus Sextus rex fundator hujus regalis collegii*," and behind his Majesty are the three estates of the realm. The Commons who are below the Lords are saying, " *Prient les Communes*," to which the Lords spiritual and temporal add, " *Et nous le prions ausi*." Foremost among the

---

[18] Louth, *Life of William of Wykeham*, p. 180. Oxon, 1777.

Peers kneels Archbishop Stafford, and immediately behind him Cardinals Beaufort and Kemp.[19]

The present seal of Eton, which represents the Assumption of our Blessed Ladye, with the Royal arms beneath her, was adopted in 1474, and apparently, says the learned historian of Eton, on political grounds.[20] The original seal, of which two examples only are known at present, represents the Assumption of our Blessed Ladye, who is borne up by eight angels; the

Original Seal of Eton College.

arms of Eton are under her feet, and kneeling on the right is the Royal Founder, Henry the Sixth. On either side is an angel supporting the arms of France and England. The arms granted by Henry the Sixth to Eton College were, "On a field, sable, three lily flowers, argent, intending that our newly founded College, lasting for ages to come, whose perpetuity we wish to be signified by the stability of the sable colour, shall bring forth

[19] *History of Eton College*, 1440–1475, by H. C. Maxwell Lyte. London, 1875 (p. 52). I have not seen the original, and I have been unable to decipher fully the inscription before the King. It appears to read "*Ad laudem gloriam et . . . tuam,*" and is evidently addressed to our Blessed Ladye.

[20] *Ibid.* p. 72.

the brightest flowers, redolent of every kind of knowledge. . . . To which also that we may impart something of Royal nobility, which may declare the work truly royal and illustrious, we have resolved that portions of the Arms, which by Royal right belong to us in the Kingdoms of France and England, be placed on the chief of the shield, per pale, azure, with a flower of the French, and gules with a leopard passant, or." [21]

Mr. Maxwell Lyte remarks that the arms of Eton, which was dedicated to our Ladye alone, only bear her lilies ; those of King's College, Cambridge, dedicated to our Ladye and St. Nicholas, bear two lilies and a mitre and pastoral staff.[22] It will be noticed that the Eton lily flowers are not the heraldric *fleurs-de-lis.* May they not be symbolical of the spotless virginity of our Ladye before childbirth, in childbirth, and after childbirth ?

The Reformation produced dire results at Eton. "It is incredible," says the learned historian, "that there should ever have been an entire absence of religious teaching at the greatest school in Christian England ; yet such, from all accounts, must have been the case at Eton until about fifty years ago."[23] Let us, therefore, hark back to the ages of faith, and see what were the observances at Catholic Winchester and Catholic Eton.

Devout clients of our Ladye like William of Wykeham and the good King Henry the Sixth would never have dreamed of omitting such important duties as morning and night prayers in the constitutions of their colleges, whereas the Commissioners of Edward the Sixth required the Winchester "scholars and children thenceforth to omit to sing or say *Stella cæli* or *Salve Regina* or any suchlike untrue or superstitious anthem."[24] No wonder, then, that the spirit of devotion soon died out, and that as a natural result there ensued the state of things to which Dean Stanley has alluded.

The Statutes, which were drawn up for Eton in 1444, prescribe that after Matins and Prime of the day, all the choristers

---

[21] *History of Eton College,* pp. 52, 53.

[22] *Ibid.* p. 54.

[23] *History of Eton College,* p. 370.

[24] Walcott, *History of W. of Wykeham and his Colleges.* Lond. 1852, p. 152 and p. 242.

shall recite the Hours of our Ladye, according to the use and ordinal of Sarum. Equally the scholars, as soon as they had arisen, and whilst making their beds, were to recite the Matins of our Ladye, which they were to finish before going to school ; and in the evening, on leaving school, they were to sing an antiphon of our Ladye, with *Ave Maria* and a collect ; and before going to supper they said the Vespers of our Ladye, according to Sarum use. After Vespers, or at another time, as the Provost might appoint, on every day excepting Maundy Thursday and Good Friday, the choristers and scholars, in surplices, were to say a *Pater Noster* before the crucifix, on their knees, and then, rising, to sing the *Salve* before the image of our Ladye. And at the end of the day, all the choristers and scholars before going to bed were, at the first peal of the curfew bell, to kneel down by their beds, those who are in each room, and to say alternately the entire hymn, *Salvator mundi Domine*, with the versicle, *Custodi nos Domine*, and the psalm, *Nunc dimittis*, the antiphon, *Salva nos Domine vigilantes*, with the *Kyrie eleison, Pater noster, Ave Maria*, and Creed. And then all were to recite in a loud and intelligible voice the antiphon, *Stella cœli extirpavit*,[25] with the usual versicle and prayer.[26] Moreover, they were to recite the whole Psalter of our Ladye.[27]

At Winchester, either the *Stella cœli* or the *Salve Regina* was always sung in the evening, and the Prior's charity boys in like manner sang an evening antiphon of our Ladye, together with the *De Profundis*.[28]

It would be well if this pious old English custom of singing an antiphon of our Blessed Ladye, after night prayers, were revived in all our schools and colleges. It already exists at St. Cuthbert's College, Ushaw, and those who have had the privilege of assisting at the College night prayers will not easily forget the solemn and impressive manner of giving the Good Night to our Ladye by singing the *Maria Mater gratiæ*.[29]

[25] This antiphon is given in all the editions of the well-known *Libellus Precum*.

[26] *Ancient Laws of the Fifteenth Century for King's College, Cambridge, and for the Public School of Eton College.* Edit. Heywood and Wright. London, 1850, pp. 552—555.

[27] *Ibid.* p. 607.

[28] S. pp. 242, 243.

[29] Lest exception may be taken to the use of this term, I may as well mention that it is an old English form.

It cannot be doubted that the Eton boys often went on little pilgrimages to Our Ladye of Windsor,[30] and other neighbouring sanctuaries of our Ladye. Our Ladye of Eton [31] is often mentioned ; and it may safely be presumed that the Winchester boys often went to greet our Ladye before her celebrated image at the Pillar in the Cathedral, where Wykeham was habitually accustomed to pray. Thus were the youths of England trained up in the love of our Blessed Ladye, and the seed thus early sown and nurtured, fructified in after life.

§ 2.—OXFORD AND CAMBRIDGE.

Primus discendi ardor nobilitas est Magistri. Quid nobilius Dei Matre ?
Quid splendidius est, quam Splendor elegit ?

St. Ambrose.[32]

The outfit for a young man going up to the University in the ages of faith differed somewhat from that which is considered necessary for a gentleman-commoner of Christ-Church in the nineteenth century. When Mabel Rich sent her son St. Edmund to Paris, the outfit which she gave him consisted of a Bible and a hairshirt : and whilst he was at Oxford she would, from time to time, forward supplies of linen, to which she invariably added a hairshirt.

It was at Oxford that St. Edmund espoused himself to our Blessed Ladye, as I have already mentioned ; and from the words of the chronicler of Lanercrost, the image on the finger of which he placed the ring, was the object of veneration of the whole University ;[33] and his example greatly contributed to increase devotion to the Glorious Mother of God. The image

---

[30] S. pp. 246, 249.

[31] *Ibid.* p. 32. After some deliberation the *Montem* was abolished in 1847. "Perhaps the most curious defence of *Montem*," says Mr. Maxwell Lyte, "was that set up by an intensely Protestant Fellow, who, having somehow got an idea that the triennial procession to Salt Hill had taken the place of a pilgrimage to the (Blessed) Virgin, desired that the ceremonies happily freed from superstition should be retained as a symbol of the Reformation, and a standing protest against Popery" (*History of Eton College*, p. 468).

[32] *De Virginibus*, Opp. t. iii. lib. ii. Paris, 1616.

[33] S. p. 121.

placed over the gate of New College, by William of Wykeham, yet remains.

In the Statutes of Magdalen College, founded by Bishop Wayneflete, provision is made for our Ladye's antiphon on Saturdays :

"Our pleasure is that on every Saturday throughout the year, and on all the eves of the Feasts of the Blessed Virgin

Gateway of New College, Oxford.

Marye, after Complin, all and each of the said Fellows and Scholars and Ministers of our chapel, do devoutly perform among themselves in the common hall by note, an antiphon of the said Glorious Virgin."

Again, in regard of the third part of the Psalter of our Ladye :

"The President and each of the Fellows are to hear one Mass

d

every day, unless they are Priest-fellows who can say it, and either at Mass, or at some other time, if prevented, they do say in honour and remembrance of the Most Blessed Virgin Mother of our Lord Jesus Christ, with all possible devotion on their bended knees, fifty times over the Angelical Salutation together with the Lord's Prayer, after every ten rehearsals of the salutation aforesaid."[34]

A similar statute in respect of the singing of an anthem of our Ladye in hall, after Complin on Saturdays, was made by Bishop Fox for Corpus Christi College.[35]

Chaucer has left the description of a poure scoler's room at Oxford:

> His almagiste, and bokes gret and smale
>
> .   .   .   .   .
>
> On shelues couched at his beddes hedde
> His presse icouered with a folding redde
> And all aboue there lay a gay Sautrie,
> On which he made on nights melodic
> So sweteley, that all the chambre rong ;
> And *Angelus ad Virginem* he song.[36]

Moreover, at Oxford the poorer students would beg from door to door, singing the *Salve Regina*, and ask a pittance for our Ladye's love, in whose sweet name nothing was ever refused.

The celebrated Alexander of Hales had made a vow never to refuse anything which it was in his power to grant, when asked of him in our Ladye's name. He was the master of St. Thomas Aquinas and St. Bonaventure, and it is quite evident that the example of the devotion to our Ladye of his English master was not lost upon St. Bonaventure. It was in consequence of this vow that Alexander of Hales joined the Order of St. Francis, of which he became such an ornament.

"A certain devout matron," says the author of the *Collectanea Anglo-Minorita*, "coming to the knowledge of this vow, and being much affected to the Carmelites and Dominicans, told

[34] *Statutes of Magdalen College*, translated by G. R. M. Ward, Esq., M.A. Lond. 1840, pp. 97, 98.

[35] *Foundation Statutes of Bishop Fox for Corpus Christi College, Oxon. A.D.* 1517, now first translated into English by G. M. Ward, Esq., M.A. Lond. 1843, c. xx. p. 93.

[36] *The Miller's Tale.* Opp. f. 12. Does this refer to the Hail Marye? When Chaucer lived the devotion of the *Angelus*, in its present form, was unknown.

some of the former the secret, bidding them to go to the Doctor Halensis and ask him, for the glorious Virgin Marye's sake, to enter into their Order, assuring them that the Doctor would grant them their request. The White Friars are surprised at the thing, considering the man, and the elevated station he was in, but relying on the devotion and integrity of the matron they go to the Doctor, who received them with all the marks of civility imaginable, and they discoursed with him on many heads for a good while, and then returned home, not once (God having otherwise appointed) so much as remembering the business they came thither for; which the good lady took for an affront, thinking that the omission was an effect of either slight, or a misbelief of what she had suggested to them, so she let the Dominicans into the secret, who soon went privately to the Doctor, and first discoursing with him about indifferent matters that they might at last usher in their address in a more courtly manner; when, behold, in comes a Friar Minor with his wallet on his shoulder, having been begging bread about the town for his brethren; and being now come hither also to beg a little bread, and having fixed his eyes upon the Doctor as he sat talking with the Dominicans, he simply addressed himself to him in these plain terms—viz., "Reverend Doctor, you are a very great scholar, and the fame of your virtue is spread far and near; you see the poor Order of Friars Minors has as yet but few learned men in it, and no Doctors. If you were in it many persons would improve by your means, and therefore I beseech you, for the love of God and the Blessed Virgin Marye, that you will take upon you the habit of our Order, for the good of your soul, and for the honour of our Institute." The Dominicans were amazed to see themselves thus prevented, and the Doctor himself at first seemed to be in a consternation, but at last recovering himself, and being inwardly touched with the grace of the Holy Ghost, and taking the words of the simple Brother to be a call from God, he made this reply, "Go your ways, Brother, for I will follow you presently and comply with your request."[37]

The statutes of King's College, Cambridge, founded by Henry the Sixth in the year 1443, are equally precise in regard of devotions to our Blessed Ladye. Chapter xli. is: "Of the

[37] *Collectanea Anglo-Minorita.* London, 1726, p. 53.

prayers to be said by the Provost, Fellows, and Scholars of the College."

"We wish that all the choristers present in the College, shall, after Matins and Prime, divided on either side of the choir, arrayed in surplices, recite alternately and without note, and in a distinct and clear voice the Matins and other Hours of the Blessed Virgin ; and also at the hour of Vespers, at or about the first sound of the bell, they shall recite among themselves in a similar manner, without note, and in a distinct and clear voice the Vespers and Complin of the Blessed Virgin, and let them finish before the bell for the Vespers of the day. We also ordain that on each and every day of the year in the evening, at a fitting time, as shall appear most convenient to the Provost, or, in his absence, to the Vice-Provost, all the choristers present of our Royal College, together with the choir-master,[38] when the bell for this service rings, excepting on Maunday Thursday and Good Friday, when the bell must not be tolled, shall come to the church, and therein with lighted candles, and arrayed in surplices, shall sing before the Image of the Blessed Virgin, solemnly, and in the best manner they know, an antiphon of our Blessed Ladye with the verse *Ave Maria* and the prayer *Meritis et precibus*. . . .

"Moreover, we ordain that all and each of the Fellows and Scholars aforesaid shall, if they can conveniently, every day hear one Mass, unless they are priests ; and that every day, at proper appointed times, they shall recite the Hours of the Blessed Virgin, and that they shall make a special commemoration at Vespers and at Matins[39] of the most holy confessor Nicholas, &c."[40]

In schools and colleges the same grace before and after meals, as is now said with us, was recited, but with the addition of an antiphon of our Ladye. Thus, after *Benedicamus Domino ; Deo Gratias;* was said *Ave Regina cælorum, Mater Regis Angelorum. O Maria Flos Virginum, velut Rosa, velut Lilium, funde preces ad filium pro salute fidelium. Ave Maria. Meritis et precibus suæ piæ Matris benedicat nos Filius Dei Patris. Amen* The shorter grace after meals was as follows : *Pro tali convivio*

---

[38] *Informator in Cantu.*
[39] Matins comprise both Matins and Lauds.
[40] *Ancient Laws,* &c., p. 107.

benedicamus Domino. Deo gratias. Mater ora filium ut post hoc exilium nobis donet gaudium sine fine. Ave Maria. Meritis et precibus, &c., as above.[41] According to the Sarum Manuale, an antiphon of our Ladye, usually that of the season, was added at pleasure after grace.[42]

Pendant in the Divinity School, Oxford.

[41] *Early English Meals and Manners.* Edited by F. J. Furnevall, M.A. Lond. 1868, pp. 367, 368.

[42] Ed. Rothomagi, 1509, f. lxii. Stonyhurst Library

CHAPTER THE FOURTH.

Universal Homage.

§ I.—KINGS.

Holde up oure yong kyng, Ave benigna,
And sende us peas in oure londe, Ave Regina
Mater, nunc *bryht bee thy beamys,*
Mooder of mercy, save bothe reamys.
From a Balade on the coronation of King Henry VI., Nov. 6, 1429.[1]

THE most substantial proofs of the love which our Catholic
monarchs bore to the Blissful Mother of God are the monasteries which they founded in her honour ; for the services which
the Religious Orders rendered in the propagation of devotion
to our Blessed Ladye in England were very great. The
Chronologia Benedictino-Mariana of Bucelin, the Annals of
St. Alban's, Evesham, and the other great Benedictine houses
contain many interesting details in this regard. Foremost
amongst the English Benedictines may be named St. Augustine,
Venerable Bede, Abbot Bennet Biscop, St. Dunstan, St. Ecgwine,
St. Oswald of Worcester, and Alewine, the preceptor of Charlemagne, all of whom were celebrated clients of our Ladye.
William of Malmesbury describing the edifying death of a
young monk of Ensham says " it is well known that the monks
of Ensham are devout to our Ladye and are beloved by her."[2]
The White Friars or Carmelites propagated throughout Europe
the devotion of the Scapular which had been revealed to
St. Simon Stock at Newenham ;[3] and were called her brothers.[4]
The Grey Friars or sons of St. Francis were ever conspicuous

---

[1] *Political Poems and songs relating to English History from the beginning of
the reign of Edward III. to that of Richard III.* Edited by T. Wright, M.A.,
F.S.A., vol. ii. p. 146. Rolls Edit.

[2] *De gestis Pontificum Anglorum,* lib. iv. p. 314. Rolls Edit.

[3] S. pp. 105, 243.

[4] S. p. 14.

for their devotion to our Ladye and her Immaculate Conception. The Black Friars, as the Friars Preachers or Do-. minicans were called, spread far and wide the Psalter of our Ladye. St. Gilbert of Sempringham[5] in the rules which he drew up for his Order desired that unless there was any urgent necessity for the contrary, all the churches of the Order were to be founded in the memory of our Ladye. Thus the Religious Orders were central schools of devotion to our Blessed Ladye ; and thus our kings by founding monasteries, proved their love for her. So many royal foundations are recorded in the second portion of this work that it is needless to dilate in this place upon that favourite expression of zeal in the service of the Queen of Heaven. From the time of the conversion of England down to the sad period of the great apostasy, there was scarcely one king who did not leave some proof of his love for our Blessed Ladye, either by building a church in her honour, or by erecting and endowing a monastery, or by large donations to her sanctuaries, or by going on pilgrimage to some celebrated spot where her power had been made manifest. A few instances of the personal devotion of English kings may be adduced.

Æthelbald the son and successor of Æthelberht, who was converted by St. Augustine, built a chapel of our Ladye at Canterbury, in which he was buried.[6] King Arthur went to Glastonbury that he might die under the protection our Ladye. Ine built the "Silver Chapel," as it was called, of our Ladye at Glastonbury. St. Eadward the Martyr instituted pilgrimages to our Ladye of Abingdon. Cnut was singularly devout to our Ladye, and profuse in his donations to her great sanctuary of Chartres. Moreover, he seems to have loved to celebrate the festivals of our Ladye in some religious house : such at least I think is the construction which his journey to Ely presupposes. St. Eadward the Confessor used no other oath than *Per Sanctam Mariam.* Edward the Third returning from France after the capture of Calais about the feast of St. Michael, was overtaken by a storm at sea, and addressed himself to our Ladye in these words : " Sancta Maria, Domina mea, quid est quod tenendo versus Franciam felici aura potior, mare placatur,

[5] Dugdale, *Monasticon Anglic.* t. vi. p. l. under the heading of Sempringham.
[6] S. p. 6.

et cuncta prospera mihi succedunt : in redeundo vero versus
Angliam mihi eveniunt infortunia et nimis adversa."[7] Henry
the Fifth, amongst other proofs of his devotion to our Blessed
Ladye, caused her life to be written by Dan John Lydgate, a
monk of Bury.

The crown worn by the Kings of England, our Ladye's
Dower, bore her image with that of her Divine Son. In the
Inventory of the English Regalia in the time of Henry the
Eighth, it is mentioned that in the Kinge's crowne there were
five flowers de luce, three of which were sett w[t] an image of
Christe, &c. ; one sett w[t] an image of our Ladye and her childe,
a balace (*i.e.* a balass ruby), a poyntid dyamont, three ples
(*i.e.* pearls), and twoo colletts w[t] oute stones; and the other
flower de luce sett w[t] Seynt George.[8] On August 15, 1649,
when the plate remaining within the upper jewel-house of the
Tower was delivered over to the trustees of Parliament for the
sale of the King's goods, the King's crown was valued, and in
the valuation this item occurs : In a flower de luce having
y[e] picture of y[e] (Blessed) Virgin Marye, two sapphires valued
at 65*l.* ; eight rubies ballaces valued at 26*l.*[9]

Bucelin, as I have pointed out under the heading of
Glastonbury, mistook the act of King Eadgar, with which he
invested the abbey by laying his sceptre on the altar, for a
solemn consecration on his part of England to our Blessed
Ladye.[10] It is, nevertheless, remarkable, that in the British
Museum there is a copy of Eadgar's foundation charter of Newminster, A.D. 966, with an illumination which represents the
King with our Blessed Ladye standing at his left side in the act
of crowning him.[11] Now this is precisely the type which appears
three years later on a gold coin of the Emperor John the First,
Zimisces, A.D. 969–975, although in this instance the busts only
are represented. Our Ladye is on the left of the Emperor, and

---

[7] Th. Walsingham, *Hist. Anglicana,* t. ii. p. 271. Rolls Edit.

[8] *Ancient Kalendars and Inventories of the Exchequer.* Edit. Palgrave. London
1836, vol. ii. p. 259.

[9] *Antiquarian Repertory,* vol. iii. p. 84.

[10] S. p. 46. The words of Bucelin are : *Edgarus lituum proprium sive sceptrum
in Ara Beatissimæ Virginis deponit, et Regnum quasi suum tantæ Reginæ offert et
consecrat* (*Chron. Benedictino-Mariana,* p. 90).

[11] Cott. MS. *Vespasian,* A. vii. This has been reproduced and printed by the
Palæographical Society.

in the act of crowning him.[12] The Empire had already been consecrated to our Ladye by Leo the Sixth who died in 911.

Four English coins bear the Annunciation of our Blessed Ladye, but they belong to the Anglo-Gallic series, and are usually called *Salutes*. Three different types in gold were struck off by Henry the Fifth, and one in silver by Henry the Sixth.[13]

§ 2.—KNIGHTS AND ORDERS OF KNIGHTHOOD.

> *Zabulo*[14] *terribilis*
> *Acies castrorum,*
> *Portus et Refugium*
> *Sis christianorum.*
>
> Little Office of the Immaculate Conception.

Holy Church applies to our Blessed Ladye those words of the Book of Proverbs : *Clypeus est omnibus sperantibus in se.*[15] St. John Damascene, Hugh of St. Victor, Richard of St. Lawrence, Bartholomew of Pisa, and others, call her our Shield, *Clypeus noster;*[16] George of Nicomedia, *Scutum eorum qui summa rerum potiuntur ;*[17] and the Emperor Theodore Lascaris, *Ensis noster,* and also, *Scutum insuperabile, spiritualium hostium phalanges repellens ab eis qui cum fide et affectu eam canunt.*[18]

Juliana Berners, Lady Abbess of St. Albans, says in her curious treatise on Heraldry :

"And bycause ye cros is the mooste worthi signe emong al signys in armys, at ye cros I woll begynne, in the wich thys nobull and mighty Prynce Kyng Arthure hadde grete truste so that he left his armys that he bore of iij. dragonys and over that a nother sheelde of iij. crownys, and toke to his armys a crosse of sylver in a felde of verte, and on the right syde an Ymage of owre Blessid Ladye, hir sofie in hir arme."[19]

---

[12] Sabatier, *Description Générale des Monnaies Byzantines,* &c. Paris, 1862, vol. ii. plate xlvii. n. 17.

[13] Ruding, *Annals of the Coinage of Great Britain.* London, 1840, vol. ii. p. 400. They are figured in vol. iii., supplement part ii. plate xiii. nn. 10, 11, 13, 14.

[14] *Zabulus* is another form of *Diabolus ;* see Du Cange.

[15] xxx. 5.

[16] Marracci, *Polyanthea Mariana, sub voc.*

[17] *Orat 3 de Præsentatione B. V.M.:* quoted by Marracci, *sub voc.*

[18] In canon, *ad SS. Dripar:* quoted by Marracci, *sub voce.*

[19] *Boke of St. Albans,* reprint, 1811, a. i. Cf. what is said in the S. pp. 103, 304.

Froissart relates that at the battle of Poictiers, Sir John Chandos and the Lord Jehan de Cleremont, bore embroidered on their surcoats, unknown to each other, an image of our Blessed Ladye, and that the accidental discovery was the cause of a personal quarrel.

" . . . it so fortuned that the Lorde John Chandos rode the same day coostyng the French Host, and in like maner the Lord of Clermont one of the frenche Marshalles had ryden forthe, and aviewed the state of the Englysshe hooste, and as these two knyghtes retourned towardes their hoostes they mette togyder, eche of them bare one maner of devyce, a blewe Ladye embraudred in a soñe beame, above on theyr apayrell. Then the Lorde Cleremont sayd : ' Chandos howe long have ye taken on you to bere my devyce ? ' ' Nay ye bere myne,' sayd Chandos, ' for it is as well myne as yours.' ' I deny that,' sayd Cleremont,' but and were it nat for the truse thys day betwene us, I shulde make it good on you incontynent that ye have no right to bere my devyce.' ' A sir,' sayd Chandos, ' ye shal fynde me to morrowe redy to defend you and to prove by feate of armes that it is as well myne as yours.' "[20]

And now I venture to offer a conjecture as to the origin of surcoats, which, so far as I know, has hitherto escaped the notice of any writers on Heraldry. It cannot, however, be expected that anything which savours of devotion to our Ladye will find favour in the eyes of Protestant Heralds. Writing many years ago to a friend, now no more, who held high office in the College of Arms, to inquire whether the figure of our Ladye occurred in any English shields, I received for answer, that the device was too puerile (*sic*) to be mixed up with the noble science of Heraldry !

Heralds seem to be generally agreed that surcoats were introduced towards the end of the reign of King John, and the earliest instance in England is the figure of the Earl of Salisbury, who died in 1226. Now at Chartres there is preserved a most valuable and well authenticated relic of our Ladye, which, from ignorance of Eastern manners, had generally been taken to be the chemise of our Ladye. The Chapter adopted it for their armorial bearings. Early in the thirteenth century, it became the custom to make linen tunics, and to lay them on the *chasse* which contained the relic. These were called *Chemi-*

[20] Froissart, Lord Berner's translation, reprint. London, 1812, vol. i. p. 197.

settes de Notre Dame de Chartres, and their manufacture formed a considerable portion of the trade of the city. All the pilgrims to our Ladye of Chartres bought them. Warriors wore them when they went to battle as a sure defence—a shield, as it were, with which knights deemed themselves invulnerable—to such a point, that in a duel, if one of the combatants wore a tunic of our Ladye, he was obliged to inform his adversary, otherwise the fight would have been unequal. An old MS. relates how the knight without fear and without reproach came to Chartres *se faire enchemiser de la chemise de Notre Dame.* Women had a great devotion to this relic from the belief that our Ladye had worn it before the Birth of our Lord ; hence arose the custom that the Chapter of Chartres, as soon as it was informed of the pregnancy either of the Queen or the Dauphiness would cause a tunic to be made of white taffetas, edged with gold lace, and placed on the *chasse* for nine days, on each of which Mass was celebrated in the crypt for the happy delivery, and then it was conveyed to the Queen or the Princess by four of the Chapter.[21] Now may not this custom of knights wearing tunics of our Ladye have been the origin of surcoats ?

Froissart also relates an amusing anecdote of Sir John Norwich, who was besieged in Angoulême, and reduced to great extremities. He trusted to our Ladye to help him out of his difficulties. On the eve of the Purification he succeeded in making a truce with the Duke of Normandy for the feast day only, out of reverence for our Ladye. The next day he and his companions armed themselves, and packed up what they had, and rode forth. The French army was put in motion, but Sir John riding up said : " Gentlemen, in faith of the truce we may ride wherever we please." This was communicated to the Duke, who replied : " Let them go in God's name whatsoever way they choose, for we cannot force them to stay ; I will keep the promise I made them." Sir John and his men rode through the whole French army, and took the way rejoicingly to Aiguillon.[22] We must remember that it is a Frenchman who tells the story.

At the battle of Azincourt the English army carried five

---

[21] *N. Dame de France, ou Histoire du Culte de la S. Vierge en France depuis l'origine du Christianisme jusqu' à nos jours,* par M. le Curé de Saint-Sulpice (M. Hamon). Paris, 1861, vol. i. p. 208.

[22] C. cxix. pp. 141, 142.

colours into action, bearing respectively, the Most Holy Trinity, St. Eadward, St. George, the Royal Arms, and our Blessed Ladye; the latter were borne in attendance upon the King, by his Majesty's command :

> Avaunt baner without lettyng
> Sant Joyrg before eny of myne,
> The banere of the Trenyte, that is Haven Kyng,
> And Sente Edward his baner at thys tyd.
> "Our Ladye," he sayd, "that is Haven Quene,
> Myn oune baner with her schall abyde."[33]

An old poem on the siege of Rouen describes the preparations made by the Duke of Exeter for the triumphant entry of the King into that city after its fall :

> & riche baneris he up sette
> Vpon the porte seint Hillare
> A baner of the Trynyte.
> & at the port Kaux he sette evene
> A baner of the quene of heven.[34]

I may mention here that the standard[35] of Joan d'Arc bore the Holy Names, 𝕵𝖍𝖊𝖘𝖚𝖘, 𝕸𝖆𝖗𝖎𝖆; and her banner the Annunciation.[36]

The ancient war-cry of the English Kings was Montjoye Notre Dame, with the name of St. George added.[37]

I know of no families in England which bear the image of our Blessed Ladye on their shields; nevertheless she appears on the arms of the ancient Catholic sees of Salisbury and Lincoln in England, and of Tuam in Ireland, which are now borne by the Protestant dignitaries who occupy them. Instances, however, occur in foreign heraldry.

The image of our Blessed Ladye often appears on swords and breastplates. I have more than one example of swords— one of the fifteenth century with our Ladye and her Divine Son on one side, and St. George on the other; and the

---

[33] Lydgate, *Battle of Axincourt.* Edit. Nicolas, p. 322.

[34] *Archæologia,* vol. xxii. p. 382.

[35] The difference between a standard and a banner is this : the banner was square and bore the arms of its owner or some other device; the standard was long and narrow, and split at the end. In the upper part by the staff was the cross of St. George; the remainder being charged with the motto, crest, and badge, but never with the armorial bearings.

[36] *Jeanne d'Arc.* Par H. Wallon. Paris, Firmin Didot. 1876, p. 62.

[37] *Curiosities of Heraldry.* By M. A. Lower, p. 154.

Meyrick collection has several breast-plates thus adorned.[28]
The sword with which Richard the First of England was
girt for his dukedom of Normandy by the Archbishop of
Rouen had been laid on the altar of our Ladye, and hallowed,
prior to the investiture.[29]

In the ages of faith challenges to perform feats of arms were
often given in honour of our Ladye. In 1390, three French
knights, Jean le Meingre de Boucicaut, Renaud de Roye, and
the lord of Sempy proposed a tournament at St. Inglevert
(near Boulogne), and to hold their own against all the knights
of England, Hainault, or Lorraine, who might present themselves. Sir John de Boucicaut had caused it to be proclaimed
in many Christian countries, in England, Spain, Aragon,
Germany, Italy, and elsewhere. After vanquishing the best
lances of England, they took no glory to themselves, but came
to offer their chargers and their trappings to our Ladye of
Boulogne.[30] After the tournament between Lord Scales and
the Bastard of Burgundy, sundry other challenges were made.
Messire Philip Braton, first esquire to the Count de Charleroys,
sent one to Louys de Brutallis, a Gascon esquire, worded thus:
*En lonneur et en la reverence de mon creature Jhu Christ, et
de la ts gloriouse Vierge Marie sa mier et madame Sainte Anne
et de mon sz Seinte George*, &c.[31]

In 1854, when the plans for the invasion of the Crimea by
the allied armies of Great Britain and France had been arranged,
Marshal de Saint Arnaud published an *Ordre Général* to the
French troops, in which, it may be noticed that the word *gloire*
does not appear.[32] In curious contrast to the above order,
Lord Raglan who commanded the British forces, issued a
memorandum requesting "Mr. Commissary-General Fielder to
take steps to insure that the troops shall be provided with a
ration of porter for the next few days."[33] But, in earlier ages,
a chronicler has recorded of the Battle of Crecy, that because
it was fought on a Saturday, the English army went into

---

[28] *Armour at Goodrich Court*, vol. i. plates 41, 59, 70.
[29] Roger of Wendover, *Flor. Hist.* Edit. Coxe, vol. iii. p. 2.
[30] For the several authorities see Haigneré, *Hist. de Notre Dame de Boulogne.*
Edit. 1864, p. 101.
[31] *Excerpta Historica*, p. 214.
[32] No. 100, dated Varna, August 25, 1854, quoted by Russell, p. 146.
[33] *The War.* By W. H. Russell. London, 1855, p. 147.

action fasting in honour of our Ladye.[34]   After this evidence who will say that English soldiers cannot fight without their breakfast !

Our Ladye's name is not yet forgotten on the battle-field. Describing the terrible scene on Mount Inkermann on the evening of November 5, 1854, after the defeat of the Russians, Kinglake says of the poor wounded soldiers : "Some found means to cry out for 'the hospital,' some for 'water,' some only for pity. Men appealed in their agonies to a common faith, and invoked the name of her who must be dear—so they fondly imagined—to all the churches of Christ."[35]

On October 27, 1396, Charles the Sixth King of France, and Richard the Second King of England met at a spot not far from Guines, a few miles from Calais. After shaking hands they proceeded to the place fixed for the interview, where it was decreed that there should be built on the spot, at the joint expense of the two sovereigns, a chapel to be called of our Ladye of Peace, in perpetual memory of their interview. And this being arranged, they shook hands and departed, each to his tent.[36] Froissart says that this chapel *seroit nommée Nostre Dame de la Grace. Je ne say se riens il en fut fait.*[37]   A few days later the marriage of Richard the Second with the Princess Isabella daughter of Charles the Sixth was celebrated at Calais.

Eleven foreign and two British Orders of Chivalry were founded in honour of our Blessed Ladye prior to the sixteenth century.

Our Blessed Ladye is the chief patroness of the Most Noble Order of the Garter.

The historian of the Order, Ashmole, says of Edward the Third, "that this religious and pious king being singularly affected to the Blessed Virgin Marye, though she was accounted the General Mediatrix and Protectress to all men and upon all occasions, yet did he more peculiarly entitle her to the Patronage of this most noble Order.

"And no less was King Edward the Fourth in a special

---

[34] *Chron. Galf. Le Baker de Swinbroke,* p. 166.

[35] *Invasion of the Crimea.* London, 1875, vol. v. p. 440.

[36] "*Ut construeretur in eodem loco, amborum sumptibus, una capella, quae vocaretur Nostræ Dominæ de Pace*" (Johis de Trokelowe et Henr. de Blaneford, monachor. S. Albani, *Chronica et Annales,* p. 191. Rolls Edit.).

[37] Liv. iv. c. 78, p. 247.   Edit. Sauvage, Lyon, 1560.

manner devoted towards the same Blessed Virgin, insomuch as he thought it necessary that some additional ceremonies within the Order should be observed by himself and the Knights and Companions to her peculiar honour : and there-upon ordained that on her five solemnities, the Knights Companions should annually (as it was wont and accustomed at the yearly feast of St. George) wear the peculiar habit of the Order, as long as Divine Service was celebrating (unless they had sufficient cause of excuse), bearing on the right shoulder a golden figure of the Blessed Virgin Marye, and further that they should go in the same manner and habit upon all the Sundays throughout the year, and lastly, that on the same days, for ever, they say five *Pater Nosters* and five *Ave Marias.*"[38]

St. George of Cappadocia is the third patron of the Order. This was the ancient form of Investiture :

" To the laud and honour of Almighty God, His Immaculate Mother, and St. George, the holy martyr, tie or gird your leg with this most noble Garter, wearing it to the increase of your honour, and in token and remembrance of this most Noble Order ; remembering that you being admonished and en-couraged in all just Battles and Wars, which only shall you take in hand, both strongly to fight, valiantly to stand, and honourably to have victory."[39]

Equally is the Order of the Thistle of Scotland under the patronage of our Blessed Ladye. The Statutes say :

" The most ancient and most noble Order of the Thistle was to consist of the Sovereign and twelve Knights Brethren, in allusion to our Blessed Saviour, and His Twelve Apostles, and that under the protection of our Blessed Ladye and His Holy Apostle St. Andrew, Patron of Scotland, the said Order being instituted for the defence of the Christian religion, &c.[40]

Thus it appears how the name and love of our Blessed Ladye were intimately associated with the chivalry of England. Whether Sir Reginald de Argentein, whose epitaph I have given, was a Knight of the *Frati Gaudenti*, or of some foreign

[38] Ashmole, p. 187. He also remarks that the Statutes were so judiciously devised that they afterwards became a precedent to other Orders particularly those of the Golden Fleece, and of Monseigneur St. Michael (*Ibid.* p. 189).

[39] *Ibid.* p. 300.

[40] *Statutes of the Order of the Thistle.* London, W. Pickering, 1828, 4to, not paginated.

Order of our Ladye, or whether he had called himself our
Ladye's Knight out of his love for her, I know not. But
Lydgate calls St. George our Ladye's Knight. Was this
because he is Patron of our Ladye's Dower.

> Helpe, Sent George, oure Lady Knyjt.[41]

This is the epitaph of Sir Reginald.

> *Reignauld de Argentein ci gist*
> *Qui cest chappell feire fist :*
> *Fut Chevalier Sainct Marie,*
> *Chescuni pardon pour lalme prie.*
>
> Regnald de Argentyne here is laid
> That caused this chappell to be made :
> He was a Knight of Seynt Marie the Virgin
> Therefor prey pardon for his sin.[42]

The Grand Priors of the Knights Templars all took an
oath to defend the perpetual virginity of our Blessed Ladye.[43]

§ 3.—SHIPMEN.

> *Alma Redemptoris Mater quæ pervia cæli*
> *Porta manes, et Stella Maris, succurre cadenti.*
>> From the Antiphon of the Church.[44]

> O sterre of sterres with thy stremys clere
> Sterre of the sea, to shipmen light and guide.
> . . . .
> Mede unto mariners that haue sailed farre.
>> Chaucer, *A Balade of our Ladie.*[45]

Dear to sailors was the Virgin Mother of God, the Brilliant
Ocean Star,[46] whom they invoked as their Guide, their Anchor,[47]
their Port of refuge, their Haven in shipwreck.[48] To her did
they raise their cry in their hour of need, when tossed on

---

[41] *Battle of Azincourt*, p. 300. So in the Battle of Otterburn, the English "Sent
George the bryght, our ladyes knyght, To name they were full fayne ;" lines 189, 190.
See Percy's *Reliques*, and Ritson, *Ancient Songs and Ballads*, p. 89, Lond. 1877.

[42] *Ancient Funerall Monuments within the United Monarchie of Great Britain
and Irdand.* London, 1631, p. 545.

[43] S. p. 90.

[44] In Breviario Romano *temp.* Adventûs.

[45] Opp. fol. 329 b. Edit. cit. 1602.

[46] Marracci gives more than one hundred instances of this title being applied to
our Ladye by the Fathers (*Polyanthea Mariana, sub voce*).

[47] St. John Damascene and many others give this title to our Ladye (*Ibid.*).

[48] *Portus Naufragantium* quoted sixty-eight times by Marracci (*Ibid.*).

the angry billow, and in danger of being wrecked, although the impious Erasmus, in the person of Adolphus, laughs at sailors for calling on our Ladye.[49] Not unfrequently would they make a vow of pilgrimage, in thanksgiving, to one of her great sanctuaries ; and many monasteries owe their foundation to a vow made at sea. Ships sailing past our Ladye of Bradstow, at Broadstairs, used to salute her by striking their top-sails, or by clewing up the top-sail sheets.[50]

The Issue Roll of Richard the Second for the year 1397 mentions the offering of a silver ship to our Ladye of Aques by John Mayhew, Master of the King's ship, called *La Trinité de la Tour*, in fulfilment of a vow made during a storm.[51]

In 1506, the English pilgrims, who had started for the Holy Land with Sir Richard Guylforde were in great danger off the island of Mylo ; " and greate pyte it was to se what trybulacion and fere the maryners hadde that nyght, and also the pylgrymes, whiche rose out of our lodgings, and drewe vs together, and deuoutly and ferefully sange *Salve Regina* and other Antymes with versicles and collettis appropred for such effecte ; and we all yaue money and vowed a pylgrymage in generall to our blessed Lady de Myraculis of Venyse, besides other perticules vowes that many pylgrymes made of theyr singuler deuocons. And in lykewyse the maryners made a pylgrymage at their awne costes and charge."[52]

A captain in the Royal Navy, Master Arthur, being in great danger of losing his ship, invoked our Ladye of Walsingham, and made a vow if she would preserve him, not to eat flesh

[49] In Colloq. de Naufragio. Opp. tom. i. col. 713. Lugd. Bat. 1703. On Wednesday, the 11th of July, 1441, Thomas Bekynton, secretary to Henry the Sixth, was becalmed at sea on his way to Bordeaux. *In mare contingebat le calm, et circiter horam VIIam in sero per astimationem, navem sequebatur piscis vocatus le Shark, qui quidem piscis percutiebatur bis cum uno harpingyren et recessit ; quibus vero percussionibus non obstantibus, incessanter navem sequebatur ; et tunc magister navis cum dicto ferro latera ejus penetravit. Demum pro vento habendo dictus Dominus meus secretarius devoto et humili corde promisit et flexit argentum beatissimæ et gloriosissimæ Virgini Mariæ de Etona ; et post votum sic factum in honore dictæ Virginis, cum cæteris in navi quos incitabat facere ut ipse fecerit ; quo facto cantaverunt antiphonale Sancta Maria. Qua finita, ventus vertit se in aquilonem, et ibi flavit magis continue* (Official correspondence of Thomas Bekynton, vol. ii. Appendix, p. 184. Rolls Edit.).

[50] S. p. 4 : I inadvertently used the word "dipping," whereas "dipping" refers to the colours only.

[51] Pell Records, Issue Roll, Easter, 21 Ric. II. p. 267.

[52] *The Pylgrymage of Syr R. Guylforde, Knyght*, p. 64, Camden Soc. 1851.

é

nor fowl until he had been on a pilgrimage to her sanctuary. The Lord High Admiral of England, Sir Edward Howard, gave him leave of absence for the purpose of fulfilling his vow; and in writing an account of it to the King recommends him highly to his Majesty, hoping that he will give him comfortable words for his bravery. The letter is dated April 17, 1513.[53]

On taking up the Royal Navy List, it appears that the various British ships of war are named either after distinguished personages or mythological celebrities of pagan history, or some animal, or bird, or beast. But in Catholic days most of the ships of the Royal Navy were named either after the Most Holy Trinity or our Blessed Ladye or a saint. Thus out of the twenty ships in the reign of Henry the Seventh four bore the name of Marye.[54] Nor was the name of our Ladye confined to the Royal Navy. In the year 1512-13, amongst the victualler ships was the *Marye Whalsyngham*, Captain Yelverton;[55] and in 1513, amongst the hired ships for the Navy were the *Maria di Loreta*, of eight hundred tons, and the *Marye of Walsingham*, of one hundred and twenty tons, and ninety-seven men.[56] In 1391, by will dated September 26, Robert de Ryllyngton of Scarborough desires those two ships called *Saintmaryeboite* and the *Katherine* to be sold, and the proceeds to be expended for the health of our souls, &c.[57]

During the London Season of 1853, I met the late Lord Bishop of Southwark on the Greenwich steamer. He was going in his usual unostentatious manner to visit two old sailors in the Greenwich Hospital, and he told me the following story of them. I regret I did not take a note of their full names, as I have now forgotten them. At Trafalgar, when the English fleet was going into action, these two Catholic bluejackets were serving at the same gun, to which eleven hands were told off. Whilst they were waiting for orders to open fire, one of them sung out to the other: "Bill, let's kneel down and say a Hail Marye; we shall do our duty none the worse for it." "Aye, aye," replied Bill, "let's do so;" and forthwith, amidst the jeers and scoffs of their messmates, these two gallant tars knelt down, and greeted our Ladye with .

[53] S. p. 187.   [54] *Battle of Azincourt*, Edit. Nicolas, Append. p. 22.
[55] *Letters and Papers*, &c. *Henry VIII.* vol. i. pp. 421, 551.   [56] *Ibid.* p. 972.
[57] *Test. Ebor.* vol. i. p. 157.   Saintmaryeboite means Saint Marye's boat.

the Angelical Salutation. Twice during the action was that gun manned, and each time every soul was sent into eternity with the exception of our Ladye's two clients, who came out unscathed.

The contrast at the present time between the names of English and French vessels is very great, as may be seen daily in Dunkirk, Calais, Boulogne, Havre, and other ports on the northern coast of France, frequented by British collier and carrier steamers, and coasting brigs and top-sail schooners, which are usually named after some heathen god or local celebrity, such as the *Neptune,* the *Ariadne,* or the *Thomas and Susan,* the *Betsy-Jane,* and the like. Now these French towns have large fishing fleets, and amongst the Boulogne fishing-boats there are very few which do not bear our Ladye of Boulogne on their mast-vanes, and the names, often repeated, of *Notre Dame, Notre Dame de Grace, Notre Dame de Miracles, Notre Dame de Boulogne, La Toute Belle sans Tache, L'Immaculée Conception, L'Etoile de la Mer, L'Etoile du Matin, La Sainte Famille, St. Joseph.* And as the Boulognese fishermen love to go on pilgrimage to our Ladye of Boulogne ere setting sail for the deep-sea fishery,[58] so did our English crews in the ages of faith visit some favourite sanctuary in our Ladye's Dower ; and amongst the offerings to our Ladye of Ardenburg at Great Yarmouth in the year 1484, are recorded some herrings, which were sold for 16*s.* 4*d.*[59]

On the coasts of England, as now in Catholic countries,[60] there were many sea-side sanctuaries of our Ladye, the especial object of devotion to sailors, as *e.g.,* Our Ladye of Ardenburg, at Great Yarmouth,[61] Our Ladye in the Rock, at Dover,[62] Our Ladye of Bradstow,[63] Our Ladye of Scarborough,[64] and Our Ladye of Grace, at Southampton.[65]

---

[58] 11 Mars, 1876. Les marins qui se disposent à partir pour la pêche aux maquereaux sur la côte d'Irlande, se rendent par centaines en pèlerinage à Notre Dame de Boulogne (*Annuaire de Boulogne-sur-Mer*, pour 1876, p. 125. See S. p. 276).

[59] S. p. 257.

[60] Cf. *Notice Historique sur la Chapelle de N. D. des Dunes à Dunkerque.* Par M. Raymond de Bertrand. Dunkerque, 1853.

[61] S. p. 257.

[62] S. pp. 28, 29.

[63] S. p. 4.

[64] S. p. 137.

[65] S. p. 140.

Lately, whilst I was crossing the Channel, a Rev. Vincentian Father related to me what follows about a fishing station on the coast of Kerry, in Ireland. These fishermen are all Catholics. After a violent storm, when all their vessels had returned in safety, one of the men was asked how it was that they never seemed to be afraid of these gales, and that they always rode them out snugly and unharmed. "We are never afraid, Father," said he. "This is our secret. Whenever it begins to blow great guns, and the sea gets up, we just put a man in the bows to look out for waves, and whenever he sees a big one towering up, he lifts his hand and makes the sign of the Cross over it, and the wave always leaves us in peace."[66]

"Our Ladye, to whom shipmen sing *Ave Maris Stella*," says the homily against the period of idolatry.[67] This, therefore, was the favourite hymn of English sailors, while the Boulogne fisher-man turns towards our Ladye of Boulogne, and sings in the fulness of his heart :

> Sur la mer en furie
> Luttant contre la mort,
> Le matelot te prie ;
> Tu le conduis au port.
> Salut, Vierge bénie,
> Dame du Boulonnais,
> Qui t'honore et te prie
> Ne périra jamais.
>
> Du haut de ta nacelle,
> Sur nous jette les yeux,
> Ta famille t'appelle,
> Marie, entends nos vœux :
> Nos pères t'ont priée
> Et tu les as benis.
> Patronne bien-aimée
> Exauce encore leurs fils.

And this is the common hymn of the French *matelot :*

> *Je mets ma confiance,*
> *Vierge, en votre secours ;*
> *Servez-moi de défense,*
> *Prenez soins de mes jours*
> *Et quand ma dernière heure*
> *Viendra finir ma sort,*
> *Obtenez que je meurs*
> *De la plus sainte mort.*

[66] Related to me, July 2, 1877.   [67] Part iii. p. 203. Edit. Oxon. 1844.

From its historical antecedents, I am fully justified in considering Boulogne-sur-Mer as intimately connected with the subject of this book, and I have accordingly included it in my list of Sanctuaries.

§ 4—SERJEANTS-AT-LAW.

A visit to the chapel of our Ladye of Pewe at Westminster formed one of the ceremonies of the creation of Serjeants-at-law, which occupied several days.[68] They are fully set out by Dugdale in his *Origines Juridicales.*

§ 5.—AUTHORS AND PRINTERS.

> *Omni die*
> *Dic Mariæ*
> *Mea, laudes, anima.*
> *Ejus festa,*
> *Ejus gesta,*
> *Cole devotissima.*

Hymn of the Anglo-Saxons (not of St. Casimir) to our Blessed Ladye.

> *Pone scribentium tot esse millia*
> *quot habent nemora frondes et folia,*
> *quot cæli sidera et guttas maria,*
> *indigne Virginis scribent præconia.*

Walter Map or Mapes.[69]

I haue none English conuenient and digne
Mine hearts Hele Ladie thee with to honour.

Chaucer.[70]

Oceleve, the disciple of Chaucer, gives his master the title of Servaunt of Maiden Marie.

> As thou wel knowest, O Blissid Virgyne,
> With louyng hert and hye deuocion
> In thyne honour he wroot ful many a lyne ;
> O now thine help and thy promocion
> To God thi Son make amocion
> How he thi seruaunt was, Mayden Marie,
> And let his loue floure and fructifie.[71]

[68] S. pp. 238, 239.

[69] *Latin Poems,* Camden Soc. pp. 191, 192. 1841. Cf. Peter Comestor, who gives the same ideas in all but the same words ; Cf. also, Lilja or Lilium, an Icelandic poem in honour of our Ladye, by Eystein Asgrimsson, c. A.D. 1350. Copenhagen; 1858, stanzas 93, 94, 95. An excellent translation has been made by Eiríkr Magnússon, M.A., and published in 1870 by Williams and Norgate, Henrietta Street, Covent Garden.

[70] *A Balade of our Ladie,* Opp. edit. cit. f. 329 b.

[71] Works, *MS. Harl.* 4866, f. 91.

There are several passages in Chaucer's poems, which are
eagerly seized by the enemies of the faith of Christ,[72] who
strive to judge of the state of religion in England in the fourteenth century by what he says, and by what appears in the
visions of Piers Ploughman, by John Longland. Perhaps this
is the reason why these authors are so popular with certain
classes.

But no less an authority than Mr. Thomas Wright, M.A.,
has shown that the Ploughman's tale, which is the most objectionable, is not the composition of Chaucer.[73] Of his sentiments
about our Blessed Ladye it is impossible for any of his readers
to entertain a doubt.

Old authors were fond of addressing our Blessed Ladye, and
of invoking her aid and assistance.

Ne scribam vanum, duc pia Virgo manum

was a common aspiration in former days.[74]

These lines appear at the end of the poems of Sedulius:

Finem carmen habet, nec lauri serta requiro;
Tu studii merces esto, Maria, mei.[75]

The author or transcriber of a book for the health of the
soul would ask an *Ave* from the reader. Thus the Ancren
Riwle concludes: "Ase oft ase ȝe readeð out o þisse boc
greteð þe lefði mid one *Ave Marie*, for him þet maked þeos
riwle, and for him þet hire wrot and swonc her abuten. Inouh
meðful ich am þet bidde so lutel"—"As often as ye read
anything in this book greet the Ladye with an *Ave Maria* for
him who made this Rule, and for him who wrote it and took
pains about it. Moderate enough am I, who ask so little." [76]

The author of the Saga of St. Thomas of Canterbury exclaims
in his prologue:

May Jesus Christ now grant by the intercession of His
Sweet Mother and Maiden Marye—sinnar sætu moþur ok
meyjar Marie—and by the merits of Holy Thomas, that this

[72] *e.g.* See *English Gilds*, note 1. p. lxxxvii. Early Eng. Text Soc. 1870, appended to Dr. Brentano's *Essay on the Hist. of Gilds.*
[73] *Political Poems and Songs relating to English History from the beginning of the reign of Edward III. to that of Richard III.* vol. ii. pp. 304—348. Rolls Edit.
[74] *Gautier. Prières à la S. Vierge d'après les Manuscripts,* p. 504. Paris, 1873.
[75] *Patrolog. Lat.* Edit. Migne. t. xix. col. 764.
[76] Pp. 430, 431.

work so begin, continue and end, that it be to the praise and
glory of Him, but for spiritual joy to those who hearken thereto,
and be worthy of the intercession of Blessed Thomas." [77]

Chaucer thus invokes our Ladye :   -

> My conning is to weake, O blisfull Quene,
> For to declare thy high worthinesse,
> That I ne may the weight sustene
> But as a child of twelve moneth old or lesse
> That can vnnethes ane word expresse
> 'Right so fare I, and therfore I you pray
> Gideth my song, that I shall of you say. [78]

In another poem he says :

> And thou that art floure of virgins all
> Of whom that Bernard list so well to write. [79]

And in his "Balade in commendation of our Ladye" he
implores her to assist him in the singing of her praises. [80]

Herodotus named the nine books of his History after the
Muses ; Robert Fabian, citizen of London, inscribed the seven
books of his Chronicles to the Seven Joys of our Blessed Ladye.
He commences by addressing our Blessed Ladye, and invoking
her assistance :

> Moste Blyssyd Ladye, comforte to such as calle
> To the for helpe in eche necessyte
> And what thou aydest may in no wyse apale
> But to ye beste is formyd in ylke degre
> Wherfore Good Ladye I praie it maie please the
> At my begynnynge, my penne so to lede
> That by thyne aid my werke may have goode spede. [81]

He concludes the first book in these words :

And in the way of a thanke to be gyven to our most blessyd
Aduocat and helper of al wretchys that to her lyste to call,
I mean that moste blessyd virgyne our Lady saynt Mary moder
of criste: For that of her grace hath fortheryd this werke
hytherto.   And for to Impetre[9] of her ye grace and ayde of her
moste mercyfull contyneance to accomplisshe this werke begon

[77] *Thómas Saga Erkibyskups*, p. 5.   Rolls Edit.
[78] The Prioresses' Prologue, Opp. ed. cit. f. 68 b.
[79] The Second Nonnes' Prologue, Opp. ed. cit. ff. 54, 54 b.
[80] Opp. ff. 329, 330 b.
[81] *The New Chronicles of England and France.*   Reprint from Pynson's edit. of
1516.   Lond. 1811 *in principio.*

as before is shewed, vnder supporte of her moste bountéous grace; here wyll I wt humble mynde salute her with the firste ioye of the VII Ioyes whiche begynne

Gaude Flore Virginali, &c.[81]

It has been well said that "if the ancient religious poetry of England should ever find an editor, readers who are accustomed to suppose that intelligible English dates from the time of Spenser, would be amazed at the power and pathos possessed by earlier writers. When we examine such poetical fragments as are yet preserved, the wonder perhaps ceases that they should have found small favour from modern editors. For the most part they are devoted to celebrate the glories of the Blessed Virgin, or the Mysteries of the Passion. The first subject has, of course, no chance of indulgence from a Protestant public, and the second is hardly more popular, when treated precisely in the same spirit as it is presented to us in the prayers of St. Bridget, or the devout productions of ancient Catholic art. To Catholics, however, it is a joy and a solace to look back into past centuries, and remember that these were days when our poets drank of a purer fount than that of Castaly; and made it their pride to celebrate in their verse, not Dian, nor Proserpine, but the Immaculate Queen of Heaven."[83] During the ten years that have elapsed since the work from which this passage is taken was written, the Early English Text Society have reproduced many old Catholic poems and documents of the highest interest.

Our Anglo-Saxon poets found in the praises of our Blessed Ladye an inexhaustible theme of song. In their metrical compositions they employed both Latin and their own language. Amongst the Latin effusions may be named the verses of St. Ealdhelm, and the smaller poems of Alcwine.[84]

Out of the vast array of poems in honour and in praise of our Ladye, I have selected a few by way of illustration.

The Collection of Anglo-Saxon poems, known as the *Codex*

---

[81] *The New Chronicles of England and France*, p. 19.
[83] *Christian Schools and Scholars.* Lond. 1867, vol. ii. p. 271.
[84] Cf. Opp. t. ii. col. 724. Edit. Migne.

Exoniensis,[85] contains much in praise of our Ladye. The poet addresses her—

> O Delight of women,
> Throughout the host of glory
> Damsel most noble
> Over all earth's region.[86]

He then commemorates her spotless virginity—

> Now thou the Glory of Majesty
> In thy bosom barest,
> and was not injured
> thy pure virginity : [87]

and calls her

> . . . the Blessed Maiden
> ever of triumph full,
> Holy Marye.[88]

In another poem on the Nativity of our Lord the poet apostrophizes our Blessed Ladye—

> O thou Marye
> of this mid-world
> the purest
> woman upon earth
> of those who have been
> throughout all ages :
> how thee with right
> all with speech endow'd
> name and say,
> men over earth,
> blithe of mood,
> that thou art Bride
> of the Most Excellent
> Lord of Heaven :

After referring to Isaias, the poet concludes—

> At least this beseech we
> dwellers upon earth,
> that thou the Comfort
> make known to people,
> thine own Son,
> that we may afterwards
> with one accord
> all exult.
> Now we before that Child
> gaze in our thoughts :
> intercede for us now
> with bold words
> that He let us not
> any longer,
> in this vale of death,
> error obey,
> but that He us convey
> into His Father's Kingdom,
> where we sorrowless,
> may after
> dwell in glory
> with the Lord of Hosts.[89]

[85] This MS. was one of the many given to the Library of his Cathedral by Leofric, the first Bishop of Exeter, under whom the see was transferred to that city from Crediton, of which he was the last bishop, in 1046. It is a moderate sized folio, in a fair and rather fine hand of the tenth century.

[86] *Ibid.* p. 5.

[87] *Ibid.* p. 6.

[88] *Ibid.* p. 8. .

[89] *Ibid.* p. 21.

One peculiar feature of Anglo-Saxon poetry was the occasional intermingling of Latin with the vernacular; and an
instance is given where five Greek terms are also interwoven.[60]

A "Song to our Ladye" of the thirteenth century shows a
similar combination of Latin with the English.

> Of all that is so fayr and brijt,
>   *velut maris stella.*
> Brijter than the day is lijt
>   *parens et puella.*
> Ic crie to the, thou se to me.
> Leuedy preye thy sone for me,
>   *tam pia*
> That ic mote come to the
>   *maria.*
>
> Of kare conseil thou ert best
>   *Felix fecundata,*
> Of alle wery thou ert rest
>   *mater honorata.*
> Bi-sek him wij milde mod,
> That for ous alle sad is blod,
>   *in cruce*
> That we moten komen til him
>   *in luce.*
>
> Alle this world was for-lore
>   *eua peccatrice*
> Tyl our lord was y-bore
>   *de te genitrice.*
> With aue it went a-way,
> Thuster nyth and comet the day
>   *salutis*
> The welle springet hut of the
>   *virtutis.*
>
> Leuedi flour of alle thing
>   *rosa sine spina*
> Thu bere ihesu heuene King
>   *gratia divina.*
> Of alle thu berst the pris
> Leuedi quene of paradys
>   *electa*
> Mayde milde, Moder
>   *es effecta.*
>
> Wel he wot he is thy sone
>   *ventre quem portasti*
> He wyl nout werne the thi bone
>   *parvum quem lactasti.*

[60] Sharon Turner, *Hist. of the Anglo-Saxons*, vol. iii. p. 201.

> So hende and so god be his
> He havet brout ous to blis
> *superni*
> That have; hi-dut the foule put
> *inferni*.[91]

These are a few lines of the address to our Ladye which Chaucer places in the mouth of the prioresse—

> Mother maiden O maiden & mother free
> O bush unbrent, brennyng in Moyses sight,
> That rauishedest downe fro the deite
> Through thin hüblesse the gost yt in the light
> Of whose vertue, whe in thine hart pight
> Conceived was the father's sapience
> Helpe me to tell it in thy presence.[92]

Several Latin hymns to our Blessed Ladye were composed in England.

The *Ave Maris Stella* is generally attributed to St. Bernard,[93] who died in the year 1153; but it must be ascribed to an earlier author, since it was known to the Anglo-Saxons, for it appears amongst the hymns of the Anglo-Saxon Church, with an interlinear Anglo-Saxon gloss, in an *Hymnale* dating probably a little later than the Norman invasion,[94] published in 1851, by the Surtees Society.

I claim for an Anglo-Saxon the authorship of the well-known hymn *Omni die dic Mariæ*, which is generally ascribed to St. Casimir, and which is usually called the hymn of St. Casimir.

Pez has already noticed that the Chartreuse of Jumiéges possessed a codex of a date anterior to St. Casimir, which contained this hymn; others attribute the authorship to Conrad, Prior of the House of the Throne of our Ladye at Jumiéges.[95] But in the British Museum there is a late eleventh century Psalter, written by an Anglo-Saxon scribe, somewhere, as it would seem, in the Province of York, shortly after the reign of St. Edward the Confessor. This is the opinion of the late Dr. Rock, to whom it formerly belonged, and it is fully con-

---

[91] *Egerton MSS.* 613, f. 2. Early Eng. Text Soc. vol. 49, 1872, pp. 194, 195.

[92] *The Prioress's Prologue.* Opp. ed. cit. f. 68.

[93] Greg. Valentianus, *Hymnodia SS. Patrum.* Genuæ, 1660, p. 369.

[94] Vol. xxiii. pp. 76, 77 and Pref. p. viii. Bonsi and Signoretti attribute it to Venantius Fortunatus. See Reithmeier, *Flores Patrum Latinorum et Hymni ecclesiastici.* Scaphusiæ, 1853, p. 374.

[95] *Thesaurus Anecdotum.* 1721, vol. I. f. xvi. præf.

firmed by Mr. Bond, the learned keeper of our national MSS. In this Psalter the hymn is given after the Psalm *Domine ne in furore tuo,*[96] and it is in the same handwriting, consequently it must have been known in England some centuries before St. Casimir flourished. Certain however it is that St. Casimir used to recite it daily; and a copy of it was found in his tomb, when it was opened for reparations in 1604. His body was incorrupt, and the hymn was lying under his right hand.[97] The Bollandists give it; and it will be seen that the version in the York Psalter runs word for word with it.

Hymn in York Psalter, c. A.D. 1070.	*Hymn found in St. Casimir's tomb,* 1604.
Omni die dic Mariae	Omni die dic Mariæ
Mea laudes anima	Mea laudes anima
Ejus festa, ejus gesta	Ejus festa, ejus gesta
Cole splendidissima.	Cole splendidissima.[98]
Contemplare et mirare	Contemplare et mirare
Ejus celsitudinem,	Ejus celsitudinem,
Dic felicem genitricem,	Dic felicem Genitricem,[99]
Dic beatam Virginem. &c.	Dic beatam Virginem. &c.

St. Simon Stock composed the *Flos Carmeli*,[100] and to him is also attributed the authorship of the hymn *Ave Mundi Medicina*.[101] Some of the Latin poems of Robert Grostete were translated into English by William de Shoreham, Vicar of Sutton, county Kent, in the time of Edward II. Of one of these translations I give four stanzas, 1, 2, 3, and 14.

> Mary, mayde, mylde and fre,
> Chambre of the Trinité,
> One wyle lest to me
>   As ich the grete wyth songe ;
> Thaȝ my fet onclene be,
> My mes thou onder-fonge.

---

[96] *Additional MS.* 21927, f. 39 b. See also *Church of our Fathers*, vol. iii. p. 5. The hymn as given in this MS. ends with the line, *Clemens audi tue laudi quos instanter aspicis*, and it is immediately followed by the next psalm. The whole codex is in the same handwriting, consequently there are no grounds for supposing that the hymn might have been inserted at a later date.

[97] *Act SS.* t. i. Martii, p. 341.

[98] This word is generally omitted in the printed versions, and replaced by *devotissima.*

[99] *Act SS.* t. i. Mart. p. 355. Edit. Palmé.

[100] S. p. 106.

[101] *Menologium Carmelitanum.* Bononiæ, 1628, p. 292.

Thou art quéne of paradys,
Of hevene, of erthe, of al that hys ;
Thou bere thane kynge of blys,
 Wythoute senne and sore ;
Thou hast y-ryȝt that was a-mys
 Y-wonne that was y-lore.

Thou ert the colvere of Noe
That broute the braunche of olyve-tre,
In token that pays scholde be
 By-tuexte God and manne ;
Swete levedy, help thou me,
 When ich schal wende hanne.

Have, levedy, thys lytcl songe,
That out of senfol herte spronge,
Aȝens the feend thou make me stronge,
 And yȝt me thy wyssynge ;
And thaȝ ich habbe y-do the wrange,
 Thou graunte me amendynge.[102]

This beautiful hymn to our Blessed Ladye is exceedingly
valuable and instructive, and with the spelling modernized it
might most advantageously take a place in the Catholic hymn-
books, and be taught to our school children, who are already
familiar with the *Omni die dic Mariæ,* or, "Daily daily
sing to Marye." And I hope this latter one will hereafter
be described by its proper name, "A hymn of the Anglo-
Saxons to our Blessed Ladye," and no longer as the hymn of
St. Casimir.

I have already exceeded my limits; but the poetry and
hymnology of Ireland claim to be mentioned.

Towards the close of the sixth century St. Cuchumneus, a
contemporary of Adamnan, composed a Latin hymn of great
length in honour of our Blessed Ladye, which soon became
celebrated, and had a place assigned to it amongst the hymns of
the Irish Church.

Cantemus in omni die
 Concinnantes varie,
Conclamantes Deo dignum
 Hymnum Sanctæ Mariæ
.Bis per chorum hic et inde
 Collaudamus Mariam,

. [102] The Religious Poems of William de Shoreham, Vicar of Chart, Sutton. Edited
by Thomas Wright, M.A., F.S.A. Percy Society, n. lxxx. November, 1849.

Ut vox pulset omnem aurem
Per laudem vicariam.[103]

Prior, however, to St. Cuchumneus flourished Cœlius Sedulius, whose reputation was widely spread abroad. In his *Carmen Paschale* he dwells on the special dignities and privileges of the Blessed Mother of God.

Et velut e spinis mollis rosa surgit acutis,
Nil quod lædat habens, matremque obscurat honore ;
Sic Evæ de stirpe sacra veniente Maria
Virginis antiquæ ut facinus nova virgo piaret ;
Ut quoniam natura prior vitiata jacebat
Sub ditione necis, Christo nascente, renasci
Possit homo, et veteris maculam deponere carnis.

Salve Sancta Parens, enixa puerpera Regem,
Qui cælum terramque tenet per sæcula,[104] cujus
Numen et æterno complectens omnia gyro,
Imperium sine fine manet ; quæ ventre beato
Gaudia matris habens cum virginitatis honore,
Nec primam similem visa es, nec habere sequentem.
Sola sine exemplo placuisti fœmina Christo.[105]

There is an old Irish hymn to our Blessed Ladye entitled, "The Protecting Corselet of Marye," which is attributed to the eleventh century. It consists of twenty-four stanzas, of which I give the two first.

Direct me how to praise thee,
Though I am not a Master of Poetry.
O thou of the angelic countenance without fault,
Thou hast given the milk of thy breast to save me.

I offer myself under thy protection,
O loving Mother of the Only Son,
And under thy protecting shield I place my body,
My heart, my will, and my understanding.[106]

Several of the poems which I have just cited were evidently intended to be sung. St. Ealdhelm, Bishop of the West Saxons,

[103] Given by the Right Rev. Dr. Moran,.Lord Bishop of Ossory. *Essays on the Early Irish Church*, Dublin, 1864, pp. 25, 27. Mone has also printed it, and has given several variations from various MSS. *Hymni Latini Medii Ævi*, Friburgi Brisgoviæ, 1854, t. xi. n. 572, pp. 383—386.

[104] This is the earliest occurrence of this couplet now so well known, amd incorporated with the Introit of Our Ladye's Mass.

[105] Lib ii. col. 595-596, 599-600, lines 28-34, 63-69. *Patrol. Lat.* t. xix. Edit. Migne.

[106] *Irish Ecclesiastical Record*, vol. vi. n. lxvii. April, 1870.

who died in 709, speaks of rhymed verse, and even his prose praises of our Ladye, seem as if meant to rhyme. Here is a specimen, which I have divided into lines.

Beata Maria	*Ac felix vernacula.*
Virgo perpetua;	*Sanctarum socrus animarum*
Hortus conclusus	*Supernorum regina civium.*
Fons signatus	
Virgula radicis	. . .
Gerula floris	*Obsidem sæculi,*
Aurora solis	*Monarcham mundi;*
Nurus patris	*Rectorem poli;*
Genitrix et Germana	*Redemptorem soli;*
Filii, simulque sponsa.	*Archangelo præmonstrante*
	Paracleto adumbrante.[107]

And Girald de Barri, surnamed Cambrensis from the country of his birth, who flourished in the latter half of the twelfth century, says that the English and Welsh are so subtle in their songs, rhymes, and set speeches, that they produce in their mother tongue ornaments of wonderful and exquisite invention, in their words and in their sentences.[108] This shows the perfection which the Anglo-Saxon gleemen and the Cambrian bards had already attained prior to the times of Girald.

[107] *De laudibus Virginitatis.*

[108] *In cantilenis rythmicis et dictamine.* In addition to the fifteen contemporary witnesses who have left evidence that Thomas à Kempis was the author of the *Imitation of Christ;* another, Adrian de But, describes him as having written it *metrice,* as Dr. Hirsch has demonstrated so clearly. This important witness was unknown until recently. The chronicle of Adrian de But commences with the year 1431, and ends with 1488, the year of his death. Under the year 1480 it says, *Hoc anno frater Thomas de Kempis, de Monte Sanctæ Agnetis, professor ordinis regularium canonicorum, multos scriptis suis ædificat; hic vitam sanctæ Lidwigis descripsit et quoddam volumen metrice super illud: Qui sequitur me.* (*Chroniques relatives à l'Histoire de la Belgique sous la Domination des Ducs de Bourgogne,* publiées par M. le Baron Kervyn de Lettenhove, Membre de la Commission Royale d'Histoire. Bruxelles, 1870, t. i. p. 547). One of the quaintest conceits in verse ever written about our Blessed Ladye was by the celebrated Eric Puteanus, or Du Puy, a disciple of Justus Lipsius. He took from the poems of Father B. Bahusius, or Bauhius, S.J., the following line:

Tot tibi sunt Dotes, Virgo, quot sidera cælo,

and produced 1,022 variations of it without changing its measure. About this time there seem to have been so many stars calculated. These lines were elegantly printed in small folio. Subsequently Father James Bernouille, S.J., showed this verse to be capable of 40,320 variations, but without preserving its measure, and Father Prestet, S.J.—they were both celebrated mathematicians—that it admitted of 3,776 variations still preserving the measure. See Erici Puteani Thaumata in Bern. Bahusii, S.J. Proteum Parthenicum unius libri versum unius versi librum sive formis MXXII. variatum. Antv. ex Off. Plantin, 1617. I have a copy of this rare book. See also De Backer, *Ecrivains de la Comp. de Jesus,* 2d Edit. sub nomm.

St. Godric's hymn is, I believe, yet sung in the north of England, but I do not know the exact form in which it is now repeated. Few, however, I ween, of those who sing it are aware that their favourite song is believed to have been taught to St. Godric by our Blessed Ladye herself. These are the words of it as recorded by Roger of Wendover.

> Seinte Maria clane vergine,
> Moder Jesu Christ Nazarene,
> Onfo, schild, help thin Go(d)rich,
> Onfang, bring heali widh the in Godes rich.
> Seinte Marie, Christes bour,
> Meidenes clenhed, Moderes flour
> Delivere mine sennen, regne in min mod,
> Bring me to blisse wit thi selfe God.[109]

One of the most popular carols of the present day is that of the "Seven Good Joys of Our Blessed Ladye," which for a very long time past has been annually reprinted by the printers of carol-sheets throughout the entire length and breadth of the land. Those printed at Newcastle extend them from seven to twelve joys.[110]

It is a pity that the street music of the present day is not under the wholesome regulation of which Alban Butler speaks, saying, " I have had in my possession an original MS. ordinance of John Talbot, Earl of Shrewsbury (who fell at Northampton in 1460), in which, by an act which is called perpetual, he commands that every musician who shall play on any instrument within the limits of his county of Salop, shall pay a small sum to a certain chapel of our Ladye, under pain of forfeiting their instruments, with other ordinances of a like nature."[111]

John Bedell, or Bydell, appears to have sold books in the year 1535, if not before ; probably he was an apprentice to Wynkyn de Worde. He first kept his shop at the sign of Our Ladye of Pitie, next to Fleet Bridge.[112] John Redman in Paternoster Row also adopted the same sign.[113]

---

[109] *Flores Historiarum*, t. xi. p. 348. Edit. Coxe. London, 1841.

[110] *Songs of the Nativity :* being Christmas Carols, ancient and modern. Edited by W. H. Husk. London, J. Camden Hotten, S.A. pp. 87—90.

[111] *Lives of the Saints.* Dublin, 1870, vol. x. p. 284, note.

[112] Ames, *Typographical Antiquities.* Edited by Herbert. London, 1785, vol. i, p. 482.

[113] Cf. *History of Sign Boards from the earliest Times to the present day.* By Jacob Larwood and John Camden Hotten. London, 1876, p. 272.

Pynson's mark or device was the monogram of our Blessed Ladye.[90]

In an old edition of the *Vitæ Patrum*, translated by Caxton, was written, "Of your charitie praye," &c.

> Moder of merci shyld him from thorrībul fynd,
> And bryng hym to lyff eternall that neuyr hath ynd.[91]

The York Manuale printed by Wynkyn de Worde in the year 1509 begins, *Ad laudem Dei et honorem, tuamque non immerito, flos Virgo Maria, ecce manuale,"* &c.

§ 6.—INNHOLDERS.

It is easy to trace old Catholic signs in many of the modern names of inns and hotels. Thus there is the Angel, which is of frequent occurrence; and the Salutation, which is represented by two persons in the act of shaking hands; yet both these signs are the remains of the Catholic representation of the Annunciation. The Virgin is to be found in several places, and was intended for the Blessed Virgin, in the ages of Faith. "Newe Inne," says Stow, "was a gueste Inne, the sign whereof was the picture of our Ladye, and thereupon it was called our Ladye's Inne."[92]

---

[90] Fosbroke, *Encyclopædia of Antiquities.* London, 1843, p. 501.
[91] Parr-Gresswell, *Annals of the Parisian Press*, p. 92.
[92] *History of Sign Boards*, p. 272.

f

PART THE SECOND.

Forms of Homage.

CHAPTER THE FIRST.

Shrines.

§ 1.—CHURCHES. ORGANS AND BELLS. WAX IMAGES.

And King David said to the assembly. . . . The work is great, for a house is prepared not for man but for God. And I with all my ability have prepared the expenses for the house of my God. Gold for vessels of gold, and silver for vessels of silver, brass for things of brass, iron for things of iron, wood for things of wood; and onyx stones, and stones like alabaster, and of divers colours, and all manner of precious stones, and marble of Paros in great abundance.

1 Paral. xxix. 1, 2.

CHURCHES.

THE Church of Sancta Maria *Trans Tiberim,* or Santa Maria in Trastevere, is the earliest one in Rome which was dedicated to God in honour of the Blessed Virgin Marye. It was built on the spot where formerly stood the Taberna Meritoria, and consecrated by St. Calixtus the First in the year 224.[1]

Glastonbury is the most ancient and venerable sanctuary of our Ladye in England. According to tradition it was originally a little oratory built of wreathed twigs, and erected by St. Joseph of Arimathea,[2] who also carved an image of our Ladye.[3] Two centuries later it was rebuilt of stone; and in the year 530, St. David added a Ladye Chapel.[4] In 708 Ine of the West

---

[1] Baronius, ad ann. 224, n. 5. For history of this church, and many authorities cited, see Gaume, *Les Trois Rome.* Paris, 1864, vol. ii. pp. 201—207.
[2] S. p. 43.
[3] S. p. 280.
[4] S. p. 44.

Saxons reconstructed the abbey and the church, and also built the " Silver Chapel " as it was called from its richness.[5]

There is a tradition that the old church at Glastonbury was consecrated by our Lord Himself in honour of His Blessed Mother; and this is mentioned in the charter of Ine, and also in that of Henry the Second,[6] so that this pious belief has existed for many centuries. It is unnecessary for me to recapitulate the various evidences in regard of the early foundation of Glastonbury: the arguments on both sides are set out in the *Dublin Review*.[7] It is admitted that Glastonbury was the earliest Christian Church in England, and that it was dedicated to God in honour of His Blessed Mother; consequently devotion to our Blessed Ladye is coeval with the introduction of Christianity into England. Therefore, also, the foundation of Glastonbury in England in honour of our Ladye is anterior to that of Santa Maria in Trastevere in Rome.

In 607, in the eleventh year after he had been sent into England by St. Gregory the Great, St. Augustine built a church in honour of our Blessed Ladye, on a spot called Cratundene, in the island of Ely.[8]

A few years later, King Æthelwald, whose father, King Æthelberht had been converted by St. Augustine, built the church of the Holy Mother of God at Canterbury, in which he was buried in 640. It was consecrated by St. Mellitus.[9] This church was subsequently called the *Sacrarium* or *Vestiarium* of our Ladye.[10]

St. Bennet Biscop built a church in honour of our Ladye in St. Peter's Monastery, Weremouth.[11]

---

[5] Gaume, p. 46.

[6] A portion of this charter I have already quoted (S. pp. 47, 48); but after enumerating the kings who were benefactors, it says: *Quorum privilegia et chartas feci diligenter inquiri et coram me presentari et legi, confirmata sunt prædictæ ecclesiæ, qua olim a quibusdam Mater Sanctorum dicta est, ab aliis Tumulus Sanctorum, quam ab ipsis discipulis Domini ædificatam, et ab ipso Domino dedicatam primo fuisse, venerabilis habet antiquorum auctoritas* (Wilkins, *Concilia*, tom. I. p. 489).

[7] New Series, n. xxi. pp. 85, seq.

[8] *Anglia Sacra*, tom. i. p. 594. *Acta SS.* tom. vi. Maii, ad diem 26, p. 371. Edit. Palmé. Giles puts the death of St. Augustine in 605, but the Bollandists prove that it took place in 608.

[9] Bede, *Hist. Eccl.* lib. ii. cap. vi. Opp. vol. ii. p. 194. Edit. Giles.

[10] S. p. 7.

[11] Bede, *De Vitis BB. Abbatum.* Opp. tom. iv. p. 375. Edit. cit. Venerable Bede uses the word *ecclesia*.

Another church in honour of our Ladye was erected at Lestingau, now Lastingham, near Whitby;[12] and in the year 675 Cyssa built a church in our Ladye's honour at Abingdon.[13]

The round church of our Ladye at Hexham, built by St. Wuilfrid of York, which Aelred describes as having four porticoes looking towards the four quarters of the earth,[14] deserves more than a passing mention. He ascribes the work to St. Wuilfrid only, but Richard, Prior of Hexham and a contemporary of Aelred, says that the Saint began it, and that it was finished by Acca.[15]

In 705, on his return from Rome for the last time, St. Wuilfrid had a sudden seizure at Meaux, and lay motionless and almost lifeless for four nights and days. All at once his speech returned to him, and calling for Acca, he described to him the wonderful vision which had been vouchsafed to him. The Archangel Michael had stood before him in the early morning, beaming with celestial light, and the bearer of a message from Heaven. He revealed to the Saint that the Blessed Virgin Mother of God had interceded in his behalf, and that four years had been added to his life on earth. "Go home," said the Archangel, "and erect a church in her honour who has won for thee thy life. Andrew has one already, let not Marye be forgotten."[16] Prior Richard adds that this church was destroyed by the Danes, but restored by a priest of the place. Its remains lie at the south-east corner of the chancel of the priory.[17]

I must say a very few words on the churches of our Anglo-Saxon forefathers, which even a well-informed writer describes as "the comparatively rude structures of the seventh century." I presume he speaks from an architectural point of view: but if the Anglo-Saxon churches, as structures, were rude, they were not ruder than those erected at Rome and elsewhere.

It should be borne in mind that from the time of the second conversion of England, the great tide of pilgrims to the *Limina*

---

[12] Bede, *Hist. Eccl.* cap. xxiii. Opp. tom. ii. p. 357. Edit. cit.

[13] S. p. i.

[14] *De Sanctis Ecclesiæ Hagustaldensis, et eorum miraculis libellus* (auctore Aelredo Abbate Rie-vallensi), cap. v. p. 183. Surtees Society, vol. xliv. 1863.

[15] *History of the Church of Hexham*, p. 15, vol. xliv. Surtees Society.

[16] Eddi, *Vita S. Wilfridi, episc. Ebor*, apud Gale, *Hist. Brit.* etc, *Scriptores* xv. Oxonii, 1691, tom. i. cap. liv. p. 83.

[17] *History of the Church of Hexham*, pp. 14, 15, notes.

Apostolorum set in, and this was not transitory, but incessant: and this constant intimacy with Rome led at once to the introduction of Roman plans and designs into this country. I am not aware that the *Basiliche,* or what remains of them at Rome, are considered as "comparatively rude structures;" Anastasius bears evidence to the immense wealth which began to be expended upon the churches in Rome as soon as the persecutions ceased, and to the magnificence of their decoration, and the richness of their altars and sacred furniture; and one of the greatest ecclesiastical attractions to the Christian architect and archæologist is the most interesting Basilica of St. Clement, and the discoveries which have been made by its worthy Prior, Father Mulhooly, O.P.

It is quite certain that whatever St. Augustine built would have been in the fashion of Rome: therefore the church, already mentioned, which he built in honour of our Ladye at Cratundene may be safely pronounced to have been in the Roman style. St. Bennet Biscop went to Rome three times; and when building the Church of our Ladye at Weremouth, he sent for masons and glaziers from Gaul.[18] Of the minster which St. Wuilfrid built from his own designs at Hexham, Eddi, his biographer and contemporary, says that he had not heard of a church erected on this side of the Alps which was its equal,[19] and Eadmer describes it as *templum mirabili operc.*[20] Venerable Bede records that the church at Lincoln, which, after the conversion of that district, St. Paulinus built, was of stone.[21] And King Eadwine, who was baptized at York on Easter Sunday— the 12th of April—A.D. 627, in the little wooden chapel which had been erected in honour of St. Peter by St. Paulinus, as soon as he was baptized, desired the Saint to build a larger and more noble church (*basilica*) of stone, within which the wooden oratory in which he had received the faith of Christ was to be inclosed.[22]

The church which the Princess Bugga, daughter of King Eadwin, built was dedicated to the Nativity of our Ladye:

[18] *De Vitis BB. Abbatum,* p. 366. Opp. tom. iv. Edit. cit.
[19] *Ubi sup.*
[20] *Act SS.* ad diem 24 April. p. 302. Edit. Palmé.
[21] *Hist. Ecclesiast.* lib. ii. cap. xvi. Opp. vol. ii. p. 241. Edit. cit.
[22] *Ibid.* lib. ii., cap. xiv. Opp. tom. ii. p. 235.

Istam nempe diem, qua templi festa coruscant,
Nativitate sua sacravit Virgo Maria.[83]

And our Ladye's altar stood in the apse :

Absidem consecrat Virginis ara.[84]

David gave three thousand talents of gold of the gold of
Ophir, and seven thousand talents of refined silver to overlay
the walls of the Temple.[85] St. Gregory the Third, A.D. 730—740,
covered the beams, which were placed over the Confession of
St. Peter, with refined silver ;[86] but our Godgifu covered the
walls of our Ladye's Church at Coventry with a sheathing of
silver ; and the church which she and her pious husband built
at Evesham is described by the chronicler as one of the finest
churches in England.[87] No wonder, therefore, that she is
recorded as having denuded herself of all that she possessed.[88]
I do not hesitate to express my conviction that in splendour
and decoration, and in richness of church-plate, altars, and
vestments our Anglo-Saxon churches were pre-eminent.

In Ireland foundations in honour of our Ladye are coeval
with St. Patrick. According to Colgan, the Abbey of Canons
Regular at Trim was founded by St. Patrick himself in the year
432, and built on a piece of ground given for that purpose by
Fethlemid, the son of Leoghaire and grandson of Niall, and
dedicated to our Blessed Ladye.[89] Wilde is of opinion that the
original abbey which was dedicated to our Ladye stood, in all
probability, upon the picturesque site of the Yellow Tower,
which, in after ages, was erected here, and is stated to be the
most lofty remnant of Norman architecture now existing in
Ireland.[90]

Under the heading of Clonfert, Archdall records that St.
Brendan the son of Findloga was a disciple of St. Finian in

---

[83] *Carmen ad Templum Buggæ*, by St. Ealdhelm, given inter Opp. Alcuini,
tom. ii. col. 1311.

[84] *Ibid.* col. 1310.

[85] 1 Paralip. xxix. 4.

[86] Anastasius Bibliothecarius. In vitâ, opp. tom. ii. Edit. Migne.

[87] S. p. 36.

[88] S. p. 21.

[89] Butler, *Trim Castle*, p. 181, quoted by Gaffney, *Ancient Irish Church*,
Dublin, 1863, p. 70.

[90] *The Boyne and Blackwater*, p. 83.

the Academy of Clonard, and that in A.D. 553 or 562 he founded an abbey here under the invocation of our Ladye.[81]

Moreover, Wilde records of Kells, Co. Meath, that Dermod the son of Fergus Kervail made a grant of this place to St. Columban, who founded a monastery here about the year 550 and dedicated it to our Ladye.[82] Here then are three instances of dedications to our Blessed Ladye, the earliest by St. Patrick, and the third not later than the middle of the fifth century; and these prove that in Ireland, as well as in England, devotion to our Ladye was coeval with Christianity.

ORGANS AND BELLS.

Many churches had a pair of organs which seem to have been used exclusively for the Marye Mass, and to have been called by our Ladye's name; thus, in the churchwarden's accounts of Ludlow there is an entry of the year 1543, "payed for a corde to our Ladye organs, 1d."[83] Formerly organs were invariably described as a pair of organs.

Some of the Ladye Altars were provided with what John Baret of St. Edmund's Bury describes as the "chymes of bells," which were rung at the sakering of the Mass. These chimes consisted of a number of small bells fixed to a wheel, which was attached to the wall, and whirled round at the proper times. At St. Edmund's Bury the wheel was set in motion by a "plomme of led," and John Baret left to the bearer of the pax brede longyng to Seynt Marie awter viiid. yerely, so that he take hede . . . to wynde vp the plomme of led as oft as nedith, and to do the chymes goo at ye sacry of the messe of Ihv, at the sacry of Seynt Marie Masse on the Sunday.[84] This was an Anglo-Saxon custom. Bishop Æthelwald, the friend of St. Dunstan, made a wheel full of small bells for Abingdon, which from their being gilt was called the golden wheel, and was to be rung on feast days to excite greater devotion.[85]

[81] *Monasticon Hibernicum*, p. 278.
[82] *The Boyne and Blackwater*, p. 144.
[83] Published by the Camden Society.
[84] S. p. 135.
[85] "Præterea fecit vir venerabilis Æthelwoldus quandam Rotam tintinnabulis plenam, quam auream nuncupavit, propter laminas ipsius deauratas quam in festivis diebus ad majoris excitationem devotionis reducendo volvi constituit" (*Mon. Angl.* t. i. p. 516). A wheel of bells of the fifteenth century at Gerona, in Spain, is figured by Lübke (*Ecclesiastical Art in Germany during the Middle Ages*. Lond. 1870, p. 152).

In 1840 I saw a similar wheel of bells at Mugnano, near Naples, which was usually whirled round before the shrine of St. Philomena was uncovered.

The large bells used for the service of the Church are baptized, and anointed with the holy oil, a godmother is given to each bell, and also the name. The ceremony is a most impressive one, as those who have assisted at it can well testify. Many bells were named after our Blessed Ladye. Thus the two great bells which were put up at Evesham by Abbot Adam, A.D. 1160—1191, were called Jesus and Gloriosa, and those cast by order of Abbot Boys for the same abbey, A.D. 1345—1367, were named Maria and Egwyn. Maria bore the inscription :

> *Me sonante, pia succurre Virgo Maria,*
> *Ecclesie genti discedant fulgura, venti.*
> > MARIA.[56]

At the church of St. Marye in Coslany, Norwich, was a bell inscribed :

> *Virginis egregie vocor Campana Marie.*[57]

The same inscription was on a bell of St. Simon and St. Jude in the same city.[58] William, twenty-second Abbot of St. Albans, gave the great bell called St. Marye to the abbey.[59]

The Marye Bells were usually rung for the Marye Mass; and several other inscriptions are recorded by Lukis. Thus at Awliscombe a bell is inscribed

> + Protege memento pia quos. . . . Sancta Maria,[60]

evidently intended for

> + Protege mente pia quos convoco, Sancta Maria :

at Pulham, Dorset,

> + Sunt mea spes hi tres, Xps Maria Johes :[61]

at Dyrham, Gloucestershire,

> + Serva Campanam Sancta Maria sanam :[62]

[56] S. p. 38.
[57] S. p. 114.
[58] S. p. 116.
[59] S. p. 131.
[60] *An Account of Church Bells,* &c. By the Rev. W. C. Lukis, M.A., F.S.A. London and Oxford, 1857, p. 69.
[61] *Ibid.* p. 71.
[62] *Ibid.*

and in Gloucester Cathedral,

> ✠ Sum rosa pulsata mundi Maria vocata ;[43]

at Hexham,

> ✠ Est mea vox grata dum sim Mária vocata, A.D. mcccciiij ;[44]

in Oxford Cathedral,

> ✠ Stella Maria Maris succurre piissima nobis ;[45]

at East Bergholt, Suffolk,

> ✠ Sonans stella Maria maris campana vocitaris ;[46]

at Bedale, Yorks.,

> ✠ Iou ego cum fiam cruce custos laudo Mariam
> Digna dei laude, mater sanctissima gaude.[47]

and at Alkborough, Lincolnshire there is a bell in the church tower inscribed,

> ✠ Jesu: for: yi: modir: sake: saue: al: the: savls: that: me: gert: make: amen.[48]

Moreover, in many churches there was a bell which was rung for the devotion called the *Angelus*, in the form in which it was recited prior to the middle of the sixteenth century, and this bell was called the Gabriel Bell. Thus the third bell of St. Gregory's, Norwich, bore,

> ✠ Gabriel ave, hac in conclave nunc pange suave ;[49]

and at Weston, Suffolk,

> ✠ Missus vero pie Gabriel fert leta marie ;[50]

at Welford, Berks,

> ✠ Missi de celis habeo nomen Gabrielis.[51]

This latter was a very common inscription for the Gabriel bell.

---

[43] *An Account of Church Bells.*
[44] *Ibid.* p. 87.
[45] *Ibid.* p. 89. This bell is said to have come from Osney.
[46] *Ibid.* p. 97.
[47] *Ibid.* p. 132. This inscription is given *verbatim.*
[48] *Instructions for Parish Priests.* By John Myrk. Early English Text Society. Edited by Edward Peacock, F.S.A. P. 76, note.
[49] S. p. 111.
[50] S. p. 239.
[51] Lukis, p. 263.

At Misterton, Notts, the Gabriel bell is inscribed,

> ✠ Personet hec celis dulcissime vox Gabrielis ;[61]

and at King's Sutton, Northamptonshire,

> ✠ Ave Maria gracia plena, dominus tecum.[62]

Bishop Grandison required that the bell which rang in the College of St. Marye, Ottery, for the Marye Mass should also be tolled for the evening Ave.[63]

The plunder of the property of God at the Great Apostacy is associated with many disgraceful scenes. When Christ our Lord was crucified the brutal soldiers cast lots for His seamless garment. Henry the Eighth, King of England, and "Defender of the Faith," cast at dice with Sir Miles Partridge for the bells of St. Paul's Cathedral, London; and with that retributive justice which invariably follows sacrilege,

> . . . . Miles Partridge fell.
> This last was hanged (in Rope of Bell
> Perhaps), for he, as Heylin tells,
> Cast Dice with old King Hal for Bells,
> And by the sacrilegious Fling,
> Won Jesus' Bells, the finest Ring
> That ever England had before ;
> The Dev'lish throw no sooner o'er
> But Partridge goes and melts 'em down
> And sells the Mettle as his own.[64]

WAX IMAGES.

During the Middle Ages wax figures were often placed in churches. These images represented benefactors, or men of position, whose memories it was wished to perpetuate; they

---

[61] Lukis, p. 88.

[62] *Ibid.* p. 85.

[63] S. p. 117. Much interesting information on bells is to be found in the *Essai sur le symbolisme de la Cloche dans ses rapports et ses harmonies avec la Religion par un prêtre du clergé paroissial.* Poitiers. Oudin, lib. ed. Rue de l'éperon 4, 1859.

[64] Ward, *England's Reformation*, canto i. p. 100. London, 1719. I have often heard it said that the two fine bells of the Gesù in Rome had formerly belonged to St. Paul's, London. In the Revolution of 1848 they were taken by the scoundrels of the period, and melted down and cast into guns. The cannon burst at the first discharge, and a good lay-brother bought back the fragments of the burst guns, and when better times returned the metal was recast into bells, which were placed again in the Gesù.

were dressed as living persons, and they remained where they were put until they perished with age.[56]

They were sent as thank-offerings.

In 1439 Isabel, Countess of Warwick, leaves her great image of wax, now in London, to Our Ladye of Worcester.[57] And in 1443 Mrs. Paston writes to her husband, who was ill in London, to say that "My mother behested another image of wax, of the weight of you, to Our Ladye of Walsingham."[58]

I have already referred to the numerous wax images which were offered to our Ladye of Caversham.[59]

In the year 1423 it was enacted that wax chandlers in England shall sell *figures et autres overaignes de cere faits pur oblation*, only three pence in the pound dearer than plain wax.[60]

§ 2.—LADYE CHAPELS. LORETO CHAPELS. OTHER LADYE CHAPELS.

LADYE CHAPELS.

Every minster and every collegiate and parish church had a chapel dedicated in honour of our Ladye, which was known as the Chapel of our Ladye. If in some of the smaller parish churches there was no Ladye Chapel, there would be at least the Altar of our Ladye. Ladye Chapels were, as I have just shown, coeval with the introduction of Christianity into England.

Moreover a priest was generally in charge of these little chapels, as at Caversham, where the Warden of the Chapel, as he was called, was a Canon of Notley Abbey, and "songe," *i.e.,* said Mass, "in the chapell, and hadde the offeringes for hys lyvinge."[61]

Without, however, venturing to express a definite opinion on the subject, it appears to me, after considerable investigation, that there was no rubric for the exact position of the Ladye Chapel in our English Churches. It should be borne in mind that, according to general belief, our Lord was crucified with

---

[56] Viollet le Duc, *Dict. Raisonné du mobilier Francais.* Paris. P. 134. Cf. also Ducange, sub. voc. *Longitudo, Statualis cereus, Statuarium.*

[57] S. p. 253.

[58] Paston Letters. Edit. Fenn, 1787. Vol. iii. p. 21.

[59] S. pp. 10, 11.

[60] Rotuli Parliamenti, t. iv. p. 453 b.

[61] S. p. 11.

His face to the West, and His back to Jerusalem, and that our Ladye stood at His right hand, and consequently on the North side; and for this reason, as I have shown under Westminster, the North Doors of Cathedrals were dedicated to our Ladye.[62] Frequently in parish churches the Ladye Chapel is on the North side of the church. On the other hand, the early Ladye Chapel at Canterbury was at the West end, and was re-erected by Lanfranc in the aisle of the North nave. It occupied the South choir-aisle at Elgin, and the North at Thetford, Hulme, Belvoir, Bristol, Oxford, Llanthony, and Wymondham, but was detached at Ely. At Waltham and Rochester it was on the North side of the nave; on the South of the choir at Ripon, where it is over the Chapter-house; in the South transept at Wimborne; at Lincoln and Gloucester it is cruciform; at Lichfield and Wells it has a polygonal apse, and at Durham it is in the Galilee.[63]

In other instances, as at York, the Ladye Chapel stands due East behind the Choir and High Altar. Dr. Rock thinks, and I fully agree with him, that the Ladye Chapel, placed at the East end, "symbolizes our Lady as the Morning Star which harbingered day in a ghostly meaning."[64] There are many passages in the Fathers which fully bear out this interpretation, and describe our Ladye as the *Aurora consurgens*, or the Rising Morn of the Day of Salvation, that is, Christ our Lord.[65]

At Mildenhall, in Suffolk, the Ladye Chapel was over the porch;[66] at St. Andrew's, Norwich, the Chapel of our Ladye of Grace was under the steeple.[67]

With the Benedictines, it seems to have been the custom to place an image of our Ladye in the centre over the High Altar; and another in a side chapel, so that the monks might not be disturbed when singing Divine Office by the crowds of people who came to implore her help.[68] Although this is mentioned

---

[62] S. pp. 223, seq.

[63] *Church and Conventual Arrangement.* By Mackenzie E. C. Walcott, M.A., F.S.A., p. 107.

[64] *Church of our Fathers*, vol. iii. p. 264.

[65] Marracci quotes one hundred and ninety-one instances of *Aurora* being applied to our Blessed Ladye (*Polyanthea Mariana*, sub voce).

[66] S. p. 102.

[67] S. p. 108.

[68] Epitome Chron. celebr. Monast. S. Nicasii Remensis O.S.B. c. x. apud Morlot. Metropolis Remensis Historia. Remis, 1679, t. i. p. 659.

in the history of a French Benedictine Monastery, *mos Bene-dictinorum* evidently refers to the usual custom of the Order.

LORETO CHAPELS.

DEIPARÆ DOMUS UBI VERBUM CARO FACTUM EST.[68]

The Holy House of the Blessed Mother of God at Loreto enjoys a singular veneration from its having been the scene of the Incarnation of the Son of God.

The Church celebrates the festival of the Translation of the Holy House on the 10th of December; and there is a proper Mass and proper Office in the Missal and the Breviary. By order of Pope Sixtus the Fifth, in 1586, Priests celebrating Mass in the Holy House say in the last Gospel, *Hic Verbum caro factum est*, instead of *Et Verbum*, etc.[70]

Engraved on a pillar in the North aisle of the Cathedral of Loreto is a narrative by R. F. Robert Corbington, S.J., entitled—

THE WUNDRUS FLITTINGE OF THE KIRK OF OUR BLEST LADY OF LAURETO,

and concluding thus—

By decree of the meikle worthy Monsignor Vincent Casal of Bolonea, Ruler of this helly place, under the protection of the most werthy Cardinal. To the praise and glorie of the most pure and immaculate Virgin.

I, Robert Corbington, priest of the Companie of Jesus, in the yeir MDCXXXV. heve trulie translated the premisses out of the Latin storie hangged up in the seyd kirk.

For the ghostly comfort of those who wished to go on pilgrimage to our Ladye of Loreto, and were prevented by circumstances, the pious custom arose of erecting in various places chapels which were exact representations of the Holy House, and in which a statue of Our Lady of Loreto was placed in the niche behind the altar. Guppenberg says the earliest Loreto Chapel so erected was at Lille, by John Luffold, who was attached to the Court of Charles the Fifth.[71]

I have shown by a comparison of the measurements that the Sanctuary of Our Ladye of Walsingham was not a model

[68] Inscription on the front of the Church at Loreto, erected by Pope Sixtus V.

[70] *Loreto and Nazareth.* By W. A. Hutchison, Priest of the Oratory, p. 47. London, 1863.

[71] *Atlas Marianus*, p. 112.

of the Holy House of Nazareth.[72] But the old tradition says that it was.[73]

Dom Richard Beere, Lord Abbot of Glastonbury, who was sent to Rome in the twenty-second of Henry the Seventh, 1506, 1507, "coming from his Embassadrie out of *Italie*, made a chapel of our Ladye *de Loretta* joining the north side of the body of the chirche," [74] at Glastonbury.[75]

At Musselburgh in Scotland there was a chapel of Our Ladye of Loreto,[76] which Tursellino describes as "a little church something like to the Sacred House of Loreto;" and there was another one at Perth, called *Allareit.* The materials of the former, when finally destroyed in 1590, were used for building the Tolbooth,[77] and what remains of Allareit at Perth is now the Police Office.[78]

Hence it appears that England and Scotland kept pace with other nations in their devotion to Our Ladye of Loreto; and if the Loreto Chapel at Glastonbury was a model of the Holy House, as it seems to be the earliest instance on record, to Abbot Beere will be due the credit of having erected the first facsimile of the Holy House of Loreto.

The Holy House at Loreto is not only faced on the outside with marble, the work of Clement the Seventh,[79] but it is inclosed within the church, which is built over it. This is an old English custom, for King Eadwine, after his baptism, ordered St. Wuilfrid to inclose the wooden church in which he had received the waters of salvation within a church of stone;[80] and the wooden sanctuary of Our Ladye at Walsingham was also inclosed within a stone chapel, which communicated with the priory church.[81]

OTHER LADYE CHAPELS.

In addition to the Ladye Chapels in churches, and Ladye Chapels on bridges, several others, which possess considerable interest, are mentioned in the *Series.* Thus the history of the Chapel of our Ladye at Wroxhall[82] is the counterpart of that

[72] S. pp. 169, 170.   [73] S. p. 157.
[74] Leland, *Itin.* vol. iii. p. 489.   [75] S. p. 48.   [76] S. p. 301.   [77] S. p. 303.
[78] So I am informed by a Rev. correspondent, letter dated February 18, 1875.
[79] Hutchison, *Loreto and Nazareth,* p. 27.
[80] Bede, *Hist. Eccl.* lib. ii. cap. xiv. Opp. vol. ii. p. 235.   Edit. cit.
[81] S. pp. 163, seq.   [82] S. p. 254.

of the foundation of the Basilica of St. Marye Major, at Rome, in the year 352.[83] The Chapel of Our Ladye of Pewe was one of the most celebrated in England.[84] The Ladye chapel at the bridge at Beccles[85] had an ankret, and those of Court-up-Street[86] and our Ladye of Grace at Quarrywell[87] each had a hermit.[88] The little Chapel of our Ladye in the Park, near Liskeard, was an early place of pilgrimage, and in 1441 Bishop Lacy granted an indulgence to those who contributed towards the repair of the road to it.[89] The Chapel of our Ladye at King's Lynn is remarkable for its architectural construction.[90]

Finally, the private Chapel of our Ladye in Berkeley Castle was of no small importance, as appears from the Bull of Urban the Fifth.[91] It seems curious, however, that indulgences should be offered to benefactors of vestments, chalices, and any other aids of charity to the private chapels in the castle of an English Baron of the fourteenth century.

§ 3.—LADYE ALTARS. INSCRIPTIONS. CANDLES. RELICS.

LADY ALTARS.

If Sixtus the Third, A.D. 432—440, gave an altar of silver weighing three hundred pounds to the Patriarchal Basilica of St. Marye Major,[92] our Ine, in 725, gave 264 lbs. of gold for the altar of the silver chapel at Glastonbury.[93] What our forefathers saw done in Rome, they themselves did in England; and the altar frontals of the Anglo-Saxon Church were often of the most gorgeous character, made of gold and silver, and adorned with precious stones. Many altars graced the Anglo-Saxon churches; they were generally of stone, which of course would be concealed by the frontals; relics were inclosed in them as

---

[83] Cf. *Breviarium Romanum* ad diem 5 Aug.
[84] S. pp. 229—239.
[85] S. p. 3.
[86] S. p. 16.
[87] S. p. 129.
[88] This is the difference between a hermit and an ankret : a hermit might leave his cell, but an ankret never went beyond the threshold of the building in which he had vowed to live and die.
[89] S. pp. 65, 66.
[90] S. p. 99.
[91] S. p. 266.
[92] Anast. Bibliothecar. in vita, t. ii. Edit. Migne.
[93] S. p. 46.

now; and there was this peculiarity with the Anglo-Saxons, that if relics could not be obtained, the most Blessed Eucharist was inclosed within the altar; and this liturgical practice lasted in England up to the time of Lyndwood, A.D. 1446.[94]

The Anglo-Saxon altars were of smaller dimensions than those which now are erected, and this appears to have been in accordance with the use at Rome, for William of Malmesbury relates that St. Ealdhelm brought back with him from Rome in the year 701, an altar the dimensions of which were one foot and a half high, four feet long, and three palms wide.[95]

The great sapphire given by St. David to our Ladye of Glastonbury was set in a *superaltare.*[96]

Images of our Ladye were set in tabernacles over the high altar in many of our large churches, as at Glastonbury[97] and Worcester.[98] In York Minster the high altar was considered the altar of our Ladye, whose gilt image stood near the south end, and whenever Mass was celebrated at that altar, two large wax candles were lit before our Ladye.[99] Moreover it was the custom at York for the *hebdomadarius* who sang the daily High Mass to carry from the sacristy a silver gilt image of our Ladye with her Divine Son in her arms, which he placed upon the high altar.[100] I have not found any evidence that a similar custom was observed in other cathedral churches in England, so it speaks well of the profound old Yorkshire devotion for our Blessed Ladye. But images of our Ladye were used to decorate altars, when they were arrayed in becoming splendour, for the celebration of festal days.[101]

The *Series* affords interesting evidence about these altars of our Ladye in the Catalogue of Shrines; and the different titles under which they were consecrated. At Coventry there was an altar of our Ladye in *Gesem;*[102] at Durham, and in many

---

[94] For all authorities and details cf. Rock, *Church of our Fathers*, vol. i. pp. 41, 42.

[95] "Sesquipedali crassitudine, quadrupedali longitudine, et latitudine trium palmarum" (*De Gest. Pont. Anglor.* lib. v. p. 372. Rolls Edit.).

[96] S. p. 44. For full details about superaltars see Rock, *Church of our Fathers*, vol. i. pp. 249—263.

[97] *Ibid.* p. 48.

[98] *Ibid.* p. 252.

[99] *Ibid.* p. 260.

[100] *Ibid.* p. 260.

[101] Cf. *Wills of Northern Counties.* Surtees Soc. p. 7.

[102] *Mon. Angl.* tom. iii. p. 188.

other churches, there was an altar of our Ladye of Pity;[103] at Evesham there were set on four different altars images of our Ladye "right well peynted and feyre arayed wyth golde and divers other colours, the whyche schewyd to the people that behylde hem grete devocyon;"[104] at Hingham there was an altar of her Nativity;[105] at Peterborough, the altar of our Ladye of Pity was known as that of our Ladye's Lamentation[106]—a title which, by the way, leaves no doubt as to the iconography of our Ladye "of Pity;" at St. Albans there was the altar of our Ladye called of the Four Candles, *Quatuor Cereorum*, because four candles offered by four of the officials of the abbey were daily lighted during the Marye Mass;[107] and at Perth the Church of St. John had forty altars, all endowed, amongst which were five of our Ladye and one of St. Joseph.[108]

There are many technical features about English altars which do not exclusively relate to those of our Ladye. But in the twelfth century, and as Dr. Rock says, perhaps earlier, there was to be found in our churches, over, but eastward to the back of the high altar, a square beam, the ends of which were let into the walls of the chancel, which was decorated in the most splendid manner; in the centre stood the Rood with Marye and John, as it is usually described, and along the beam, on either side, were placed reliquaries and "texts," and holy books, which had belonged to, or had been written by, sainted men.[109] But these reliquaries must not be confounded with the greater shrines of the Saints of England, which occupied a fixed position in their various churches. These shrines made of the precious metals were adorned with images of our Blessed Ladye and the Saints. On the west side of the shrine of St. Albans was an image, in high relief and decorated with gems, of our Ladye with her Divine Son seated on her lap,.[110]

The shrine of St. Edward was adorned by a silver image of our Ladye, which was placed there by Queen Eleanor of Provence, and in 1243—1244 Henry the Third caused an emerald and a ruby to be set in the forehead of that image. Affixed also to this shrine was an ivory image of our Ladye which had been offered by St. Thomas of Canterbury.[111]   In the

---

[103] S. p. 29.   [104] *Ibid.* p. 37.
[103] *Ibid.* p. 54.   [106] *Ibid.* 127.   [107] S. p. 133.   [108] *Ibid.* p. 303.
[109] *Church of our Fathers*, vol. iii. p. 471.   [110] S. p. 130.   [111] S. p. 222.

g

year 1355, Elizabeth de Clare, daughter of Gilbert, Earl of Gloucester, made this bequest :

Je devise a Seint Thomas de Hereford un ymage de nre dame d'argent surorré d'estre taché sur son fiertre.[112]

INSCRIPTIONS.

The Council of Celchyth held on the 27th of July in the year 816, under Wuilfrid, Archbishop of Canterbury, and at which Ceonuulf of Mercia assisted, issued the following mandate to each bishop, viz. : *Ut habeat depictum in pariete oratorii aut in tabula, vel etiam in altaribus, quibus Sanctis sunt utraque dicata.*[113] These words, evidently refer to paintings, and not to inscriptions; and *tabula*, or "picture,"[114] means the reredos, or altar-piece, in this instance, and not the frontal of the altar. The Constitutions of William de Bleys, Bishop of Lincoln A.D. 1229, require inscriptions on the altars.[115]

The poems of Alcwine contain two or three or four lines or so, adapted to altars of our Ladye,[116] and many other equally short ones, to altars of the Saints; but none of these appear to have been written for England. Whatever may have been the practice in Anglo-Saxon times, inscriptions on altars were in fashion shortly after the Norman invasion.

Weever has preserved several other inscriptions which were near or on Ladye altars. A few examples may be—

> *Ora mente pia pro nobis Virgo Maria.*
> *Virgo Dei Genitrix sit nobis Auxiliatrix.*
> *Virgo Maria tuos serva sine crimine servos.*
> *Liberet a pena nos cæli porta serena.*
> *Virga virens Jesse nos verum ducat ad Esse.*
> *Nos ditet venia Sanctissima Virgo Maria.*
> *Nos rege, summe Pater, nos integra protege Mater.*
> *Nos jungat thronis veri Thronus Salomonis.*
> *Ad fontem venie ducat nos dextra Marie.*[117]

[112] Nichols, *Royal Wills*, p. 31.
[113] Labbe, tom. viii. col. 1485.
[114] Cf. Martial, *Encaustus Phæton tabula depictus in hac est.*
[115] *In ecclesiis dedicatis, annus et dies dedicationis, et nomen dedicantis, et nomen Sancti in cujus honore dedicata est ecclesia, distincte et aperte scribantur circa majus altare, in loco ad hunc idoneo : idem fiat circa minora altaria* (Wilkins, *Conc.* tom. i. p. 624).
[116] Opp. t. ii. n. 53, col. 743; n. 121, col. 757; n. 173, col. 771; n. 203, col. 774. Edit. Migne.
[117] *Ancient Funerall Monvments.* London, 1631, pp. 119, 120.

Moreover, according to the same authority "Organs, pulpits, portals, crosses, candlesticks, roods, crucifixes, and what else of that kinde were likewise thus inscribed, all of which with the rest, were erazed, scraped, cut out, or taken away by the Commissioners, and instead of them certaine sentences of the Holy Scripture appointed to be painted or dispensild in every Church."[118]

VOTIVE CANDLES.

Laudare præterea reliquias, venerationem et invocationem sanctorum; item stationes peregrinationesque pias, indulgentias, jubilæa, candelas in Templis accendi solitas, et reliqua hujusmodi pietatis ac devotionis nostræ adminicula.[119]

It is a very old and universal custom to burn candles before images of our Blessed Ladye.[120] The story of the Abbot John, quoted by many different writers, may be mentioned here with advantage. It was related in the seventh Œcumenical Council, the second of Nicæa, A.D. 787, by Dionysius, priest of the church of Ascalon, who took it from the Ecclesiastical History of Evagrius.[121]

At Sicchus, twenty short miles from Jerusalem, there lived in a cave an ankret, by name John. Here he had an image of our Blessed Ladye with her Divine Son in her arms, before which he always kept a candle burning. Whenever he was going away on a journey, either into the desert or to Jerusalem, or to make his prayer on Mount Sinai, or to other sanctuaries of the martyrs, he would go to our Ladye, and say to her : *Sancta Domina Deipara, quandoquidem restat mihi longum iter conficiendum, candelam tuam cura, eamque inextinctam juxta meum propositum serva. Nam ego, tuo fretus subsidio, longum iter ingredior.* And on his return he invariably found that the candle which he had lighted was still burning.[122]

This pious custom was most common in England. In the year 1225, William, Earl of Salisbury, otherwise known as

---

[118] *Ancient Funerall Monuments,* p. 123.

[119] Reg. VI. regular. ut cum orthodoxa Ecclesia sentiamus. *Exercitia Spiritualia* S. P. Ignatii Loyolæ, cum versione literali ex autographo Hispanico. Lond. 1837, p. 331.

[120] On the use of lights see Rock, *Hirurgia,* Lond. 1851, pt. ii. ch. xi. pp. 391—411.

[121] Lib. iv. cap. xxvi. Labbe, ubi infra.

[122] Labbe, *Concilia,* t. vii. col. 808, 809.

Long-Sword,[123] was nearly lost at sea in a violent storm on his
return to England. When they were in the uttermost despair,
suddenly a large wax taper, burning with a brilliant light,
was seen at the mast-head by all who were thus in danger
on board the ship ; by the side of the candle they beheld a lady
of wondrous beauty standing, who protected the light of the
candle, which brilliantly illumined the darkness of the night
from the violence of the squalls and the heavy downpour of the
rain. Whereupon, from this vision of heavenly brightness the
Earl, as well as all the crew, feeling assured of their safety,
acknowledged that Divine assistance was with them. And
whilst every one on board was ignorant of the portent of this
vision, Earl William alone attributed the favour of this kindness
to the Blessed Virgin Marye, because from the day when he
was first girt with the belt of knighthood, he had assigned one
wax taper before the altar of the most Blessed Mother of God,
which should burn during the Mass which was sung every day
in honour of the said Mother of God, and during the Canonical
Hours, and thus exchange the temporal for the Light eternal.[124]

The Earl died in the following year. It was said that poison
had been administered to him. Feeling his end drawing near,
he retired to his castle at Salisbury, and sent for the Bishop,
from whom he received the last sacraments of the Church,
and died an edifying death. It happened, continues Wendover,
that whilst his body was being carried from his castle to the new
church, about a mile distant, for burial, the lighted candles,
which were borne with the cross and thurible, according to
custom, gave, amidst the heavy rain and gusts of wind, a continued light throughout the journey, so as to make it clearly
evident, that the Earl, who had been so penitent, already
belonged to the sons of Light.[125]

Throughout the *Series* there is a constant record of lights
and lamps kept burning before images of our Ladye ; and it
seems to have been an universal custom throughout England to

---

[123] This was his epitaph :

> *Flos comitum Willelmus obit, stirps regia, Longus*
> *Ensis vaginam cepit habere brevem.*

(Rog. de Wendover, *Flores Hist.* Edit. Coxe. Lond. 1842, vol. iv. p. 117, note.)
[124] Wendover, edit. cit. vol. iv. p. 105, ad ann. 1225.
[125] *Ibid.* p. 126, ad ann. 1226.

burn lamps or candles before her principal image at least ; and
the foundations and endowments made for this object were
on no niggardly scale.[126] Lands given for this purpose were
called lamp-lands and light-lands,[127] and bequests of this nature
and in money occur at an early date.[128] Lands were held by the
service of providing lights to burn before our Ladye, as at East
Herling and Plympton. At Chobham, Norton, and Wyke,
sheep, and at Chevington and Felsham cows, were left for the
support of our Ladye's light ; whilst at Ixworth Thorpe, in
1524, Golfrey Gilbert leaves to our Ladye's light one skeppe of
bees to be delyvered to the fermor, and he to delyver it to the
next fermor, wt all the increase at his departyng.[129]

Moreover, in various parish churches there were lights named
after the different classes of those who kept them burning, such
as the Common Light,[130] the Married Men's Light,[131] the
Bachelors' or Singlemen's Light,[132] and the Plough Light.[133]
Mention often occurs of the Jesus Light,[134] of the Rood Light,[135]
and of the Ladye Light. One of the Ladye altars at St. Albans
was called that of the Four Tapers.[136] In many churches,
Ladye lights were supported by the gilds, some of which were
founded for this very object.

It was not only in rural districts that candles were kept
burning before our Ladye. Thus Henry the Eighth used to
keep candles, called the King's Candles, before our Ladye
at Doncaster, and at Walsingham,[137] and the Earl of Northumberland maintained candles at the same sanctuaries all the
year round.[138]

On festal days the candles burning before our Ladye were

---

[126] S. p. 65 for Lincoln, and p. 118 for St. Mary Ottery.

[127] Money expended in wax lights was called wax-shot (*General History of Norfolk*, p. 968, note).

[128] S. p. 61.

[129] S. see under the different places named.

[130] S. p. 144.

[131] *Proceedings of the Suffolk Archæological Institute*, vol. ii. p. 140.

[132] S. p. 144.

[133] S. p. 152.

[134] S. p. 246.

[135] S. p. 61.

[136] S. p. 133.

[137] S. pp. 28, 195.

[138] S. pp. 28, 191.

wreathed with flowers,[139] and on some occasions shields with armorial bearings were attached to them.[140]

Candles burnt in honour of the five joys of our Ladye were called Gaudes or Gawdyes, and also "Joys." William Berdewel, senior, of West Sterling in Norfolk, c. 1445, leaves to the feywe joys afore our Ladye xs.[141]

RELICS.

The mention of shrines and reliquaries naturally calls attention to some relics of our Blessed Ladye which were venerated in England.

Relics may be divided into two classes, Real and Sanctified. Sanctified ones are those which have touched the real relics, and may or may not be copies of the originals. Such were "the handkerchiefs and aprons which had touched the body of St. Paul cast out devils, and cured all diseases."

At the Church of the Holy Cross in Jerusalem, at Rome, one of the Nails of our Lord is preserved ; models or copies of it are made, and they each have an authentication under seal, declaring that they are only copies of the original Nail which they have touched. In the Wardrobe books of the twenty-eighth year of Edward the First is mentioned *unus pannus linteus qui tetigit sudarium Christi.*[148] This was a sanctified relic.

I shall speak about the Relics of the True Cross, and of the so-called "Milk of our Ladye," in the *Series* under Walsingham.

Our Anglo-Saxon forefathers held holy relics in the highest veneration. When the decrees of our Bishops and Provincial Synods, and the fact that relics cannot be bought or sold for money, and cannot be exposed for public veneration, unless they are sealed by proper authority and duly authenticated, are taken into consideration, the watchful care of the Church at once becomes manifest ; and the oft-repeated and as often refuted charges about "manufactured relics," which Anglicans so frequently adduce, merely prove the ignorance—if nothing

[139] S. p. 131.
[140] S. p. 70.
[141] S. p. 42 ; also Blomefield, vol. i. p. 204.
[148] *Liber quotidianus contrarotulatoris garderobæ anno Regis Edwardi I. vicesimo octavo.* Lond. 1787. pp. 347.

worse—of those who make these accusations. At the same
time, in qualification of what I have just said, I may observe
that the treasuries of churches often contain relics which are
not, and cannot be exposed for public veneration, because the
authentications have been lost ; and moreover, that unprincipled
lay-sacristans occasionally, I fear, amuse themselves by "selling"
Anglican travellers with some stupendous tale, in the hope of
a larger "mancia," knowing well that their victims will "swallow"
any story, however preposterous, provided they can use it, as
they hope, to the detriment of the Church.

The Letters relating to the Suppression of the Monasteries,
edited for the Camden Society by Mr. Thomas Wright, mention
some curious "relics," such as "Malcom's ear that Peter struck
off." Now items of this sort do not figure in any of the genuine
English lists of venerable relics ; there is not a tittle of evidence
that these objects were ever exposed for veneration—indeed, how
could they have been ?—and the explanation of them is of the
simplest and the most natural, viz., that they were "properties,"
(I believe this is the correct term in theatrical parlance) belonging to, and used by the various gilds in their sacred pageants
and processions. Moreover, in some churches, representations
of the festival itself, *e.g.,* the Annunciation, were given, as in
the Church of St. Jacques at Bruges. At Seville I believe there is
a large wing of feathers labelled as that of the Archangel Gabriel.
In 1462, by his will dated May 9th, William Haute says : "I
bequeath one piece of that stone on which the Archangel Gabriel
stood, when he descended to salute the Blessed Virgin Mary,
to the image of the Blessed Virgin Mary in the church of
Bourne, the same to stand under the foot of the same image."[143]
And amongst the relics preserved at St. Albans there was one
described as *De loco ubi Christus Annunciatus est Virgini Gloriosæ.*[144] The nature of these two relics is obvious ; they
were fragments from the floor of the Holy House of Loreto,
which was the scene of the Annunciation. Sixtus the Fourth,
1471—1484, repaved the Holy House with marble, the ancient
pavement having been carried off as relics by pilgrims.[145]
Layton or Leighton, one of the Commissioners, in 1537 sends
to Cromwell "strange things . . . part of God's Supper *in cœna
domini, pars petræ super quam natus erat Jesus in Bethlehem,*"

[143] S. p. 4.   [144] *Mon. Angl.* tom. ii. p. 234.   [145] S. p. 161.

from Maiden Bradley. In the former, "table" was evidently omitted wilfully; the second would have been a bit of stone from the Chapel of the Nativity. The table of the Last Supper is at St. John Lateran's in Rome.

In the early days of the Christian era, the hair of the martyrs was carefully collected and preserved.[146] It is natural to suppose that some portions of our Ladye's hair would be treasured up carefully; indeed, relics of her hair are mentioned at a very early period, and like all the principal relics of our Ladye, they appear to have come from Constantinople.

There was a relic of our Ladye's hair at Croyland in the time of Abbot Turketul, who died A.D. 975; it was the gift of the Emperor, Henry the Second, who had received it from Hugh Capet, King of France.[147] King Æthelstan gave some of our Ladye's hair—*of hire feaxe*—to Exeter, as is mentioned in the list of relics at Exeter, in Anglo-Saxon, in a MS. in the Bodleian Library.[148] Some of our Ladye's hair was also preserved at Canterbury.[149] From these and other instances it appears that relics of our Ladye's hair have been venerated for many centuries.[150]

The principal relics of our Blessed Ladye are those consisting of portions of her garments and her *Zona* or girdle. They were brought from Jerusalem to Constantinople at the desire of the Empress Pulcheria. She converted the synagogue of the Jews ἐν τοῖς χαλκοπρατίοις, or the *Forum Fabrorum*, as Lang construes it, into a magnificent church in honour of our Ladye, in which she placed the Zone, and the tomb, as it is called, of the Blessed Mother of God; but it is most probable that tomb or sepulchre is used to express the coffin, or else some portion of the sepulchre of our Ladye[151] which many years later Venerable Bede saw in the Valley of Jehosaphat.[152] In con-

---

[146] *Disquisit. Relig.* Auct. J. Ferrando, S.J., l. iv. c. iv. § 4.

[147] *Mon. Angl.* t. ii. p. 94.

[148] *Ibid.* p. 528.

[149] *Iter Leonis de Rosmital* (Bibliothek des Literarischen Vereins in Stuttgart, vol. vii. 1844) p. 39.

[150] Cf. Mabillon, *Analecta Vetera.* Paris, 1723, p. 433; Locri. *Maria Augusta.* Atrebati, 1608, lib. v. ch. 22, p. 525; Baronius, ad ann. 1123; *Annales*, tom. xii. p. 152. Antv. 1609.

[151] On this point see Baronius, ad ann. 48; and Locri, *Maria Augusta*, lib. v. ch. 39, pp. 352—355.

[152] *De locis Sanctis*, ch. v. opp. tom. iv. p. 416. Edit Giles.

sequence this church was called that of the Holy Tomb—'Αγία Ζαρός.[158]

The festival of the Deposition of the Girdle of our Ladye is kept in the Greek Church on the 31st of August.[154] The festival of the Girdle of our Ladye is celebrated throughout the Augustinian Order on the Sunday within the Octave of St. Augustine.[155] Pulcheria also built the church of our Ladye Τῶν 'Οδηγῶν, in which she placed the picture of the Blessed Virgin painted by St. Luke, which had been sent to her by her sister Eudoxia.[156] The Greek Church celebrates the deposition of this picture on the 26th of August. A third church of our Ladye built by Pulcheria was that of the Blacherna, in which the robe of our Ladye was placed.[157] The festival of its deposition is kept in the Greek Church on the 2nd of July.[158]

It is from this venerable store that the various relics of our Ladye which are preserved in many churches of Europe have come. One of the most authentic is the mantle-veil of our Ladye at Chartres, which has always been called the *camisia*. It was brought from Constantinople by Charlemagne, who had received it from the Emperor Leo the Fourth, and given to Chartres by Charles the Bald in the year 826.[159]

At Peterborough there was a super-altar made of a fragment of the tomb of our Ladye,[160] and a piece of the same relic was also preserved at St. Albans.[161] At Windsor, beneath the high altar, there was a relic of the same, described as *de tumba Beatæ Mariæ*,[162] and a fragment of the same was found with the other relics inclosed in the head of the statue of our Ladye at

---

[158] Nicephorus Callixtus, *Hist. Ecclesiastica.* Edit. J. Lang. Paris, 1574; col. 972.
[154] *Ephemerides Graco-Mosca*, apud *Act. SS.*; tom. i. Maii, f. xlii. *Menologium Græcum Basilii Maced. Imp.*, Urbini, 1727, ad diem 31 Aug. *Menologium Græcum.* Edit. Sirlati, ad diem 31 Aug. Colvener, *Kalendarium Marianum*, ad diem 31 Aug. § 1.
[155] Miechoviensis, *Discursus prædicabiles super Litanias Lauretanas.* Neapoli, 1857, tom. ii. p. 57. Note of Editor.
[156] Nicephorus, ubi sup. col. 972.
[157] *Ibid.* col. 973.
[158] *Ephemerides Graco-Mosca*, f. xxxiv. Colvener, *Kalendarium Marianum*, ad diem 2 Julii, § ii.
[159] Capgrave, *De Illustribus Henricis*, p. 10. Rolls Edit. For the relics at Notre Dame de Chartres, see Haman, *Notre Dame de France*, pp. 200—211.
[160] Rock, *Church of our Fathers*, vol. i. p. 256.
[161] *Mon. Angl.* tom. ii. p. 254.
[162] *Ibid.* t. vi. p. 1365.

Thetford.[163] In the list of the relics at Windsor, there is one described as *de una candela B. Virginis.*[164] Evidently this was a candle from Arras, which had either touched the Holy Candle there, or was one of the facsimiles made of it, and having a few drops from the original incorporated in it. Only twenty candles are recorded to have been thus made, the first in the year 1105, the last some time about 1720; but there is no mention of one having been sent to England.[165] Space will not allow me to give the history of the Holy Candle still preserved in the Church of Notre Dame-des-Ardents at Arras.[166]

Relics of our Ladye's robes were preserved at St. Albans;[167] and at Exeter relics of her robe and of her veil.[168]

Another great relic of our Ladye was her girdle. So many girdles of our Ladye are enumerated both in England and elsewhere, that it is evident they either contained a bit of the Constantinople relic, or were copies which had touched the original and become "sanctified" relics. Lord Herbert of Cherbury, in his Life of Henry the Eighth, says that our Ladye's girdle was shown in eleven several places in England, and her milk in eight, but he has not given the names of the localities.[169]

In the list of relics under the high altar at Windsor is mentioned *una zona alba S. Johis Evangelistæ quam dedit Beatæ Mariæ;*[170] at London, Leo de Rosmital saw a girdle of the Virgin Mother of God which she is said to have made with her own hands;[171] a relic of the girdle of our Ladye was preserved in the Cluniac Abbey at Thetford,[172] and a portion of the same was found inclosed in the head of the statue of

---

[163] S. p. 149.

[164] *Ibid.*

[165] Cf. *Sanctuaires de Notre-Dame-des-Ardents, ou notices sur les saints cierges provenant de la Sainte Chandelle d'Arras.* Par M. l'Abbé Proyart, 1872. The list of the candles is given by Cavrois, Append. n. xxxvi. pp. 242—244.

[166] Cf. *Cartulaire de Notre-Dames-des-Ardents à Arras.* Par Louis Cavrois, Chev. de l'Ordre de S. Grégoire-le-Grand. Arras, 1876.

[167] *Mon. Angl.* t. ii. p. 234.

[168] *Ibid.* p. 528.

[169] *Life and Reign of Henry VIII.* p. 431. Lond. 1649.

[170] *Mon. Angl.* t. vi. p. 1365.

[171] *Iter.* &c. p. 41.

[172] *Mon. Angl.* t. v. p. 148.

our Ladye of Thetford;[173] and in the Church of the Holy Trinity at Dublin there was a relic of our Ladye, which in the Martyrology is described as "of our Ladye's vest," but in the Book of Obits, which was written after 1461, in which year many of the relics were destroyed by the fall of the west window, it is called the "zone of our Ladye."[174] Moreover, by will dated August 26, 1463, Eufemia Langton, wife of Sir John Langton of Farnley, near Leeds, bequeathed to Margaret Meyryng, her daughter, a silver-gilt cross, an Agnus Dei, and *sonam Beatæ Mariæ Virginis*.[175] To my mind this is evidence that these girdles of our Ladye were only either "sanctified" girdles, or that they contained at most but a thread of the great relic of the Girdle of our Ladye.

I have mentioned elsewhere that ladies were recommended for safe delivery to wear a girdle with the *Magnificat* inscribed upon it; chemisettes of our Ladye of Chartres were also sent to ladies for the same intention, and the girdle of our Ladye at Westminster, if not taken habitually to ladies expecting their confinement, was at least conveyed to Elizabeth of York, for in the book of her privy-purse expenses, the following entry occurs on the 13th of December, 1502.

"*Item.* to a monke that brought oure Ladye gyrdelle to the quene in rewarde, vis. viiid."[176]

One of the commissioners, R. Layton or Leighton, writing in 1537 to Cromwell, says: "I send you also our Ladye's girdle of Bruton, red silk, a solemn relic, sent to women in travail."

Ferrand mentions, from what he had seen when a boy, that a relic of the girdle of our Ladye was taken by the Canons of Le Puy to ladies "in bedgang," and that a portion of it was also conveyed to the Queen of France, who was expecting her confinement.[177]

Many bequests of girdles were made to images of our Blessed Ladye: thus in 1490, Sir Gilbert Stapylton leaves to the Abbess of Aston church a girdle of silver-gilt to hang at an image of

[173] S. p. 149.
[174] *Book of Obits and Martyrology of the Cathedral Church of the Holy Trinity, commonly called Christ Church, Dublin,* p. lxvii. Printed for the Irish Archæological Society, 1844.
[175] *Test. Ebor.* vol. ii. p. 258.
[176] Nicolas, *Privy Purse Expenses of Elizabeth of York,* p. 78. Lond. 1830.
[177] *Disquisit. Reliq.* p. 85.

our Ladye in the said church;[178] in 1442, Richard Cotingham bequeathed a red belt well adorned with silver to the image of our Ladye in the little chapel near St. Marye's Abbey, York;[179] and John White, who had been Mayor of Dublin in the years 1424, 1431, and 1432, left a girdle of the price of 20s. to the image of our Ladye in Christ Church.[180] It is possible that these girdles attached to images of our Ladye were also known as "our Ladye's girdles."

There is also another girdle of our Ladye at Prato, in Tuscany, which never was at Constantinople, and which is wholly distinct from the girdle of our Ladye in the Chalcoprateion, but Mrs. Jameson has confused the one with the other.[181]

Its legendary history is briefly this. It purports to be the girdle which our Ladye is said to have let fall to St. Thomas at her Assumption.[182]

This legend is pronounced utterly apocryphal by St. Antonine of Florence,[183] Molanus,[184] Baronius,[185] and others.[186] Nevertheless, in the large engraving of the Assumption which faces the Office of the festival in the Dominican Breviary, printed at

[178] S. p. 2. I can find no trace of any convent at Aston. In France the care of the Ladye altars is intrusted to three maidens, who are called *Les Reines de Notre Dame.* Cf. Haigneré, *Hist. de N. D. de Boulogne,* p. 283. Was "abbess" the English name for those who fulfilled this duty?

[179] S. p. 268.

[180] S. p. 307.

[181] *Legends of the Madonna,* pp. 344—347. Edit. 1852.

[182] Cf. *Notizie istoriche intorno alla sacratissima cintola di Maria Virgine, che si conserva nella città di Prato in Toscana descritte dal Dottore Giuseppe Bianchini, di Prato.*

[183] *Historiarum,* p. 3, tit. 8, c. 4, parag. 2, quoted by Locri ubi infra.

[184] C. 73, quoted by Locri.

[185] Ad ann. 48.

[186] Locri says: Dimisit, scilicet, in cœlos scandens Diva, cingulum, atque in Beati Thomæ manus delapsum est; incredulitatis, quod a morte Dei Filius surrexisset, mnemosynon futurum. Id figmentum est, nec tolerandum; adeoque a B. Antonino, Molano, Baronio, aliisque ex pictorum officina recte explosum. Affero Antonini, ut antiquioris, verba a Molano repetita: *Nec etiam,* scribit, *laudandi sunt pictores, cum Apocrypha pingunt; ut obstetrices in partu Virginis; et Thomæ Apostolo cingulum suum a Virgine Maria, in Assumptione sua, propter dubitationem dimissum* (Maria Augusta, lib. v. c. 17, p. 520). Locri was parish priest of St. Nicholas at Arras, and his work is dedicated to his Bishop, John Richardot. Peter de Natalibus who composed his *Catalogus Sanctorum* between 1369 and 1372—it was finished on the 26th of May of that year—says: Quod autem dicitur de Thoma qui abfuit, et resurrectionem virginis credere voluit; zonamque ipsius ex aere delapsam recepit: delusorium et frivolum reputatur (lib. vii. cap. lxv. fol. 193. Lugduni, 1508). At fol. 193 he says that the story is found in an apocryphal book ascribed to St. John the Evangelist. But the Golden Legends mention it under the heading of the Assumption.

Venice in 1514, our Ladye is represented as giving her girdle to St. Thomas, who is on a hillock raised above the eleven other Apostles.[187]

The learned John Chrysostome Trombelli has carefully examined the history of the girdle at Prato, as set forth by Bianchini. He fully admits the authenticity of the Constantinople girdle, and that relics of it have been brought to various churches in Europe, but he considers that the Prato girdle is only a sanctified relic which has touched or contains a thread of the precious girdle of Constantinople.[188] But Bianchini mentions an instance of a girdle which had been made, and had touched the zona at Prato.[189] Thus there is evidence of the practice of multiplying girdles of our Ladye, which became "sanctified" relics; and this custom gives the explanation of the many "girdles of the Blessed Virgin."

It should also be borne in mind that pilgrims have long been accustomed to carry away pieces of the veils of venerated images of our Ladye. Even the relics of our Ladye's hair might, in some cases, be so explained. Statues of our Ladye which were robed had also false hair; and the "cootes, cappe, and *here*" of our Ladye of Caversham are mentioned.[190] Veils of our Ladye of Loreto have been cut into pieces, and distributed, for years; and in the year 1749, Benedict the Fourteenth issued a Bull on the subject, by which, in order to prevent any controversy or dispute, the three priests *custodes* were alone empowered to put on to the image of our Ladye the new veils, to take them off, and to authenticate them. The authentications are to bear only the print of our Ladye, and the writing. No money is to be taken for them on pain of suspension. The Penitentiaries are also allowed to distribute them, but the attesting paper must be signed by their rector.[191]

[187] Fol. 315 b.

[188] *De reliquiis B. Virginis Mariæ*, sect. iii. capp. l. li.

[189] *Notizie*, &c. p. 43.

[190] S. p. 11.

[191] *Bullarium Benedicti PP. XIV.* tom. iii. 54. On relics of our Blessed Ladye, Cf. Fereol Locri, *Maria Augusta*. Atrebati, 1608, lib. v. cap. xix.—xlvi. pp. 521—567; *Inventaire des Sacrées Reliques de Nostre Dame*, par le R. P. Antoine de Balinghem, S.J. Douay, 1626; Ferrando, *Disquisitio Reliquiaria*; Surius, ad xxxi. Aug.; B. P. Canisius, S.J., *De Beata Maria Virgine Incomparabili et Dei Genitrice.* Ingolstadii, 1577, lib. v. cap. xxiii.; Joan. Bonifacius, S.J., *De Diva Virginis Mariæ vita et miraculis*, Coloniæ, 1628, lib. ii. cap. ix. pp. 289—294; Trombelli, *De reliquiis B. Virginis Mariæ.*

CHAPTER THE SECOND.

Associations.

§ I.—GILDS.

MANY Gilds are mentioned in the *Series*. I do not believe that in the ages of faith there existed a single church or parish in England which had not one or more Gilds.[1]

These brotherhoods had their origin in England, and in the time of our Anglo-Saxon forefathers; they existed in the days of Ine, A.D. 688—725.[2]

They may be divided into two classes: (1) Secular, (2) Religious; and the former may be subdivided into (1) Frith Gilds; (2) Merchant Gilds, which were the origin of our municipal corporations; (3) Trade or Craft Gilds, which are represented by our civic companies.

Now one common feature in all the English Gilds was, that quite irrespective of the particular object for which they were instituted, certain religious observances were invariably enforced by their statutes; the principal of which were: (1) The celebration of the Gild-festival, and of Holy Mass at the Gild-altar by the Gild-chaplain; (2) compulsory attendance of the brethren and sisters, under pain of a fine of wax tapers, or a small sum of money; (3) the burial of the dead; (4) prayers for the dead; and (5) the keeping of the obits of the deceased members. Thus, although all Gilds were not instituted solely for religious objects, the observance of religious duties formed an essential portion of their statutes.[3]

---

[1] For the derivation of the name, see Rock, *Church of our Fathers*, vol. ii. p. 395, and the *English Gilds*, published by the Early English Text Society, vol. xl. pp. xiv.—xvi. lxi.

[2] *Ancient Laws and Institutes of England.* Edit. Thorpe, pp. 16—21.

[3] The volume of the constitutions of more than a hundred of the old English Gilds was prepared by the late Mr. Toulmin Smith, on whose premature death the final editorship devolved upon his accomplished daughter, Miss Lucy Toulmin Smith,

Every Gild had its chaplain.[4] The Latin Christ's Book or Gospels written by an Anglo-Saxon scribe, which formerly belonged to Sherborne, and is now preserved at York, contains the Anglo-Saxon Bidding prayer, in which Gilds and Gild priests are enumerated : "þittan þe gebiddan . . . for, ure gildan 7 gilds preostra."

Moreover, in the Canons enacted under King Eadgar, a priest is forbidden to deprive another of anything, either "in his minster, his shrift-shire, or his gild schipe."[5] If, however, as sometimes was the case, trade Gilds did not keep a Gild-priest,

whose valuable introduction is for general readers the most interesting portion of the book. The President of the Society, Mr. Furnivall, who has added some notes, and Mr. Toulmin Smith object to any Gilds being called "religious," they prefer the term "social;" they discussed the subject together, and their united wisdom on the subject is thus recorded by Mr. Furnivall : "To have called them 'religious,' because of their ornament of a saint's name, would have seemed to him and me a monstrous contradiction, in the days of Chaucer and Wycliffe, of William, who had the vision of Piers the Plowman, and others who have left us records of what Romanism, with its monks and friars, practically then was in England" (*English Gilds*, p. lxxxvii. note 1). Mr. Furnivall caused to be inserted in this volume a learned essay on the subject of Gilds by Lujo Brentano, of Aschaffenburg, I.U.D. et Phil, a Catholic gentleman, but Miss Toulmin Smith adds "that this gentleman had no communication whatever with my father, to whom he was quite unknown, and who therefore will not be held responsible for views differing much on some points from his own" (*Ibid.* p. xiv. note 1). Dr. Brentano, very properly, retains the correct appellation of "religious" for some Gilds, a fact not pleasing to Mr. Furnivall, as Dr. Brentano has recorded in a supplemental passage when he says, "as Mr. Furnivall thought that my reasons (for so doing) were to be sought for in connection with the fact of my being a Roman Catholic, *and as he has even asked me to state this fact to my readers, in order to caution them against any prejudices,* I wish only, while doing this, to add a few words more on the real reasons for calling these Gilds 'religious'" (*Ibid.* p. lviii.). The italics are mine. Therefore, according to Mr. Furnivall, a Catholic archæologist is unfit to write on Catholic institutions, and Catholic matters, and these can be more ably described and explained by Protestants, imbued with Protestant prejudices, whose writings are disfigured by ignorance and bigotry. I may remark that reference is made several times to Dr. Rock, yet the *Church of our Fathers* gives many documents about Gilds, which are fatal to some of the assertions and inferences contained in the "English Gilds," and it is no wonder, therefore, that they should have been passed over unnoticed.

⁴ Miss Toulmin Smith has noted, in her introduction, that the Gild of the Annunciation at Cambridge "excludes priests altogether" (*English Gilds*, p. xxix.). The statutes will not bear out this assertion. The Latin original is *nullus capellanus . . . in dicta gildâ recipiatur,* which Mr. Toulmin Smith construes : "No parson . . . shall come into the Gild." "Parson," *persona,* is the old term used in England, in the ages of faith, for a priest ; but in this instance of the Cambridge Gild, *capellanus* evidently applies to a priest who is *already* a "chaplain" of some other Gild or institution.

⁵ *Ancient Laws,* &c. Edit. Thorpe, vol. ii. p. 247.

they paid a sum of money to have a daily remembrance, or "certain" made at Mass for all their members, living and dead. Thus the *Valor Ecclesiasticus* mentions "the certent of iii. gylds."[6]

Every Gild, also, had its own arrangements in regard of its general meetings; they took place once, or thrice, or oftener in the year. This was the ceremonial observed. They assembled in their Gild-hall, and then went to the church, in which they had their chapel, or altar, at which Holy Mass was celebrated by the Gild-priest. Then the general meeting—the Mornspeche, or the spekyng to-gedyr—was held, which generally began with a prayer, such as five *Paters* and five *Aves*;[7] and then the affairs of the Gild were discussed, and arranged for the year, after which the members had a refection together in the Gild-hall,[8] and on the following morning the Mass of Requiem was celebrated. The allowances of ale and other items were generally fixed by the statutes; and it was at these festive meetings that the *poculum charitatis*, or grace cup, or loving cup, was passed round the festive board.[9]

The English Gilds were invariably placed under the protection of our Blessed Ladye or some saint; and in those Gilds which bear the name of a saint, our Ladye is usually included amongst those to whose honour, or under whose guardianship the Gild was established.[10] This is fully proved by the nine

---

[6] Cf. tom. vi. p. iv. For the meaning of "certain," cf. Rock, *Church of our Fathers*, vol. iii. pp. 126—131. May not "certain" have taken its name from a "certain" sum of money being left for the object. Thus in the tale of the Chanons yemen, the

> Chanon came upon a daie
> Unto this priestes chamber, where he laie
> Beseching him to lene him a certain
> Of gold . . .
>
> (Chaucer, Opp. Edit. 1602, fol. 59).

[7] *English Gilds*, p. 37.

[8] *Ibid. passim.* Cf. Brentano, *ibid.* p. lxxxii.; and Labbe, tom. viii. col. 572. Edit. cit. For the *Eulogia*, cf. Labbe, tom. i. col. 1523, 1524; and Rock, *Church of our Fathers*, vol. i. pp. 135—139.

[9] The *caritas*, or a single draught of wine, in pledge of mutual kindness was in use with our Anglo-Saxon forefathers. Want of space allows me only to refer to it, but full and most interesting details are given by Rock, *Church of our Fathers*, vol. ii. pp. 335—342.

[10] Mr. Toulmin Smith thought that he had succeeded in finding a Gild which was an exception to this general rule—in the Gild of the Smiths of Chesterfield (*English Gilds*, p. 168, note), but it seems to have escaped his notice that it had already become incorporated with the Gild of the Holy Cross of the Merchants of Chesterfield in 1387, consequently, any previous title which it might have borne had merged into the new one (see Dr. Brentano's note, p. lxxxiii.).

hundred and nine Gilds which existed in Norfolk alone, and of which one hundred and seventy-seven were Gilds of our Ladye.[11]

Some Gilds were founded solely for religious purposes, such as the Salve Gild in the Church of St. Magnus near London Bridge, so called because the members assembled together every evening to sing the *Salve Regina*.[12] Stow particularly mentions that most other churches had theirs, *i.e.* Salve Gilds; and legacies of candles were often left to burn before the image of our Ladye, whilst the *Salve* was being sung.[13] The object of the Gild, called the Little Fraternity of our Ladye, in the Church of St. Stephen, Coleman Street, was to provide candles to burn before the image of our Ladye in that church.[14]

At Bodmin there was a Gilde of our Ladye of Walsingham.[15]

At Carbrooke Magna the Gild of our Ladye had its chapel, and maintained a priest to sing there.[16] At Caston the Gild of our Ladye kept a light constantly burning before her image;[17] as likewise did the Ladye Gild at Cheveley,[18] and the Ladye Gild at Griston.[19] The Gild of the Annunciation had its altar in St. Paul's, London.[20] The Drapers' Company maintained its Ladye-light in St. Marye Woolchurch;[21] and Sir Simon Eyre, a famous merchant, and Mayor of London in 1445, made a rich endowment for a Gild of our Ladye in the Church of St. Marye Woolnoth.[22] The Gild of our Ladye at Lynn was founded in 1329.[23] In the Church of St. Andrew's, Norwich, there was a Gild of Our Ladye of Grace.[24] At Oxford, the Gild of the Cordwainers built the chapel of our Ladye in the Church of All Hallows;[25] and the barbers of Oxford, on their incorporation, agreed to keep a light before our Ladye Chapel, in the Priory of St. Frideswithe, and fixed the sum which each member should contribute during the year.[26] The object of the Ladye Gild at Silverton was to find a Gild-priest to pray for its members and its benefactors.[27] At Tottington the Gild of the Nativity of our Ladye kept a candle burning continually before her image during the time of Divine Service.[28]

---

[11] S. p. 2. I inadvertently stated the number as one hundred and seventy-eight.
[12] S. pp. 87, 88.   [13] S. p. 115.   [14] S. p. 89.
[15] Lysons, *Magna Britannia*, Cornwall, p. 35.   [16] S. p. 9.   [17] *Ibid.*
[18] S. p. 15.   [19] S. p. 50.   [20] S. p. 73.
[21] S. p. 77.   [22] *Ibid.*   [23] S. p. 99.   [24] S. p. 108.
[25] S. p. 119.   [26] *Ibid.*   [27] S. p. 139.   [28] S. p. 152.

h

These few instances, which are taken from all parts of England, are quite sufficient to prove what was the universal custom with the secular Gilds at least.

All the possessions of the thousands of Gilds in England, became vested in the Crown by the Acts of the 37th Henry the Eighth cap. 4, and of the 1st Edward the Sixth, cap. 14. The great Livery Companies of London escaped, being trading Gilds, and the Corporations of London had to redeem their property with £18,700.[29] The act of spoliation Mr. Toulmin Smith describes as a "case of pure, wholesale robbery and plunder, done by an unscrupulous faction to satisfy their personal greed, under cover of the law."[30] In another place he says that "the unprincipled courtiers, who had devised and helped the scheme, gorged themselves out of this wholesale plunder of what was, in every sense, public property."[31] He thinks, however, that for the seizing of the property of monasteries some excuse can be made. Monasteries in truth were quite as much public property as Gilds, in fact, even more so : and it should be borne in mind that the *only* evidence against the religious houses is the report of Cromwell, who was *employed to provide a cause for confiscation;* but the original printed copies were destroyed before the death of Henry the Eighth, and the six versions of the report still extant, and each professing to be the original, all differ in most important details.[32]

What the monasteries did on a large scale, the Gilds did on a smaller one and in a different sphere ; still acts of charity to their neighbours and the poor of Christ, and prayers for deceased members and benefactors, were common to both. Parkins, the continuator of Blomefield, speaking of the suppression of the Gilds at Tebenham, one of which was of our Ladye, says : "But as the poor of the parish were always partakers with them, I much question whether their revenues were not better spent than they have been since they were rapaciously seized from the parishes to which they of right belonged."[33] The same

---

[29] Brentano, *English Gilds,* p. clxiii.
[30] *English Gilds,* p. xlii. note 1.
[31] *Ibid.* p. xliii.
[32] See a most interesting little book, *The Monastic Houses of England ; and their accusers and defenders.* By S. H. B. pp. 1, 2. London : Richardson and Son, 1869.
[33] *Hist. of Norfolk,* sub. nom.

might, with greater justice, be said of the monasteries and convents.

§ 2.—THE SODALITY.

The Great Sodality of the Blessed Virgin Marye Mother of God does not, strictly, come within the limits I had laid down; nevertheless, as it had a brief existence in England in the latter part of the seventeenth century in the College of the Society of Jesus in the Savoy, London,[84] it deserves to be appended to the list of old English Catholic devotions to our Ladye.

The Sodality of the Blessed Virgin may be called the special devotion of the Society of Jesus, just as the White Friars confer the Scapular, and the Black Friars propagate the Psalter of our Ladye, and the Passionists, devotion to the Passion of Christ crucified. In every College of the Society there is a Sodality.

The Society of Jesus cannot but be devoted in an especial and pre-eminent manner to the Blessed Mother of Jesus, our God and Lord; and a reference to De Backer[85] will show how many works the Fathers of that illustrious Society have written in her honour and praise. It was divinely revealed to Blessed Alphonsus Rodriguez, that one of the objects for which the Society had been instituted was to obtain the promulgation of the dogma of the Immaculate Conception.[86]

This is, briefly, the history of the origin of the Sodality.

Father John Léon, born at Liège, was admitted into the Society at Rome; in 1563 he taught grammar in the Roman College.

Each day, after schools, he assembled the most pious of the scholars, selected from his own and the other classes, around a little altar which he had erected in honour of our Blessed

---

[84] In the *Catholic Miscellany* for the year 1825 a "Constant Reader" inquires: "In what part of London was the Sodality of our Ladye of Power held, of which Lord Cardigan was Prefect?" (vol. iv. p. 126). The query was not answered. Lord Cardigan probably was Robert Brudenell, second Earl Cardigan, 1664—1703. I have found no mention of this Sodality, and Rev. Father Morris, S.J., tells me that he knows nothing of it. *Ita ad me,* February 26, 1876.

[85] Cf. *Écrivains de la Compagnie de Jésus.* Second Edition.

[86] Ant. Natali, S.J. *De Cælesti Conversatione.* Brunæ, 1721, p. 251.

Ladye, to say a few prayers, and to make a spiritual reading in common. On Sundays and festival days they sang Vespers.

It soon became noticed that these spiritual pupils of Father Léon were remarkable for their virtuous conduct and example; they became models of good behaviour, and many others sought to join this little body. In 1568 a few very simple rules for its organization were drawn up with the approval of the Sovereign Pontiff; and in 1584, Gregory the Thirteenth, on hearing of the excellent results of this Sodality or Congregation, and of the good example which the members universally gave, issued the Bull *Omnipotentis Dei*, December 5, 1584, which established this Sodality in the Church of the Annunciation of the Roman College, and under the same title, and granted many privileges and indulgences. It was named the Mother Sodality or *Prima Primaria*[87] of all the other Sodalities erected or to be erected.

Passing over the other Papal Bulls relating to the Sodality, it is only necessary to say that on the 27th of September, 1748, Benedict the Fourteenth issued what is called the Golden Bull, *Gloriosæ Dominæ*. In virtue of this Bull, the altar of every Sodality is a *privileged* one for every priest, secular or regular, who says Mass there for a deceased Sodalist. Moreover, every priest who is a Sodalist can say Mass with the same privilege for a deceased Sodalist at any altar in any church.

The Sodality of our Blessed Ladye at Stonyhurst is a branch of the *Prima Primaria*, and represents that affiliation which was established in the English College of the Society of Jesus at Louvain, about the year 1617. The College began in 1613, and was removed to Liège in 1622. The first Prefect was Sir Thomas Leeds, Knight of the Bath; the second Sir Ralph Babthorpe; and the third Dr. Horton, a secular priest who subsequently entered the novitiate of the Society.[88]

The suppression of the Society in 1773 did not affect it, for the ex-members, who continued to hold the College under the name of the English Academy, kept up the Sodality until

---

[87] This is the inscription over the doors of the *Prima Primaria* in the Roman College:

PRIMA · PRIMARIA
CONGREGATIO
OMNIVM · CONGREGATIONVM
TOTO · ORBE · DIFFVSARVM
MATER · ET · CAPVT.

[88] *Ita ad me*, Rev. Father Morris, S.J.

they were driven out of Liège in 1794, in which year they came
to England, and established themselves at Stonyhurst. Consequently the Stonyhurst Sodality, tracing an unbroken descent
from the year 1617, is, perhaps, the oldest existing branch in
the world of the *Prima Primaria.*[39]

Whenever I revisit our venerable Alma Mater, it is always
a subject of grief to me that the old Sodality chapel exists no
longer as a sanctuary of our Blessed Ladye. There were, doubtless, good reasons for the change. Nevertheless it was a
hallowed spot, dear to many who have gone before us with
the seal of faith, and sleep the sleep of peace. It was the great
College sanctuary; it was, so to say, of ancestral interest, and
associated with the *fasti* of many of the old Catholic families
which, yet existing in unbroken male line, have had the glorious
privilege of surviving the days of persecution, and of being the
connecting links in the chain of faith between the old and the
restored English Church; we knelt at our dear Ladye's altar,
on the step whereon our fathers, and even our grandfathers,
had knelt before us, when we solemnly consecrated ourselves
to her service, as they before us had done; it had a sort of
hallowed atmosphere, such as one experiences at Loreto, at
Einsiedlen, and in the chapel of our Ladye *della Strada* in the
Gesù at Rome. As was said of the Chapel of Allinges, so might
have been said of it: "Poor and plain, simple to ruggedness,
naked to austerity, dark and lone was that chapel . . . there
was about it the same peculiarity that has been noticed about
other places of frequent pilgrimage and constant devotion. The
walls seem to be impregnated with and redolent of prayer:
there appears to be a whisper of prayer breathing around the
place, and the walls seem to give out and to surround you
with an atmosphere of prayer . . . the very stones appear to
have been mesmerized by the power of human supplication, and
to cry to one, as one enters, 'Great is the power of prayer, great
the peace to be obtained here by prayer.'"[40]

I admit that the old Sodality chapel was irregular in form,

---

[39] One of the old Sodality Register Books at Stonyhurst contains the copy of
a letter from the Rev. Father Thorpe to the Rev. Father Howard, which gives the
history of the legitimate continuation of our Sodality. The letter is dated September 5,
sine anno, but was written some time after 1773.

[40] *Month,* vol. iv. p. 48.

and somewhat inconvenient in other respects, but these very
irregularities added to the hallowed interest which haunted it,
because they carried one back to the days of the Penal Laws,
and, in imagination, almost to the "Church of the Hiding
Places." How many vocations to a religious life date from that
chapel? How many lives have been wholly influenced and
guided by the advice given in that chapel, and the resolutions
made before our Ladye's altar, and faithfully carried out?

It is the rule for the English Sodalists to recite daily either
the Little Office of the Immaculate Conception or the beads;
and on Sundays and holidays to sing the longer office, called
Officium Parvum B.M.V. I look back with joy and gladness
to my happy College days as a Sodalist; the chanting of the
hours of our Ladye seems to me more melodious than any
minstrelsy I have ever heard:[41] perhaps it was that those who
then sang were *innocentes manibus et mundo corde;* and although
years have rolled by, and good fellows have passed away, and
tongues, which then sang our Ladye's praises, are now mute
in the grave, the echo of what Dante calls

> The sweet strain of psalmody,

of the dear old Sodality chapel, still rings in my ears as I am
penning these words; friends and schoolfellows now scattered
over the wide world, or

> Carried into Heaven's light,

appear before me once more in their accustomed places, and I
seem to myself to be a Sodalist again, at Alma Mater. And if
it be that dying men see, *in ictu oculi,* displayed before them
the book of their whole lives, in which their every word and
action are set down, what a consolation to a dying Sodalist—
if he has proved himself worthy of the name—must be that
white page, standing out clearly before his memory, in which
is recorded the day and the hour of his solemn consecration to
our Ladye, every day since then remembered and daily repeated
according to his rule. And how great will be the peace of his
soul, as for the last time, with failing utterance, but with his

---

[41] Thomas, thirtieth Abbot of St. Albans, A.D. 1349—1396, is described as
"*multum gaudens modulatione suorum monachorum quibus æstimabat optimos cantores
comparari non posse*" (*Gesta Abbatum Monast. S. Albani,* vol. ii. p. 401, Rolls Edit.).

stout English heart, he invokes our Ladye in the words of Holy
Church—

Maria Mater gratiæ
Dulcis Parens clementiæ
Tu nos ab hoste protege
Et mortis hora suscipe.

There is a Sodality in the Colleges of Mount St. Marye's,
of St. Stanislaus, Beaumont, and of St. Francis Xavier's, Liverpool, and one was established some years ago at Farm Street,
London. One entry in the *Fasti* of the Sodality at Stonyhurst
shows how highly its membership was valued. The late Mr.
Peter Middelton of Stockeld Park, who during a long life was
conspicuous for his piety, was admitted into the Sodality at
Stonyhurst on the 8th of December, 1798. Several years later,
he applied to have his name again inscribed on the Roll, and
his reason is set forth in the book. *Eodem die* (8 Dec.) *Dom.
Petrus Middelton, olim hujus collegii alumnus, pie timens ne inter
nomina sodalium ipsius nomen fuerit omissum, in desiderio habuit
iterum inscribi; sit igitur.* PETRUS MIDDELTON, SERVUS
PERPETUUS B.M.V. Every Sodalist, on admission, signs his
name on the Roll as *Servus Perpetuus Beatæ Mariæ Virginis.*

It cannot be denied that Stonyhurst has received signal and
manifest proofs of our Ladye's favour and protection. There
was a sad period, many years ago, when discord and disaffection
arose; mischievous spirits were at work, and authority was set
at defiance. If a mistaken act of kindness had not led to the
violation of one of the principal conditions of admission to the
College, the evil would have been insignificant. I may allude
to this period, since unfortunately it was of public notoriety.
There was serious cause for apprehension, as the welfare and
reputation of the College were at stake. It was an anxious time.
Venerable Fathers of the Society, held to be experienced in
government, were summoned to the rescue; but with varying
success, for ever and anon the flames of disaffection burst forth
again. It was disheartening. Then a young Father, blithe of
mood, yet stedfast and resolute, over whose placid brow thirty-
nine winters had not passed, was named Rector, and the result
proved the wisdom of his nomination. He was the right man
in the right place. The clouds disappeared, the storm blew

over; his nomination was the dawn of a day of brilliant sun-shine. *Esto perpetua!*

But how was this change brought about? Wherein lay the secret of his success?

Father Rector was a devout Sodalist, who could say what Justus Lipsius wrote of himself: *A prima adolescentia Divæ Virginis amorem et cultum indui, eamque Patronam mihi et ducem in periculis, in molestiis, in omni vitæ cursu elegi.*[a] What wonder, then, that our Ladye should have chosen him to be her especial champion? Evidence is not wanting to confirm this belief. Born upon one of her great festivals, his name stands forth in single and grand pre-eminence in the annals of our Sodality, for during his college career he was *five times* elected its Prefect by the Sodalists.

William of Malmesbury, writing of Abbot Ælfric about the date 947, says: *Hic est Ælfricus qui omnem curam ad Beatam transferens Mariam, possessionem et nomen monasterii ejus delegavit ditioni, ut, tacito interim beatissimi Petris nomine, ipsa sola loco videatur imperare. Nec fastidivit gloriosa Domina illustris et prædicandi viri munus.*[b] Even so did Father Rector. He placed the College of Stonyhurst under the especial protection of our Blessed Ladye; and one of his first acts was to erect, in what was then called the "Dancing Gallery," a statue of our Blessed Ladye. It was a plain image of plaster, and stood on a simple bracket of stained wood affixed to the wall, not far from the door of the Sodality chapel; yet it was the first image of our Ladye that hitherto had been erected in any public part of the College. What a sudden change ensued! and certainly not wrought by the hand of man! In this gallery, thenceforth named after our Ladye, and which had been the scene of the last manifestation of disaffection—I remember well the day and the hour—there might constantly be seen, kneeling on the bare stones, Sodalists and others, who habitually, and of their own accord, resorted thither on their way to schools or to recreation to greet our Ladye with an *Ave*, and perhaps to offer a candle to her.

This, then, was the origin of the sanctuary now put up in our Ladye's gallery, and in which her venerated image is placed

---

[a] *Diva Virgo Hallensis.* Antv. Ex Off. Plantin, 1616, cap, i.
[b] *De gestis Pontificum Angl.* vol. v. p. 405. Rolls Edit.

in its beautiful marble tabernacle, raised some years later. And from the date of the erection of that poor and simple statue, the history of the College is a series of success, prosperity, and triumph. Truly our Blessed Ladye loves those who love her, and repays with heavy interest whatsoever is done in her honour.

Several years have passed since the old Sodality chapel has been disused ; and it is possible that in a year or two hence the shrine of our Ladye may be removed to a more noble and spacious locality. Hence, for every reason, the old Sodality chapel and our Ladye's gallery and shrine at Stonyhurst deserve a place amongst these records.

THE "ENFANTS DE MARIE," OR CHILDREN OF MARYE.

In many convents there are congregations or confraternities of our Blessed Ladye, the members of which are called *Enfants de Marie*, or Children of Marye ;—in Italian, *Figlie di Maria.* Those which are erected by a diploma of the General of the Society of Jesus are branches of the great *Prima Primaria* Sodality, and enjoy all the privileges and indulgences attached to it, in common with all other Sodalists. A distinction, therefore, must be made between the *Enfants de Marie*, or Lady-Sodalists, who are affiliated to the *Prima Primaria*, and those *Enfants de Marie* who are members of some local or conventual confraternity which has no connection with the *Prima Primaria*.

On the 7th of January, 1837, the Congregation or Association of the *Figlie di Maria*, erected in the Convent of the Sacred Heart of Jesus in the Convent of the Trinità de' Monti at Rome, was affiliated to the *Prima Primaria* in the Roman College.[44] The Sodality of Girls erected at St. Marye's, Hampstead, was affiliated to the *Prima Primaria* by Letters of Aggregation of the General of the Society of Jesus, dated Rome, December 5, 1874.

[44] *Regole della Congregazione delle Figlie di Maria che vivono in mezzo al secolo.* Roma : Typ. A. Monaldi, 1844, p. 21.

CHAPTER THE THIRD.

Devotions and Good Works.

§ I.—PILGRIMAGES. PROCESSIONS. ALMS. FASTING.

> *O Benigna*
> *Mediatrix nostra*
> *Quæ es post Deum spes sola*
> *Tuo Filio nos repræsenta*
> *Ut in poli aula læti jubilemus.   Alleluya.*
>
> Missal of Arbuthnot.[1]

PILGRIMAGES.

PILGRIMAGES, which are now so well understood in consequence
of their happy revival in England, were a favourite form of
devotion with our forefathers.   The *Servitium Peregrinorum*,
that is, the form of the blessing of the staff, and the pilgrim
Mass, is given in the Sarum *Manuale*.[2]   Heretics, have always
manifested their especial dislike to the practice of them.   Thus,
about the year 1389, the Wiclefites "preched openly ageyn
pilgrimage, and specially Walsingham and the rode of north
dore.[3]   The bischopps of this lond saide right nowt to this
but kept hem in here houses, and opened no mouth to berk
ageyn these erroneous doggis."[4]   The Lollards maintained
that "God is lyk presentli everywhere, and therefore he is lyk
readi for to ȝeve hise gracis and ȝiftis everywhere, where ever
a man sechith after hem ; and therefore no place in erthe is
holier than an other place is, and noon ymage is.   Wherefore
it is a vein waast and idil for to trotte to Wa(l)singham rather
than to ech other place in which an ymage of Marie is, and
to the rode of the north dore at London rather then to ech

---

[1] Reprint, p. 352.   Burntisland, 1864.
[2] Rothomagi, 1509 ff. liiii—lviii ; cf. also the Sarum Missal.
[3] The rood at the north door of St. Paul's, London.   S. p. 70.
[4] Capgrave, *Chronicle of England*, p. 252.   Rolls Edit.

other roode in what ever place he be."[5] Cranmer, as might readily be supposed, adopted similar views.[6]

The great and unceasing stream of pilgrims to the Holy Places, and to the Tomb of the Apostles at Rome, commenced almost with the dawn of Christianity. Other great sanctuaries in the course of time became famous, as St. Martin of Tours, and St. James of Compostella. The Irish were particularly conspicuous for their love of pilgrimages. Walfrid Strabo says that their custom of going on pilgrimages was almost a second nature,[7] and Richmarch, in the *Life of St. David*, speaks of their insatiable ardour of making pilgrimages.[8] Their faith was strong, yet it must be admitted that their zeal led them to undertake pilgrimages in a somewhat reckless manner, and occasionally without any apparent definite object, provided, as the Saxon Chronicle says, "they were in a state of pilgrimage for the love of God." Under the year 892 it records that :

"Three Scots came to King Ælfred in a boat without any oars from Ireland, whence they had stolen away, *because they desired, for the love of God, to be in a state of pilgrimage, they recked not where.* The boat in which they came was wrought of two and a half hides, and they took with them food for seven nights, and on the seventh night they came to land in Cornwall, and they went straightways to King Ælfred. Thus were they named, Dubslane, Macbetha, and Maclinmum."[9]

Pilgrims were held in reverence. Charlemagne wrote to Offa, King of the Mercians, freeing English pilgrims on their way to the *Limina Apostolorum* from all tolls and customs.[10] In Ireland the law protected from distress a member of a tribe who had gone on pilgrimage, or to obtain Holy Communion or a physician for a person on the point of death.[11] In the

---

[5] *The Repressor of over-much blaming of the Clergy.* By Reginald Peacock, D.D., sometime Lord Bishop of Chichester, vol. i. p. 194. Rolls Edit.

[6] S. p. 57.

[7] In *vita S. Gall.* lib. ii. cap. xlvi ; Gretzer, t. iv. pt. ii. p. 69.

[8] *Insatiabilis ardor peregrinandi* (Gretzer, *Ibid.*)

[9] Ad ann. 892. Rolls Edit. These wandering pilgrimages on sea were not unusual in Ireland. For the expedition of the sons of the Corra and the wandering pilgrimage of Snedhgus and MacRiaghla in the seventh or early in the eighth century—See O'Curry, *Lectures on the MS. Materials of Ancient Irish Hist.* Dublin, 1861, pp. 292, 293, 333.

[10] Gretzer, t. iv. pt. ii. p. 86.

[11] *Senchus Mor.* p. 267. Rolls Edit.

year 1399 an Englishman was taken prisoner by the French
soldiers at Cahors, but immediately set at liberty when they
discovered that he was on pilgrimage to Our Ladye of Roc-
Amadour.[12] The English acted in like manner in regard to
pilgrims; but to insure this international privilege it was
necessary to wear one of the pilgrim signs of Roc-Amadour.[13]

A proof of the multitude of pilgrims from Great Britain
and Ireland who crossed the Channel into France, was the
establishment of a special cemetery for them at Wissant about
the year 1130.[14] Wissant is a little to the east of Cape Gris-Nez.

The Pilgrimages of Devotion may be divided into two
classes: (1) Greater ones to sanctuaries across the sea, or in
distant countries; (2) lesser ones to some sanctuaries nearer
home; and these were common to all classes. Then there
were also *vicarious* pilgrimages, made by deputy to sanctuaries
both at home and abroad; and these differ from *spiritual*
pilgrimages often made by religious communities which have
inclosure.

In the Council of Calne, A.D. 978, it was decreed that it
should be lawful for the people to make pilgrimages to
St. Marye of Abingdon.[15] The English royal pilgrims to Our
Ladye of Walsingham are given under that name in the Series.

Henry the Second, on recovering from a severe illness,
went on pilgrimage, as he had vowed, to Our Ladye of Roc-
Amadour, in 1170,[16] or according to Robert du Mont in 1171.
Henry the Third visited the Sanctuary of Our Ladye of
Boulogne.[17] Edward the Second went to Our Ladye of
Boulogne, where he was married.[18] After his victory off Sluys
Edward the Third went on pilgrimage to Our Ladye of Arden-
berg.[19]

Many of the sanctuaries of our Ladye to which pilgrimages
were made were little out-of-the-way chapels. Leland records

---

[12] *Hist. Critique et religieuse de Notre Dame de Roc-Amadour.* Par A. B. Caillu.
Paris, 1834, p. 113.

[13] Forgeais, *Collection de Plombs Historiés.* Paris, 1863, pp. 52—60.

[14] *Hist. de N. Dame de Boulogne.* Par le R. P. Alphonse de Montfort, Capucin.
Paris, 1634, pp. 67, 68.

[15] S. p. i.

[16] Roger de Hoveden, *Annales.* Ad ann. 1170.

[17] Haigneré, *Hist. de N. Dame de Boulogne.* Boulogne, 1864, p. 41.

[18] Le Roy, *Histoire de N. Dame de Boulogne.* Paris, 1682, p. 54.

[19] S. p. 257.

that not far from Edon Water is a village "cawlled Burgham, and ther is a gret pilgrimage to our Ladye."[20] To the little chapel of Our Ladye of Caversham there "wasse great pilgremage."[21] At Newcastle-on-Tyne, Pilgrim Street still records the piety of our ancestors.[22] Near Liskeard, in a wood, there was a chapel of our Ladye, "caullid our Ladye in the Park, where was wont to be gret pilgrimage."[23] At Norwich there was our Ladye atte Oke, or of the Oak, so named because her image was placed in an oak tree,[24] a practice which is still so common in Catholic countries. Near Southampton the chapel of Our Ladye of Grace was "hauntid with pilgrimes,"[25] whilst "the fame of Southwick stoode by the Priory of the Blake Chanons there, and a pilgrimage to our Ladye."[26] Indeed, it is very probable that other towns besides Walsingham owed much of their prosperity to the pilgrimages to sanctuaries of our Blessed Ladye.

It was by no means unusual to make a vow of pilgrimage for the recovery of a sick friend or relative. Thus, on September 28, 1443, Mrs. Margaret Parton writes to John Parton, saying, "I have behested to go on pilgrimage to Walsingham and St. Leonards for you."[27] When Henry the Sixth was lying ill the principal members of his Court sought leave to make pilgrimages to sanctuaries in foreign countries for his recovery. One of them was John Mowbray, Duke of Norfolk, whose request the King graciously granted by writ tested at Westminster on the 14th of August, A.D. 1457.[28]

Not long after this date the Duke was on pilgrimage at Walsingham, and in the year 1471 the Duke and the Duchess together were on pilgrimage to Our Ladye of Walsingham on foot.[29]

Cardinal Wolsey ordered a yearly pilgrimage to be made to Our Ladye of Grace at Ipswich.[30] There exists in the Vatican a letter from Wolsey to Pope Clement the Seventh, dated London, April 16, 1526, returning thanks to His Holiness for the Indulgences which he had granted to this sanctuary; . . . *quia dive Marie de Ipswico sacellum hujus regni ob sacra miracula*

[20] S. p. 5.   [21] S. p. 11.   [22] S. p. 59.
[23] S. p. 65.   [24] S. pp. 112, 113.   [25] S. p. 140.   [26] S. p. 142.
[27] *i.e.*, Our Ladye in the priory of St. Leonard's, Norwich. S. p. 112.
[28] Rymer, *Fœdera*, t. i. pt. xi. p. 78; Hagæ Comitum, 1740.
[29] S. p. 175.   [30] S. p. 57.

fulgentissimum lumen, ac meum natale solum decorare dignata fuit.[31] Evidently the Cardinal was proud of his native place.

By a regulation made in 1268 the Canons of Senlis were allowed fifteen days of non-residence to go to visit Our Ladye of Boulogne.[32] By the "Consuetudines" of Hereford Cathedral, presumed to have been drawn up c. A.D. 1250, no canon was allowed to make more than one pilgrimage across sea in his life; for a pilgrimage to St. Denis he had leave of absence for seven weeks; to St. Edmund of Pontigny, eight; to Rome, and St. James in Galicia, sixteen; and to Jerusalem, one year. By the same constitutions he was given three weeks of absence every year to go on pilgrimage in England.[33]

VICARIOUS PILGRIMAGES.

As their name implies, these pilgrimages were made by deputy in accordance with a wish expressed by will or otherwise.

In 1310 Marguerite de Dampierre, wife of Gaucher the Fourth, of Châtillon, by will dated the 16th of January, left ten *livres* for the pilgrimages which she owed to Our Ladye of Boulogne, and other sanctuaries which she named, and desired that a pilgrim should be sent to each of them for her.[34] Formerly it was the custom at Boulogne to offer the *Vin d'honneur* to distinguished pilgrims.[35]

In 1471, William Ponte makes a bequest "to any one of those who will pilgrimage for me to Blessed Marye of Walsingham."[36] William Ecopp, rector of Hellerton, by his will dated September 6, 1472, desires that a pilgrim, or some pilgrims, be sent immediately after his burial on pilgrimage for him to Our Ladye of Walsingham, Our Ladye of Lincoln, and five more sanctuaries of our Ladye, and at each to offer 4d.[37] Robert Agas of Thurston mentions Our Ladye

---

[31] Theiner, *Vetera Monumenta Hibernorum et Scotorum Historiam Illustrantia*. Romæ. Typis Vaticanis, 1864, p. 554, n. 982.

[32] *Chartulary of Notre Dame de Senlis*, quoted in the MS. of Dom Grémier, Bib. Imperiale, Paris, t. clxiii. f. 64; quoted by Haigneré, *N. D. de Boulogne*, p. 47.

[33] *Archæologia*, v. xxxi. pp. 251, 252, notes.

[34] Du Chesne, *Histoire de la Maison de Châtillon-sur-Marne*. Paris, 1621, p. 360; Haigneré, ubi sup. p. 62; cf. also p. 67.

[35] S. p. 270.

[36] *Testamenta Vetusta*, p. 42.

[37] S. p. 42.

of Woolpit as one of the seven local pilgrimages which he directed his son to "go or do gon."[38] The various offerings of Elizabeth of York, which I have recorded under the different sanctuaries of our Ladye, were all made for her by deputy; and on the 26th of February, 1503, there is an entry of payment to a man that went on pilgrimage to Our Ladye of Willesden, by the Queen's commandment, of iii*s*. iiii*d*.[39] John Parfay, draper, of St. Edmundsbury, says in his will dated May 28, 1509: "I bequeth to a honest pst (priest) seculer (that) wyll go for me to our Lady off Park n' Lyskard in Cornewall, to Seynt Mychell Mount, and to Seynt Jamys in Galys ye next yer off grace aftr my dyscesse x marcs."[40] Legacies were also left to pay pilgrims to repair to Our Ladye of Pitye at Horstead.[41]

PENITENTIAL PILGRIMAGES.

These deserve a longer notice than my space will allow me to give. In the ages of faith penitential pilgrimages were very common. They may be divided into two classes: (1) Those undertaken in a penitential spirit, like that of Henry the Second, King of England, to the tomb of the Blissful Martyr, St. Thomas of Canterbury; (2) Pilgrimages made by order of a judicial sentence. It is with these latter that I shall occupy myself; because English sanctuaries are mentioned amongst those to which judicial pilgrimages were made.

Our Ladye of Boulogne was one of the celebrated sanctuaries of our Ladye to which pilgrimages of this sort were directed to be made. About the year 1273, Margaret Countess of Flanders, condemned a citizen of Ypres, who had stabbed another with a knife, to make a pilgrimage to Our Ladye of Boulogne. The ceremony, according to the terms of the sentence, was solemn. The condemned was to receive publicly in the church the pilgrim-staff and belt; and on his return he was to bring back an attestation, under seal, that he had fulfilled his sentence.[42] This is the earliest instance known of a judicial pilgrimage to Our Ladye of Boulogne.

[38] S. p. 249.
[39] S. p. 239.
[40] *Bury Wills and Inventories.* Camden Society, p. 109.
[41] S. p. 54.
[42] The charter of the Countess Margaret is preserved in the Archives of the Département du Nord, France; Haigneré, ubi sup. pp. 48, 50.

This practice formed a part of the penal law in France for the lay tribunals, as well as for ecclesiastical justice.[43]

Pilgrimages to different shrines of our Ladye were often imposed by the Inquisition in France. In the seventeenth century the Registers of the Inquisition of Carcassonne were transcribed by the Commissary Doat; and these volumes form one of the most curious collections in the Bibliothèque[44] at Paris. In one of these Registers there is a list of the principal sanctuaries in Christendom, classified according to the importance which they then enjoyed. There were four greater ones, the Tomb of the Apostles in Rome, St. James of Compostella,[45] St. Thomas of Canterbury, and the Three Kings of Cologne. The lesser ones were Our Lady of Boulogne, Vauvert, Puy, Chartres, Roc-Amadour, and many others.

Often pilgrimages to these shrines were imposed in commutation of a more severe sentence, and might be performed by deputy for a fixed sum of money.

These are the prices for deputy judicial pilgrimages from Ghent to the English sanctuaries of our Ladye—[46]

	Livres.		
Our Ladye at Salisbury	5	0	0
Our Ladye at Walsingham	4	0	0
Our Ladye in the Church of St. Katherine at Lincoln	5	0	0
Our Ladye of Lincoln	5	0	0

The celebrated old pilgrim-hymn to Our Ladye of Boulogne is now out of use : this is the first stanza—

> Roine qui fustes mise
> Et assize
> Là sus ou thron' divin,
> A Boulogne vostre église
> Sans faintise
> Sui venus ce matin
> Comme vostre pèlerin ;
> Chief inclin

[43] *Collect. MS. de Camps.* n. 39, f. 347, Bib. de Paris ; Haigneré, ubi sup. pp. 68, 69.

[44] I believe that at the present time, 1877, the proper name is Bibliothèque Nationale ; but its designation varies according to the dynasty which for the moment is supreme.

[45] By some, Compostella is considered to be another form of San Giacomo Apostolo, Giacomo Apostolo, Como Postolo, Compostol, Compostella.

[46] Cannaert, quoted in the Series under the respective names.

Humblement je vous présente
Mon âme et mon corps, affin
Qu' à ma fin
Vous veuilliés (estre présente) etc.[47]

It consists in all of eighty-four lines.

PROCESSIONS.

Congregatim de domibus confluebant, publica supplicatione obsecrantes.

2 Mach. iii. 18.

The processions in Catholic England must have been carried out on a magnificent scale. Processions were formerly called *Litaniæ*, and subsequently *supplicationes*. The first great procession in Rome, the *Litania Septiformis*, so called because the people assembled in seven divisions, was the celebrated procession organized in the year 591, to avert the scourge of the plague which had attacked the city of Rome with excessive violence. The Station was held at St. Marye Major. On the third day, according to the old *Libri Rituales,* the procession went to St. Peter's, carrying the miraculous picture of our Ladye by St. Luke, and the plague ceased as it was borne through the streets. When they arrived at the Tomb of Hadrian—now the Castle of Sant' Angelo—an angel was seen standing on the summit, in the act of sheathing his sword, and angels were heard singing, *Regina Cæli lætare, Alleluia. Quia quem meruisti portare, Alleluia, Resurrexit, sicut dixit, Alleluia :* to which St. Gregory added *Ora pro nobis Deum, Alleluia.*[48]

At Glastonbury there was a fair image of the Blessed Mother of God. In the course of time, Abbot Chinnock, A.D. 1374—1420, clad it very becomingly in gold and silver, and adorned it with precious stones. He also placed many relics in it. This image, together with the other relics, was carried with vene-

---

[47] From MS. 11,066, Bib. de Bourgogne, Brussels. See Haigneré, hist. cit. pp. 128—132. But Mone has given another text from a different MS., consisting of one hundred and thirty-two lines.

Royne, qui fustes mise
Et assise
Lapsus on throsne divin,
Devant vous en ceste eglise,
Sans faintise, etc.

Hymni Latini Medii Ævi. Friburgi Brisgoviae, 1854, t. ii. pp. 214—216.
[48] Baronius, t. x. pp. 493, 494, quoting from St. Gregory of Tours.

i

ration in the processions which were made on the more solemn festivals of the year.[49]

At Ipswich, a procession was celebrated every year in honour of Our Ladye of Grace, on the 8th of September.[50] At Leicester, in the annual procession of our Ladye, her image was carried under a canopy by four bearers,[51] and preceded by twelve persons representing the twelve Apostles.[52] At Stamford, in the procession of the Gild of our Ladye, five torches were carried in her honour,[53] evidently in commemoration of her Five Joys; and at St. Albans, the weekly procession in honour of our Ladye, the monks wearing albs, was a very old custom. Badulf, the seventeenth Abbot, A.D. 1146—1154, obtained that it should be made to the altar of our Ladye.[54]

The first great public procession in honour of our Ladye celebrated in England after the repeal of the penal laws, took place at Stonyhurst, on the 26th of May, 1842.

ALMS.

Da tua, dum tua sunt; post mortem nulla potestas Dandi: si dederis, non peritura dabis.[55]

No one could ever refuse a poor person who besought alms for our dear Ladye's love.

At Blois, the Hotel Dieu is described, in its earliest documents, as *L'Aumône de Notre Dame*, as if to show that it was the love of our Ladye which prompted the support of this charitable institution.[56]

Maild, the mother of the Blissful Martyr St. Thomas, used to place her son when young into a scale, and fill up his weight[57] in bread, meat, clothes, coins even, and other things, which were

---

[49] John. Glaston. ubi sup. p. 46.

[50] *History and Description of the Town and Borough of Ipswich.* By G. R. Clarke. Ipswich and London, 1830, p. 178.

[51] The image of our Ladye of Puy in France is carried in procession by four of noble birth, and the four who bear the canopy are called the "Barons" of our Ladye.

[52] S. p. 61.

[53] S. p. 143.

[54] S. p. 130.

[55] Over the door of a hospital in the town of Opolia or Oppela, near the frontiers of Poland. Migne, *Dict. des Pèlerinages*, t. ii. p. 1311.

[56] Hamon, *Notre Dame de France*, p. 135. Cf. *Recherches sur l'Hotel Dieu.* Par M. Dupré, Bibliothécaire de la ville de Blois.

[57] Cf. Ducange, voc. *ponderare.*

of use to the poor, and then she would distribute them to the needy, endeavouring thereby more earnestly to commend him to the Divine Mercy, and to the protection of the Blessed Marye ever Virgin.[58]

In 1254, Walter de Suffield, Bishop of Norwich, left to Walter de Calthorpe his nephew sundry articles, for which he required him, as long as he lived, to feed one hundred poor on the Assumption of the Blessed Virgin, and to give a dinner to a poor person every day in the year.[59]

Archbishop Winchelsey of Canterbury was accustomed on the four more solemn feasts of our Blessed Ladye, and on their vigils, and on the feasts of her Conception, to distribute one hundred and fifty pennies to an equal number of poor persons, in the praise of our Ladye.[60]

Bread and meat given in our Ladye's love were called Saint Marye's loaf,[61] and Ladymeat.[62]

It may be that the chapel of our Ladye of Alingtre *prope furcas*, or near the gallows, took its name from the custom of giving a cup of ale to criminals as they passed on their way to execution.[63]

By his will, dated February 25, 1506-7, John Stockdall, alderman of York, bequeathed to "my wiff Ellen my new house in Petergait as long as she keepeth her soul and unmarried, so y* she yerly on Candilmesse day mayk a dyner to thirteen men and a woman, in the honour of Christ and His twelve Apostells, and ye woman in the worschipe of oure Ladye, and to keep oure Ladye Masse wekely on ye Saturday."[64]

The Privy Purse expenses of the Princess Mary, afterwards Queen Mary, contains this entry in the month of August, 1544:

"*Itm*, delyured to Mr. Lathom to distribute in almes on O. Lady daye, thassumption, xx *s.*"[65]

---

[58] In *Vita*, auct. Rogerio de Pontiniaco. *Patrol. Lat.* t. cxc. col. 59. Edit. Migne.
[59] S. p. 107.
[60] *Anglia Sacra*, t. i. p. 13.
[61] S. p. 138.
[62] S. p. 104.
[63] S. pp. 51—53.
[64] *Test. Ebor.* vol. iv. p. 257.
[65] P. 162.

FASTING.

The laws of King Æthelred say: "Let all Saint Marye's feast-tides be strictly honoured, first with fasting, and afterwards with feasting."[66]

John Peckham, Archbishop of Canterbury, A.D. 1278—1294, who was a Franciscan, kept the Lent of his Order, which consists of a fast of forty days in preparation for the feast of the Assumption of our Ladye.[67] He also wrote a pastoral letter on the subject, in which he recommended this Franciscan fast, and granted an indulgence of ten days to all who should observe it.[68]

Fasting in honour of our Ladye, and sometimes on bread and water, especially on Saturdays, is an old custom, and was much practised by our forefathers. There is a proverb which says: *Qui non indiget Divæ Virginis ope, ejus Sabbato non jejunat.*[69]

In 1397 Hugh MacMahon recovered his sight by fasting in honour of the Holy Cross at Raphoe, and of the Blessed Virgin Marye at Ath-Trim.[70]

The Saturday fast in honour of our Ladye was sometimes called "drinking with the duck and dining but once." Thus in Piers Ploughman, our Ladye is thus addressed:

> Lady to py leve sone, lowte for me nouthe
> That he have pyte on me putour, of his pure grace and mercy
> Whit þat ich shal quath þat shrewe, Saterdayes for thy love
> Drynke bote wᵗ þe douke, and dyne bote ones.[71]

Fordun, an old Scottish writer, alluding to this custom, says that, "in the days of our fathers the Saturday was held in the greatest veneration in honour of the (Blessed) Virgin, chiefly by the devotion of the women who, fasting every Saturday, were most devoutly content with one refection of bread and water only."[72]

---

[66] *Ancient Laws and Institutes of England.* Edit. Thorpe, 1840, folio edit. p. 131.
[67] Wadding, *Annales*, t. v. p. 85, n. xxv. Romæ, 1741.
[68] Wilkins, *Concilia*, t. ii. pp. 94, 95.
[69] Wichmans, *Brabantia Mariana.* Antv. 1632, vol. i. p. 121.
[70] *Annals of the Four Masters.* See S. p. 311.
[71] *Passus Septimus*, p. 96. Edit. Whitaker. London, 1813.
[72] Johis de Fordun, *Scotichronicon.* Edit. W. Goodall. Edinburgh, 1759, lib. vii. cap. xlii. p. 422.

He then notices some little peculiarities of the gratification of self-will in regard of fasting in honour of our Ladye. "Prelates are deserving of blame who allow the people to vary the days of fasting in honour of our Blessed Ladye, since, for the reasons already given, the Saturday is dedicated to her. But now you will find both men and women, who take good suppers, eating even eggs on Saturday, who on Tuesday or Thursday would not touch a crust of bread lest they should break the fast of our Ladye. Thus they transgress, without fear, the fasts prescribed by the Church, either on the Ember Days, or the vigils of the Apostles, whilst neither for God nor man would they break a fast which they have undertaken of their own will, on days when meat is allowed. O self-will! enemy of the soul! opposed to God and pleasing to the foul fiend."[73]

I cannot help thinking that these voluntary fasts on Tuesdays and Thursdays in honour of our Ladye must have reference to some particular Scottish devotion, the memory of which has perished. In some places, according to Spinelli, even the feast of the Annunciation itself was kept a fast, out of profound reverence to the great mystery of the Incarnation. Fast was equally kept in some places on Tuesdays, in honour of Our Ladye of Constantinople, and on Wednesdays in honour of Our Ladye of Mount Carmel.[74]

Thomas of Cantimpré, who wrote in the thirteenth century, notices that the fasting on Saturdays, in honour of our Ladye, obtained for many the grace of a sincere repentance, and a good confession, together with the last sacraments of the Church, before they died.[75]

In Scotland, six feasts of our Ladye were kept with fasting on the eve, as was also the festival of St. Thomas of Canterbury.[76]

On the other hand, some extra portions were given to the sick in honour of our Ladye on Saturdays. Thus Geoffrey, sixteenth Abbot of St. Albans, A.D. 1119—1146, endowed the

---

[73] *Scotichronicon,* cap. xlviii.

[74] *Pietas ac Devotio quibus B. Virgo Deipara Maria a nobis colenda est.* Auct Pet. Anton. Spinelli, S.J. cap. v. § viii. apud *Summam Auream de Laudibus B. V.M.* t. v. col. 101. Edit. Migne.

[75] *Bonum universale de apibus in quo ex mirifica apum repub. universa vitæ bene et Christiane instituendæ ratio traditur.* Duaci, 1627, lib. ii. c. 28.

[76] *Breviarium Aberdonense,* reprint, in Kalendario.

infirmary with the church of St. Peter in the town, so that the refectory of the infirmary might be supplied with a "charity" of wine or meat every Saturday, or on another day of the week instead of the Saturday, when the commemoration of our Ladye was kept, which Abbot Geoffrey ordained to be made in albs.[77]

HAIR-SHIRTS.

Corporal mortifications and austerities in honour of our Ladye were also much practised, and one very favourite one in England consisted in wearing a hair-shirt. As every one may not know what exactly a hair-shirt is, I may add that it is a garment composed of horse-hair twine, netted, like the horsehair gloves which are used in bath-rooms. One which I saw from a monastery in Germany had arms, and was about four feet long.

St. Thomas of Canterbury clothed himself with an "hard heyre, full of knottes, which was his sherte, and his breche was of the same;" and St. Edmund's mother "were herde heyre for our Ladye's love."[78] This sainted matron included a hair-shirt in the outfit which she gave her son on going to the University, as I have already mentioned.

After Antony Widvile, Earl Rivers, had been beheaded, a hair-shirt was found on his body. It was known that he had worn it for some time before his death. It was subsequently hung up before the celebrated image of our Ladye in the White Friars' church at Doncaster.[79]

"When Sir Thomas More was about eighteen or twenty years old he used oftentimes to weare a sharp shirt of hayre next his skinne, which he neuer left of wholy; no, not when he was Lo: Chancellour of England. . . . He added also to this austeritie a discipline euerie fryday and high fasting dayes. . . . He used also much fasting and watching, lying often either vpon the bare ground, or vpon some bench, or laying some logg vnder his head, allotting himselfe but foure or five howers in a night at the most for his sleepe, imagining with the holie Saints of Christ's Church that his bodie was to be

[77] *Gesta Abbatum Mon. S. Albani*, vol. i. p. 76. Rolls Edit.
[78] This is stated in a life of St. Edmund, in an imperfect black-letter volume in the library of St. Beuno's College.
[79] Bentley, *Excerpta Historica*, p. 245, see S. p. 28.

vsed as an asse, with strokes and hard fare, least prouender
might pricke it, and so bring his soule like a headstrong iade
into the bottomelesse pitt of hell."[80]   I can bear testimony that
an illustrious descendant of his, who now sleeps in Christ,
followed the example of his great ancestor in all these practices
of mortification ; and that after he had reached the patriarchal
age of eighty years, he still continued to fast on bread and
water on the Saturdays, in honour of our Blessed Ladye.

§ 2.—THE MARYE MASS.

Salve Sancta Parens, enixa Puerpera Regem,
Qui cælum terramque regit per sæcula.
Introit of our Ladye's Mass, Sedulius, *Carmen Paschale.*

Mention is frequently made in the *Series* of the Mass of our
Ladye, often called the Mass of St. Marye, or the Marye Mass.

In most of, if not in all, the cathedrals, collegiate churches, and
abbeys in England, it was the daily custom to sing a Mass of
our Ladye, which was celebrated at an early hour, and quite
independently of the festival of the day.   Generally one particular priest was appointed for this special duty, and he was
known as the Seynt Marye priest, a title which is often
mentioned in old wills.[81]   And his residence would be called
St. Marye priest's house.[82]   I have found no record of the
origin of this pious custom,[83] but it was not confined to England.

The Mass said on these occasions was the votive Mass of
our Ladye composed by our Alcuin, to whom, according to
general opinion, belongs the honour of having composed the
first Mass of our Ladye, which was inserted in the Missal
where it still is.[84]

The daily morning, or Marye, Mass was the same throughout
the year, even on festivals of our Ladye.   The Sarum Missal
gives it under the rubric *Ordinatio Misse quotidiane beate virginis*

[80] *The Life and Death of Sir Thomas Moore, Lord High Chancellour of England,*
written by M.T.M. s. l. v. a. pp. 27, 28.   The hair-shirt of Sir Thomas More is now
preserved in the convent at Spettisbury.
[81] *Bury Wills,* pp. 6, 16, 56, 74, 831.
[82] S. p. 265 sub voc. *Arlingham.*
[83] Cf. *Act. SS.* ad diem 14 April, p. 241 ; also the *Statutes of the Abbey of Cluny.*
[84] Alcuin, *Liber Sacramentorum,* c. vii. Opp. t. ii. col. 455.   Edit. Migne.

que dicitur salve:[85] hence I am inclined to believe that chapels
described as Salve Chapels were so called, because the Marye
Mass was celebrated in them.[86]   The Sarum Missal also gives
a Mass for women before childbirth: *Missa ad honorem virginis
gloriose pro mulieribus pregnantibus, aut alias in partu labor-
antibus.*

There can be no doubt that the Marye Mass was, in addition
to those I have already mentioned, celebrated in every church
in England, where the number of priests allowed of one being
told off for this pleasing duty without interfering with the
parochial and other claims incumbent on their services.   Thus,
at St. Andrew's, Norwich, and the Charnel-house, there was a
daily Marye Mass.[87]   And in the Northumberland Household
Book, there is a list of "my lordis chapleins and preists in
Household.   Which be not appointed to attend at no tymes
but at service tymes and meallis," they are eleven in number,
and one of them is a "priest for singing of our Ladies Mass
in the chappell daily."[88]

In 1136, mention is made of the Marye Mass at Gloucester,
where it was celebrated, as usual, very early in the morning.[89]
Within less than a century later, it had become general in all
the greater churches of England.   Walsingham says that at
St. Albans the Marye Mass was sung with four candles, and
a chalice of gold and beautiful vestments ; it had been instituted
by Abbot William de Trumpington, 1214—1235.[90]   At Evesham,
twenty-four candles of wax and thirty-three lamps were to be
lighted daily, and to burn during the Marye Mass.[91]   Early
in the reign of Henry the Third, St. Marye Mass in St. Paul's,
London, is mentioned.[92]   There was also a daily Mass of our
Ladye in the Tower, and payments to the chaplain for its
celebration are mentioned in the Liberate Rolls.[93]   Both at
St. Paul's,[94] at Salisbury,[95] and elsewhere, there were foundations
for the Marye Mass.   At Ely, the custos of our Ladye's altar
received all the offerings there, and provided the Missal, chalices,
vestments, and candles required for the celebration throughout

[85] Edit. Paris, 1554, f. xxiii. in fine lib.
[86] As at Barking, S. p. 3.   [87] S. pp. 108, 109.   [88] P. 323.   [89] S. p. 49.
[90] S. pp. 130, 131.   [91] S. p. 37.   [92] S. p. 68.
[93] 24 & 25 Henry III. p. 13.   [94] S. pp. 68, 69.   [95] *Valor Ecclesiasticus,* vol. ii. p. 85.

the year.[96]   At Magdalēn College, Oxford, Wayneflete ordained that the second Mass every day should be that of our Ladye after the custom of the Church of Sarum.[97]

Elizabeth de Juliers, Countess of Kent, wife of John, Earl of Kent, second son of Edmund of Woodstock, who died in the 26th of Edward the Third, was solemnly veiled a nun at Waverley by William Edendon, Bishop of Winchester. Subsequently she quitted her profession, and was privately married without licence to Sir Eustace Dabricescourt, Knight, on the feast of St. Michael, 1360. The Archbishop of Canterbury imposed on them a penance, one part of which was that they should find a priest to celebrate daily service in Our Ladie's Chapel in Wingham Church, and another priest to do the same in their own private chapel.[98]

The Marye Mass was invariably sung. When Cardinal Wolsey issued his ordinances for all the houses of Canons Regular throughout England, by which he strictly forbade the use of *cantus fractus et divisus*, commonly called Prick-song,[99] in their choirs, he still allowed it during the Mass of our Ladye and the Mass of Jesus, which were sung outside of the conventual choirs in almost all the monasteries of the kingdom.[100]

In 1463, John Baret left a house to the "Seynt Marie priest of Seynt Marie Chirche here."[101] The accounts of St. Marye Hill, in London, for 1531, contain an entry of "Three gallonds and six pynts of malvesy for a year for Lady's Mass, 3s. 9d."[102] that is about two pints and a half a month.

The Provincial Council of Worcester, held under Walter de Cantilupe in 1240, made a decree against the priests of our Ladye's service going out for the day, after saying early Mass, and not being present at Divine Office.[103]   In the fifteenth

---

[96] Bentham, *Hist. and Antiq. of the Conventual and Cathedral Church of Ely*, p. 129. Lond. 1812.

[97] *Statutes*, p. 119.   Cf. also the *Descript. of the Ancient Rites of Durham*.

[98] Nichols, *Royal Wills*, pp. 215, 216.

[99] This was also expressed by *figuraliter*. *Singulis diebus in Aurora Missa de Domina nostra* figuraliter *decantatur*. Colvener, *Liturgia Mariana* c. ii. § 3, apud Summ. Aur. t. iii. col. 629.

[100] Wilkins, *Conc.* t. iii. p. 686.

[101] S. p. 135.

[102] Nichols, *Illustrations of manners and Expenses of ancient times in England*, p. 109. Lond. 1798.

[103] Labbe, t. xi. pt. cap. xii. col. 577.

century an abuse seems to have crept in of celebrating a very
early Mass on the five festivals of our Ladye, so as to leave
a long day free for enjoyment and pleasure. This was called
the "Gloton Masse," and it was at once prohibited. In 1418,
the commissary of the Bishop of Lincoln issued a monition
addressed to the Archdeacon of Leicester against those who
celebrate the Glutton Mass within the Archdeaconry, peremp-
torily forbidding it under pain of excommunication.[104]

§ 3.—OFFICE. LITTLE OFFICE OF THE IMMACULATE CON-CEPTION. ANTHEMS. SATURDAYS.

THE OFFICE OF OUR BLESSED LADYE.

*Cum in psalmodia studiis et divinis laudibus te vigilanter exerceas,
hortor, venerande frater, et moneo, ut quotidianum Beatæ Mariæ Virginis
officium non omittas.*

St. Peter Damian to the Monk Stephen.[105]

THE laity in Britain began centuries ago to recite the Office of
our Blessed Ladye. St. Margaret of Scotland used to recite
this office every day ; it would have been of the primitive form,
since she died in 1093.[106] In the ancren Riwle there are minute
prescriptions about the method of reciting the Office of our
Ladye.

It seems that each anchoress had to copy or transcribe the
Hours of our Ladye for her own use, as the Riwle continues :
"Let every one say her Hours as she has written them, and
say every service (tide, time, season of prayer) separately, as far
as you can in its own time, but rather too soon than too late,
. . . at the one psalm you shall stand if you are at ease, and at
the other sit, and always rise up at the *Gloria Patri* and bow ;
whosoever can stand always in worship of our Ladye, let
her stand in God's name ; "hevo se mei stonden euer on vre
Leafdi wurschipe, stonde a godes halve," and at all the seven
hours say *Pater noster* and *Ave Maria.*[107]

The *Miroure* of oure Lady, which is a devotional treatise on

[104] *Book of Memoranda of Philip Repingdon, Bishop of Lincoln,* Wilkins; *Concilia,* t. iii. p. 389.
[105] Lib. vi. ep. 29, opp. t. i. col. 419, *Patrol. Lat.* t. cxliv. Edit. Migne.
[106] *Act. SS.* ad diem 13 Jun. p. 328. Edit. Palmé.
[107] P. 21.

the Divine Offices, with a translation of these offices as used by the Sisters of Sion in the fifteenth and sixteenth centuries, contains some interesting instructions on the Office of our Ladye, and assigns various mystical significations to the several Hours in close conformity with what Durandus gives in his *Rationale.*[108]

The general arrangement of subjects for contemplation during the recital of the Office of our Ladye is as follows: at Matins, the Annunciation; Lauds, the Visitation; Prime, the Nativity of our Lord; Tierce, the Circumcision; Sext, the Purification; None, the Adoration of the Three Kings; Vespers, the Flight into Egypt; Complin, the Assumption. In all the Sarum Prymers these subjects are engraved at the beginning of the different Hours, but they are not invariably given in this order.

Up to the Great Apostacy the Office of our Blessed Ladye used in England was generally after the ancient and venerable use of Sarum, which office differs in some respects from the Roman. There was also an Office of our Ladye of the use of York, printed by Ursyn Milner in or about 1516.[109] Only one copy of it was known to exist some years ago, and I have not ascertained where it now is.[110]

These prayer-books, which were called Prymers, contained the Office of our Ladye, of the Dead, the Little Offices of the Holy Ghost and the Holy Cross, the Seven Psalms, and the Litanies of the Saints, the Passion of our Lord, together with many other fine old prayers, which may be looked for in vain in modern English books of devotion. Before printing was invented, these Books of Hours were often magnificently illuminated. Bequests of them often occur in wills: thus, in 1429, Ralph Avirley leaves his red Primer to Thomas Stone,[111]

---

[108] *Rationale*, lib. v. c. i. n. viii. Edit. Barthélemy, vol. iii. pp. 6, 7. Paris, 1854.
[109] Ames, *Typog. Antiq.* vol. iii. p. 1431.
[110] *Memoir of the York Press.* By Robert Davies, F.S.A. Westminster, 1868, p. 20. Among the valuable MSS. in the Public Library at Boulogne-sur-mer there is a fine MS. Horæ of our Ladye, which I take to be of the York use. It differs from the Sarum with which I have compared it. The Litany contains amongst others the names of Saints Alban, Oswald, Edmund, Augustine, Paulinus, John, Wilfred, Cuthbert, Swythin, Edmund, Edward, Leonard, Sampson, Austreberta, Hilda, Everildis, Etheldreda.
[111] *Test. Ebor.* vol. ii. p. 30.

and in 1443, Henry Markett of York, merchant, left his second best primer to Henry, his son.

The great number of existing MS. *Horæ* prove how general was the custom with the upper classes in England of reciting the Office of our Blessed Ladye. Henry the Sixth recited it daily.[112] Many of the *Horæ* contain the armorial bearings, and not unfrequently the portraits of the owner and his wife, attended by their patron saints, and on their knees before our Blessed Ladye. The so-called Bedford Missal is in reality the *Horæ* of our Ladye, executed for the Regent of France. Until the time of Louis the Fifteenth it was the custom in France to include in the *trousseau* of a bride a pair of beads and a copy of the Hours of our Blessed Ladye.[113]

When the Sarum rite ceased to exist in England, the Office of our Ladye of the Roman use was introduced. Thousands and thousands of copies were printed abroad, principally in the Low Countries. They found their way to England, and were well used, as I can testify from several old family ones in my possession, one of which bears the names of four generations by whom it was used.

It is also evident that our ancestors learned the Office of our Ladye by heart in their childhood, and a peculiar feature with them was that they recited it together, of which there is evidence of the fifteenth and sixteenth centuries. They even recited it whilst dressing. The Boke of Curtesay admonishes Lytyl John—

> While that ye be aboute honestly
> To dresse your self and do on your arraye
> With felowe wel and tretably
> Our lady matyns loke ye that ye say.[114]

And at Eton, chapter xxx. of the Statutes prescribes that the scholars of the same royal college in the mornings as soon as they shall have arisen, and whilst making their beds, shall say the Matins of our Blessed Ladye after Sarum use.[115]

---

[112] Agnes Strickland, *Life of Margaret of Anjou*, p. 217.

[113] Egron, *Culte de la S. Vierge.* Paris, 1842, p. 174.

[114] Caxton's *Boke of Curtesay.* Early English Text Society, 1868. Extra series, vol. iii. p. 5.

[115] *Ancient Laws, &c., for King's College and Eton*, p. 552. By their ancient rules the Carthusians were allowed to say the Office of our Ladye whilst they were at work : Horas B. M. omnibus diebus dicimus in cellis, vel ubi *sumus in opere* extra

Ladies were equally fervent in saying the Office of our Blessed Ladye, and bequests of primers are often found in their wills. Thus, in 1446, by will dated the 15th of August, Matilda, Countess of Cambridge, leaves " to my kinswoman (*consanguinea*) Beatrix Waterton, a gold cross which belonged to my mother, and my green [bound] prymer and a diamond, &c., to Katherine Fitzwilliam a small black [bound] prymer, and to Alesia, Countess of Salisbury, my cousin, my large best prymer."[116]

Cardinal Fisher says of the Countess of Richmond, mother of Henry the Eighth, that " First in prayer every daye at her uprysynge, which comynly was not long after five of the clok, she began certain Devocyons, and so after them, with one of her gentlewomen, the Matynes of our Ladye."[117]

It will be noticed that this excellent princess recited the Office of our Ladye with one of her gentlewomen in accordance with the usual custom in England, which made such an impression on the Venetian Ambassador that he considered it of sufficient importance to be mentioned in his relation to his Government.

" They are all present at and hear Mass every day . . . and if any can read they take the Office of our Lady to church, and recite it in a low voice in alternate verses, after the manner of religious orders."[118]

Queen Katherine also daily recited the Office of our Ladye, and on her knees.

The Martyr Lord High Chancellor of England, Sir Thomas More "vsed euerie day to say our Ladie's Mattins, the Seauen psalmes and letanies, and manie times the Graduall psalmes, with the psalme *Beati immaculati in via* and diverse other pious praiers, which he himself composed."[119]

cellas (Pars i. Stat. Antiq. cap. xxxvi. n. 13. Basileæ, 1510). Cassian says that the ancient monks of Egypt were allowed to sing their psalms as they worked (Opp. Edit. D. Alardus Gazæus, O.S.B. Attrebati, 1628. Lib. iii. *de Diurnis orationibus*, cap. ii. pp. 41, 42.

[116] *Test. Ebor.* vol. ii. p. 121.

[117] A mornynge remembrance had at the moneth mynde of the noble prynces Margarete, Countess of Rychemonde and Darbye, moder vnto Kynge Henry the VII. and grandame to our soverayne lorde that nowe is, uppon whose soule Almyghty God have mercy. Emprynted at London. in Flete Strete, at the sygne of the Sonne, by Wynkyn de Worde (1521). Not paginated. Stonyhurst Library.

[118] *Italian Relation of England.* Camden Society, p. 23.

[119] Christopher Cresacre More, *Life and Death of Sir Thomas More*, p. 31.

LITTLE OFFICE OF THE IMMACULATE CONCEPTION.

Few prayer-books are now printed which do not contain the Little Office of the Immaculate Conception of our Blessed Ladye, beginning with the hymn *Salve Mundi Domina.* Nevertheless, strange as it may appear, with a very few exceptions, those notably being the editions of 1730, 1802, and 1823, of the celebrated *Libellus Precum,*[1] either the condemned version which was put upon the Index in 1678, or a portion of it, is generally given instead of the approved Office of 1679. The history of this Little Office is evidently, in these days, quite unknown.

For the advantage of those who were unable to assist at Divine Office, a shorter form of Office consisting usually of versicles, hymns, and prayers to correspond with the seven Canonical Hours was prepared.

It is mentioned in the life of Alban Butler that he disapproved of these Little Offices, which he attributed chiefly to the Fathers of the Society of Jesus, and reference is made to the well-known *Cæleste Palmetum,* by Father Nakateni, which has gone through innumerable editions. I cannot, however, but think that his biographer is at fault, because the learned hagiographer must have known full well that Little Offices were in common use from the middle of the thirteenth century, at the latest. St. Bonaventure, who died in 1274, composed a Little Office of the Passion of our Lord ;[2] and a shorter one of the Compassion of our Blessed Ladye.[3] Another Little Office of the Compassion of our Ladye is attributed to Pope Clement the Fifth, A.D. 1305—1314, who granted forty days of indulgence to all who recited it.[4] Any one who has examined MS. *Horæ,*

---

[1] *Libellus Precum et Piarum Exercitationum in usum pie vivere et feliciter mori desiderantium.* St. Omers, 1730. The Liverpool edition of 1823 is a verbatim reprint, with the addition of the *Officium Parvum* of our Blessed Ladye and that of the dead. This most excellent prayer-book is given to every sodalist at Stonyhurst and the other Colleges of the Society of Jesus in England. Abroad, most of the sodalities had their own prayer-book in Latin, varying more or less, but containing many devotions common to all. Having examined a large number of them, I do not hesitate to say that our *Libellus* is not excelled by any of them.

[2] *Opusc.* t. i. pp. 439—442. Lugd. 1619.

[3] *Ibid.* pp. 486—490.

[4] *Hortulus Animæ,* Moguntie. 1511, not paginated ; also Marrucci, *Pontifices Mariani,* c. lx.

and the early printed prayer-books, and Offices of our Ladye, and the Sarum *Horæ* and Prymers, cannot have failed to notice the number of Little Offices which they contain. In many of these books the Hours of the Little Offices of the Holy Cross and the Holy Ghost are inserted after the corresponding Hours of the Office of our Ladye, thus showing that they were recited daily, as well as those of our Ladye. A reprint of the Sarum Prymer, with the magnificent prayers which our forefathers loved to recite, but which have been replaced in many instances with modern insipid and sensational compositions, would be a great boon. All the early printed *Horæ* and Prymers, and all the *Officia* of our Ladye printed at Antwerp, Douay, St. Omer's, and Rouen,—many of those which came from the presses of the three latter places are in English and Latin—contain the Passion of our Lord and a prayer to our Ladye, *Obsecro te Domina*. This was called of yore the *Obsessio*, or "Besieging prayer of our Ladye," those who recited it feeling sure that our Ladye could never refuse a petition made in such earnest words. A rubric in the Sarum Prymer of 1534 prescribes its recital before an image of Our Ladye of Pity ; [5] that is, a representation of our Ladye seated, with her Divine Son dead and lying on her knees.[6] The old English devotion to Our Ladye of Pity was very great ; and I do not believe that there existed a church in England in which an image of Our Ladye of Pity was not to be found. The Thirty Days' Prayer is the modern form of the *Obsessio;* and it was a common practice with our forefathers to read a Passion daily for the souls in Purgatory ; a pious custom which was observed by the Anglo-Saxons, as appears from a document of

[5] "To all them that be in the state of grace that dayly say devoutly this prayer before our blessyd ladye of pitie she wyll shewe them her blessyd vysage and warne them the daye and the houre of dethe, and in theyr laste ende the angelles of God shall yelde theyr sowles to heven, and he (they) shall obteyne v. hondred yers and soo many lentes (*i.e.* quadragenes or forty days) of pardon graunted by v. holy fathers popes of Rome." In the Stonyhurst Library. I cannot give the page, since the pagination in many leaves of this splendid edition has been cut away.

[6] *Tabulam depictam, in qua est Pietas, id est, Deipara in gremio tenens mortuum filium. Acta SS.* ad diem 2 Junii, p. 489, ad ann. 1421. The title of our Ladye of Pity is applicable to this type or representation alone. A magnificent image of our Ladye of Pity, of English work, two feet six inches in height, was recently discovered in Breadsall Church, Derbyshire. Photographs may be had of Mr. Richard Keene, Fine Arts Repository, All Saints, Derby.

about the year 805, which is given by Kemble in the *Codex Diplomaticus Ævi Saxonici.*[7]

The institution of the festival of the Conception of our Ladye in England is attributed to St. Anselm ; the earliest evidence in favour of St. Anselm is a Constitution of Simon Meopham, Archbishop of Canterbury, in the Provincial Synod of London, held in St. Paul's in February, 1328.[8] For many years it had no proper Office ; the Office used was that of the Nativity of our Ladye, "Conception" being substituted for "Nativity."

This substitution of "Conception" for "Nativity" was made in consequence of the alleged vision of Elsi, described in the apocryphal letter of St. Anselm, which is printed amongst his spurious works.[9] As this vision occupies a prominent place in several of the Offices of the Conception, it is as well to give its history, which is, briefly, as follows :

"After the Norman invasion it was rumoured that the Danes were preparing to fight the invaders, on the pretext that England was theirs by right. Wherefore William sent a prudent envoy, Elsi, Abbot of Ramsey, to Denmark to find out the real state of the case. After having accomplished his mission, and whilst on his return to England, he was overtaken by a dreadful storm at sea. In his danger he invoked our Blessed Ladye, when lo! a venerable old man, robed as a bishop, was seen walking on the troubled waters towards the ship. He thus addressed Elsi : ' Know that I am Nicholas, sent to thee by the Blessed Mother of God, whom thou hast invoked. Wouldst thou be saved ? Promise to God and to me that thou wilt celebrate and cause to be celebrated the festival of the Conception of the most pure Mother of God : the Office shall be that of her Nativity, Conception being substituted for Nativity.'"[10]

There are different versions of this alleged vision. Peter de Natalibus says that it occurred to St. Anselm whilst Abbot of Bec,[11] and crossing the straits on his way to England on affairs

---

[7] Vol. i. p. 93.
[8] Labbe. *Concilia.* t. xi. c. ii. col. 2478. Paris, 1672.
[9] Opp. t. ii. coll. 319—321, 323. Patrol. Lat. t. cxlix: Edit. Migne.
[10] *Ibid.*
[11] Catalogus Sanctorum, l. i. c. xlii. f. ix. Lugduni, 1508. St. Anselm was born A.D. 1033, entered the Order of St. Benedict in 1060, became Abbot of Bec in 1078, Archbishop of Canterbury in 1093, and died in 1109 (*Acta SS.* t. ii. Aprilis ad diem 21 Apr. p. 865).

of his Order. The *Cursor Mundi*, a poem of the fourteenth century, a copy of which is in the British Museum, describes the apparition to Elsi as that of an angel, and not of St. Nicholas,[12] or one vested in episcopal robes.

The lessons of the Office of the Conception of our Ladye, which Langebek quotes from a MS. Breviary which he does not name, describe the apparition as that of an angel arrayed in pontifical robes. Langebek, however, gives their date as A.D. 1042, but as the fifth lesson describes the victory of William the Norman over Harold, which occurred twenty-four years later, there is clearly a mistake somewhere. According to Langebek, these lessons were originally in a MS. written in the year 1042, and belonging to the Academic Library of Copenhagen, which MS. perished in the fire of 1728. They had, however, been copied out, together with other legends of saints, by Thomas Bartholinus, and inserted in Tom. A. of his collections. These extracts were also burnt in the same fire, but the charred fragments were partially restored by Arnas Magnaeus and others; and it was from the charred fragments of Bartholinus that Langebek published these lessons.[13]

With reference to the authenticity of the vision, St. Bernard alludes to it in his letter to the Canons of Lyons, written A.D. 1140, but gives no credence to it.[14] Gerberon, the Benedictine editor of the edition of the works of St. Anselm which I have used, expresses his opinion very plainly. Mgr. Malou, the late learned and venerated Bishop of Bruges, does not hesitate to say : "*Le récit de la vision de l'abbé Helsin est apocryphe. Il fourmille d'incohérences, d'anachronismes, et de contradictions.*"[15] The venerable Lord Bishop of Birmingham, Dr. Ullathorne, who has written an interesting book on the Immaculate Conception of our Blessed Ladye, entertains a different opinion.[16]

The authenticity of this alleged vision is a question with

---

[11] MS. Cott. Vespasian A. iii. f. 139, col. 1.

[13] *Scriptores rerum Danicarum medii ævi.* t. iii. pp. 253, 254.

[14] Epist. 174. Opp. t. i. coll. 333—335. *Patrol. Lat.* t. clxxxii. Edit. Migne.

[15] *L'Immaculée Conception de la B.V.M. considérée comme Dogme de Foi*, par Mgr. J. B. Malou, evêque de Bruges, vol. i. p. 114; vol. ii. pp. 429—439. Bruxelles 1857.

[16] *The Immaculate Conception of the Mother of God.* An Exposition by the Right Rev. Dr. Ullathorne, Bishop of Birmingham. London, 1865, pp. 168—170,

J

which I do not, and need not, here occupy myself. Domesday Book, as the Great Survey made by order of William the Norman is called,[17] was unknown to Dom Gerberon,[18] and to Malou. The former was evidently misled by an error in the old edition of the Monasticon, which assigns the date A.D. 1080 to Elsi,[19] whose successor is stated to have been the celebrated Herbert de Losinga, subsequently Bishop of Thetford; and Malou, in all probability, accepted this mistake. Now it is proved by the Ramsey Register[20] that Elsi was a witness to a charter of St. Eadward the Confessor,[21] and also to a deed of William the Norman, A.D. 1070.[22] Moreover, Domesday Book records the absence of Abbot Elsi in Denmark.[23] I need say no more about Elsi. Two other visions of our Ladye, which are also considered apocryphal,[24] are mentioned in the spurious letter of St. Anselm; yet they, together with the vision of Elsi, are commemorated in the original version of the Little Office of the Immaculate Conception.

The earliest Office for the festival of the Immaculate Conception of our Ladye was that of her Nativity, "Conception" being substituted for "Nativity"[25] wherever it occurs. The next Office was that of the Nativity of our Lady, but the first six lessons at Matins are taken from the apocryphal letter of St. Anselm, and give the history of Abbot Elsi. The lessons of the third nocturn are from St. Jerome. Another Office of the Conception of our Ladye is styled *Officium Conceptionis Beatæ Mariæ Virginis ex Concilio Basiliensi;* the lessons of the first nocturn are from the decree of the Council, A.D. 1431; and those of the second and third from the apocryphal letter of

---

[17] This priceless national record, the equal of which is possessed by no nation, used to be preserved at Winchester, in the Chapter House, which was called the *Domus Dei*, hence it was known as the *Liber Domus Dei*, whence the name Domesday Book.

[18] Cf. his *Censura* on the works of St. Anselm, tom. i. coll. 42—45. Edit. cit.

[19] Cf. Mon. Angl. vol. ii. p. 548 of the modern edition.

[20] MS. Cott. Vespasian, E 11.

[21] *Ibid.* f. 9.

[22] *Ibid.* f. 16 b.

[23] *Sed cum abbas esset in Danemarca*, &c. vol. i. f. 208. Cf. also Ellis, *Introduction to Domesday Book*, vol. ii. pp. 99—104. London, 1833.

[24] See the *Censura* of Gerberon, *loc. cit. ubi sup.*

[25] *E.g.* Nativitas *est hodie Sancta Maria Virginis*. Conceptio *est hodie Sancta Maria Virginis*, &c. as in the *Brev. Rom. in fest. Nativ. B.M.V.*

St. Anselm.[95] Hitherto the Offices were of the Conception of our Ladye.

A few years later the Offices of the Immaculate Conception appear. The first is the celebrated *Sicut Lilium* Office, so named from the first anthem at Vespers—*Sicut lilium inter spinas, sic amica mea inter filias Adæ.* It was composed by Leonard Nogaroli, a protonotary apostolic, and approved by Sixtus the Fourth. The lessons make no mention of Elsi; the collect is as follows :

Deus qui per immaculatam virginis conceptionem dignum filio tuo habitaculum præparasti, concede quæsumus, ut sicut ex morte ejusdem filii tui prævisa, eam ab omni labe præservasti, ita nos quoque mundos ejus intercessione ad te pervenire concedas. Per eundem, &c.[97]

It was followed almost immediately by another Office of the Immaculate Conception, which was composed by Bernardine de Busti of Milan, a friar minor of St. Francis. It is the most copious of all the Offices of the Immaculate Conception, for it contains nine new lessons for every day of the octave. Sixtus the Fourth approved of it, first verbally, and then by Brief under the ring of the Fisherman, dated St. Peter's, October 4, 1480; and later, *vivæ vocis oraculo*, attached to it the same indulgences with which he had enriched the *Sicut Lilium* Office of Leonard Nogaroli.

The fifth and sixth lessons of the fourth day of the octave give the history of Abbot Elsi, but St. Nicholas is not mentioned by name; the apparition is described as that of a venerable man wearing an episcopal mitre.

This Office never attained the celebrity of the *Sicut Lilium;* it was little used, and is rarely to be met with. F. Bernardine de Busti also composed a Mass of the Immaculate Conception.[98]

---

[95] For many interesting particulars cf. *L'Immaculée Conception de la Bienheureuse Vierge Marie considerée comme Dogme de foi*, par Mgr. J. B. Malou, evêque de Bruges. Bruxelles, 1857, vol. i. pp. 141, seq.

[97] Breviarium Romanum, f. ccclix. Lugduni, 1509. [This collect is used in the latest Office of the Immaculate Conception, ordered to be used generally by Pius IX. in 1863.]

[98] This Office and Mass are given in the *Mariale* of B. de Busti, Nuremberg, 1503, not paginated, in folio, from which I have taken all these details. Cf. Wadding, Annales, ad ann. 1480, n. 38.

As these preliminary observations contain all that is requisite for the history of the Little Office of the Immaculate Conception, it is unnecessary for me to say anything about the Breviary compiled by Cardinal de Quignonez, and of the subsequent Offices of the Immaculate Conception. During the glorious pontificate of the Sovereign Pontiff Pius the Ninth of happy memory, three new Offices of the Immaculate Conception, the one superseding the other, have been inserted in the Breviary.

Two at least of the Sarum Prymers—those of 1531[29] and 1534[30]—contain a Little Office called that of the Conception of our Ladye, but being, in reality, of the Immaculate Conception. They are both different. The Office in the Prymer of 1531 had been given twenty-three years previously in the *Hore Beate Marie Virginis*, printed by Kerver at Paris in 1508, a copy of which I have seen in the Museum at Maidstone.[31]

Some years later another Little Office of the Immaculate Conception appeared, the *Salve Mundi Domina*, which is now in almost universal use throughout the Church.

Its author is unknown. Alegambe, Southwell,[32] and De Backer,[33] attributed it to Blessed Alphonsus Rodriguez, of the Society of Jesus ; but the Bollandists do not consider that the education which he had received would have enabled this holy lay-brother to have composed it.[34] Moreover, Father Colin, S.J., who was his disciple in spiritual matters, and afterwards wrote his life,[35] is of opinion that it may have been taken from the Large Office of Bernardine de Busti, or have been composed by him, because in the Little Office, as recited by Blessed

---

[29] F. cxxvii. Stonyhurst Library. According to the index, this Little Office is included amongst some prayers newly added to this edition.

[30] F. lxxxi. Stonyhurst Library.

[31] *The Hore B.M. ad usum FF. Predicator. Ord. S. Dominici*, printed by Kerver in 1529, also contains it. A copy is in the Bib. Royale at Brussels. De Alva et Astorga gives it, pp. 145, 146.

[32] *Bibliotheca Scriptorum Soc. Jesu, sub nomine.* Antv. 1643.

[33] *Écrivains de la Compagnie de Jesus, sub nom.* 2 ed.

[34] Most obligingly communicated by the learned writer of his life in the forthcoming volume of the *Act. SS.*

[35] *Vida, hechos, y milagros del Venerable Hermano Alonso Rodriguez, Religioso de la Compañia de Jesus.* Despuesta por el Padre Francisco Colin, Rector del Colegio de Manila, Madrid, 1652. This is a work of considerable rarity. A copy is in the Bollandist Library; and another in the Library of the Fathers of the Oratory, South Kensington.

Alphonsus, the three apparitions described in the apocryphal letter of St. Anselm are given.

But be the author who he may, it is certain that Blessed Alphonsus recited this Little Office daily for the last forty years of his life, and since he died in 1617, this takes it back to 1577 at least. At the earlier part of this period, the Little Office cannot have been in print, because Colin records, that in consequence of injunctions received from our Blessed Ladye herself, the good lay-brother, who fulfilled the onerous duties of a *janitor*, or door-porter in the College of Palma in Majorca, occupied all his spare moments in transcribing copies of it for distribution amongst the students who frequented the College, and others.[86]

Although Blessed Alphonsus recited it in its original form until his death, two years at least, if not more, before that event, the Little Office underwent a change; the three visions were omitted, and it assumed almost its present form, and in such form was approved of by Paul the Fifth in 1615. The Office in this form continues Colin : *es el mismo que dos anos antes de su felis transito, approvò la Santidad de Paulo Quinto, a instancia del Reverendissimo Padre Fray Antonio de Trejo, entonces Vicario General de la Orden del Serafico Padre San Francisco, y despues dignissimo Obispo de Cartagena.*[87] The importance of this evidence will presently appear.

After the death of Blessed Alphonsus Rodriguez, the revelation of our Blessed Ladye to him in regard of this Little Office was made known, and contributed immensely to its popular diffusion and recital. It was spread far and wide, and printed in many parts of Europe.[88] Colvener mentions an

---

[86] Describing the various daily devotions and prayers of Blessed Alphonsus to our Blessed Ladye, one of which was this Little Office, Colin says: *Estas devociones aprovò la Reyna de los Angeles, y mandò a su siervo Alonso que las escriviesse y communicasse à otros, y animasse con su exemplo a usarlas. Y como el, por su humilidad se recogiesse y recelasse, que no huviesse en aquello algun engaño, bolviò la Virgen à mandarle lo mismo, y le quito todo reselo, y assi desde entonces persuadia a los Hermanos de casa, y estudiantes seglares, que con el tratavan, que reusassen cada die este oficio y paras mas facilitarlo, se lo dava escrito de su mano* (*Vida*, &c. cap. xx. ff. 72, 72 b). Alegambe gives the following as the prayers composed by Blessed Alphonsus: *Corona carissimæ et amantissimæ Dominæ Matris Mariæ; Litaniæ ejusdem; Sanctissimum Officium Purissimæ et Immaculatæ Conceptionis ejusdem Deiparæ* (*Bib. Scriptor. Soc. Jesu, sub. nom.*).

[87] *Vida*, &c. ff. 72, 72 b.

[88] *Ibid.*

edition of the year 1613, but does not say whether it was the original or the amended version.[39]

It was printed in large type at the Plantin Press in Antwerp in 1621, in a book of Little Offices, entitled *Exercitivm Hebdo-marivm, collectore Joanne Wilsono, Sacerdote Anglo, in gratiam piorvm Catholicorvm,* which was reprinted *verbatim* at the Plantin Press in 1630. It has the approbation of four bishops and one archbishop, which is undated, but must have been given, at the latest, early in 1618, since James Blaze, Bishop of St. Omer's, died on the 21st of March of that year.[40] Now at page 126, immediately after the Commendation, *Supplices offerimus Tibi, Virgo pia,* &c., there is a rubric as follows : *Sequens Ana. a Paulo V. Pont. Max. approbata est ; qui eandem vna cum oratione de immaculata Virginis Conceptione recitantibus centum dierum Indulgentias concessit.*

Ana. *Hæc est virga,* &c.

V. *In conceptione tua,* &c. R. *Ora pro nobis Patrem, &c.* Oratio. *Deus qui per immaculatam Virginis Conceptionem, &c.* as is given at the end of the Little Office.

Father Colin fully confirms this evidence. After repeating what I have already quoted of Paul the Fifth, he says that the Brief was *expedido a instancia del muy Reverendo Padre, Fray Antonio de Trajo, Vicario General de la Orden del Serafico Padre San Francisco, dada en Roma en Santa Maria la Mayor, a 27 Julio de 1615. Y tiene cien dies de indulgencia para los que la rezeren, añadiedo la antiphona.* Hæc est virga, &c. *con su versiculos y oracion,* Deus qui per Immaculatam Virginis Conceptionem, &c. *La qual,* continues Colin, *se añadira a la fin del oficio que aqui pödremos, para que gozen del tesoro de la indulgencia los que le rezeran.* He then gives the Little Office as approved of by Paul the Fifth, and also in its original form, as recited by Blessed Alphonsus.[41]

[39] Kalendarium Marianum, cap. iii. § 3.

[40] This is the license. *Imprimatur: Petrus, Episcopus, Prorex, et supremus Inquisitor hæreticæ pravitatis in Regno Lusitaniæ ; Michael Archiepiscopus Vlyssiponensis ; Alphonsus Episcopus Conimbricens ; Fr. Jacobus Episcopus Audomarens ; Joannes Episcopus Antverpiensis. Cum Privilegio Serenissimorum Belgicæ Principum. De Witte.* A rare little book, in red and black, entitled *Officium Purissimæ et Immaculatæ Conceptionis Deiparæ Virginis* (Antv. apud Gulielmum Lesteenum, M.DC.XXXV. p. 72), contains the following APPROBATIO : *Hoc Officium immaculatæ Conceptionis Deiparæ Virginis Mariæ est pium, et dignum ut ab omnibus in pietate legatur : merito ergo imprimi debet. Quod testor,* 6 *Martii anni* 1621. Egbertus Spülholdius Pleb. Antverpiensis. A copy of this book, but *apud Joannem Knobaert,* is in the Bollandist Library.

[41] Vida, &c. ff. 215—217.

Thus from Father Colin, and from the two Antwerp editions of 1621 and 1630, with the approbation of one archbishop and four bishops, there is positive evidence that the indulgence of one hundred days was attached, *not* to the Little Office itself, but to the antiphon, versicles, and prayer added to it at the end of the commendation. Moreover, Colin gives the date of the Brief—July 27, 1615—which is very important.

In this form, with the indulgence of one hundred days attached to the antiphon, versicles, and prayer at the end of the commendation, but *not* to itself, the Little Office was spread far and wide, and translated into various languages. I have seen translations into Flemish, French, Greek,[42] Italian, Portuguese, Polish, and Spanish. The earliest English translation of which I know was printed at Rouen in 1669.[43]

John Wilson's *Exercitium Hebdomarium* of 1621 and 1630,[44] Father de Balinghem, S.J.,[45] the *Typus Prædestinationis*,[46] and Colin,[47] all quote the Little Office "*ut habetur in quibusdam horis valde antiquis.*" It is probable that one took the authority from the other. On this point I can offer no explanation, but this much I may say, that for the last twenty-six years I have examined MS. and early printed *Horæ*, and other prayer-books, without number, and have not found the slightest trace of this Little Office, *Salve Mundi Domina.*

Suddenly, on the 17th of February, 1678, Fra Raymond Capizucchi, Master of the Sacred Apostolic Palace, issued a

---

[42] τὸ τῶν Καθολικῶν Εὐχολόγιον. By Aloysius Perrault Maynand. Paris, Preisse 1838, pp. 558—586. But the Latin text used is the condemned version of 1678.

[43] *Primer, &c., with six new Offices added.* Edited by Thomas Fitzsimon, Priest. Printed at Roven by David Mavry, 1669. This translation has been frequently reprinted. Other English translations have been made by the late Provost Husenbeth, R. Fr. Aylward, O.P., the late Rev. E. Caswall, Edmund Waterton, and an anonymous translator, with the approbation of the Bishop of Clifton. An excellent translation which I once saw was made at Stonyhurst in 1843, by the late Rev. Henry White, S.J., but the only MS. copy known has unfortunately been lost. I have heard of two other translations which have never been published.

[44] *Ubi. Sup.* p. 104.

[45] Parnassus Marianus, seu Flos hymnorum et rhythmorum de SS. Virgine Maria ex priscis tum Missalibus, tum Breviariis plus sexaginta, collectore A. de Balinghem, S.J. Duaci, 1624.

[46] Typus prædestinationis et conceptionis Mariæ filiæ Dei immaculatæ. *In fine.* Antv. 1630.

[47] *Vida, &c.* ff. 215.

decree by which the recital of the Little Office of the Immaculate Conception was prohibited, and the Little Office itself was placed upon the *Index Librorum prohibitorum.* The edition or copy of the Little Office referred to in this decree was printed at Milan by Francis Vigone;[48] and Capizucchi issued this decree on the sole information of D. Michael Angelo Ricci who was one of the consultors of the Holy Office. A reference to the *Index* shows that Capizucchi included the antiphon, versicle, and prayer, at the end—to which *alone* the indulgence was attached—as *a portion* of the Little Office.

Offizio dell' Immacolata Concezione della S. Vergine Nostra Signora, approvato del Sommo Pontefice, Paulo V. il quale a chi lo recitarà concede Indulgenza di cento giorni. Quod Officium incipit : Eja mea labia nunc annunciate. *Et desinit cum orat :* Deus qui per Immaculatam Virginis Conceptionem, etc. *Decret.* 17 *Febr.* 1678.[49]

The plea named for this decree, as will be seen presently, was, that it was falsely asserted that Paul the Fifth had approved of this Little Office, and that it contained an apocryphal indulgence. Evidently Capizucchi knew nothing of the Brief of Paul the Fifth, of the 27th of July, 1615, of which Colin has given such precise details. What the "other reasons" (*aliæ causæ*) may have been is not recorded. But from the decree it would appear that Capizucchi himself, by including the antiphon, versicles, and prayer, as a *portion* of the Office had thereby construed the indulgence really granted by Paul the Fifth to them only, as affecting the *entire* Office, and had thus committed the very mistake which was adduced as the main cause of the prohibition.

This decree of the too zealous Master of the Apostolic Palace caused universal consternation and dismay, more especially in Germany and in Spain.

The Emperor of Austria, Leopold the First, wrote to the Holy Father to have the decree of Capizucchi revoked. On the 18th of December of the same year, 1678, Pope Innocent

---

[48] St. Dominic was the first Master of the S. Apostolic Palace, and was so created by Honorius the Third in 1216—1217, and in consequence this post has always been held by a Black Friar (Butler, *Lives of the Saints*, vol. viii. p. 84. Dublin, 1780).

[49] Plazza, *Causa. Imm. Concept.* p. 262, n. 216.

the Eleventh replied to the letter of the Emperor in these terms:
"Most dear son in Christ . . . A few months ago a certain
Office of the Immaculate Conception was prohibited because
it contained an apocryphal indulgence, and because it was
falsely asserted that it had been approved of by Our predecessor
Paul the Fifth of happy memory, and for other reasons which
it was necessary to consider lest the Faithful might be deceived.
But that Office, *i.e.*, the *Sicut Lilium*, which, by permission of
the Holy See, has been recited from most ancient times, is not
included in that prohibition. For We do not desire in any way
to diminish devotion to the Mother of God, but rather, as much
as it can be done, to increase and augment it. This is Our
answer to your Majesty upon that question. But you will
learn all farther details by word of mouth from the Ven. F.
Francis, Archbishop of Thessalonica, Our Nuncio. In the meanwhile We give you the praises due to the noble zeal which your
letter expresses, and We impart to your Majesty our Apostolic
benediction." [50]

This document is abundantly significant.

Charles the Second of Spain also wrote to Innocent the
Eleventh to the same effect as the Emperor Leopold had done. [51]

The Holy Father having thus had his attention fully drawn
to the decree of Capizucchi, lost no time in causing the question
to be fully examined, and this duty was given to five consultors
of the Holy Office, amongst whom were D. Michael Angelo
Ricci, and Father Capizucchi himself. The result of their
deliberations was that the Little Office of the Immaculate
Conception was taken off the Index, the Holy Father, of his
own accord, causing *Immaculatam* to be added after *Sanctam*
in the prayer, and the Master of the Sacred Apostolic Palace,
Capizucchi, *ne vana prohibitio videretur*, made a few other
changes in the text. [52] In this revised and approved form it
was first printed at Lucca in the following year, 1679, with the
approbation of the Master of the Sacred Apostolic Palace. [53]
A copy of this edition was sent to Charles the Second of
Spain. [54]

[50] *Index libr. prohibitor.* Mechliniæ, 1860, pp. 233, 234.
[51] Gravois, *op. cit.* p. 45, n. 19. Plazza, *Causa. Imm. Concept.* p. 447.
[52] Malou, op. cit. vol. i. p. 200; vol. ii. p. 323.
[53] Gravois, *op. cit.*; *Summarium in fine operis*, p. 45; Plazza, p. 262, n. 217.
[54] Plazza, n. 218.

I give the prohibited version of 1678, and the corrected and approved text of 1679 in parallel columns.

LITTLE OFFICE, &c.

Version put on *Index* 1678.	Corrected and approved version 1679.

Invitatory.

V. Eja mea labia, etc.
R. Laudes et præconia Virginis beatæ.

R. Laudes et præconia Virginis immaculatæ.

AT MATINS.

Salve plena gratia
Clara *lux divina.*

Clara *luce divinâ.*

. . . .
Te pulchram ornavit
Sibi sponsam *in qud*
Adam non peccavit.

Sibi Sponsam *quæ in*
Adam non peccavit.

Versicle, throughout the Little Office.

V. Domina *exaudi* orationem meam.

V. Domina *protege* orationem meam.

The Prayer.

. . . ut qui nunc tuam *Sanctam Conceptionem* devoto affectu recolo.

. . . ut qui nunc tuam *Sanctam et Immaculatam Conceptionem* devoto affectu recolo.

AT PRIME.

V. Ipse creavit illam in Spiritu Sancto.
R. Et *effudit* illam *super* omnia opera sua.

R. Et *exaltavit* illam *inter* omnia opera sua.

AT COMPLINE.

V. Benedicamus Domino.
R. Deo Gratias.
V. Fidelium animæ per misericordiam Dei requiescant in pace.

V. Benedicat et custodiat nos Omnipotens et misericors Dominus Pater, et Filius, et Spiritus Sanctus.

R. Amen.

R. Amen.

Commendation.

Supplices offerimus,
Tibi, Virgo Pia,
Has horas canonicas.

Hæc laudum præconia.[44]

By the Constitution *Creditæ Nobis* of the 7th of June, 1680, which confirmed the Statutes for Ecclesiastics in Bavaria, Innocent the Eleventh ordained that the young clerics who, on account of their tender age, did not recite the *Officium*

---

[44] Gravois, *Summarium*, p. 45; Plazza, p. 262, n. 217.

Parvum of our Blessed Ladye, should say instead the Little Office of the Immaculate Conception as approved of by the Holy See, principally to preserve their chastity.[56]

Such, then, is the history of the Little Office of the Immaculate Conception of our Blessed Ladye. I hope that, for the future, censors of prayer-books will examine the text, wherever it is submitted to them, and see that they do not give their · *Imprimatur* to that version of it which was put on the *Index.*

ANTIPHONS.

Another favourite devotion of our ancestors was the evening antiphon, or anthem, of our Ladye, which was sung in the cathedral and collegiate and other churches in England. It was also sung at other times. Thus, in 1365, John Barnet, Bishop of Bath and Wells, made a large donation to the Dean and Chapter of St. Paul's, London, requiring them every day after Matins to sing an anthem of our Ladye, *Nesciens Mater,* or another one, before our Ladye at the pillar, in the nave, commonly called Our Ladye of Grace.[57]

Many bequests occur of candles to be lighted during the *Salve.* At Barking there was a chapel of Our Ladye de Salue, or *Salve,* so called, I infer, either because the Salve was usually sung in it, or because the Marye Mass was celebrated there.[58] At St. Peter's Mancroft, in Norwich, the *Salve* was sung in the Ladye Chapel.[59]

In the Church of St. Magnus, in London, near London Bridge, there was, as Stow Records, "a most famous Gild of Our Ladye *de Salve Regina* ;"[60] and he adds that "most other churches had theirs."[61] Hence it appears how universal they were in England. The oft-quoted foundation charter of Whittington College, dated December 14, 1424, requires that, on each day of the week, at or after sunset, when the artisans residing in the neighbourhood have returned from their work, a special little bell shall be rung for the purpose, and the chaplains, clerics, and choristers of the college shall assemble in the Ladye Chapel, and sing an anthem of Our Ladye.[62]

---

[56] Bullar. Rom. tom. viii. p. 135, n. 12. Edit. Romæ, 1743.
[57] S. pp. 68, 69.   [58] S. p. 3.   [59] S. p. 115.   [60] S. p. 87.
[61] *Monasticon Angl.* t. vi. p. 741.   [62] *The Prioresses' Tale.* Opp. f. 68 b.

According to Chaucer the anthems of our Ladye were taught in the schools to children.

But the anthems of our Ladye were not confined to the church ; her liegemen delighted to sing them at all hours, and whether journeying by sea or land, or going forth in quest of alms for our dear Ladye's love.

The dear little clergion, the widow's brave child, who preferred to risk a thrashing three times within an hour rather than not learn the *Alma Redemptoris Mater*, having been taught it by his fellow :

> than he song it wel and boldely
> Fro word to word, according to the note,
> Twise a day it passeth through his throte,
> To scoleward and homeward when he went,
> On Christ's mother set was all his entent.
>
> As I haue said, throughout the iewry
> This litel child, as he came to and fro,
> Full merely then would he sing and cry,
> O Alma redemptoris Mater, ever mo
> The swetenesse hath his hert persed so
> Of Christes mother, that to her to pray
> He cannot stint of singing by the way.

The custom of singing our Ladye's anthems and hymns by those who were on journeys, seems to have been very common. Henry de Knyghton mentions that on one occasion certain clerics on a journey being overtaken by a thunderstorm as they were singing the *Ava Maria Stella*, were preserved from danger by our Blessed Ladye.[a]

The poor would sing the *Salve Regina* as they went about in quest of alms. To this custom Sir Thomas More alludes. After resigning the Chancellorship, and having dismissed his retinue, he found his income so seriously diminished that he called his family together and thus spake :

" I have been brought vp at *Oxford*, at an Inne of *Chancery*, at Lincoln's Inne, and also in the King's Courtes, and so forth, from the lowest degree to the highest, and yet I have in yearly reuenewes left me at this present little above one hundred poundes by the yeare. So that now we must hereafter, if we will live together, be content to become contributours to ech

[a] Apud Twisden, *Decem Scriptores*, t. ii. p. 2368. For a good instance of the happy results attending on this practice, see *Chronicle of Lanercrost*, p. 31.

other; but by my counsell it shall not be best for us to fall to
the lowest fare first. We will not therefore descend to *Oxford*
fare, nor the fare of *New Inne*, but we will begin with *Lincolne's
Inne* dyet, where many right worshipful of good yeares do live
full well; which, if we find not our selues the first yeare able
to mayntayne, then will we the next yeare go one steppe
downe to *New Inne* fare, wherewith many an honest man is
well contented. Then if that exceed our abilityes will we the
next yeare after descend to *Oxford* fare, where many grave,
learned, and ancient doctours be continually resident, which
if our powers be not able to mayntayne neyther, then may we
yet with bagges and wallets go a-begging togeather, hoping
that for pitty some good people will giue vs their charity at
their door, to sing *Salve Regina*, and so still may keepe company
togeather, and be as merry as beggars."[64]

In his confutation of Tyndall Sir Thomas says "that he
forbiddeth folk to pray to her (our Blessed Ladye), and specially
misliketh her deuoute anthem of *Salve Regina*."[65]

THE SATURDAY.

*Septima quæque dies quod sit sacrata Mariæ
Cælitus ostendit pluribus illa notis.*[66]

Those who care to investigate the reason why Saturday was
dedicated to our Blessed Lady will find the question treated
of at length by Wichmans,[67] Colverer,[68] Benedict the Fourteenth,[69] Trombelli,[70] Justin of Miechow,[71] Locri,[72] Durandus,[73]
and others.

---

[64] Roper, *The Mirroure of Vertue in Worldly Greatnes, or the Life of Syr Thomas
More, Knight, sometime Lo. Chancellour of England.* At Paris, MDCXXVI. p. 86, 88.

[65] Opp. Edit. cit. p. 488.

[66] Wickmans, *Brabantia Mariana*, vol. i. p. 134.

[67] Wickmans, *Sabbatismus Marianus, in quo Origo, Utilitas et Modus colendi
hebdomatim Sabbatum in honorem Sanctissimæ Deiparæ explicantur.* Antv 1628.

[68] *Generales aut quotidianæ commemorationes B. M. in princip. Kalendarii
Mariani,* c. vii. viii.

[69] *De Festis B. M. V.* c. xviii.

[70] *De culto publico ab Ecclesia B. Mariæ exhibito.* Dissertatio XVIII.

[71] *Discursus prædicabiles super Litanias Lauretanas.* Discursus CCXXXII.
l. xi. pp. 60, 61. Neapoli, 1857.

[72] *Maria Augusta.* Atrebati, 1608, l. vi. c. xxiii.

[73] *Rationale divinorum Officiorum.*

The Sarum *Missal* gives five reasons why the Saturday is dedicated to our Blessed Ladye.[74]

Alcwine, in the distribution of the various offices which he drew up for each day of the week, assigns the Saturday to our Blessed Ladye. This he did for the Abbey of St. Vedastus, and writing to the monks about the year 796 he says that he has taken the Masses from our *Missal,* to which he has added a Mass of our Ladye to be sung on some days.[75] And writing to the monks of Fulda about the year 801, he tells them that he has also sent them a *Cartula Missalis,* with a Mass of our Blessed Ladye.

The Office of our Ladye, which the Council of Clermont, A.D. 1094, required to be recited daily together with the Divine Office, was ordained to be celebrated with solemnity on Saturdays.[76]

St. Godric, the hermit of Finchale, made it a custom every Saturday to give an alms in our Ladye's honour."[77]

In his beautiful farewell poem to Aran, St. Columbkille says that

> . . . Angels come from Heaven,
> To visit it every day in the week,

and names the leading angel each day, but—

> Marye, Mother of the Son of God, comes,
> And her train along with her,
> And angels among her host,
> To bless it on Saturday.[78]

In all the Colleges of the Society of Jesus the Litanies of our Ladye are solemnly sung on Saturdays. Those who have lived in Rome will remember the Saturday instruction at the Gesù in the chapel of Our Lady *della Strada.*[79]

---

[74] Edit. Paris, 1554, f. xxiiii. in fine lib.

[75] "Missas quoque aliquas de nostro tali Missali. . . . Postea sancta Dei Genitricis semperque Virginis Mariæ missam superaddidimus per dies aliquot, si alicui placuerit, decantandam." Ep. li. Ad Monach. Vedastinos, opp. t. i. col. 215. Edit. Migne.

[76] Durandus, *Rationale,* l. vi. c. ii. n. vii. Edit. Barthélemy, v. iii. p. 106.

[77] *Libellus de vita,* &c. Surtees Soc. p. 358.

[78] Archdall, *Monasticon Hibernicum,* vol. ii. pp. 192, 193. Edit. Dublin, 1876.

[79] Cf. *Sabbati del Gesù di Roma, overo Esempii della Madonna.* Dal P. Giovanni Rho, D.C.D.G. Bologna, 1694.

Becon, who sneers at all the practices of the Catholic Church, mentions some of the old English customs, including a practice for each day of the week.

" Seventhly and finally, on the Saterday cause a Masse to be song or sayde in the honour of our Ladye and al vergines. Ligten v. candles. Fede v poore men, or geue v almosses. Jesu mercy. Lady help."[80] These were evidently in honour of the Five Joys of our Ladye.

In Scotland the same idea took a very practical form : " En Ecosse on voit le pieux roi Guillaume (I.) allié d'Innocent III., afin de donner une preuve de son amour pour l'Eglise et la Sainte Vierge ordonna que le pauvre peuple se reposerait de ses travaux tous les Samedis depuis midi " (1202).[81]

The singing of our Ladye's anthem at Magdalen College, Oxon, on the Saturday, and other instances of old English devotion to our Ladye on this day have been already noticed.

§ 4.—THE ANGELUS.

Vespere et mane et meridie clamabo et annuntiabo.

Psalm liv. 18.

The devotion called the Angelus, as it is now universally recited, was unknown in Catholic England. It did not assume its present form until towards the close of the sixteenth century, and the earliest instance of it in this form with which I myself have met, is in the *Manuale Catholicorum* of Blessed Peter Canisius, S.J., printed in the year 1588.[82]

Pope John the Twenty-Second had made an order that each evening at the pealing of the *ignitegium*—the couvre-feu, or curfew bell—three Hail Maryes were to be recited; and the Thirteenth Canon of the Council of Paris in 1346 requires the uninterrupted observance of this regulation.[83]

In England it was the custom to say one Our Father and five Hail Maryes, as is evident from the Mandate of Thomas

[80] *Reliques of Rome*, p. 206, A.D. 1563.
[81] Montalembert, *Hist. de Ste. Elisabeth*, Introd. Paris, 1861, p. 43.
[82] Antv. ex off. Christoph. Plantini, p. 30.
[83] Labbe, *Conc.* t. xiii. col. 1915. It is mentioned in the Acts of the Canonization of St. Bonaventure that he exhorted his brethren to salute our Ladye when the bell rang after Complin, since it is believed that the angel saluted her at that hour (in fini Opusc. Lugduni, 1619, p. 813).

Arundel, Archbishop of Canterbury, in 1399, issued at the special desire of the King (Richard the Second) for the promotion of the greater veneration of the Mother of God, which enjoins the ringing of the bell and the recitation of the same prayers at the break of day as are said in the evening, viz., one *Pater* and five *Aves*, and gives a pardon of forty days, *toties quoties.*[84]

The following rubric appears in the *Horæ* of Sarum use of 1523 and 1534.[85]

"Our holy father the pope Sixtus hath graunted at the instaunce of the hyghe moost and excellent princesse elizabeth late qwene of englonde and wyf to our souerayne lyege lorde Kynge hēre the seuenth. god haue mercy on her swete soule and all cristen soules, that euery day in the mornynge after. thre tollynges of the ave bell say iii. times the hoole salutacyon of our lady. Aue maria gratia plena. that is to say. at vj. the clocke in the mornyng. iij. Ave maria. at. xij. the clocke at none. iij. Ave Maria. & at. vj. the clocke at euen for euery tyme so doynge is graunted of the spirituall tresour of holy chyrche. iij. C. dayes of pardon totiens quotiens. And also our holy father the archebysshop of cantorbery and yorke wit other ix. bysshoppes of this reame haue graunted. iij. times in the day. xl. dayes of pardon to all them that be I the state of grace able to receue pardon / the whyche begonne the xxvi. daye of Marche. Anno. M.CCCC.XCII. anno henrici vii. And the summe of the indulgence & pardon for euery. Ave maria. viii. hondred dayes &. lx. totiēs quotiēs. Thys prayer shall be sayde at the tollynge of the aue bell.

"*Suscipe verbum Virgo Maria quod tibi a Domino per angelum transmissum est. Ave Maria . . .* ending, *fructus ventris tui Jesus. Amen.*

"§ Say thyss. iii. tymes & afterwarde say thy col. (collect) folowynge.

"V. *Dilexisti justitiam et odisti iniquitatem.* R. *Propterea unxit te Deus, Deus tuus oleo lætitiæ præ consortibus tuis. oratio. Deus qui de Beatæ Mariæ Virginis utero, &c. Amen. Pater noster. Ave Maria.*

"§ Say thys prayer deuoutly at the tollinge of the aue bell

[84] Wilkins, *Concilia*, tom. iii. pp. 246, 247.
[85] In the Library of Stonyhurst College.

at none for a memory and remēbraunce of the passion and deth of cryste.

" R. *Tenebre facte sunt dum crucifixissent iesum iudei, et circa horam nonam exclamavit iesus voce magna. Heli heli lamaza-bathani : hoc est, Deus meus, deus meus vt quid me dereliquisti ; et inclinato capite emisit spiritum. Tunc unus ex militibus lancea latus ejus perforavit : et continuo exivit sanguis et aqua. Et velum templi scissum est a summo usque deorsum : et omnis terra tre-muit. Et inclinato capite emisit spiritum.*

" V. *Proprio filio suo non pepercit Deus.*

" R. *Sed pro nobis omnibus tradidit illum.*

" Oratio.

" *Domine Jesu Christe fili Dei vivi qui pro salute mundi in cruce felle et aceto potatus es: sicut tu, consummatis omnibus in cruce expirans, in manus patris commendasti spiritum tuum, sic in hora mortis mee in manus tue pietatis commendo animam meam, ut eam in pace suscipias, et in electorum tuorum choris aggregari precipias. Qui vivis, etc. Pater noster. Ave Maria.*"

Such was the old English form of the Angelus.[86]

The bells which usually tolled the Angelus were called Gabriel bells and Ave bells. Many yet exist, and may be known by the appropriate inscriptions which they bear :

+ Missi de celis habeo nomen Gabrielis,[87]

at Welford, Berkshire ;

+ Personet hec celis dulcissime vox Gabrielis,[88]

at Misterton, Notts ;

+ Gabriel ave, hoc in conclave nune pange suave,[89]

formerly at St. John the Baptist, in the Maddermarket, Norwich, and the like.

---

[86] The prayers recited at the ringing of the Ave bell seem to have varied in different countries. Cf. *Hortulus Anime.* Moguntii, 1511. The *Manuale piarum orationvm ex antiqvis et Catholicis Patribus, in vsvm fidelium* (per Patres Soc. Jesv. revisvm emendatum et avctum. Veneliis, apud Iuntas, 1572, f. 37) makes no mention of the Angelus, but gives a form of prayers to be said at the morning, noon, and evening bell ; those in the morning in memory of our Lord's Resurrection ; at noon in memory of His Death ; and at the sound of the evening bell in memory of the Incarnation.

[87] Lukis, *Church Bells,* p. 63.

[88] *Ibid.* p. 88.

[89] Blomefield, *Hist. of Norfolk,* vol. ii. p. 698. Vide ante, pp. 73, 74.

k

Blomefield mentions one at Diss inscribed :

+ Sancte Gabriel ora pro nobis,

and adds : "They call this the Kay bell, being a corruption for the Gabriel bell.[90]　In the *Times* of the 21st December, 1876, a correspondent mentions that the curfew bell is still rung at Sandwich, in the county of Kent, as well as a bell at 5 o'clock a.m. called the "Cow" bell.　Is this a Kentish corruption for the Gabriel bell ?

At King's Lynn the largest bell of the principal church is still tolled at six o'clock, both morning and evening, and serves as a signal to labourers and artisans.[91]　I have been told that a similar custom prevails at Great Billings in Northamptonshire. These two bells hallowed with the sacred chrism and the blessings of Holy Church still raise their notes, which in Catholic days gladdened the ears alike of the rich and poor by reminding them of the Incarnation, and inviting them to repeat to the Blessed Mother of God the greeting of Hail full of Grace, first conveyed to her by the Archangel Gabriel *ex ore Altissimi*, but those sacred tones now principally fall on ears made deaf by heresy and consequent ignorance, and are associated only with the commencement and end of the day's toil.　Even to the gentle poet Gray, the Gabriel bell only

Toll'd the knell of parting day,

when the world was left to "darkness and to me ;" whilst from the venerable ivy-mantled church tower the moping owl made her complaint to the moon of those who wandering near her secret bower molest her ancient solitary reign.　Certainly no one in the ages of faith would have thought of calling the house of God the "bower of the owl," or said that she alone was to hold there "her ancient solitary reign."

In many places to this day the Gabriel bell rings out its joyous notes from the church steeple in the evening, and the morning, and at midday.　Moreover to those who have any acquaintance with the large manufacturing towns of England, it is well known that hundreds of Catholic girls and young women lead the lives of angels in those hotbeds of iniquity and vice, are shriven and houselled weekly, preserve their white robe of baptismal inno-

---

[90] *Hist. of Norfolk.* vol. i. p. 14.
[91] *Promptorium Parvulorum*, sub voce *Curfu*.　Camden Society.

cence unstained and a spotless reputation. They turn the factory bells to good account, and to their pealing at six, twelve, and six o'clock, they respond by reciting the *Angelus.*

I may observe that in the list of Indulgences granted by Gregory the Thirteenth for all places beyond the Alps, the Angelus at noon is not mentioned : " 13. *Qui . . . B. M. Virginem mane et vespere salutaverit.*"[92]

§ 5.—THE BEADS.

THE AVE-PSALM-PSALTER.

Omnis homo omni horâ
Ipsam ora, et implora
  Ejus patrocinia.
Psalle, psalle, nisu toto
Cordis, oris, voce, voto,
  AVE PLENA GRATIA.

           Portiforium ad usum Sarum.[93]

The Hail Marye in its present form, consisting of two parts, salutation and petition, was not used in England before the year 1531.[94] Towards the end of the fifteenth century some words of petition began to be added to the salutation after the name of Jesus, as the *Myroure of our Ladye* says : "Some say at the begynnyng of this salutacyon Aue benigne Iesu, and some saye after, Maria Mater dei, with other addycyons at the ende also. And such thinges may be sayde when folke saye theyr Aues of theyr owne devocyon. But in the seruyce of the chyrche, I trowe it be moste sewer and moste medefull to obey to the comon use of saynge, as the chyrche hathe set, without all such addicions."[95]

The earliest mention of the Hail Marye as a salutation in daily use is made by Baldwin, who became Bishop of Worcester in 1180, and Archbishop of Canterbury four years later. These are his words :

[92] Public Record Office, *Dom. Eliz.* Addit. vol. xxv. n. 66 (*Records of English Catholics,* Douay Diaries. London, 1878, pp. 366, 367).

[93] Edit. A.D. 1551, e sequentiis Missæ quotidianæ B.M.V. These lines are from the hymn *Hodiernæ lux diei,* attributed by the Saga to St. Thomas of Canterbury. See *infra,* p. 152. For the hymn see Mone, vol. ii. p. 53.

[94] *Sarum Breviary,* Paris, 1531.

[95] Early English Text Society, p. 79.

Huic Angelicæ salutationi, says he, *qua per singulos dies Beatissimam Virginem ea quæ datur devotione salutamus, adjicere solemus "et benedictus fructus ventris tui," quam clausulam Elizabeth post, a Virgine salutata, quasi finem Angelicæ salutationis repetens adjecit, dicens, Benedicta tu inter mulieres, et benedictus fructus ventris tui. Hic est ille fructus de quo Isaias dicit: In illa die erit germen Domini in magnificentia et gloria, et fructus terræ sublimis* (iv. 2).[96]

Used as an antiphon, the first part of the Hail Marye is found at a much earlier date in the Mass of the Fourth Sunday of Advent, which is given in the *Sacramentale* of St. Gregory.

The Hail Marye, still only as a salutation, was ordered to be recited after the Our Father in Divine Office by the Council of Paris, A.D. 1195. Therefore, when Dr. Rock speaks of the Hail Marye as unknown in England before the year 1172, it is perhaps only doing him justice to suppose that he denies its use in the sense of a prayer formally recognized by the Church.[97]

Speaking of the Catholic versions of Scripture in general, and of Dr. Challoner's translation in particular, Cardinal Wiseman observes that

"There is another alteration of more importance, especially when it is considered in reference to the present times, and the influence it has had upon established forms of Catholic speech. In the first edition, in conformity to Catholic usage in England, the word ' Dominus ' is almost always translated by ' *Our* Lord.' The amended text changed the pronoun into an article, and says ' *The* Lord.' In the *Ave Maria* Catholics have always, till lately, been accustomed to say, ' *Our* Lord is with thee ;' as it is in that version, and as it was always used in England, even before that translation was made. But, in conformity with the change of the text, we have observed of late a tendency to introduce into the prayer a similar variation, and to say, ' *The* Lord is with thee :' a change which we strongly deprecate as stiff, *cantish,* destructive of the unction which the prayer breathes, and of that union which the pronoun inspires between the reciter and her who is addressed. We have no hesitation

---

[96] *Tractatus de Angelica Salutatione. Patrol. Lat.* t. cciv. col. 469. Edit. Migne.

[97] For a fuller history of the Hail Marye, see Rock, *Church of our Fathers,* vol. iii. pp. 314—320; also, *Act. SS. ad diem,* 16 Oct. pp. 1108—1113, for an exhaustive article on the subject; also Coppenstein, O.P., *Clavis prædicandi rosarium,* Heidelburgæ, 1630, cap. xii.

in saying that this difference, trifling as many will consider it, expresses strongly the different spirits of our and other religions. It has never been the custom of the Catholic Church to say, '*The* Redeemer, *the* Saviour, *the* Lord, *the* Virgin ;' 'Redemptor *noster*, Dominus *noster*,' and so '*our* Saviour, *our* Lord, *our* Lady,' are the terms sanctioned, and, therefore, consecrated by Catholic usage since the time of the Fathers. We own it grates our ears and jars upon our feelings to hear the former essentially un-Catholic forms used by preachers and writers ; they want affection ; they are insipid, formal ; they remind us of Geneva caps, and smack of predestination. The Rheims translators have explained their reason for their translation in a note (p. 585), as follows : 'We Catholics must not say *The Lord*, but *Our Lord ;* as we say *Our Lady* for His Mother, not *The Lady*. Let us keep our forefathers' words, and we shall easily keep our old and true faith, which we had of the first Christians.' Nor is such a modification of the word 'Dominus' peculiar to the English Catholics ; the Syriac version, and after it the Syriac Church, calls Christ not simply *moryo*, '*the* Lord,' but *moran*, '*our* Lord,' even where the Greek has ὁ Κύριος. If, therefore, it be considered too great a departure from accuracy in translation to restore the pronoun in the text of our version, let us at least preserve it in our instructions, and still more in our formularies of prayer."[98]

The year 1216 is generally given as the date of the "invention" of the Psalter—or, as it is now called, the Rosary—of our Blessed Ladye.

The word *psalterium*, or psalter, from ψαλτήριον—literally a musical instrument of ten strings,

in psalterio decem chordarum psallite[99]—

is used by the Fathers as a term for the hundred and fifty psalms of King David : thus St. Augustine describes the Psalms as *Codex Psalmorum qui Ecclesiæ consuetudine Psalterium nuncupatur*.[100]

This term Psalter is also applied to three different forms of devotion to our Blessed Ladye, which are :

1. A prayer consisting of one hundred and fifty strophes,

---

[98] *Essays on Various Subjects*, vol. i. pp. 76, 77.
[99] Psalm xxxii. 2.　[100] In Psalm cxviii. Opp. t. iv. col. 1505. Edit. Migne.

each beginning with *Ave*, and with each of which a verse from one of the psalms is worked up. This is the earliest form of these Ladye-Psalters which are numerous; the stanzas of the later ones of this class commence with *Ave*, but are not composed from the Psalms. The former I shall call the *Ave-Psalm-Psalters;* the latter, the *Ave-Psalters*, merely to distinguish them.

2. The second form, in chronological order, of the Ladye-Psalters consists of one hundred and fifty *Aves*, *i.e.*, the Angelical Salutation, or prayer Hail Marye, &c., and fifteen Our Fathers. It is called the Psalter of the Blessed Virgin Marye, says Sixtus the Fourth, in his Constitution *Ea quæ*, of the 9th of May, 1478, because it contains as many Angelical Salutations as there are psalms in the Psalter of David.[101] This is the explanation usually given, but it points to an earlier meaning, and the invention of this form of the Ladye-Psalter is generally attributed to St. Dominic. To distinguish it from the others, I shall call it the *Bead-Psalter.*

3. The third form of Ladye-Psalter is the abbreviated paraphrase of David, in honour of our Ladye, which is attributed to St. Bonaventure, the disciple of the renowned Alexander of Hales.[102] This Psalter does not enter into my argument. St. Bonaventure also composed an Ave-Psalter, which is called his *Psalterium minus.*[103]

From what has been said it would appear that the *Ave-Psalm-Psalter* was the original of the *Bead-Psalter*, or Rosary, so that this was rather a simplification of an existing form of prayer than a completely new invention. The word *Psalter* necessarily implies some connection with the Psalms of David.

St. John Damascene, who died in the year 780, composed, for the festival of the Annunciation, a homily which contains the mystic numbers 15 and 150. The exordium is composed of fifteen sentences, of which the last ends with these words: "Hail, full of grace, our Lord is with thee; blessed art thou amongst women, and blessed is the fruit of thy womb."[104]

The Homily itself consists of one hundred and fifty salu-

---

[101] *Bullarium Romanum.* Romæ, 1743, t. iii. pt. i. pp. 172, 173.

[102] *Act. SS.* t. iii. Julii, ad diem 14, p. 781.

[103] Opusc. t. i. p. 499.

[104] Opp. Edit. F. P. Mich. Lequien, Ord. Fr. Præd. Paris, 1742, t. ii. pp. 835—841.

tations or greetings of our Ladye, each of them beginning with χαῖρι or χαίροις. Therefore evidence exists that in the eighth century St. John Damascene saluted our Ladye with 150 *Aves ;* and also that the Hail Marye, in its then form, was not unknown to him. Still the *Aves* of the Homily were not 150 Hail Maryes.

Having traced the familiar *Rosary* to the *Ave-Psalm-Psalter*, we must next inquire, who was the first in the West to compose an Ave-Psalm-Psalter? It is a satisfaction to find that this glory belongs to one of two names illustrious in English history St. Anselm or St. Thomas of Canterbury.

St. Anselm entered the Order of St. Benedict in the year 1060. He became Prior of Bec in 1063, Abbot of the same abbey in 1078, Archbishop of Canterbury in 1093, and died in 1109. Whilst at Bec he composed many prayers for the use of his friends, and at their request.[105] In one of his letters to Gundulf he mentions a long prayer in three parts to our Ladye which he had thus composed.[106] Eadmer, his biographer, does not state what these prayers were ; but amongst them Gerberon gives an Ave-Psalm-Psalter.[107] A MS. of the year 1200 in the British Museum gives another Ladye-Psalter with the name of St. Anselm ;[108] and a second MS. of the same date contains one without his name.[109] But the text of neither agrees with the version of Gerberon.

The Saga of St. Thomas of Canterbury says :

"He was of all men the first to find, as far as hath become known here in the north, how to draw some meditation out of every psalm in the Psalter, *out of which meditations he afterwards made verses of praise to our Ladye.* Following his example, Stephen Langton did the same in England, and later still the same was done by three masters in the west of Scotland, at the request of Queen Isabel."[110]

This evidence leaves no doubt as to the origin of the Ave-Psalm-Psalter of our Ladye. Moreover, these "verses of praise"

---

[105] *Act. SS.* t. ii. Aprilis, ad diem 21, p. 896.
[106] Opp. t. i. Epist. xx. col. 1086. *Patrol. Lat.* vol. clviii. Edit. Migne.
[107] *Ibid.*
[108] Arundel, 157.
[109] *Cott. MS.* Titus, A. xxi.
[110] *Thómas Saga Erkibyskups*, or a Life of Archbishop Thomas Becket, in Icelandic, with English translation, notes, and glossary. Edited by Eiríkr Magnússon, sub-librarian of the University Library, Cambridge, 1875, pp. 20—23. Rolls Edit.

made from the Psalter show by their very name of Psalter that they were to be sung, whereas the Bead-Psalter of St. Dominic was composed for recitation ; a most essential difference, for the word psalter necessarily implies psalmody and music ; consequently a Psalter of one hundred and fifty Hail Maries is a misnomer, and evidently refers to the earlier form of the devotion.

But it will at once be objected to me, on the faith of Herbert of Bosham, that St. Thomas had never learned to make verses. In the sense of hexameters and pentameters and odes in Horatian metres,[111] granted. But St. Thomas had composed the hymn of the Seven Joys of our Ladye ; and no greater scholarship was required for the composition of the Ave-Psalm-Psalter.[112]

Secondly. Why do not his other biographers refer to it ? and how is it that the Ave-Psalm-Psalter is attributed to St. Anselm ?

What is stated is this, viz., that St. Thomas habitually used a book containing prayers composed by his predecessor, St. Anselm ;[113] and nothing is more probable than that St. Thomas had written, or caused to be transcribed, in this very book the verses which he had composed in praise of our Ladye. It is equally probable that in course of time these verses may have been considered as the production of St. Anselm, and in consequence, attributed to him.

But the Saga proves the widely-spread early belief on the subject.

This is the earliest Ave-Psalm-Psalter, which I take to be

---

[111] *Qui versificandi nec etiam sub scholari disciplina artem attigisset, vel in modico.* Herib. de Boseham, *Vita S. Thomæ,* l. v. cap. xxx. *Patrol. Lat.* t. cxc. col. 1248. Edit. Migne.

[112] Father Morris mentions that St. Thomas is not known to have left any writings, except his letters, and that the hymn of our Ladye's Seven Joys is attributed to him (*Life and Martyrdom of St. Thomas à Becket,* p. 383). The Saga, on the other hand, says 'it is also averred by all folk that the blessed Thomas composed the Prose, *Imperatrix gloriosa,* and another, a lesser one, *Hodiernæ lux diei* (l.c.). Cf. Mone, vol. ii. pp. 53, 78.

[113] "When Mass is being sung through down to the Gospel, he readeth the prayers which his predecessor Archbishop Anselm of blessed memory had composed (Thomas Saga, &c. cap. xx. p. 103). "Et frequentius ea hora habebat in manibus quemdam orationum libellum quem unus prædecessorum suorum . . beatus Anselmus, &c. (*Vita S. Th. Cant. Archiep. et Mart.* ab anonymo quodam scriptore ex aliorum scriptis compilata. *Patrol. Lat.* t. cxx. col. 356. Edit. Migne).

the one mentioned in the Saga, although it sometimes appears with the name of St Anselm.

> 1. *Ave Mater advocati,*
> *Qui beatus concilio,*
> *Aula ventris incorrupti,*
> *Processit ut ex thalamo.*

Beatus vir qui non abiit in concilio impiorum, et in via peccatorum non stetit, et in cathedra pestilentiæ non sedit (Psalm i. 1).

> 2. *Ave Mater, cujus partus*
> *Postulavit Deum Patrem,*
> *Et accepit, quas redemit*
> *Gentes in hæreditatem.*

Postula a me et dabo tibi gentes hæreditatem tuam, et possessionem tuam terminos terræ (Psalm ii. 8).

And in like manner, through the Psalms. Some few of the strophes consist of eight lines.

I have not been able to meet with the Psalter composed by Archbishop Stephen Langton, A.D. 1207—1228. St Edmund of Canterbury wrote one, the introduction of which commences:

> *A Maria Mater pia,*
> *O Benigna, laude digna,*
> *Plena Dei lumine.*
>
> *Me dignare te laudare*
> *Verbis dignis, sanctis hymnis*
> *Et psalmorum carmine.*

Then the Ave-Psalter begins.

> *Ave virgo, lignum mite,*
> *Quæ dedisti lignum vitæ*
> *Salutis fidelium.*
>
> *Genuisti Christum Jesum,*
> *Sed pudoris non est læsum*
> *Nec deflexit folium.*

I have found no traces of the Ladye-Psalm-Psalters composed, according to the Saga, by the three unnamed masters in the west of Scotland.[114]

---

[114] Cf. Mone, vol. ii. pp. 233—260, who gives several Ave-Psalters and Psalm-Psalters, some beginning with *Ave*, others not, *e.g.*,

> Beatus vir, *qui in lege meditatur,*
> . *de Maria quid dicatur*
> *quæ regina coronatur,*
> *dum in cælo collocatur.*

(From a MS. of the fifteenth century, p. 253.)

This Ave-Psalm-Psalter was not suited for general popular use ; and in the time of St. Anselm and St. Thomas of Canterbury, the *Ave*, as a prayer, was not known ; whereas in Spain it had been in use from the ninth century, and consequently could not but have been most familiar to St. Dominic Gusman ; and at the very time that he was "thinking out under the inspiration of the Holy Ghost" an easy method of prayer, St. Mary of Oignies, who died on the 23rd of June, A.D. 1213, was in the habit of reciting the whole Psalter standing, and she used to say a Hail Marye on her knees at the end of each Psalm.[115] This early adaptation of the Hail Marye to the Psalter probably would not have been recorded if it had not been somewhat unusual.

The evidence adduced goes to show that the composition and use of these Ave-Psalm-Psalters and Ave-Psalters originated in England ; and therefore that the original seed of the Beads or Rosary germinated in the Dower of our Ladye long anterior to the days of St. Dominic.

METHOD OF RECITING THE PSALTER.

I think there can be no reasonable doubt that, in what he wrote of the modes of reciting the beads, Alan de Rupe has recorded the traditional practice of his order in that regard. He compiled his Compendium for the use of the Members of the Confraternity of the Rosary, and says that St. Dominic taught the following method of reciting the Psalter, which was revealed to him by our Blessed Lady ; to wit, that the first *quinquagene* should commemorate the articles of the Incarnation of our Lord ; the second, those of the Passion ; and the third,

Another commences—

> *Ave Virgo virginum*
> *per quam vir beatus*
> *visitavit nos miseros,*
> *nobis ex te natus*
> *tuis mater meritis*
> *nostras miseratus*
> *releva miserias*
> *felix advocatus.*
>
> (p. 257).

[115] *Totum psalterium super pedes stando, legens, per singulos psalmos flexis genibus, Beatæ Virgini Salutationem Angelicam offerebat (Act. SS. t. v. Junii, p. 553, ad diem 23. Edit. Palmé. Cf. Vincent of Beauvais, Speculum Historiale, l. xxx. cap. xxiv ; Benedict XIV, Votum, ubi. sup.).*

those of His Resurrection and Glory, meditating on one article at each Hail Marye. The *quinquagenes* may be repeated together or separately, one in the morning, a second at noon, and a third in the evening, or as can best and most conveniently be arranged.[116] Another method, also drawn up by St. Dominic —and several are mentioned—is propounded by Michael de Insula. Prescribing the use of the Psalter to a nun, the saint desired her to recite the first *quinquagene* in thanksgiving for the Incarnation, meditating on the infancy and childhood of our Lord ; the second in memory of the Passion, meditating on the principal scenes of it ; and the third for the remission of her sins, past, and daily ones, invoking the assistance of her patron saints.[117]

Alan de Rupe proposes many other methods. All the different writers on the subject are agreed that the pious God-gifu, Countess of Mercia, is the first who is recorded to have recited her prayers upon a string of beads or gems,[118]—that is, on beads strung upon a cord—but no trace exists of what these prayers were. St. Godric used stones for the same object,[119] but Reginald, his biographer, has not recorded whether they were strung on a cord, or loose after the manner of the solitaries of the desert. No mention of the Psalter of our Ladye is made in the *Ancren Riwle ;* although at the end of the *Alma Redemptoris* in the Devotion of the Five Psalms it prescribes : "Here say fifty or a hundred *Aves*, more or less, according as you have time."[120] Apart from the evidence of the Paternostrers in London of the year 1277-8, the earliest trace of the Bede-Psalter of our Ladye in England with which I have met is in the life of Robert of Winchelsey, Archbishop of Canterbury, who died A.D. 1295. Stephen Birchington, his biographer, describes his great love of our Blessed Ladye, and says that as soon as he had finished his daily occupations he

[116] *Compendium Psalterii Beatissime Trinitatis*, Magistri Alani de Rupe ordinis Predicatorum. Colonie, 1479, cap. ii. p. 3.

[117] *Quodlibet de utilitate fraternitatis rosarii seu psalterii beate marie virginis conventus coloniensis ordinis predicatorum provincialus colonie.* In scola arcium tempore quodlibetorum. Anno M.CCCC.LXXVI. per fratrem michaelem de insula sacre theologie professorem ejusdem ordinis. Colonie, 1479, p. 35.

[118] S. p. 24. Of course I do not take the Mohammedan practice into consideration, and therefore need not inquire into its antiquity.

[119] *Libellus*, &c., ubi sup.

[120] P. 43.

invariably recited the Angelical Salutation on his fingers.[121] This seems to imply that the Archbishop said his beads in this manner, for the practice to which allusion is made was certainly adopted as a convenient mode of computation. William of Waynflete always recited his beads on bended knees.

It is admitted that the Bead-Psalter of our Ladye had fallen into almost total disuse on the Continent, prior to the revival of the Confraternity at Cologne in the year 1475 ;[121a] whereas in England it was the popular devotion to our Ladye, and its use universal with all classes. This is satisfactorily proved by numberless wills and inventories of the fourteenth and fifteenth centuries. One remarkable feature in these wills is, that in the very minute description which the testators give of their beads, the Our Fathers are often called *Gawdyes.*

Now this term Gaudye gives clue to what, in my mind, was the general manner of saying the beads in England. They were said in honour of our Ladye's Five or Fifteen Joys, according as one or three *quinquagenes* were recited. Indeed, Michael de Insula says that the old books of devotion contain the Fifteen Joys of our Ladye, in honour of which these fifteen *Pater nosters* may be referred, since they are followed by ten *Aves.*[122]

The Sarum Manuals and Prymers contain the following method of saying the Rosary, which is often to be found in MS. and printed *Horæ* of our Ladye both in England and abroad. It is described as a Compendium of the Life of Jesus, and is called the Golden Rosary.

Suscipe rosarium, Virgo, deauratum :
Jesu per compendium vita decoratum.
    Ave Maria . . . fructus ventris tui.   Amen.
Quem virgo carens vitio de flamine concepisti,
Dum Gabrieli nuntio humillime consentisti.
    Ave Maria.

---

[121] "Salutationem Angelicam . . . per numerum dignitorum suorum, quocumque se diverteret, semper dixit " (Wharton, *Anglia Sacra*, t. i. p. 13.)

[121a] Coppenstein, *De frat. rosarii*, capp. xvi.—xviii. Heidelbergæ, 1269.

[122] M. de Insula says fifteen *Aves*, which must be a misprint. *Solent eciam in antiquis libris devocionalibus scribi quindecim Virginis gaudia in quorum honorem hec quindecim Pater noster referre possent quia eis eciam XV Ave Maria superadduntur* (Quodlibet, p. 40). Possibly fifteen may refer to decades.

Quo impregnata citius cognatam visitasti ;
Johannemque celerius in ventre sanctificasti.
Ave Maria.[123]

and so on throughout the five decades. This rosary could be sung, like the original Ave-Psalm-Psalter.

Another form given in the Sarum *Hore* of our Ladye of 1512 consists of an addition to each *Ave* after the name *Jesus Christus*, thus :

Ave Maria . . . ventris tui Jesus Christus, Quem de Spiritu Sancto, Angelo nunciante, concepisti.

Ave Maria . . . Jesus Christus, Quo concepto in montana perrexisti.[124]

There is one remarkable fact connected with the Bead-Psalter of our Ladye, and its division into mysteries by St. Dominic. The Black Friars were numerous and popular in this country. They had eighty-six houses in England, Wales, Scotland, and Ireland,[125] yet, so far as my researches enable me to speak, there is not the slightest trace of the Dominican arrangement or distribution of the Rosary into mysteries, as it now exists, to be found in England prior to the great apostacy. Indeed, I doubt very much whether the actual arrangement of the Joyful, Sorrowful, and Glorious Mysteries is to be found in any printed book prior to the year 1560. Moreover, I have never found any trace of the Confraternity of the Psalter or Rosary in Catholic England.

THE NAME OF BEADS.

I thought King Henry had resembled thee
In courage, courtship, and proportion :
But all his mind is bent to holiness
To number *Ave-Maries* on his Beads.
Queen Margaret to Suffolk.
Henry the Sixth, Part ii. Act i. Scene 3.

Bead or Bede is, as I presume every educated Englishman knows, an Anglo-Saxon word, *bidde* or *beade*, which means a

---

[123] Mone, *Hymni Latini*, xx. vol. ii. pp. 263—265. He also gives other forms, but none are older than the fifteenth century (*ibid.* pp. 266, 267). *Hore beatissime Virg. Mariæ secdm. usum Sarum.* Paris, 1526, f. xlviii, and several others of various years (Stonyhurst Library). The same is given in the *Hore* of our Ladye *ad usum Romanum*, printed in Paris in 1522.

[124] F. cxcvii (Stonyhurst Library).

[125] Echard, *Scriptores Ord. Prædicator.* Paris, 1719, t. i. ff. x. xi.

prayer, and is derived from *biddan* or *beodan*, to pray ; in German *beten*, hence the response in the Litanies, in German *bete für uns*, and in Flemish, *bid voor ons.* Consequently, to bid one's beads is the old form of expressing to say one's prayers. Thus in *Piers Plouhman :*

> Ich bidde my bedis.

And an English hymn to our Ladye of about the year 1430 runs thus :

> Heil be thou marie that art flour of alle,
> As roose is eerbir so reed !
> To the, ladi, y clepe and calle,
> To the y make my beed.[126]

The *Promptorium Parvulorum*, A.D. 1400, gives bede or bedys, *numeralia, deprecula ;* bede or prayer, *oracio, supplicacio.*[127] Hence the term Bede or Bead-roll, a list of persons to be prayed for ; Bedesmen were those who prayed for their benefactors and others, and in Catholic days a most common form of subscribing letters was " your poor bedesman " or " bedeswoman."

Many writers assign the devotion of the beads of our Ladye to the early ages of Christianity, and say that Venerable Bede greatly propagated it ; and derive the word beads from him ! Heath suggests with more plausibility that Venerable Bede received his name from his assiduity at prayer. Mabillon also conjectures that bead might be derived from *beltis.*[128]

This has reference to one of the Canons of the Council of Celchyth or Chalkhyth, A.D. 816, respecting obsequies of bishops, which contains the following words : *Et septem beltidum Pater noster pro eo cantetur ;* the meaning of which is evidently : " Let the Our Father be sung seven times for him."[129] This has been

---

[126] Early English Text Society, vol. xxiv. 1867, p. 6.

[127] Edited for the Camden Society by Albert Way, M.A.

[128] " Huc id torquent quod Rosarium apud Anglos Bedes nomine appellatur tanquam a Bede auctore. At potuit alia de causa sic vocari—puta in beltide " (Præf. in Sæc. V. *Act. SS. O.S.B.* n. 125). It is remarkable that Alan de Rupe (*Compendium,* cap. vii.), Michael de Insula (*Quodlibet,* p. 33), Juan de Lopez (*Rosario de Nuestra Señora, Salamanca,* 1589, fol. 10 b), Coppenstein (*B. Alani de Rupe redivivi Apologia,* Neapoli, 1632, part i. p. 20, and part ii. p. 86), all Dominican writers on the Rosary, attribute the propagation of the Psalter of our Lady to Venerable Bede. Bucelin, O.S.B. (*Chronologia Benedictino-Mariana,* p. 43) follows their opinion. Cf. also *Libellus perutilis de fraternitate sanctissima Rosarii et Psalterii beate Marie Virginis,* Auguste Vindelicorum, 1507, pp. 86, 87.

[129] Labbe, tom. vi. col. 1588.

strangely misunderstood and misconstrued by Benedict the Fourteenth,[130] Spelman,[131] Grancolas,[132] Butler,[133] Rock,[134] and others, who take it to mean : " Let seven *belts* of *Pater nosters* be sung for him." The Bollandists saw the difficulty, and finally gave it up as inexplicable.[135] Haddan and Stubbs have hit upon the most probable meaning ;[136] and hence it appears that the theory of the Anglo-Saxon "belts of *Pater nosters*" cannot for a moment be supported."

The practice of counting prayers by stones is a very old one. Palladius mentions that the hermit Paul used to recite three hundred *Pater nosters* every day, which he counted by as many little pebbles ; he also speaks of a penitent lady who daily recited seven hundred, and of the Abbot Macarius who recited one hundred.[137] The earliest example of counting prayers by beads strung on a cord is that of Lady Godgifu, who bequeathed the celebrated string of gems, which she used for that purpose, to the Image of Our Ladye of Coventry.[138] But there is no clue as to what the prayers were which she thus recited.[139] St. Godric, who died in 1172, counted his usual prayers by stones, but Reginald, his biographer, describes neither the prayers, nor whether the *lapides calculares* were strung on a cord.[140]

---

[130] *Votum*, written A.D. 1726 ; *Analecta Juris Pontificii*, tom. ii. col. 1398. He gives another reading—*triginta diebus canonicis horis ex plena synaxi*—quoting from Hen. Kelmann (Spelman), tom. i. *Concil. Anglor.* p. 331 ; but Spelman, whom I have tested, gives the same text as Labbe. Possibly the *Analecta* may have made a typographical error.

[131] Glossarium, sub voce *beltis*.

[132] *Annales Liturgiques*, vol. ii. p. 418.

[133] *Lives of the Saints*, vol. x. p. 24, note. Dublin, 1780.

[134] *Church of our Fathers*, vol. iii. p. 8.

[135] *Act. SS.* ad diem 4 Aug. p. 232. How can *septem beltidum* be the nominative to *cantetur?*

[136] They say of *beltidum* : "This word is explained by Spelman as meaning a Rosary, but Ducange remarks that Rosary is of much later invention. Schilter proposed to read *beltidum*, and explain it 'of the singing of prayers' from *biddan* to pray, and *leoth* a song. It seems now natural to derive the word from Bel (Anglo-Saxon) a bell, and Tid (Anglo-Saxon) 'time,' and explain it in reference to the seven Canonical Hours at which the prayer bell rang" (*Councils and Ecclesiastical Documents*, Oxford, 1871, vol. tii. p. 585, note).

[137] *Hist. Lausiaca*, cap. xxiii. Sozomena has the same, lib. vi. cap. xxiv.

[138] S. pp. 24, 25.

[139] *An inter orationes illas, quas tactis singulis circuli gemmeis globulis recitabat Galdina (Godgifu), censenda sit salutatio Deipara Virginis non satis liquet* (Mabillon, *Act. SS. O.S.B.* sæc. v. præf. n. 126).

[140] *Libellus de vita et miraculis S. Godrici*, p. 225. Surtees Soc.

In progress of time the little round balls strung together for this purpose became named *beads*, hence the origin of the term.

THE NAME OF ROSARY.

Ave, salve, gaude, vale,
O Maria! non vernale
Sed de Rosis spiritale
Tibi plecto nunc crinale
De Rosarum flosculis.

St. Bernard.[141]

The name Rosary was never applied to the Beads themselves, but exclusively to the devotion. It was not known in England in the beginning of the fifteenth century, according to the *Promptorium Parvulorum.*[142]

In his will, dated A.D. 1385, Sir William Walworth, the loyal Mayor of London, mentions *unum Rosarium;*[143] but the word occurs in the list of his books. *Rosarium* was a very common title for books, and as such, dates certainly from the thirteenth century. A celebrated *Rosarium* was composed by Arnold de Villanova, in Catalonia, a renowned physician, and doctor to Pope Boniface the Eighth A.D. 1294—1303.[144] Chaucer refers to it in the tale of the Chanon's yeman :

Lo thus saith Arnold of the new toun
As his rosarie maketh mencion.[145]

Guy de Basio, Archdeacon of Bologna, composed a commentary on the Decrees, called *Rosarium;*[146] and the inventory of the Cathedral of Aberdeen taken in 1436 enumerates a copy of it : *Rosarium archidiaconi super Decretum.*[147] I have a *Rosarium sermonum predicabilium,* by Bernardine de Busti.[148]

The term Rosary, however, as applied to the devotion of the beads was originally used to designate a third part, or five

---

[141] Mone, *Hymni Latini,* vol. ii. p. 268 ; but his version gives a different reading.

[142] Rose, *rosa,* Rosiere (rosiziere), *Rosetum,* a bed of roses.

[143] Bentley, *Excerpta Historica,* p. 136.

[144] Cf. Catalogue of MS. in the Bibliothèque at Paris, nn. 7147, 7149, for two codices of this work.

[145] Opp. fol. 61. Edit. 1602.

[146] Hain, n. 2715.

[147] *Registrum Aberdonense.* Spalding Club, p. 130.

[148] Cf. also *Mon. Angl.* tom. vi. p. 1362, for a Rosarium amongst the books at Windsor, in the list taken in the 8th of Richard II. 1384, 1385.

decades of the Psalter: consequently a Psalter was composed of three Rosaries. The name of Psalter has become obsolete, and is replaced by that of Rosary, which is now accepted in the same sense as Psalter formerly was. The Confraternity of the Rosary in France was known as that of the *Sertum* or *Chaplet*.[149]

OTHER NAMES.

Psalter is the original name applied by Alan de Rupe, Michael de Insula, and others to the Beads, and was used in England until the days of the so-called Reformers.[150] Rosary I have already explained. *Patriloquium* and *Patriolum* are also two early names for the Beads.[151] *Sertum* is the Latinized form of the French *Chaplet*, corresponding with the Flemish *Roosencrans*, or *Roosenhoet*,[152] a chaplet of roses. *Capellina* also occurs.[153] These, however, were not employed in England.

Paternosters, Bedes, Preculæ, Par precularum, or *precum*, were the common terms in England.

PATERNOSTERS.

This appears to have been the primitive appellation of the Beads in England; it was also used on the Continent.

In France it sometimes appears as *Patenotre*. Benedict the Fourteenth[154] and Ducange[155] quote examples from a *Compotus*, A.D. 1333 to 1336.

English evidence is of an earlier date. The making of bead-psalters was a considerable trade, and the tradesmen exercising this craft were called *Paternostrers*. In the year 1277-8, mention occurs in the Rolls of the City of London of Roger de Bury, Paternostrer; Richard le Bryd, Paternoster; and John Grethened, Paternostrer. They would, probably, be

---

[149] Quodlibet, p. 20.
[150] *Certain Sermons or Homilies appointed to be read in Churches in the time of the late Queen Elizabeth.* Oxford, 1840. Third part of Sermon on Good Works, p. 52.
[151] *Act. SS.* t. i. April. Pp. 107, 121.
[152] Sasbout, *Dictionaire Flameng-Francoys.* Anvers, 1576.
[153] *Act. SS.* t. ii. Mart. P. 244.
[154] Votum, n. 43, apud *Analecta Juris Pontif.* t. ii. c. 1395.
[155] Glossarium, sub voce.

l

residing in Paternoster Lane.[156] And in the year 1295 William le Paternostrer occurs.[157] In 1317 I find mention of one pair of *paternostres* of pearls, value twenty shillings.[158] I may remark that this is the earliest English evidence respecting the Beads with which I have met.

By his will, dated August 2, 1400, Richard, Lord Scrope of Bolton, leaves to his most dear son and heir a pair of paternosters of coral, "which formerly belonged to my lord father, as well as a cross of gold, which I have used and worn; with the blessing of Almighty God, of the Most Glorious Virgin Marye, St. Anne, All Hallows, and mine own."[159]

Roger, Lord Scrope of Bolton, was the son and heir mentioned as the legatee of the paternosters of coral; he was thus the third to whom they had descended in succession, and by his will, dated September 23, 1403, he, using the words of his father's will, bequeaths the pair of paternosters to his son and heir Richard.[160] This is evidence of the reverence and value in which a pair of beads were held in Catholic England, descending from father to son for four generations. If the *pocula patrum trita labiis* were valued by the pagans in the days of old, what wonder that a pair of beads, worn away, *patrum digitis*, in our Ladye's honour, should be highly prized by a succession of her devout liegemen?

PRECULÆ, PAR PRECULARUM, PAR PRECUM.

These names are of very frequent occurrence, and the four volumes of Yorkshire wills, and the Wills of the northern counties are full of examples. The *Promptorium Parvulorum* gives for bedes or bedys *numeralia, depreculæ;* and the will of Lady Jane Haselrigg, dated December 1, 1400, contains a bequest of *unum par preculum,* Anglice, *bedys.*[161]

A *par precum,* however, does not always mean a pair of beads consisting of five decades; it is used as well for the

---

[156] *Memorials of London and London Life in the Thirteenth, Fourteenth, and Fifteenth Cent.* Extracted from the Early Archives of the City of London. By H. T. Riley, M.A. Published by order of the Corporation of London, 1868, p. 20.

[157] *Ibid.* p. 30.

[158] *Ibid.* p. 124.

[159] *Test. Ebor.* vol. i, p. 275.

[160] *Ibid.* p. 329.

[161] *Ibid.* vol. i, p. 266.

Corona of six tens; thus, by will dated July 9, 1444, John Brompton leaves to Margaret, daughter of Nicholas Brompton, *i par precum de argento et corall continens VI^xx* (six tens) *absque gaudes, et V sunt de auro.*[162] *Par precularum* was also used to express a single decade of beads.

I have not as yet been able to explain the full meaning of the word *par* to my satisfaction.[163]

THE CORONA, OR CROWN OF OUR LADYE.

This is composed of sixty-three *Aves*, says Cardinal Bona, in accordance with the number of years which the Blessed Virgin is believed to have lived upon earth, according to the more probable opinion.[164]

This was a favourite devotion with Margaret, Countess of Richmond, the mother of Henry VII. Cardinal Fisher says that kneeling was very painful to her :

"And yet, nevertheless, dayly, when she was in helth, she faylled not to say the Crowne of our Ladye, whiche, after the manere of Rome, conteyneth LX. and thre Aues ; and at euery *Ave* to make a knelynge."[165]

BEDE RINGS

are rings with ten small knobs, or bosses, and a large one for the Paternoster. They occur of gold, silver, base metal, and ivory ; and their use certainly dates as far back as the fourteenth century in England and Ireland.

HOW THE BEADS WERE WORN.

According to Alan de Rupe, St. Dominic carried a pair of beads attached to his girdle.[166] St. Francis recited the Psalter,

---

[162] *Test. Ebor*, vol. ii. p. 104.

[163] Henry de Knighton says that St. Edmund of Canterbury "per singulos dies *tria* dixit horarum *paria* : de die de Domina, de Sancto Spiritu, cum officio defunctorum. . . Post primum somnum de nocte surgens sinazim dixit." (*De Eventibus Angliæ*, apud Twisden. Decem Scriptores, col. 2433.)

[164] *Horologium Asceticum*, cap. v. § 7, p. 164. Paris, 1866 ; cf. also B. de Busti. *Mariale*, pt. xii. Serm. i. pt iii., not paginated. Nuremberg, 1503.

[165] *A Mornynge Remembrance*, &c., not paginated. Stonyhurst Library. In Cambridge Edit. of 1841, p. 114.

[166] *Compendium*, p. 11.

and enjoined his Order to do so as well, and to wear it.[167]   Alan de Rupe also says that the faithful of every state should carry in their hands, or at their belt, these manual-psalters—*psalteria hæc manualia*—as wonderful signs of the Divine things of God,[168] and Michael de Insula exclaims: "Alas, they are now worn for vanity's sake, although originally instituted for piety and devotion.[169]

Chaucer, in the only original portrait which has been preserved of him, is shown as holding in his left hand a pair of beads, consisting of ten *Aves*, which are black and strung upon a red cord.[170]

Among the woodcuts in the folio edition of the Canterbury Tales printed by Caxton, the Clerke of Oxenforde wears his beads slung beltwise over his shoulder as he rides, and the wyf of Bathe carries hers upon her right arm.   Dame Eglentine, the accomplished Prioresse,

> Of small corall about her arme she bare
> A paire of bedes, gauded all with grene,
> And thereon hong a broch of goldfull shene,
> On which there was first writ a crowned A,
> And after, *Amor vincit omnia*.[171]

Brooches, or ouches, and rings are often mentioned as attached to pairs of beads, their object evidently being to enable the wearer to fasten his beads to his girdle.   William of Wykeham in 1404 bequeathes *unum par precum de auro appensum ad unum monile de auro habens hæc verba inscripta* 𝕴𝖍𝖈. 𝕬𝖒𝖔𝖗. 𝕸𝖊𝖚𝖘.[172]

Beads are often figured in monumental brasses; and many examples yet exist. I have noticed that whilst ladies are represented with beads consisting of six or ten decades, men are generally given with short beads of one decade.   Thus in the church of North Creak, Norfolk, there is the figure of a man, c. 1500.   He is represented with one decade, having a ring at one end and a tassell at the other, and on each of the

---

[167] *Compendium*, p. 10.
[168] *Ibid.* p. 16.
[169] Quodlibet, p. 33.
[170] *MS. Harl.* 4866, f. 91, quoted by Rock, iii. 329.
[171] Prologue, n. iiii. Opp. Edit. cit.
[172] Louth, *Life of Wykeham*, Appendix, f. xxxvi.

ten beads is engraved 𝔄𝔟𝔢.[173] Haines enumerates many other examples on tombstones of figures with beads.[174]

Stow also records that on a field to the east side of Houndsditch one of the Priors of the Holy Trinity had erected some small cottages two stories high for poor bed-rid people. "In my youth," says he, "I remember devout people, as well men as women, of this city were accustomed oftentimes, especially on Fridays weekly, to walk that way purposely, and there to bestow their charitable alms, every poor man or woman lying in their bed within their window, which was towards the street, open so low that every one might see them ; a clean linen cloth lying in their window, and a pair of beads : to show that there lay a bed-rid body, unable but to pray."[175]

A beautiful custom ! In those days, then, it was the "correct thing" for good people to wend their way, on certain days, towards Houndsditch, where the attractions were, not a meet of the Four-in-hand, and Coaching Clubs, or a muster of well-mounted fathers and a bevy of daughters, attended by smart grooms irreproachably turned out, in quest of grooms of another description,—but the blessed poor of Christ, bed-ridden, awaiting charity for the love of our Blessed Ladye, whose beads laid out upon a napkin, made the silent yet irresistible appeal to the hearts of her liegemen and for her love.

The evidence which I have produced shows that it was the usual custom in England, in Catholic days, for our forefathers to carry their beads about with them. Many, now-a-days, wear their beads round their necks ; but as every layman does not habitually peruse the *Ritual*, I think it may be of advantage to add the concluding words of the Blessing of Rosaries :

"*Eisque tantam infundas virtutem Spiritus Sancti*, ut quicumque horum quodlibet secum portaverit, atque in domo sua reverenter tenuerit, *ab omni hoste visibili et invisibili semper et ubique in hoc sæculo liberetur, et in exitu suo ab ipsa Beatissima*

---

[173] These must be correct representations, for the Venetian Ambassador, Sir Francis Capello, mentions that the Englishwomen carry about long strings of beads in their hands : "Et in publico dichino molti Pater noster, de i quali le donne portano lunghe filze in mano" (*Italian Relation*, p. 23, Camden Society).

[174] *Manual of Monumental Brasses*, &c. By the Rev. Herbert Haines, M.A. Parker, 1861, p. 123. Cf. *Monumental Brasses of England*. By Rev. C. W. Bontell, M.A.

[175] S. p. 94.

Virgine Maria Dei Genitrice, Tibi plenas bonis operibus præsentari mereatur.

When Burleigh wanted Queen Mary to employ him in her Government, one of the hypocritical means by which he tried to cheat her into the belief of his friendly feelings towards the old faith, was to walk about Stamford with a pair of beads in his hands. "Truly," says Rock, "did the future unprincipled Minister of Elizabeth exemplify the remark of Polydore Vergil, who, in speaking of the beads, said : *Hodie tantus honor ejusmodi calculis accessit, ut non modo ex ligno, succino et corallio, sed ex auro argentoque fiant, sintque mulieribus instar ornamenti et hypocritis præcipua fucosæ bonitatis instrumenta.*[176] In the *Memorial of a Christian Life*, by Father Lewis de Granada, printed at St. Omer's by John Heigham in 1625, there is an engraving which represents both men and women wearing a decade of beads hanging from their waists.

OF WHAT MATERIALS THE BEADS WERE MADE.

The pairs of beads which our forefathers used were of great value, as appears from the old wills and inventories. Michael de Insula,[177] and the *Libellus Perutilis*,[178] both say that the beads of value, and made of gold and silver and precious stones, may be worn, not for the sake of vanity or display, but rather to the praise and glory of our Blessed Ladye, and to symbolize her virtues, which are more brilliant and precious than all gold and silver and gems.

The Compotus of A.D. 1333—36, referred to by Ducange, which I have already quoted,[179] mentions pairs of beads made of amber, glass, and crystal. But in the *Memorials of London*, in the year 1317, one pair of *paternostres* of pearls, value of twenty shillings, is mentioned.[180] These Memorials also give a most interesting inventory and valuation of stock in a jeweller's shop of the year 1381, 5th Richard the Second.

"One forcer (*i.e.*, coffer or box), value 6*d.*, with divers jewels in the same contained—namely, 4 sets of *paternostres* of white amber, value 2*s.*; 16 sets of *paternostres* of amber, 20*s.*; 5 sets of *paternostres*, namely, 4 of coral, and one of *geet* (jet), 10*s.*;

---

[176] *De rerum inventoribus*, lib. v. cap. ix. p. 337. Amstelodami, Elzevir, 1671.
[177] Quodlibet, p. 43.   [178] P. 84.
[179] See ante, p. 161.   [180] P. 455.

6 sets of *aves* of *geet*, and *paternostres* of silver gilt, of one
pattern, 8*s.*; 38 sets of *aves* of *geet*, with *gaudees* of silver gilt,
of another pattern, 38*s.*; 14 sets of *aves* of blue glass, with
paternostres silver gilt, 3*s. 4d.*; 28 sets of *paternostres* of *geet*,
3*s. 4d.*; 15 sets of *paternostres* of mazer (*i.e.*, probably of wood
inlaid with metal), and 5 of white bone for children, 5*s.*;
20 necklaces of silver gilt, 5*s.*; 46 rings of silver gilt, 10*s.*;
14 necklaces of *geet*, the tongues of silver, 3*s. 4d.*; and two
crucifixes of silver gilt, 3*s.*"

In contrast with these evidences of the ages of faith in
England, I may observe that occasionally a pair of beads may
be seen in the window of a London goldsmith, but as an object
of curiosity or vertù.

In the Yorkshire wills, and the *Testamenta Vetusta*, there
are numerous descriptions of pairs of beads; a few of which are
sufficient as illustrations.

In 1430, *unum par preculum de aumbre ;*[181] in 1432, *optimum
meum par precularium de nigro gete, et tria flammeola de fils ;*[182]
in 1452, *unum par precum de pomoder ;* another, *de mistylltyn ;*[183]
in 1459, i payre of bedes gete with gawdes of silver, and i
crucifix, and i Saynt James shell hangyng at the same bedes.[184]

John Baret of St. Edmundsbury is very precise in the description of his beads. He says:

"*Item*, I yeue and beqwethe to the seid Dame Margaret Spo
(Spurdance of Norwich) a peyre of bedys with pater ñris of gold
and on each side of the pat^r ñris a bede of coral and the Ave
Maryes of colour aftir marbil with a knoppe othir wyse called a
tufft of blak sylke, and ther in a litil nowche of gold with smal
perle and stoonys, be sekyng the seid Dame Margarete to prey
for me, and that she wil vowchsaf if hire daughter leve longer
than she to have the said bedys aftir hire dissees."[185]

Frequent mention is made of beads consisting of fifteen
decades. Thus, in 1486, Isabella Wilson leaves to her daughter
Marion,

"i payr of bedis of corall conteigning thre times l. with all
the gaudis of silver and gilt, and of every side of the gaudis a
bede of silver."[186]

[181] *Test. Ebor.* vol. ii. p. 13.   [182] *Ibid.* p. 23.   [183] *Ibid.* p. 160.
[184] *Ibid.* p. 237.
[185] *Bury Wills*, p. 36.   [186] *Test. Ebor.* vol. iv. p. 17.

Sir Thomas More speaks of his wife's gay girdle and her beads of gold.[187]

The *Libellus Perutilis* speaks of pairs of beads made of horn of animals. Beads made of wood were used by poor bedesmen at funerals.[188] A pair of beads was sometimes given as a New Year's gift.[189] A magnificent pair of gold beads, which formerly belonged to the unfortunate Mary, Queen of Scots, is now in the possession of my friend Mr. Howard, of Corby Castle.

§ 6. OUR BLESSED LADYE'S LITANIES.

Litaniæ, or Litanies, a word derived from the Greek λιτανία, from λίσσομαι, is a form of earnest prayer and supplication to obtain the mercy of God through the intercession of the Blessed Virgin Marye and all the saints. The earliest Litany is that of the Saints, which was composed by St. Gregory the Great, and which is known as the *Litania Major*, or greater Litany. But *Litanies*[190] must not be confounded with *Acclamations*.

Only three Litanies have the approbation of the Church, *i.e.*, are liturgical : (1) The Litany of Jesus ; (2) the Litany of Loreto ; (3) the Litany of the Saints, which is indubitably the most ancient.[191] The Litany for a departing soul, which is in the Ritual is an abbreviation of the *Litaniæ Majores*.

In the Litany of the Saints as used by the Anglo-Saxons, the name of our Blessed Ladye stands invariably before that of any angel or saint ; and it is worthy of notice that it is repeated three times. So it appears in the Pontificale of Ecgberht, Archbishop of York, A.D. 732—766,[192] and in the Litany of Alcwine ;[193] in the early Anglo-Saxon Litany quoted by

[187] Cresacre More, *Life of Sir T. More.* Edit. Hunter. London, 1827, p. 322.
[188] *Test. Ebor.* vol. ii. p. 187.
[189] Bentley, *Excerpta Historica*, p. 150.
[190] Mrs. Jameson has fallen into a singular mistake about the word "Litanies." Speaking of the Immaculate Conception, she says : "We must be careful to discriminate between the Conception, so styled by ecclesiastical authority, and that singular and mystical representation which is sometimes called the ' Predestination of Mary,' and sometimes the ' Litanies of the Virgin ! '" (*Legends of the Madonna*, p. 51. London, 1872).
[191] *Ferraris, Bibliotheca Prompta.* Paris, 1854, t. v. p. 177. Edit. Migne.
[192] Surtees Society, vol. xxvii. p. 27 ; cf. also p. 32.
[193] Opp. *Officia per ferias*, vol. ii. col. 522. Edit. Migne.

Mabillon ;[194] in the Anglo-Saxon Pontificale,[195] which formerly belonged to the Monastery of Jumiéges, and is now in the public library at Rouen ; and in the short Litany which follows the blessing of the palms on Palm Sunday, in the Missal of Leofric,[196] which was one of the 11 *fulle maesse bec* given by Bishop Leofric in the time of St. Eadward to Exeter Cathedral.[197] But in the Caroline Litany, so called because it is believed to have been composed in the reign of Charlemagne, and during the Pontificate of Hadrian, the name of our Ladye is only given once.[198]   Hence it would seem that the triple invocation of our Ladye was peculiar to the Anglo-Saxons ; and it was not con- fined exclusively to the Litany, as is proved by a prayer in the Book of Cerne, which is of the eighth century.[199]   Nevertheless, there is no trace of any Litany of our Ladye in Anglo-Saxon times.

But the Irish have a very ancient Litany of our Blessed Ladye, which is preserved in the Leabhar-Mor now deposited in the Royal Irish Academy.   Professor O'Curry says that it differs in many ways from the Litany of our Ladye in other languages, clearly showing that although it may be an imitation, it is not a translation.[200]   It is much to be regretted that the learned Professor did not add in what languages, and where were to be found the Litanies of our Ladye, of which the Irish Litany might be an imitation.

Professor O'Curry believes this Litany to be as old at least as the middle of the eighth century.   No earlier Litany of our Ladye seems to be known ; therefore to the Island of Saints is due the glory of having composed the *first* Litany of their Immaculate Queen.   " The Litany of our Ladye," says Cardinal Wiseman, "is not a studied prayer, intended to have logical con- nection of parts, but is a hymn of admiration and love, composed of a succession of epithets expressive of those feelings, the recital of which is broken into, after every phrase, by the people or

---

[194] *Vetera Analecta.* Paris, 1723, p. 168.
[195] *Archæologia,* vol. xxv. p. 18.
[196] Bib. Bodley, Oxonii, n. 579.
[197] *Cod. Dip. Ævi. Sax.* vol. iv. p. 275.
[198] *Vet. Analect.* pp. 170, 171.
[199] The Gospels of Æthelwald, Bishop of Sherborne, A.D. 760, formerly belonging to Cerne Abbey in Dorset.   It is in the Cambridge Library, Ll. i. 10.
[200] MSS. of Irish History, p. 380.

chorus, begging the prayer of her to whom they are so worthily applied."[201] "It is a hymn, a song, of affectionate admiration, and, at the same time, of earnest entreaty."[202] The Cardinal then refers to St. Cyril of Alexandria, and says : " Hear him apostrophize the Blessed Mother of God in the following terms : ' Hail, Marye, Mother of God, Venerable Treasure of the entire Church, Inextinguishable Lamp, Crown of Virginity, Sceptre of True Doctrine, Indissoluble Temple, Abode of Him Who is Infinite, Mother and Virgin. . . . Thou through whom the Holy Trinity is glorified ; thou through whom the precious Cross is honoured ; thou through whom Heaven exults ; thou through whom angels and archangels rejoice ; thou through whom evil spirits are put to flight. . . . Thou from whom is the oil of gladness ; thou through whom, over the whole world, churches were planted ; thou through whom Prophets spoke ; thou through whom Apostles preached ; thou through whom the dead arise ; thou through whom kings reign, through the Blessed Trinity.'[203] " Now here," continues the Cardinal, " is a Litany not unlike that of Loreto, and we have only to say *pray for us* after each of the salutations to have a very excellent one. This intercalation would surely not spoil, nor render less natural, or less beautiful, that address of the holy patriarch."[204] Hence it appears that whilst these and other homilies suggest the formation of a Litany of our Ladye, the Irish were the first who did form a Litany ; that is, a prayer to our Ladye in the shape of what is now understood by a Litany. This old Irish Litany of our Blessed Ladye has an indulgence of one hundred days granted to all who recite it by Pius the Ninth ; it consists of fifty-eight invocations, from which I have selected the following :

LITANY.

O Great Marye,
O Marye, greatest of Maryes,
O Greatest of Women,
O Queen of the Angels,
O Mistress of the Heavens,
O Mother of the Heavenly and Earthly Church,
O Gate of Heaven,
O Destruction of Eve's disgrace,
O Regeneration of Life,
O Mother of God,
O Mistress of the Tribes,
O Mother of the Orphans,
O Breast of the Infants,
O Queen of Life,
O Ladder of Heaven,

Hear the petition of the poor, spurn not the wounds and groans of the miserable.

[201] *Essays on various Subjects.* London, 1853, vol. i. pp. 419, 420. [202] *Ibid.* p. 418. [203] Labbe, *Conc.* t. iii. col. 584, 585. [204] *Essays,* &c., ubi. sup. p. 419.

A *Mariale* by an English scribe of the year 1200, or thereabouts, which I have quoted elsewhere, contains a Litany of
our Ladye.[205] Then may be mentioned the Litany composed
by St. Bonaventure, who died on the 14th of July, 1274.[206] But
although the *Mariale* affords evidence of the existence of a
Litany of our Ladye in England at the commencement of the
thirteenth century, it does not appear that this or any other
Litany of our Ladye had been raised to the position of a
liturgical prayer.

The Litany of Loreto.—This beautiful Litany, which is now
one of the three approved of by the Church for public worship,
and is recited daily through the length and breadth of Christendom, was unknown to Catholic England. Liturgical and other
writers are provokingly silent about its origin, but none of them
claim a high antiquity for it. I doubt if it can be traced back
so far as the year 1560.[207]

On the 13th of September, 1601, Clement the Eighth ordered
that no one should sing or recite in public without his permission,
or that of the Sacred Congregation of Rites, any other Litanies
than the very old ones ordinarily inserted in the Missals,
Breviaries, Pontificals, and Rituals, and the Litanies of the
Blessed Virgin Marye which are sung in the Holy House of
Loreto.[208]

§ 7.—OTHER DEVOTIONS.

THE JOYS OF OUR BLESSED LADY.

This is the appropriate place for a remark which is suggested
by nearly every detail of the devotion of our forefathers to her
whom they loved to call the "Blissful Mother of God."

It cannot fail to strike the Catholic mind that everything
connected with the service of our Ladye is pre-eminently of
a joyful character. The Introit of the Mass of the Assumption
says, *Gaudeamus omnes in Domino diem festum celebrantes sub
honore Beatæ Mariæ Virginis de cujus Assumptione gaudent*

---

[205] Cott. MS. *Titus A.* xxi.
[206] Opusc. ed. cit. t. i. p. 519.
[207] Cf. *Discursus Prædicabiles super Litanias Lauretanas*, studio et opere P.F.
Justini Miechoviensis, O.P. Neapoli, 1857, p. 14. He wrote in the year 1628.
[208] Bourassée, *Bullarium Marianum*, in Summa Aurea, t. vii. col. 151. Edit.
Migne.

Angeli, et collaudant Filium Dei. Digby justly says that "it is very remarkable, bearing in mind the gloomy sadness of those who reject the intercession of Marye, that the Church whenever she invokes the Blessed Virgin's aid, seems invariably to have in view the deliverance of men from sadness, and the attainment of present as well as of eternal joy, *a præsenti liberari tristitiâ et æterna perfrui lætitia,* being her words conformable to those of the sweet hymn—

> *Iter para tutum*
> *Ut videntes Jesum*
> *Semper collætemur.*[209]

She is the true Cause of our Joy.

The most common and homely of all the old English devotions were the Five Wounds of our Lord and the Five Joys of our Blessed Ladye. There were, however, several series of our Ladye's Joys; her Five Joys; her Seven Earthly and Seven Heavenly Joys; her Twelve Joys, and her Fifteen Joys.[210] Lansperg composed a Rosary of the Fifty Joys of our Ladye.[211] I have met with many variations of these Joys, and therefore I only give those which were commemorated by our forefathers.

I. The Five Joys are: (1) the Annunciation; (2) the Nativity; (3) the Resurrection; (4) the Ascension; (5) the Assumption.

The Ancren Riwle calls the Five Joys our Ladye's Five Highest Joys—*hire vif hexte blissen.* It gives five prayers, one of each of the Five Joys, which are embodied with the devotion of the five Psalms in honour of our Ladye's Name.[212]

Ames quotes a prayer from the *Speculum Christiani*:

> Ladye for thy Joyes Fyve
> Gete me grace in thys lyve

---

[209] *Compitum,* vol. ii. p. 145. This title of "Blissful" was also applied to St. Thomas à Becket. So in the Prologue to the *Canterbury Tales,* the host of the Tabarde says—

> Ye goon to Caunterbury; God you speede,
> The blisful martir quyte you youre meede.

[210] Léon Gautier, *Prières à la S. Vierge d' après les Manuscrits du moyen age.* Paris : V. Palmé, 1873, pp. 347—352; Pelbart de Temeavar, *Stellarium.* Hagenaw, 1501, lib. x. pt. iv. art. iii.; Drexellius, *Rosæ selectissimarum virtutum.* Antv. 1636, pp. 99—102 ; Mone, *Hymni Latini medii ævi,* vol. ii. hymns nn. 454 to 484.

[211] *Divini Amoris pharetra variis orationibus ignitisque aspirationibus referta,* auctore Joanne Lanspergio. Antverpiæ in ædit. Joan. Steelsii, 1550, f. 111. b.

[212] Pp. 42, 43.

> To knowe and kepe over all thyng
> Christen feith and Goddes byddyng.
> And trewly wynne all that I nede
> To me and myn clothe and fede.
> .   .   .   .
> Swete ladye full of wynne
> Full of grace and God withynne.[213]

There are many evidences of the popularity of this devotion. At Hull, in 1453, Robert Golding leaves five nobles to five poor virgins to buy five cows when they shall be married, in honour of the Blessed Virgin Marye:[214] evidently in honour of her Five Joys. In 1463, John Baret of Bury St. Edmunds wills to have at his interment and dirge and messe v. men clade in blak in wurshippe of J'hus v. woundys, and v. women clad in white in wurshippe of oure ladyes fyve joyes, eche of them holdyng a torche of clene vexe."[215] In 1475, John Weryn left an alms of 10d. in worship of the Five Wounds of our Lord and the Five Joys of our Ladye.[216] On Candlemas Day the Earl of Northumberland, if at home, offered five groats for the Five Joys of our Ladye.[217] In 1531, William Keye gave half an acre of land to provide "five Gawdyes for ever to burn before our Ladye at Garboldesham, at every antiphon of our Ladye, and at the Mass on all her feasts."[218]

II. The Seven Earthly Joys are: (1) The Annunciation; (2) the Nativity; (3) the Adoration of the Wise Men; (4) the Finding of our Lord in the Temple; (5) the Resurrection; (6) the Ascension; (7) the Assumption.

III. The Seven Heavenly Joys: (1) Our Ladye's surpassing glory; (2) her brightness, which lights the whole Court of Heaven; (3) all the Host of Heaven obeys and honours her; (4) her Divine Son and she herself have but one will; (5) God rewards at her pleasure all her clients both here and hereafter; (6) she sits next to the Most Holy Trinity, and her body is glorified; (7) her certainty that these Joys will last for ever.

The Seven Heavenly Joys are associated with the memory of St. Thomas of Canterbury, to whom our Ladye revealed this devotion, and by whom this hymn was composed—

---

[213] *Typographical Antiquities.* Edit. Herbert. London, 1785, vol. ii. p. 14.
[214] S. p. 55.   [215] *Bury Wills.* Camden Society, p. 17.
[216] S. pp. 73, 74.   [217] *Northumberland Household Book.* London, 1770, p. 333.
[218] S. p. 42.

> *Gaude flore Virginali*
> *Quæ honore principali*
> *Transcendis splendiferum.*[119]

It is also related that a similar vision was vouchsafed to B. Arnulph of Corniboult, a lay-brother of the Abbey of Villiers, who died in the year 1228.[120]

There is a corresponding hymn of the Seven Earthly Joys of our Ladye—

> *Gaude Virgo Mater Christi*
> *Quæ per aurem concepisti*
> *Gabriele nuntio, &c.*

Although there is no evidence that St. Thomas wrote this hymn, it certainly looks as if it comes from the same hand which wrote the Heavenly Joys. Jacopone of Todi composed a *Stabat Mater gaudiosa.*

In one of the great windows of Canterbury Cathedral the Seven Joys of our Ladye were represented, together with the "Blissful Martyr," and the patron Saints of England. This magnificent window was not destroyed until the Commonwealth.[121] In the absence of positive proof it is impossible not to hazard a conjecture that the great veneration, in which the glorious martyr St. Thomas was held by the English people, and throughout Christendom, may have contributed to spread and make popular the devotion of our Ladye's Joys.

The Fifteen Joys vary very much in different lists. In some they consist of the Seven Earthly, and the Seven Heavenly Joys, with the addition of the Visitation ; and in one set I have found the Crucifixion included as a victory over hell.[122]

John of Gant by his will leaves to the Carmelites of London xv. *marcs dargent en lonur des* xv. *ioies de Nostre Dame.*[123]

Other Seven Joys of our Ladye as they are called, are yet commemorated in popular song in some of the English counties.[124] Sometimes Twelve Joys are sung.

[119] Morris, *Life and Martyrdom of St. Thomas à Becket.* London, 1859, p. 384. For an old translation of this hymn see *Political, Religious, and Love Songs,* Early English Text Society, 1866, vol. xv. p. 145.

[120] Colvener, *Kalendarium Marianum* ad diem 7 Maii, § 3.

[121] For full description see Northcote, *Sanctuaries of the Madonna,* pp. 281, 282.

[122] Cf. MS. Cott. Nero, c. ix. ; Léon Gautier, *ubi sup.;* Drexellius, *ubi sup.*

[123] *Test. Ebor.* vol. i. p. 223.

[124] *Journal of British Archæological Association,* vol. viii. p. 238 ; Husk, *Songs of the Nativity.* London : Camden Hotten, s. a. pp. 87—90.

THE FIVE PSALMS.

It was an old and pious custom to recite five of the Psalms which begin with the five letters composing our Blessed Ladye's Name.

> M. *Magnificat.* (St. Luke i.)
> A. *Ad Dominum cum tribularer.* (Psalm cxix.)
> R. *Retribue servo tuo.* (Psalm cxviii.)
> I. *In convertendo Dominus.* (Psalm cxxv.)
> A. *Ad te levavi oculos meos.* (Psalm cxxii.)

The first who is related to have practised this devotion is Blessed Joscio, a monk of the celebrated Abbey of St. Bertin at St. Omer's, who died in 1163.[225] They were also sung daily by another monk, Josbert, who died in 1186;[226] and by many others, among whom may be named Blessed Jordan of Saxony, the successor of St. Dominic, who took up the Devotion.[227] There are several variations of it, but I confine myself to the English form.

In England the five Psalms were said in honour of the Five Joys of our Blessed Ladye. The Ancren Riwle says: "These psalms are according to the five letters of our Ladye's name. Whoso pays attention to this name MARIA may find it in the first letters of these five psalms aforesaid, and all those prayers run after these five. After her five highest joys, count in the antiphons, and thou shall find in them five salutations. Cause to be written on a scroll what you do not know" (by heart). The prayers I have omitted, excepting the last.

In the form given by the Ancren Riwle a prayer is prefixed to each psalm. It says: "Whoso cannot say these five prayers, should say always one, and who thinketh them too long, may omit the psalms.

"Sweet Ladye Saint Marye, for that same great joy which thou hadst within thee at the very time when Jesus God, the Son of God, after the salutation of the Angel, took flesh and

---

[225] Th. Cantimpré de apibus, lib. ii. cap. xxix. par. xv.

[226] Colverer, *Kalend. Marian.* ad diem 30 Nov. § ii. nn. 3, 4.

[227] The form used by B. Jordan is given in the *Daily Manual of the Third Order of St. Dominic.* By the Rev. F. James D. Aylward, O.P. Dublin, 1862, pp. 284 —290. The *Raccolta* gives this Devotion in the indulgenced form. Authorised Edit. London, Burns and Oates, 1873, pp. 169—173.

blood in thee and of thee, receive my greeting with the same
Ave, &c.   Hail Marye, to the end, five times." A different
prayer, with the same number of Hail Maryes, accompanies
each of the other four psalms, and at the end of the last comes
the versicle, *Spiritus Sanctus*, and the prayer, *Gratiam tuam*,
&c., with the antiphons, *Ave Regina cœlorum*, *Gaude Dei Genitrix*, *Gaude Virgo*, and *Alma Redemptoris*. " Here say fifty
Aves, or a hundred, more or less, according as you have time.
Lastly, this versicle, *Ecce ancilla Domini*, and the prayer,
O Sancta Virgo. Whoso will, may stand up immediately after
the first prayer, and then say her number of *Aves*." [228]

St. Bonaventure gives another version of the Five Psalms,
which he called the Crown of our Blessed Ladye. [229]

THE SCAPULAR.

This most widely spread Devotion is one of the glories of
our Ladye's Dower. The history of its foundation I have given
under Newenham [230] and Winchester. [230] Among the members
of the confraternity the *Menologium* names King Edward of
England with his wife and children, Henry, Duke of Lancaster,
miraculis clarus, the King of Scotland with all his family, the
" Earl of Ireland " with his wife and children, and Henry, Earl
of Northumberland, whose names are taken from the Annals of
the Order. [232]

NIGHT HYMN.

This is an old hymn to our Blessed Ladye, which our forefathers would recite before retiring to rest :

> Upon my ryght syde y may ley :
>   blessid Lady to the y prey
> Ffor the teres that ye lete,
>   vpon your swete Sonnys feete ;
> Send me grace for to slepe
>   and good dremys for to mete ;

[228] Pp. 39—43.
[229] Opusc. vol. i. p. 491. Edit. cit.
[230] S. pp. 105, 106,
[231] S. pp. 243—246.
[232] *Menologium Carmelitanum.* Auct. R.P. Petro Thoma Saraceno de Bononia,
Carmelita. Bononiæ, 1628, p. 293.

Slepyng, wakyng til morrowe day be :
Our Lord is the freute, our Lady is the tre,
Blessid be the blossom that sprang, Ladye, of the,
In nomine Patris et Filii et Spiritus Sancti. Amen.[223]

The following is written on a fly-leaf of the Sarum *Horæ*, 1530, in the Stonyhurst Library :

Uppon my right side I lay me
as Jesus did on Maries knee ;
Now Jesus for thy holly name
shield me from sin and shame.
Witt and wisdome vnto me geve
as longe as I in this world live,
Sweet Jesus. Amen.

§ 8.—COMPARISON OF OLD AND NEW.

Those who have ever looked into the subject cannot fail to be struck with the great contrast between the old manuals of devotions and modern prayer-books. The former teem with milk and honey, and are full of unction for the soul, whilst in the latter, quantity and novelty are the characteristic features. Occasionally, well-meaning editors completely spoil a prayer of some standing, because they have not understood it. Old prayers are frequently remodelled by those who have not caught their meaning, and brought out in a new shape and with a new name. Thus the Thirty Days' Prayer in its original form was called the *Obsessio*, or the "Besieging," of our Ladye, as if it were felt that she could not refuse a prayer made in such earnest language.

It is more than a century since an edition of the Prymer was brought out. This was the favourite prayer-book of our fore-fathers. It contains the *Obsessio* of our Ladye, and other fine · prayers, and also the Passion of our Lord according to the four Evangelists. It is an old English custom to recite one of these Passions daily. My late father did so every day of his life, although he never told me his reason or his object. In the times of our Anglo-Saxon forefathers, the Passions of our Lord were read for the souls of the faithful departed ; thus in the Codex about the year. 805 :

[223] *Harl. MS.* 541, f. 228 b.

m

" ic bidde . . . ðæt . . . æghwilc diacon arede twa passione fore his sawle."[234]

This love of the old prayers which their fathers had used was one of the characteristics of the civil martyrs of the penal laws. Miss Dorothy Daniel, who became the wife of Mr.William Bell, of Temple-Broughton—he died in 1598—is described as "delighting in the abnegation of herself and corporal austerities, and in the same instructing her children : being so much given to prayer, as besides the Office of our Blessed Ladye, of the Dead, the Gradual and other Penitential Psalms, Hymns, Litanies, Office of the Holy Ghost and Holy Cross, prayers of the Manual which were her daily exercise; in the time of Lent she would never sleep before she had read over the whole Passion of our Saviour according to one of the four Evangelists, in Latin, which she understood well."[235]

Our forefathers loved to offer to our Ladye various "garments." Many old metrical prayers to our Ladye were in the form of acrostics, and took their name from some key-word, e.g., *Amictus*, or Mantle—*Annulus, Thronus, Crinale.*[236]

> *Est* titulus *talis, probat ut series capitalis.*
> Sit Thronus iste pia tibi gratus Sancta Maria.[237]

Then a "ring" may be offered to our Ladye, the key being the words, *Annulus Beate Virginis Marie :*[238] and also a "hairpin," or *crinale*, which consists of ten strophes, each of five lines, and commences, *Ave, Salve, Gaude, Vale, O Maria,*[239] each word being the beginning of every strophe in the respective five decades. Lastly, there are the "Alphabets," or "Staverows "[240] of our Ladye, the verses of which commence with the letters of the alphabet in succession.

---

[234] *Codex Diplomaticus ævi Saxonici*, t. i. p. 293. Among the prayers usually given in the old Prymers is one to our Lord by St. Bernard, *O Bone Jesu, O Piissime Jesu*, which I once found described in an illuminated copy of the Horæ of our Ladye as *Orison pour faire enragier le deable*, as no doubt it did whenever it was recited.

[235] *Catholic Miscellany*, vol. iv. p. 391. In the Indulgences granted by Gregory XIII. for all places beyond the Alps is mentioned *Quicumque . . . legerit passionem Christi . . .* &c., Douay Diaries, ubi sup, pp. 366, 367.

[236] Mone, *Hymn. Lat. medii ævi*, v. ii. pp. 239, 268, 442, 445.

[237] *Ibid.* p. 442.

[238] *Ibid.* p. 445.

[239] *Ibid.* p. 268, see ante, p. 48.

[240] *Ibid.* p. 449.

In no feature, perhaps, do English Catholics of the present day differ more from their forefathers than in their want of a *liturgical* spirit. They are present at the services of the Church without joining in the words of the Liturgy. During Mass they prefer to say other prayers rather than those of the Missal. There are many excellent methods of assisting at Mass, but they all fall short of the prayers used by the priest. Any one who attends the parochial High Mass in France cannot fail to be struck with the liturgical spirit of the congregation, for the greater part, if not all of them, join in the singing and follow the priest.

Cardinal Wiseman most appropriately says : "There can be no doubt that, while the ancient Christians had their thoughts constantly turned towards God in private prayer, the Church took care to provide for all the regular and necessary discharge of this duty by her public offices. These were not meant to be holiday services, or mere clerical duties, but the ordinary, daily, and sufficient discharge of an obligation belonging to every state and class in the Church. It never was understood that *besides* the public offices there should be certain long, family or private prayers, as necessary to discharge the duty of morning and evening spiritual sacrifice. Unfortunately, those offices have, for the most part, been reduced to a duty, discharged by the clergy in private, and have thus come to be considered by us as a purely ecclesiastical obligation superadded to, not comprehending, the discharge of ordinary Christian duty. One is apt to forget that Prime is the Church's morning prayer, and Compline her evening devotions. Yet so the two manifestly are. But what greatly helps to make us overlook this fact is, that we have been accustomed to consider morning and evening prayers as necessarily consisting of a specific form, composed of certain definite acts of devotion arranged in a formal order, and have lost sight of that model which characterizes all the offices of the Church, and is and must be far the most perfect. Let us observe the principal difference between the two classes of prayers.

" 1. It will at once strike us, that the modern ones are almost entirely composed for recital by one person. That this is not with a view to private devotion, appears from the few responses which are introduced, just sufficient to show that

congregational or family worship, as it is called, is intended.
Yet the great body of assistants must be mere listeners while
one person recites a long series of prayers. Every one knows
how difficult it is to keep up prolonged attention under these
circumstances, how easily the mind wanders and is finally lost,
till recalled mechanically by a response. Now this shows the
advantage of frequency in such interruptions; nay, how expedient it would be to have them come in almost every moment.
In the more solemn liturgy, or Mass, where the principal actor
is the priest, having a ministry exclusively his, the rest must
be content to join their prayers mentally with his, or rather
with the sacred rite performed by him. And so in some other
functions, wherein the priestly character alone has efficacy to
act. But in all other daily Church offices the service is especially choral; all join in nearly equal parts—psalms, hymns,
versicles, antiphons, belong to the entire company of fellow-
worshippers. All therefore become equally sharers, equally
interested, in the holy exercise, and the attention is kept alive
or easily recovers itself. Surely this is a great advantage, and
gives at once immense superiority to the ancient over the
modern form of prayer."

The same high authority goes on to say: "The Church
offices are always full of life and cheerfulness. This, in fact,
seems to be a marked characteristic of the Catholic Church:
she ever prays in hymns, making 'a joyful noise to God with
psalms.'" Moreover, "in the Church offices, everything is prayed
for that ought to enter into the exercises for which they are
intended; but they being composed of 'psalms, hymns, and
spiritual canticles,' most beautifully selected, the various peti-
tions run blended through the entire office, according as the
various portions of the chosen parts express them. This pre-
vents weariness: it is like a variety of modulations in music,
full of passages through various keys, with occasional apparent
and momentary dissonances, that only give zest to surrounding
harmonies. On the other side, our modern devotions have each
petition, and each act of virtue accurately distinct; no room is
left for a varied play of feeling; there are no contrasts, no
light and shade. The former is the language of nature; the
latter that of art."[241]

[241] *Essays, ubi. sup.* pp. 389—390.

Now in the list of Old English Devotions to our Blessed Ladye, it will be noticed that all of them, including the Psalter or Rosary, in its primitive form, and before it was simplified by St. Dominic, are adapted to general as well as to private use, and may be sung as well as recited. The Hymns of our Ladye's Joys, the Litanies, the Marye Mass, the Five Psalms, the Psalter, the Antiphons, and the Night Hymn all partake of that spirit which the Cardinal describes.

Some there are who consider the recent introduction of the grand old Gregorian chant into our churches as an innovation. Probably they are unaware that this was the chant used by our Anglo-Saxon forefathers, and Venerable Bede relates that some years after the coming of St. Augustine, John, the Arch-chaunter of Rome, was sent to England to teach the true principles of sacred music.

CHAPTER THE FOURTH.

Things Consecrated.

§ I.—CITIES AND MUNICIPAL CORPORATIONS.

Gloriosa dicta sunt de te, CIVITAS DEI.

Psalm lxxxvi.

Salve Præsidium Urbanum, tu mœnibus hostes
Arces, et moles concutis horrificas.

Johannes Geometra.

IN every nation of Europe there are many cities which are placed under the special protection of our Blessed Ladye, and others which bear her name.

In England may be mentioned Ottery St. Marye's,[1] and St. Marye's Cray. The name Evesham, or Eovesham, records the vision of our Ladye to Eoves the swain,[2] represented on the seal of the abbey.[3] Lincoln was dedicated in a special manner to her after the victory of the citizens over the Earl of Chester, in 1147,[4] just as Siena was consecrated to her in thanksgiving after the battle of Arbia. Aberdeen was under the patronage of our Ladye, and in consequence the armorial bearings are a pot of lilies.[5] Florence, for a similar reason, bears a lily.

Our Ladye, between St. Peter and St. Paul, with the City arms under her feet, was formerly represented on the old seal of London, which was made in the time of William Walworth.[6] She yet appears on the corporation seals of Rye,[7] Leith,[8] and Newhaven.[9] The seal of Rye is a splendid piece of engraving. It represents our Ladye with her Divine Son in her arms, standing in a beautiful tabernacle ; the legend is—Aue · Maria gracia · plena · dns · tecum · benedicta · tu · in · mulieribus.

---

[1] S. p. 117. [2] S. p. 33. [3] *Archæologia*, vol. xix. p. 43. [4] S. p. 63.
[5] S. p. 287. [6] S. p. 67. [7] I have seen an impression.
[8] S. p. 300. [9] S. p. 302.

TOWN GATES.

*Alma Redemptoris Mater quæ pervia cæli
Porta manes.*

Antiphon of the Church.

Many town gates were dedicated to our Blessed Ladye, whom the Church invokes as the Gate of Heaven. Images of our Ladye stand over the Porte de Calais, and the Porte des Dunes at Boulogne-sur-Mer: over the former is inscribed—VRBIS · ET · ORBIS · DECVS · ET · DOMINA. At the Monastery of St. Laura on Mount Athos there is by the gate a little chapel dedicated to "Our Ladye the Portress," in Romaic πορταίτισσα; or more properly, θυρωρος, the door-keeper.[10] Chaucer addresses our Ladye—

To hem that rennen thou art itenerarie.[11]

At Arundel there was a gate called the Marye Gate, which was erected at the close of the thirteenth century, and over it was a chapel served from the College, in which Mass was daily celebrated.[12] The images of our Ladye and the Archangel Gabriel yet grace their niches in the Stonebow at Lincoln. Over the New Gate of London stood an image of our Ladye, which Father Campion saluted from his hurdle as he was dragged under the arch on his way to martyrdom.[13]

Other images of our Ladye are also mentioned, which from their names show where they were erected, and they must have been as commonly placed in house-corners and in walls, as they are yet to be seen in Catholic countries. Thus there was our Ladye in the Wall at Calais, and our Ladye in the Rock at Dover, at both of which sanctuaries Henry the Eighth made his offerings.[14] There was also our Ladye in the Tower at Coventry,[15] and our Ladye of Grace in the Wall at Northampton.[16] The Series gives the history of our Ladye at

[10] Didron, *Annales Archéologiques*, vol. iv. p. 84. Cf. also Marracci, *Polyanthea Mariana* sub voce, Janitrix, Janua, Porta.

[11] *A Balade in commendacion of our Ladie* Opp. Edit. cit. f. 329 b.

[12] S. p. 266.

[13] S. p. 281.

[14] S. pp. 5, 29. I searched in vain at Calais, in 1875, for this shrine. No traces exist, and the very memory of our Ladye in the Wall has perished.

[15] S. p. 27.

[16] S. p. 107.

the Cross in West Cheap, London.[17] When her image with that of her Divine Son was finally removed, it was replaced by "an alabaster image of Diana.[18] The "Reformers" considered that an indecent statue of a heathen divinity was a more fit ornament for the base of the emblem of man's Redemption at West Cheap than the image of the Virgin Mother of God with her Divine Son in her arms. How truly were the words of Horace borne out in succeeding generations—

Ætas parentum pejor avis tulit
Nos nequiores.[19]

I have long noticed an image of our Ladye over a shop in London; and the image of our Ladye now in the Church of the Sacred Heart in Edinburgh was found over a shop in Peterborough.[20]

BRIDGES.

Maria . . . Pons periculosi hujus mundani fluminis.

Bernardine de Busti.[21]

The more the principles of Christian art by which our forefathers were influenced are studied, the more the beauty of their symbolism becomes manifest. It did not escape them that St. John Damascene calls our Blessed Ladye the Bridge which leads to the Creator; St. Proclus, the Bridge by which God descends to man; St. Andrew of Crete, the Bridge conducting mortals to heaven. Marracci quotes many other similar expressions from the writings of the Fathers.[22]

The river, too, was the emblem of the fleeting and transitory life of man, and thus the bridge became the symbol of her whose prerogative it is to lead us through this mortal life to God.

Thus it is that so many bridges exist in Great Britain which either yet are or formerly were called by the name of our Blessed Ladye. As the bridge was the great thoroughfare, it presented a most fitting site for a chapel, or an image of our

---

[17] S. p. 93.
[18] Stow. Edit. Strype, bk. iii. p. 35.
[19] Lib. iii. od. 6.
[20] S. p. 299.
[21] Mariale, Serm. ii. *De Coronat. B.M.V.* in fine. Nuremberg, 1503, not paginated.
[22] *Polyanthea Mariana*, sub voce.

Ladye, which would offer to the pilgrim and wayfarer of all classes the opportunity of breathing an *Ave* to our Blessed Ladye, as her liegemen were taught to do from their infancy.

At Sheffield there was St. Marye's Bridge, on which was a chapel where Mass was celebrated.[23] At Leicester there was a chapel of our Ladye on the Brig, which is mentioned in the will of William, Lord Hastings, dated June 27, 1481 : "Also I woll that myne executors do make new and edify the chapell of our Ladye called the chapell on the Brigge, at Leicestre ; and for the making thereof *cli.*, also that they finde a preste in the same chapell by the space of seven years next, after my decese, to say daily Masse, &c., in the same chapell, and other prayers as shall be ordeigned by myne executors."[24] Thus Mass was constantly celebrated in the various Ladye chapels on bridges. At Lynn-Episcopi, now King's-Lynn, a chapel of our Ladye stood at the east end of the bridge.[25] At Blythe, there was either an image or a chapel, for in 1347 Alice, wife of John Henriot, bequeaths to the light of our Ladye on the bridge of Blye her green tunic with its hood.[26] At Wakefield the chapel of our Ladye on the bridge is one of the gems of Yorkshire ; its vicissitudes are described later.[27] At Bradford, York-shire, there is a bridge which, although dedicated to St. Osith, is called the Ivy Bridge. I have pointed out that in Stow's map of London, Ave Maria Lane is given as Ivy Lane, consequently the Ivy Bridge of Bradford may be considered as the modernized form of Ave Bridge. On the farm of Drax Abbey, near Snaith, there is a lane formerly known as Ave Maria Lane, but the unlettered rustics, who know nothing of our Ladye, now call it Hairy Mary Lane. Leland mentions our Ladye chapell on Avon Bridge, at Bristol.[28] At Aberdeen there were chapels of our Ladye at the Brig of Dee, and our Ladye on the Brig.[29] At Perth the remains of the chapel of our Ladye at the Brig[30] are now transformed into the Police Office. In Catholic days gilds were sometimes founded for the repairing of bridges, or the making of roads, and it may safely be con-cluded that due attention and care was paid to our Ladye's chapels and images.[31]

---

[22] S. p. 138. [24] *Test. Vet.* p. 371. [23] S. p. 100. [26] S. p. 269.
[27] S. p. 154. [25] S. p. 4. [29] S. pp 287, 290. [30] S. p. 303.
[31] See Leland, *Itin.* vol. ii. p. 67 ; vol. iv. p. 27.

HOSPITALS AND BEDE HOUSES.

In London or the suburbs there were five hospitals named after our Blessed Ladye: (1) St. Marye Barking, for poor priests and men and women of the city of London; now suppressed.[32] (2) St. Marye Bethlem, founded in 1247, by Simon Fitz-Marye, who had been one of the sheriffs in the preceding year.[33] It is now transferred to Southwark. (3) St. Marye Spital, or the New Hospital of our Ladye, founded by Walter Brune, a citizen of London, and Rosia his wife, in 1197. It surrendered to Henry the Eighth, when it was found to contain nine score beds well furnished for the receipt of the poor of charity.[34] (4) St. Marye within Cripplegate, founded in 1329, by William Elsing, mercer, for one hundred blind men of the city of London.[35] (5) St. Marye Rounceval, near Charing Cross, founded in the thirteenth century.[36] It was pulled down, and Northumberland House was erected on its site, and out of the ruins; and now Northumberland House no longer exists.

The celebrated Sir Richard Whittington founded a College of the Holy Ghost and our Blessed Ladye, and a God's House for thirteen poor men, who were daily to pray for the founder and his wife.[37] Walter, Lord Montjoy, by his will in 1474 endowed a God's house for the maintenance of seven old folks of his estates, and required that each of them should recite twice each day the Psalter of our Ladye in their chapel.[38] A similar God's house for five poor men was founded by Lord Marney in 1523.[39] Many other similar foundations might be enumerated.

The indomitable energy and perseverance which characterized their forefathers, are equally to be found in the leading British merchants of the present day—

Fortes creantur fortibus et bonis ;

but too many of the religious thoughts and pious practices which graced the earlier generations, to whom a possible peerage was not the *summum bonum,* may be looked for now

---

[31] S. p. 95.   [33] *Ibid.*   [34] S. p. 97.   [35] S. p. 98.   [36] *Ibid.*
[37] S. p. 94.   [38] Test Vet. p. 271.   [39] *Ibid.* pp. 610, 611.

in vain. In Catholic times men knew what it was to be poor in spirit, and to live for eternity. They cared very much to secure a remembrance in the prayers of the Church and those of their poor bedesmen.

§ 2.—CONSECRATION OF LAND.

In the illuminated charter of privileges of Eton the royal founder, Henry the Sixth, is represented on his knees offering the foundation deed to our Ladye.

It may be said that in the ages of faith very few Englishmen who had it in their power to give some practical proof of their love of God and His Blessed Mother, omitted to do so.

Thus, owners of ancestral estates and lords of manors would give to our Ladye their seigneurial or manorial rights, like Richard Beauchamp, Earl of Warwick, who died at Rouen in the year 1439. In his will he left directions for a chapel of our Ladye to be well, faire, and goodly built, in the middle of which his tomb was to be made. He then orders that, "in the name of *Herryott* to our Ladye there be given myne image of gold, and that of our Ladye there to abide for evermore."[40] Now a heriot is the best beast or other chattel which, by the custom of some copyhold manors, the lord has a right to seize on the death or alienation of his tenant, but more usually on his death. However, the right of the lord is now confined to such a chattel as the customary law will enable him to take.[41] In many manors upon the death of a copyholder, even though he was only tenant for life, the lord becomes entitled to his best beast or chattel, whether consisting of a jewel, a piece of plate, or anything else, or to some pecuniary compensation thereof. A heriot is only due on the death of a legal tenant, not on the death of the person entitled to an equitable estate in a copyhold.[42] Therefore there can be no doubt as to the act of the Earl of Warwick ; and it may with safety be presumed that this was not a solitary instance.

Then in regard of the tenure of land. Thomas Winchard held lands in Conington, County Leicester, *in capite*, by the

[40] S. pp. 220, 221.
[41] Haliday, *Digests*, &c. Edit. Badham. London, 1872, p. 182.
[42] *A Compendium of the Law of Real and Personal Property*, &c. By Josiah W. Smith, B.C.L., D.C. London, 1870, vol. ii. p. 969.

service of saying daily for the souls of the King's progenitors, and the souls of all the faithful departed, five *Pater nosters* and five *Ave Marias.*[43]   Richard Paternoster, for his relief, said three times before the present Barons (of the Exchequer) the Lord's Prayer, with the Salutation of the Blessed Marye, as John his brother had done for his relief.[44]   This John Paternoster held one yard-land with the appurtenances, in East Hendred, in the county of Berks, by the serjeanty of saying for the soul of our lord the King one *Pater noster* daily, and it was worth 5s. yearly.[45]   And Alice Paternoster held one yard-land in Pusey in the same county, *in capite*, of our lord the King by the service of saying every day five *Pater nosters* for the souls of the King's ancestors.[46]   Did this family take their surname from their service ?

Lands were also held by the service of providing lights to burn before images of our Blessed Ladye.   William Strode held two tenements with gardens of the Priory of Plympton by the payment of wax to the value of four shillings and sixpence to be burnt before the image of our Ladye in the Conventual Church.[47]   And at East Herling, in 1510, Robert Banham purchased a messuage and six acres of land, held of the manor of East Herling, by 8d. a year, to find a wax candle burning in that church before the image of our Blessed Ladye.[48]

Those who know Bavaria and Belgium will remember the numerous way-side sanctuaries, and crucifixes, and images of our Blessed Ladye, sometimes of a rude description, but nevertheless all recalling the great mystery of the Incarnation, and of our Redemption, and inviting the peasants and those who pass by to greet our Ladye with the Angelical Salutation, or salute the Five Wounds of our Lord.   Thus, in *Dives and Pauper* : " For this reason ben crosses by ye waye, that whan folke passynge see the crosses, they sholde thynke on Hym that deyed on ye crosse, and worshyppe Hym aboue all thynge."[49]

[43] Blount, *Fragmenta Antiquitatis*, or *Ancient Tenures*. Edit. Beckwith. London, 1815, p. 281.

[44] *Rot. Fin. Easter*, 31 Edw. III.   Blount, p. 282.

[45] Blount, *Ibid*.

[46] *Ibid.*

[47] S. p. 127.

[48] S. p. 53.

[49] *A Compendiouse Treatyse, or Dialogue of Dives and Pauper*, &c. Imprynted in Fletestrete by me, Thomas Berthelet. 1536.

From Chaucer it is quite evident that, in the ages of faith,
similar way-side roods and images of our Ladye were thickly
spread over the length and breadth of England, because school
children were taught to salute our Ladye whenever they passed
by her image, as the wedow taught her son, the litel clergion.[50]

And frequently under these way-side images the lines of
St. Bonaventure, which are quoted in the Sarum Prymer, would
be written or painted :

Hac ne vade viâ nisi dixeris Ave Maria.
Sit semper sine væ, qui tibi dicat Ave,

as in the corner of the garden wall of the Cluniac abbey at
Paisley.[51]

In the third year of Henry the Sixth, 1424-5, a tenant of
the Abbot of St. Albans, by name William, being at Marford,
and afflicted with blindness, in a spirit of devotion caused a
wooden cross to be erected by the road leading to Codicote, and
near to it he placed an image of our Ladye in alabaster.[52] Sometimes these crosses represented our Lord on one side and our
Ladye on the reverse, as in the celebrated cross erected within
the area of Merton College, Oxford,[53] and at Somersby, county
Lincoln, where, I believe, the cross still exists.[54] And the
names of many of the sanctuaries I have given explain their
position. Our Ladye in the Wood, near Epworth ; Our Ladye
prope furcas, near Hereford ; Our Ladye in the Island of
Hilbury, which "is sandy, and hath conies;" Our Ladye at the
Oak, Islington, and Our Ladye in the Park, at Liskeard.[55]
The images of our Ladye in many of her great sancturies, such
as at Montaigu, in Brabant, have been found attached to trees,
which was the history of Our Ladye of Fernyhalgh.

Dr. Rock says : "If every large town has yet its St. Marye's
Church ; if every, however small, parish once had its St. Marye's

[50] See *ante.* p. 25.
[51] S. p. 303.
[52] S. p. 100.
[53] S. p. 123.
[54] S. p. 139. For other evidence on way-side crosses, Cf. Leland, *Itin.* vol. i.
p. 42 ; *Ibid. Collectanea*, vol. ii. p. 438 ; Camden, *Britannia.* Edit. Gough, t. ii.
p. 245 ; t. iii. p. 33 ; *Chronicon sive Annales Prioratus de Dunstable*, Edit. Hearne,
vol. ii. p. 586 ; Walsingham, *Hist. Anglicana.*
[55] S. pp. 31, 51, 54, 58, 65.

altar, almost every district had its Ladye grove, its Mary-field, its Mary-well, its Lady-mead, besides other patches of ground by wood and stream, with other such-like denominations."[56]

The Manor of Tacabré, or Takkabere, formerly belonging to the Abbey of St. Marye of Graces, acquired the name of Merrifield, a corruption probably of Mary-field.[57] The Cathedral at Salisbury was built on a piece of ground once called Miryffeld, or Maryfield.[58] And near Sowerby, in Yorkshire, a considerable portion of land was called Ladyland.[59] Camden speaks of a place in the county of Glamorgan, called Margam, perhaps Mairgwm, or *vallis Mariæ*, because the church is dedicated to our Ladye, and lies in a bottom.[60] At Ashurst, in Kent, there is a fine old chestnut tree commonly called our Ladye's tree.

A ceremony, which is called "Beating the Bounds" of parishes is yet observed in England. This is the remnant of the Catholic custom of blessing the fields and the crops on the three days preceding the festival of Holy Thursday, or the Ascension of Christ our Lord. These are called the Rogation Days in the Missal; they were known to our Anglo-Saxon forefathers as the "Gang Days." On these days a solemn procession was made through the streets of towns and the fields of a country parish; the relics of the saints were taken out of the churches and carried round, and the Litanies of the Saints, commonly called the Greater Litanies were sung, to implore the blessing of God upon the new crops and farm-stock. The Anglo-Saxon homilist, Aelfric, admonishes "how we also in those days (the gang days) should offer up our prayers, and follow our relics out and in, and with fervour praise Almighty God."[61] On these solemn occasions our Ladye was specially invoked.

Now comes the day wherein they gad
abroad with cross in hand,
To bounds of every field, and round
about their neighbour's land ;

[56] *Church of our Fathers*, vol. iii. p. 288.
[57] Lysons, *Magna Brittania*. Cornwall, p. 45.   [58] S. p. 136.
[59] S. p. 142.   [60] *Britannia*. Edit. Gough, t. ii. p. 150.
[61] *Homilies*. Edit. Thorpe. Vol. i. p. 247.

And as they go, they sing and pray
To every saint above,
But to our Ladye specially,
whom most of all they love.[61]

In these days of rinderpest and potatoe disease, and the probability of the invasion of the Colorado beetle, the processions of the Gang days according to the ritual of Holy Church, might well be revived.

The first Monday after the Epiphany is yet called by its old Catholic name of Plough Monday. On this day the ploughmen used to go round from house to house to seek for alms wherewith to buy candles to burn before images of our Ladye and the saints, to implore a blessing on their agricultural labour. Thus in the chapel at Tunstead there were images of the Most Holy Trinity, and Our Ladye of Pity, and the Ploughlight, as it was called, of Upgate and Hungate.[63]

Those who have been to Rome will remember well the long trains of hay carts which arrive in the city from the Campagna, and they will not have failed to notice that the leading *biroccio* is drawn by a magnificent pair of oxen, with bells at their necks, and that fixed into the pole there is an upright shaft with a picture of our Ladye, and a canopy over it. This pious custom must be of very ancient origin; I do not know if it was observed in England.

As to the religious foundations, royal or otherwise, which covered the land, abundant evidence is contained in the *Series* which forms the second part of this book.

§ 3.—LADYE WELLS.

All the host of angels, and all holy things,
Say and sing that thou art of life the well-spring.
A Good Orison of our Ladye, thirteenth century.[64]

Innumerable in England, Scotland, and Ireland are holy wells, and wells dedicated to our Blessed Ladye, as is evident

---

[61] For many interesting details, see *Instructions sur la Liturgie*, &c. By M. Noel Vicaire Général du Diocèse de Rodez. Paris: Perisse frères. 1861. Vol. v. pp. 341, 371.

[63] S. p. 152. Cf. also Blomefield, *Parkin' Cont.* v. iv. p. 325.

[64] *Old English Homilies of the Twelfth and Thirteenth Centuries.* First Series. Early English Text Society, vol. xxxiv. p. 190, n. xx. lines 71, 72.

from their name of Ladye wells ; and many of them are renowned
for their sanitary properties.   Certain it is that the water which
they supply is invariably the best in the neighbourhood.[65]   It
is impossible not to believe that at some period these Ladye
wells had been placed under the protection of the " Well-spring
of Life," the Blessed Mother of God, and hallowed with the
blessing of Holy Church.   The same may be said of wells
dedicated to particular saints.   Miraculous cures are yet wrought
in St. Winefride's Well, which gives its name to the town—
Holywell.   And it must be noticed that Protestants as well as
Catholics are yet in the habit of resorting habitually to these
Ladye wells.   The principal ones which I have named are under
the headings of Eccles, Fernyhalgh, Jesmount, *i.e.,* Jesus-Mount.
Muswell, Scarborough, Sowerby, Walsingham, Woolpit, and
Stowe and Tarbat in Scotland.   Norden, who was a Protestant,
mentions the miraculous cure of a King of Scotland by the
water of the spring of Our Ladye of Muswell, and says very
significantly : "absolutely to denie the cure I dare not, for that
the High God hath giuen virtue vnto waters to heale infirmities,
as may appeare by the cure of Namaan the leper, by washing
himselfe seauen times in Jordan, and by the poole Bethseda,
which healed the rest that stepped thereinto after it was mooued
by the Angell."

The Church, however, was ever ready to check any undue
devotion which might arise from visits to wells not hallowed.[66]

---

[65] At the Sanitary Congress at Leamington, on Friday, the 5th of October,
Archdeacon Denison read a paper on the supply and storage of water at East Brent,
in which he said, " that when he went to East Brent in 1845 there was no pure
water to be had, except what was held in two shallow wells near the foot of the
knoll—the Lady Well, or ' Well of the [Blessed] Virgin :' (the church being dedicated
to the [Blessed] Virgin), and the Dripping Well, both of them on the foot of the
knoll at some considerable distance from the village, and of limited supply, though
never wholly failing " (*Times,* October 6, 1877).

[66] In the year 1240 the Council of Worcester forbids "superstitiosas fontium
adorationes, et populorum collectiones apud Cerne, et apud fontem Rollæ, apud
Gloverniam, et in aliis locis similibus, quoniam ex hoc animabus fidelium multa
novimus pericula provenisse, per sacerdotes vicinos præcipimus prohiberi, et per
substractionem panis benedicti et aquæ benedictæ, coerceant eos quos in hoc de
cætero noverint deliquisse " (Cap. xv.   Labbe, t. xi. pt. I. col. 574).

§ 4.—FLOWERS.

Quæ peperit florem det nobis floris odorem.

Breviary of Aberdeen.

It should not escape notice how often in the old English prymers, prayers, and poems, our Blessed Ladye is called by the name of some flower or plant. In the early part of the eighth century the Irish invoked her in their ancient litany as the Enclosed Garden, Branch of the Root of Jesse, Cedar of Mount Lebanon, Cypress of Mount Sion, Crimson Rose of the land of Jacob, Blooming like the Olive tree. Alcwine addresses her as the Flower of the fields, the Lily of the world, the Garden enclosed :

> *Tu Regina poli, campi flos, lilia mundi*
> *Hortus conclusus, vitæ fons, vena salutis.*[67]

In the Sarum Prymer she is hailed as the Rose without thorns, the lofty plant of the Lily of chastity, the deep Violet of the valley of humility, the wide-expanding Rose of the field of Divine charity.[68]

In an old hymn to our Ladye, we find—

> Heyle plesaunt lyly, most goodly in bewty,
> O plesaunt olyve with grace circundate.[69]

In the Life of St. Werburga written by Henry Bradshaw, a monk of the abbey of Chester, our Ladye is called the Flower of womankind :

> Nexte in ordre suynge, sette in goodly purtrayture
> Was our blessed Lady flowre of femynyte.[70]

Many of the plants and flowers which now bear the name of our Blessed Ladye were, in pagan times, called after Venus. The scandix, or *Pecten Veneris*, is now our Ladye's comb. In the north of Europe, before the Christian faith had been intro-duced, the name of Freyja, the "frau"-mother and queen of the northern gods, was used, and is still to be met with. Thus in

---

[67] Opp. t. ii. coll. 771. Edit. Migne.

[68] Edit. 1556, not paginated.

[69] *Political, Religious, and Love Songs.* Early English Text Society, vol. xv. pp. 81, 82.

[70] *Life of St. Werburga.* Cheetham Society, 1848, p. 61 (a reprint of Pynson's edition of 1521, in 4to.)

Iceland one species of the *Adiantum* is known as Freyja's hair;
the lady-bird, the German Marienvoglein, was once Freyja's bird;
and the constellation of Orion's belt, known in Zealand as
Mariärok—Marye's spindle—is still Freyja's spindle in Sweden.[71]

In the old English Herbals many plants and flowers are
mentioned in connection with the different feasts of our Ladye,
and several are named after her garments.   For the affectionate
love which our forefathers had for the Blessed Mother of God
was borne out in the most minute details. The snowdrop
was called our Ladye of February, and afterwards the Fair
Maid of February, or Purification flower.[72] Lungwort, from the
feast of the Annunciation, at which time it is in full flower, has
been called our Ladye's milk-wort.[73] The marygold belongs to
nearly all the feasts of our Ladye, and the name seems to allude
to the rays of glory round her head.

> Long years ago, ere faith and love
>   Had left our land to sin and shame,
> Her children called my blossoms bright
>   By their sweet Mother's gentle name.
> And when amid the leaflets green
>   They saw sweet " Mary-buds " unfold,
> In honour of the Angels' Queen
>   They plucked the Royal Marygold.
>
> I was the favourite of the poor,
>   And bloomed by every cottage door,
> Speaking of Heaven's Fair Queen to men,
>   They loved me for the name I bore.
> There is no love for Marye now,
>   And faith died out when love grew cold,
> Men seldom raise their hearts to Heav'n,
>   Though looking at the Marygold.
>
> But Marye from her throne on high
>   Still looks on England and on me ;
> The namesake of the Queen am I,
>   The Ladye of the Land is she.
> And surely she must win once more
>   Her heritage to Christ's True Fold ;
> Then to her children, as of yore,
>   Will preach again the Marygold.[74]

[71] King, *Sketches and Studies.* London, 1874, p. 68.
[72] *The Catholic Annual,* containing the Circle of the Seasons, and the key to the
Calendar. By Thomas Forster, M.D., F.R.A.S. London, 1830, p. 32.
[73] *Ibid.* p. 20.
[74] *Legends of our Ladye and the Saints.* London, 1870, pt. i. p. 77.

Our Ladye's smock at our Ladytide,

says an old English verse. The ladysmock, *Cardamine Pratensis*, is a corruption from our Ladye's smock. Shakespeare alludes to it in his Spring Song :

> When daisies pied and violet blue,
> And lady-smocks of silver hue.

Black Bryony, *Tamus Communis*, was called our Ladye's seal. It is in flower till August, when it bears large berries. It is mentioned by Lord Bacon in his *Sylva Sylvarum*. It was formerly a medicinal herb, and known by the name of *Sigillum Beatæ Mariæ Virginis*.[75] Many varieties of *clematis*, or Virgin's-bower, come into flower about Visitation-tide ; they are in full blow at the Assumption, and fade about the 8th of September. Hence their name.[76] The lily is the especial emblem of that "fayre mayd that was flowre of all maydens, for righte as the lylie is whyte and fair among bryers and other flowres ; ryght soo was our Ladye among other maydens."[77]

> From Visitation to St. Swithin's showers
> The lily white reigns Queen of the Flowers.[78]

"The lily," says Malou, "is a simple yet evident symbol of the Immaculate Conception of our Blessed Ladye, because, in the language of Holy Scripture, thorns denote sin and sinners, whilst the lily is the image of innocence and purity.

"After the fall of our first parents, God cursed the earth, and said that in punishment of the sin of Adam it should produce briars and thorns. Thorns are therefore, as it were, a sort of monument of the fall of the first man. The comparison of our Blessed Ladye to the lily which grows among the thorns recalls the perfect holiness which she preserved among sinners. It is, virtually, an admission that all mankind are accursed plants (*i.e.*, inasmuch as they are born in original sin) with the exception of the Blessed and Immaculately-conceived Virgin Mother

---

[75] *The Herball*, or General Historie of Plants. Gathered by John Gerarde. Enlarged by Thos. Johnson. London, 1636, p. 871 ; *Catholic Annual*, p. 159.

[76] *Catholic Annual*, p. 183.

[77] *Liber Festivalis*, De Nat. B.M.V. f. calvi., quoted by Rock, vol. iii. p. 248.

[78] *Catholic Annual*, p. 56. Cf. also Marracci, *Polyanthia Mariana*, voce *Lilium*, for the Fathers who have applied this word to our Blessed Ladye.

of God, who alone, on this earth, preserved a spotless innocence, and the sweet perfume of all virtues." [79]

This is expressed in the hymn of Vespers in the Little Office of the Immaculate Conception.

> *Lilium inter spinas*
> *Quæ serpentis conterat*
> *Caput.*

The white-flowered, or wild Virgin's bower,[80] and our Ladye's bedstraw (*Galium molugo ;* the upright is the *Galium erectum*[81]) belong by the time of their blooming to the feast of the Visitation.   There seems to be some difference of opinion whether this should be written bed-straw or bead-straw.[82]   In the middle of August we find our Ladye's traces, or tresses, *Spiranthus,* or *Neottia spiralis.*[83]   The white or wild Virgin's bower is recorded also as the Assumption flower.[84]

> When Marye left us here below,
> The Virgin's bower is in full blow.[85]

The Assumption was sometimes called the *Festum Herbarum.*[86] Barnaby Googe has the following lines upon this day in his English version of the *Popish Kingdome,* by Naogeorgus.

> The Blessed Virgin Maries feast hath here his place and time,
> Wherein, departing from the earth, she did the heavens clime ;
> Great bundles then of hearbes to church the people fast do beare,
> The which against all hurtfull things the priest doth hallow theare.[87]

Our Ladye's fringes, *Gentiana ciliata,* flowers for her Nativity.[88] A few other flowers may be named.

Our Ladye's thistle.   This is the purple-flowered Ladye's thistle, *Carduus Marianus,* called also the milk thistle, the leaves of which are beautifully diversified with numerous white

---

[79] *Iconographie de l'Imm. Concept.* p. 105.

[80] *Catholic Annual,* p. 189,

[81] *Ibid.* p. 193.

[82] Cf. *Old English Wild Flowers.* By J. F. Burgess. London, 1868, p. 68 ; and Brand, *Popular Antiquities.* London, Bohn, 1849, vol. ii. p. 66.

[83] *Catholic Annual,* p. 208.

[84] *Ibid.* p. 228.

[85] *Ibid.* p. 56.

[86] Harris Nicolas, *Chronology of History.* London, 1835, p. 116.

[87] P. 55, quoted by Brand. Edit. cit. vol. i. p. 349.

[88] *Catholic Annual,* p. 252.

spots. It derived its name from our Blessed Ladye, some of whose milk is said to have fallen upon the leaves of the plant, and to have caused the white spots.[99] The tradition is of no modern date, as appears from the name given to this thistle by early botanists of different countries: *Carduus Mariæ, Carduus Sanctæ Mariæ, Carduus Marianus, Cardo di Santa Maria, Chardon Notre Dame, Chardon Marie, Marie Distel, Frauen Distel, Onzer lieve Vrauwen Distel.*[00]

The common maiden-hair fern, *Asplenium trichomanes,* is said to have been previously called our Ladye's hair;[01] but Gerard is of opinion that it was originally named Venus's hair, *Capillum Veneris,* and then changed into our Ladye's hair, and *Chevaux de Notre Dame.*[92]

Our Ladye's slippers, *Cypripedium*; in French, *Sabot* or *Soulier de Notre Dame;* in Dutch, *Vrouweschoen;* and in Portuguese, *Calçado de Nuessa Senhora.*[03] Our Ladye's Costus, or Costmary; in German, *die Frauenmünger,* and in Spanish, *Hierba de Santa Maria.*[04] Our Ladye's fingers, *Anthyllis vulneraria;* our Ladye's mantle *Alchemilla vulgaris,* in Swedish *Mariä Kåpa;*[05] and the common yellow buttercup is called our Ladye's bowl. Our Ladye's laces, or lace-grasses, *Gramen striatum.*[00] Amongst the mosses and plants found about Whitsand Bay, Cornwall, there is one called Saint Marye's fan, from its resemblance to a fan. The beautiful little blue forget-me-not is called in France the eyes of our Ladye, *les yeux de Notre Dame.*[07]

D'Herbelot mentions a plant, *Bokhur Miriam,* the perfume of Marye, *i.e.,* the *Cyclamen odoratum.*[08] The Persians call it *Tchenk Miriam,* and *Penchch Miriam, i.e.,* the hand of Marye, and say that our Ladye, having laid her hand on this plant, it took the form of her five fingers, and gave a most delightful

[99] Brand, *Popular Antiquities.* Edit. cit. vol. i. p. 48.
[90] Loudon, ut sup. p. 681.
[91] *Catholic Annual,* p. 30.
[92] *Herball,* p. 1144.
[93] Loudon, *Encyclopedia of Plants.* London, 1855, p. 766.
[94] *Ibid.* p. 696.
[95] *Ibid.* p. 88.
[96] Gerard, p. 26.
[97] Montalembert, *Vie de Ste. Elizabeth,* Introd. p. 14c. Edit. 1861.
[98] *Bibliothèque Orientale.* Paris, 1697, p. 209.

fragrance.   The Arabs call it *Arthanita ;* in France it is named
the gloves of our Ladye, *les gants de Notre Dame.*[99]

Fortunatus, Bishop of Poictiers, who flourished in the sixth
century, mentions the custom that then prevailed of hanging
flowers and garlands over the altars :

> *Texistis variis altaria festa coronis,*
> *Pingitur ut filis floribus ara novis.*[100]

They were also suspended round the walls of churches, as
appears from St. Gregory of Tours, who mentions that the
priest St. Severus had attached lilies to the walls of one of the
churches which he had built.   *Solitus erat flores liliorum tempore
quo nascuntur colligere, ac per parietes hujus ædis appendere.*[101]
And St. Paulinus says :

> *Ferte Deo pueri laudes, pia solvite vota ;*
> *Spargite flore solum ; prætexite limina sertis :*
> *Purpureum ver spiret hyems : sit floreus annus*
> *Ante diem : sancto cedat natura diei.*[102]

This custom was practised in the old English churches, and
happily it is now being revived.   It is still observed on the
Continent.   Those who have visited Rome will remember the
beautiful mosaic-like carpets of flowers which are sometimes
made before the Confessions of the saints on their festal days.
Flowers are also strewed or placed on the tombs of the martyrs.
St. Augustine, in his treatise *De Civitate Dei,* mentions that
Martial, the most considerable man in the city of Calama, in
Africa, was miraculously converted by the application of a
flower taken from the tomb of St. Stephen.[103]   Flowers were
also worn as chaplets or garlands by the canons of some of our
old Cathedrals, and the parish priests in the great processions ;
and this practice was not confined to England.   Dr. Rock gives
many interesting details and examples.[104]   Flowers form a most
appropriate offering to the altar, and before the images of our
Ladye.

---

[99] *Ibid.* p. 584 b.
[100] Quoted by Pugin, Glossary, sub voce.
[101] De Gloria Confessorum c.l. col. 866.   *Patrol. Lat.* t. lxxi.   Edit. Migne.
[102] Quoted by Pugin, ubi. sup.
[103] Lib. xxii. cap. viii. col. 766.   Edit. Migne.
[104] *Church of our Fathers,* vol. ii. pp. 72—77.

The illustrious Augustus Welby Pugin, to whom the Church in England owes so much, makes some very pertinent observations. "The custom," says he, "of decorating churches with flowers is not only most ancient, but it is truly admirable, as proceeding from the beautiful principle of making all the creatures of God contribute, in their season, to increase the solemnities of His worship: *Benedicite universa germinantia in terra Domino*—'All things that bud forth on the earth, bless ye the Lord.'[105]

"It should however be remarked,"—and to what follows, I wish to draw particular attention,—"that each quarter of the year in succession produces a fresh variety for this purpose; nor less beautiful is the red-berried holly, fresh and bristly, among the tapers of a Christmas night, than the roses of the Assumption. While nature then supplies the richest stores for each succeeding festival, how monstrous is the *modern practice* of resorting to paper leaves and tinsel flowers, standing like faded trumpery throughout the year, a mockery and a disgrace to the sacred edifices where they are suffered to remain. The English churches were decorated several times in the course of the year;"[106] and it will be seen from the following extracts from the parish accounts of St. Marye Outwich, London, for the years 1524, 1525, that branches of birch, holly, yew, and broom, were used for the decoration of churches and altars.

" *Item*, for byrch at midsomer, ii*d.*

Item, for holly and ivy at Chrystmas, ii*d.*

1525.   Paid for Korks-flowers and yow, ii*d.*

Paid for brome ageynst Ester, i*d.*

Paid for byrche and bromys at Midsomer, iii*d.*

Paid for rose garlands on Corp[s] Xti daye, vi*d.*"

I hope this old Catholic custom may be fully revived, and that the altars and churches of God will no longer be disfigured by artificial flowers. When the great expense which is lavished in these days, in the hire of flowers to adorn window-conservatories, balconies, the dinner-table, and ball-rooms, is taken into consideration, it seems wonderful that a few flowers cannot be sent as well to the house of God—new plants and fresh, and not second-hand ones, which have already done duty at a banquet or a ball, for that would be giving to God that which has budded

[105] Cant. trium puer.   [106] Pugin, Glossary, sub voce.

forth at His command, after man had no longer any use for it. Even the *Epergne* which, now-a-days filled with flowers, occupies the centre of the dinner-table, is the old Catholic alms-dish, as its very name indicates.[107]

A few zealous and active "Queens of our Ladye" in every congregation would soon change the aspect of things, and see that proper attention was paid to the floral decorations of the houses of God and the altars of the Lord, and the shrines and images of the Blissful Mother of God, "that Rose of most transcendant beauty, that most fragrant Rose, to whom flew the Heavenly Bee, Who feeds amongst lilies, and dwells in the flower-bearing country of the angels, on whom He settled, to whom He clove."[108]

But who are the "Queens of our Blessed Ladye?"

OUR BLESSED LADYE'S QUEENS.

In the former diocese of Boulogne, now incorporated with that of Arras, there exists a very ancient and beautiful custom, of which I have found no traces in Catholic England, but which might be introduced most appropriately into the Dower of our Ladye. In nearly every parish church the care of our Ladye's altar is intrusted to three young ladies, or three maidens, for the space of two or three years. Their duty is to look after the decorations of the altar, and the altar linen. In country churches they attend to the decoration of the church for great festivals. They keep burning before the altar of our Ladye large wax candles, wreathed with flowers—as was the custom in England—and adorned with ribands, which they carry in processions. Their place is at the head of the maidens of the parish.[109] These young ladies are usually called the Queens of our Ladye—*les Reines de Notre Dame.*[110] There is a large field for their services in England.

---

[107] From *épergne.*

[108] *Liber fraternitatis Rosaceæ coronæ.* Without date, pagination, or place, but c. 1500. Library of the Oratory, London.

[109] Cf. Haigneré, *Hist. de N. D. de Boulogne,* p. 283.

[110] See ante, p. 93, note 182.

§ 5.—HOUSEHOLD FURNITURE.

A most favourite object in the houses of our forefathers was an image of our Blessed Ladye. St. Edmund of Canterbury had constantly an ivory image of our Ladye on his table ; and in 1493, Thomas Wilmott, Vicar of Ashford, bequeathed to the chapel of St. Nicholas the image of our Ladye which used to stand in his study.[111] Moreover, from the numerous examples of diptychs and triptychs beautifully carved in ivory, which represent, in the case of triptychs (or polyptychs), our Ladye, with scenes from her life, and in diptychs, the crucifixion on one leaf, and our Ladye with her Divine Son on the other, that these were intended for private use, and in many instances to serve as portable oratories, because it is sometimes added that they had cases. Thus in the Wardrobe book of the 28th of Edward the First are enumerated, an image of the Blessed Virgin Marye of ivory, with a tabernacle of ivory, in a case—*in uno coffino ;* [112] and four images of our Blessed Ladye with tabernacles, and sundry images.[113] These latter were evidently triptychs or polyptychs. Little portable images of our Ladye were also made in gold and silver. From the constant mention which occurs of them and from the different inventories it would seem as if the Kings of England kept *jocalia* of this kind for presents. Amongst the jewels in the Treasury in the time of Henry the Eighth was a tabernacle of gold with Our Ladye of Pity,[114] and others of a like nature.

In the decorations of houses, representations of our Ladye and of her life often occur. Thus, in 1266, by a royal writ tested at Westminster on the 11th of February, the Constable of Winchester Castle is ordered to make a certain window of white glass, and to cause the Nativity of the Blessed Virgin Marye to be painted in it.[115] Amongst the accounts of works at Windsor in the time of Henry the Third, there is a notice

---

[111] S. p. 2.

[112] "*Coffinus* or *cophinus*, a little chest ; those in the Royal Treasury in the thirteenth and fourteenth centuries were of wood " (*Promptorium Parvulorum*, sub voce. See also note, *Ibid.* p. 128, under *Dowcet Mete*).

[113] Lib. Garderob. Edw. I. pp. 351, 352.

[114] *Ancient Kalendars and Inventories of the Exchequer*, vol. ii. p. 274.

[115] S. p. 242.

of the insertion of a glass window in the gable of the Queen's chamber, on which was depicted the Root of Jesse, a favourite pictorial subject of the time ; it was provided with a wooden shutter.[116]

Then, again, may be named mural paintings, remains of which may still be found in old houses.[117]

BEDS.

By will, dated July 9th, 1444, John Brompton of Beverley leaves, *inter alia*, to his son a bed of arras-work with the image of our Blessed Ladye and the Three Kings.[118] And John Baret of Bury St. Edmunds says in his will :

"*Itm*, I yeue and qwethe to John Aleyñ my chyld, &c. &c. *Itm*, if he will be a preist or a prentys to a craft, I wil my executors helpe hym therto with my good[s], and there is a tester with ii costers small palyd of bukram blew and bett[s] blew with an ymage of oure ladye in gold papyr that I vsed to trusse with me, I wil he heue hem and the selour longyng therto."[119]

He also by his will gives to his niece "the steynyd clooth of the coronacōn of our Ladye with the clothes of my that longe to y[e] bedde that she hath loyen in."[120]

PAINTED CLOTHS.

Our Blessed Ladye also formed the subject for painted cloths, probably intended for the decoration of walls. Thus John Tidman, chaplain, by his will dated August 4, 1458, leaves to Alice, the wife of William Philipp, a cloth painted with the history of the Five Joys of our Blessed Ladye ; and to Isabella, daughter of Jane Byddus, a cloth painted with a large image of the Blessed Virgin Marye.[121] And by his will dated July 19, 1464, John Burton, chaplain of the infirmary of the poor in the Hospital of St. Leonard's, York, leaves to his sister Ellen a small stevened cloth with an image of the Blessed Virgin Marye, and the legend, 𝕻𝖆𝖙𝖊𝖗 · 𝖉𝖊𝖎 · 𝖒𝖊𝖒𝖊𝖓𝖙𝖔 · 𝖒𝖊𝖎.[122]

[116] Rot. Comp. Pipæ 20 Henry III.
[117] *Journal of the Archæological Association*, vol. iv. p. 93.
[118] *Test. Ebor.* vol. ii. p. 99.
[119] *Bury Wills and Inventories.* Camden Society, p. 34.
[120] *Ibid.* p. 23.
[121] *Test. Ebor.* vol. ii. p. 213.
[122] *Bury Wills and Inventories.* Camden Society, vol. ii. p. 262.

GOLD AND SILVER PLATE.

1. *Cups and Mazer-bowls.*—In 1368, Richard Colier of Nottingham leaves to his daughters Alice and Isabella his two large *scyphi murrei*, or mazer-bowls; the one with the Trinity in the centre to Alice; the other with an image of our Ladye in the centre to Isabella.[123] John Charlton, prebendary of Riccall in the church of York, by his will dated July 18, 1438, leaves to Master Robert Gilbert, Dean of York, "a gilt cup covered like a chalice with an image of the Blessed Virgin on the base, out of which in preference to other ones I used to drink, and rejoiced, so that at the sight of this little present he may remember me."[124] William Nawton of Grimston, near Settrington, Esquire, by will dated March 19, 1453, amongst other bequests to John Nawton, his son and heir, leaves him a covered cup of silver called the "Standing Piece," with an image of our Blessed Ladye on the summit.[125] And in 1463, by will dated August 26, Eufemia, wife of Sir John Langton, leaves to her son Henry Langton a silver cup with an image of the Blessed Virgin Marye on the top.[126]

2. *Dishes, or shallow basins* (pelves).—In 1426, by will dated August 8, Peter del Hay, of Spaldington, leaves to his wife Elizabeth two silver dishes with the Annunciation in the centre,—*cum Salutatione Angelica in fundo situata.*[127] This is evidently the construction in this instance of *Salutatio Angelica.*[128]

3. *Spoons.*—Anne Wood of Bury St. Edmunds, in 1525, mentions in her will a spoon knopped with the ymage of our Ladye.[129] I have a very beautiful spoon, silver gilt, with the image of our Ladye and her Divine Son on the end, about A.D. 1500.

The old wills also include occasional bequests of what

---

[123] *Bury Wills and Inventories,* vol. i. p. 85.
[124] *Ibid.* vol. ii. p. 14.
[125] *Ibid.* p. 58.
[126] *Ibid.* p. 259. On the silver-gilt rim of a late fifteenth century cup belonging to the Ironmongers' Company, the Angelic Salutation is inscribed.
[127] *Ibid.* vol. ii. p. 11. See also *Surrey Archæol. Collections,* vol. iii. p. 161.
[128] Cf. remarks thereon, S. p. 190.
[129] *Bury Wills and Inventories,* p. 258, note.

are described as "Maidenhead" spoons :[130] thus William of Wykeham bequeathes some spoons *cum Maydens hedd*.[131]

Maidenhead, or rather Maidenhede, signifies *virginitas*.[132] The typical representation of virginity or maidenhood, or maidenhede, as it was formerly written, was a young maiden with her hair loose and flowing over her shoulders.[133] But there is no evidence that the representation of the Maidenhede was ever intended for our Blessed Ladye. I have seen several of the spoons so called, and they quite bear out what I have said.

BANQUETS.

A favourite dish at the great banquets of our forefathers was a "subtlety."[134] This was an elaborate piece of confectioner's art, adorned with figures, and representing a scene or group having reference to the occasion of the festival. The modern representation of a "subtlety" is a richly adorned wedding-cake. Such was, I take it, the object I have described under the heading of Canterbury, at the enthronization feast of Archbishop Wareham. He had been promoted to the Mastership of the Rolls; and as there was doubtless, a celebrated image of our Ladye, in the Chapel of the Rolles, these two circumstances afforded a scope for the ingenuity of the Procurator, and the Maister Cooke. Accordingly, in the device, "the King presented my lorde in his doctor's habit unto our Ladye at Rolles, sytting in a towre with many rolles about him, with comfortable words of his promotion, as it appeareth in the verse following :

> *Est locus egregius tibi Virgo Sacrata dicatus,*
> *Publica servari quo monumenta solent.*
> *Hic primo hunc situ dignabere, dignus honore :*
> *Commendo fidei scrinia sacra sua*.[136]

[130] *Bury Wills and Inventories*, p. 134.

[131] *Journal of the Royal Archæological Institute*, vol. x. p. 235.

[132] *Promptorium Parvulorum*, sub voce. Also Halliwell, *Archaic and Provincial words*, sub voce.

[133] Cf. Herbert, *The Twelve great Livery Companies*, vol. i. pp. 225, 226.

[134] For full particulars see the Forme of Curie, a Roll of ancient English Cookery, by the Master Cook of King Richard II. Edited by S. Pegge. London, 1783. Many curious details of cookery are given in the *Opera di M. Bartolomeo Scappi, cuoco secreto di Papa Pio Quinto*, Venetia, 1596, a work of considerable rarity.

[136] *Forme of Curie*, p. 112.

Locus egregius evidently refers to the religious house of converts in New Street, now Chancery Lane, known by the name of the Rolles. It was founded by Henry the Third c. A.D. 1236, for Jews, converts, and to be converted, to the Christian faith. Edward the Third appointed this house for the custody of the Rolls and Records of Chancery. John Yong, I.U.D., and Master of the Rolls was buried in the chapel A.D. 1516.[136] There was also a house of converts dedicated to our Ladye at Rolles, near Canterbury.[137]

§ 6.—DETAILS OF COMMON LIFE.

Unius vita omnium disciplina.

St. Ambrose.

MODESTY AND DISCRETION.

Our Ladye's modesty in dress is commended. In a "Litelle short ditey agayne hornes"—referring to the period when ladies disfigured themselves by wearing horned head-dresses—the poet begins by saying that all beauty is natural, and that beauty needs no horns, and adduces the example of our Blessed Ladye.

> Grettest of vertues is humilite,
>   As salamon sayth, sön of sapience,
> Most was accepted to the deite.
>   Take hede here-of gefe to thys word credence,
> How maria, which had a preeminence
>   Aboue alle women, in bedlam whan she lay,
> At cristes byrth, no cloth of gret dispence,
>   She weryd a keuerche ; hornys were cast away.
>
> Moder of ihesu, myrrour of chastite,
>   In word nor thought that never did offence ;
> Trew exemplire of verginite,
>   Hede-spryng and welle of perfyte continence !
> Was neuer clerk by retoryk or science
>   Cowde alle hyr verteus reherse to this day.
> Noble princesse of much beniuolence,
>   By example of hyr joure hornys cast away.[138]

Walsingham gives some amusing details of the importation of French fashions into England after the taking of Calais by

[136] S. p. 7.
[137] S. p. 232.
[138] *Political, Religious, and Love Songs.* Early English Text Society, vol. xv. pp. 45, 46.

Edward the Third, in 1347,[139] which shows that the English matrons of those times were not exempt from some little failings which prevail now-a-days. Conversation on fashions frequently leads to what is, unkindly, no doubt, called gossip, savoured occasionally with a *soupçon* of "scandal." In the ages of faith idle talk was severely reprehended; and our Ladye was held up as the model for discretion in speech. The Ancren Riwle, which has a delightful quaintness and humour about it, although it was written for Anchoresses, contains much that might be read and put into practice by many of the daughters of Mother Eve. "Eve," it says, "in Paradise, held a long conversation with the serpent, and told him all the lesson that God had taught her and Adam concerning the apple; and thus the fiend, by her talk, understood at once her weakness, and found out the way to ruin her. Our Ladye, Saint Marye, acted in quite a different manner. She told the Angel no tale, but asked him briefly that which she wanted to know. Do you, my dear sisters, imitate our Ladye, and not the cackling Eve. Wherefore, let an anchoress, whatsoever she be, keep silence as much as she can and may. Let her not have the hen's nature. When the hen has laid, she must needs cackle. And what does she get by it? Straightway comes the chough and robs her of her eggs, and devours all that of which she should have brought forth her live birds. And just so the wicked chough, the devil, beareth away from the cackling anchoresses, and swalloweth up, all the good they have brought forth, and which ought, as birds, to bear them up toward heaven, if it had not been cackled."[140]

Instances also occur of peculiar dresses, or devices on them, being worn in honour of our Ladye. Thus in the College of Ottery St. Marye all the collegians were to eat together on the festival of the Assumption, and, "in token of the spotless virginity of the Dear Dove of Paradise," they had to wear surplices during dinner, without which no one, unless he were

---

[139] "The spoils which the English brought from France were dispersed all over England. . . . *Nam nullius nominis erat fæmina, quæ non aliquid de manubiis Cadomi, Calesiæ, et aliarum urbium transmarinarum, vestes, furruras, culcitras et utensilia possidebat. . . . Tunc superbire cæperunt matronæ Anglicanæ in apparatibus matronarum Galliæ Celticæ, et ut illæ dolebant de rerum suarum amissione, sic istæ gaudebant de rerum dictarum adquisitione*" (*Historia Anglicana*, vol. i. p. 272. Rolls Edit.).

[140] P. 67.

a religious man, should be permitted to eat.[141] The Knights of the Order of the Garter had to bear on the right shoulder of their mantle a golden figure of the Blessed Virgin Marye, on her five festivals, and on all Sundays of the year.[142] And by his will, dated January 13, 1518, Richard Cloudesley gave and bequeathed to two poor men of the parish of Islington, two gowns, and the same gowns to have 𝕸𝖆𝖗𝖎𝖆 upon them, in honour of our Blessed Ladye, every gown to be of the price of 6*s.* 8*d.*"[143]

Among the various articles of dress may be included :

GIRDLES.

To what has been already said about our Ladye's girdles, it is only necessary to add that in difficult cases of childbirth ladies were also recommended to wear in honour of our Blessed Ladye a girdle or scroll with the *Magnificat* written on it ; or as a MS. of the fifteenth century, entitled "The Knowyng of Woman Kynde," has it, "to wryte the salme of Magnificath in a long scrow and gyrdet abowte her, and sche shall be delyvert."[144] It appears to have been a custom for young ladies to wear hallowed girdles as a protection from insult ; and these belts seem to have been called Girdles of our Ladye.[145]

It was, as I have mentioned elsewhere, a most common practice, both with men and women, to wear a pair of beads, or a decade, pendant from their girdles.

GARTERS.

An example of a leather garter of the fifteenth century, on which is stamped 𝕬𝖇𝖊 𝕸𝖆𝖗𝖎𝖆, 𝖌𝖗𝖆𝖈𝖎𝖆 𝖕𝖑𝖊𝖓𝖆, is preserved in the Roach-Smith collection of antiquities found in the city of London,[146] and now in the British Museum. The letters being

---

[141] S. p. 118.

[142] Ashmole, ubi sup. p. 189.

[143] *History, Topography, and Antiquities of the parish of St. Marye, Islington.* By John Nelson. London, 1811, p. 302.

[144] *Privy Purse Expenses of Elizabeth of York*, p. 197, note.

[145] Cf. *Our Ladye's Girdle*, a border ballad. *The Local Historian's Table Book*, &c. By M. A. Richardson. Legendary division, vol. iii. pp. 161—199. Newcastle-upon-Tyne, 1846.

[146] *Catalogue of the Museum of London Antiquities collected by Charles Roach-Smith*. Printed for subscribers only, 1854, n. 645.

stamped, prove that this was a common form of garter. During the middle ages, prophylactic virtues were often attributed to inscriptions worn on *fibulæ* and rings, such as + 𝕵𝖊𝖘𝖚𝖘 · 𝖓𝖆𝖏𝖆𝖘 𝖗𝖊𝖓𝖚𝖘 · 𝖗𝖊𝖝 · 𝖏𝖚𝖉𝖊𝖔𝖗𝖚𝖒, or + 𝖆𝖚𝖊 · 𝖒𝖆𝖗𝖎𝖆 · 𝖌𝖗𝖆𝖈𝖎𝖆 · 𝖕𝖑𝖊𝖓𝖆. It is not improbable that these garters may have been worn against the cramp. One of the old English "charms" against the cramp bears evidence to our Ladye's immunity from sin.

> Cramp be thou painless
> As our Ladye was sinless
> Whan she bare Jesus,
> And quickly leave us.[147]

GYPCERES,

or bag-purses, attached to the belt, were much worn; and the clasps often bear the monograms of our Lord or of our Blessed Ladye; and an inscription which frequently occurs on them is + 𝖆𝖚𝖊 · 𝖒𝖆𝖗𝖎𝖆 · 𝖌𝖗𝖆𝖈𝖎𝖆 · 𝖕𝖑𝖊𝖓𝖆, and sometimes in capital letters.[148]

RINGS AND FIBULÆ OR BROOCHES.

There is one class of rings peculiar to England, examples of which I have never met with elsewhere. They have figures of our Blessed Ladye and the Saints engraved on them, sometimes on the bezels, and in signet rings on the shoulders. Rings of this description must have been very common, for they are often mentioned in wills.[149] Rings also occur inscribed + 𝕸 · 𝖒𝖆𝖙𝖊𝖗 · 𝖉𝖊𝖎 · 𝖒𝖊𝖒𝖊𝖓𝖙𝖔 · 𝖒𝖊𝖎, and with the Holy Names + 𝕵𝖍𝖊𝖘𝖚𝖘 · 𝕸𝖆𝖗𝖎𝖆: and occasionally with + 𝖆𝖚𝖊 · 𝖒𝖆𝖗𝖎𝖆 · 𝖌𝖗𝖆𝖈𝖎𝖆 · 𝖕𝖑𝖊𝖓𝖆, an inscription which is often found on *fibulæ*.

---

[147] *Journal of the British Archæological Association*, vol. xxiv. p. 287. In the 5 Richard II., 1382, Robert, Clerk of Wandlesworth, was punished for pretending to be a physician; on examination, he "was found to be an infidel, and altogether ignorant of the art of physic or surgery." He hung about folks' necks a piece of parchment inscribed, *Anima Christi Sanctifica me; Corpus Christi, salva me; in isanguis Christi nebria me* (sic.—for, *Sanguis Christi inebria me*); *cum bonus Christus tu, lava me* (Riley, *Memorials of London*, p. 465).

[148] *Archæologia*, vol. xxiv. p. 353; *Ibid.* vol. xviii. p. 115; Whitaker, *History and Antiquities of the Deanery of Craven, co. York.* London, 1805, p. 169.

[149] *Fœdera.* Edit. 1740, t. iv. pt. ii. p. 134. Also *Test. Ebor.* passim.

JEWELS.

These may be divided into three classes: (1) those for personal wear; (2) portable ornaments described as jewels; (3) morses and jewelled mitres, which come under the head of church ornaments.

1. Jewels adorned with the image of our Ladye are often mentioned in wills. In the Inventory of the treasures in the Exchequer, *temp.* Henry the Eighth, sundry items occur, such as "a lytell tablett of golde wᵗ our Ladye grauen in a garnett, and a lytyll ple (pearl), a cheyne and a hooke wayinge ii oz. iii qts. di."[150]

2. Of portable ornaments :

"*Itm*, a tabernacle of golde wᵗ our Lady techyng her Sonne, wᵗ an angel bearing an ouche, &c. xvi oz."[151]

"*Itm*, a tabernacle of golde wᵗ our Lady of Pyty wᵗ her sonne in her lappe, wᵗ ii angells behynde, &c. x oz."[152]

Jewels of this description used to be sent by the Kings of England as New Year's gifts.[153]

SEALS.

Seals form a subject of great historical interest,[154] but my space only allows me to make a brief mention of them. It must be borne in mind that, as far as is known, seals were not used by the Anglo-Saxons,[155] whose charters were given *cum sigillo sanctæ crucis, i.e.,* with a cross, or, as they called it, Christ's Rood Token,[156] prefixed to their names, and not *sub sigillo.* Nevertheless, instances of some six or seven Anglo-

---

[150] *Ancient Kalendars and Inventories of the Exchequer,* vol. ii. p. 265.

[151] *Ibid.* p. 274.

[152] *Ibid.* 275.

[153] Nichols, *Excerpta Historica,* p. 149.

[154] Those who are interested in British sphragiology may consult with advantage Laing's *Scottish Seals,* the *Monasticon,* and the Transactions of the different Archæological Societies, *passim.*

[155] "*Anno ab incarnatione Domini MIV. indictione II. tempore Æthelredi Regis Angliæ, patris S. Edwardi Regis et Confessoris, quidam nobilis Wlfricus, cognomento Spot, construxit abbatiam Burtoniam vocatam, deditque ei omnem hæreditatem paternam appreciatam septingentas libras.* Et quia nondum utebantur sigillis in Angliâ, *fecit donum suum his confirmari subscriptionibus prout in charta continetur*" (Annals of Burton. *Annales Monastici,* vol. i. p. 183. Rolls Edit.).

[156] Cf. the Codex Dipl. aevi Sax. *passim.*

O

Saxon *matrices* are known, but they appear to have been employed exclusively for foreign correspondence.[157]

Our Ladye occurs on abbey, collegiate, and corporation seals ; and also on those of private individuals.

A common form is the image of our Blessed Ladye with her Divine Son, and the owner of the seal in a suppliant attitude before her ; and with a label bearing the invocation : + 𝔐ater · 𝔇ei · memento · mei. And in the case of the owner being entitled to coat-armour, a shield of the armorial bearings is added, as in the instance of John de Shareshulle, precentor of Exeter, whose seal is affixed to a charter dated the 7th of June, 1355.[158] I may add one or two examples of the inscriptions or legends on these seals. The *General History of Norfolk* gives one : + 𝔐ater · sancta · dei · sit · tibi · cura · mei.[159] Another is given in the *Monasticon :* + 𝔙irgo · roga · pro · me · totum · semper · tibi · do · me.[160]

The seal of the Monastery of our Ladye of Graces, near the Tower of London, which was founded by Edward the Third, represents our Blessed Ladye with her Divine Son, and the King praying to her on the dexter side, and divers other persons also praying on the left ; underneath are the royal arms, on account of its royal foundation.[161] The seal of Eton represents the Assumption of our Ladye, attended by six angels, with the royal arms beneath her, as was customary in royal foundations. It may be presumed that the seal of the Black Friars of Oxford commemorates the act by which St. Edmund of Canterbury espoused himself to our Blessed Ladye.[162]

---

[157] See the subject fully discussed in a most interesting article by the late Sir Frederick Madden, K.H., *Journal of the Royal Archæol. Inst.* vol. xiii. pp. 355—371.

[158] *Journal of the Royal Archæol. Inst.* vol. xviii. p. 362.

[159] Pp. 547, 624. Norwich, 1829.

[160] T. ii. p. 346.

[161] *Ibid.* t. v. p. 717.

[162] S. p. 122.

§ 7.—DEATH AND BURIAL.

For though, in feudal strife, a foe
Hath laid our Ladye's Chapel low,
Yet still, beneath the hallowed soil,
The peasant rests him from his toil,
And dying, bids his bones be laid
Where erst his simple fathers prayed.

Marmion.[163]

During the fourteenth and fifteenth centuries few wills were made by which the testators do not bequeath their souls to God and our Ladye. These wills teem with proofs of the love of our forefathers for our Blessed Ladye.

The will of Henry the Seventh affords an interesting example. After recommending his soul into the most merciful hands of his Redeemer, he says:

"My moost mercifull redemer, maker, and salviour, I truste by the special grace and mercy of thi most Blissid Moder evir Virgyne, oure Lady Saincte Mary ; in whom, after the in this mortall lif, hath ever been my moost singulier trust and confidence, to whom in al my necessities I have made my continuel refuge, and by whom I have hiderto in all myne adversities, ever had my special comforte and relief, wol nowe in my moost extreme nede, of her infinite pitie take my soule into her hands, and it present unto her moost dere Son. Whereof swettest Lady of mercy, veray Moder and Virgin, welle of pitie and surest refuge of all nedefull, moost humbly, moost entierly and moost hertely I beseche thee."[164]

One feature is well deserving of notice—the common desire to be buried in the Ladye Chapel, or before some favourite image of our Ladye. It is not unlikely that these frequented spots were selected for interment as being the more sure of securing a greater share of the prayers of the faithful, and of candles and alms for the repose of their souls. Thus an old

[163] Edinb. 1808, pp. 68, 69. This refers to the Chapel of St. Marye of the Lowes (de Lacubus), which gives its name to the lake : "By lone St. Marye's silent lake" (*Ibid.* p. 67). It was laid waste by the clan of Scott in a feud with the Cranstouns (*Ibid.* p. xxxix. note).

[164] London, 1775, p. 2.

poem recounts that Mold Nevill was buried in the Ladye Chapel at Worksop Priory :

Afore our Blessed Ladye, next the stall side
There may she be seene, she is not to hyde.[165]

St. Augustine[166] and St. Maximin of Tours[167] bear witness to the desire of the early Christians to have their sepulchres joined to those of saints and martyrs as expecting greater security to their souls thereby. Thus King Arthur, after receiving his mortal wounds, caused himself to be removed to Glastonbury, so that he might die under the protection of our Blessed Ladye, to whom he was so devoted.[168] There is something truly noble and majestic in the death of the brave old Earl Sigwearth, the friend of Leofric and Godgifu. Feeling his last end at hand, he retired to die in the celebrated Abbey of St. Marye at York, which he had founded. When death seized his extremities, he desired once more to be arrayed in martial panoply with his shield, sword and spear, that, as a loyal soldier to the last, he might thus appear in the presence of his Creator. Truely did he die a *Bonus Miles Christi*.

As William the Norman lay dying in his camp at Rouen, he heard a bell tolling at an early hour. He asked what bell it was ; his attendants replied that it was the bell for Prime in the Cathedral of our Ladye. Then the King, with the greatest devotion, raised his eyes to Heaven, and stretching out his hands, exclaimed : "I commend myself to my Ladye Saint Marye the Mother of God, that she with her prayers will reconcile me to her most dear Son our Lord Jesus Christ," and then expired.[169]

It is recorded that Leofric and Godgifu were buried in the porches of their great Abbey Church at Coventry. This seems to have been an Anglo-Saxon custom.[170] Leland mentions many instances of persons buried before our Ladye ;[171] and the

---

[165] S. p. 254.

[166] Lib. *De cura pro martyr*, cap. xviii.

[167] Hom. *De martyr*.

[168] S. p. 45.

[169] *Ord. Vitalis*, lib. vii. p. 661.

[170] Cf. Bede. Opp. t. ii. pp. 181, 189, and t. iii. p. 179. Edit. Giles. Rock notices that *porticus* is not used for porch, but for the aisle of the church (vol. ii. p. 309).

[171] *Itin.* vol. iii. pp. 78, 79 ; vol. iv. pt. ii. pp. 61, 153.

Series abounds with similar notices. Thomas de Cobham, Bishop of Worcester, who died on August 20, 1327, in his great desire to ensure being buried before our Ladye, bequeathed to the altar before which he should be interred a silver gilt image of the Blissful Mother of God, which he had received as a present from the Abbot of St. Augustine's, Bristol.[172]

Then there were the Chantry chapels. A chantry was an endowment either in land or in money for the support of one or more priests to celebrate Mass daily for the soul of the founder, and on certain days to give a dole to the poor.[173]

Chantries were of two kinds; either for a limited period, or perpetual, according to the terms of the foundation.[174] With the Anglo-Saxons, and down to the great apostasy, "singing" was the word usually employed to signify the celebration of Holy Mass.[175] Hence the endowment for a Mass was called a chantry. Often illustrious personages would build a chapel in which their bodies were to be buried, and in which the Mass for their soul was to be celebrated; and for this reason they were named chantry chapels. The number of chantries which existed in England is unknown, but Fuller says that "if Hercules may be measured from his foot, a probable conjecture may be made of them, from those which we find founded at St. Paul's Cathedral in London," which were returned to be of the number of forty-seven.[176] Many of these chantry chapels yet exist, as at Ely, Wells, Winchester, and elsewhere. One of the gems of Yorkshire is the Waterton Chapel at Methley, built by Sir Robert Waterton, the elder, in 1424.[177] He was a Privy Councillor

[172] S. p. 254.

[173] Cf. *Valor Ecclesiasticus*, t. i. p. 63.

[174] Cf. *Wills of the Northern Counties.* Surtees Society, pp. 20, 47, 50, 52, 105, 111, 112. Also *Test. Ebor.* i. passim; Dugdale, *St. Paul's*, p. 19, 20, 21, 335; also S. pp. 8, note, 138; also *Test. Vetust.* p. 143, for the chantry founded at Leicester in the new Church of our Ladye by John of Gant; also *Ibid.* pp. 215, 257, 581.

[175] *Ancient Laws and Institutes of England.* Edit. Thorpe, vol. ii. p. 404. The Accompt of the Prioress of Bray contains an entry: " Paid for howseling brede, syngyng brede and wyne vd." (*Mon. Angl.* t. iii. p. 359). Hence it appears that altar breads were called singing breads, and the particles used for the communion of the faithful houseling breads.

[176] Taylor, *Index Monasticus Dioc. Norv.* Introd. p. xv.

[177] Before succeeding to his brother, Sir John Waterton of Waterton and Methley, who had been Master of the Horse of Henry V. at Agincourt, he had been Governor of Pontefract Castle. He is the Sir Robert mentioned in *Richard II.* Act ii. Sc. 1.

and a distinguished statesman.[178] He made a provision for the support of three chaplains for ever, for to sing for the health of the souls of himself and of Cecily, his wife, and King Richard the Second, and King Henry the Fourth, one of whose executors he was.[179] Their recumbent figures yet exist, and both he and Lady Waterton wear collars of SS.[180]

Our forefathers eagerly sought the intercession of our Blessed Ladye at their funerals. John Lord Scrope of Masham, by his will dated July 1, 1441, desired to be buried in the Chapel of St. Stephen, in York Minster,[181] adding these directions: " My corpse to be preceded by twenty-four men clothed in white gowns with hoods, each of them carrying in his hands a new pair of wooden beads for the occasion, being all alike, without carrying any lights ; and that the said twenty-four poor men . . . shall recite both during the Dirige[182] and during the Mass, the Psalter of the Blessed Virgin Marye, beseeching God that He would grant to my soul life everlasting."[183]

John White, cloth merchant of Beverley, by his will dated September 10, 1453, leaves to thirteen poor men a white gown and hood and a pair of shoes each, on condition that they kneel round his corpse on the day of his burial, and recite the Psalter of our Ladye, and that for the eight days following they shall stand or sit around his grave, and recite the aforesaid Psalter.[184]

Anne Buckenham of St. Edmund's-bury in 1539, "leaves 1d. to a poore body by the space of an whole yeare that wolde saye yᵉ psalter of oure Ladye everie Saturdaye."[185] And Sir John Milborne, draper, Lord Mayor of London in 1521, founded a God's house for thirteen bedesmen near the Church of the Crutched Friars, who were to attend daily the Mass at eight o'clock to be sung at the altar of our Ladye, in the middle aisle

---

[178] *Pell Records,* pp. 291, 335, 379 ; and *Fœdera,* t. iv. passim. Hagæ Comit, 1740. Also Acts of the Privy Council, *passim.*

[179] *Fœdera,* t. iv. pt. ii. p. 30. Edit. cit.

[180] *Churches of Yorkshire,* vol. i. p. 11. Leeds, 1844. Cf. Whitaker, Loidis and Elmete, where his tomb is figured.

[181] See S. p. 261.

[182] In Catholic England the Vespers and Matins of the Dead were called *Placebo* and *Dirige,* being the words with which the antiphons commence : hence the term Dirge, which included also the Mass of *Requiem.*

[183] *Test. Ebor.* vol. ii. p. 187.

[184] *Ibid.* p. 167.

[185] *Bury Wills,* p. 138.

of the church, and that before the beginning of the said Mass they should stand round the tomb of Sir John, and severally, two and two of them together, shall say the psalm *De Profundis*, and a *Pater*, *Ave*, Creed, and Collect for the prosperous estate of the said Sir John and Dame Johan, their children and friends now living, and for their souls when dead.[186] This evidence proves how highly our forefathers valued the prayers of the blessed poor.

At great funerals it was customary to carry banners bearing the image of our Ladye. Among the banners delivered out of the Tower in the 33rd of Henry the Sixth, "for y⁰ entierments of the iii. Queenes were iiij. banners beten of our Ladye."[187] At that of Elizabeth of York banners of our Ladye, of her Salutation, Assumption, and Nativity were borne near the car by knights and esquires.[188] Sir David Owen, knight, by will dated February 20, 1529 desires "my body to be buried in the Priory of Esseborne, after the degree of a banneret, that is, with helmet and sword, my coat-armour, my banner, my standard, my pendant, and set over a banner of the Holy Trinity, one of our Ladye, and another of St. George."[189] And at the "great and solemne obit kept at Paules in London, on June 7, 1539, for the Empresse, late wyf to Charles the Fifte, there were foure other harrouldes houldinge foure other banners of white sarcenet richly guilded with the images of our Ladye and St. Elizabeth, in their mourninge gownes and coate armours."[190]

The tombstones of our forefathers were proof of the love of those whose remains they covered for the Blissful Queen of Heaven. John Fabian, giving directions for his tombstone to his executors, says that : "On the upper part of that gravestone I will be sett a plate, and thereyn graven a figur of our Ladye with her Child sitting in a sterr, and under that ii. figurys with the children before specified, and either of the said ii figures holding a rolle wheron upon the mannys part I will be graven 𝕾tella 𝕸aría 𝕸arís. And upon the wommannys rolle

[186] Stowe. Edit. Strype, bk. ii. p. 74. Cf. Herbert, *Great Livery Companies of London*, vol. ii. p. 193, note. London, 1836.

[187] *Archæologia*, vol xvi. p. 124.

[188] *Privy Purse Expenses*, Introd.

[189] *Test. Vet.* p. 700.

[190] *Chronicle of England during the reign of the Tudors*, 1485—1559. By Charles Wriothesley, *Windsor Herald*, vol. i. p. 97. Camden Society.

Succurre piissima nobis."[101]   John Denham, citizen of
London, and draper, in his will dated April 5, 1532, says:
" Also I wil that my executors buy and provide for me a
stone of the value of five marks to lie upon my grave with an
image of myself, and over the head of the same image a picture
of the Assumption of our Blessed Ladye."[102]   The brass monumental plate of Geoffrey Fyche, dean of St. Patrick's, Dublin,
represents him on his knees before Our Ladye of Pity.[103]   At
Northleach there is the effigy of William Lawnder, from whose
mouth issues a label bearing this invocation to our Blessed
Ladye :

O Regina poli mediatrix esto Lawnder Willi.[104]

Panel from the Tomb of Lady Montacute in Oxford Cathedral.

A tombstone in the Church of St. Lawrence, Norwich, was
inscribed :

Mater Jhesu Christi post hoc exilium nobis donet gaudium sine fine,[105]

Several of the female figures round the tomb of Richard

<hr />

[101] *New Chronicles of England and France.*   Reprint, vol. i. pref. p. x.   Cf.
Blomefield, *Hist. of Norfolk*, vol. ii. p. 728 for another interesting tombstone.
[102] Stowe.   Edit. Strype, bk. iii. p. 269.
[103] Figured in Mason's *Hist. and Antiq. of the Collegiate and Cathedral Church
of St. Patrick's, Dublin*, p. 146 ; and in the new edition of Archdall's *Monasticon*,
vol. ii. p. 88.
[104] Haines, *Manual of Monumental Brasses*, p. 100.
[105] Blomefield, vol. ii. p. 678.

Beauchamp, Earl of Warwick, hold a pair of beads in their hands, all with tassels at the end.[196]

Weever has preserved from oblivion many old English epitaphs, which usually request a *Pater noster* and an *Ave Marie* for the departed; one or two examples will suffice :

> Of your cherite say a *Pater noster* and an *Ave*
> For the soul of William Pratte, sometym of Pekerle,
> On whos soul Jesu have mercy.[197]
> William Goldhirst and Margaret his wife
> .   .   .   .   .
> Vpon whos sowls Jesu have mercy,
> That for vs say a *Pater noster* and an *Ave.*[198]

Robert Trappes was twice married, he died in 1526, and was buried in St. Leonard's, Foster Lane, London. This was his epitaph :

> When the bells be merely roung,
> And the Masse deuoutly soung,
> And the meate merely eaten,
> Then sall Robart Trappis his wyffs and
>   his chyldren be forgotten.
> Wherfor Jesu that of Marye sproung,
> Set their soulys thy Saynts among,
> Though it be vndeservyd on their syde,
> Yet good Lord let them euermor thy mercy abyde.
>   And of your cheritie
> For their soulys say a *Pater noster* and an *Ave.*

"The pictures of Robert, Agnes and Joan (his wives), inlaid in brasse," says Weever, "seeme thus to speake," *i.e.*, labels, thus inscribed, issued from their mouths :

> *Sancta Trinitas unus Deus miserere nobis.*
> *Et ancillis tuis sperantibus in te.*
> *O Mater Dei memento mei.*
> Jesu mercy, Ladye help.[199]

Here is another one of the year 1514 :

> Marye moder mayden clere
> Pray for me William Goldwyre,
> And for me Isabel his wyf.
> Ladye for thy Ioyes fyf.
> Hav mercy on Christian his second wyf,
> Swete Jesu for thy woundys fyf.[200]

---

[196] *Description of the Beauchamp Chapel at Warwick.* London, 1804, plate vi.
[197] *Ancient Funerall Monuments.* London, 1631, p. 430.
[198] *Ibid.* p. 404.
[199] *Ibid.* p. 392.
[200] *Ibid.* p. 618.

The Lord of St. John, William Weston, the brave old Lord
Prior of the Knight Hospitallers in England, who had been one
of the heroes of Rhodes, died of grief the day his noble Order
was suppressed. "Vpon the seventh day of May, 1540," says
Weever, " being Ascension day, and the same day of the dissolution of the house (the Priory at Clerkenwell), he was dissolued
by death, which strooke him to the heart, at the first time when
he heard of the dissolution of his Order."   On a brass plate over
his tomb were inscribed the lines more pious than artistic :

> *Ecce quem cernis tuo nomini semper devotum*
> *Suscipe in sinum, Virgo Maria, tuum.*
> *Spes me non fallat quam in te semper habebam,*
> *Virgo da facilem . . .*[201]

Very different were the dying thoughts of one whom Englishmen have cause to execrate. Henry the Eighth, of whose early
devotion to our Blessed Ladye many proofs have been given
in this book, begins his will : " In the name of God and of the
Glorious and Blessed Virgin our Lady Seinct Marye, and of all
the Holy Company of Heaven."   He says : " Also we do
instantly requyre and desire the Blessed Virgin Marye His
(God's) Mother with all the Holy Company of Heaven continually to pray for us and with us whiles we lyve in this
Woorld, and in the Time of passing out of the same, that we
may the sooner atteyn everlasting Lief after our departure out
of this transitory Lief, which we do both hope and clayme by
Christes Passion and Woord."[202]

The "Defender of the Faith " sits in his chair of death, for
recline on a couch he cannot,

> *Monstrum horrendum, informe, ingens,*

with the leaves of his life's book unfolded before him.   They do
not tell of rich foundations to the glory of God and the honour
of His Blessed Mother, like those of his royal predecessors.

---

[201] *Ibid.* p. 430. The rest of the line is missing. The Order of the Knights
Hospitallers, not being a monastic order, was not included in the Act of Dissolution
of 1539, it was dissolved by a special Act of May 7, 1540, Stat. 32, Hen. VIII.
c. xxiv. The Lord Prior, as Lord of St. John, sat in the House of Lords as premier
lay-baron, after the viscounts, and before the barons.

[202] Given in *The Life and Death of the Renowned John Fisher, Bishop of Rochester.*
By Thomas Bailey, D.D. London, 1740, pp. 256—260 ; also in *Dodd's Church
History of England.* Edit. Tierney. London, 1839, vol. i. Append. p. 454.

They do not tell of lavish expenditure on the houses of God or zeal for their beauty, after the example of Ine of the West Saxons. He trembles as he reads the black and damning register of plundered shrines. No priest of God is at his side to whisper words of repentance, and of supplication to our Ladye, or to administer the last rites of Holy Church and the sin-forgiving Sacrament of Extreme Unction. He was excommunicate; he had put away his sainted Queen, and had first married and then put to death his own natural daughter, Ann Boleyn;[203] he had stolen the property of the house of God,[204] and had desecrated the sanctuaries of the Blessed Mother of God, and caused her venerated images of Walsingham and other places to be burnt; heedless of the maledictions invoked by the pious donors on the sacrilegious robber—be he who he might[205]—he had seized the rich endowments of the religious houses which constituted the patrimony of the blessed poor of Christ; he had caused numberless poor to be executed for following his royal example, by thieving[206]—but then he had driven them to it by robbing them himself of their patrimony; finally, on him lay the innocent blood of Cardinal Fisher, of his trusty and loyal

---

[203] Sanderus, *De Origine ac progressu schismatis Anglicani.* Col. Agripp, 1585, Lewis's translation. London, 1877, Introd.; also Bailey, *Life of Bishop Fisher,* ch. vii.

[204] In the Bodleian Library, Oxford, there is a roll of parchment fifty-four feet long containing a list of the royal thievings of Henry VIII. entitled, "The Declaration off Thaccompte of Sir John Williams, Knight, late Master and Treasurer of the Jewelles and Plate which were the late Kinge's Henrye the Eighth, and found in sundri monasteries, priories, cathedrals, churches, and colleges at his Majestie's visitation."

[205] Cf. *e.g.*, the charter of Æthelberht, the first Anglo-Saxon Christian King, to Rochester Cathedral A.D. 604: *Si quis . . præsumpserit minuere, aut contradicere, in conspectu Dei sit damnatus et sanctorum ejus, hic et in æterna sæcula, nisi emendaverit ante ejus transitum quod inique gessit contra Christianitatem nostram (Cod. Dipl. ævi Sax.* tom. i. p. 1). The undated charter of Earl Leofric to Evesham says : *Si qui sunt qui huic meæ donationi nocere volunt, vel adversari moliuntur, in profundum inferni descendant viventes et perpetuis pænis mancipati judicium ultionis percipiant cum impiis, nisi ante mortem ad satisfactionem venerint, et reatum suum agnoscentes, pænitentiam egerint (Ibid.* vol. iv. p. 272, ch. dccccxxxiii.). His son, Ælfgar, is more terse : *Si quis de æcclesia retraxerit, de regno Christi retrahatur (Ibid.* p. 297, ch. dccccxliii.); and in another: *Si aliquis ei abstulerit, cum diabolo Beelzebub, nisi pænituerit, permaneat (Ibid.* p. 298, ch. dccccxliv.). For the fate of those who have held abbey lands, cf. Spelman, *History of Sacrilege.* All the children of Henry VIII. died without issue.

[206] Holinshed says that during the reign of Henry VIII. no fewer than twenty-two thousand persons were executed for theft.

Lord High Chancellor, Sir Thomas More, of the Carthusians, of Sir David Gonson[207] and Sir Adrian Fortescue, Knights of St. John, and many other martyrs—these were "the works that were to follow him." In his last sickness he was always muttering about "monks and friars."[208] When he was told that he was at the point of death, he called for a goblet of white wine, and turning to one of his horrified attendants exclaimed, "All is lost!"[209] As Ward expresses it:

> Black Sacriledge, Blood spilt, Blood stain'd,
> And Schism brought into his Nation,
> Stern Conscience, and black Desperation,
> Affrighted his expiring Ghost,
> And his last words were ALL IS LOST !
> A fearful exit ![210]

His corpse was carrried from London to Windsor for burial; and it rested the first night at the Monastery of Sion, which he had suppressed. The leaden coffin burst, and the next morning when the attendants went with the plumbers to repair it, a dog was found lapping and licking up the King's blood, as it befell King Achab.[211]

So died by the just judgment of God the despoiler of

ENGLAND THE DOWER OF MARYE.

---

[207] His name often occurs in the *Procès Verbaux* of the English Language of the Order, and generally with the addition of "ye goode knyghte."

[208] Sander. Edit. Lewis, p. 164, note 2.

[209] *Ibid.* text.

[210] *England's Reformation*, canto i. p. 62. London, 1719. Not less horrible was the death of the Emperor Constantine Copronymus, who had despoiled the great sanctuaries of our Ladye in Constantinople. For the dreadful account see Cedrenus, *Compendium historiarum.*

[211] Sander, ubi sup. p. 112, note 5.

PART THE THIRD.

The Iconography of our Blessed Ladye in England.

Et dicis nos lapides et parietes ac tabellas adorare. Non est ita, ut dicis, Imperator, sed ut memoria nostra excitetur, et ut stolida et imperita crassaque mens nostra erigatur et in altum provehatur per eos quorum hæc nomina et quorum appellationes, et quorum sunt imagines; et non tanquam Deos, ut tu inquis; absit, non enim spem in illis habemus. Ac si quidem imago sit Domini, dicimus Domine Jesu Christe Fili Dei succurre et salva nos : sin autem Sanctæ Matris ejus, dicimus Sancta Dei Genitrix Domini Mater, intercede apud filium tuum verum Deum nostrum, ut salvas faciat animas nostras.

St. Gregory to the Emperor Leo the Isaurian, A.D. 787.[1]

§ I.—PRELIMINARY REMARKS.

Sit vobis tanquam in imagine descripta virginitas vitaque Beatæ Mariæ, de quâ, velut speculo, refulget species castitatis et forma virtutis. Hinc sumatis licet exempla vivendi.

St. Ambrose.[2]

THERE was an image of our Ladye at Glastonbury which was traditionally said to have been wrought by St. Joseph of Arimathea.[3] King Arthur also is related to have brought an image of our Ladye from Jerusalem, as I have mentioned in the Series under Stowe, formerly called Wedale.[4]

When St. Augustine and his companions came into the presence of Æthelberht, King of Kent, in the year 597, they bore a silver cross, and the image of our Lord and Saviour painted on a board,—*imaginem . . . in tabulâ depictam,*[5]—but

---

[1] Second Council of Nicæa. Labbe, t. vii. col. 14. Epist. i.
[2] Lib. ii. *De Virgin.*
[3] S. p. 280.
[4] S. p. 304.
[5] Opp. vol. ii. p. 103. Edit. Giles.

Venerable Bede says nothing about any image or picture of our Ladye, although modern artists introduce one when portraying the arrival of St. Augustine, and omit the historical image of our Lord as described by Ven. Bede.[6]

In 672, or seventy-five years after the arrival of St. Augustine in England, Abbot Bennet Biscop went to Rome, whence, as Ven. Bede records, he brought back with him pictures or sacred representations—*imagines*—to adorn the Church of St. Peter which he had built—namely, an image of the Blessed Mother of God and Ever Virgin Marye, and of the Twelve Apostles, with which he intended to adorn the central roof of the nave, on boarding placed from one wall to the other, also some representations from ecclesiastical history for the south wall, and others from the Revelations of St. John for the north wall "—here Ven. Bede explains the reasons why Abbot Biscop brought these images—" so that every one who entered the church, even if they could not read, wherever they turned their eyes, might have before them the amiable countenance of Christ and His saints, although but in a picture, and with more watchful mind might reflect either upon the benefits—*gratiam*—of the Incarnation of our Lord, or having as if before their eyes the peril of the Last Judgment, might remember to make a more strict examination of conscience—*districtius se examinare meminissent.*"[7] So that the earliest introduction of images into England was for the purpose of instructing the ignorant.

Although Ven. Bede has left no record of the type of this picture of our Ladye, it is evident from his words that it must have been of the Greek School ; that is, of the St. Luke design, as it is called. It was "a picture of the Blessed Mother of God and Ever Virgin Marye"—consequently it represented her as Mother of God with her Divine Son in her arms—" to recall to the beholders the benefits of the Incarnation," since it was through her that God the Son became Incarnate, and took flesh of her.

Now at the time when Abbot Biscop was in Rome, the Greek, or St. Luke, type of our Blessed Ladye was all prevalent, and it was evidently one of these pictures which St. Bennet

---

[6] *Pictorial Bible and Church History.* By the Rev. H. Formby, vol. iii, p. 275.

[7] *Vita BB. Abbatum.* Opp. vol. iv. p. 368. Edit. Giles.

Biscop brought with him to England.[8] Happily an example of an Anglo-Saxon representation of our Blessed Ladye with her Divine Son in her arms has been preserved, and it is of the St. Luke type. It is a rude figure, in incised lines, on the lid of the coffin of St. Cuthberht, presumed to be the work of Eadfriŏ, Bishop of Lindisfarne, in the year 698. Here, accordingly, is an image of the St. Luke type executed in the North, and by a North-countryman, twenty-six years after the introduction of the prototype into England by St. Bennet Biscop in 672. The unskilfulness of the hand which traced a figure so grotesque does not diminish its value ˙in point of evidence.

The celebrated Book of Kells in Ireland, which is assigned to the year 700 or thereabouts, contains a most valuable illumination of our Blessed Ladye with her Divine Son ; and the limner could not but have taken his outlines from an original of the St. Luke type, although the treatment presents all the rude characteristics of early Irish art, and the right hand of our Lord is not raised in the usual attitude of blessing. The traditional colours of the garments have yielded to the Celtic ideas of the beautiful.

She wears a purple garment, *semēed* with leaves of Shamrock, reaching to her feet, which are bare ; the sleeves are blue ; above is another robe ; and her head is surrounded by an elaborate nimbus. Our Lord has no nimbus. He is seated on His Mother's knee, His right hand resting on hers, and His left placed on her breast, and He is looking towards her. He is clothed in a green upper tunic with a red border reaching to His knee, and under it a yellow garment is displayed which falls to his feet, which, like those of His Mother, are bare.[9]

Thus the earliest evidence extant bears out what has been said, that the St. Luke type of our Ladye was the prevailing one in England ; and consequently proves that England closely followed Rome in Christian art.

---

[8] By the St. Luke type I mean the form exemplified in the celebrated picture in the Basilica of St. Marye Major in Rome, which is attributed to St. Luke. Cf. *Act. SS.* t. viii. oct. p. 295. Also Plazza, *Christianorum in Sanctos*, &c., *devotio vindicata*, part ii. c. 5, p. 572. Panormi, 1751.

[9] Figured in plate 57 of the Facsimiles of the Paleographic Society ; also in chromo-lithograph, by Westwood, *Palæographia Sacra Pictoria.* London, 1845.

In an illumination of the ninth century in the Psalter of Æthelstan, which gives the Ascension of our Lord, our Blessed Ladye is represented standing with her arms extended, but not raised ; she wears a blue robe, with red sleeves, and a green mantle-veil. The nimbus is red, and the name MA-RIA is added.[10] This seems to have been suggested by the *orante* type.

In the foundation charter of Newminster, of Eadgar, now in the British Museum, of the year 966, our Ladye is represented in the act of crowning the King ;[11] a type which appears three years later on a gold coin of the Emperor John I. Zimisces.[12]

The illuminations of the Benedictionale of St. Æthelwald represent our Ladye with the large mantle-veil, and are Byzantine in character.[13]

The great image of our Ladye of silver and gold put in the church of Ely by Abbot Elsi, prior to A.D. 1016, was seated, as well as all the images at Evesham, and the great silver one at Lincoln.

After the arrival of the Normans sphragistic evidence begins; the earlier seals represent our Ladye seated, with the large mantle-veil, and our Lord on her lap before her, frequently in the act of blessing. Later, our Ladye appears seated, with a mantle-robe, but no longer placed over the head, like the Greek type. Her hair flows over her shoulders, sometimes she wears a kerchief, and usually a crown ; indeed, images of our Ladye not crowned, after the twelfth century, are the exception.[14] In the fourteenth century standing images of our Ladye began to prevail. Instances occur, though rarely, of our Ladye being represented alone, and without her Divine Son. Thus she is figured in the large seal of Thomas de Melsanby, appointed

---

[10] MS. Cott. *Galba*, A. xviii. It is figured in Westwood, ubi sup. In the *orante* type our Blessed Ladye is represented standing with her arms extended.

[11] *Ibid. Vespas.* A. vii. ; also Paleographic Society, plate 47.

[12] Sabatier, *Description générale des Monnaies Byzantines.* Paris, 1862, vol. ii. p. 141, and plate xlvii. n. 17. See ante, p. 40.

[13] *Archæologia*, vol. xxiv.

[14] The following seals, chosen at random, all vary in the treatment of the subject, which is the same, our Blessed Ladye seated, with her Divine Son in different attitudes : Kelso, Prioress and Convent of Clerkenwell, Worcester, Coventry, Glastonbury, Cheshunt Nunnery, Suffield, Humberstayn, St. Neots, Spalding, Binham, Pershore, Bardney, Shaftesbury, Walsingham, Arbroath, and Haddington (*Mon. Angl.* sub nomm. ; Laing, *Catalogue of Scottish Seals.* Edinburgh, 1850).

Prior of Coldingham A.D. 1233. She is seated, crowned, her right hand lies on her breast, and in her left she holds a globe surmounted by a cross. In order that there may be no mistake as to her identity, a scroll or label, on the right side of her head, bears her name MARIA.[15] The addition of the name proves that this representation of our Ladye alone was unusual.

Although I have not ventured as yet to form a decided opinion, I think there are very good grounds for believing, as the different seals all vary, that they represented the principal image of our Ladye in their various localities.

When it is borne in mind that the earliest painting of our Ladye extant represents her as seated, with her Divine Son on her knee,[16] and that this seated type prevailed generally, but not exclusively, until the fourteenth century, and taking into consideration that the seated attitude implies dignity, authority, and power,[17] it would seem as if the representation of our Ladye in this posture implies a direct acknowledgment of the transcendent dignity of the Mother of God, whom our Anglo-Saxon forefathers called the Queen of the whole world. The Great Seals of England from that of St. Eadward to our most Gracious Queen (whom God preserve), represent the sovereigns seated ; whereas I cannot remember an instance of a non-official personage in that attitude on his seal.

Such are the general outlines of the early Iconography of our Blessed Ladye in England.

Before coming to the several types under which our Ladye was represented in England, I must say a few words on the names and types of her different images in general.

Many have arbitrary titles given them by the devotion of the faithful. Thus *Notre Dame des Vertus* is the old name of Our Ladye of Miracles, as used in the fourteenth century.[18] A celebrated but ungraceful modern image at Paris is called Our Ladye of Victories ; so is the votive picture of our Ladye at Siena, offered by the Sienese after the battle of Arbia, under

[15] *Priory of Coldingham.* Surtees Society, vol. xi. 1851, f. xviii. n. 1.
[16] See Northcote, *Roma Sotterranea.* Lond. 1869, pp. 258, 259.
[17] *E.g.*, as in the Consular diptychs. Cf. Gori, *Thesaurus veterum Diptychorum Consularium et ecclesiasticorum.* Florentiæ, 1759.
[18] Hamon, *Notre Dame de France*, p. 101.

p

the title of Our Ladye of Victory. Nevertheless the title of
Our Ladye of Victory alone, does not represent any fixed type
or form; and the same may be said of many more titles of
that sort.

The mediæval type of our Ladye "the Cause of our Joy"
represents her as holding a bunch of grapes in her hand.[19]

Elizabeth, Queen of Edward the Fourth, in her will, dated
April 10, 1492, calls the Blessed Virgin Mother of God, "oure
blessed Ladye Quene of comforte."[20]

Many images again have the name of their sanctuaries, as
Our Ladye of Loreto, Our Ladye of Walsingham, and these of
course, if copied, are known under the same appellations. Such,
doubtless, were Our Ladye *de Populo,*[21] Our Ladye of Millain,[22]
and our Ladye of Ardenberg.[23] Our Ladye of Boulogne is
always represented in a boat. Others are named from some
object in the picture, as the *Vierge au panier,* by Correggio, in
the National Gallery; the *Virgen de la Servilleta,* or "of the
Napkin," in allusion to the dinner-napkin on which it was
painted.

Images of our Ladye which have a fixed type, are those of
Pity, of Good Counsel, of Perpetual Help, and a few more.
And although they have a fixed type and name, they have
frequently another local title conferred by the piety of the
neighbourhood. This, I believe, explains the common old
English title of Our Ladye of Grace.

In the Series, several names occur which speak for themselves, and are local: such as Our Ladye in the Rock, at Dover;
in the Tower, at Coventry; of the Oak, at Islington; in the
Park, at Liskeard; at the Oak, in Norwich; at the Pillar, in
St. Paul's, London; at the Red Ark, at York, and at Beverley.[24]

With these general *data,* I now proceed to examine some
of the details of the English Iconography of our Blessed Ladye.

[19] *Nouveaux Mélanges d'Archéologie,* &c. Par le P. Ch. Cahier de la Cie de Jesus.
Paris, 1877, p. 209.

[20] Nichols, *Royal Wills.* London, 1780, p. 350.

[21] S. p. 38.

[22] S. p. 115. May not Our Ladye of Millain have been a copy of Our Ladye *della
Scala* at Milan? Lucy, Countess of Kent, and widow of Edmund Holland, Earl of
Kent, K.G., by her will dated 2 Hen. VI., left to the Provost and Canons of Our
Ladye *de la Scale* at Milan 1000 crowns (*Test. Vet.* p. 205).

[23] S. p. 257.

[24] S. under the names.

§ 2.—THE IMMACULATE CONCEPTION.

A "table of the Conception" stood on the high altar of the Church of St. Margaret, Westminster.[25]

The Conception of our Ladye has been treated in two ways : historical and symbolical.

I. The historical supposes the representation of events and circumstances under which the mystery was operated, and these visible circumstances denote the hidden mystery. Of these historical representations there are four types :

1. The first is designed from the account of the Conception of our Ladye which is supplied by the apocryphal gospel of her nativity, and the proto-gospel of Jacob.[26] It represents St. Anne, in her garden at prayer, receiving by the mouth of an angel the promise of the birth of the Blessed Virgin Marye, her daughter, and St. Joachim receiving the same promise in the mountains whither he had retired. The "Guide of Painting" of Mount Athos follows this ancient narration almost word for word ;[27] and it appears also in the poem of Hrotsuitha, the learned nun of Gandersheim, who died A.D. 999.[28] The German translator of the Guide remarks that, in Northern art, St. Anne is represented in her house, and not in her garden, in consequence of the difference between the customs of the North and those of the East, where people live more in the open air than in their houses.[29]

This representation is the most ancient.

2. The Greek and Sclavonic diptychs give another representation, which is less happy. St. Joachim and St. Anne meet, after having received the blessings and promise of the angel, and tenderly embrace each other. This, according to the Bollandist,

---

[25] S. p. 228.

[26] *Evangelia apocrypha.* Edit. C. Tischendorf. Lipsiæ, 1853, pp. 1, 106. Quoted in the *Iconographie de l'Immaculée Conception de la Très-Sainte Vierge Marie.* Par Mgr. J. B. Malou, évêque de Bruges. Bruxelles, 1856, p. 16.

[27] Didron, *Manuel d'Iconographie Chrétienne,* p. 279. Cf. St. John Damascene. *Clamaverunt justi, Ubinam? In proprio horto . . . consentaneus justorum precationis locus. In horto preces fundentes, hortum priore longe feliciorem genuerunt* (Orat. ii. *De Nativ. B.M.V.* Opp. t. ii. n. 5, p. 852).

[28] Schafer, *Das Handbuch der Malerei vom Berge Athos.* Trier. 1855, p. 276. Quoted by Malou, ubi sup.

[29] *Historia Nativitatis laudabilisque conversationis Intactæ Dei Genitricis.* Edit. Migne, *Patrol. Lat.* t. cxxxviii. coll. 1067, 1068.

Father Papebrooch, was the Greek type of a chaste marriage.[30] Malou justly remarks that this was of all the most difficult feature, and the least necessary to portray. Consequently, from an iconographic point of view, this type is not deserving of praise. Although these diptychs are not earlier than the seventeenth century,[31] this representation appears to be the reproduction of a type earlier than the conversion of the Slavonic nation, and consequently anterior to the ninth century. Malou says that it might go back even to the early ages of the Church.

The meeting of St. Joachim and St. Anne is given in one of the windows of Fairford Church.[32]

3. The third type Malou describes as simply hideous. It represents our Ladye under the form of a little child, nude, and placed in the calix of a flower, to denote the instant of her creation. He attributes this composition of design to Father Peter de Alva et Astorga, who gives this representation at the head of his *Monumenta Antiqua* printed in 1664,[33] and of his *Radii Solis*, in 1666.[34] But Bourassée says that this type has often been reproduced, and is of a much earlier date.[35] Under this heading may be classed the stained glass window in Waddington Church.[36]

4. The fourth historical representation of the Immaculate Conception, that of the miraculous medal, is modern.[37]

II. Symbolical.

From a doctrinal point of view, the Immaculate Conception is the mystery of the original holiness of the Blessed Virgin Marye Mother of God. In a word, what has to be represented is the *immaculateness* of our Ladye's conception.

Now I wish emphatically to point out that the mere representation of our Ladye, standing, and alone, without any symbol

---

[30] *Acta SS.* t. i. Maii, plate lviii.

[31] *Notice sur l'Iconographie sacrée en Russie.* Saint Pétersbourg, 1849, p. 45. Quoted by Malou, ubi sup.

[32] Joyce, *Fairford Windows*, p. 67. Arundel Society.

[33] *Monumenta Antiqua Imm. Conceptionis SS. Virg. Mariæ, ex novem auctoribus collecta.* Lovanii, 1664.

[34] *Radii solis zeli seraphici cœli veritatis pro Immaculatæ Conceptionis mysterio Virginis Mariæ, discurrentes per duodecim classes auctorum.* Lovanii, 1666.

[35] *Summa Aurea de Laudibus B.M.V.* t. ii. col. 950, note. Edit. Migne.

[36] S. p. 282.

[37] Malou, ubi sup. pp. 20, 21.

or attribute of the mystery, does not, and cannot express her Immaculate Conception. Thus Murillo's so-called Immaculate Conception is nothing else than a fanciful representation of our Ladye, but not one of our Ladye immaculately conceived. Add the serpent under her feet, and the mystery of the Immaculate Conception becomes at once symbolized. Indeed I do not hesitate to express my conviction that, wherever the dragon is represented at the feet of our Ladye, no matter under what " type " she is figured, it has a direct allusion to her Immaculate Conception. The Annunciation is given in the old gate at Lincoln called the Stonebow. Our Ladye and the Archangel occupy tabernacles on either side of the gate. Our Ladye is standing, her hands are folded across her breast, and under her feet is the dragon. I have carefully examined this statue.

This is abundantly manifest. Our mother Eve sinned by eating of the apple, and so brought death on her posterity. The Fathers constantly call our Ladye the second Eve, who was to undo the work of the first Eve, and bring life to man. The second Eve was to be in the state of the first Eve before the Fall, that is, without sin. It is in this sense that Cornelius à Lapide explains those words of the Canticles, *Nigra sum sed formosa.*[88] Our Ladye was dark, as a daughter of Eve, yet *formosa*, or beautiful, because she was free from original sin; *singulari Omnipotentis Dei gratiâ, et privilegio, intuitu meritorum Christi Jesu Salvatoris humani generis*, as it is defined in the Bull *Ineffabilis.*

Now this is most beautifully expressed in the celebrated window of the time of Edward the First in the Church of St. Margaret, Oxford, but curiously enough the iconographic importance of this representation seems, hitherto, to have escaped notice. It is of the utmost value. The Maiden Mother of God, the second Eve, is seated, looking with an ineffably sweet expression towards her Divine Son, Who, with His right hand raised, blesses His Mother, and with His left places an apple—no longer the *pomum noxiale*[89]—into her right hand, as if saying : " Hail! My sweetest Mother, full of grace,

[88] *Commentaria in Scripturam Sacram.* Edit. Crampon. Paris, 1860, t. vii. pp. 495, 496.

[89] *Quando* pomi noxialis, *In necem morsu ruit*, &c. From the Hymn *Pange lingua gloriosi lauream certaminis*, in the Missal, for Good Friday.

thou art the second Eve, I am the Blessed Fruit of thy womb—
fructus ventris generosi,[40]—I give thee the apple, of which *thou*

From the window of St. Margaret's Church, Oxford, temp. Edward I.

mayest eat, since by My merits and blessing I have preserved
thee from original sin. In thee I have made to live again that

[40] From the Hymn *Pange lingua gloriosi corporis mysterium*, in the Missal, for
Maundy Thursday.

which Eve killed. I, the Son of God and thy Son am the cause of thy Immaculate Conception."

What is this but a literal, early English, pre-realization of the words of the Definition in the Bull *Ineffabilis*? In this composition the serpent was unnecessary. I do not, however, wish to be understood as maintaining that the apple *alone*, which our Ladye sometimes holds in her hand, as in the tale of St. Mary's Abbey, York, ought to be thus interpreted; but that it bears this construction, when our Lord is represented in the act of blessing His Maiden Mother and giving her an apple.

Another symbolical representation of the Immaculate Conception occurs in two, at least, of the Prymers of Sarum Use,[41] and although it was adopted in England, there is, unfortunately, no evidence that it was designed by an English artist. Malou attributes it to Henry Stephanus, or Stephens, the celebrated Parisian printer, who gives it as a frontispiece to the work of Josse Clichtoue, *De Puritate Conceptionis beate Marie Virginis*,[42] published in Paris in 1513; but it occurs in the *Hore dive virginis marie secundum verum usum romanum*, printed at Paris in 1508 by Thielmann Kerver, now in the Museum at Maidstone,[43] and consequently five years previously to the celebrated picture of the Immaculate Conception by Gerolamo da Cottignola,[44] dated 1513, to which Malou attaches such importance.[45] In this composition our Ladye is standing, arrayed in an ample robe, her hair flowing over her shoulders, with no veil, and her hands joined, but not clasped before her. Above her is God the Father, of Whom only the bust appears, crowned, holding a globe surmounted by a cross in His left, and blessing her with His right hand. Beneath Him is a scroll containing the words, TOTA PULCHRA ES, AMICA MEA, ET MACULA NON EST IN TE. Our Ladye is surrounded by numerous symbols, each named :—the sun, *electa ut sol;* the

---

[41] Those of 1531, Paris, Regnault, f. cxxvi. b, and of 1534, Stonyhurst Library.

[42] A copy of this rare book is in the Library of the Fathers of the London Oratory.

[43] *Archæologia Cantiana*, vol. ix. p. 196.

[44] Now in the collection of Mr. Bromley Davenport, M.P., Wootton Hall, Staffordshire. It is fully described by Mrs. Jameson, *Legends of the Madonna*. Edit. 1872, p. 53. Cf. also *Del Rio*.

[45] Ubi sup. pp. 131, 132.

moon, *pulchra ut luna;* a gateway with turrets, *Porta cœli;* a cedar, *cedrus exaltata;* a rose-tree, *plantatio rosæ;* a well, *Puteus aquarum viventium;* a branch bearing flower, *Virga Jesse floruit;* a square garden with a hedge, *hortus conclusus;* the lily, *sicut lilium inter spinas;* a star, *stella maris;* the Tower of David, *turris Davidica cum propugnaculis;* a mirror, *speculum sine macula;* an olive tree, *oliva speciosa;* a fountain, *fons hortorum;* a city with gates, towers, and buildings, *civitas Dei.* Passaglia, who has fully explained many of these symbols, develops them as evidences of the Immaculate Conception;[46] and this, says Malou, is sufficient to persuade us that artists of the fifteenth and sixteenth centuries may have had recourse to them.[47]

Now from this evidence it appears most probable that representations of our Blessed Ladye with God the Father blessing her, or with her Divine Son blessing her and presenting her with an apple, or with the serpent under her feet, all have direct reference to her Immaculate Conception. The Mortuary Roll of John de Wygenhale, Abbot of West Dereham, Norfolk, represents at the head, God the Father on a throne, with His right hand raised in the attitude of blessing; in another compartment immediately below Him is our Ladye, arrayed in a mantle, her hair flowing, and her hands joined before her; and lower again is depicted the burial of the Abbot.[48] But, although the Abbot is represented as a diminutive figure on his knees at the right of the Throne of God the Father, it is evident that the blessing is given not to him, but to our Ladye, and consequently, that her Immaculate Conception is here signified.

Thus there is evidence that the Immaculate Conception of our Blessed Ladye was represented at an early period in England; and such are the types in which it was figured prior to the year 1540.

About the year 470, St. Pulchronius, Bishop of Verdun, on his return from Rome, built a new church in honour of our Ladye, and caused to be sculptured an image representing her with

---

[46] Cf. *De Immaculato Deipara semper Virginis Conceptu, Commentarius.* Auct. Carolus Passaglia, S.J. Sac. Romæ, 1854.

[47] Ubi sup. p. 136.

[48] Norwich vol. of the Royal Arch. Institute, p. 99.

the serpent under her feet.[49] The Earl of Warwick, when he was Governor of Calais, presented to our Ladye of Boulogne an image of her with the devil under her feet, of silver gilt.[50]

At the portal of the Chapter House at York is an image of our Blessed Ladye with her Divine Son in her arms. She is standing on a lion and a dragon.

The serpent is also represented under the feet of our Blessed Ladye in the Angels' Choir at Lincoln; which Professor Cockerell so much admired.

Richard Fitz Alan, fourth Earl of Arundel, by his will, dated March 4, 1392, leaves to his daughter Alice, the wife of John Charleton, Lord Powis, a diptych of gold enamelled *ove un ymage de la incarnacioun de notre dame dedeins*, *i.e.*, of the Nativity of our Ladye.[51]

§ 3.—THE ANNUNCIATION.

Ingressus Angelus ad eam dixit : Ave gratia plena, Dominus tecum;
Benedicta tu in mulieribus.

St. Luke.

In the *Benedictionale* of St. Æthelwald, our Ladye is seated and wears the large mantle-veil; the Archangel is barefoot.[52] In another Anglo-Saxon MS. she is standing up, holding in her left hand a scroll with the words, ECCE ANCILLA DNI FIET M SCDM VBU TUUM.[53] In the MS. *Horæ* of the York Use in the public library at Boulogne-sur-mer,[54] the Annunciation represents the Archangel kneeling on one knee, our Ladye rises from prayer as if disturbed by his words —*in sermone ejus*—she has flowing hair, and no veil, before her is a vase with a lily bearing three flowers. This appears

[49] *Act. SS.* ad diem 17 Febr. pp. 12, 13.
[50] Haigneré, *Notre Dame de Boulogne*, p. 118.
[51] Nichols, *Royal Wills*, p. 133.
[52] *Archæologia*, vol. xxiv. plate x. p. 50.
[53] Cott. MS. *Caligula*, A. vii. Figured by Strutt, *Manners and Customs of the English*. London, 1774, vol. i. plate xxvi. fig. 2.
[54] Marked MS. 44.

to have been the usual English form.[65]   On English seals, which represent the Annunciation, our Ladye is generally standing.

The seated attitude of our Ladye is held to be the most correct, for the Jews did not kneel habitually at prayer. Moreover, she was in her room—*ingressus Angelus ad eam*—therefore the scene should be laid in the Holy House, and not large halls with pillars, or the open air.

Anything less inspired than the Annunciation designed by Flaxman was never beheld by mortal eyes. Nevertheless Mrs. Jameson has considered it worthy of admiration.[66]

Several altars of the Annunciation are mentioned in the Series.

In the English representations of the Annunciation a vase of lilies is generally represented in the foreground. Modern artists figure it as well, but they often destroy the symbolism from knowing no better. The correct representation is one stalk with three flowers, symbolising the spotless maidenhood of our Ladye, before childbirth, in childbirth, and after childbirth.[67]

§ 4.—OUR LADYE IN GESINE, BEDGANG, OR CHILDBIRTH.

Quod ex te nascetur Sanctum, vocabitur Filius Dei.

St. Luke.

This title is intended in reality for the Nativity of our Lord. In the *Benedictionale* of St. Æthelwald our Ladye is represented as veiled and lying in bed, a female attendant veiled is placing an ornamented pillow under her head, St. Joseph is sitting on a chair at her feet, lower down, at the right of our Ladye, her

---

[65] Cf. Will of Cardinal Beaufort, Bishop of Winton, A.D. 1446 (Nichols, *Royal Wills.* P. 324).

[66] *Legends of the Madonna.* Edit. 1872, p. 183. By mistake it is numbered 97 instead of 98. See list of illustrations, p. xi. For some excellent remarks on the artistic treatment of the Annunciation, cf. Wiseman, *Essays,* &c. vol. i. p. 517.

[67] For full account Cf. *Act. SS.* t. iii. April ad diem 23, p. 239.

Divine Son, arrayed in swaddling clothes, lies in a manger, between which and our Ladye's couch are the ox and the ass.[58] The wood-cut only gives our Ladye.

In another page of the same MS. our Lady is represented on a couch, with her Divine Son on her lap. He has a cruciform nimbus, whilst His Virgin Mother has none.[59]

In 1325-6, Roger de Waltham erected in the Cathedral of St. Paul's, London, "a glorious tabernacle which contained the image of the Blessed Virgin, sitting as it were in childbed, as

---

[58] *Archæologia*, vol. xxiv. plate xii. p. 56.
[59] *Ibid.* plate xv. p. 59. Cf. also Strutt, *Manners and Customs of the English.* London, 1774, plate xxvii. fig. 3.

also of our Saviour in swaddling clothes lying betwixt the ox and the ass, and St. Joseph at her feet."[60]

Thus this representation of our Ladye was known to the Anglo-Saxons; and it often appears in carved ivories and illuminated MSS. It was described as that of our Ladye in *gesine,*[61] both in England and elsewhere; nevertheless, this mode of representing our Ladye is manifestly incorrect. The pains of labour were the consequence of the sin of Eve; the Mother of God, the second Eve, being exempt from original sin, suffered them not, and St. Jerome says that "no midwife nor woman with tender care was present."[62] Indeed this is evident from the words of the Evangelist: *Pannis involvit infantem, et collocavit eum in præsepio.*[63] Hence pictures and sculpture which represent our Lord as nude, and lying on the ground,—in fact, in any other way than wrapped in swaddling clothes and in a crib or manger, are directly at variance with the account given in the Gospel. The ox and sheep are found in a representation of the Nativity on a tomb bearing the date A.D. 343.[64]

§ 5.—THE ASSUMPTION.

In the English representations of the Assumption, our Ladye is usually represented as standing, with her hands joined

[60] S. p. 71.

[61] *Gesina,* in French *gesine,* from the old verb *gesir,* to be in childbirth (Roquefort, *Glossaire de la langue Romaine*). *Calix quæ est de Capella* Gesinæ *Dominæ nostræ;* also *Ibid. Pro imaginibus Dei et Beatæ Virginis matris suæ* à la gesine (*Inventory of the Church of Noviomagum,* A.D. 1419, quoted by Ducange, sub voc. *gesina.* Noviomagum may mean Nimegue, Lisieux, Noyon, Nuits, or Spires, I know not which). Among the jewels of the Royal Chapel at Windsor was *unum tabernaculum pulchrum cum imagine S. Georgii . . . et* gesina *Beatæ Mariæ, cum imagine Joseph,* &c. (*Mon. Angl.* t. vii. p. 1364). In June or July, 1419, Henry V. made at Maunt certain ordinances for the government of his army. One was, For women that lye in Gesem. "Also that no manner of man be so hardy to goe into no chamber or lodging wher that any woman lieth in gesem" (Nichols, *Excerpta Historica,* p. 29). Cf. also Halliwell, *Archaic and Provincial Words.* Bedgang is the corresponding old English word. See *Lost Beauties of the English Language.* By Charles Mackay, LL.D. London, Chatto and Windus.

[62] Contra Helvidium; also S. Cyprian, *Sermon on Nativity of our Ladye.*

[63] S. Luc. ii. 7. Cf. also Locri, *Maria Augusta,* lib. iv. cap. xiv. p. 511; Molanus, *De Hist. SS. Imaginum.* Edit. Paquot. Lovanii, 1771, pp. 78, et seq.; Fordun, *Scotichronicon.* Edinburgh, 1759, lib. ii. capp. xxi. xxii. pp. 56, 57.

[64] De Rossi, *Inscriptiones Christianæ,* vol. i. p. 54.

together before her, but not clasped, and her hair flowing down over her shoulders: borne up by angels, and frequently crowned. Thus is she figured on both of the seals of Eton College.[65]

She is not however invariably crowned. The illuminated charter of privileges to Eton of 1447, represents our Ladye in

The Assumption of our Blessed Ladye in Fownhope Church.

her Assumption, with her arms extended, and the Most Holy Trinity in the act of crowning her. In the centre boss over the entrance into the choir from the nave and transept in York Minster, our Ladye is represented in a *vesica piscis*, which is

[65] See ante, p. 29. Cf. also *Yorkshire Archæological Journal*, 1870, p. 109, for Assumption in window of Thornhill Church.

borne up by four angels, but she is not crowned.[66] I have often heard this particular figure spoken of as intended for the Immaculate Conception, but, in the absence of the requisite symbols, it can only be intended for the Assumption.

The representation of the Assumption which depicts our Ladye as throwing down her girdle to St. Thomas is apocryphal;[67] it may be seen in the Dominican Breviary of 1514, in the Office of the feast.[68]

Our Ladye of Pity was pre-eminently the favourite old English representation of the Blessed Mother of God.

§ 6.—OUR LADYE OF PITY.

O vos omnes qui transitis per viam, attendite et videte si est dolor, sicut dolor meus.

Our Ladye of Pity must not be confounded with Our Ladye of Mercy.   The title of Our Ladye of Pity is applicable solely to one type, or representation ; that of Our Ladye of Mercy to several.   At the Ladie of Pitties altar in the Galilee at Durham, the picture represented our Ladye "carryinge our Saviour on hir knee as He was taiken from the Crosse, a very dolorouse aspecte."   An old inventory at Melford says that in the tabernacle at the south end of the Jesus' aisle "there was a fair image of our Blessed Ladye having the afflicted Body of her dear Son, as He was taken down, off the Cross, lying along in her lapp, the tears, as it were, running down pitifully upon her beautiful cheeks, as it seemed, bedewing the said sweet Body of her Son, and therefore named The Image of our Ladye of Pitty."[69]   In Latin this representation of our Ladye is

---

[66] Browne, *History of the Metropolitan Church of St. Peter, York.* London, 1847, plate 121.

[67] Locri, *Maria Augusta*, lib. v. cap. xvii. p. 520.

[68] Fol. 315 b.

[69] *Views of the most interesting Collegiate and Parochial Churches in Great Britain.* By John Preston Neale. London, 1825, vol. ii. sub Melford, not paginated. "From the Moûte of Calvery," says the *Pylgrymage of Syr R. Guylforde, Knight, in* 1506, "we descendyd and come to ye place assygnyd by a whyte stone, where our Blessyd Lady moste dolorous Mother sat, hauynge in her lappe the deed body of her dere son new taken downe from ye cross" (p. 27. Camden Society, 1851). Amongst the Royal Jewels in the Treasury, *temp.* Henry VIII., was "a tabernacle of golde wᵗ our Ladye of Pyty, wᵗ her sonne in her lappe," &c. (*Kalendars and Inventories of the Exchequer*, vol. ii. p. 274).

expressed by *Pietas*,[70] or *Domina nostra de Pietate;*[71] in Italian, *la Pietà;* and in French, *Notre Dame de Pitié.*[72]

Pity in this use signifies compassion, *i.e.*, fellowship in suffering, and not mercy.

In the old English poem, *Quia amore langueo*, of about the year 1430, our Blessed Ladye appeals to mankind. She says—

> Moder of mercy Y was for thee made :
> Who nedith mercy but thou a-loone ?
> To jeve grace and merci y am more glade
> Than thou to aske.   .   .
>
> .   .   .   .   .   .
>
> My sone hath grauntide me for the sake
> Every merciful praier that y wole haue,
> For he wol no veniaunce take
>   If y aske mercy for thee, but that y schal haue.
> Therfor axe thou merci, y schal thee saue,
>   With *pitee* y rue upon thee so,
> I longe for *merci* that thou schuldist craue.
>   *Quia amore langueo.*[73]

Hence Our Ladye of Pity has a twofold meaning. She compassionates and suffers with her Divine Son. And she is in this type the object also of our compassion. This is well expressed in a poem of the fourteenth century, entitled Our Ladye's Lamentation, which represents our Ladye as speaking to some happy mother, between whose joys and her sorrow she draws a contrast.

[70] ". . . Tabulam depictam in qua est *Pietas*, id est, Deipara in gremio tenens mortuum filium" (*Act. SS.* t. i. Junii, p. 489, ad ann. 1421, in Vit. S. Rosselniæ).

[71] The silver image of Our Ladye of Pity given to the Cathedral of Aberdeen in 1499, is described, in the Visitation of the Jewels in that year, as *imago dive Virginis Marie de Pietate inscripta cum ymagine filii sui crucifixi*, *crucifixus* being here used to denote the dead Body of our Lord after the crucifixion, as in the Response of the first lesson in the Office of Easter Sunday—*scio enim quia* crucifixum *quæritis*—not in the crucifixion. The Visitation of 1496, which enumerates two *jocalia*, one *cum ymagine crucifixi et pietatis*, the other *ymago crucifixi cum ymagine pietatis*—this latter one appearing in the Visitation of 1464 as *ymago pietatis* only—includes a Pax-brede of silver gilt, *cum ymaginibus crucifixi, beate virginis et Sancti Johannis.* Here *crucifixus* refers to the actual crucifixion, and consequently our Ladye is described as *Beata Virgo* and not *de Pietate*.

[72] "On appelle N. Dame de Pitié la représentation de la Vierge tenant son fils mort sur ses genoux" (Furretiére, *Dict. universelle.* La Haye, 1690, sub voc. *Pitié*).

[73] *Political, Religious, and Love Songs.* Early English Text Society, vol. xv. 1866, pp. 149, 150, lines 25—28, 57—64.

Of all women that ever were bore,
　　That bare children, abide and see
How my Son lieth me before,
　　Upon my skirt, taken from the tree.
Your children ye dance upon your knee,
　　With laughing, kissing, and merry cheer.
Behold my child, behold well me,
　　For now lieth dead my dear Son dear.

．　　．　　．　　．　　．　　．

Thou hast thi sone ful whole and sounde,
　　And mine is ded upon my kne;
Thi child is lose, and myn is bounde;
　　Thi child is lyf, and myn——ded is He.
Whi was this, doghter, but for the?
　　For my Childe trespast never here;
Me think ye be holden to wepe with me,
　　For now lies ded my dere Sone dere.[74]

Thus in the inventory taken in 1468 of the goods and chat-
tels of Elizabeth, widow of William Sywardby of Sywardby,
Esquire, which were not included in her will, is *j imago Beate
Marie Virginis lamentabilis.*[75] And at Peterborough the altar
of Our Ladye of Pity was called that of our Ladye's Lamentation.[76] At Hull, Our Ladye of Pity was called the Mother of
Pity.[77]

No possible doubt can, therefore, exist as to the representation of our Ladye of Pity. From the great mass of evidence
on the subject which I have collected, I do not hesitate to say
that the image of Our Ladye of Pity was, not only the most
popular and homely in England, *but that there was scarcely one
church in our Ladye's Dower in which an image of Our Ladye of
Pity was not to be found.* Three old English images of Our
Ladye of Pity yet exist. One occupies one of the *sedilia* in
Battlefield Church, Shropshire;[78] the other, a magnificent image
in alabaster, two feet six inches in height, was recently found
buried under the pavement in Breadsall Church, near Derby;
the third is over the porch of Glentham Church, in Lincolnshire,
and below is a shield with the armorial bearings of the Tournays,
the former lords of Caenby.

[74] *Chester Plays.* Edit. Wright, vol. ii. p. 204.
[75] *Test. Ebor.* vol. iii. p. 166.
[76] S. p. 127.
[77] S. p. 55.
[78] *Archæologia,* vol. xiv. pl. xlviii. fig. 1, p. 272.

One proof of the ubiquity of the image of Our Ladye of Pity in England is supplied by the Sarum Prymer of 1534. Prefixed to the prayer, *Obsecro te Domina Sancta Maria*, which was commonly called, as I have shown elsewhere, the *Obsessio* or Besieging of our Ladye, is the following rubric :

" To all them that be in the state of grace that dayly say deuoutly this prayer before our blessed ladye of pitie, she wyll shewe them her blessyd vysage and warne them the daye and the houre of dethe, and in theyr laste ende the angelles of god shall yelde theyr sowles to heuen, and he (they) shall obteyne v. hondred yers and soo many lentes of pardon graunted by v. holy fathers popes of Rome." [79]

Our Ladye of Mercy is of a different type, and usually represented standing with her mantle extended, and covering many of her clients who are on their knees around her. At Verviers in Belgium there is a celebrated image of our Ladye venerated under the title of Our Ladye of Mercy. She is standing by our Lord, Who is on a bench, and is placing a sceptre in His hand. As I have found no mention of Our Ladye of Mercy in England, it is needless to say more on the subject.

A representation of our Lord seated, or standing, in the sepulchre, as He was visibly seen by St. Gregory, is called the *Pietas Sancti Gregorii.*[80] Mary the Miserable, who is buried in the chapel of Our Ladye of Woluwe-Saint-Lambert, near Brussels, is called *Maria Dolorosa,*[81] and must not be confounded with our Ladye, *Mater Dolorosa.*

At Telgetana an image of Our Ladye of Pity is venerated under the title of *Consolatrix afflictorum.*[82]

Our Ladye seated alone at the foot of the Cross, is called our Ladye at the foot of the Cross—*al pié de la cruz*—and not

---

[79] Sir William Weston distinguished himself at Rhodes, and at the departure of the Order from their island home, was appointed to the command of the great ship, commonly called the "Carrack of Rhodes." His flag bore the image of our Ladye with her dead Son in her arms, and the legend : AFFLICTIS ' TV ' SPES ' VNICA ' REDVS (Bosio, *Istoria della Sacra Religione et Illma. Militia di San Giovanni Gierosolimitano.* Napoli, 1684, t. iii. pp. 5, 9).

[80] Cf. Sarum Missal, 1555, f. 1.

[81] *L'Innocence Opprimée.* Bruxelles, 1872, passim; also *Act. SS.* ad diem 18 Junii.

[82] In an old engraving *penes me.*

Our Ladye of Pitye. Sometimes our Ladye is represented as standing alone, in an attitude of grief, or bearing the Crown of Thorns. Thus figured she is called *Nuestra Señora de la Soledad.*

§ 7.—OUR LADYE OF GRACE.

Ave gratia plena.

Under this title, many images of our Ladye were venerated in England, as at Beeston, Cambridge, Heigham Potter, Ipswich, Northampton, St. Andrew's in Norwich, Quarrywell, Southampton, Great Berkhampstead,[83] and elsewhere. In St. Paul's Cathedral, London, there was an image of Our Ladye "at the Pillar," in the nave, commonly known as Our Ladye of Grace.[84] The only clue to the type, under which our Ladye may possibly have been thus represented, is at Perth, where one of the five altars dedicated to her is called that of the Visitation, or Our Ladye of Grace.[85] At Tamworth a barn and a croft were left for the perpetual maintenance of a priest to celebrate the Mass of Our Ladye of Grace.[86] In 1478 a Gild of English merchants trading in Ireland was established in the chapel "Del Marie du Grace," at the bridge end, in Dublin.[87]

The beautiful image of Our Ladye of Graces, near the Tower of London, took its name, in all probability, from the abbey founded by Edward the Third in the year 1350, under the title of *B. Maria de Graciis*,[88] which might also be construed as Our Ladye of Thanks.[89]

It is most probable that these images of Our Ladye of Grace were so named on account of the favours obtained at

[83] S. sub nomm.
[84] S. pp. 68—70.
[85] S. p. 303.
[86] *History and Antiquity of the Collegiate Church of Tamworth, co. Stafford.* By C. Ferrers R. Palmer, O.P. Tamworth, 1871, p. 39.
[87] Gilbert, *History of Dublin*, vol. i. p. 324.
[88] S. pp. 91, 92.
[89] The Dominican Priory at Youghal, founded A.D. 1268—1271, was called that of St. Marye of Thanks (Archdall, *Monasticon Hibernicum.* Edit. 1873, vol. ii. p. 150). The version of the Hail Marye in Kentish dialect in the Ayenbite of Inwyt, A.D. 1340, begins, Hayl Marie of thonke uol, lhord by mid the, &c. (Early English Text Society, vol. xxiii. p. 262).

these sanctuaries, rather than because they were of any fixed type. I incline the more to this opinion since the picture of our Ladye of the St. Luke type presented by Fourey de Bruille, A.D. 1450, to the collegiate church dedicated in her honour in Cambrai, is variously called *Notre Dame aux Neiges, Sainte Marie Majeure, Notre Dame de Saint Luc,* and *Notre Dame des Graces.*[90] Formerly in Constantinople there were fifty-nine churches dedicated in honour of our Ladye, each of which had a distinguishing name ; one was called that of Our Ladye full of Grace (κιχαριτωμίη).[91]

A representation of the Visitation was sometimes called the Magnificat ;[92] and this explains what is to be understood by the "Story of the Magnificat" which was depicted in the window of the church of the Blackfriars at Norwich. John Baret of St. Edmund's Bury "bequeathed x marks to the peyntyng rerdoos and table at Seynt Marye avter of the Story of the Magnificat.[93]

§ 8.—OUR LADYE OF PEACE.

Quasi oliva speciosa in campis.

At Winfarthing, Norfolk, there was an image of Our Ladye of Peace.[94] This is the only instance I know in England of our Ladye being venerated under this title. Our Ladye of Peace usually holds an olive-branch in her hand, or, occasionally, a piece of fruit, signifying thereby that she was the New Eve who produced the Fruit Which has given peace to the world.[95] The image of Our Ladye of Peace in the Church of St. Michael, at Antwerp, represents her standing, with her Divine Son, Who is holding a crown over her head, in her arms, and a sceptre in her right hand.[96] At Brussels, in the Church of St. Nicholas, Our Ladye of Peace holds an olive-branch in her right hand.[97]

[90] Speelmans, *Belgium Marianum.* Tournai, 1859, p. 178.
[91] *Martyrologe Universel.* Paris, 1709, p. 838.
[92] Pascal, *Institutions de l'Art Chrétien.* Paris, 1856, vol. i. p. 232.
[93] S. p. 135.
[94] S. p. 249.
[95] Cf. *Le Saint Pélerinage à N. Dame de Paix à Enneticres-en-Wappes.* Par le R. P. Possoz, de la Comp. de Jesus. Tournai, 1859, p. 7.
[96] In an old engraving *penes me.*
[97] *Id.*

Thus, whilst the Blessed Virgin may be invoked anywhere as Our Ladye of Peace, she cannot be represented under that type except with the appropriate symbol of peace. In a modern and highly valued picture of Our Ladye of Peace, she holds both the sceptre and a branch of olive in her right hand, and our Lord holds a globe and an olive-branch in His left, His right being raised in the attitude of blessing. But there is only one step from the sublime to the ridiculous, and this painting is a fair instance of the carelessness of a modern artist. Our Ladye is represented as standing on a small globe, in a boat which is one-fifth shorter than her figure, and deep in the water. The waves are rough, and one is breaking over the stern. It is surely an extravagance of folly to depict our Ladye as balancing herself, like an acrobat, on a globe loose in a boat, in a rough sea! Such like absurdities are not uncommon in modern French art. The French say, in justification, that *il leur faut des émotions.* Heaven save England from these emotion-producing frivolities, not to use a stronger expression.

§ 9.—BEAUTY OF ENGLISH IMAGES OF OUR LADYE.

Tota pulchra es, et macula non est in te.

The English images and pictures of our Ladye were pre-eminently conspicuous for their great beauty. Our old artists and sculptors bore in mind that Christ our Lord was *speciosus forma præ filiis hominum*,[98] and that His Virgin Mother was "all fair—TOTA *pulchra*—the beloved of God, and in whom there was no stain,"[99] consequently they endeavoured to represent her as lovely and beautiful as it was in their power to do ;[100] and their handiwork yet excites an admiration which modern art cannot call forth.

Much has been written about the celebrated text, *Nigra sum sed formosa*,[101] which forms one of the antiphons in the Vespers

---

[98] Psalm xliv. 3.

[99] Cant. iv. 7.

[100] Dante alludes to the resemblance between our Lord and His Virgin Mother—

Riguarda ormai nella faccia ch' a Cristo
Piu s' assomiglia.

[101] See a paper in the *Month*, vol. xxix. p. 455, by Lord Arundell of Wardour.

of our Ladye. Many believe that sundry black images of our Ladye owe their origin to these words ; and there exist several images of our Ladye called *Vierges noires*, as La Vierge noire at Dijon, at Beaune, and in the Cathedral of Puy-en-Velay[102]; but the more probable explanation is that their colour is more commonly due to their antiquity. Tursellino describes the venerable statue of Our Ladye of Loreto as a cedar image of our Blessed Ladye standing. " Her face is varnished with amber, giuing a silver glasse [*sic*], but darkened with the smoke of the lights, yet this very darkening (a token of antiquity and religion) doth exceedingly increase the majesty of her virginall countenance."[103] Moreover, the Ethiopians and Abyssinians, and other dark nations, represent our Blessed Ladye of the colour of the nation, so to say, and like themselves, whilst in contra-distinction they paint the 'hell-devil' white.[104] I have a small painting on vellum of our Ladye of the St. Luke type, from Magdala, which represents her as dark. The traditional description of our Ladye recorded by St. Epiphanius, and quoted by Blessed Canisius, says : " Her complexion resembled the colour of ripe wheat ; her hair was golden, her eyes bright with light coloured pupils of an olive hue. She had dark and gently curved eyebrows.[105]

Nigra sum sed formosa, so far as it is applicable to our Ladye, must be taken in a mystical sense, as Cornelius à Lapide explains.[106]

The artists of the ages of faith did not use models for sacred subjects :[107] that was a practice of pagan origin, and revived at the fall of Christian art—a period commonly misnamed the Renaissance. Christian artists painted from inspiration. Thus in the curious document purporting to be issued by the three Bishops in the year 1291, Prince Edward was ordered in his

---

[102] De Caumont, *Abécédaire d' Archéologie.* Caen, 1859, p. 283.

[103] *History of our Blessed Ladye of Loreto.* Douay, 1608, pp. 15, 16.

[104] Pascal, *Institutions de l'art Chrétienne,* vol. i. p. 252.

[105] *De B. Maria Virgine.* Ingolstadii, 1577, lib. i. cap. xiii. p. 95.

[106] *Commentaria in S. Script.* Paris, 1860, t. vii. pp. 495, 496.

[107] Agnes Strickland says, "It is well known that the portraits of the lovely young Philippa (of Hainault) and her princely boy (Edward the Black Prince) formed the favourite models for the [Blessed] Virgin and Child at that era." (*Lives of the Queens of England.* Philippa of Hainault, p. 255) ; but unsupported as this statement is by any authority or references, it is of no weight. Barnes, however, says that the Queen suckled all her children, like Blanche of Castile, the mother of St. Louis of France (*Life of Edward the Third.* Cambridge, 1688, p. 44).

dream to go to "the most cunning limner in the whole world, Marlibrun the Jew, of Billingsgate, who would paint the picture of our Ladye and her Divine Son by Divine inspiration."[108] The "Stacions of Rome" in the Vernon MS. A.D. 1370, says that in the portrait of our Ladye by St. Luke, her face was filled in by angel hands.

> An ymage sikerly,
> Wonder feir, of vre ladi.
> Seint Luik, while he lyuede in londe,
> Wolde haue peynted hit with his honde.
> And whon he hedde ordeyned so,
> Alle colours that schulde ther to,
> He fond an ymage, al a-pert,
> Non such ther was, middelert,
> *Mad with angel hond*, and not with his,
> As men in Rome witnesseth this.[109]

Southey's "pious painter of Catholic days" is represented on the wall of the Ladye Chapel at Winchester as painting our Ladye from inspiration.[110]

The several images of our Ladye at Evesham were "right well peynted and feyre arayed wyth golde and diuers other colours, the whyche schewyed to the people that behylde hym grete deuocyon.[111] Professor Cockerell, R.A., describes the group on the south side of the choir of Angels, in Lincoln Cathedral, which represents our Ladye with her Divine Son, in terms of the highest admiration, and bears witness to the religious spirit which had inspired this work.[112] One of the images at St. Alban's, carved by the celebrated sculptor Master Walter of Colchester, in the beginning of the thirteenth century, was known as Our Ladye the Beautiful—*Sancta Maria Pulchra.*[113] Dr. Wilhelm Lübke speaks of "the Grand Madonna statue" at the portal of the Chapter House, York, saying: "She is holding her Child towards the spectator with motherly pride, and in doing so her slender figure is strongly curved, and the drapery with its broad folds is executed with masterly power." The date of this statue is c. 1300. "The splendid Madonna and Child at the main portal of Wells Cathedral, is a work of grand beauty, nobly conceived, and with free and

[108] S. pp. 79, 80. [109] Early English Text Society, 1867, pp. 16, 17.
[110] S. p. 241. [111] S. p. 37. [112] S. p. 64.
[113] S. pp. 131, 133.

flowing drapery."[114]   And Leo de Rosmital, in 1465—1467, was profoundly struck by the beauty of the English images.   "At Reading, in the abbey church," says he, "there is an image of the Mother of God so exceedingly elegant that, in my opinion, I have never beheld, nor shall see one to be compared to it, even were I to go to the extreme ends of the earth.   Nothing more beautiful nor lovely could be executed!"   He next halted at Andover, where he saw "a most beautiful statue of the Blessed Virgin sculptured in alabaster," and at Salisbury "he had never beheld more elegant images;" those of our Ladye with her Divine Son, and the Resurrection of our Lord, appeared to him "not as handiwork, but alive.'[115]

The silver image of Our Ladye of Pity at Aberdeen, is described in the Visitation of 1516, as *Pulchra imago*.[116]

The beauty of the English illuminations of our Ladye is equally remarkable ; and Dr. Waagen draws particular attention to three MSS. in the British Museum.   One is a Psalter of the first half of the eleventh century, with an illumination of our Ladye enthroned;[117] the second is the celebrated autograph history of Matthew Paris, which Dr. Waagen mentions "chiefly in order to call attention to the picture of the [Blessed] Virgin, which is one of the best miniatures of the thirteenth century known to me, and a striking proof of the excellence which the art had attained at that time."[118]   The third are the miniatures in an English religious poem A.D. 1420—1430.[119]

What then was the secret of this great beauty in the early pictures and images of our Blessed Ladye?   Simply this: Religious art was under the direct influence and control of the Church ; and the artists undertook their work in a proper religious spirit.   "It is good, and very advantageous to paint holy and venerable images," says the Fourth Council of

[114] *History of Sculpture from the earliest ages to the present time.*   London, 1872, vol. ii. p. 98.   Of this image Drake says, "that it bears a mark of those times which made even stone statues feel their malice" (*Eboracum*.   London, 1736, p. 476).

[115] Iter Leonis de Rosmital, A.D. 1465—1467, *Bibliothek des Literarischen Vereins in Stuttgart*, vol. vii. pp. 44, 46.   1844.

[116] *Registrum Episcopatus Aberdonensis*, vol. ii. p. 173.   Spalding Club.

[117] Harl. MS. 603.

[118] Royal MS. 14, ch. vii.

[119] Cott. MS. *Faustina*, B. vi. ; *Treasures of Art in Great Britain.*   By Dr. Waagen.   London, 1854, vol. i. pp. 145, 158, 183.   Letter vi. of vol. i. is well worth reading.

Constantinople, A.D. 869; "but it is neither good, nor by any means advantageous, that they should be executed by unworthy men," that is, by any under the anathema of the Church. Hence the Council defines that "whoever, thus censured, shall, after this definition, attempt to paint holy images in churches, shall, if a cleric, be liable to degradation from his rank, and, if a layman, he shall be separated and deprived of the communion of the sacred mysteries.[120] This Cardinal Frederic Borromeo inculcated at a later period, saying: *Pietatem pictori in primis esse necessariam.* Of Beato Angelico, Vassari says: *Che fa cose di Cristo, con Cristo deve sempre stare.*[121] He would paint his Christs on his knees. It was not his ambition to excel in the science of the nude; and on rare occasions when he had to paint the human body, faults in anatomy may be found. He never used models,[122] and would receive Holy Communion before venturing to depict the lovely majesty of our Ladye.[123] And Sassoferrato, in later times, did the same.[124]

Catholic artists were not men who would paint a Leda or a Venus one day, and a picture of our Ladye the day after, from the same model. All the pictures of our Ladye by Andrea del Sarto have the features of his handsome but vulgar wife; those of Rubens and Albano the portraits of their wives; those of Allori and Van Dyck are portraits of their mistresses, after the example of Praxiteles.[125] There exists a fresco— it is needless to say more—which represents Giulia Farnese as our Ladye, and Alexander the Sixth kneeling at her feet. But the greatest abomination of this description was executed in France. There existed in the Church of St. Stephen at Caen, a Holy Family. Our Ladye and St. Joseph were portraits of Gabrielle d'Estrées and Henri the Fourth, and their bastard son, the Duc de Vendôme, represented our Lord![126] Other later im-

---

[120] Act. x. Can. vii.; Labbe, t. viii. coll. 1130, 1131. Edit. cit.

[121] In Vita.

[122] *Vie de Frà Angelico di Fiesole.* Par E. Cartier. Paris, 1857, p. 101.

[123] *May Papers.* By Edw. Ignatius Purbrick, S.J. London, 1874, p. 57.

[124] *Summa Aurea*, t. ii. col. 965, note.

[125] *Praxiteles autem, ut declarat Possidipus in libro de Cnido, Cnidiæ Veneris effingens simulacrum Cratina, quam amabat, formam in eâ expressit, ut haberent miseri unde amicam Praxitelis adorarent* (Clement Alexandr. Opp. Lut. Parisior, 1641, p. 35). *Cum floreret autem Phryne meretrix Thespiaca, pictores omnes Veneris imagines ad Phrynes pulchritudinem imitatione referebant (Ibid.).*

[126] Pascal, ubi sup. p. 259. Happily this picture is now destroyed.

pieties need not be mentioned.[187] Such were the unchristianizing results of the Renaissance. From the time of Raffaele, I know of no picture or statue of our Ladye which inspires devotion like those of the ages of faith; and although, of late years, Christian art has made great progress in the right direction, much is yet to be desired. Chateaubriand says of himself that *Une Madone coiffée d'un couronne gothique, vetûe d'une robe de soie bleue, garnie d'une frange d'argent m' inspire plus de devotion qu'une Vierge de Raffael.*[128] Evidently when he wrote these lines he had in his mind some venerated image of our Ladye carved and painted in the ages of faith. For my part, I do not see how Raffaele's pictures can inspire devotion to any excepting to those who know nothing of his history. There is a print of him which represents him in the act of sketching the *Madonna della Seggiola;* but so far from trusting to inspiration, the scene is laid in the courtyard of an *osteria.* The model, a handsome *contadina* with her child, is seated at an open window, and Raffaele is painting her likeness on the end of an empty wine cask tilted up! Rio frankly allows that several of the "Madonnas" of Raffaele were not painted as objects of devotion.[129]

Artists considered those as happy days which were occupied in painting our Blessed Ladye; as Guido of Siena has recorded at the foot of his celebrated picture executed in 1221: ME GHVIDO DE SENIS DIEBVS DEPINXIT AMENIS; and then, as if imploring the mercy of his Redeemer, for the sake of His Virgin Mother, he adds: QVEM XPS LENIS NVLLIS VELIT ANGERE PENIS. In a word, the Christian artists and sculptors of the ages of faith, considering that the execution of an image or picture could be properly worked out only by *innocentes*

---

[187] Pascal, *ubi sup.* p. 219.

[128] *Mémoires d'Outre Tombe.* Paris, 1860, vol. i. p. 47.

[129] On Raffaele's return from Urbino to Florence, "ce qu'il faisait pour les Florentins avait plutôt pour but de flatter leur amour-propre par la possession d'un trésor admiré d'avance, ou de leur procurer des jouissances esthétiques où la piété proprement dit entrait pour peu de chose. C'était encore le culte du beau, mais ce n'était plus cet idéal religieux qui avait exalté les imaginations en épurant les ames, et je crois que *la Vierge à l'œillet*, la Vierge *au linge* du Musée du Louvre, *la Vierge* du Palais Nicolini, et *la Vierge* du Palais Colonna exécutées toutes vers cette même époque peuvent légitimement être soupçonnées de n'avoir jamais été traitées comme des images de dévotion" (*Michel-Ange et Raphaël.* Par A. F. Rio. Paris, 1867, pp. 124, 125).

manibus et mundo corde, endeavoured to render themselves worthy of undertaking their pious labour of love, by being shriven and houseled, and by prayer. What Montalembert says of the early German artists is eminently applicable to our old English painters and sculptors. *Déjà la popularité de cet art naissant était si grande que l'on ne cherchait plus l'idéal de la beauté dans la nature déchue, mais bien dans ces types mystérieux et profonds, dont d'humbles artistes avaient puisé le secret au sein de leurs comtemplations religieuses.*[180] It is from this source alone that Catholic art can raise itself to the perfection of the ages of faith.[181]

§ 10.—THE ROBING OF STATUES OF OUR BLESSED LADYE.

Mrs. Jameson ascribes this practice to the "influence of Jesuitism on art"! "This Order," says she, "kept alive that devotion for the Madonna, which their great founder Loyola "— as she calls St. Ignatius, *more Scotico*—"had so ardently professed when he chose for the 'Lady' of his thoughts, 'no princess, no duchess, but one far greater and more peerless.' The learning of the Jesuits supplied some themes not hitherto in use, principally of a fanciful and allegorical kind, and never had the meek Marye been so decked out with earthly ornament as in their church pictures. If the sanctification of simplicity, gentleness, maternal love, and heroic fortitude were calculated to elevate the popular mind, the sanctification of mere glitter and ornament, embroidered robes and jewelled crowns, must have tended to degrade it. It is surely an unworthy and foolish excuse that, in thus desecrating with the vainest and most vulgar finery the beautiful ideal of the [Blessed] Virgin, an appeal was made to the awe and admiration of vulgar and ignorant minds, for this is precisely what, in all religious imagery, should be avoided. As, however, this sacrilegious millinery does not come within the province of fine arts, I may pass it over here."[182]

[180] *Vie de S. Elizabeth,* pref.

[181] Cf. Carove, quoted by Digby, *Broad Stone of Honour,* vol. iv.; Orlandus, pp. 341—343. Edit. London, 1876.

[182] *Legends of the Madonna,* Introd. pp. xxxvii. xxxviii. Edit. cit.

Carove is more to the point. "In observing," says he, "the splendid robes with which the artist adorns holy persons, we should remember the intention which prompted his hand, that as the poor as well as the rich, in these times, often and gladly gave their best and most beautiful robes to ornament altars and holy images, the painter, with similar piety, expended his utmost skill in worthily adorning those saints whom he painted and honoured with religious honour; by means of the wide and flowing drapery, it was the intention, not only to clothe the body, but also to keep it completely out of the view and thought of the observer, and to confine the attention solely to the spiritual countenances of the heavenly."[133]

In the year 833, Uuitlaf, King of Mercia, gave his coronation mantle to Croyland to be made into a chasuble or a cope; and Harold the First (Harefoot) followed his example.[134] Matilda of Flanders, wife of William the Norman, gave her tunic and mantle to the Abbey of the Holy Trinity for the same object, and one of her girdles of gold for the suspending of the lamp before the altar.[135]

It may be a question whether, in earlier days, the custom of robing statues took any other form than that of attaching a mantle to the shoulders. It will be remembered by those who have visited the Basilica of St. Peter in Rome, that on festal days the bronze seated statue of St. Peter, which was cast in the time of St. Leo the Great from the bronze of Jupiter Capitolinus, is arrayed in a cope and tiara. The antiquity of this custom I have not ascertained. At Glastonbury, the image of our Ladye, of which William of Malmesbury speaks, had a veil on its head, which was not consumed by the fire,[136] yet it will be observed that he makes no allusion to robes.

The many instances of "coats" for our Ladye and her Divine Son, which are mentioned in the Series, prove how universal was the custom of robing images of our Ladye in England. At Caversham the image of our Ladye had false hair.[137]

---

[133] Quoted by Digby, *Broadstone of Honour*, vol. iv.; Orlandus, pp. 342, 343.

[134] *Mon. Angl.* t. ii. p. 90.

[135] Agnes Strickland, *Lives of the Queens of England*, vol. i. p. 92. London, 1851.

[136] S. p. 48.

[137] "Cootes, cappe, and hers" (S. p. 11).

It should be borne in mind that from the eighth century it was a custom to cover venerated images made of wood with a sheathing of gold or silver plates, and to adorn them with gems, ornaments, and precious stones. The treasury of Conques contains a magnificent seated image of Sainte Foi of this description, of the ninth century. The body is of wood sheathed with gold, the head is of gold alone, *repoussée*. Affixed to it are engraved and plain gems, and many interesting pieces of jewelry of various dates. Through the courtesy of M. Poussiélgue I was able to examine this statue not long ago.

§ 11.—COLOURING OF STATUES.

Statues of our Ladye, not sheathed with gold and silver or made of precious metals, were invariably coloured and gilt. This was an early custom in England, as is proved at Glastonbury and Thetford. Those at Evesham are described in 1196 as "right well peynted and feyre arayed wyth golde and divers other colours." The Series mentions many bequests for the object of painting various images of our Ladye. Thomas Barsham, called Thomas of Yarmouth, acquired considerable reputation during the early part of the fifteenth century as a painter and *imagier*, or maker of images; to him, probably, are due many interesting specimens of mediæval art which still remain on the altar screens of some of the Norfolk churches.[128]

As all the images in England, excepting those made of gold or silver, or sheathed with precious metals, were painted, it may have been that it was sought to give them a more festal character by robing them in rich garments of textile fabric, which were so often bequeated in wills. Moreover, the robing of images afforded the means of displaying to advantage the numerous offerings and bequests of girdles, brooches, rings, pairs of beads, and the like. At Melford, according to the Inventory of 1529, three rings were fastened to the apron of our Ladye. There is no evidence that the English statues of

---

[128] A curious list of prices paid to workmen for the painting of images in Westminster Abbey from the 6th to the 26th of Edward III. is given in the *History of Ecclesiastical Architecture in England.* By G. Ayliffe Poole, M.A. p. 284.

our Blessed Ladye were arrayed in those stiff pyramidal robes which disfigure her images at Loreto, Einsiedlen, in Belgium,[139] and elsewhere.

Now, considering that the Society of Jesus was instituted only in the year 1554, it is impossible to understand how Mrs. Jameson could assign to "Jesuit influence" the origin of a custom which had already existed for many centuries. Random assertions, such as these, deprive works, otherwise meritorious, of much of their value and authority.

A decree of the Sacred Congregation of Rites, dated April 11, 1840, forbids different mantles for summer and winter wear to be placed on images of the saints.[140]

§ 12.—VEILS.

The Anglo-Saxons represented our Ladye with the Byzantine mantle-veil, the use of which disappears shortly after the Norman invasion; the mantle is worn on the shoulders, and a kerchief is added, reaching to the mantle, or falling slightly over it. The kerchief or little veil was no doubt, as I have already observed, the earliest form of applying textile fabrics to images of our Ladye, as at Glastonbury, where it was used in the thirteenth century. In the inventory of the jewels and other objects belonging to Our Ladye of Miracles, at St. Omer's, taken in the year 1383, are mentioned xxii *galmata, gallicé kevvrekiefs pro imagine Beate Marie;*[141] yet no robes for the image of our Ladye appear in the inventories until nearly a century later.

There are many details about the images and pictures which represent our Ladye with flowing hair and with and without the veil, into which it is impossible here to enter. I am inclined to believe that there was no general rubric on the subject, and that artists were influenced in some degree by the customs of their country; that is, by the manner in which maidens wore

---

[139] Cf. *Etudes sur les types de la Sainte Vierge à l'époque Romano-Byzantine.* Par l'Abbé Hyacinthe de Bruyn, vicaire aux Minimes (Bruxelles), Président du Comité archéologique de Brabant. Brux. 1870, p. 28.

[140] *Manuel d'Archéologie pratique.* Par l'Abbé Th. Pierret. Paris, 1864, p. 366.

[141] Didron, *Annales Archéologiques,* vol. xviii. pp. 257—264. These inventories are of much interest.

their hair, and whether they wore the veil or not. Our Ladye
of Pity recently found at Breadsall does not wear the usual
great mantle-veil over her head—it hangs from her shoulders—
but the kerchief which falls on it. But in the Assumption in
English art, our Ladye is usually represented as young, with
her hair flowing over her shoulders, and no veil.

§ 13.—OUR LADYE'S FEET.

It was not until the commencement of the Renaissance, or
fall of Christian art, that our Ladye is represented with bare
feet. They came in with *robes collantes,* and *phainomerides*
tunics, and other artistic extravagances, which are utterly to
be condemned.[142] In the frescoes of the Catacombs, in Anglo-
Saxon illuminations,[143] and the early English and Italian schools
of painting and sculpture, Our Ladye is invariably represented
with shoes on her feet—at least with her feet covered—whilst
our Lord usually has bare feet, and occasionally sandals. I
know of only one solitary exception. In the very remarkable
illumination in the Book of Kells, A.D. 700, our Ladye is
depicted with bare feet, probably in accordance with the
national custom in Ireland, otherwise it seems impossible to
explain this exception to the general rule.[144]

Sometimes the feet of images of our Ladye were fitted with
silver shoes. The Visitation of the treasury of the Cathedral
at Aberdeen, March 1, 1496, enumerates *duo sotulares nostre
domine cum duobus berillis.*[145] At Limerick, in the 30th of
Henry the Eighth, the Commissioners "did take off the image
of our Ladye showes of silver, weighing six unces with divers
stones, and fifteene buthons of silver valued at 3*s.* 9*d.* sterling."[146]

[142] Cf. Pacheco, quoted by Mrs. Jameson, *Legends of the Madonna,* pp. ii. lii.
Edit. 1872.

[143] See the *Benedictionale* of St. Æthelwald, *Archæologia,* vol. xxiv.

[144] Lest it may be objected to me that the seal of Kelso (S. p. 299) as given in
Gordon's *Scottish Monasticon* (Glasgow, 1868, p. 441), represents our Ladye with
bare feet, I ought to say that the bare feet are an invention of the engraver's, and
that the seal itself represents her with shoes (See Laing, *Catalogue of Scottish Seals,*
p. 189, n. 1057).

[145] *Regist. Episcopatus Aberdon.* vol. ii. p. 169. Spalding Club, 1845.

[146] S. p. 308.

And in the inventory of York Minster taken 1420, are mentioned *ii plates de argento pro pedibus ymaginis Beate Marie.*[147] These were probably "frontals"—if I may use this word—for our Ladye's feet, and intended to represent the upper parts of the shoes.

§ 14.—THE CROWNING OF STATUES OF OUR BLESSED LADYE.

Veni, dilecta mea, veni, coronaberis.

Mrs. Jameson attributes the origin of "jewelled crowns" on the head of our Ladye to the influence of Jesuitism! The following evidence will prove what her statement is worth.

Anastasius, Librarian of the Church, proves that the practice of crowning images of our Blessed Ladye was observed in Rome in the first half of the eighth century. He relates that Pope Gregory the Third, A.D. 731—741, had built a chapel in honour of our Ladye, with an altar and an image, which is described as a statue of the Holy Mother of God, having a golden crown, set with precious stones, and a necklace of gold with pendant gems and ear-rings set with six hyacinths.[148]

In the *Benedictionale* of St. Æthelwald, Bishop of Winchester, A.D. 948—963, one of the illuminations represents the death of our Ladye. She is lying on her couch, and a hand, holding a crown, is issuing from a cloud.[149] The anecdote of Cnut, who placed his crown on the head of the great image of our Lord crucified, at Winchester, will be remembered.[150] In a MS. in the British Museum, assigned to the years 1012—1020,[151] there is a miniature of our Blessed Ladye seated, with God the Father and her Divine Son, the Holy Ghost is hovering over her: she is crowned.

Within two centuries the practice of representing images of our Blessed Ladye, with her Divine Son, crowned, had become almost universal in England. Frequently crowns of gold and silver were placed upon her images. The great image of Our

---

[147] *York Fabric Rolls,* p. 296. Surtees Society, 1859.
[148] *Hist. de Vitis Rom. Pontificum,* t. ii. col. 1025. *Patrol. Lat.* Edit. Migne.
[149] *Archaeologia,* vol. xxiv. plate xxxi. p. 106.
[150] Henry of Huntingdon, *Francofurti,* 1601, p. 364.
[151] Cott. MS *Titus,* D. xxvii.

Ladye of Lincoln, which was an early one, and of silver, had a crown of silver gilt.[162] Isabel, Countess of Warwick, bequeathed a crown of gold with precious stones, weighing 20 lbs., to Our Ladye of Caversham.[163] Several crowns for the image of our Ladye and her Divine Son in the Royal Chapel at Windsor are enumerated in the inventory of the 8th of Richard the Second.[164] Lambeth Simnel was crowned with the crown of Our Ladye of St. Marye's Abbey, Dublin;[165] and many other instances are given in the Series.[166] The image of our Lady in the Herbert Chapel at Abergavenny is singularly interesting, because she is represented with a triple crown, which evidently is intended to designate her as Queen of the Church Triumphant, the Church Militant, and the Church Suffering.[167]

St. John Chrysostom and other Fathers of the Church often give to the saints the title of Princes, because, compared with the faithful in this world, they have, in consequence of the predilection which God bears them, and the glory which they enjoy, a vast superiority over them. Our Blessed Ladye is the Queen of all these Princes of Heaven. It is impossible to refuse her the title of *Queen of All Saints*, without denying that she surpasses all other saints in merit, in grace, and in influence with God. Hence it appears that the crowning of images or statues of our Blessed Ladye is a public acknowledgment of her glory and a mysterious representation on earth of the act of God in elevating her above all the other saints, and of her coronation in Heaven—*Veni, dilecta mea, veni, coronaberis*—which is so beautifully expressed in an old English poem entitled "A Song of great sweetness from Christ to His Daintiest Damme."

VENI CORONABERIS.

Surge mea Sponsa, swete in siȝt,
　And se thi sone thou ȝafe souke so scheene;
Thou schalt abide with thi babe so briȝt,
　And in my glorie be callide a queene.
Thy mammillis, moder, ful weel y meene,
　Y had to my meete that y miȝt not mys;
Aboue alle creaturis, my moder clene,
　　Veni, coronaberis.

---

[162] S. p. 63.　　[163] S. p. 10.　　[164] S. p. 247.　　[165] S. p. 305.
　　　[166] S. pp. 63, 135, 137.　　[167] S. p. 283.

Come clenner than cristal to my cage ;
Columba mea, y thee calle,
And se thi sone that in seruage
For mannis soule was made a thralle.
In thi palijs so principal
I pleyde priuyli withoute mys ;
Myn hiȝ cage, moder, haue thou schal ;
  Veni, coronaberis.
For *macula*, moder, was neuere in thee,
Filia Syon, thou art the flour,
Ful sweteli schalt thou sitte bi me,
And bere a crowne with me in tour,
And all my seintis to thin honour
 Schal honoure thee, moder, in my blis,
That blessid bodi that bare me in bowur,
  Veni, coronaberis.
Tota pulchra thou art to my plesynge,
 My moder, princes of paradijs,
Of thee a watir ful well gan sprynge
 That schal aȝen alle my riȝtis rise ;
The welle of mercy in thee, moder, lijs
 To bring thi blessid bodi to blis ;
And my seintis schulen do thee seruice,
  Veni, coronaberis.
Veni electa mea, meekili chosen,
 Holi moder and maiden queene,
On sege to sitte semeli bi him an hiȝ
 Thi sone and eek thi childe.
Here, moder, with me to dwelle,
 With thi swete babe that sittith in blis,
There in ioie and blis that schal neuere mys,
  Veni, coronaberis.
Veni electa mea, my moder swete,
 Whanne thou had me, babe, be ful stille,
Ful goodli oure lippis than gan mete,
 With briȝt braunchis as blosmes on hille.
Fanus distillans, it wente with wille
 Oute of oure lippis whanne we dide kis,
Therfore, moder, now ful stille,
  Veni, coronaberis.
Veni de libano, thou loueli in launche,
 That lappid me loueli with liking song,
Thou schalt abide with a blessid braunche,
 That so semeli of thi bodi sprong.
Ego flos campi, thi flour, was solde,
 That on calueri to thee cried y-wys :
Moder, thou woost this is as y wolde ;
  Veni, coronaberis.
Pulchra ut luna, thou berist the lamme,
 As the sunne that schineth clere,

r

Veni in ortum meum, thou deintiest damme,
　　To smelle my spicis that here ben in fere.
My palijs is pijt for thi pleasure,
　　Ful of brijt braunchis and blosmes of bliss ;
Come now, moder, to thi derling dere !
　　　　Veni, coronaberis.
Quid est ista so uertuose
　　That is euere lastyng for hir mekenes ?
Aurora consurgens, graciouse,
　　So benigne a ladi of such brijtnes,
This is the colour of kinde clennes
　　Regina celi that neuere dide mys ;
Thus endith the song of greet sweetlnes,
　　　　Veni, coronaberis.[158]

§ 15.—BIRDS.

King Henry the Fourth gave to the Royal Chapel of Windsor a statue of our Ladye of silver gilt ; on her right arm she bore her Divine Son, Who is playing with a bird—*ludentem cum volucre.*[159] Mrs. Jameson, with her Egyptian proclivities, sees in birds thus represented the symbols of the soul of man. I quote her opinion for what it may be worth, merely observing how unlikely it is that our Lord would be described as "playing with a bird " if it were understood to represent the soul of a man whom He had redeemed. The emblem of Saint-Cyr represents our Ladye in a boat, and our Lord "flying" a dove with a string fastened to its leg, and the end of which He is holding.[160] Barocci painted our Blessed Ladye holding her Divine Son and St. John the Baptist in her arms. St. John is rescuing a bird from a cat, which is at our Ladye's feet. This is *La Vierge au chat ;* and Pascal cannot decide whether or not the artist had some mystical signification in his mind.[161] I do not, however, remember to have met with the cat as used to

---

[158] *Hymns to Christ and our Blessed Ladye.* Early English Text Society, vol. xxiv. 1867, p. 1.
[159] S. p. 247.
[160] Haigneré, *Étude sur la légende de N. Dame de Boulogne,* p. 32.
[161] *Institutions de l'Art Chrétien,* vol. i. pp. 249, 250.

symbolize the devil. It would, however, not be out of keeping
with the wretched symbolism of the Renaissance. I think it is
said of Cornelius Agrippa, or some other proficient in magic arts,
that his familiar demon used to appear to him under the form
of a black cat.

The seal of Plympton Priory represents our Ladye seated
with her Divine Son on her knee, and holding on her hand a
hawk, belled and hooded.[162] A hawk was the symbol of the
highest nobility. *Præcipuum erat accipiter primæ nobilitatis
insigne*, says Cancellieri ;[163] and one of the distinctions of the
Anglo-Saxon nobles was to appear in public with their hawks
on their wrist.[164] For the benefit of those who are not cunning
in the noble science of Falconry, I may observe that a hawk has
attached to his legs two little leather straps a few inches in
length, to which is fixed a swivel through which the leash is
passed. When taken from their blocks or perches, they are
hooded, and carried on the hand by the two little straps from
which the leash has been removed. Now these little straps are
called *jesses*. Is the hawk in the Plympton seal intended as a
playful allusion to our Ladye the *Virga de radice Jesse?*[165] The
Tree of Jesse was a favourite subject for stained glass windows,[166]
and *tabulæ*,[167] and copes in England.

In some of the early seals of the Kings of England a bird
is represented on the top of the sceptre which they hold ; and
in like manner, some of the early British monastic seals of our
Ladye represent the sceptre which she holds surmounted by a
bird—as in the seal of Kelso.

The great silver-gilt image of our Ladye of Lincoln bore in
her hand " a scepter with one flower set with stones and pearls,
and one bird on the top thereof."[168]

[161] S. p. 127.

[162] Quoted by Oliver, *Mon. Diœc. Exon.* p. 132.

[164] Sharon Turner, *History of the Anglo-Saxons.* Paris, 1840, vol. ii. p. 38,
note 5.

[165] *Egredietur virga de radice Jesse*, &c. (Isaias xi.). The Lady Abbess of
St. Albans, Dame Juliana Berners, in her Processe of Hawkynge, says that
"Hawkys have abowte their leggys *gesses* made of leddyr most commynly." *Book
of St. Albans*, sig. b. iii. Cf. *Promptorium Parvulorum*, sub. voc. Iesyz.

[166] Cf. *Memoirs illustrative of the Art of Glass Painting.* By Charles Winston,
M.A. London, 1865, p. 238.

[167] *Priory of Finchale*, fol. ccccl. Surtees Society.

[168] S. p. 63.

§ 16.—OPENING STATUES.

At Durham the image of Our Ladye of Boulton was "madde to open with gimmers (*i.e.* hinges) from her breastes downwards."[169]

These statues, called in French, *Images ouvrantes*, were in great vogue during the fourteenth and fifteenth centuries. As their name implies, they were made to open and form a triptych, containing either relics or carved representations. A very beautiful example is now in the Louvre at Paris;[170] and several others of the year 1480 are mentioned.

§ 17.—RELICS IN STATUES.

It is an ancient custom to inclose relics in statues of our Blessed Ladye ; and instances are mentioned of such images at Barking Abbey,[171] Glastonbury,[172] and Thetford.[173] It was also observed abroad.[174] Relics were also placed in the figures of our Lord crucified, as was done in the Great Rood at St. Edmund's Bury, A.D. 1102.[175]

§ 18.—OFFERINGS TO SANCTUARIES OF OUR LADYE.

And the people rejoiced when they promised their offerings willingly, because they offered them to God with all their heart ; and David the King rejoiced also with a great joy.

1 Paralip. xxix, 9.

I have merely one or two observations on this point to add to what appears in the Series.

Only a few votive hearts, which are so common abroad, are

---

[169] Viollet le Duc, *Dict. raisonné de Mobilier Francais.* Paris, 1868, p. 131.

[170] Migne, *Dict. d'Orfèvrerie,* col. 1042. In the Inventory of the Duke of Burgundy, A.D. 1420, n. 4238, is *Ung petit ymage dor de Nostre Dame ouvrante par le ventre ouquel est la Trinité dedans,* &c. (*Ibid.*).

[171] Sir Thomas More, *A Dialogue concerning Heresies and Matters of Religion.* Written A.D. 1518, bk. ii. ch. ix. Opp. Edit. cit. p. 192.

[172] The image mentioned in S. p. 48 contained relics.

[173] S. pp. 148, 149.

[174] Viollet le Duc, *Dict. raisonné de Mobilier Francais,* p. 133; *Gallia Christiana.* Paris, 1715, t. xiii. p. 102.

[175] Batteley, *Antiquitates S. Edmundi Burgi.* Oxon. 1745, p. 57.

mentioned as offerings to English sanctuaries of our Ladye.[176]
They were symbols that the donors had given their hearts to
our Ladye the *Raptrix cordium*,[177] and, perhaps, in thanksgiving
for some favour received through her intercession. Thus Chaucer
in a ballad addresses our Ladye :

> Mine hart I yeue you Lady in this entent,
> That ye shal holly thereof haue gouernaunce,
> Taking my leaue with hart's obeisaunce,
> *Salve Regina* singing last of all
> To be our helpe when we to thee call.[178]

The heart was considered the *pars melior pro toto corpore.*
Isabella, Countess of Gloucester, died A.D. 1239, and was buried
at Beaulieu.

> Postrema voce legavit cor comitissa,
> Pars melior toto fuit huc *pro corpore* missa.[179]

'What can be more touching," says a recent writer, "than
to read of a great and good man bequeathing his heart to the
place or person of his affections?"[180]   Our Richard the Lion-
Heart gave his heart to Our Ladye of Rouen, whom he heartily
loved—*quam præcordialiter dilexerat.*[181]   In 1387 John the
First, Count of Auvergne and Boulogne, left his heart to Our
Ladye of Boulogne ;[182] and Antony Widvile, Earl Rivers,
bequeathed his to Our Ladye of Pue.[183]   Truely might these
good men exclaim in the words of St. Bonaventure : *O Domina
quæ rapis corda dulcedine! Nonne cor meum, Domina,
rapuisti ?*[184]
   On two occasions Sir Robert Wingfield, who was Ambassador
at the Court of the Emperor Charles the Fifth, asked leave of
absence of his sovereign that he might offer his beard, which he

---

[176] A silver votive heart is mentioned at Aberdeen.   Cf. *Archæologia Cantiana,*
vol. ix. p. lxii. for a votive heart of wax.

[177] St. Bonaventure, *Opusc.* t. ii. p. 235.   Edit. cit.

[178] *Works.* London, 1602, fol. 330.

[179] *Mon. Ang.* vol. ii. p. 55.

[180] *Enshrined Hearts of Warriors and Illustrious People.* By Emily Sophia
Hartshorne. London, 1861, p. 5, proeme.

[181] S. p. 83.

[182] Haigneré, *Nostre Dame de Boulogne.* Edit. cit. p. 99.

[183] *Opusc.* Edit. cit. t. ii. p. 240.

[184] S. pp. 128, 235.

had already vowed to Our Ladye of Walsingham.[185] I have
not space to enter into details on the subject of beards, which
would explain the importance of this offering of Sir R. Wingfield ; but it will be remembered that when Sir Thomas More
was on the scaffold, "laying his head vpon the blocke, he bad
the executioner stay vntill he had removed aside his beard,
saying, that 'that had never committed anie treason.' "[186]

§ 19.—TABERNACLES.

It will be noticed that in the Series frequent mention is
made of " Tabernacles " for the images of our Ladye.

Tabernacles were canopied niches. In ancient contracts
they were also called *maisons*, habitacles, hovels, and howsings,[187]
all reverting to the original derivation of the word. The Latin
tabernaculum signifies a booth, or small *taberna* of boards,
capable of being put together or taken asunder, as a tent is
pitched. In the Vulgate it is thus employed for the portable
Temple of the Jews, "the Tabernacle in the Wilderness." Hence
the word came to signify any small cell or other place in which
some holy and precious things were deposited, and thus was
applied to the ornamental receptacle over the altar for the
Blessed Sacrament. Sepulchral monuments, the stalls in a
choir, and the *sedilia*, being surmounted by rich canopy work
—all this was called tabernacle work. Inigo Jones applies it
to the niches of Roman architecture.[188]

Sometimes these tabernacles for our Ladye's images were on
a magnificent scale, as at Bridlington and Peterborough ; others
were of silver, as at Caversham ; whilst at Walberswick the
tabernacle of Our Ladye of Pity was in 1474 to be painted and
gilt, according to the form of Our Ladye of Pity at Southwold.[189]
Sometimes they were of smaller dimensions, and portable ;
thus, in the Wardrobe book of the 28th Edward the First are

[185] S. p. 192.
[186] *Life and Death of Sir T. More.* By M. T. M. s. d. p. 335.
[187] S. pp. 134, 135.
[188] *Glossary of Architecture*, p. 451.
[189] S. p. 155.

enumerated, an image of the Blessed Virgin Marye of ivory with
a tabernacle of ivory in a case—*in uno coffino*, and four images
of our Blessed Ladye, with tabernacles and sundry images.[100]
Evidently these were small polyptychs. In the jewels in the
treasury of Henry the Eighth was a tabernacle of gold with
Our Ladye of Pity.[101]

MY labour of love is finished. Most deeply grateful am I to
the Blissful Queen of Heaven for that by her favour it has
been vouchsafed to me—an unworthy but hereditary liegeman
of her Dower—to collect and publish these evidences of the
affection which our forefathers bore her. They prove that in
devotion to her Catholic England was second to no nation in
the world.

A nation which has once lost the faith has never till now
regained it. Yet there is a world-wide belief that England
will be restored to the Church of Christ, and that at her second
conversion she will do more for religion than at her first.
Among the many "signs of the times," it is impossible not
to notice the restorations which are being made in all our old
desecrated churches, as if to prepare them to be once more
Houses of God; and the commencement of devotion to our
Blessed Ladye in the Protestant Establishment.

Our gracious Queen, whom may God long preserve, counts
millions of loyal Catholic subjects within the limits of her vast
Empire, on which the sun never sets; and within which—a
thing that cannot be said of any other nation that has ever
existed—from the rising to the setting of the sun, the unbloody
Sacrifice of the Mass is celebrated[102] on British soil.

The might and prestige of the British Empire is already
in some degree at the service of the Church. Under the
protection of the glorious national banner, charged with the
cross of St. George, our Ladye's knight, missionaries go forth
to preach the Word of God, and announce the praises of His

[100] Lib. Gard. Edw. I. pp. 351, 352.
[101] *Kalendars and Inventories of the Exchequer*, vol. ii. p. 274.
[102] Malachi i. 11.

Maiden Mother, whose sweet name will soon be heard in the
far-off regions of Central Africa.

England, like Rome of old, after having persecuted the
Church of Christ, is ready to become a powerful instrument
for her exaltation, and for the propagation of the praises of the
Mother of God.[103]

Upon us, the Catholics of England, the restored or hereditary
liegemen of our Ladye's Dower, it devolves as a sacred duty
to endeavour to revive, in fervent practice, the grand old
English love of the Blissful Mother of God. British hearts
and British tongues do not stand in need of foreign phraseology;
we cannot improve upon the terms in which our forefathers
addressed our Ladye. We need not go to the language of
Italy to tell her of our dutiful affection.

In these pages I have endeavoured in brief terms to give
an idea of the *universality*, and of the minute details of the
old English love of our Ladye, and how it was carried out.
Some of the pious practices are known to us; others are
forgotten; some again are considered old-fashioned. Can anything in the service of our Ladye be considered old-fashioned?
Shall we ever have restored to us the venerable Uses of Sarum
and York, with the daily Marye Mass? Will bedesmen be
summoned, as of yore, to attend funerals and recite the Psalter
of our Ladye? Will the present generation learn to rejoice
habitually with the joys of the Blissful Mother of God, or to
pity the woes of our Ladye of Pity?

I hope that there is no Catholic Church in England in which
the image of our Ladye is not so placed as to be the object
of popular devotion. May we again see in all our churches
candle-beams and "perks," and votive candles, and "gawdyes"
and "joyes" burning in honour of her five joys, as heretofore.
May the charitable once more give "our Ladye's meat," and
"our Ladye's loaf" as alms on Saturdays in our dear Ladye's
love. May the Gabriel bell again peal forth, where it is not now
habitually tolled. May the evening anthem of our Ladye
become a popular usage. Cannot our school children be taught
regularly to greet our Ladye with an *Ave* whenever they pass

---

[103] "The Empire of Rome was the most decided enemy of the early Church, yet
that very Empire, in God's hands, became a mighty instrument for the exaltation of
the Church" (Rev. George Porter, S.J.).

by her image? Every congregation might easily supply three Queens of our Ladye to look after the Marye-altar.

The memory of some, at least, of the celebrated sanctuaries of our Ladye might be most appropriately revived; and little pilgrimages made to them in commemoration of the old ones so ruthlessly plundered and destroyed. This is what has been done in France. The time-honoured statue of our Lady of Chartres was destroyed at the Revolution, but a new image has replaced the original; Our Ladye of Miracles at St. Omer's is mutilated, yet in this state she is the object of popular devotion; whilst at Boulogne-sur-mer her new sanctuary, rebuilt on the ancient site, is the great pilgrimage in the north of the *Regnum Galliæ, Regnum Mariæ,* as heretofore; and in these, and many other renewed sanctuaries, our Ladye loves to bestow her graces and favours as of yore. Might not devotion to our Ladye of Pewe at Westminster, so dear to the Kings of England, and so celebrated throughout their realm, be appropriately revived at St. Marye's, Horseferry Road? What church more suitable to restore the cultus of Our Ladye of Graces by the Tower than that of the English Martyrs? or that of St. Marye's, Moorfields, for the foundation of a Salve Guild?

Happy, indeed, shall I be if these my humble and feeble labours in our Ladye's love shall, with the blessing of God, be the means of reviving some of the old English devotions in her honour. And as I have been writing of Catholic times, I may well conclude in the beautiful words penned in the ages of faith:

"Royne des angeles je te preng pour mon moïen, confort et ayde, et te prie et requierez humblement quil te plaise, par ta clemence et doulceur, deffendre et garder de tous dangiers et adversitez ceulx et celles quy ce present traittié, par bonne intention et pour lonneur et révérence de toy, glorieuse Vierge, volront lire et recorder. Amen."[194]

Gloria, laus et honor Tibi sit, Rex, Christe Redemptor :
Gloria fine carens sit tibi Virgo Parens.

---

[194] *Légende de N. Dame de Boulogne.* MS. XV. cent. Edited by Haigneré, Boulogne-sur-mer, 1863, p. 53.

BOOK THE SECOND.

*Catalogue of Shrines, Sanctuaries, Offerings,
Bequests, &c.*

Old English Devotion to our Blessed Ladye.

ABINGDON.   In 675 Cyssa founded here a church in honour of our Blessed Ladye, and a monastery for twelve Benedictine monks. It became richly endowed, for our Anglo-Saxon forefathers dearly loved—to use their own affectionate form of language—"to make God and our Ladye their heirs."[1] And the charters of donations in land were not sent by a messenger, but the pious donor would go to the church attended by his friends and relations, all of whom had approved of, or concurred in, the donation, and reverently lay the deeds upon the altar of our Lady. Thus Lullan, a noble Saxon, who had received a gift of the vil of Estun from Brihtric, King of Wessex, 784—800, desired to make God his heir, and gave Estun to Him and our Ladye, and laid the charter upon the altar, saying, "Al mine richte that ic hædde in Estun ic gife to Sæinte Marie in Abbedun."[2]

St. Eadward the Martyr and St. Dunstan ordained that it should be lawful for the people to make pilgrimages, for the sake of devotion, to the church of our Ladye of Abingdon.[3]

AILMERTON, NORFOLK.   Here was a light of our Blessed Ladye.[4]

ALDBURGH, NORFOLK.   Here was a celebrated image of our Blessed Ladye in the church.[5]

---

[1] Chron. Monast. de Abingdon, pp. 15, 27. Edited by order of the Master of the Rolls.

[2] *Ibid.* p. 15.

[3] Spelman, Concilia, vol. i. p. 493.

[4] *General History of Norfolk*, p. 148. Norwich, 1829.

[5] *Ibid.* p. 135.

B

ASHBY DE LA ZOUCH.   1503, November 22. Katharine Lady Hastings desires by her will to be buried in the Ladye Chapel of Ashby de la Zouch, between the image of our Ladye and the place assigned for the vicar's grave.[6]

ASHFORD.   Thomas Wilmott, perpetual vicar of the parish church of Ashford, in his will dated April 25, 1493, says :

"I will that the image of St. Marye now standing in my study be placed at my expense in the said chapel of St. Nicholas."[7]

ASHILL, NORFOLK.   Here was a statue of our Ladye of Pity.[8]

In 1458, 17 May, Jeffrey Coo was buried before the altar of St. John the Baptist here. He gave legacies to all the gilds, and 5 lbs. of wax to our Lady of Pitie's light.[9]

Note.—Prior to the Reformation nearly every parish in England had one or more gilds, each with their own chapel and chaplain. Some of these gilds were for the especial purpose of keeping up our Ladye's light. Some churches had the married men's light and the single men's light. In Norfolk alone there existed nine hundred and nine gilds, of which one hundred and seventy-eight were gilds of our Blessed Ladye. These were for the most part suppressed by the Act of Henry VIII. which his successor put into execution.[10]

ASTON, BUCKS.   By his will, October 28, 1490, Sir Gilbert Stapylton leaves :

"to the Abbess of Aston Church, in Buckingham, a girdle of silver gilt, to hang at an image of our Ladye in the said church." [11]

BANHAM, NORFOLK.   In 1437, John Ropere, of Banham, gave 12s. to the lamp that burns before the image of the Blessed Virgin in the church.[12]

---

[6] Testamenta Vetusta, p. 450.   [7] *Ibid.* p. 450.   [8] Blomefield. ii. 349.   [9] *Ibid.* i. 613
[10] Taylor, *Index Monasticus of the Diocese of Norwich*, p. 71. London, 1821.
[11] Test. Vetust, p. 398.   [12] Blomefield, i. 242.

BARKING.
This convent was founded by Erconwald, Bishop of London, in honour of our Blessed Ladye. The charter of foundation is dated 677.[13]

Here was the chapel of our Ladye de Salue, called also La Chapele de Salue, and the chapel of Nostre Dame de Salue en larche.[14]

Amongst the burials are named,

Dame Yolente de Sutton qe gist deuant lauter Nostre Dame de Salue.

Dame Katharine Sutton gist en la chapele de Nostre Dame de Salue en larche.[15]

There was a "Gylde or Fraternite in the Worschipp of our Ladye (St. Marye atte Naxe) in the chapell of our Ladye in the cemetorie of Berkyng Church of London," which is mentioned in an Act of the 1st Henry VII.; and John, Earl of Worcester, is described as being the late master thereof.[16]

Many oblations were made to our Ladye of Barking.

In the household accounts of Elizabeth of York, March 24, 1502:

Offering to our Lady of Berking. i *s.* vi *d.* February 26, 1503.[17]

"To Sir William Barton, preest, singyng at our Ladye of Berking. vii *l.* vi *s.* viij *d.*[18] And on the 25th July, 1508, the Duke of Buckingham made "oblation to our Ladye of Barking. 20 *d.*"[19]

BECCLES, SUFFOLK.
Here was a chapel of our Ladye, with an anchorite, at the foot of the bridge.[20]

In 1374, Reginald de Ikelyngham leaves xi *d.* to the altar of our Lady in the Church of St. Michael.[21]

BEESTON, NEAR THE SEA, NORFOLK.
Many legacies were given to our Ladye of Grace, and our Ladye of Pitie.[22]

---

[13] Dugdale, Mon. Angl. i. p. 436.   [14] *Ibid.* p. 441.   [15] *Ibid.* p. 441.
[16] Rot. Parl. vi. p. 343, b.   [17] Privy Expenses, p. 3.   [18] *Ibid.* p. 102.
[19] Letters and Papers, Henry VIII. vol. iii. pt. i. n. 1285.
[20] Suckling, *Antiquities of Suffolk*, vol. i. p. ii. London, 1842.   [21] *Ibid.* p. 15.
[22] *Index. Mon. Dioc. Nor.* p. 21.

BOSTON.

Our Ladye in the Church of St. Botolph.

Here was the pardon of the *Scala Cœli* at Rome, a privilege which existed in England only in the chapel of our Ladye of the Scala Cœli, in the church of the Austin Friars at Norwich, and the chapel of the same name at Westminster.[23]

BOURNE.

May 9, 1462. William Haute, esquire, desires to be buried in the Austin Friars, Canterbury. In his will he says :

"I bequeath one piece of that stone on which the Archangel Gabriel descended when he saluted the Blessed Virgin Mary, to the image of the Blessed Virgin Mary in the church of Bourne, the same to stand under the foot of the same image."[24]

BOULOGNE.

Henry VIII. made several offerings to our Ladye of Boulogne.[25]

BRADLEY,
Co. LEICESTER.

Sir John Skevington, alderman of London, and merchant of the Staple of Calais, by his will, leaves

"To our Ladye of Bradley in Leicestershire a white damask vestment with my arms on the cross, worth 53*s.* 4*d.*[26]

BRADSTOW,
KENT.

Our Ladye of Bradstow at Broadstairs. Here was a much venerated image of our Ladye; and according to very old traditions, ships sailing past used to salute her by lowering, or "dipping" their topsails.[27]

BRIGHTSTOW ON
AVON, OR BRISTOL.

Leland enumerates "Our Ladye Chapell on Avon Bridge."[28]

2. Our Ladye in the Monastery of St. Austin's.
April 6, 1508. The Duke of Buckingham made an "oblation in the Monastery of St. Austin's, Bristow, to our Lady in one crusady. 4*s.* 6*d.*"[29]
3. Our Ladye of Belhouse.
In January, 1521, the Duke of Buckingham gave to our Ladye of Belhouse 4 *s. d.*[30]

[23] Blomefield, ii. p. 552.
[24] Test. Vetust, p. 300.
[25] N. Harris Nicolas, Privy Purse Expenses of Henry VIII, introduction, f. xx. London, 1827 ; also Hall, p. 791, ed. 1809.
[26] Letters and Papers, Henry VIII. vol. iv. p. i. n. 952.
[27] A very old tradition ; quoted on the authority of the late Right Rev. Dr. Grant, Lord Bishop of Southwark, and of others.
[28] Itin. vi. p. 86.
[29] Letters and Papers, Henry VIII. vol. iii. pt. i. n. 1285.
[30] *Ibid.*

BUCKINGHAM, NORFOLK.

1429. Peter Payne of Barham left to the chapel of the Blessed Virgin at Thetford 6*s.* 8*d.*, and to the chapel of the Blessed Virgin at Buckyngham 13*s.* 4*d.*[31]

BURGHAM, Co. WESTMORELAND.

Leland says :

"There is an old castel on the . . . side of Edon Water cawlled Burgh. About a dim from the castel is a village cawlled Burgham, and ther is a gret pilgrimage to our Ladye."[32]

CALAIS.

In the Privy Purse expenses of Henry VIII. is this entry :

"1520, June. Offering at our Ladye at St. Peter's Church without Calais, at the King's coming from, 6*s.* 8*d.*"[33]

"1532, November 12. Item. Paied to my lorde Chamberlayne for the King's offering at our Ladye in the wall at Calais, v *s.*"[34]

CAMBERWELL, SURREY.

Richard Skynner, in his will dated 1492, gives 12*d.* for a light before the image of the Blessed Virgin Mary.[35]

CAMBRIDGE.

There was a much venerated image in the church of the Black friars, which formerly stood on the spot now occupied by Emmanuel College. Concerning it, John Bishop of Rochester, wrote to Cromwell that "there hath of long time been an image of our Ladye in the said house of friars, the which hath much pilgrimage unto her, and specially at Sturbridge fair ; and for as much as that time draweth near, and also that the said prior cannot bear such idolatry as hath been used to the same, his humble request is that he may have commandment by your lordship to take away the said image from the people's sight."

The Atlas Marianus[36] enumerates our Ladye of Cambridge, described as *Imago B. V. miraculosa Liberatrix*, and quotes a story from a MS. in the Vatican, about a young student named William *Vidius* (query, White?). It may be summed up briefly as follows—

[31] Blomefield, i. p. 241. [33] Letters and Papers, Henry VIII. vol. ii. pt. ii. p. 154. [34] Privy Purse, Henry VIII. p. 272. [35] Manning, *Hist. of Surrey*, iii. p. 423 [36] P. 1028, n. cmlxxii, ed. Monachii, 1672.

A young student by name William Vidius, led an irregular life, but never laid aside his devotions to our Ladye, and was accustomed daily to honour her, by reciting before her image certain prayers. He had a comrade, James by name, who shared his room, and one night as they slept, James was awakened by the groans of his companion, who, he observed, was trembling and covered with sweat, as though he was suffering from great terror. With some difficulty James succeeded in awakening him. "Well is it for me," exclaimed William, "that I have been used to honour the image of the Blessed Virgin, for otherwise I should have perished eternally. For this night I have stood before Christ the Judge, who required of me a strict account of my life. The enemy was about to seize my soul, when I beheld the Blessed Mother of God, and, according to my custom invoking her aid, she put the demon to flight, and obtained for me a further respite."

William might have thought that it was a mere dream, if he had not found in his hand a paper in writing unknown to him, which contained all the crimes of his life, and many things known to himself alone. The next day he went and threw himself at the feet of his spiritual father, and made a full confession, and thenceforth reformed his manner of life. His friend James subsequently became a priest.

CANTERBURY.

1. St. Augustine's monastery in Canterbury was founded by King Æthelbert and St. Augustine in 608.

His son and successor, Æthelbald, built a chapel here in honour of our Blessed Ladye, in which he was buried in 640, as also his wife Emma.[87]

This was the chapel in which St. Dunstan had his visions.

"At the east end of the monastery was the oratory of the Blessed Marye which King Æthelbald built, and in which reposed the bodies of many saints. So pleasing to the Queen of Heaven

[87] Mon. Angl. p. 120.

was this oratory, that, according to the English proverb, it was called the *Sacrarium* or *Vestiarium* of Marye. In it did the Mistress of the world often appear; in it was the brightness of miracles made manifest; in it the voices of angels and the melodious strains of holy virgins were frequently heard; in it did the Blessed Dunstan see manifestly St. Adrian amongst the choirs of heavenly spirits, with the Queen of the world herself, praising God; in it did he see with his very eyes, and hear with his ears, the Blessed Mother of Christ singing, with her virgins, in alternate voices, the verses of Sedulius.

> Cantemus, sociæ, Domino, cantemus honorem
> Dulcis Amor Christi personet ore pio."

The chronicler continues that Abbot Wulfric, wishing to extend the buildings of the monastery, pulled down the west end of this chapel, and removed the cemetery of the community, and gave that space to the new buildings. The abbot, however, came shortly to a sudden end, and which, by some, was considered in the light of a judgment from heaven, in consequence of his having demolished the ancient sanctuary of our Blessed Ladye.[88]

2. Our Ladye at Rolles.

At the feast given at the enthronization of William Wareham, Archbishop of Canterbury, "in my Lord's table in ye Gret Hall.

"In the seconde boorde of the same warner the King presented my Lorde in his doctor's habit unto our Ladye at Rolles, sytting in a towre with many rolles about hym, with comfortable words of his promotion, as it appeareth in the verse folowynge.

> Est locus egregius tibi Virgo Sacrata dicatus,
> Publica servari quo monumenta solent.
> Hic promo hunc, si tu dignabere, dignor honore :
> Commendo fidei scrinia sacra suæ."[89]

This must have been the representation of some image of our Ladye, known as our Ladye at Rolles, but no other particulars have as yet been found.

---

[88] Chron. W. Thorne ap. Twisden, col. 1785.   [89] Mon. Angl. i. 115.

3. Our Ladye Undercroft.

The celebrated chapel of our Ladye Undercroft, or in the crypt, was exactly under the high altar. The statue of our Ladye stood in a canopied niche, or as the old name was, a " tabernacle," on a rich pedestal, on which were sculptured in relief subjects from her life. Even in its present ruined state it displays remains of its former splendour. On the vaultings may be seen traces of brilliant blue colourings, on which appear small convex gilt mirrors and gilded quatrefoils. The royal arms are painted in the centre, and forty other shields of coat armour are emblazoned on the lower part of the arches. This chapel was much enriched by Prior Goldstone, and the shields of arms, which mostly belong to the Lancastrian noblemen of the Court of Henry VI. would seem to have been placed there as memorials of notable offerings at the shrine of our Ladye.

Giraldus Cambrensis mentions a great miracle wrought at our Ladye of Canterbury in his time.[40]

The Black Prince desired by his will to be buried "in the Cathedral Church of the Trinity of Canterbury, where the body of the true martyr Monsire St. Thomas reposes, in the centre of the chapel of our Ladye Undercrofte, right before the altar so that the end of our tomb may be ten feet from the altar." But with these directions the executors did not comply; they erected his tomb in the chapel of St. Thomas, immediately to the south of his shrine.[41]

Numerous offerings were made to our Ladye Undercroft.

In the accounts of Elizabeth of York :

24 March, 1502. Offering to our Ladye of Undercroft by Richard Milner, of Bynfeld, v. s.[42]

25 December. Item. Delivered to Doctour Attoure for the Queene's offerings to our Ladye of Undercroft, Canterbury, iij s. iiij d.[43]

---

[40] Opp. vol. ii. Gemma Ecclesiastica, dist. i. c. xxxiv.   Rolls Ed.

[41] Cardinal Morton, who died in 1500, desired to be buried before the image of the most Blessed Virgin Marye, commonly called our Ladye of Undercroft, whom he so dearly loved. Two monks were to say each one Mass a day for twenty years, together with the *Placebo* and *Dirige* for his soul (Anglia Sacra i. 64).

[42] Privy Expenses, p. 3.

[43] *Ibid.* p. 81.

In those of Henry VIII. :

September, 1514. Offering at our Ladye Undercroft, 6 *s*. 8 *d*.[44]

May, 1520. Offering at our Ladye Undercroft, Canterbury, 6 *s*. 8 *d*.[45]

Erasmus, in his *Peregrinatio religionis ergo*, gives a brief description of the chapel of our Ladye Undercroft : " From the shrine of St. Thomas, we returned to the crypt. Here the Virgin Mother has an abode, but somewhat dark, inclosed within a double screen of iron, for fear of thieves, for indeed I never saw a thing more laden with riches. When lamps were brought, we beheld more than a royal spectacle, which in beauty far surpassed that of Walsingham. This is only shown to men of high rank, or great friends."[46]

CARBROOKE MAGNA, NORFOLK.   Opposite to the south side of the church was the chapel of our Blessed Ladye, whose altar and image were also in it ; this belonged to the gild of our Blessed Ladye, which maintained a priest to sing there.[47]

CARLTON COLVILLE, SUFFOLK.   Here, in the Church of St. Peter, was a chapel of our Blessed Ladye, and a provision for finding a light to burn before her image.[48]

CASTON, NORFOLK.   At Caston there was a gild of our Blessed Ladye, and a light constantly burning before her image.[49]

CAVERSHAM, BUCKS.   The image of our Ladye of Caversham stood in a chapel attached to the church of Caversham, which, in 1162, was granted by King John to the Austin Canons of Nutley or Notcele Abbey, in the same county. The chapel was then in existence, and was held of sufficient importance to be named separately in the deed of gift. Subsequently, the canons came into possession of a manor at Caversham, and erected a cell to their monastery, which was much enriched by the offerings made in the chapel of our Ladye. Gilbert Marshal, Earl of Pembroke, granted to

[44] Letters and Papers, Henry VIII. vol. ii. pt. ii. n. 1465.   [45] *Ibid.* p. 1541.

[46] Erasmi Colloquia. Amstelodami, 1644, p. 418.

[47] Blomefield, i. 602.   [48] Suckling, ii. p. 241.   [49] Blomefield, i. 564.

the canons the tithes of all his mills and fisheries at Caversham, together with the annual sum of twelve shillings, for the maintenance of two lamps to burn continually before our Ladye, for the health of his soul, and the soul of his brother.[60]

In her will, Isabel, Countess of Warwick, says: "To our Ladye of Caversham I bequeath a crown of gold, made of my chain and other broken gold in my cabinet, weighing twenty pounds."[61]

Many offerings were also made here.

In the accounts of Elizabeth of York:

1502, March 24. Item. Delivered to Sir William Barton, priest, for the offering of the Queen to our Ladye of Caversham, ii s. vi d.[62]

In the accounts of the King:

1517, September 6–13. Offering by the King at our Ladye of Caversham, 18 s. 4 d.[53]

1520, August. Offering at our Ladye of Caversham on Ladye-day, 6 s. 8 d.[54]

Sir Robert Wingfield, writing to Wolsey from Easthampstead, on the 17th July, 1532, says, in a postscript to his letter: "This morning the King rode forth right early to hunt, and the Queen is ridden to our Ladye of Cawssam."[55]

The fate of our Ladye of Caversham has been preserved to us.

Dr. London, writing to Cromwell, says:

"In my most humble maner I have me comendyd unto yower gude lordeschippe acertenyng the same that I have pullyd down the image of our Ladye at Caversham, wherunto wasse great pilgremage. The image ys platyd over wyth sylver, and I have putt yt in a cheste fast lockyd and nayled uppe, and by the next bardyge that comythe from Reding to London yt shall be browght to your lordeschippe. I have also pullyd down the place sche stode in, with all other ceremonyes, as lightes, schrowdes, crowchys, and imagies of wax hangyng abowt the chapell, and have defacyd the same thorowly in exchuyng of any farther resort thedyr. Thys chapell dydde belong to Notley Abbey, and ther

---

[60] Northcote, *Shrines of the Madonna*, p. 258.   [61] Test. Vestut. 240.
[62] Privy Expenses, p. 3.   [53] Letters and Papers, Henry VIII. vol. ii. pt. ii. n. 1476.
[54] *Ibid*, vol. iii. pt. ii. p. 1545.   [55] Letters and Papers, vol. iv. Henry VIII, n. 2393.

always wasse a chanon of that monastery which wasse callyd the warden of Caversham, and he songe in the chapell, and hadde the offeringes for hys lyvinge."[56]

In another letter, possibly to Sir Richard Rich, Dr. London says more on the subject of his sacrilegious proceedings; his letter is very valuable evidence of the popular devotion to our Ladye of Caversham.

"I have pullyd down the image of your Ladye at Caversham, with all trynkettes abowt the same, as schrowdes, candels, images of wax, crowches brochys, and have thorowly defacyd that chapell in exchuyng of any farther resortt, ffor even at my being ther com in nott so few as a dosyn with imagies of wax. The image is thorowly platyd over with sylver. I have putt her in a cheste fast lockyd and naylede, and by the next bardge that comythe uppe it schall be browyt to my lorde, with her cootes, cappe and here, with dyvers relykes, &c."[57]

In a third letter Dr. London adds:

"I have also sent iii. cotes of the image, with such thinges as I fownde upon them."[58]

CHATHAM.

1. In the will of Symon Fagge. c. 1535.

"I bequeath a taper of a pound of wax to our Ladye in St. Gyles' chapel."[59]

2. Our Ladye of Chatham.

3. The celebrated image of our Ladye of Chatham is believed to have stood in a niche over the entrance arch to the north porch of the old Norman church, now no longer existing.

William Lambarde, an eminent lawyer and antiquary, born 1536, and who died 1601, was the author of several learned books, one of which was *A Perambulation of Kent*, written in 1570, and published six years later. He gives in it the following account of our Ladye of Chatham:[60]

"Although I have not hitherto at any time read any memorable things recorded in historie

---

[56] *Letters relating to the Suppression of the Monasteries*, Camden Society, 1843, p. 221.
[57] *Ibid.* p. 224.   [58] *Ibid.* 226.   [59] Test. Vetust. 670.
[60] Lambarde, p. 324. ed. Chatham, 1826.

touching Chatham itselfe, yet, for so much as I have often heard (and that constantly) reported, a Popish illusion done at the place, and for that also it is as profitable to the keeping under of fained and superstitious religion, to renew to mind the priestly practices of olde time (which are now declining to oblivion) as it is pleasant to reteine in memorie the monuments and antiquities of whatsoever other kinde, I think it not amisse to commit faithfully to writing what I have received credibly, by hearing, concerning the idols, sometime knowen by the name of our Ladye and the Roode of Chatham, and Gillingham.

"It happened (say they) that the dead corpse of a man (lost through shipwracke belike) was cast on land in the parish of Chatham, and being there taken up, was by some charitable persons committed to honest buriall within their churchyarde : which thing was no sooner done, but our Ladye of Chatham, finding herself offended therewith, arose by night, and went in person to the house of the parishe clearke (which then was in the streete a good distance from the church), and making a noise at his windowe, awaked him. This man at the first (as commonly it fareth with men disturbed in their rest) demanded somewhat roughly, who was there? But when he understoode by hir own answer, that it was the Ladye of Chatham, hee changed his note, and most mildely asked the cause of her good Ladiship's comming. She told him, that there was lately buried (near to the place where she was honoured) a sinfull person, which so offended hir eie with his ghastly grinning, that unlesse he were removed, she could not but (to the great griefe of good people) withdraw her selfe from that place, and cease her wonted miraculous working amongst them. And therefore she willed him to go with her, to the end that (by his helpe) she might take him up, and cast him again into the river.

"The clerke obeied, arose, and waited on her toward the church; but the good Ladie (not wonted to walke) waxed wearie of the labour, and therefore was inforced for very want of breath to sit downe in a bush by the way, and there to rest her. And this place (forsooth), as also the whole tracke of their iournay (remaining ever after a green path) the towne dwellers were wont to shew.

"Now after a while, they go forward againe, and comming to the churchyarde, digged up the body, and conveied it to the waterside, where it was first found. This done, our Ladye shranke againe into her shrine, and the clerke peaked home to patch up his broken sleepe, but the corpse now eftsoones floted up and down the river, as it did before. Which thing being at length espied by them of Gillingham, it was once more taken up and buried in their churchyard. But see what followed upon it, not only the Roode of Gillingham (say they) that a while before was busie in bestowing miracles, was now deprived of all that his former vertue, but also the very earth and place where this carcase was laide, did continually for ever after settle and sinke downeward.

"This tale, receaved by tradition from the elders, was (long since) both commonly reported and faithfully credited of the vulgar sort; which although happily you shall not at this day learne at every man's mouth (the image being now many years sithence defaced) yet many of the aged number did lately remember it wel, and in the time of darknesse. *Hæc erat in toto notissima fabula mundo.* But here (if I might be so bould as to adde to this fable, his ἐπιμύθιον (or *Fabula significat*), I woulde tell you that I thought the morall and minde of the tale to bee none other, but that this clerkely μυθοπλάστης, this talewright (I say) and fable-forger, being either the Fermer or owner of the offerings given to our Ladye of Chatham, and crossing the common haunt and pilgrimage to the Roode of Gillingham (lately erected *Ad nocumentum* of his gaine), devised this apparition for the advancement of the one and defacing of the other.

"For (no doubt) if that age had beene as prudent in examining spirits as it was prone to beleeve illusions, it should have found that our Ladies path was some such greene trace of grasse as we daily behold in the fields (proceeding indeede of a naturall cause, though by olde wives and superstitious people reckoned to be the dancing places of night spirits, which they call fayries). And that this sinking grave was nothing else but a false filled pitte of Maister Clearks owne digging.

"The man was to blame, thus to make debate between our Ladye and her Sonne, but since the whole religion of Papistrie it self is Theomachia and nothing else, let him be forgiven, and I will go forward."

CHESTER.

Here was a celebrated statue of our Blessed Ladye in the Church of St. Werburga, and many miracles were wrought. It stood in the south side of the choir, over the head of the tomb of Goddestald the hermit.

Father Daniel à Virgine Maria relates what follows respecting our Ladye of Chester:

"In this city there were some people who were envious of the Carmelites, and said that the special title of servants of Marye belonged to the other religious orders rather than to them; for which the divine indignation fell upon them. For almost all the detractors of the Carmelite Order died of a sudden death. Wherefore Thomas, the abbot of the monastery of St. Werburga in the same city, determined that a general procession should be made to St. Werburga's, in which monastery, in the south part of the choir, at the head of the tomb of the hermit Goddestald, stood an image of the Blessed Virgin Marye by which God wrought many miracles. Whilst the procession was moving on, and the Carmelites had arrived at the image, and were venerating it, in presence of a large assembled multitude, the image, extending its hand towards them, said in the hearing of all present, 'Behold my brothers, behold my brothers, behold my beloved and chosen brothers !'"[61]

Henry de Sutton, nineteenth abbot, died May 8, 1413, and was buried in the broad aisle, close to the north side of the south pillar, next to the entrance into the choir, before a painting formerly called our Ladye of Pitie.[62]

[61] Speculum Carmelitanum per R.P. F. Danielem à Virg. Maria, Carmelit. Antv. 1680, n. 790, f. 179.

[62] Mon. Angl. ii. 374.

Old English Devotion to our Blessed Ladye. 15

CHEWE.

In May, 1508, the Duke of Buckingham made an " oblation to my Ladye of Chewe. 20 d."[63]

CHEVELEY, CAMBRIDGESHIRE.

Here was a gild of our Ladye which kept a light burning in the parish church, the bracket of the image being still in existence on the pier of the tower.

In old wills there are many bequests to this gild.[64]

CHOBHAM, SURREY.

In 1488 a sheep was given by will to the light of our Blessed Ladye.[65]

Note.—Animals were occasionally left for the support of lights. Thus in 1520 Christopher Travers, of Chaldon, Surrey, leaves a sum of money to provide an image of St. Roch, together with a cow for the support of a taper, to be kept burning before the image.[66]

COKETHORPE.

Here was a celebrated image of our Ladye, to which numerous offerings were made.

In the accounts of Elizabeth of York:

" 1502, March 24. Item. Delivered to Sir William Barton, preest, for thofferinge of the Queene to our Ladye of Cokthorp, xx d." [67]

COLTON, NORFOLK.

Had a light of the Blessed Virgin Marye, and two others, of St. John the Baptist and St. Andrew.[68]

CROWHAM.

In the accounts of Elizabeth of York:

" 1502, March 24. Item to Richard Mylner, of Bynfield, for money to be offered for the Quene, to our Ladye of Crowham, ii s. vi d."[69]

CABROKE, OR COLNBROOK, NEAR WINDSOR.

Mentioned in the accounts of Elizabeth of York:

" 1502, July 12. Item. Delivered to the Quene for hire offring at oure Ladye of Cabroke, viii d.

" Item. The same day, to the hermite there in aulmous, xii d.

" Item. The same day, to a poure man that guyded the Quene's grace thider, iiij d."[70]

[63] Letters and Papers, Henry VIII. vol. iii. pt. i. p. 497, n. 1285.
[64] *Proceedings of the Suffolk Archæological Institute,* vol. i. p. 247.
[65] Manning, *Hist. of Surrey,* iii. p. 353.
[66] *Surrey Archæological Collections,* iii. p. 353.   [67] Privy Expenses, p. 3.
[68] Blomefield, i. 664.   [69] Privy Expenses, p. 3.   [70] *Ibid.* p. 31.

COURT UP STREET,
KENT.

Leland says:

Court up Street "is a bowte a Myle fro *Lymme Hille*, and at this day yt is a Membre of Lymme Paroche. Howbeyt, ther is a Chaple for the Howses that now remayne, and this is the Chaple communely cawlled *Our Ladye of Court up Streate*, wher the Nunne of Cantorbiry wrought al her fals miracles." [71]

This sanctuary was long held in veneration, but it obtained celebrity in the reign of Henry VIII., by being the scene of the pretended revelation of Elizabeth Barton, Maid of Kent.

Here was a hermit in the chapel of our Ladye.

About 1528 Dame Isabel Poynyngs of Smeethe in the County of Kent, bequeathed

"To our Ladye Chapel of Curt of Strete a yard and two nails and a half of cloth of gold for a vestment.

"To the hermit of Curt up Strete vi *s.* viii *d.*" [72]

COVENTRY.

The celebrated image of our Blessed Ladye of Coventry is imperishably associated with the name of that perfect model of an Anglo-Saxon lady, Godgifu, Countess of Mercia, the peerless sister of Thorold, shire-reeve of Lincoln, and wife of that faithful lover of his country, wise statesman, loyal subject, and devoted husband, Leofric, Earl of Mercia. Lovely as Godgifu was, the beauties of her soul and her virtues far eclipsed her personal charms. Ingulph, who had many opportunities of seeing her, when he was with his father, who held a position at the Court of St. Eadward, describes her as *tunc fœminarum pulcherrima, sic corde sanctissima.* [73] The old historians vie with each other in her praise. Orderic Vitalis, and the chronicler of Evesham, call her the *religiosa comitissa.* [74] Roger Hoveden describes her as *Dei cultrix et Sanctæ Mariæ semper Virginis amatrix devota.* [75] Henry of Huntingdon says that she *nomine perpetuo digna, multa probitate viguit.* [76]

[71] Itin. vii. pp. 132, 133.
[72] Test. Vetust. p. 634.
[73] Scriptores Rerum. Anglicarum, pp. 892, 895. Francofurti, 1601.
[74] Vol. ii. p. 183. Edit. Paris, 1840; Chron. of Evesham, p. 85. Rolls Edit.
[75] Ad ann. 1057, vol. i. p. 103. Rolls Edit.
[76] Scrip. Rer. Angl. ad ann. 13 Eadw. Conf. p. 366.

And John of Oxenedes, who uses the same words, adds, *et laude.*[77] Richard of Cirencester names her *ancilla Christi devotissima.*[78] And Henry de Knyghton, *Beatæ Mariæ cultrix.*[79]

Indeed, her·"memory is like the composition of a sweet perfume made by the art of a perfumer. Her remembrance shall be sweet as honey in every mouth, and as music at a banquet of wine."[80] Most appropriately may those words of the Royal Psalmist be applied to her, *Zelus Domus tuæ comedit me,* for her life was in accordance with them. Truly was she the Godgifu, the Good Gift, as Aelred says, "who most magnificently put into execution the signification of her name, for it is translated as the Good Gift, either because God brought her into existence as a Good Gift to be of advantage to His Church, or that she continually offered to God a most acceptable gift of faith and devotion."[81] Happy, thrice happy, was Leofric to have such a wife—"happy is the husband of a good wife, for the number of his years is double" —happy Godgifu, to be united to a husband whose privilege it was when kneeling by the side of Eadward, his sainted sovereign, to see visibly Christ our Lord.

> In this abbey (Westminster)
>
> . . . .
> One day it chanced that King Eadward
> Heard Mass; on the other side
> Earl Leofric in this monastery
> Heard Mass at this altar.
> This earl was of good life,
> Of great honour and lordliness,
> Founder of several monasteries,
> As were his ancestors ;
> And Godiva, the countess,
> His wife, who there heard Mass.
> Well agreed they with the behaviour
> Of King Eadward, who was there before.
> In deep devotion were they,
> In tears and in prayers ;
> The King prayed intently
> For his kingdom and for his people,
> And that he might so reign in this life
> That in the other he perish not.

[77] Chron. p. 28. Rolls Edit.
[78] Spec. Hist. de Gestis Regum Angliæ, iv. c. 26, vol. ii, p. 267. Rolls Edit.
[79] Ap. Twisden, p. 2334.
[80] Ecclus. xlix.
[81] Vita S. Eadwardi Regis, vol. 195, col. 760. Edit. Migne.

c

When the chaplain raised
The Body of God between his hands,
Lo! a very beauteous Child
Pure, bright, and like a spirit,
Appeared to King Edward.
The earl looks on his side,
And his heart well understands
That this is Almighty Jesus,
The heavenly King of all kings ;
Now that his right hand has raised
The Child, the King vows to Him,
Begs for medicine for his sins ;
To the King He gives His blessing,
*And this same vision
The earl sees,* and to the King
He turned ; he says, "Quiet thee,
Thou seest, it seems to me, what I see ;
This is Jesus in Whom I believe."
The King to Jesus bows and prays ;
With joy of spirit weeps,
Ceases not tenderly to weep,
As long as lasted the Mass.
  After the Mass, says the King—
"Leofric, friend, this secret,
As a loyal knight and earl,
I pray you relate not to man ;
For you will not be believed,
Or will be considered foolish.
Let it not be known in my life,
That it appear no hypocrisy ;
Since it is better to follow the example
Of our Lord, Who commanded silence
To the three who came to the Mount
Tabor with Him, and had the sight,
Peter and his two companions,
Of the Transfiguration."
  Then went the earl to Worcester,
To a holy man who was monk and priest,
And related to him the vision
In secret confession,
And prayed him to put it in writing,
In order to keep it in remembrance,
That at any time it may be known
By the letter which would be read ;
And he said, "So be it after my days,
When you shall be assured of my death ;
I give you assurance of the circumstance
That you may conceal it as I have done."
He answered that he might be confident
That through him it should never be discovered.
All this adventure he wrote,
The writing placed in a chest,
Which was in a holy and safe place ;
Then a long time, after the days
Of King Eadward and the earl,
As history relates it,
The chest opens of itself,
And the secret was made known.[88]

Aelred says of Leofric : *Hic a latere regis,
paululum tamen semotus, astabat, dignus per omnia*

[88] La Estoire de Seint Aedwarde le Rei, lines 2514—2597. Rolls Edit.

qui tanti talisque miraculi conscius et testis existeret.[83]
These words have much significance in reference
to a miracle of the Blessed Sacrament, and bear
full testimony to the great sanctity of the Earl of
Mercia. In the sixth century, St. Gregory of
Tours describes a miracle of the Blessed Sacrament,
which took place at the moment when the deacon
was bearing the ciborium in his hands. Out of
the people assembled, but four saw It; a priest
and three women, one of whom was the mother of
St. Gregory. *Aderam fateor,* continues the Saint,
*et ego, tunc temporibus, huic festivitati, sed hæc
videre non merui.*[84]

In the Sarum Breviary there is a prayer in
which reference is made to this miracle.

*Deus qui unigenitum Filium tuum Dominum
nostrum Jesum Christum glorioso Regi Eduardo in
forma visibili demonstrasti; tribue quæsumus, ut
ejus meritis et precibus ad æternam ipsius Domini
nostri Jesu Christi visionem pertingere mereamur.
Qui, &c.*[85]

The date of the marriage of Leofric with
Godgifu is not given; it took place, probably,
between 1005 and 1010, for their only son Ælfgar
appears as a witness to a charter of Cnut in 1032.[86]
Brought up, as he had been, in times of wars,
turbulence, and pillage, it would appear, that, in
his early years, Leofric had not always proved
himself a devout son of Holy Church; witness
his assisting his own nephew Æthelwine to
upset the will of his father, and thereby to
obtain possession of Salewarp, which Godwine
had restored to Worcester;[87] and his support to
Earngate, the son of Grim, against Wulstan,
Bishop of Worcester.[88] But the sad fate of
Æthelwine in 1014, and the untimely deaths of
the children of Earngate, the son of Grim, would
not have been without effect on the mind of
Leofric; they were probably the turning-point of

[83] Vit. St. Eadwardi, vol. 195, col. 760. Edit. Migne.
[84] De Miraculis, lib. 1, c. 86, vol. 71, col. 781. Edit. Migne.
[85] Acta SS. 1, p. 302.
[86] Cod. Diplom. Ævi. Sax. iv. p. 4. Ch. dccxlviii.
[87] Heming Chartular, Eccl. Wigorniensis. Edit. Hearne. Oxon. 1723, p. 259.
[88] *Ibid.* pp. 260, 261.

his life, and may have been the means used by God to develope the inherent piety of the truly noble Earl of Mercia.

Indeed all the old historians bear testimony to the piety of Leofric, and his munificence in whatever would promote the greater glory of God. I have only alluded to these acts of his younger days, in order that his real character may be more strongly brought out, and the sincerity of his repentance more manifest. No evidence more conclusive of his virtuous disposition can be adduced than the fact that he, the noblest of the great Earls of the nation, should have remained the loyal subject and faithful adviser of Cnut, who shortly after attaining the crown of England had caused Leofric's brother, the Duke Northman, to be executed, and, according to the general recorded opinion, without cause. What a glorious example of a mind wholly in accordance with the divine precepts of the Gospel.

Shortly afterwards he became on intimate terms of friendship with Æfic, a monk of Evesham, subsequently prior, and then named dean of Christianity for the vale of Evesham. Æfic was much beloved and respected by Cnut and the leading men of the land, on account of his sanctity. He was brother to Wlsi or Wulsi, the holy hermit; and, according to Ingulph, he was related to Leofric.[89] By Æfic's exhortations, continues the chronicler, the Earl Leofric and the Countess Godgifu—for he was their confessor—(*eo quod pater erat suarum confessionum*) most prudently despising the world in many things, and diligently devoting themselves to alms and prayers, built in a glorious manner the Abbey of Coventry, and many other churches, for the love of God, and enriched them with lands, and possessions, and most magnificent ornaments.[90]

Coventry or Conventria[91] was a vill so named because a convent, of which St. Osburga formerly was abbess, had existed there; it appears to have been burnt down when Eadric ravaged the

[89] Rer. Angl. Scriptores, p. 892.
[90] Chron. Abb. de Evesham, p. 83. Rolls Edit.
[91] Camden Britannia, ii. p. 330. Lond. 1789.

country. This place, or township, described in
the Latin charters[92] as *villa*, and *lǎnd* in Saxon
ones, had become the property of Leofric.
Whether from old associations, or from the
beauties of the locality, he choose the site of the
ruined convent for the magnificent abbey which
he and his wife had determined to found. Ingulph,
however, if credence may be given to him,
ascribes this pious resolution to the instigation of
Godgifu.[93]

Their project once formed, the munificent
founders lost no time in carrying it into execution.
The pious Countess Godgifu, says Orderic Vitalis,
whose evidence is worthy of belief, gave to the
church of the monastery all her treasures, and
sending for goldsmiths, devoutly distributed all
the gold and silver that she possessed to make
the sacred books and Gospels, and crosses, and
images of the saints, and other marvellous church
ornaments.[94] In a word, for the love of God and
the service of the Church, she, literally, *denuded
herself* of all her personal property.

Unfortunately, no precise date exists as to
when the erection of the church and monastery
commenced. Æfic, the noble dean,[95] died in
1037, according to the Saxon chronicle, but that
of Evesham puts his death in 1038;[96] consequently
he did not live to see the completion of the
magnificent work which he had suggested. He
was buried at Evesham in the new Church of the
Holy Trinity, which Leofric and Godgifu had
built, and in the presence of Lady Godgifu, who
had gone thither to pay the last tribute of regard
to her venerated spiritual father, "who whilst he
lived, ever bore her in memory."[97] But Ægelnoth,
surnamed the Good, Archbishop of Canterbury,
on his return from Rome in 1024, whither he had
gone for the *pallium*, passed through Pavia,
where he bought the arm of St. Augustine for a

[92] Compare Charter dcclxvi. in the Cod. Dipl. Ævi. Sax. iv. p. 73.
[93] Ut supra, p. 822.
[94] Edit. Paris, 1840, xi. p. 183.
[95] So called in the Sax. Chron. ad ann. 1037.
[96] Chron. Abb. de Evesham, 83.
[97] *Ibid.* p. 84.

hundred talents of silver and one of gold ; and, out of his love for Leofric, he gave this precious relic to the church of Coventry. Ægelnoth died on the 29th of October, 1038 ;[98] but the Peterborough chronicle records the gift of the arm of St. Augustine under the year 1024.[99] Hence it is probable that the church and monastery had already been begun. There can be no doubt that the erection and decoration of such a pile of buildings must have occupied many years. Fourteen years were consumed in. building Westminster Abbey, under the eyes of the King, and in the capital of the nation, where the services of skilful workmen, cunning in their various crafts, could readily be commanded ; whereas goldsmiths, and it may equally be presumed, masons, and sculptors, and carpenters had to be sent for to Coventry. The church was solemnly dedicated on the 4th of the Nones of October, 1043.

The charter of Leofric[100] endows the monastery with twenty-four *vills* situated in seven different counties, and half of the vill of Coventry, for the support of an abbot and twenty-four monks. He gives them sac and sôc, toll and teâm, and liberty, and all the customs everywhere as he had ever held them of St. Eadward, whose name, with many others, appears as a witness.

St. Eadward also gave a charter[101] confirming the above, and freeing the property of the church from all taxes, including the usual Saxon *trinoda necessitas,* and all payments of any kind to the King, his lieutenant, the bishop, or any other person, and to make it more stringent, he incorporated the confirmatory bull of Alexander the Third (Benedict the Ninth.)[102]

[98] Godwin de Præsulibus Angliæ, p. 55.
[99] Chron. Angliæ Petroburgense. Edit. Giles, Lond. 1845.
[100] Ch. dccccxxxix. Cod. Dip. Ævi. Sax. vol. iv. p. 73.
[101] Ch. dccccxvi. *Ibid.* vol. iv. p. 253.
[102] These charters are perfectly genuine, but the name of Pope Alexander is introduced. He reigned from 1061 to 1073, consequently it is evident that they are copies of the original ones, and made by some scribe in the time of Alexander the Third. It was by no means unusual in those days, for safety's sake, to have double and even triple copies made. I have followed the authority of the Propylæum of Papebrochius in the Acta SS. in regard of Benedict the Ninth.

Never before had so splendid a church been raised in England; it contained every ornament and decoration wrought by the art of man that boundless wealth, spent with lavish and pious hands, could supply. It was so enriched with gold and silver, that the very walls seemed too confined to contain the treasures. William of Malmesbury adds, that the eyes of the beholders were dazzled, as though what they saw was not a reality, but something supernatural.[103] The beams supporting the shrines were covered with a sheathing of precious metals; and in the time of William Rufus, Robert de Limesey, Bishop of Chester, whose avarice induced him to transfer his see to Coventry, in 1094, stripped off from one beam alone as much silver as was valued at 500 marks.

There cannot be the slightest doubt that the "devout client of Marye," Lady Godgifu, took especial care that the great image of our Blessed Ladye should not be the most insignificant object in the abbey church. No description of it remains, but by analogy, as will be seen under Ely, Evesham, and Lincoln, in this series, it must have been fully in accordance with the munificence of Godgifu, who had "denuded herself" of all her treasure for the making of the sacred images.

At his own vill of Bromley, in the shire of Stafford, on the 11th of the kalends of October (September 30), 1057, where the venerable Earl Leofric, whom the chroniclers describe as having attained a good old age, was then residing,[104]

> came
> death the bitter,
> and so dear a one seized;

and it may fervently be trusted that,

> This noble from earth
> Angels carried,
> steadfast soul,
> into heaven's light.

Where should the Venerable Earl of the Mercians, as the charter of St. Eadward calls him,[106] more

---

[103] Gest. Pont. Ang. p. 309. Rolls Edit.

[104] Sax. Chron. ad ann. 1057. Rolls. Edit. And the other chroniclers, ad ann. 1057.

[106] Ch. dccccxvi. Cod. Dip. Ævi. Sax. vol. iv. p. 253.

deservedly repose, in expectation of the day of
doom, than in his beloved monastery at Coventry?
He was buried beneath one of the porches of the
church.[106] I cannot refrain from quoting the words
of Aelred, which form a monument worthy of his
memory :

"Cum omni reverentiâ spiritusque dulcedine
nominandus, Comes Leofricus, cujus memoria in
benedictione est, cum uxore Godgiva, interpreta-
tionem sui nominis magnifice rerum executione
complente. . . . Cum tali ergo sui lateris sociâ
Comes Sanctissimus, in Dei opere semper intentus,
multorum cœnobiorum fundator existit, et sobrie,
et juste, et pie, in omnibus vivens, possessionum
suarum et thesaurorum Christum fecit Hæredem."[107]

His peerless wife Godgifu survived her pious
husband. She outlived their high-spirited son
Ælfgar, who had succeeded to his father's earldom
of Mercia, and died in 1063.[108] She lived to see her
grandsons, Eadwine become Earl of the Mercians,
and Morkere Earl of the Northumbrians. She
saw the Normans invade—

> The dear realm
> Of Engle land,

and one of her granddaughters, Ealdgyth, already
the widow of Gruffudd, King of North Wales,
become again a widow, when her second husband,
the gallant Harold, the last of our Saxon kings,
fell at Hastings. It is not known where Godgifu
passed the latter years of her life ; probably with
Ealdgyth, the widowed queen of Gruffudd and of
Harold, at Chester,[109] or in retirement at Coventry.
But before the Survey in 1084—1086,[110] she had

> sent her steadfast
> soul to Christ,
> in God's protection,
> spirit holy.

She possessed a rich chaplet of precious gems
which she had strung on a cord, and on which she

---

[106] W. Malms. De Gest. Pont. Angl. c. iv. p. 311. Rolls Edit.

[107] Vit. S. Eadw. vol. 195. col. 760. Edit. Migne.

[108] Sax. Chron. ad ann. 1057.

[109] Eadwine and Morkere, on hearing of the death of Harold, came up to London
and sent their sister to Chester (Flor. of Worcester, ad ann. 1066).

[110] Domesday, pp. 231b, 239b, 280b.

used to repeat her prayers. On her death-bed, she desired that this chaplet should be hung round the neck of our Ladye of Coventry, whom she had so dearly loved. It was valued at one hundred marks.[111]

She was buried in the other porch of the church of Coventry, and not far from the image of our Ladye, to whom her dying thoughts and affections had been given.[112] It does not require any stretch of the imagination to believe that the death-song of the pious Godgifu was the hymn of St. Ambrose—

> Maria Mater gratiæ
> Mater misericordiæ,
> Ab hoste tu nos protege
> Et mortis hora suscipe.

Sad is it to think that, of the magnificent abbey church of Coventry founded by Leofric and Godgifu—once the glory of England—not one stone now remains. About the year 1670, the oundations were dug up, and the site was turned into a bowling alley; and afterwards into a garden, as it was about 1718. The new Cathedral of Lichfield, which was raised by Roger de Clinton in 1140, is supposed to have been built on the model of Coventry, as erected by Leofric and Godgifu.

NOTE.—The memories of the Earl Leofric and the Countess Godgifu, commonly known as Lady Godiva, are perpetuated, even to our day, by a procession held periodically at Coventry, in commemoration of a fable which is, simply, a disgrace to English history. If Lady Godiva had ever ridden through Coventry as she is said to have done, mention of so remarkable an event would most certainly have been made by some of the many early writers, but they are all silent on the subject. The Saxon chronicler, Ingulph, who knew her, Orderic Vitalis, almost a contemporary, Henry of Huntingdon, Simeon of Durham, the Chronicle of Mailros, Florence of Worcester, and William of Malmesbury, say nothing of it; whilst

---

[111] W. Malms. ut supra loc. cit.   [112] *Ibid.*

the latter, when describing the monastery of Coventry, would not have omitted to record the ride, if it had taken place.

The fable is first mentioned by Roger of Wendover, who flourished in the first half of the thirteenth century. According to him, the people of Coventry were to be assembled in the market-place to behold Lady Godgifu ride through the midst of them, in a state of nudity, which she did, attended by two soldiers! She had luxuriant tresses of hair, which she unloosened, and thus formed a mantle which completely covered her body. Roger of Wendover adds that she was seen by no one.[113] Matthew of Westminster, who wrote his history about fifty years later, mentions the fable. His work is a copy of Roger Hoveden, who wrote about 1204, and says nothing of it, consequently Matthew of Westminster must have taken it from Roger of Wendover. In his version, which differs very little from that of Wendover, he seems to hint that Lady Godgifu was supernaturally shrouded from mortal eyes, for he says that she, having ridden through the assembled multitude *a nemine visa, ad virum gaudens, hoc pro miraculo habentem reversa est.* And by recording that the people of Coventry had assembled to see Lady Godiva take her ride, Matthew of Westminster equally, and most satisfactorily, disposes of the legendary " Peeping Tom, the tailor of Coventry."[114] But Rapin mentions him.[115]

Ralph Higden,[116] the monk of Chester, who died in 1363, Henry de Knyghton,[117] and John of Brompton,[118] who were later writers, mention the ride, on the authority, no doubt, of Roger of Wendover, and Matthew of Westminster. But John of Brompton had the wisdom not to pledge himself to the authenticity of the story;

[113] Flores Historiarum. Edit. Coxe, London, 1841, p. 497.
[114] Flores Historiarum per M. Westmonasteriensem collecti. Francofurti 1601. Ad ann. 1057, pp. 216, 217.
[115] Hist. d'Angleterre, vol. i. p. 452. Edit. La Haye, 1749.
[116] Polychronicon Rad. Higden apud Gale, p. 282, ad ann. 1057.
[117] Hen. de Knyghton de Eventibus Angliæ apud Twisden, col. 2334.
[118] Chron. Joan de Brompton apud Twisden, col. 949.

he openly says, "de dictâ Comitissâ Godivâ *legitur*."

In an account of payments in the fifth of Richard the Second, 1381—1382, the altar of our Blessed Ladye in Coventry Church occurs, with a lamp burning night and day before it.[119]

2. There was also an image of our Blessed Ladye in the Tower at Coventry, to which offerings were made.

In the King's Book of Expenses, August 31 1511: The King's offering at our Ladye in the tower there, . . . sum not given.[120]

COVERHAM, YORKSHIRE.

Offerings were made to our Ladye of Coverham. In the Middleham Household Book of Richard the Third is this entry, but without date: "xv*s.* for my Lord Prince offering to our Ladye of Gervaulx, Coverham, and Wynsladale."[121]

CROME.

Offerings were made to our Ladye of Crome. February 10, 1519:

"For my lord's (Henry of Courtenay, Earl of Devon) offering to our Ladye of Crome, 4 *d.*[122]

CROWNTHORPE, NORFOLK.

There was a constant light in the church before the image of our Blessed Ladye.[123]

CROYLAND.

Berhtuulf of Mercia, in his grant to the Abbey of Croyland, dated Friday, March 27, 851, thus describes this venerable spot: "Hæc est hæreditas Dei, dos æcclesiæ Christi, solum Sanctæ Mariæ."[124]

Richard Barderey, Abbot of Croyland, who died in 1247, gave a hundred shillings a year from the fee of his church at Whaplode, so find a light perpetually burning before the altar of our Blessed Ladye.[125]

---

[119] Mon. Angl. iii. p. 188.
[120] Letters and Papers, &c. Henry VIII. vol. ii. pt. ii. p. 1452.
[121] Harl. MSS. 433, f. 118.
[122] Letters and Papers, &c. Henry VIII. vol. iii. pt. i. p. 51, n. 152.
[123] Blomefield, i. 650.
[124] Codex Diplom. Ævi Sax. ii. p. 41, Ch. cclxv.
[125] Mon. Angl. ii. p. 102.

DONCASTER.

In the church of the Carmelites, who were established here in 1350, was the celebrated image of our Lady in the White Friars, sometimes called Our Ladye of Doncaster. Frequent offerings were made here.

In the Expenses of Henry the Eighth :

"1517, April. Sir Geoff. Wren, clerk of the closet, for a taper of wax burning before Our Ladye of Doncaster four years, 4 *l.*"[126]

The Earl of Northumberland used yearly to burn candles here.

The Northumberland Household Book has the following entry :

"Item. My lord useth and accustomyth to paye yerly for the fyndynge of a light of wax to birne befor our Ladye in the Whit-Frers of my lordis foundation at every Mastyme daily throwout the yere sett before our said Ladye there. To be paid to the prior of the said hous for the hole yere for fyndynge of the said light. To be paid ounes a yere, xiii *s.* iiii *d.*"[127]

Our Ladye of Doncaster is mentioned in a letter of Roger Townsend to Lord Cromwell.

DOVER.

Our Ladye of Pitye.

A little to the east of Ardcliffe fort, along the shore, according to tradition, formerly stood a small chapel built by a foreign nobleman, who during a storm was wrecked, and cast ashore at Dover. In gratitude for his preservation, and in accordance with the religious custom of those days, he erected the chapel which was dedicated to the Blessed Virgin, and called Our Ladye of Pitye. At the dissolution of the monasteries, this also shared their fate, and not a stone remains to tell of its whereabouts. In 1576, at which time it formed the hut of a fisherman, one of those fearful gales that sometimes visit the Channel swept away all the remaining vestiges.[128]

In the Expenses of Elizabeth of York :

"1502, March 24. Offering to Our Ladye of Dover, xx *d.*"[129]

[126] Letters and Papers &c. Henry VIII. vol. ii. pt. ii. p. 1474.   [127] P. 338. Edit. 1827   [128] Dover Guide, printed at the *Chronicle* office.   [129] Privy Expenses, p. 4.

Query. Was this shrine the same as that of our Ladye in the Rock?

Henry the Eighth landed at Dover, coming from Calais, on the 14th November, 1532. In the Privy Purse Expenses is the following entry:

" 1532, November. Itm. the xiiii. daye paied to the King's own hands for his offering to our Ladye in the Rocke at Dover, iiii *s.* viii *d.*"[180]

DURHAM.

1. Our Ladye of Pitye, in the Galilee. "On the north syde of the saide Galliley was an alter called the Ladye of Pitties Alter, with her pictur carryinge our Saviour on hir knee as He was taiken from the Crosse, a very dolorouse aspecte." The Ladye-Mass was always said at this altar.[181]

2. Our Ladye of Boulton.

In the south alley of the lantern stood the altar of Our Ladye of Boulton. It was the second of the three altars. "Over the which altar was a merveylous lyvely and bewtifull immage of the picture of our Ladie, so called the *Lady of Boultone*, which picture was made to open with gimmers (two leaves) from her breastes downwards. And within the said immage was wroughte and pictured the immage of our Saviour, merveylouse finelie gilted, houldinge uppe his handes, and holding betwixt his handes a fair large CRUCIFIX OF CHRIST, all of gold, the which crucifix was to taiken fourthe every Good Fridaie, and every man (another MS. says, moncke) did crepe unto it that was in the church at that day. And ther after yt was houng upe againe within the said immage. And every principall daie the said immage was opened that every man might se pictured within her the Father, the Sone, and the Holy Ghost, most curiouslye and fynely gilted. And both the sides within her (were) verie fynely vernyshed with grene vernishe and flowers of goulde, which was a goodly sighte for all the behoulders therof. And upon the stone that she did stand on, in under, was drawen a faire crosse upon a scutchon, cauled the Neivells' cross, the

[180] Privy Purse Expenses of Henry VIII. p. 273.
[181] Monastical Church of Durham, Surtees Society, p. 38.

which should signyfye that the Neivells hath borne the charges of ytt." [133]

ELTHAM.

Mention occurs of an image of our Blessed Ladye which had been taken at sea, and brought hither in 1376.

Issue Rolls of the Exchequer:

"50 Edward the Third, February 5.

"In money paid by the hands of Robert Sybthorpe, one of the Chamberlains of the Exchequer, for the carriage and safely conducting an image of the Holy Marye, lately taken by John de Ryngborne, in a certain ship upon the sea, from Westminster to the King's manor at Eltham, delivered to the Lord the King, by direction of the Treasurer and Chamberlains of the Exchequer, 6 *s.* 8 *d.*"[133]

ELY.

After the Norman invasion, Hereward, with a small body of Saxons, fortified the island of Ely, and held out against the invaders. Irritated at their stubborn resistance, William the Norman caused all the property of the monks without the island to be sequestrated and divided amongst his needy followers. Whereupon the monks, consulting together, made their submission to William, at Warwick, and undertook to pay a fine of one thousand marks for the restitution of their lands and liberties. To raise this money, they were obliged to take all the gold and silver plate and ornaments of the church, together with the magnificent image of our Blessed Ladye, seated in a throne, with her Divine Son in her arms, which had been wrought in a marvellous manner, in silver and in gold. The image had been placed in the cathedral by Elsi, the second abbot, who died in 1016 or 1017.[134] Probably it stood in the south side, which had been consecrated to our Blessed Ladye in the time of Brithnoth, the first abbot, who died in 981, after ruling the monastery for eleven years.

Cnut was a devoted client of our Blessed Ladye, as is shown by his rich donations to Our Lady of Chartres, during the lifetime of St. Fulbert,

---

[133] Monastical Church of Durham, Surtees Society, p. 26.
[133] Pell Records 201.   [134] Anglia Sacra. i. p. 610.

who was Bishop of Chartres, and an intimate friend of the King of England. Fulbert had a constant desire to do honour to the Blessed Virgin. He extolled her, says William of Malmesbury, in musical modulations, and one may in some degree imagine with what an intense desire he was animated in his veneration of our Ladye by listening to those canticles of his composition, in which the music seems to swell with sounds that are echoes of prayers in heaven.

Cnut was proceeding up the river to celebrate the festival of our Ladye's Purification at Ely, where the beautiful seated image of our Blessed Lady had lately been placed in the church by Abbot Elsi. The voices of the monks so sweetly singing our Ladye's praises were wafted across the water, and, in the heartfelt joy which he experienced, the King burst forth into the well known Anglo-Saxon ballad—

> Merrie sungen the muneches binnen Ely
> Tha Cnut ching reu ther by
> Roweth Cnites noer the land
> And here we thes muneches saeng.

EMMETH, NORFOLK.

1. Our Blessed Ladye.
2. Our Ladye of Pity.

In this church was the chantry of the Blessed Virgin Marye, founded by Sir Adam de Hakebeach, and also the lights and images of our Blessed Ladye, Our Ladye of Pity, and St. Edmund."[135]

EPWORTH, LINCOLN.

In the chapel of Our Blessed Ladye in the Wood, in the Isle of Axholme, there was the Indulgence of Portiuncula, granted by Boniface the Eighth, by a brief dated Rome, the kalends of June, in the eighth year of our Pontificate, 1302. This chapel was, subsequently, incorporated with the Priory of the Visitation, founded in the nineteenth of Richard the Second, by Thomas Mowbray, Earl of Nottingham, Earl Marshall, and subsequently Duke of Norfolk, K.G., who dedicated it to our Blessed Ladye, St. John the Evangelist, and St. Edward the Confessor.[136]

[135] General History of Norfolk, p. 486.   [136] Mon. Angl. vi. p. 25.

2. Our Ladye of Pity.

William Marquess Berkeley founded a perpetual chantry for his soul, at the altar of Our Ladye of Pity, and endowed it with lands to the value of ten marks, by his will dated February 5, 1491.[137]

ETON.

In the Expenses of Elizabeth of York :
" 1502, March 24.
" Offering to Our Lady of Eton, xx *d.*"[138]
In the accounts of the Duke of Buckingham :
" 1521, April 14.
" To Our Ladye of Eyton, near Windsor, 6 *s.* 8 *d.*"[139]

EVESHAM, formerly EOVESHAM.

This was a renowned sanctuary of our Blessed Ladye. Its name perpetuates the vision of our Blessed Ladye to a poor herdsman called Eoves.

One of the great saints of the Anglo-Saxon Church was Ecgwin, who was appointed Bishop of Worcester in 692. The chronicler calls him the father of the orphans, the supporter of widows, the just judge of the oppressed, and consoler of the desolate, whence he became dear to God and to men. A few years later he became the victim to popular outcry and detraction ; he was driven from his see, and his calumniators sent accusations against him to the King, and to Rome. In 700 he went to the Eternal City, to defend himself ; but, before leaving England, he bound his feet in iron fetters, and fastened them with a lock, and threw the key into the Avon. He made his pilgrimage to Rome in chains, and straightway on his arrival he cast himself at the tomb of the Apostles, where he made a long watch in tears and fervent prayer. In the meanwhile, his attendants went in quest of food ; they passed a fish stall, and bought a fish which had just been taken in the Tiber. Lo ! on cleansing it, they found in its belly the key of Ecgwin's chains which he had cast into the Avon. The fame of this miracle

---

[137] Test. Vetust. 407.　　[138] Privy Expenses, &c. p. 3.
[139] Letters and Papers, &c. Henry VIII. vol. iii. pt. i. p. 501, n. 1285.

soon spread through the city; Ecgwin, who had been considered a vile and contemptible man, was now proved to be holy and venerable.[140] He was most graciously received by Pope Constantine; the calumnies were disproved, and he returned to England, where he was reinstated in his see, and taken into new favour by King Æthelred.[141]

The spot where Ecgwin had cast the key into the Avon, was called Hethomme; and very naturally, after the miracle, he desired to obtain possession of it. The account cannot be given better than in Ecgwin's own words, which are recorded in the foundation charter, dictated by himself.[142]

" In the name of the Saviour Christ our Lord. I, Ecgwin the humble Bishop of the Wicci, wish in this charter to make manifest how I first, by the inspiration of the Holy Ghost, chose this spot, and built the monastery in Homme (Hethomme) in honour of Almighty God and the Blessed Virgin Marye. To be brief in my narration, it happened, at one time, that I was frequently favoured with visions. Wherefore, by the inspiration of the Holy Ghost, I conceived an ardent desire in my mind, if God would prosper my longings, to build a place to the praise of our Lord and the Blessed Virgin Marye, and all the elect of God, as well as for my own eternal reward, before I departed from this mutable life. After my return, therefore, from Rome, where I found in the belly of the fish the key which I had thrown into the river at Hethomme, considering this to be a holy spot, I wished for it; and as I was living in the reign of Æthelred, King of the Mercians, I besought him that he would be pleased to bestow Hethomme upon me. Willingly did he grant my request, for he was a friend of God, and zealous for the salvation of his own soul. In this place the Blessed Virgin Marye had appeared to a herdsman by name Eoves (in consequence of his sanctity I have named it Eoves-ham), and he related the vision to me. Immediately, therefore, after fasting and prayer, I went barefoot to visit the spot, taking with me,

[140] Chron. Abb. de Eves. p. 7, Rolls Edit.   [141] *Ibid.* p. 8.   [142] *Ibid.* p. 9.

D

sinner as I am, three companions; and I was privileged to see manifestly the glorious Virgin, who when she had blessed me with a golden cross which she carried in her hand, disappeared. It thus being evident that the spot was favourable for my intention, I immediately purified it, and began the work which was designated by God."

He then enumerates the donations he received from King Æthelred, and Coenred and Offa, and many others, amounting to one hundred and twenty hides of land. He describes how he went again to Rome in the company of Coenred and Offa, and how, wishing to obtain the Apostolic confirmation of his foundation, he had accompanied them at the especial desire of Coenred. They were cordially received by Pope Constantine, to whom they stated the object of their visit. The next words must be given in the original—

"Audivimus optata dignationis ejus responsa, et ex condicto quæ disposueramus vota et dona Deo sub testimonio tantæ dignitatis offerentes, donavimus Deo et Sanctis Apostolis ejus et ecclesiæ Romanæ, sub manu et dispositione Romanæ papæ, cœnobium Eoveshamense quod extruxeramus multis possessionibus ampliatum : totumque liberum coram Deo et Sanctis Apostolis Ejus, et coram Summo Christianitatis pontifice, ipsum locum concessimus, fecimusque apostolica et regia corroborari auctoritate donationes et privilegia, quæ illi loco concesseramus."

The Pope confirmed everything by a Bull, and St. Ecgwin continues—

"Our desires being thus accomplished, and having received the Apostolic blessing, we began our journey homewards with the greatest joy. Then, shortly after our return, a Witangemote was assembled at Alcester, by Apostolic mandate, and Coenred the King made known to all what we had done at Rome, to the eternal retribution to ourselves and our successors. We greeted every one heartily, and imparted the Apostolic blessing under the seal of the Pope. The Witan joyfully confirmed it, *verbi et fidei jussione*, and Archbishop Beorhtuuald, in the name of all, drew up a description of the land of the place and its liberty. Then the Witan resolved that the Lord Bishop Wuilfrid and I should carry the privilege to Evesham. The day of our arrival there was All Hallows, and on the same day Bishop Wuilfrid and I consecrated the church which I had built to God and to St. Marye, and all the elect of God, and we laid upon the altar the charter of the cxx. hides and of the liberty of the place, and, in the presence of all assembled, thus spake we :

" ' Lord God Who dwellest in the heavens, and hast created everything, preserve him who shall give peace to and preserve this place, and this inheritance of God, and this liberty which we have offered unto God. Moreover, in the name of God Almighty, and of all the heavenly virtues, we command that neither king, nor prince, nor minister, nor man of any condition, shall make less this holy place, nor make any claim into his private power; but that this place shall continue, as we desire, for the use of the flock and the shepherds of God, and well ordained in the power of its own abbot, according to the Rule of God and of Blessed Benedict. But if any one, *quod absit*, carried away by the spirit of avarice, shall decide to turn aside this our injunction, may he be judged before the tribunal of God, and never be remembered by Christ, and may his name be erased for ever from the book of life; and may he be bound by the bonds of eternal punishment in hell, unless he makes amends in this life. But whosoever shall well preserve these things, may the Lord God and all His saints preserve him, and gladden his soul in the land of the living, and give him eternal rewards, both in this life and in the next.' " [148]

Between the years 941—946, the monks had been expelled from the abbey by Aldhelm who introduced canons. In the year 960, the church which St. Ecgwin had built fell in, but the relics of the saint were miraculously preserved. During the vicissitudes of the next fifty-six years the ruins remained undisturbed. Finally, in 1014, Godwine who had twice seized the lands, was expelled by

[148] Chron. Abb. de Eves. pp. 17—20.

the Abbot Ælfward, and fell two years later in the battle of Assandun.

Some years afterwards the noble Earl of Mercia, Leofric, and his incomparable Countess Godgifu, came forward with their usual munificence, and built a church for the abbey. "They greatly loved and honoured this abbey," says the chronicler, "and built a fine church in honour of the Holy Trinity, in which they caused to be placed a large crucifix (*crucem non modicam*) with an image of Marye the holy Mother of God, and of St. John the Evangelist, beautifully wrought of gold and silver; they also gave a green chasuble, and a smaller black cope, and many other precious ornaments."[144]

The charter of Leofric sets forth that he gives the estate (*terram*) called Heamtun to the monastery of Evesham, and to the church, which he and Godgifu his wife had built there, in honour of the Holy and Undivided Trinity, and for the good of their own souls. He also adds that Heamtun had belonged to his brother Northman, and that he himself had received it in gift from Cnut. The charter is without date, but Leofric cites as a witness Brichtegus, Bishop of Worcester, 1033—1038.[145]

If this was the abbey church, and there seems to be no reason to doubt it, from the wording of the charter, it did not stand many years; it was gradually pulled down by Abbot Walter, 1077—1086;[146] the chronicler remarking that it was one of the finest churches in England; as would naturally be the case, since Leofric and Godgifu had built it. To raise the necessary funds for the rebuilding of their church, two of the monks travelled through England with the relics of St. Ecgwin. It is to this new church that the description in the Revelation to the Monk of Evesham in 1196 applies.[147]

"Sothely there were in thys same chyrche iii. or iiii. ymagys of our blessyd lady Sent Marye hauyng in her lappys the ymage of our Sauyur

---

[144] Chron. Abb. de Eves. p. 84.
[145] Cod. Dipl. Ævi Sax. vol. iv. p. 272, ch. dccccxxxviii.
[146] Chron. Abb. de Eves. p. 55.   [147] *Ibid.* l. c.

ihesu cryste yn fourme of a lytyl babe, and they were sette at euery auter on right well peynted and feyre arayed wyth golde and diuers other colours, the whyche schewyd to the people that behylde hym grete deuocyon. And before euery ymage hynge a lampe, the whyche, after the custome of that same chyrche, were wonte to be lyghted at euery pryncypale feste thorowe alle the yere, bothe by nyghte and by daye enduryng fro the fyrst ensonge unto the second ensonge afore the forseyde ymages of oure blessed lady Seynte Marye. And alsoo thylke lampys lyghtnyd alle the chyrche abowte."[148]

According to ancient custom, the sacristan had to supply one lamp by day, and one cresset,[149] to burn from night till morn, before our Ladye's altar in the crypt. By the new regulations, one wax light and one lamp are to burn there continually, and one cresset by night, as formerly. Incense was, moreover, to be supplied daily at Mass. At the celebration of the Marye-Mass twenty-four wax lights were to burn daily. Of these the sacristan finds six, the seneschal of Evesham one, and the altar-keeper the rest. At the same Mass thirty-three lamps were to be lighted up, which lamps the altar-keeper is to supply.[150]

Thomas Marleberge, or Marlbarew, prior of Evesham, 1218—1229, bought two shops in the centre of the high street, of Richard, the son of Hugh of Warwick, and gave them to the support of the lights of our Ladye in the crypt. Whilst he was sacristan he arranged with the Chapter so that the lamps before the high altar and the altar of our Ladye in the crypt should be continually burning.[151] He also, when prior, bought of Adam Peterel a piece of land, the half of which he devoted to alms, and the other half to the lights of our Ladye in the crypt.[152]

[148] *The Revelation to the Monk of Evesham*, 1196, p. 195. Edited by Edward Arber, F.R.G.S. London, 1869.
[149] Cressets were torches fixed on poles.
[150] *History and Antiquities of the Abbey and Borough of Evesham*, p. 103. By W. Tindal, M.A. Evesham, 1794.
[151] Chron. Abb. de Eves. p. 267.
[152] *Ibid.* 270.

William Boys, abbot 1345—1367, endowed the keeper of the chapel of our Ladye in the crypt with 4*l.*, the proceeds of divers tenements acquired by him at Stowe, Donington, and other places.[153] He died on the 6th June, 1367, and was buried by Ludovic, Bishop of Hereford,[154] before the Image of the Glorious Virgin in the nave. He caused to be cast the two great bells, named Marye and Ecgwin, which were baptized by Richard, Bishop of Nazareth. They bore the following inscriptions[155]—

O pater Egwyne, tibi consono nocte dieque !   } Will.
Me fugiant digne tonitrua mala fulgura quæque}   Boys
                                EGWYN.   nos
Me sonante, pia succurre Virgo Maria !   } fieri
Ecclesiæ genti discedant fulgura venti.   } fecit.
                                MARIA.

The two greater bells, Jesus and Gloriosa, had been supplied by Adam, who was abbot 1160—1191. They were thus inscribed—

Christus vincit, Christus regnat, Christus imperat.
                                         JESUS.
Ave ! gloriosa virginum regina,
Vitis generosa, vitæ medicina.   GLORIOSA.

There was also an image of our Blessed Ladye adjoining the chapel commonly called the Charnelhous;[156] and William de Chiriton, abbot 1316—1344, built the noble abbey gate, which was crenellated, and which he adorned with stone statues of our Blessed Ladye and St. Ecgwin.

EYE,
SUFFOLK.

1. Here was an altar of our Blessed Ladye, and a gild in her honour; there was also her image painted with gold at the charge of Joan Busby. In 1473, John Yestes of Eye bequeathed to the altar of the Blessed Marye ever Virgin viii marcs.[157]

2. Our Ladye *de Populo.*
At the east end of the north chancel aisle is a small chapel, now the vestry. This is probably the chapel of Sir John Porter, who, by his will dated August 8, 1501, desires that his executors

---

[153] Chron. Abb. de Eves. p. 298.   [154] *Ibid.* 299.   [155] *Ibid.* 297.   [156] *Ibid.* 300.
[157] *Proceedings of the Suffolk Archæological Institute,* vol. ii. p. 140.

build, as they receive his debts and sell his house, a chapel in the worship of *Sancta Maria de Populo*, within the churchyard of Eye.[158]

This may have been a copy of the miraculous painting of Sancta Maria de Populo at Rome.

FAKENHAM, NORFOLK.   An image of Saint Marye de la Pity.[159]

FERNYHALGH, LANCASHIRE.

The following traditional account of Ladywell was given in 1723 by Mr. Christopher Tootell, of Fernyhalgh.

"A virtuous and wealthy merchant, in great distress upon the Irish sea, had recourse for safety to Him Whom the winds and the sea obey, and made a vow, in case he escaped the danger, to acknowledge the favour of his preservation by some remarkable work of piety. After this, the storm began to cease, and a favourable gale wafted his ship unto the coast of Lancashire, where, whilst he landed, he thankfully reflected on his merciful deliverance, and was in pain to know by what pious work his vow might be acceptably fulfilled, a miraculous voice admonished him to seek a place called Fernyhalgh, and there to build a chapel where he should find a crab-tree bearing fruit without cores, and under it a spring. In compliance with this direction, he spared no pains in travelling about and seeking for the place called Fernyhalgh; but all in vain, until at last he came to Preston, where, having taken up his lodgings late at night, the housemaid came in from milking, and excused her late return, occasioned by loss of time in seeking and following the strayed cow as far as Fernyhalgh. This accidental notice of the place he sought for revived the weary traveller, and sent him full of joy to take his rest. In the morning a guide conducted him to Fernyhalgh, where he continued his search until he found the crab tree and the spring foretold him, as also an unexpected, and, until then, undiscovered image of the Blessed Virgin Marye, which occasioned the spring to be called our Ladye's Well, and the

[158] *Proceedings of the Suffolk Archæological Institute,* vol. ii. p. 140.
[159] Index. Mon. Dioc. Norv. p. 72.

chapel he built by it to be dedicated in her name to God's honour and service, and likewise to be called Our Ladye's Chapel in Fernyhalgh. But after the suppression of chantries and chapels the chapel was pulled down. . . . Yet ancient neighbours have, and do affirm, that in their youth its platform and rubbish were sufficiently discernable in the hollow place on the west side of the footway, in the meadow adjoining to the walk above the well; and from its flourishing condition to this present day, Simpson's house and the close belonging to it have been, and are called and known by the name of the Chapel House, Chapel Wood, Meadows, Mass, &c., as it is manifest in ancient deeds, late conveyance, and common speech. Nevertheless, the ancient devotion of the neighbouring Catholics did not fail with the old chapel, but survived its ruins, and continued in their constant assemblies and praying together at the well on Sundays and Holidays, and especially on feasts of our Ladye, even in the severest times of persecution. Of these devotees, several have piously believed and thankfully acknowledged special benefit and help received, by means of their frequent visiting and constant prayer at Our Ladye's Well."

In 1684-5, a new chapel or house of prayer was built. This was principally the work of Mr. Cuthbert Hesketh, of White Hill, in Goosenargh, who for sixteen years paid the rent of the house, and in 1701 paid to Mr. Tootell, the pastor, also the fine or purchase-money for the ground on which it stood. Mr. Tootell was a near relative of Mr. Hesketh.[160]

It was at Fernyhalgh, near the chapel and Ladye Well, that the celebrated Dame Alice, otherwise Alice Harrison, opened her school, which soon was filled with children from the neighbourhood, from Preston, the Fylde, Liverpool, Manchester, London, and all other parts of England, and she reckoned from one to two hundred pupils. Every day she took the Catholic children to chapel, and always stopped to say a *Pater, Ave,* and *Credo* at Our Ladye's Well.[161]

[160] *Catholic Magazine and Review,* 1832, vol. ii., pp. 481-82.   [161] *Ibid.*

In an article in the Preston chronicle by "Atticus," quoted in the *Weekly Register* of July 23, 1870, the writer says :

"When the old chapel was originally erected at Fernyhalgh is not known; it is mentioned as far back as 1448 in a document in the Office of the Duchy of Lancaster."

FOSTON,
YORKSHIRE.

In regard to our Ladye of Foston, there exists a very remarkable piece of evidence, which shows that the bishops of the Church were ever ready then, as they are now, to repress indiscreet devotion in regard of certain localities until a searching investigation had been made.

It is a mandate of William Grenefeld, Archbishop of York, addressed to the Dean of Pickering, against undue reverence (*adoratio*) paid to the Image of the Blessed Virgin Marye in the parish church of Foston—

"William, by the divine permission Archbishop of York, Primate, to our dear son our Dean of Pykering, health, &c. . . .

"Sane nuper ad aures nostras pervenit quod ad quandam imaginem beatæ Virginis in Ecclesia parochiali de Foston noviter collocatam, magnus simplicium est concursus, ac si in eadem plus quam in aliis similibus imaginibus aliquid numinis appareret : sicque simplices ex concursu hujusmodi, in idolatriam et erroris devium de facili trahi possent ; fueruntque super imagine prædicta inter religiosos viros . . . priorem et conventum de Bridelington, et Johannam relictam Thomæ de Poyngton lites et contentiones variæ prius motæ, ac periculosi conflictus habiti, et alia mala quamplurima, quibus etiam pejora successura fore in posterum formidantur, nisi eis opportunis remediis occurrabatur.

"Volentes igitur, ut teneamur, hujusmodi tam animarum quam corporum periculosis dispendiis, quatenus possumus obviare, tibi firmiter injungimus et mandamus, quatenus tam in dicta ecclesia de Foston, quam in aliis ecclesiis collegiatis et parochialibus infra dictum decanatum ubilibet constitutis, omnibus parochianis nostris, tam clericis quam laicis, singulis diebus dominicis, et festivis, publice et in genere, auctoritate nostra inhibeas, sed facias inhiberi, ne quis de cetero pro adoratione dictæ imaginis ad præfatam ecclesiam, vel alibi, ubi eam transferri contigerit, accedat, vel ipsius imaginis prætextu, oblationes in pecunia, seu rebus aliis quibuscumque facere præsumat, donec de causis, rationibus, et motivis, ex quibus ad eandem imaginem hujusmodi habitus est concursus, inquisitionem fieri fecimus diligentem, sub pœna excommunicationis majoris, et aliis pœnis et districtionibus canonicis, quas in contrarium facientes, pro loco et tempore curabimus exercere. Valete.

" Datum apud Burton juxta Beverl. 5 id Apr., 1313."

I have as yet found no traces of the result of inquiry. Neither have I met with any bequest to our Ladye of Foston in the Yorkshire wills.

GARBOLDESHAM, NORFOLK.

William Keye, in his will dated May 1, 1531, says :

" *Itm.* I gif half an acr of Lond lying in Lopham Furlong to find yerely evermore v. Gawdyes Brennyng before our Ladye in the Chancel of St. John the Baptist ; at every antiphon of our Ladye and at every Feste of our Ladye, at Maesse of the same Feste evermore."[161]

NOTE.—Candles which were burnt in honour of the five joys of our Ladye were sometimes called *gawdys.*

GISBRO'.

William Ecopp, Rector of Heslerton, in his will dated September 6, 1472, says :

" *Item.* I will that a pilgrim, or some pilgrims, be sent immediately after my burial on pilgrimage for me to . . . Our Ladye of Walsingham . . . Our Ladye of Lincoln, Our Ladye of Doncaster, Our Ladye of Scardeburgh, Our Ladye of Gysburgh, Our Ladye of Jesmount, Our Ladye of Carlell . . . and shall offer to each iiii *d.*"[162]

To this will the learned editor, the Rev. James Raine, M.A., has appended the following note:

" I am not aware of the existence of any

[161] Blomefield, i. 182.
[162] Testamenta Eboracensia. Surtees Society, vol. iii. p. 201.

other document from which we can ascertain that some of these shrines were places of fame. This passage therefore is of singular interest."

GLASTONBURY.   This is the most ancient and venerable sanctuary of our Blessed Ladye in England. In its original form it was a little oratory built of wreathed twigs, and said, traditionally, to have been the work of St. Joseph of Arimathea. It is needless here to examine the various arguments on the question, the more especially since the Bollandists[163] and Tillemont[164] have proved that St. Joseph of Arimathea never was at Glastonbury. About two centuries later the oratory was rebuilt of stone, and a larger one added to it. The apocryphal charter of St. Patrick the elder, of the year 430,[165] which is given by William of Malmesbury, describes it as "a holy and ancient spot, chosen and sanctified by God in honour of the Immaculate Virgin Marye, Mother of God ;" and it also mentions that St. Patrick had been shown the writings of SS. Phaganus and Diruvianus, which state that the church had been divinely consecrated by our Lord Himself in honour of His Blessed Mother.

In 530, after the Synod of Victory, St. David of Menevia, accompanied by seven of his suffragans, came to Glastonbury, invited thither by the sanctity of the place. He formed, says William of Malmesbury,[166] the resolution of solemnly consecrating the ancient church there erected in honour of the Blessed Virgin Mother of our Lord. Having, therefore, provided all the things necessary for the performance of that sacred ceremony, on the night immediately preceding the intended dedication, he, as nature required, yielded to sleep, in which our Lord Jesus appeared to him, and demanded of him the reason of his coming thither. This, without hesitation, St. David declared to Him. But our Lord presently turned him from his resolution

---

[163] AA. SS. vii. p. 509 ad 17 Mart.

[164] *Memoires Ecclesiastiques*, vol. i. p. 210.

[165] De Antiq. Glaston. Eccl. p. 300. Ed. Gale. See also Todd, *St. Patrick, Apostle of Ireland*, Dublin, 1864, p. 484. note.

[166] *Ibid.* p. 299.

of dedicating the church, saying to him, "That must not be done." And taking the bishop's hand, He told him that many years ago He Himself had dedicated it to the honour of His Mother, and therefore, that this holy ceremony ought not to be profaned by any man's repeating it. And having said this, with His finger He pierced through the Bishop's hand, telling him that this should be a sign that what He Himself had already anticipated ought not to be again renewed. And, withal, He promised Him that the next day, when, in reciting the canon of the Mass, he was to pronounce those words, *Per ipsum, et cum ipso, et in ipso,* he should have restored the integrity and soundness of his hand. The terror of this vision quickly drove sleep from the Bishop's eyes, whereupon, with great earnestness, he examined whether that were indeed real which our Lord seemed to have done to him. And having found it so, he wondered at it, and expected (*i.e.,* awaited) what would be the issue. The next day all that were present with admiration saw and touched the prodigious wound. Hereupon all the preparation for the consecration came to nothing, and the miracle divinely wrought, being made known publicly to all the hearers, increased their admiration. And, in conclusion, when Mass was celebrated, the Bishop's hand was restored to its former soundness.[167]

St. David added on a chapel to the east side of the church, which he consecrated to the honour of our Blessed Ladye, and adorned the altar with a sapphire of inestimable value, which was called the Great Sapphire of Glastonbury.[168] From the description given, it would appear that this sapphire formed a *super-altare.* This precious gem was subsequently hidden for security's sake and its existence forgotten. It was discovered by the Abbot, Henry Swansey, who had it magnificently set in gold and silver, and surrounded by precious stones, "as it is now to be seen," adds William of Malmesbury.[169] Its fate is

[167] *Church History of Brittany.* By R. F. S. Cressy, O.S.B., 1668, bk. ii. c. vi. ad ann. 63.

[168] Spelman, *Concilia,* i. 19.

[169] *Ut sup.* pp. 305–6.

recorded. On the 15th May, 1539, "delyvered unto the King's maiesty a *super-altare*, garnished with silver and gilte and parte golde, called the Great Saphire of Glasconberye."[170]

Twelve years later, in 542, the good King Arthur, nephew to St. David, being mortally wounded in the battle of Camlan, was carried to Glastonbury that he might prepare himself more perfectly, under the protection of our Blessed Lady, for his departure out of this world for life eternal. In 1189 Abbot Swansey wrote his epitaph—

> Hic jacet Arthurus, Flos regum, Gloria regni
> Quem morum probitas commendat laudi perenni.

William of Malmesbury particularly notices that kings and the leading men of the land eagerly sought to be buried at Glastonbury, so that they might await the day of doom under the protection of our Blessed Ladye;[171] and he gives a list of many who were buried here.

In 708, Ine, of the West Saxons, rebuilt the monastery and the old abbey church, when he gave a charter of privileges, which he reverently laid upon the altar.[172] In 725 he gave his great charter of privileges, from which I shall only quote the commencement of the grant.

"Therefore I, Ine, relying on my royal dignity from the Lord, with the advice of Sexburga the queen and the licence of Beorhtuuald, Archbishop of Canterbury, and of all his suffragans, and also the exhortation of the *subreguli*, Baldred and Æthelhard, grant . . . to the ancient church situate on the spot called Glasteia, which the High Priest and Chief Pastor made known to Blessed David by many and unheard-of miracles, that of old He had, with the service of the Angels, consecrated to Himself and the ever Virgin Marye," &c.

This is early evidence of the popular opinion in regard to Glastonbury, and of the ancient tradition of its divine consecration. The charter, however, is marked by Kemble as doubtful.

---

[170] Mon. Angl. i. p. 65. [171] W. Malmesbury, *ut supra* 306.
[172] Cod. Dip. Ævi Sax. vol. i. p. 85, ch. lxxiii.

Ine also built the "Silver Chapel," as it is called, out of his love for God and His Mother the Blessed Virgin Marye. The value of the gifts, at our present standard, amounts to something prodigious. To the construction of the chapel he gave 2,640 lbs. of silver; 264 lbs. of gold for the altar; 10 lbs. of gold for a chalice and paten; 8 lbs. and 20 mancases of gold for a censer, or thurible; 12½ lbs. of silver for candlesticks; 20 lbs. and 60 mancases of gold for covers for the Gospels; 17 lbs. of gold for vases for the altar—*i.e.*, cruets, &c.; 8 lbs. of gold for *pelves*—*i. e.*, shallow basins;[173] 20 lbs. of silver for a holy water stoup; and 175 lbs. of silver and 38 lbs. of gold for images of our Lord and our Blessed Ladye and the Twelve Apostles.[174]

The next principal benefactor to Glastonbury was Eadgar, surnamed the Peaceable. The learned Benedictine writer, Bucelin, states,[175] that Eadgar laid his sceptre on the altar of our Blessed Ladye, and consecrated his kingdom to her; and this statement has misled many writers. I give a portion of Eadgar's great charter of Privilege, given in the year 971; and William of Malmesbury proves that the King laid his sceptre on the altar of our Blessed Ladye as an act of investiture, and in accordance with the common usage of the time.

"In the name of our Lord Jesus Christ. Although the decrees of Pontiffs and the words of priests are like unto the foundations of mountains that are fixed down by indissoluble ligatures, still it frequently occurs amidst the storms and tempests of worldly affairs that the religion of the Holy Church of God is disputed and broken by the polluted touch of reprobate men. Therefore it is that we have determined, and as a matter that is certain to be useful to succeeding generations, that those points which have been defined by salutary counsel, and by common consent, should be affirmed and corroborated by these our letters. Wherefore it seems fitting that the Church of the most Blessed Mother of God, and ever

---

[173] *Vide Journal of Royal Archæological Institute*, vol. x. p. 236, note.

[174] W. Malmesbury, *ut supra*, 311.

[175] Chronicon Benedictino-Marianum, p. 90, ad ann. 944.

Virgin Marye of Glastonbury, as it has, from ancient times, obtained the principal dignity in this our kingdom, so should it be honoured by us with some singular and especial privilege."[176]

William of Malmesbury then continues :

" When therefore, by the common consent, as has been said, of his prelates, abbots, and nobles, he determined to grant these privileges to the place aforesaid, he laid his own *lituus—i. e.,* staff or sceptre — beautifully formed of ivory, and adorned with gold, upon the altar of the holy Mother of God, and by that donation confirmed to the same holy Mother of God, and her monks, to be possessed for ever. Soon after he caused this sceptre to be cut in two in his presence, that no future abbot might give or sell it to any one, commanding one portion of it to be kept on the spot for a testimony of the aforesaid donation."

Eadgar then sent the charter to Pope John the Thirteenth.

"The Pope, kindly receiving the embassy, with the assenting voice of the Roman Council, confirmed what had already been done, by writing an apostolic injunction, ·terribly hurling on the violators of them, should any be so daring, the vengeance of a perpetual curse. This confirmation, therefore, of the aforesaid Pope, directed to the same place, King Eadgar, of worthy memory, laid upon the altar of the holy Mother of God, for a Perpetual Remembrance, commanding it to be carefully kept in future for the information of posterity."[177]

During the reign of Henry the Second the church was burnt to the ground, and he determined that it should be rebuilt by himself or his heirs more magnificently than ever, as he says in his charter. He then confirms to the aforesaid church, which is called by some the Mother of Saints, and by others the Tomb of Saints, and which, built by the very disciples of our Lord, was first of all dedicated by our Lord Himself—according to venerable ancient authority—all the privileges granted by his predecessors, William the

---

[176] Cod. Dipl. Ævi Sax. t. ii. p. 67, ch. dlxvii.
[177] De Gest. Reg. Angl. l. ii. c. viii. p. 57. ed. 1601.

First and William the Second, and Henry, his grandfather, and by the more ancient kings, Eadgar, the father of St. Eadward, and Ælfred, Centwine, Baldred, Ine, the Noble Arthur, and many other ancient kings, as well as King Cenwalh, a pagan. And these privileges he had caused to be read in his presence.[178]

Thus there is a long series of regal evidence showing the profound veneration in which the Church of Our Blessed Ladye of Glastonbury was held; and the devotion of our Catholic kings to the great Mother of God.

William of Malmesbury makes special mention of an image of our Blessed Ladye in the church. "Here," he says, "is an image of the Blessed Virgin Marye. When the great fire consumed all the altar cloths and ornaments, it neither touched the statue, nor the veil which was on its head. Nevertheless, the fire caused several blisters to rise on its face, as if on a living man, which long remained there, a proof to the beholders of the divine power."[179]

Abbot Adam de Sodbury, or Solbury, or Sobbury, 1322—1335, adorned the high altar with a large image of our Blessed Ladye, which was placed in a tabernacle of excellent workmanship.[180]

Here was also a chapel of Our Ladye of Loretto. Leland says:

"Bere coming from his Embassadrie out of *Italie*, made a chapelle of Our Ladye de *Loretta*, joining the north side of the body of the chirche."[181]

Abbot Richard Beere, who was installed on the 20th of January, 1493, built the lodgings for secular priests and the clerks of our Blessed Ladye at Glastonbury. He was sent to Italy as ambassador in the twenty-second of Henry the Seventh, 1506—1507. The chapel of Loretto was no doubt a *fac simile* of the Holy House.

---

[178] Wilkins, Concilia, t. i. p. 489.
[179] De Antiq. Glast. Eccl. 305.
[180] Joh. Glaston. Historia. Ed. Hearne, p. 263.
[181] Itin. v. iii. p. 104.

GLOUCESTER.

In 1306 John de Gamages, Abbot of Gloucester gave to the church an ivory image of our Blessed Ladye.[182]

Under the year 1136, it is recorded in the history that Walter de Lacy having come to the church very early in the morning, devoutly assisted at the Marye-Mass.[183]

GORLESTON.

Our Ladye.

About 1650, the Earl of Manchester, when commanding the associated counties for the Parliament, issued a commission under which Francis Jessope of Beccles removed from Lowestoft Church all inscriptions in brass commencing with the usual *Orate pro anima*, &c. Jessope has thus recorded his sacrilegious doings at Gorleston Church, which lies on the opposite side of the river to Great Yarmouth :

"In the chancel, as it is called, we took up twenty brazen superstitious inscriptions, *ora pro nobis*, &c., broke twelve apostles carved in wood, and cherubims, and a lamb with a cross, and took up four superstitious inscriptions in brass in the North chancel, *Jesu fili Dei miserere mei*, &c., broke in pieces the rails, and broke down twenty-two Popish pictures of angels and saints. We did deface the font and a cross on the font, and took up a brass inscription there with *Cujus animæ propitietur Deus;* and 'Pray for ye soule,' &c., in English. We took up thirteen superstitious brasses. Ordered Moses with his rod and Aaron with his mitre to be taken down. Ordered eighteen angels off the roof, and cherubims to be taken down, and nineteen pictures on the windows. The organ I brake, and we brake seven Popish pictures on the chancel window—one of Christ, another of St. Andrew, another of St. James, &c. We ordered the steps to be levelled by the parson of the town, and brake the Popish inscription, "*My Flesh is meat indeed, and My Blood is drink indeed.*" I gave orders to break in pieces the carved work, which I have seen done. There were six superstitious pictures, one crucifix, and

[182] Hist. et Cartular. Monast. S. Petri Gloucestriæ, vol. i. p. 40. Rolls Edit.
[183] *Ibid.* p. 16.

E

the Virgin Marye with the Infant Jesus in her arms, and Christ lying in a manger, and the three Kings coming to Christ with presents, and three bishops with their mitres and crosier staffs, and eighteen Jesuses written in capital letters, which we gave orders to do out. A picture of St. George, and many others which I remember not, with divers pictures in the window, which we could not reach, neither would they help us to raise ladders; so we left a warrant with a constable to do it in fourteen days. We brake down a pot of holy water, St. Andrew with his cross, and St. Catherine with her wheel, and we took down the cover of the font, and the four Evangelists, and a triangle for the Trinity, a superstitious picture of St. Peter and his keys, an eagle and a lion with wings." [184]

GRISTON, NORFOLK.

Here were four gilds, one of which was the gild of our Blessed Ladye, and there was a light called St. Marye's light. [185]

HALES OWEN, SALOP.

Sir William Lyttleton, knight, who died in December, 1507, by his will desires:
"My body to be buried before the image of the Blessed Virgin in the monastery of Hales Owen, near the place and grave where my first wife lieth." [186]

HEIGHAM POTTER, or POTTER HEIGHAM.

1. Our Ladye of Grace.
2. Our Ladye of Pity.
Here in the Church of St. Nicholas were the lights of Our Ladye of Grace, and Our Ladye of Pity. [187]

In August, 1517, Wolsey writes to the King that he proposes to · start for Walsingham on Monday next, and from thence to Our Ladye of Grace, in fulfilment of his vow. [188]

HEMINGBOROUGH, YORKSHIRE.

Was originally a parish church, and was erected · into a college by royal license, October 26, 1426, 5 Henry VI. [189]

[184] Manship, *History of Great Yarmouth*, Palmer's continuation, pp. 125-6, note.
[185] Blomfield, i. 570.   [186] Test. Vetust. p. 467.   [187] Gen. Hist. of Norfolk, p. 728.
[183] Letters and Papers, &c. Henry VIII. vol. ii. p. 1538, n. 38.
[189] Burton, Monasticon Eboracense, p. 442.

William de Hemyngburg, by his will dated October 6, 1409, and proved in January, 1410, orders his body to be laid before the image of Our Ladye of Pity.[190]

Katherine, widow of Sir John Hastings, knight, by her will dated February 25, 1506–7, bequeaths:

"To Our Ladye of Hymmyngburgh a piece of cremel and a lace of gold of Venys sett wt perl."[191]

HENLEY.

The will of John Andrew of Henley-on-Thames, in 1503, contains this bequest:

"Also I bequeath to our Ladye's coat in the chapel of Henley, a gold ring which was William Wylde's, to hang on the said coat."[192]

HEREFORD.

Leland says, "There is a suburbe without Wye Gate, and therein is a chapell of our Ladye of Alingtre *prope furcas*.[193]

Desirous of obtaining some clue to the meaning of Alingtre, I wrote to the Very Rev. Prior of St. Michael's, Hereford, Dom P. W. Raynal, O.S.B., who most obligingly sent me the following very interesting information :—

"The quotation from Leland gives us the precise locality of the chapel of our Blessed Lady, and it may be that its situation will afford some clue to its devotional uses.

"*Our Lady of Alingtre* is said to be in a suburb beyond Wye Gate, and is denoted as being *prope furcas*.

"A reference to Ducange (v. Furca) will show you that the chapel of our Blessed Lady stood near *The Gallows* (*prope furcas*).

"To this day there is a spot about half a mile from where the Wye-Bridge Gate stood, which is called *The Gallows-Tump*. The place is referred to in the *Acta SS.* October 2, n. 93 (p. 573. Edit. V. Palmé).

"The late Mr. B. Phillipps of Longworth left us a collection of valuable MSS., which contain the material for a history of Herefordshire. The latter was begun by Duncumb, but still needs

---

[190] Burton, Mon. Ebor. p. 448. [191] Test. Ebor. vol. iii. p. 275.
[192] *History of Henley*, p. 125, quoted in *Notes and Queries*, 3 ser. vol. iii. p. 137.
[193] Itin. iv. pt. ii. p. 82.

E 2

completing. Mr. Phillipps greatly increased the
value of the collection by his labours in the
pedigrees of county families, and by transcribing
many parish registers now lost.

"A London barrister named Hill first started
this collection in the seventeenth century.

"Duncumb (vol. i. p. 374) says 'Two small
chapels stood also in this suburb;' the site of
one is unknown, but that of the latter was on
the branch of the suburb which leads towards
Ross. Each had a garden, and a small bell of
the value of two shillings and eight pence.

"Hill, from whose MS. the above is taken,
adds that 'One of the chapells stood, as Silas
Taylor was informed, upon a bank on the left
hand on the east side of Blackmeston, on the
way to the Callowe.'

"This extract he gives from the MS. of Silas
Taylor, which is, I believe, amongst the Harleian
MSS.

"The above information seems to me to be
a clue to the place where our Lady of Alingtre
stood. Near *The Gallows Tump* there is a bank
which answers to the description given by the
Hereford people to Silas Taylor, and the singular
conformation of the roads indicates that at one
time some building must have stood on that
spot. In all probability, our Blessed Lady of
Alingtre was a chapel used for the immediate
preparation for death by those who were led to
execution. May be, that it was also used as a
kind of mortuary chapel.

"Silas Taylor lived in the seventeenth century, just a hundred years after the desecration
of the chapel, and his entry would lead us to
conjecture that in his time the building had
disappeared. Even its site seems to have been
known but to the old folks, as is always the
case with ancient buildings which disappear.

"One query there is which I wish to submit
to you. Is the title *Alingtre* in any way connected with the Gallows which stood hard by
the chapel?

"*Ailing Tree*, or *Tree of Pain*. There is no
place called Ailing in Herefordshire.

"It could scarcely be from a tree where the culprits sat to take a drink of *ale* before being suspended! We learn from the Gospel the very ancient practice of giving drink to those led to execution.

"P. W. RAYNAL, O.S.B."

The subject of Gallows is a curious one. It is sufficient, however, to remark that the *Rotuli Hundredorum* mention many places in the kingdom which had the right to gallows, and that they were generally at a distance from the town to which they belonged.[194]

Queen Maud, consort to Henry I., who died in 1118, built a hospital for lepers in St. Giles's, which she endowed. Here was a gild or brotherhood of our Blessed Ladye, Corpus Christi, and St. Giles. And at this hospital it became a custom to present the malefactors carried to execution at Tyburn with a great bowl of ale, to drink of it as they pleased for their last refreshment in this life.[195]

HERLING (EAST) NORFOLK.	In 1510, Robert Banham purchased of William Banham a messuage and six acres of land in East Herling, held of the manor of East Herling, by 8*d.* a year, to find a wax candle burning before the Image of the Blessed Virgin Marye in that church.[196]
HERLING (WEST).	C. 1445. William Berdewelle leaves 10*s.* to our Ladye at West Herling and 10*s.* to our Ladye in Thetford.[197]
HEVORE.	Sir John de Brunby, Knight, evidently fell in the battle of Shrewsbury. Of him nothing is known. By his will, dated June 23, and proved October 11, 1403,[198] he left four pounds of wax for four candles to burn before the Image of the Blessed Virgin Marye in the church of Hevore.

[194] *History of Bradford*, by John James; p. 51. London, 1841.
[195] Entick, *Hist. and Survey of London*, 1766, vol. i. p. 93.
[196] Blomefield i. 225.   [197] *Ibid.* i. 204.
[198] Test. Ebor. vol. i. p. 303.

HEXTILDESHAM,
or HEXHAM.

Robert Cooke, of Hextildesham, in his will, dated Friday before the feast of the Annunciation, 1396, leaves to the light of our Blessed Ladye in her church outside the abbey, 1s.[199]

HILBURY (Island),
off CHESHIRE.

Hilbré, *i.e.*, St. Hildeburga's ea, or isle.

Leland describes this island thus : " It is about a mile in cumpace, and the grounde is sandy and hath conies. There was a Celle of Monkes of Chestre, and a Pilgrimage of our Lady of Hilbiri.[200]

Here was found, not long ago, a leaden pilgrim sign of our Ladye of Roc Amadour, with the legend—

✠ SIGILLVM . DEATE . MARIE . DE . ROC . AMADOVR.[201]

HINGHAM, NORFOLK.

Our Ladye of Pity.

The church is dedicated to St. Andrew. In it there was an altar of our Blessed Ladye in the south aisle ; another altar, of her Nativity ; a chapel of our Ladye by the Rood loft, and a chapel of our Ladye of Pity.

There were eight gilds here, each having a stipendiary chaplain. " Without doubt," says Blomefield, "this church must make a fine appearance in those times."[202]

Radulph Fulloflove, Rector of West Herling, who died September 16, 1479, gave two pounds of wax to St. Marye's light at Hingham.[203]

HOCHAM, NORFOLK.

The same Radulph Fulloflove, by his will, left a legacy to the Tabernacle of our Blessed Ladye at Hocham, for prayers for Alice, his mother.[204]

HORSTEAD, NORFOLK.

Our Ladye of Pitye.

Many pilgrimages were made hither ; and legacies were occasionally left to pay pilgrims to repair to this sanctuary.[205]

HOWE ON HOO,
NORFOLK.

There was here an image of our Blessed Ladye with a light.[206]

---

[199] Test. Ebor. vol. i. p. 214.   [200] Itin. v. 52.
[201] South Meols, p. 283.   [202] Vol. i. 666, 667.
[203] *Ibid.* i. 208.   [204] *Ibid.* i. 280.   [205] Index Mon. Dioc. Norv. p. 66.
[206] *Gen. Hist. of Norfolk,* p. 92.

HULL.

1. Church of the Most Holy Trinity.

John Swan, of Kingston-on-Hull,[207] merchant, by his will, dated November 2, 1476, desires to be buried in the Church of the Holy Trinity, at Kingston-on-Hull, in the south aisle, between the choir and our Ladye the Mother of Pity.

2. St. Michael of the Carthusians. Robert Golding, by will dated September 1, 1453, desires to be buried in this church, and leaves to the Prior 4*l.* for the erection of a stained-glass window of three lights :[208] in the centre one to contain the image of our Blessed Ladye ; and as a memorial of himself, and out of his devotion, his own figure is to be represented kneeling below the feet of the image of our Ladye. He also leaves five nobles to five poor virgins, to buy five cows when they shall be married, in honour of the Blessed Virgin Marye.

IPSWICH.

There were four churches of our Blessed Ladye at Ipswich.

St. Marye at Elm,
St. Marye at Quay,
St. Marye at Stoke,
St. Marye at Tower,

each of which had doubtless an image of our Ladye and the usual light.

But the celebrated and miraculous image of our Blessed Ladye called Our Ladye of Ipswich was in St. Marye's chapel called Our Ladye of Grace, which was situated at the north-west corner of the lane without the West gate opposite to the George Inn, and which to this day goes by the name of Lady Lane. It was a great pilgrimage, and many great miracles were wrought here.

Sir Thomas More says—

"And as for the point that we spake of, concerning myracles done in our dayes at divers images, wher these pilgrimages be, yet could I tel you sōe such done so openly, so farre from all cause of suspicion, and thereto testified in suche sufficient wyse, that he might seme

[207] Test. Ebor. vol. iii. p. 225.   [208] *Ibid.* vol. ii. p. 166.

almoste madde that hyring the whole matter,
wil mistruste the miracles. Amōg which I durst
boldly tell you, for one, the wonderful work of
god, that was within these few yeres wrought, in
yᵉ house of a right worshipful knight syr Roger
wentworth, upon divers of his children, and
specially one of his doughters a very faire yong
gentlewoman of xiį. yeres of age, in meruailous
maner vexed and tormented by our ghostly enemy
the deuįll, her mind alienated and rauing with
despysyng and blasphemy of god, and hatred of
all halowed thinges, with knowledge and par-
ceiving of the halowed from the unhalowed, al
wer she nothing warned thereof. And after that
moued in her own mind and monished by the
will of god, to goo to our Lady of Ippiswitche.
In the wai of which pilgrimage, she prophesied
and tolde many thinges done and said at the
same time in other places, whiche were proued
true, and many thinges said, lying in her traunce of
such wisdome and learning, that right conning mē
highly merueiled to hyre of so yonge an vnlearned
maiden, whan her self wist not what she saide,
such things vttered and spoken, as well learned
mē might have missed with a lōg study, and
finally being brought and laide before the image
of our blessed Lady, was there in yᵉ sight of
many worshipful people so grieuously tormēted,
and in face, eyen, loke, and countenaunce so
griselye chaunged, wᵗ her mouth drawen aside,
and her eyen laid out upon her chekes, that it
was a terrible sight to behold. And after many
merueilous thinges, at yᵉ same time shewed upō
divers p̄sons by yᵉ deuil thorowe goddes suffer-
aunce, as wel al the remenaunt as the maiden
her self in the presence of all the companye
restored to theyr good state perfectly cured, and
sodeinly. And in this matter no pretext of
begging, no suspicion of faining, no possibilitie
of couterfeityng, no simplenes in the seers, her
father and mother right honorable and rich, sore
abashed, to see suche chaunces in their children,
the witnesses, great noumbre, and many of great
worshippe, wisdom, and good experience, the
maide her selfe to yonge to fayne, and the

fashion it self to straunge for any man to faine. And the ende of the matter virtuous, the virgine so moved in her minde with the miracle, that she foorth with for ought her father coulde do, forsoke the world and professed religion in a very good and godly company at the mynoresse, where she hath lived well and graciously ever sins.[209]

This was one of the great sanctuaries of our Blessed Ladye to which our forefathers used to make yearly pilgrimages. Cranmer says :

"Your owne fathers they themselfes wer greatly seduced to certeyne famouse and notoriouse ymages, as by our lady of Walsingham, oure ladye of Ippeswiche, saynt Thomas of Canterbury, sainct Anne of Buckestone, the rood of grace, and suche lyke, whom many of your parentes visitide yerely, leauinge their owne houses and familyes. To them they made vowes and pilgrimages, thinkyng that God would heare their prayers in that place rather than in another place. They kissed their feete deuoutly, and to theim they offred candles, and ymages of wax, rynges, beades, gold and sylver aboundantly."[210]

Cardinal Wolsey ordered a yearly pilgrimage to be made to Our Ladye of Ipswich.[211]

In the thirtieth of Henry the Eighth the image of Our Ladye of Ipswich was carried up to Chelsea and burnt : the rich offerings and jewels went, as a matter of course, to the King's treasury.

A curious letter of Thomas Dorset to the "right worshipful Mr. Horsewell, maior," and others, has been preserved.

". . . I toke a whery at Pawlis wharffe, wherein also was allredye a doctour, namyd doctor Crewkehorne, which was sent for to come to the byshope of Canterbury. And he before the iii bishopis of Canterbury, of Worcetre, and Salesbury, confessed that he was rapte into heven, where he see the Trinite settyng on a pall, or

---

[209] *A Dialogue concerning Heresyes and matters of Religion made in the year of our Lorde mdxxviij.* By Sir Thomas More. Book i. c. 16. Opp. : London, 1557. P. 137.

[210] *A Short Instruction into Christian Religion,* being a Catechism set forth by Archbishop Cranmer in 1548. Reprint, Oxford, 1829, p. 23.

[211] Ind. Mon. Dioc. Nor. p. 117.

mantell, or cope (call it what you pleese), of blew color, and from the middle upward they were thre bodyes, and from the midle they were closied all thre into on bodye, they were but on, havyng also but ii feete, nor but ii legges; and he spake with Our ladye, and she toke hym by the hande, and bad hym serve her as he had doon in tyme passed, and bad hym to preche aborde (abroad) that she wold be honorid at Eppiswhiche and at Willisdon as she hath bee in old tymes, *neforte;* this he said he wolde abyde bye.   Then my lord of Canterbury opposed hym nerre, and he made but weke aunswer, and was bade to departe and come agayne the second day aftre.   So did he, but at the laste he denyed his vision." [212]

ISLINGTON.   This was a celebrated image of our Blessed Ladye.   It was burnt at Chelsea in 1538.   Burnet says : "Then many rich shrines of Our Ladye of *Walsingham,* of *Ipswich,* and *Islington,* with a great many more, were brought up to London and burnt by Cromwell's orders." [213]

2. Our Ladye of the Oak.

Was the image of Our Ladye of Islington the same as Our Ladye of the Oak?

There exists an original proclamation of Henry the Eighth as follows :

"A proclamation yt no pson interrupt the King's game of partridge or pheausant.

"*Rex majori et vicecomitibus London'.*   *Vobis mandamus,* &c.

"Forasmuch as the King's most royall matie is much desirous to have the games of hare, partridge, phesaunt, and heron pserved in and about his honor att his palace of Westm. for his own disporte and pastime; that is to saye from his said palace of Westm. to *St. Gyles in the Fields,* and from thence to *Islington,* to *Or Ladye of the Oke,* to *Highgate,*" &c. [214]

IXWORTH THORPE.   The will of Golfrye Gylbert, of Ixworth Thorpe, in 1524, contains this bequest:

[212] *Letters relating to the Suppression of the Monasteries,* p. 36.

[213] *Hist. of the Reformation.* Lond. 1681, bk. iii. pt. i. 243.

[214] In the collection of original proclamations in the Library of the Society of Antiquaries, vol. i. p. 210.

" Itm. I give to the Tenement longing to our ladye's lyght in Thorpe aforesayd to the reparacōn of the sayd ten-te tenne peces of hewne tymber lyeing in my house.

" Itm. I give to the sayde lighte of Our Ladye one skeppe of bees to be delyvered to the Fermor, and he to delyver yt to the next fermor wt all the increase at hys departing."[215]

The fermor was the renter of the hives, from *ferme*, a rent ; hence the word farmer, a hirer of land.

JERVAULX.

Our Ladye of Gervaulx, mentioned under Coverham.[216]

JESMOND.

About a mile from Newcastle-on-Tyne. Here was a well called Saint Marye's Well, to which there was a great resort of pilgrims.[217]

Pilgrimages to this well, and to the chapel at Jesmond, were so frequent, that one of the principal streets in Newcastle-on-Tyne is supposed to have taken its name partly from having an inn to which the pilgrims, who flocked thither for the benefit of the holy water, used to resort. This well is said to have had as many steps down to it as there are articles in the Creed.[218]

KELLOW.

John Trollop, Esquire, of Thornley, by his will dated October 30, 1476, leaves to the light of the Blessed Virgin Marye in the church of Kellow, vi *s.* and viii *d.*, and one pound of wax.[219]

KENILWORTH.

John Beaufilz, of Balsall, in the county of Warwick, says, in 1488 :

" I . . . doe make my Testament. My body to be buried in the church of the abbey of Kenilworth before the image of the Blessed Virgin Marye in the passage to the door of the choir, or wherever Dom John Yardley, abbot of the said monastery, shall consider most expedient."[220]

[215] *Proceedings of Suffolk Arch. Inst.* vol. i. p. 105.
[216] See *ante*, p. 27.
[217] *Statistical Account of Scotland*, vol. ii. p. 381.
[218] Brand, *Hist. of Newcastle-upon-Tyne*, vol. i. p. 339.
[219] *Wills and Inventories of the Northern Counties.* Surtees Society, pt. i. p. 97.
[220] *Kenilworth Illustrated.* Chiswick, 1821, p. 10.

KESSINGLAND,
SUFFOLK.

In the church of St. Edmund, the altar of Our Ladye stood in the chancel, and over it her image, with a light burning perpetually before it.[221]

KIMBERLEY,
NORFOLK.

There was a chapel of our Blessed Ladye in the churchyard here; at the altar of this chapel was the image of our Blessed Ladye, with a lamp burning before it, and there was an endowment for a priest to say a daily Mass. It was founded before 1370, but the lands were not settled on the chantrey-priest till 1401, and then Henry the Fourth passed a licence of mortmain for the purpose.[222]

KINGSTON,
SURREY. ,

Clement Milam, of Kingston, by his will dated November 11, 1498, left :
  " To Our Lady Lyght, 1 *d.*
  " To Our Lady Lyght of Pety, 1 *d.*"[223]

KINGSWOOD.

In the accounts of the Duke of Buckingham, 1520, there is an entry :
  " The duke's oblation of 6*s.* 8*d.* to Our Ladye of Kyngeswode.
  " Lord Stafford gave 1*s.*"[224]

KIRKBY FLETHAM,
YORKSHIRE.

August 10, 1445 :
  " Richard Barton, Esquire, leaves to owre Ladye light iii *s.* iiii *d.*"[225]

KIRKBY.

Giraldus Cambrensis relates what follows, as having occurred in his day : "In the diocese of Coventry, and during the episcopate of Robert Pecthe, or Peche, in Latin, *Peccatum,* 1117—1127, some thieves came by night to the church of St. Marye, in the village of Kirkby, near the castle of Bridelawe, they broke in the door and robbed the church of a silver chalice, the books, and all the ornaments which they found of service for their own use, or rather, abuse. Lastly they went to the image of the Blessed Virgin, which was fairly adorned with gold and silver, and despoiled it of

[221] Suckling, p. 258.   [222] Blomefield, i. 748.
[223] Manning, *Hist. of Surrey,* vol. i. p. 370.
[224] Letters and Papers, &c. Henry VIII. vol. iii. pt. i. p. 500, n. 1285.
[225] Test. Ebor. ii. p. 215.

the gems and gold ornaments; and preparing to depart, they attempted to carry away the figure of the Child which was seated in His Mother's lap, whose arms were, as usual, stretched forward. Suddenly she closed her right arm round her Son, and held Him to her. This they saw by the light of a lamp which was burning outside. They fled in alarm, carrying off the spoils which they had placed in sacks. Vainly, all night, did they attempt to escape; when morning dawned they went back to the door of the church, and were unable to depart. They then entered the church with the priest, and restored all that they had stolen, and admitting their guilt, they clove to the altar, and thus, through the refuge and protection afforded them by the church, they escaped the death which they deserved. And even to this day, in proof of this great miracle, our Ladye enfolds her arm around her Divine Son."[226]

KIRKLINGTON.

October 2, 1472 :
" Eleanor Wandesford of Kirklington, widow, leaves to the support of the lights called Rudlith and Ladylith (the Rood-light, and the Ladye-light), in the church of Kirklington, iij*s*. iiij*d*."[227]

LAPWORTH.

In the sixth of Edward the First, 1277–8, Ivo Pipard settled a messuage and lands, and 24 *d.* a year, for the maintenance of two wax candles, and two lamps in the church of Lapworth; viz., one candle to burn before the altar of St. James on Sundays, the other to burn before the relics, and one lamp before the altar of our Blessed Ladye in the chancel.[228]

LAUNCESTON.

Richard, Earl of Cornwall, son of King John, left five shillings for the support of a light in the chapel of our Blessed Ladye.[229]

LEICESTER.

There was a solemn procession annually from the church of St. Marye to St. Margaret's, in which the image of our Blessed Ladye was carried under a canopy borne by four persons, with a quinstrel,

[226] Gemm. Eccl. Dist. 1. c. xxxiii. Rolls Edit.   [227] Test. Ebor. iii. 202.
[228] *Notices of the Churches in Warwickshire.* Warwick, 1847, vol. i. p. 16.
[229] Monasticon Diocesis Exoniensis. By George Oliver, D.D. London, 1846, p. 27.

harp, and other music, before her, and twelve persons representing the twelve Apostles, each of them bearing the name of the Apostle he represented in his bonnet. There were also four persons bearing banners, with the virgins of the parish attending.

In the church, the image of our Blessed Ladye was adorned with a crown on its head, and placed in a tabernacle, with a candlestick and light before it, and a table (*i.e.*, *tabula*, or reredos) representing her consecration.[230]

John of Gant bequeaths to the new collegiate church of our Ladye of Leicester, "moun rouge vestiment de velvet embroudez de solales dor ovecque trestout l'apparail a ycelles vestiment appartenant, et a cella trestoutz mes messalx et autres livres de ma chapelle qui sount del use et ordinal de la eglise Cathedrales de Sarum."[231]

LEYTON, or LOW LEIGHTON.

"In this parish church, dedicated to St. Mary, there was," says Stow, "in the Popish times, a taper of wax containing three pounds, and the wick to contain half an ounce, that was burnt before the image of our Blessed Lady on her five holy days. And a glass lamp, and a gallon of oyl to burn in the said lamp within the said church, before the crucifix or the rood there. As also one pound of frankincense every year, *ad Laudem Dei & omnium Sanctorum ibidem in eadem Ecclesia in diebus Festivalibus per totum annum thurificand*, as the record mentions it. And that the Abbot of Stratford, parson of the church *Beatæ Mariæ de Leyton* in 35 year of Henry 6 did sue an assize and set forth,"[232] that he and his predecessors were to have half an ounce of cotton wick and three pounds of wax, to make a candle, or taper, to burn in the said church before the image of the Blessed Mary, yearly, on five festival days, viz., her Annunciation, Conception, Purification, Assumption, and

---

[230] *Hist. and Antiquities of the ancient Town of Leicester.* Attempted by John Throsby. Leicester, 1794, p. 220.

[231] Test. Ebor. i. p. 223.

[232] *A Survey of the Cities of London and Westminster*, &c. By John Stow. Ed. John Strype, M.A. London, 1720. Appendix, p. 114.

Nativity.[233] All this is stated in the Year Book of the 35 Henry VI.[234]

LINCHLADE.

August 5. 1502.
"Itm. For thoffering of the Quene to Oure Ladye at Linchelade, ii *s.* v *d.*"[235]

LINCOLN.

Our Blessed Ladye was chosen as the Patroness of Lincoln on the occasion of the victory of the citizens over the forces of the Earl of Chester in 1147, which they ascribed to her intercession.[236]

In the inventory of the treasures of the cathedral appropriated by Henry VIII., which was made in the twenty-eighth year of his reign, 1536, there is a description of the image of our Ladye.

"Itm. A great image of our Ladye sitting in a chair, silver and gilt, with four polls, two of them having arms on the top before, having upon her head a crown, silver and gilt, set with stones and pearls, and one bee with stones and pearls about her neck, and an owche depending thereby, having in her hand a scepter with one flower set with stones and pearls, and one bird on the top thereof; and her child sitting upon her knee, with one crown on His head, with a diadem set with pearls and stones, having a ball with a cross, silver and gilt, in His left hand, and at either of His feet a scutcheon of arms."[237]

Mention is also made of an ivory statue of our Blessed Ladye which was in the treasury of the cathedral.

"Itm. A tabernacle of ivory standing upon four feet, with two leaves, with one image of our Ladye in the middle, and the Salutation of our Ladye in one leaf, and the Nativity of our Ladye in the other leaf."[238]

The easternmost portion of Lincoln Cathedral is commonly called the Choir of Angels, from the conspicuous elegance of the winged figures in

---

[233] Newcourt, Repertorium Ecclesiasticum Parochiale. Lond. 1708, v. ii. p. 380.

[234] Stow, *ut sup. loc. cit.*

[235] Privy Expenses, &c. p. 37.

[236] Rog. de Hoveden, *Annales*, vol. i. p. 209. Rolls Edit.; also, Atlas Marianus, n. DCLXXI., p. 735.

[237] Mon. Angl. vi. p. 1279.

[238] *Ibid.*

high-relief which adorn the spandrils of the tri-
forium arches.

On the south side is a group, of singular
purity of design, representing our Blessed Ladye
and her Divine Son, which was thus described in
1848 by Professor Cockerell, R.A. : "The artist
has relied wholly on the idea, form and grace of
the composition and of the parts ; eschewing
every extraneous ornament.   No hair, scarcely
the flesh, the 'nude,' or accessory of any kind,
appears ; an austere but noble plainness characterizes the whole, and we are captivated by the
intrinsic beauty of the conception and execution,
unaided by the common resources sought by the
vulgar in after-times, when the religious spirit, by
which these works were inspired, had declined.

"The Godhead of the Child Jesus appears in
the dignity of His attitude and gesture, especially
as contrasted with the angelic boy acolyte, who
ministers incense to Him with officious zeal. With
one hand upon His mother's breast, and standing
on her lap, He seems affectionately to confess
the taking of our human nature upon Him ; while
with the other He unveils her whom all generations shall henceforth call *Blessed.* Her nobility,
modesty, graciousness, and youth fulfil all the
idea of the Virgin Mother.

"Under her feet is the serpent, according to
the prediction that 'her seed should bruise its
head.'

"It may safely be proposed to compare this
composition with any other known of this or of
any other previous Christian epoch."[239]

This elongation of the church was effected
about 1282 for the reception of the relics of
St. Hugh, which were enclosed in a golden shrine
of exquisite workmanship.

Of St. Hugh his biographer says : "But not
to mention the more authoritative opinions of
others concerning these great miracles of Almighty
God, let it suffice for the present to commend the
following consideration to the faith of all simple
minded p:rsons : that it was not without good
reason that so joyous a display of light was seen

to shed lustre on the funeral procession of one, (to do honour to him) who, for the glory of the ever-Virgin Mother of the True Light, had himself crowned the lights which usually burned in her church with the gift of a host of others. For he endowed the treasury of Lincoln with ample revenues for this very purpose, that the lustre of the tapers with which the immense area of its huge cathedral was illuminated during the offices of the night might vie with that of the rays of the sun, with which it was lit up by day.[240]

In the fifteenth century pilgrimages were often imposed as a punishment, just as a magistrate, now-a-days, would pronounce a sentence of four-teen or twenty-one days, or more. And the great peculiarity of being sentenced to a pilgrimage of this sort was, that the penalty might be worked out by deputy. In the municipal archives of Ghent there is a MS. described as the "Witten-bouc," which contains a long list of the pilgrimages in Europe thus inflicted at Ghent, and the prices for which they can be bought off, or made by deputy. This list was evidently drawn up prior to 1422. The pilgrimage from Ghent to Our Ladye of Lincoln—*t'ons Vrauwe Lincole*—is put down at five *livres*.[241]

2. Our Ladye in St. Catherine's Church is also named in the list of the *Witten bouc; t'ons Vrauwe en t' Sente Katheline, te Lincole*, and the pilgrimage from Ghent is put down at five *livres*.[242]

Our Ladye in the Park.

LISKEARD.

Leland says: "About half a mile, or I cam to Liskard, I passed, in a wood, by a chapel of our Lady caullid Our Lady in the Park, where was wont to be gret pilgrymage."[243]

This was an early and a celebrated pilgrimage. In the reign of Edward II. it was determined

---

[240] Magna Vita S. Hugonis Lincoln epis. p. 366. Rolls Ed.
[241] Cannaert. Bydragen tot de kinnis van het oude Strafrecht in Vlaenderen. Ghent, 1835, p. 354.
[242] *Ibid.*
[243] Itin. vol. iii. p. 27.

F

that the vicar of the parish church had no right to the oblations made at this chapel.[244]

On the 1st November, 1441, Bishop Lacy granted an indulgence to penitent persons who contributed to the repair of the road to this chapel.[245]

It is also mentioned that there were "certen lands gyven to ye said chappell, a garden with an orchard, and one halfe acre of grownde. And in the said chappell was great oblacons sometyme."[246]

LONDON.

London in Catholic times may vie with any city in the world in practical devotion to our Blessed Ladye. A volume would not suffice to enumerate all the foundations and pious acts of the citizens of old in her honour. But in the present series a few examples must suffice. The charities, gilds, hospitals, and God's-houses prove that, in their successes, the Catholic citizens of London were ever mindful of our Blessed Ladye. They sought the greater glory of God, the honour of His Immaculate Mother, and their own salvation. Their ambition was to be inscribed in the Book of Life. They strove to acquire riches, but not with the sole object of founding a family: they loved to make the poor of Christ—the Blessed Poor, as they were called in Catholic days—partakers of their wealth; and in the endowment of alms-houses, commonly named Houses of God, they sought to provide refuges for a succession of Blessed Poor, or *Bedesmen*, whose prayers should daily be offered up for the repose of their souls.

First of all I will begin with
The City Seal.

Stow says : "In the 4 of Richard II., 1380-1, in a full assembly made in the upper chamber of the Guildall, summoned by William Walworth, then Mayor, as well of Aldermen as of the

244 Rot. Parl. iii. p. 505 ; and Lysons, Magna Britannia, Cornwall, p. 202.
245 Mon. Dioc. Exon, p. 72.
246 *Ibid.* p. 448.

Common Council in every ward, for certain affairs concerning the King, it was there by common consent agreed and ordained, that the old seal of the office of the mayoralty of the city being very small, old, unapt, and uncomely for the honour of the city, should be broken, and one other new should be had. Which the said Mayor commanded to be made artificially and honourable for the exercise of the said office thereafter in place of the other. In which new seal, besides the images of Peter and Paul, which of old were rudely engraven, there should be, under the feet of the said images, a shield of the arms of the said city perfectly graved, with two lions supporting the same, with two serjeants-of-arms, on either part one and two tabernacles, in which, above, should stand two angels, between whom (above the said images of Peter and Paul) should be set the glorious Virgin. This being done, the old seal of the office was delivered to Richard Odiham, Chamberlain, who brake it, and in place thereof was delivered the new seal to the said Mayor, to use in his office of mayoralty as occasion should require."[247]

It is generally believed that the sword which is borne in the arms of the city is in commemoration of Sir William Walworth's loyal conduct. Stow, however, disposes of the question thus:

"This new seal seemeth to be made before William Walworth was knighted. For he is not intitled there Sir, as he afterwards was. And certain it is that the same new seal then made is now in use, and none other, in that office of mayoralty. Which may suffice to answer the former fable, without showing any evidence sealed with the old seal, which was the cross and sword as now be of St. Paul, and not the dagger of William Walworth."[248]

The City arms are, argent, a plain cross gules, a sword of St. Paul in the first quarter.

St. Paul's Cathedral.

1. The Marye Mass and Office of our Blessed Ladye.

[247] Bk. ii. p. 186.   [248] Bk. ii. p. 186.

"Shortly after the beginning of King Henry the Third's time,'" says Dugdale, "an assignation is made by Eustace de Fauconbridge, Bishop of London, of the church of Bumstead, which the prior and convent of Stoke, at his request, had granted to this cathedrall for the behoof of poor clerks frequenting the quire and celebrating the Holy Office of Our Ladye; and, moreover, of v. marks issuing out of the church of Finchingfeld; so that six clerks should be made choice of every day, with one priest of the quire, to be at the celebration of the Mass of Our Ladye, and also to say mattens and all other canonical hours at her altar.

"And in *anno* MCCXCIX. (29th Edward the First) the prior and convent of Thetford gave four marks *per annum* to be distributed likewise amongst the clerks which should celebrate the Mass of the said Blessed Virgin at her altar."[249]

2. Our Ladye in the Ladye Chapel.

"Which altar," continues Dugdale, "was doubtless it that stood in a certain chapel dedicated to the honour of our Ladye in this church, whereunto I finde that the executors of Hugh de Pourte, in 2nd Edward the Second, gave xviii. *sol* yearly rent to maintain one taper of three pounds weight to burn before it every day whilst her Mass should be solemnizing; and at every procession of the quire before the same altar."[250]

3. Our Ladye at the Pillar in the Nave, commonly known as Our Ladye of Grace.

"But in the body of the church stood the glorious image of the Blessed Virgin, fixt to the pillar at the foot of Sir John de Beauchamp's tomb (viz., the second pillar on the south side from the steeple westwards.) Before which that there might be a lamp burning every night I find a grant made to the dean and chapter of this cathedrall in *anno* MCCCLXV. (39th Edward the Third) by John Barnet, then Bishop of Bathe and

---

[249] *History of St. Paul's Cathedral in London.* By William Dugdale. London, 1658, pp. 18, 20.
[250] *Ibid. loc. cit.*

Wells, of one water-mill, lxxvi. acres of arable land, v. acres of meadow, ix. acres of pasture, viii. acres of wood, and xliii *s.* yearly rent lying in Nastoke, in the county of Essex: In which grant he appointeth that after mattens celebrated in the Quire every day, and those present thereat gone out, an antheme of our Ladye, *scilicet*, Nesciens Mater, or some other one suitable to the time, should be sung before the said image, with a versicle: which being performed, the gravest person then present to say a collect of the said Blessed Virgin; afterwards the Psalm of *De profundis* for the souls of all the faithfull, with the versicle and prayer, *Deus cujus miseratione*, &c.: and then the same person to say, *Animæ omnium fidelium defunctorum per Dei misericordiam requiescant in pace.*

"Many and frequent were the oblations which were made to this image by devout people and pilgrims, as by the accompts of the church officers appeareth, in so much as the bishop expected some advantage thereby; but to this the dean and chapter not yielding, the difference was referred to the arbitration of Thomas Arundell, Archbishop of Canterbury, who by his award, bearing date xv. February, *anno* MCCCCXI. (13th Henry the Fourth) adjudged them totally to the dean and canons resident; forasmuch as it was then proved that those oblations had been formerly received by their substitutes, viz., the chamberleins and bell-ringers of the church; who giving their daily attendance therein, and taking notice of those that offered their tapers burning, having extinguisht the light, carried them to a roome below the chapter-house, and there caused them to be melted to the use of the said dean and canons. And as for the oblations of money, which were put into an iron box fixt to the same pillar, under the feet of that image; they were then also decreed by the before-specified Archbishop, to the same dean and canons and their successors for ever."[251]

When the mayor, sheriffs, and aldermen of London had been dismissed their offices conse-

[251] *Loc. cit.*

quently upon the disturbances caused by the Wycliffites, and their successors appointed, the King sent privately, and commanded the city officers to assemble, and make a wax candle, or taper, with the Duke of Lancaster's arms upon it, and carry it, in a solemn procession, to St. Paul's Church, there continually to burn before the image of the Blessed Virgin Marye, at the expence of the City, which was punctually performed.[252]

In the accounts of Elizabeth of York, March 24, 1502—

"Offering to Our Ladye of Grace in Poules, xx *d.*"[253]

December 24, 1502—

"Itm for thofferinge of the Quene to the roode at the north dore of Polles, iii *s.* viii *d.* ; and to Our Ladye of Grace there iii *s.* viii *d.*

"Summa, vii *s.* iiii *d.*[254]

NOTE.—As the anthem, *Nesciens Mater*, has disappeared from our modern prayer-books, I think it as well to insert it here—

> Nesciens Mater Virgo virum perperit
> sine dolore Salvatorem sæculorum,
> ipsum Regem Angelorum sola Virgo
> lactabat ubere de cœlo pleno.[255]

> A Maiden-Mother pure, who never man did know,
>   The Saviour of all times, with pangless travail bare
> The Angel's King Himself, from breasts which heaven
>   made flow,
>   Alone a Virgin fed, His Maiden-Mother fair.

4. Our Ladye in the New Work.

"But," continues Dugdale,[256] "besides the before-specified chapell or altar of our Ladye in the body of the church, as before said, there was another in the New Work (viz., above the quire), whereof the first mention that I have found is in *anno* MCCCXXIX. (3rd Edward the Third), the then dean (said John de Everdon) and canons granting seven tapers, each weighing two pounds,

---

[251] Entick, *Hist. of London*, vol. i. p. 282.
[253] Privy Expenses, p. 3.   [254] *Ibid.* p. 81.
[255] Schneidt, Olivetum Marianum. Col. Agrip. 1735, p. 97.
[256] *Ut supra, loc. cit.*

to burn at the celebrations therein to the honour
of God, our Ladye, and St. Lawrence ; and
appointed that the charge of those tapers should
be supported out of the oblations made by good
people thereto ; who either for reverence of those
saints, or the images of St. Lawrence and St. John
Baptist, standing about that chapell, or of St.
Mary Magdalen, on the outside thereof to the
east, had recourse thither.

"So likewise there was an image of our Ladye
in the said part called the New Work : for it
appears that in 19th Edward the Third, 1345,
Thomas Hatfield, Bishop of Durham, granted an
indulgence of xl. days' pardon to all such as
being truely penitent and confest of their sins,
should come thither and say a *Pater noster* and an
Ave, with a pious intent, or give in books, vestments, or other ecclesiastical ornaments, &c., any
considerable matter thereto."

5. Our Ladye "in Gesem," or *de Puerperio.*

"In the 19th Edward the Second, 1325–6,
Roger de Waltham, canon of this church, amongst
many other good works, founded out of his
piety a certain oratory on the south side of the
quire of this cathedrall, towards the upper end
thereof, to the honour of God, our Ladye, St.
Lawrence, and all Saints ; and adorned it with
many images and pictures of the celestial hierarchy, the joys of the Blessed Virgin, &c. And
lastly, in the south wall opposite to the said
oratory, erected a glorious tabernacle which contained the image of the said Blessed Virgin,
sitting as it were in childbed, as also of our
Saviour in swadling clothes, lying betwixt the ox
and the ass, and St. Joseph at her feet. Above
which was another image of her standing with the
Child in her arms. And on the beam thwarting
from the upper end of the oratory to the before-
specified childbed, placed the crowned images of
our Saviour and His Mother sitting in one tabernacle ; as also the images of St. Katherine and
St. Margaret, virgins and martyrs. Neither was
there any part of the said oratory or roof thereof,
but he caused it to be beautified with comely

pictures and images; to the end that the memory of our Blessed Saviour and His saints, and especially of the glorious Virgin His Mother, might be always the more famous. In which oratory he designed that his sepulture should be."[257]

6. Our Ladye in Sir John Pultney's chapel.

Sir John Pultney, who had been four times Mayor, desired to be buried in the Church of St. Lawrence, in Candlewyck Street. In his will, dated November 14, 23rd Edward the Third, he says:

"I will and ordain that in the Church of St. Paul, in London, which as my mother I desire to honour with a filial affection, there be three priests celebrating divine service in a certain chapell newly to be built at my cost in the north part thereof. In which chapell it is my desire that one of those priests shall every day say the Mass of the Blessed Virgin for my soul," &c, and for those of his parents and relations, &c.

"And for the solemn performance of his anniversary assigned particular yearly pittances to the principal canons; so also to the petty canons, the vicars-chorall, and officers of the church, appointing that the Lord Mayor being thereat should have vi *s.* viii *d.*; the recorder, v *s.*; the two sheriffs, vi *s.* viii *d.*; the common cryer, iii *s.* iv *d.*; the Lord Mayor's sergeants, vi *s.* viii *d.*; and the master of the College of St. Lawrence, vi *s.* viii *d.* But if any of these should be absent, then their portion to be distributed to the poor. And furthermore bequeathed the yearly sum of xx *s.* to the almoner of this church to be by him bestowed on the summer habits of the choristers; upon condition that they, the said choristers, should every day, after compline ended in the quire, go into the before-specified chapel, as intended by him to be built, and sing an anthem of the Blessed Virgin before her image there being, solemnly with note, which being ended, one of them to say the prayer of the said Virgin, next the Psalm *De profundis*, and then the prayer for the dead, and lastly these words, *Anima Johannis de Pultoney fundatoris hujus capellæ, et animæ omnium*

[257] Dugdale, p. 29.

*fidelium defunctorum per Dei misericordiam requies-
cant in pace.*"[258]

7. Our Ladye of the Annunciation.

In the 34th of Edward the Third, 1360, John
King of France, lays down at the Annunciation
xii. nobles.[259] This was the altar of the Gild of
the Annunciation.[260]

PATERNOSTER ROW lies close to St. Paul's on
the north. "It was so called," says Stow, "because
of stationers or text-writers that dwelled here, who
wrote and sold all sorts of books then in use,
namely A B C, or *Absies*, with the *Pater noster*,
Ave, Creed, Graces, &c. Turners of beads also
dwelled there, and they were called Pater noster
makers; and as I read in a record of one Robert
Nikke, Pater noster maker and citizen in the
reign of Henry the Fourth, and so of others. At
the end of this Pater noster Row is Ave Mary, or
Ave Maria Lane, so called upon the like occasion
of text-writers and bead-makers then dwelling
there.[261] In the plan it is called Ivy Lane.[262]

In the twenty-six wards of London there were
a hundred and fourteen parish churches, thirteen
of which were dedicated in honour of our Blessed
Lady. Stow's list agrees with the one given in
the London *City Press* of the 15th July, 1871,
excepting that St. Marye Axe does not appear.
He gives the sad reason: "This parish, about
the year 1565, was united to the parish church
of St. Andrew Undershaft. And so was St. Mary
at the Axe suppressed, and letten out to be a
warehouse for a merchant." Here was afterwards
a Free School kept.[263]

I. St. Mary Abchurch.

The parish church is called of St. Mary
Abchurch, Apechurch, or Upchurch, as I have
read it, says Stow.[264]

In 1475, John Weryn, citizen and goldsmith,
desired to be buried in the church or church-

[258] Dugdale, pp. 30, 31.   [259] *Ibid.* p. 22.   [260] Stow, bk. iii. p. 145.
    [261] *Ibid.* bk. . p. 174.   [262] *Ibid.* bk. ii. p. 124
    [263] *Ibid.* p. 86.   [264] *Ibid.* bk. ii. p. 183.

hawe (yard) of St. Mary Abchurch, and bequeathed
10 *d.* among the people in worship of the five
wounds of our Lord Jesus Christ and of the five
joys of our Ladye.[205]

Many bequests were made to this church.

II. St. Mary Aldermanbury.

So called from its situation in Aldermanbury
Street.[266]

III. St. Mary Aldermary,

Was the oldest of all the churches of our
Ladye in the city, and consequently called the
elder, or Alder Marye.[267]

IV. St. Mary Axe, or Pellipar,

Commonly called St. Mary at the Axe, from
the sign of an axe over against the east end
thereof; or St. Mary Pellipar, from a plot of
ground lying to the north side thereof pertaining
to the Skinners of London.[268]

V. St. Mary Bothaw, or Boat-haw.

This church, being near unto Downgate on
the river Thames, has the addition of Bothaw
or Boat-haw, of near adjoining to an haw or
yard, wherein (of old time) boats were made
and repaired. This seems of old to be called
also St. Mary de Bothache.[269]

VI. St. Mary Bow,

Called *De Arcubus*, from the stone *arches* or
bows on the top of the steeple or bell tower
thereof. Which arching was as well on the old
steeple as on the new. This church in the reign
of William the First, being the first in this city
built on arches of stone, was therefore called the
New Mary-church, or St. Mary *de Arcubus, ad
Arcus,* or le Bow, in West Cheaping.[270]

In 1469, it was ordered by a Common Council
that the Bow bell should be rung nightly at nine
o'clock. In 1472, John Dunne, mercer, by his
will gave to the parson and churchwardens of

---

[265] Stow, bk. ii. p. 184.   [266] *Ibid.* bk. iii. p. 71.   [267] *Ibid.* p. 18.
[268] *Ibid.* bk. ii. p. 86.   [269] *Ibid.* bk. ii. p. 198.   [270] *Ibid.* bk. iii. pp. 20, 21.

St. Mary Bow, two tenements with the appurtenances in Hosier Lane, then so called, for the maintenance of Bow Bell.

One William Copeland, churchwarden, gave the great bell, which is rung nightly at nine of the clocke, which had this inscription cast in the metale in 1515—

> Dudum fundabar Bowbel campana vocabar
> Sexta sonat, bis sexta sonat ; ter tertia pulset.[271]

St. Mary *ad Arcus* is mentioned in the *Atlas Marianus*.[272]

It is from the Church of St. Marye-le-Bow that the *Court of Arches* derives its name. Blackstone says :

" The Court of Arches is a court of appeal belonging to the Archbishop of Canterbury ; whereof the judge is called the *Dean of the Arches*, because he anciently held his court in the church of St. Mary-le-Bow (*Sancta Maria de Arcubus*), though all the principal spiritual courts are now holden at Doctors' Commons. His proper jurisdiction is only over the thirteen peculiar parishes belonging to the Archbishop in London ; but the office of Dean of the Arches having been for a long time united with that of the Archbishop's principal officer, he now in right of the last-mentioned officer (as doth also the official principal of the Archbishop of York) receives and determines appeals from all the sentences of all inferior ecclesiastical courts within the province."[273]

VII. St. Mary Colechurch.

Named of one Cole that builded it, says Stow.[274]

In the first year of his reign Henry the Fourth gave licence to William Marshall and others to found a brotherhood of St. Katherine in this church, because St. Thomas à Becket, and St. Edmund, King, were baptized there. It is thus expressed in the Record: *In Eccles. de S. Maria*

---

[271] Wever, p. 402.
[272] N. DXXXVIII. p. 629. [273] Commentaries, bk. iii. c. 5, § 1. p. 64. Oxford, 1770.
[274] Stow, bk. iii. p. 34.

de Colechurch juxta magnum aqueduct in qua ecclesia S. Thomas de Cantuar, et B. Edmund, Rex, baptizati fuerunt. This gild was confirmed in the twenty-fifth of Henry the Sixth.

VIII. St. Mary Hill, or atte Hill.

So called because it is on the ascent from Billingsgate.[275]

By the churchwardens' accounts of 1353, John Causton, mercer, left the rents of certain tenements for one priest, and five tapers to burn before the image of our Ladye at the high altar of the Salutation.

The great festival here was the Assumption.

In 1489, there is an entry for "ale and brede on our Lady Day, the Assumption, 3d."

And amongst the annual quit-rents :

"To the brotherhood of our Lady and St. Thomas in St. Magnus' church, for Hugh Brownham for the *Salve* per annum, xii *s.*

To the brotherhood of our Ladye in the same church, for T. Cawston, vi *s.*[276]

IX. St. Mary Mounthaw, Monthaut, Mounthaut, De Monte Alto. A very small church, and was originally built for the Monthauts, who had their house there.[277]

X. St. Mary Somerset; sometimes called Summer's-hith.[278]

XI. St. Mary Staining.

Apparently so called from being in Staining Lane,[279] which lane took its name, as may be supposed of painter-stainers dwelling there. But others say that the word steining is derived from stein, or stan which is the Saxon for stone, and signifies as much as a stone church.[280]

---

[275] Stow, bk. ii. p. 168.
[276] Nichols, *Illustrations of the manners and expenses of ancient times in England.* Lond. 1798, p. 89.
[277] Stow, bk. iii. p. 212.
[278] Newcourt, vol. i. p. 451.
[279] Stow, bk. iii. p. 96.
[280] Newcourt, vol. i. p. 457.

XII. St. Mary Woolchurch.

So named "from a beam placed there ever in
the churchyard, as it seemeth; for the same was
therefore called Woolchurch Haw, of the Tronage,
or weighing of wooll there. And to verify this,
I find amongst the customs of London written
in French in the reign of King Edward the
Second, a chapter entitled, *Les Customes de
Woolchurche Haw,* wherein is set down what
was then to be paid for every parcel of wooll
weighed."[281]

In the Ordinances of the Drapers' Company,
under the date of the sixth year of Henry the
Sixth this entry occurs:

"*For the manteyninge of oure lighte.*

"Also ordeyned hyt is that there schull be v
tapers of wax of resonable wheight sette on a
candelstyke of laton, as ordeyned of old tyme at
Wol-chyrche in the worchipp of th' assumpcyon of
oure Lady, and they to brenne at due tymes, as
the custom ys, the which lyght schull be well and
honestly ordeyned and mainteyned."[282]

XIII. St. Mary Woolnoth.

"There is in the high street," says Stow, "a
proper parish church of St. Mary Woolnoth, of
the Nativity, the reason of which I have not yet
learned. Probably, because this church was
dedicated to the Blessed Virgin Marye with
the Infant Jesus in her arms, as she is often
pictured."[283]

Sir Simon Eyre, a famous merchant, sometime
an upholsterer, then a draper, and Mayor of
London in 1445, the founder of Leaden Hall, and
a fair chapel there, gave the Cardinal's Hatt
Tavern, in Lombard Street, with a tenement
annexed on the east part of it, and a mansion
behind the east tenement, together with an alley
from Lombard Street to Cornhill, with the appurtenances, all which were by him new built, towards
a Brotherhood of our Ladye in this church, in
which he was buried.[284]

[281] Stow, bk. ii. p. 195.
[282] *Journal of Royal Archæological Institute,* vol. vi. p. 156. [283] Survey, bk. ii. p. 160.
[284] Newcourt, vol. i. p. 461.

XIV. All Hallows, Barking.

There were eight churches of All Hallows in London; this one, which is near the Tower, became the property of the Abbess and Convent of Barking, and was converted into a vicarage about 1389. Hence it was called All Hallows, Barking, to distinguish it from the other churches of that title. It was formerly surrounded by a large churchyard or cemetery, on the north side of which stood the celebrated chapel of Our Ladye of All Hallows, Barking, frequently described as Our Ladye Barking, which was founded by Richard the First.[285]

Newcourt, in the appendix to his Repertorium,[286] gives a very remarkable document about this chapel, but I at once saw that his version must be inaccurate, so I collated it with the Register of Gilbert, Bishop of London, 1436–1446, from which he took it; and had it again verified by one of the transcribers at the Public Record Office.

The entries in the Register extend for a few lines on fol. 194; the remainder of the leaf is left blank; and the entries commence again on fol. 195. The last entry on fol. 194 is dated 18 January, 1440, and the first on fol. 195, 4 March, 23 Henry (VI.) *i.e.* 1445. On the blank space of nearly two pages thus intervening, the document in question is entered, evidently at a later date, and by a different hand, and in very bad ink.

Newcourt gives it thus :

"Universis &c.   Nos miseratione divina Adrianus Tartarorum *episcopi*, Domini Papæ *legati* &c."

The correct reading is as follows :

"Universis Sancte Matris ecclesiæ filiis presentes literas inspecturis, nos miseratione divina . . . Civitatis novæ, Johannes Carpentorañ, Adrianus Tartarorum episcopi, Domini Pape Legati, salutem &c.

"To all the sons of Holy Mother Church who shall see these present letters, We, by Divine Mercy . . . Bishop of Cittanova, John, Bishop

---

[285] Maitland, *Hist. and Survey of London*, 1756, p. 1053.   [286] V. 1, p. 765.

of Carpentras, Adrian, Bishop of the Tartars, wish
eternal health in the Lord.

" It has been given to us to understand by the
most illustrious King of England, Edward, the
son of King Henry, that the chapel in the
cemetery of Barking Church situated in London,
was founded in a wonderful manner by the brave
Richard, formerly King of England; as also how
the Welsh invaded England, in spite of the
precautions of the said Henry, and laid waste
the country on all sides, slew men and women,
and children in their cradles, and horrible to tell,
killed with their swords women lying in childbirth ;
moreover that they took the Isle of Ely in a
hostile manner, and held it with a strong force
for a year, and at last, when the time suited them,
returned unmolested to Wales. The same Edward,
at that time a youth, at the sight of so many
disasters, wrongs, and insults, tending to the
disinheritance of his father, and the destruction
of the whole of England, wept bitterly, and gave
way to such a flood of bitter grief and anguish
of heart, that his body was more especially
affected, and throwing himself half dead on his
couch, he believed that he would never entirely
recover his health. But one night asking the
aid of Marye, the Mother of God, he devoutly
besought her in her loving clemency to inspire
him by some divine revelation, through some
vision during the night, how the English might
most quickly be revenged on the Welsh. And
as it came to pass, whilst he slept, a most lovely
Maid adorned with the flowers of all virtues,
the Glorious Virgin Mother of God, by whose
prayers the Christian people are helped, who by
the ineffable cooperation of the Holy Ghost
brought the Unfading and Eternal Flower,
appeared to him as if in a vision of the night
saying : 'Edward, friend of God, why dost thou
cry out ?   Know for certain that during the
lifetime of thy father the Welsh cannot be entirely
checked or conquered by the English ; and this
on account of the vile sin and heavy extortions
of thy father.   But do thou go very early to-
morrow morning to a certain Jew, by name

Marlibrun, the most cunning limner (picturæ artificem) in the whole world, who dwells at Billingsgate in London, and engage him to make thee a portrait of me as ·thou seest me now; by divine inspiration he will paint two countenances in the picture, one he will limn exceedingly like to my Son Jesus, the other resembling me in every feature, so that no one will be able with truth to point out any defect whatsoever in it. This picture when it is thoroughly finished, I would have thee endeavour to send, as soon as possible, to the chapel in the cemetery of Barking Church, situated near the Tower of London, and cause it to be fairly framed on the north side. If thou dost so, know with certainty that greater wonders in thy favour will forthwith be seen. For as soon as the said Marlibrun shall have gazed thoughtfully on the expression of the faces within the said chapel, he will soon be so drawn to the love of heavenly things, that together with his wife Juda, he will be converted to the Catholic Faith, and afterwards will reveal to thee many secrets of the Jews for which they are to be punished. And do thou, Edward, on beholding this miracle make thy vow to Almighty God, that as long as thou livest and art in England, thou wilt, five times every year, visit this said picture in honour of the Mother of Christ, and that as often as it needs it, thou wilt repair this same chapel, and support the same. And this spot deserves indeed thy homage. For as soon as thou shalt have made this vow on bended knee, and fulfilled it substantially, according to thy ability, in whatever part of the world thou mayst be, thou wilt become most victorious over all people, and invincible; and at the death of thy father, thou wilt be King of England, conqueror of Wales, and lord of the whole of Scotland. Moreover, believe me, that any righteous monarch of England, or perchance any one else, who shall devoutly make this vow, and substantially fulfil it according to his power, will ever be victorious over the Welsh and Scots, and invincible.' With these words she disappeared. The Prince on awaking and coming to himself, bethought him of his dream, and, as it were, almost ravished in spirit, began to wonder. Nevertheless he fulfilled everything that had been prescribed to him during his sleep. Moreover, in our presence, and in that of many nobles both of England and Scotland, the aforesaid Edward, of his own accord, made oath, that up to this time he had found everything, that had been shown him in his sleep, come to pass exactly as it was foretold. Wherefore, desirous that the said chapel be attended with fitting honours and perpetually venerated by the faithful of Christ, to all who shall be truly penitent, and having confessed their sins, shall go to this chapel for the sake of devotion and prayer, and shall make donation towards the lights, repairs, and ornaments of the same ; and, moreover, to all who shall say the Lord's Prayer and Angelic Salutation for the souls of the noble Richard, formerly King of England, whose heart lies buried under the high altar in that chapel, and for those of all the faithful departed, as often as, and whensoever they shall say the same, We trusting in the mercy of God Almighty, and the merits and authority of His Blessed Apostles, Peter and Paul, do each of us mercifully grant in the Lord a several pardon of forty days (*singuli singulas quadragenas dierum*) of the penance enjoined them, provided the local Diocesan shall ratify this our indulgence.

"In witness of all which we have thought fit to confirm this present letter with our seals.

"Given at Norham, where the Parliament of England, as of Scotland, is held, the 20 day of May, in the year of our Lord one thousand two hundred and ninety-one." [287]

I give this document as I find it. The name of the Bishop of Civitas-nova has perished in the Register, but Gams mentions Simon as Bishop of Cittanova, in Istria, in 1284–1293 ; [288] and after much research, I am unable to identify either John, Bishop of Carpentras, or Adrian, Bishop of the Tartars. The latter would have

[287] Bishop Gilbert's Register, fol. 194.
[288] Series Episcoporum, p. 770 : also for Carpentras, p. 530 ; and Gallia Christiana, t. l. col. 905 : Paris, 1715.

G

been a Franciscan, but although Wadding and the *Orbis Seraphicus* give copious details about the Tartar missions of that period, they do not mention Adrian.

In 1288, Argon, King of the Tartars, sends to Pope Nicholas, as envoys, Bersauma, bishop *in partibus*, the Noble man Sabedin, Thomas de Anfusis, with Ugues as interpreter.[289] On the 23rd of August, 1290, Nicholas the Fourth writes from Civita Vecchia to Argon, King of the Tartars, respecting the recovery of the Holy Land, and says that he is exciting all the Catholic Kings and Princes of the earth to a new crusade, &c., and that his most dear son Edward, the illustrious King of England, has already assumed the Cross, &c.[290] On the 2nd of December he writes to King Edward to receive kindly Andrew, formerly called Zaganus Bascarellus de Gisulfo, a a citizen of Genoa, and Moracius, the messengers of Argon, the illustrious King of the Tartars, &c.[291] On the 31st of the same month, there is another brief from Nicholas the Fourth to the King, asking him to receive kindly Sabedin, messenger of Argon, King of the Tartars.[292]

I have been unable to find any mention of the three bishops, Legates of our Lord the Pope, but that fact does not disprove their mission; whereas the evidences I have cited would go far to establish that Nicholas the Fourth had sent legates to Edward the First and other Princes.

This document exhibits a confusion of ideas in regard of actual facts, but due allowance must be made for impressions formed by foreigners, even men of position and education, during a hurried visit to England in the thirteenth century. Even two centuries later, Leo de Rosmital, brother of the Queen of Bohemia, one of the most distinguished men in that country, where he was Chief Justice, and who spent two years on his travels through Europe, from 1465—1467, has left a

[289] Orbis Seraphicus per Fr. Dominicum de Gubernatis a Sospitellia. Romæ, 1689, t. i. p. 365.
[290] *Ibid.* p. 371.
[291] Fœdera, vol. i. pt. iii. p. 76.
[292] *Ibid.*

most interesting account of England, but from which it appears that Dover Castle was the strongest citadel in Christianity, and had been built by devils—*a cacodæmonibus extructa !* [293] Yet his account of the building of Dover Castle does not necessarily invalidate his other statements.

Testing this document by collateral evidence, it appears that :

1. The Welsh never held Ely for a year, and then left it at their own convenience. They were constantly making predatory incursions across the borders during the reign of Henry the Third, and many good lives were lost,[294] but Ely was held in 1263—1265 by the barons and their outlawed followers, commonly known as the "Disinherited," who ravaged and laid waste the counties of Huntingdon and Cambridge.[295]

2. Edward the First finally conquered the Welsh in 1281—1282.

3. Stow, even, mentions the tradition about the heart of Richard the First being buried in this chapel underneath the high altar.[296] It is impossible to conjecture what foundation there was for this fable, unless it were the very document in question.

Richard desired to be buried at Fonteverault, and bequeathed his heart to the cathedral of Rouen : " Ecclesiæ Rothomagensi quia Normanniam præcordialiter diligebat, cor suum inexpugnabile delegavit," says Matthew of Paris.[297] Gervase of Dover, a contemporary historian, describing the obsequies of Richard, relates that "cor ejus grassitudine præstans, Rothomagum delatum est, et honorifice sepultum."[298] It was enclosed in a magnificent shrine of silver and gold, according to Guillaume le Breton :

" Cujus cor Rothomagensis ecclesiæ clerus argento clausit et auro, sanctorumque inter cor-

[293] *Iter Leonis de Rosmital,* 1465—1467, Bibliothek des Literarischen Vereins in Stuttgart, 1844, c. vii. p. 37.

[294] Brady, *Complete History of England.* London, 1685, vol. i. p. 605, et seq.

[295] *Ibid.* vol. ii.

[296] *Survey,* bk. ii. p. 32.

[297] Abbrev. Chron. t. iii. p. 218. Rolls Edit.

[298] Ap. Twisden, Decem Scriptores, col. 1628.

pora, in æde sacrata compositum, nimio devotus honorat honore ; ut tanta ecclesiæ devotio tanta patenter innuat in vita quatum dilexerat illum."[299]

The Chroniques de Normandie say that the Sepulture Royale d'Argent, called in the edition by Le Misgissier, the Chasse, which had contained the heart of Richard "pour la rançon du Roy Sainct Loys de France quant il fut prisonnier aux Sarrazins, fut despecée et vendue."

The heart, however, never left Rouen. On the 31st July, 1838, it was found enclosed within two boxes of lead ; the inner one was lined with a thin leaf of silver, that time had in a great part decayed, and thus inscribed within, in rudely graven characters—

> + HIC : IACET :
> COR : RICAR
> DI : REGIS :
> ANGLORUM.[300]

4. The date of this document is correct. On the 10th of May, 1291, a Parliament of England and Scotland met at Norham. The subject of debate was the accession to the crown of Scotland. It continued, by adjournments, until the 2nd of June, and was then prorogued till the 14th of October.[1] Norham is given in the document as Northm, which Newcourt mistook for Northampton !

According to this account, the celebrated image of our Ladye of Barking must have been a painting or picture ; for *picturæ artifex* cannot be construed as a *statuary*.

Edward the Fourth gave licence to his cousin John Tiptoft, Earl of Worcester, to found there a Brotherhood for a master and brethren, which he richly endowed, and appointed it to be called the King's chapel or chantry, *in capella Beatæ Mariæ de Barking.*[2] This brotherhood, together with two offerings to Our Ladye of Barking, were inadvertently inserted under Barking.[3]

---

[299] In Vita Phil. Arg. Depping, Hist. de la Normandie.   Rouen, 1835, t. ii. p. 393.

[300] Archæologia, vol. xxxix. p. 202, et seq.

[1] Parry, *The Parliaments and Councils of England.*   Lond. 1839, p. 35.

[2] Stow, bk. ii. p. 33.

[3] See ante, p. 3.

On the 27th January, 1310, three Templars, one of whom was Brother John de Stoke, a serving brother of seventeen years' standing, were examined by the inquisitors in the chapel of our Blessed Lady of Barking Church.[4]

In the Privy Purse expenses of Henry the Seventh :

" For offering at Our Lady Berking, 6*s.* 8*d.*"[5]

In this churchyard was buried the martyr Bishop of Rochester, John Fisher. "He was martyred," says his biographer, "on Tuesday the 21st of June, 1535, the feast of St. Alban, the proto-martyr of England. His body, after laying nude all day on the scaffold, was, towards eight of the clock in the evening, carried on a halberd by two of the watchers, and buried in a churchyard there, hard by, called All Hallows Barking, where on the north side of the church, hard by the wall, they digged a grave with their halberds, and tumbled the body of this holy prelate, all naked and flat upon his belly without either shirt or other accustomed things belonging to a Christian man's burial, and so covered it quickly with earth."[6] Subsequently the remains of this holy martyr were moved from the churchyard to St. Peter's, in the Tower of London.[7]

It is either to Our Ladye of Barking or Our Ladye of Graces, but most probably to the former, that the following letter written by Sir Thomas More, shortly after he had been made a Privy Councillor, to Bishop Fisher refers. Both are described as near the Tower. "Most unwillingly did I come to Court, as every one knows, and the King himself sometimes tells me in joke. And to this day I seem to sit as awkwardly there, as one who never rode before sits in a saddle. But our Prince, though I am far from being in his especial favour, is so affable and kind to all, that every one, let him be ever so diffident, may find some reason for imagining that he loves him, after

---

[4] Addison, *History of the Knights Templars.* London, 1842 ; p. 230.

[5] Excerpta Historica, p. 130.

[6] Baily, *Life and Death of the Reverend John Fisher, Bishop of Rochester.* Third Edition. Lond. 1740, p. 231.

[7] Weever, p. 500.

the manner of the London matrons, who are persuaded that the image of our Blessed Ladye near the Tower smiles upon them, as they look closely at it whilst they pray before it. I am neither so fortunate, in reality, to perceive such favourable tokens, nor of so sanguine a temperament as even to flatter myself that I do so. Yet such are his Majesty's virtues and learning, and such his daily increasing industry in both, that the more and more I see his Majesty make progress in good and truly royal accomplishments, the less and less do I feel this Court life to hang heavily upon me."[8]

XV. Our Ladye *de Clypeo*.

In the Atlas Marianus, Guppenberg enumerates Our Ladye *de Clypeo* in London. This is the image of our Ladye which King Arthur had painted on his shield, and which Guppenberg conjectures to have been "exposed somewhere, probably in London."[9] I shall describe it in its proper place.

XVI. Our Ladye of Cony-Hope Lane.

There is Cony-Hope Lane, of old time so called, of a sign of three conies hanging over a poulterer's stall, at the end of the lane. In this lane anciently was a chapel dedicated to the Blessed Virgin. So in the Bishop of London's Register of Wills : *Capella Beatæ Mariæ de Conyng Hope Lane*. [10]

XVII. St. Dunstan's in the East.

Sir Bartholomew James, alderman, mayor in 1479, desires in his will that, after his month's mind, the four great tapers which he had given should be broken and made into small tapers, every piece weighing one pound, which he willed should be set before the images of the Holy Trinity and of our Blessed Ladye, in the church of St. Dunstan, to burn at due and convenient times and seasons.[11]

---

[8] Stapleton, Tres Thomæ. ed princeps. Duaci. 1588 in Vit. T. Mori, p. 97.
[9] No. DI. p. 593.   [10] Stow, bk. iii. p. 33.   [11] *Ibid.* bk. ii. p. 43.

XVII. St. Dunstan's in the West.

In this church there was a celebrated gild of our Ladye, as appears from donations made by Henry VIII.

11 Henry VIII. 1519.

August. To the Fraternity of Our Ladye's Gild at St. Dunstan's in the West, 40s.[12]

12 Henry VIII. 1520.

October. To the Fraternity of Our Ladye's Gild at St. Dunstan's in the West, 2l.[13]

XIX. St. Magnus, near London Bridge.

In this church (as most other churches had theirs) was a most famous gild of our Ladye *de Salve Regina.* An account whereof was brought into the King, upon an Act of Parliament in the reign of King Edward the Third, when some special cognizance was taken of these gilds or fraternities throughout England. And that we may see a little, continues Stow, the manner and intent of these devotions, I shall show what this gild was from the certificate thereof offered by this fraternity as I found it in the Tower Records.

"La Fraternité de nôtre Dame de Salve Regina, et de Seint Thomas en Eglise de Seint Magne sur le Pount de Loundres, donct les Mestres sount a present John Sandherst, Walter atte Well, Gilbert Sporiere, et Estephen Bartelot."

17 Edward III. 1343—1344, in English thus:

"Be it remembered that Rauf Capelyn du Bailliff, Will. Double, fishmonger, Roger Lowber, chancellor, Henry Boseworth, vintner, Stephen Lucas, stockfishmonger, and other of the better of the parish of St. Magnus, near the Bridge of London, of their great devotion, and to the honour of God and His glorious Mother our Ladye Marye the Virgin, began, and caused to be made, a chauntry, to sing an anthem of our Ladye, called *Salve Regina*, every evening. And thereupon ordained five burning wax lights at the time of the said anthem, in the honour of the five principal joys of our Ladye aforesaid; and for exciting the people to devotion at such

---

[12] Letters and Papers, &c. Henry VIII. v. iii. pt. 2. p. 1537.   [13] *Ibid.* p. 1543.

an hour, the more to merit to their souls. And thereupon many other good people of the same parish, seeing the great honesty of the said service and devotion, proffered to be aiders and partners to support the said lights and the said anthem to be continually sung, paying to every person every week a halfpenny. And so that hereafter, with the gift that the people shall give to the sustentation of the said light and anthem, there shall be to find a chaplain singing in the said church for all the benefactors of the said light and anthem. And after the said Rauf Chapelyn, by his testament made the 18th June, the year of the said King the 23 (1349), devised 3 *s.* by quit rent issuing out of one tenement in the parish of St. Leonard of Eastcheap."[14]

But the piety of the citizens did not always wax fervent. About the year 1498, there was a visitation; and Stow has recorded

"How matters stood in one parish, namely, that of St. Magnus, with relation to the above mentioned Articles of Enquiry, the presentment following will declare; where, at a visitation of the Ordinary, were fourteen substantial parishioners made inquisitors, who found these articles.

.   .   .   .

"*Item.* We fynde, that for defaute of good provysion, both of the chirchwardeyns and also of the masters of the *Salve,* neyther the preystys nor clarkys that ben retayned for the chyrche will not come to our Lady Masse, nor *Salve.*

"Nor the clarkeys and preystys that ben retayned by the maysters of the *Salve* wil come to Masse or Matins in the quyer, where it might be wel brought about of the maysters of the *Salve* and the wardeyns of the chyrche wolde, for the mayntenyng of Goddys servyce, at the time of the receyvynge of such preystys and clarkys, gyve them charge, for as moche as they have so profytable and reasonable salery, that they al sholde as wel attende upon Masse, Matins, and Evensong, as unto our Lady Masse and *Salve,* and other servyce; the whych to do sholde encrease

[14] *Survey,* bk. ii. p. 175.

in the preystys and clarkys gud custume of vertu, and grete encrease of dyvyne servyce."[15]

XX. St. Martin.
11 May, 1259.

Master John of Gloucester, the King's mason, and the wardens of the works at Westminster, are ordered to supply five figures of kings, cut in free-stone, and a certain stone to be placed under the feet of an image of the Blessed Virgin Marye, to the wardens of the works of the church of St. Martin, London, for the same works, of the King's gift.

Writ tested Westminster. May 11.[16]

St. Stephens.

In 1368—43 Edward III.—a gild, called the Little Fraternity of our Ladye in the church of St. Stephen, in Colman Street, was founded by William Molton, mason, John Lenham, brewer, John Mushach, smith, John Smith, currier, Thomas Belchamber, leather-dyer, and other good people of the said parish, of their great devotion, and in honour of our Ladye, to find five wax candles upon one branch, of 31 pounds of wax, hanging before an image of our Ladye in the said church upon the beam; each brother and sister paying 12 *d.* yearly.

This is the first constitution of the gild: "Fyrst. All the bretheren and sustren everich yer ayenes the self Feste of the Assumption of our Ladi Seint Marye shul ben clothed of one sute of covenable clothings that falleth to her astat. But yif ony shall be of the kompaignee, because of poortee, ne may noyht make gree, yet he shal have atte lest a hode of the suyte, in token that he is a broder of the fraternite, so that he be holden broder or suster of gode condicion and honeste. The which day of the Assumption the foresaid bretheren and sustren shall have a solempne Messe in the honour of the foreseid Marye songen in the church of St. Stephen foreseid. At which Messe al the foreseid brethren and sustren up peine of two

[15] *Survey*, bk. v. p. 29.   [16] Close Roll. 43 Henry III.

pound wax shalle be present, fro the begynnyng of the foreseid Messe to the end : and at the Messe in dew tyme everych broder and suster a penye shal offre. The which Messe y-songen al the foreseyd bretheren and sustren shal go togydren to a certeyn place be her Maistres which be for the tyme assigned. In the which place alle schullen ete togedryn, on her owne purse, or at leste drinkes. And after the etyng and drinkyng (whether it be) the foreseid maistres his accompte for the time shall yelde up in gode manner and honeste."[17]

The Temple Church. ·

This beautiful church was consecrated by Heraclius, the Patriarch of Jerusalem, during his visit to England in 1185, and who died at the siege of Acre, in 1190. The following inscription was placed over the door leading into the cloister :

✠ ANNO ' AB ' INCARNATIONE ' DOMINI ' MCLXXXV
DEDICATA ' EST ' HEC ' ECCLESIA ' IN ' HONORE
BEATE ' MARIE ' A ' DOMINO ' ERACLIO ' DEI ' GRATIA
SANCTE ' RESURRECTIONIS ' ECCLESIE ' PATRIARCHA
IIII ' IDVS ' FEBRVARII ' QUI ' EAM ' ANNATIM ' PETEN-
TIBUS ' DE ' INIVNTA ' SIBI ' PENITENTIA ' LX ' DIES
INDVLSIT.[18]

The English Knights Templars formed a distinguished part of this noble and gallant order. The Rule of the Poor Fellow-Soldiers of Jesus Christ and of the Temple of Solomon was drawn up by St. Bernard, and sanctioned by the Council of Troyes in 1127.[19]

The Grand Priors, or Provincial Masters, took an oath to defend with their lips, by force of arms, with all their strength and their life the mysteries of the Faith, &c. . . . and the perpetual virginity before childbirth, in, and after childbirth, of the Blessed Virgin Marye, the

---

[17] Stow, bk. iii. p. 62.

[18] A facsimile of this inscription is given by Stow, bk. iii. p. 272 ; and by Addison, *History of the Knights Templars* : London, 1842, frontispiece.

[19] Labbé, *Concilia*, t. x. col. 923.

daughter of Joachim and Anne of the tribe of Juda, and of the race of King David.[20]

The Tower of London.

1. St. Peter *ad Vincula.*

In 1241 the King commands the keeper of the Tower works to have whitewashed the chancel of St. Marye in the Church of St. Peter, &c.; and the image of our Blessed Ladye (Mariola), with its tabernacle, to be coloured anew, and refreshed with good colours.

Tested Windsor, 10 December 25 Henry III., 1245.[21]

2. Chapel of St. John the Evangelist.

The same to the same.

"We command you . . . to whitewash the whole chapel of St. John the Evangelist in the great tower. And to make in the said chapel three glass windows, one, to wit, on the north part, with a certain small figure of Marye holding her child."

Tested, same place and date.[22]

3. The White Chapel.

Similar orders are also given for a glass window with our Blessed Ladye.[23]

Our Ladye of Graces, near the Tower.

In 1348 there was a great plague in London. It increased to such an extent, that, for want of space in the churchyards to bury the dead, one John Cory, clerk, procured of Nicholas, Prior of the Holy Trinity without Ealdgate (Aldgate) a toft of land near East Smithfield, for the burial of those who died, with the condition that it should be called the churchyard of the Holy Trinity. By the aid of devout citizens it was enclosed with a wall, and consecrated by Ralph Stratford, Bishop of London. Innumerable bodies were buried here, and a little chapel was erected to the honour of God.

---

[20] Henriquez, *Menologium Cisterciense.* Antv. 1639, p. 171; also Manrique, *Annales Cisterc.*: Lugd. 1942, p. 187.

[21] Librate Roll. 25 Henry III. m. 20.

[22] *Ibid.*

[23] *Ibid.*

During a storm at sea, and when in great danger, Edward the Third made a vow to build a monastery to the honour of God and Our Ladye of Graces, if God would grant him to come safe to land. He therefore built on this spot a monastery, which he caused to be called East-Minster, and placed in it an abbot and community of the Cistercian Order.

To them he gave all the messuages and appurtenances at Tower Hill which he had of John Cory aforesaid, in pure and perpetual alms, desiring this house to be called the Royal Free Chapel of St. Marye of Graces, by letters patent, tested at Westminster March 20, in the twenty-fourth year of our reign in England, and the eleventh of our reign in France—1350.[24]

They are to this effect:

"Edward, &c.

"Whilst with devout consideration we reflect on the various dangers to which on sundry occasions, as well by land and on sea, we have been, to all human appearance, exposed without any hope of escape, and on the lavish favours, with which, in these perils, the clemency of Christ on our invoking Him and the most Glorious Virgin His Mother, has mercifully prevented us, our heart burns within us, and we are inflamed with love for Jesus Christ our Lord Himself, and our Ladye His most beloved Mother Mary aforesaid. Desiring humbly to arrange something to their praise and glory, in memory of such favours, hoping that He, Who with so great favours mercifully prevented us, will always, through the affectionate mediation of His Mother, mercifully follow us up with an infusion of heavenly graces. Out of this consideration therefore, we have determined to found and endow, in the new cemetery of the Holy Trinity near our Tower of London, a House for the Monks of the Cistercian Order, which we will to be called the Free Chapel of Blessed Marye of Graces, to offer the sacrifice of praise and thanksgiving to God and our chief Protectress, the aforesaid most Blessed Marye, in a special manner. Know ye therefore," &c.

[24] Mon. Angl. V. p. 717.   [25] *Ibid.*

Those letters patent are recapitulated in the charter of Richard II., dated Nottingham, July 3, apparently in 1388; in which he confirms the foundation of his grandfather Edward, and recites and confirms the other donations.[25]

Sir Nicholas de Lovaigne, knight, by his will dated 20th September, 1375, wills his body to be buried in the Abbey Church of Penshurst, otherwise in the Abbey of Our Lady of Grace, in London, near the Tower.[26]

Our Ladye in West Cheap.

A cross used to stand in West Cheap, of which Stow says: "In the year 1581, the 21st of June, in the night, the lowest images round about the same cross (being of Christ's resurrection, of the Blessed Virgin Marye, King Edward the Confessor, and such like) were broken and defaced. Whereupon proclamation was made, that whoso would bewray the doers thereof should have forty crowns, but nothing came to light. The image of the Blessed Virgin, at that time, robbed of her Son, and her arms broken, by which she staid Him on her knees, her whole body was also haled with ropes and left ready to fall; but was in the year 1595 again fastened and repaired. And in the year 1596, about Bartholomew tide, a new son, misshapen (as born out of time) all naked, was laid in her arms, the other images remaining broken as before. On the east side of the same cross, the steps being taken thence, under the image of Christ's resurrection defaced, was then set up a curious wrought tabernacle of grey marble, and in the same an alabaster image of Diana."...[27]

About the 5th January, 1601, the image of our Lady was again defaced, by plucking off her crown, and almost her head, taking from her her naked child, and stabbing her in the breast.[28]

God's Houses.

One example must suffice.

II. Sir Richard Whittington, who was four times Lord Mayor, built a College of the Holy

Ghost and Saint Marye, and a God's House for thirteen poor men, one of them to be the tutor. The MS. Constitutions are in the archives of the Mercer's Company.

This is the ordinance in regard of prayers—

"Every tutour and poor folk, every day first whan they rise fro their bedds, kneeling upon their knees, sey a *Pater noster* and an *Ave Maria* with special and herty recommendacion-making of the foreseid Richard Whyttington and Alice to God and our Blessed Ladye Maidyn Marye. And other times of the day whan he may best and most commody have leisure thereto, for the staat of al the souls abovesaid, say three or two sauters of our Lady at the least : that is to say, threies seven *Ave Marias*, with XV *Pater nosters*, and three *Credes*. But if he be letted with febleness or any other reasonable cawse, one in the day at the least, in case it may be : that is to say, after the Messe, or whan Complyn is don, they come togidder within the College about the tomb of the aforesaid Rich. Whyttington and Alice, and then they that can sey, shal sey for the souls of the said Richard and Alice, and for the souls of all Christen people, this psalm *de Profundis*, with the Versicles and Oriosons that longeth thereto. And they that can shal sey three *Ave Marias*, three *Pater nosters*, and oon *Crede*. And after this doon, the tutour, or oon of the eldest men of theym, shal sey openly in English, God have mercy on our founders' souls and al Chrysten. And they that stond about shal answer and sey Amen."[29]

ALMSGIVING.

On a field to the east side of Houndsditch there were some small cottages two stories high, and little garden plots behind, for poor bed-ridden people—for in that street dwelt none other—built by some Prior of the Holy Trinity, to whom that ground belonged. "In my youth," continues Stow, "I remember devout people, as well men as women, of this city were accustomed often-times, especially on Fridays, weekly, to walk that

[29] *Survey*, bk. iii. p. 4.

way purposely, and there to bestow their charitable alms, every poor man or woman lying in
bed within their window, which was towards the
street, open so low that every man might see
them : a clean linen cloth lying in their window,
and a pair of beads, to show that there lay a
bed-rid body, unable but to pray only."[30]

HOSPITALS.

In London and the suburbs there were five
hospitals called after our Blessed Ladye.

1. St. Mary in Barking

Was provided for poor priests and others,
men and women in the city of London that were
fallen into frenzy or loss of their memory, until
such time as they should recover.   It is now
suppressed.[31]

2. St. Mary Bethlehem.

The magnificent hospital in Southwark, commonly called Bedlam, commemorates the pious
foundation of Simon Fitz-Marye in 1247.   He
had been one of the sheriffs of London in the
preceding year.   It was originally founded for a
priory of canons with brethren and sisters ; and
Edward the Third, in the fourteenth year of his
reign, 1340—1341, granted a protection for the
brethren *militiæ Beatæ Mariæ de Bethlehem* in the
City of London.   It was after a hospital for dis-
tracted people.[32]

This is the foundation deed as given by Stow :

" To all, &c., Simon the son of Marye sendeth
greeting in our Lord.

" Where among other things, and before other
lands, the high altitude of the heavenly counsels,
marvelously wrought by some readier devotion, it
ought to be more worshipped : of which things
the mortal sickness (after the fall of our first
father Adam) hath taken the beginning of this
new repairing.   Therefore, indeed, it beseemeth
worthy that the place in which the Son of God is
become Man, and hath proceeded from the
Virgin's womb, which is increaser and beginner of

---

[30] *Survey*, bk. ii. p. 23.   [31] *Ibid.* Appendix, p. 20.   [32] *Ibid.* bk. ii. p. 94.

man's redemption, namely ought to be with reverence worshipped, and with beneficial portions to be increased. Therefore it is that the said Simon, son of Marye, having special and singular devotion to the Church of the Glorious Virgin at Bethlehem, where the same Virgin of her brought forth our Saviour Incarnate, and lying in the cratch (*i.e.*, manger), and with her own milk nourished; and where the same Child to us then born, the chivalry of the heavenly company sang the new hymn, *Gloria in excelsis Deo.* The same time, the increaser of our health (as a King, and His Mother as a Queen) willed to be worshipped of kings; a new star going before them at the honour and reverence of the same Child and His most meek Mother, and to the exaltation of my most noble Lord, Henry King of England, whose wife and child the foresaid Mother of God and her only Son have in their keeping and protection: and to the manifold increase of this City of London in which I was born; and also for the health of my soul, &c. Have given, granted, and by this my present charter have confirmed to God and to the Church of St. Marye of Bethlehem all my lands, &c." (here follows the enumeration). The foresaid church of Bethlehem to have and to hold in free and perpetual alms. And also to make there a priory, and to ordain a prior and canons, brothers, and also sisters, when Jesus Christ shall enlarge His grace upon it. And in the same place the Rule and Order of the said Church of Bethlehem solemnly professing, which shall bear the token of a star openly on their copes and mantles of profession, and to say Divine Service then for the souls aforesaid, and all Christian souls. . . . And in token of subjection and reverence, the said place in London without Bishopsgate, shall pay yearly in the said city a mark sterling at Easter to the Bishop of Bethlehem, his successors or his messengers, in the name of a pension. And if the faculties or goods of the said place (our Lord granting) happen to grow more, the said place shall pay more in the name of pension, at the said term, to the mother church of Bethlehem. This gift and confirmation of my deed, and the putting-to of my seal for me and mine heires I have steadfastly made strong, the year of our Lord one thousand two hundred forty seven, the Wednesday after the feast of St. Luke the Evangelist; these being witnesses, Peter the son of Allen, then Mayor of London, and many more."[33]

The spot on which this hospital stood was called Old Bethlehem ; now Liverpool Street.

In 1644, it was under consideration to enlarge the old hospital, but the situation was judged unfavourable : in 1675 the new hospital of Bethlem was commenced near London Wall, to the south of the lower quarter of Little Moorfields; subsequently it was transferred to the other side of the river, where it now forms one of the chief features of Southwark.[34]

The ancient seal represented the Assumption of our Blessed Ladye.[35]

3. St. Mary Spital, or the New Hospital of Our Ladye.

This Priory and Hospital of our Blessed Ladye, commonly called Saint Marye Spittle, or Spital, was founded by Walter Brune, a citizen of London, and Rosia, his wife, in 1197. It was dedicated by William, Bishop of London, to the honour of Jesus Christ, and His Mother, the perpetual Virgin Marye, by the name of Domus Dei et Beatæ Mariæ extra Bishopgate. In 1235 it was refounded, and as a work *de novo*, and not relatively to any other foundation, received the title as above.[36] It surrendered to Henry VIII., and besides the ornaments of the Church, and other goods pertaining to the Hospital, there were found standing nine score beds well furnished for the receipt of the poor of charity. For, continues Stow, it was a hospital of great relief.[37]

In the yard of St. Mary Spital stood the celebrated Pulpit Cross.

The later common seal represents our Blessed

[33] Bk. ii. p. 94. I have been unable to collate Stow's version with the original.
[34] Mon. Angl. vi. 621.
[35] Hearne's MS. Diaries, vol. cxxii. in the Bodleian Library, Oxford.
[36] Mon. Angl. t. vi. p. 623.   [37] Bk. ii. p. 97.

H

Ladye under a canopy, between two religious men, and surrounded by Cherubim.[38]

4. St. Mary within Cripplegate was founded in 1329 by William Elsing, mercer, as a Hospital for one hundred blind men of the City of London.[39]

5. St. Mary Rounceval, or Roncevalles, near Charing Cross.

William Marshal, Earl of Pembroke, having amongst other estates, given several tenements near Charing Cross to the Prior of Rouncevall, or *de Rosida Valle*, in the diocese of Pampeluna in Navarre, *temp*. Henry III., a Hospital or Chapel of St. Marye which was the chief house in England belonging to that foreign priory was erected on the site.[40]

In 1614, Northumberland House, now a mansion of the past, was erected, and according to Newcourt, out of the ruins of this Hospital.[41]

THE TWELVE GREAT LIVERY COMPANIES.

Our Blessed Ladye was the Patroness of four of them; to wit:

1. The Skinners' Company, which was incorporated in the first year of Edward III., 1327, and made into a Brotherhood in the eighteenth of Richard II., 1394—1395.[42]

2. The Clothworkers' Company, which was incorporated April 12, 1482, by the appellation of the Fraternity of the Assumption of the Blessed Virgin Marye of the Sheermen of the City of London.[43] Their annual feast and entertainment of meat and drink was held in a competent place on the festival of the Assumption of our Blessed Ladye.[44]

[38] Mon. Angl. t. ii. p. 97.
[39] Stow, Append. p. 20.
[40] Mon. Angl. c. vi. p. 677.
[41] Repertorium v. i. p. 693.
[42] Herbert, *History of the Twelve Great Livery Companies of London.* Lond. 1836, v. ii. p. 299.
[43] *Ibid.* p. 643; and Stow, Bk. v. p. 198.
[44] Herbert, p. 651.

3. The Drapers, as the Mother of the Lamb. They were incorporated in 1430.[45]

4. The Mercers.[46]

LUDGERSHALL CASTLE.

In 1250 the Constable of Marlborough Castle is ordered . . . to place an image of Blessed Marye, with her child, in the King's chapel, in the Castle of Ludgershall.

Writ tested Clarendon, July 19.[47]

In 1251 the Constable of Marlborough Castle is ordered . . . to make an image of Blessed Marye, with her child, in the chapel of St. Leonard in Ludgershall Castle.

Writ tested Marlborough, July 3.[48]

LUDLOW.

There was a very remarkable example of a pendant pix or ciborium at Ludlow, which is described as "an image of our Ladye of Pytte for yᵉ Sacrament."[49]

LYNN EPISCOPI, now LYNN REGIS, or KING'S LYNN.

1. Our Ladye on the Mount.

Many offerings were made to the image of our Ladye, in her chapel on the Mount of Lynn, by pilgrims who visited it on their way to Walsingham.[50]

This chapel is described as a very remarkable specimen of architecture; extreme length 17 feet, and width 14. The perfect form of a cross is preserved, although it stands within an octagonal wall; and another curious feature was that every one was obliged to make a complete circuit of the chapel before entering it.

Our Ladye's Gild at Lynn was founded in the third year of Edward III., 1329.

Great was the resort of pilgrims to this sanctuary, and the profits and offerings at the Chapel on the Mount are accounted as 16*l.* 10*s.* in the compotus of George Elyngham, prior of St. Margaret, in the first year of Henry VIII.[51]

[45] Herbert, v. i. pp. 67, 391. [46] *Ibid.* p. 226.
[47] Liberate Roll, 34 Henry III. [48] *Ibid.* 35 Henry III.
[49] *Transactions of the London and Middlesex Archæological Institute*, v. iv. p. 373.
[50] *Index. Mon. Diœc. Norv.* p. 66; and Preface, xx.
[51] *General History of Norfolk*, pp. 429—431.

2. Our Ladye on the Bridge.

Some small remains of this chapel converted into a little dwelling stood, till very lately, on the eastern side of the bridge.[52]

MAYFIELD.

In 1471 William de Ponte bequeaths "towards a new picture of St. Marye of Maghfield xx*s*., if the parishioners are willing to repaint the same.[53]

MALTON.

Not far from Malton was a celebrated sanctuary of our Blessed Ladye, called Mount Grace. It is mentioned in the MS. account of the martyrdom of Father John Taylor, S.J., in 1642.[54]

MANCHESTER.

The Cathedral.

Hollingworth mentions a large statue of St. George in the chapel called by that name, "the horse from which was," he says, "lately in the saddler's shop. The statues of the Virgin Marye, St. Dyonyse, the other patron saints, were upon the two highest pillars next to the quire; unto them men did bow at their coming into the church."[55]

MARFORD, near ST. ALBAN'S.

In the third of Henry VI., 1424–5, one William, a tenant of the abbot's, being at Marford, and afflicted with blindness, in a spirit of devotion caused a wooden cross to be erected on the right hand side of the high road leading to Codicote over Marford Bridge; and near to it he placed a statue of our Blessed Ladye in alabaster.[56]

MARLBOROUGH.

The Constable of Marlborough Castle is ordered to make . . . in the Queen's chapel a crucifix there with Marye and John, and Marye with her child.

Writ tested Clarendon, July 19.[57]

MELFORD.

In the inventory of the ornaments belonging to the Church of the Holy Trinity are enumerated "coats belonging to our Ladye."

[52] *General History of Norfolk*, p. 431.　　[53] Test. Vetust. p. 326.
[54] MS. Varia S.J. Cart. 29, in Bib. Reg. Bruxell.
[55] *Journal of British Archæological Association*, v. iii. p. 197.
[56] *Chron. Mon. S. Albani*, v. i. p. 6. Rolls Edit.
[57] Liberate Roll, 34 Henry III.

1. A coat for the good days, of cloth of tissue bordered with white; and for her Son, another of the same, in like case.

2. A coat of crimson velvet, and another for her Son, in like case.

3. A coat of white damask, and another for her Son, in like case, bordered about with green velvet.[58]

I find this entry in the second of Edward VI., "*It.* Sold to Mr. Clopton the altʳ alebastʳ in our ladye's chapell vi *s.* viii *d.*"[59]

MESSINGHAM PARVA, NORFOLK.
John l'Estrange, third son of Henry l'Estrange, of Hunstanton, by his will in 1516 bequeaths his body to be buried, if he died within five miles of Messingham, before our Blessed Ladye, in the chapel on the south side of the chancel of this church.[60]

METTINGHAM, SUFFOLK.
A piece of land called Nolloths was left to the College of Mettingham, to find a wax light, for ever to be burnt before the image of our Blessed Ladye in the choir of the chapel.[61]

About the year 1414, an image of our Blessed Ladye was sculptured, for which the wood appears to have been provided by Sir William Argentein; and Thomas Barsham, of Yarmouth, who is also called Thomas de Jernemuta, received in several payments, for making and painting two images, with tabernacles, and a *tabula* for the high altar, not less than 37 *l.* 4 *s.* 8 *d.*[62]

MIDDLEBOROUGH.
In 1453, Thomas Lynehouse of Leventhorpe, in Cleveland, leaves a support for the light of our Ladye in the parish church of St. Hilda of Middleburg.[63]

MILDENHALL.
1. The image of our Ladye was by the high altar. In 1477, Thomas Chylderston bequeathed

---

[58] *Notes and Queries* 3 Series, v. iii. p. 179.
[59] *Proceedings of Suffolk Archæological Institute*, v. ii. p. 81.
[60] *General History of Norfolk*, p. 472.   [61] Suckling, v. i. p. 177.
[62] *Proceedings of Royal Archæological Institute*, v. vi. p. 67.
[63] Test. Ebor. vol. ii. p. 171.

to the image of the most glorious Virgin Marye by the said altar, vi *s.* vii *d.*[64]

2. The chapel of our Ladye over the porch.

In 1519, Thomas Marchanter of Mildenhall bequeathed "to the reparacon of the chapell of owre Ladye ovyr the porch, xx*d.* ;" and in 1527, Alice Bateman left xii*d.* for the same object.[65]

MISSINDEN, BUCKS.

In the King's expenditure, July 27, third Henry the Eighth: "To Mast. Egerton for offering at our Ladye at Myssenden Abbey, 6*s.* 8*d.*"[66]

MOLESCROFT.

By will dated February 25, 1498, Agnes Hilyard leaves to the image of our Blessed Ladye at Mollescroft, 3*s.* 4*d.* in gold to hang round her neck.[67]

MOLSA.

Agnes, wife of William Bird of Beverley, by will dated the feast of St. Lambert, 1398, leaves half a piece *velorum de sipirs* to the image of the Blessed Virgin Marye over the door of the chapel in the woods of Molsa.[68]

MOULTON S.MICHAEL, *or* GT. MOULTON. NORFOLK.

Here was a chapel of our Blessed Ladye with an altar, image, and light.[69]

MOUNT BADON.

Guppenberg mentions in the *Atlas Marianus* a miraculous image of our Blessed Ladye under the title of *Imago B. V. M. miraculosa Regia de Monte Badonico.*[70] It was, however, the image of our Blessed Ladye which King Arthur had painted on his shield, and carried at the battle of Mount Badon ; and which Guppenberg describes in another place as our Ladye *de Clypeo.* I have already referred to it.[71]

The account of the battle is thus given by Matthew of Westminster :

"The Saxons Colgrin, Bardulf, and Cheldric, repented of having made a truce with King Arthur, and assailed Mount Badon. The King ordered

---

[64] *Proceedings of Suffolk Archæological Institute*, vol. i, p. 271.   [65] *Ibid.*
[66] Letters and Papers, &c. Henry VIII. vol. ii. pt. ii. p. 1452.
[67] Test. Ebor. vol. iv. p. 133.
[68] Test. Ebor. vol. i. p. 240.   [69] *General History of Norfolk*, 106.
[70] No. ccccxxxxix. p. 591.   [71] Vide p. 86.

his troops to arms; he himself put on his coat of mail, and donned his dragon-crested helmet. He slung on his shoulder his shield named Pridwen, in which the image of the Holy Mother of God painted thereon perpetually recalled her to his thoughts. He girded on his brave falchion Caliburn, and seized his lance called Iron with his right hand. Drawing up his forces, he boldly attacked the Pagans. They fought bravely, but when much of the day had been spent in fighting, at last King Arthur, drawing Caliburn, and invoking the name of the Blessed Virgin Marye, dashed into the serried ranks of the foe; whomsoever he struck needed no second cut. He did not cease until eight hundred and forty of the enemy had fallen beneath his sharp-edged blade! Colgrin and Bardulf perished, with many thousands of their followers; Cheldric saved himself by flight."[72] This victory the pious King attributed to the intercession of our Blessed Ladye.

MUSWELL.

On the hill which separates Hornsey from Finchley Common, and not far from the Alexandra Park stood the celebrated shrine of our Ladye of Muswell to which there was a continual resort of pilgrims. It was attached to the Priory of the Knights Hospitallers of St. John of Jerusalem at Clerkenwell, by Richard de Beauvais, Bishop of London in 1112.

In his *Speculum Britanniæ*, Norden says:

" There formerly stood at Muswell Hill, called Pinsenall, a chappell, sometime bearing the name of our Ladie of Muswell, where now Alderman Row hath erected a proper house; the place taketh the name of the hall (Mousewell Hill) for there is on the hill a spring of faire water which is now within the compass of the house. There was for some time an image of the Ladye of Muswell, whereunto was a continued resort in the way of pilgrimage, growing as is (though as I take it) fabulously reported, in regard of a great cure which was performed by this water upon a King of Scots, who, being strangely diseased, was by

[72] Flores. Hist. per M. Westm. collecti. Francofurti 1601, pp. 96, 97. Roger of Wendover gives the name of Arthur's lance as Ron, vol. i. pp. 64, 65. Ed. Coxe. Lond. 1841.

some divine intelligence advised to take the water of a well in England, called Muswell, which, after long scrupulation and inquisition, this well was found, and performed the cure ; absolutely to deny the cure, I dare not, for that the High God hath given virtue unto waters to heale infirmities, as may appear by the cure of Naaman, the leper, by washing himself seven times in Jordan, and by the Poole Bethseda which healed the rest that stopped there, after it was moved by the Angell."[73]

MUTFORD, SUFFOLK. Here the church had a gild and a light of our Ladye.

In 1401, Dame de Mutford, widow of Sir Edward de Hengrave, gave by her will vi *s*. viii *d*. to the light of our Ladye in Mutford church.[74]

NEWARK. John Burton, S.T.P., Vicar of Newark, says in his will, dated 29th September, 1475 :

"I desire that certain collars, pairs of beads, rings, gems, crucifixes, and other jewels which appear in a list in the keeping of the churchwardens, remain for ever for the adorning of the image of the Blessed Virgin Marye and her Son, in the chapel beyond the south doors of the aforesaid church, in the honour of God, the Blessed Virgin Marye, and all the Saints.[75]

NEWBURGH MONAS- Every day there was given and distributed to
TERY, YORKSHIRE. the poor an alms called *Ladymete*, and a measure of beer.[76]

NEWENHAM, CAM- Although I have found no mention of any
BRIDGESHIRE. shrine of our Blessed Ladye, or of lights and offerings at this place, still Newenham must not be omitted from this series, because here it was that the Scapular was instituted.

In 1249, Michael Malherbe gave the Carmelites a habitation at Newenham, just outside Cambridge, where they remained forty-two years. In 1291 they removed into the parish of St. John-Miln-Street, where they received great benefac-

---

[73] Vol. i. p. 653.   [74] Suckling, v. i. p. 276.
[75] Test. Ebor. vol. iii. p. 218.   [76] *Valor Ecclesiasticus*, t. v. p. 93.

tions from King Edward I., Sir Guy de Mortimer, and Thomas de Hertford.[77]

Born in 1165, St. Simon Stock was admitted into the Carmelite Order in 1212; and in 1245 was named General by the Chapter held at Aylesford.

The celebrated vision occurred on the morning of the 16th July, 1251, before the break of day, and in the Carmelite Chapel at Newenham.

The principal authority is Father Peter Swanyngton, a Carmelite, and the confessor, companion, and secretary of St. Simon. He wrote the relation of the vision as dictated to him by the Saint, and on the day of its occurrence.

These are his words:

"The Blessed Simon, broken down by a lengthy old age and rigorous penance, and by bearing the troubles of his brethren in his heart, was diligently watching in prayer through the night, even until morning. And whilst thus making his prayer, he received a consolation from heaven, which he thus narrated to us in community:

"'Most dear Brothers, Blessed be God, Who does not abandon those who hope in Him, nor despise their prayers! Blessed, the most Holy Mother of Christ Jesus our Lord, who, mindful of the days of old, and of the tribulations which have found many of you exceedingly (not considering that all who desire to lead a devout life in Jesus Christ suffer persecutions), sends you a message which you will receive in the joy of the Holy Ghost: may He direct me that I may make it known to you in the manner in which it behoves me to speak.

"'Whilst I was pouring out my soul in the sight of the Lord, dust and ashes as I am, and praying with full confidence to our Ladye the Blessed Virgin Marye, that, since she wished us to be called her brothers, she would show herself a Mother to us, by delivering us from the danger of temptations and recommending us by some SIGN of favour to those who were persecuting us, saying to her with sighs—

[77] *Mon. Angl.* vi. p. 1570.

Flos Carmeli,
Vitis florigera,
Splendor cœli,
Virgo puerpera
Singularia.
Mater mitis,
Sed viri nescia,
Carmelitis
Da privilegia.
Stella maris.

"'She appeared to me attended by a great retinue, and holding in her hands the habit of the Order—*habitum ordinis*—said :

"'*Hoc erit tibi et cunctis Carmelitis privilegium. In hoc moriens æternum non patietur incendium.*'"

Swanyngton continues :

"He sent this same message to the brethren who were in other places very sorrowful, as a letter of consolation, which I, undeserving as I am, wrote at the dictation of the man of God, so that they might return thanks altogether by prayer and perseverence. At Cambridge, on the morrow of the Separation of the Apostles (16 July), 1251."[78]

St. Simon Stock died in 1265, at the age of a hundred years, in the house of his Order at Bordeaux. His death-song was the Angelic Salutation. When the controversies about the Carmelite Order were started in the seventeenth century, an autograph copy of Father Swanyngton's letter was found in the archives of the convent at Bordeaux.[79]

NORTHAMPTON.

Our Ladye of Grace.
In the accounts of Elizabeth of York.
March 24, 1502.
Offering to our Ladye of Grace at Northampton, ij *s.* vi *d.*[80]
August 5, 1502.
Item. Delivered to M. Xpofre Plommer, for

[78] *Vinea Carmeli,* n. 751, pp. 390 *et seq.*: *Speculum Carmelitanum,* t. ii. p. 429, n. 1515: *Menologium Carmelitanum,* p. 292. Bononiæ, 1628.
[79] Benedict XIV. *De Festis,* l. ii. c. vi. § 8. De Festo B.M. de Monte Carmelo.
[80] P. 3.

thoffering of the Quene at hir being sikke at Woodstock to oure Lady at Northampton ij *s.* vi *d.*[81]

In the King's book of payments, 3 Henry VIII. August 3-9, 1509.

Offerings at the Rood of the Wall in Northampton.

At our Ladye of Grace there. Sum not given.[82]

NORTON, SUFFOLK. Frequent bequests of sheep, wheat, barley, malt, &c., were made here at the altar of our Blessed Ladye, for the support of her light.[83]

NORWICH. I. The Cathedral

1. In 1244, Bishop Walter de Suffield founded the chapel of the Blessed Virgin at the east end of the Cathedral, before the high altar of which he was buried. It is now demolished.[84] By his will, amongst other bequests, he left to the light of our Ladye on the altar in her chapel by him founded, the tithes in his demesne lands in Thornham for ever, and twenty marks to purchase more annual rents for its support. Also, to Walter de Calthorpe his nephew, sundry articles, for which he required him, as long as he lived, to feed yearly one hundred poor on the Assumption of the Blessed Virgin, and to give a poor person a dinner every day in the year. To his faithful and beloved William de Whitewell he bequeathed the image of our Blessed Ladye given him by Master Roger de Reveningham.[85]

2. Our Ladye of Pity.

The chapel of our Ladye of Pity was in the ante-choir; her image was under the rood loft.[86]

In 1423, John Crispyng, Esquire, was buried here; and amongst other legacies he gave 40 *s.* to find a light burning before our Ladye of Pity.[87]

3. There was also another image described as the great image of the Blessed Virgin; in 1401 there was a charge of ij *s.* vi *d.* for painting on the wall before it.[88]

P. 37. [82] Letters and Papers, &c. Henry VIII. v. ii. pt. ii. p. 1452.
[83] *Proceedings of Suffolk Archæological Institute,* v. ii. p. 290.
[84] Blomefield, vol. ii. p. 345. [85] *Ibid.* p. 347.
[86] *Ind. Mond. Diœc. Norv.* p. 66. [87] Blomefield, vol. ii. p. 509.
[88] Norwich vol. of the Royal Archæological Institute, p. 208.

II. St. Andrew's.

1. Our Ladye of Grace.

The chapel of our Ladye of Grace was under the steeple; in it was her image, with a light always burning before it, on her altar, and a gild to her honour was held here.[88]

Numerous bequests were made to this sanctuary.

In 1504, Agnes Est leaves to our Ladye in the steeple a pair of beads of silver. In 1505, Edmund Wright bequeathed 20s. to the church lights to be set before the images in the chapel of Our Ladye of Grace. In 1508, Robert Gardiner, alderman, desires to be buried in our Ladye's chapel in the steeple, and gave £6 for a pair of gilt chalices; he also willed a well-disposed priest to go to Rome, to sing there thirteen weeks, for himself and his wives; and the rest of the year in St. Andrew's, and he to have twenty marks.[90] In 1510, John Chirche left a legacy to gild the image of Our Ladye of Grace in her chapel.[91]

2. Our Ladye in the Churchyard.

In 1476, Thomas Cambridge, mercer, desired to be buried in the churchyard before the image of our Ladye. He left several legacies of vestments, and gave a donation towards the maintenance of the daily Mass of Jesus and the Marye Mass.[92]

3. There was also a tabernacle with the image of the Visitation of our Blessed Ladye.[93]

III. St. Augustine's.

In 1418, Sir John Corpusty, rector of this church, on the presentation of the Prior of Norwich, founded a light before the image of the Blessed Virgin in her chapel here.[94]

IV. Church of the Austin Friars.

1. Our Ladye of Pity.

2. In this church was the celebrated chapel of our Lady called the *Scala Cæli*, to which there was a continual resort of pilgrims, who made their offerings at the altar. It was richly endowed

[88] Blomefield, vol. ii. p. 703.   [90] *Ibid.* p. 702.   [91] *Ibid.* p. 703.
[93] *Ibid.* p. 702.   [92] *Ibid.* p. 703.   [94] *Ibid.* p. 832.

with indulgences by various Popes; most folks desired to have Masses sung for them here, or to be buried in the cloister of the *Scala Cæli*, that they might be made partakers of the many pardons and indulgences granted by the Popes to this place; this being the only chapel in England, except that of the same name at Westminster, and that of Our Ladye in St. Botulph's, at Boston, which had the same privileges as the chapel of the *Scala Cæli* at Rome.[95]

V. The Charnel House, now the Free School.

Ralph Pulvertoft, principal or custos of the Charnel House, by his will dated March 27, 1525, desired to be buried in our Ladye's chapel at the end of the presbytery, and left a taper of five pounds of wax to be set before the image of our Ladye in the chapel in which he was buried, and a candle of half a pound of wax to be kept for a year burning on his grave daily, whilst the Ladye Mass was being sung there.[96]

VI. The Carmelites, or White Friars.

The Carmelites were established in Norwich about the year 1256. Their founder was Philip, the son of Warine, the son of Adam Arnold, or Ernold, of Cowgate, in Norwich, a merchant who assumed the name of Cowgate; he bestowed his messuage, and the buildings and yards belonging to it, on the order; the friars, by the gift of their founder and other good people, erected a noble church, and dedicated it to the Holy Virgin; which being finished, Philip entered the order and died in the house of his own foundation on the 23rd April, 1283. He appointed no patron, and consequently they continued without one until 1485, when the prior, Thomas Waterpitte, S.T.B., and his convent, supplicated the mayor, aldermen, sheriffs, and citizens of Norwich, that, as their founder was a merchant and a fellow-citizen, and had assigned to them no patron, they would henceforward be patrons, which they accepted; and it was confirmed in the General Chapter of

---

[95] Blomefield, vol. ii. p. 552; and *Index. Mon. Diæc. Norv.* pp. 43, 66.
[96] *Ibid.* p. 529.

their order held at Burnham, on the Feast of the Assumption, 1486, and Brother John, Prior Provincial of the said order, decreed in open chapter, that the Corporation should be prayed for in all divine services in the monastery as their patrons, and should be partakers of all the benefit of the prayers of all the brethren of the order throughout England; and in token hereof, the convent confirmed it under the common seal to the mayor, and the mayor, under the city seal, to the order.[97]

In 1498, the mayor and sheriffs granted to the prior and brethren, under their common seal, that they should be for ever free from all toll and custom of the city, and all fees due to the city officers.[98]

The image of our Blessed Ladye stood in the north side of the church, and several persons were buried before it.[99]

The seal of the Carmelites at Norwich bore a castle, showing the city to be their patrons, under it our Blessed Lady holding her Divine Son in her arms, on each side two friars in their proper habits, two of whom have labels issuing from their mouths bearing these words :

1. Ave Fili Mater.
2. Virgo divina, Mater.[100]

VII. St. Edmund, K.M.

The image of our Blessed Ladye, with its light, stood in the south chapel. In 1467, John Moor was buried in that chapel, and before the image of our Ladye.[101]

VIII. St George of Colegate.

In this church there was a light before the image of our Blessed Ladye.[102]

IX. St. George at Tombland.

In 1491, Agnes Petyte, widow, was buried in this church; she gave wax lights to burn before Our Ladye of Pity.[103]

---

[97] Blomefield, p. 789.   [98] *Ibid.* p. 790.   [99] *Ibid.* p. 791.   [100] *Ibid.* p. 895.
[101] *Ibid.* p. 783.   [102] *Ibid.* p. 829.   [103] *Ibid.* p. 744.

X. St. Giles.

Here was an altar of Our Ladye of Pity, and its gild; a light was also kept burning before the image of our Blessed Ladye. Several persons were buried before Our Ladye of Pity.[104]

XI. St. Gregory.

On the north side was the chapel of our Ladye, which was dedicated to her Assumption. Here was our Ladye's altar and her image, with a light always burning before it. At this altar the Jesus Mass was celebrated.[105]

There were five bells here; the third bore the inscription—

Gabriel abe, hac in conclabe nunc pange suabe.[106]

XII. St. James.

There is in this church, at the upper end of the aisle, a chapel dedicated to our Ladye, whose image stood by the altar, with a light burning before it.[107]

XIII. St. John the Baptist, or the Friars Preachers.

An image of our Ladye stood in the choir of this church.[108]

In 1452, Edmund Segeford, mercer, was buried in the upper end of the north aisle, in the chapel by the window glazed with the history of the *Magnificat.*[109]

XIV. St. Julian.

In 1421, Robert Steynton of Wilton was buried in the chancel before the image of our Blessed Ladye at the south-east corner of the high altar.[110]

XV. St. Lawrence.

1. Our Blessed Ladye.

In 1508, John King by his will leaves two dozen wax candles to burn before this image, in her chapel.[111]

[104] Blomefield, p. 657.   [105] *Ibid.* p. 680.   [106] *Ibid.* p. 681.   [107] *Ibid.* p. 795.
[108] *Ibid.* p. 730.   [109] *Ibid.* p. 727.   [110] *Ibid.* p. 545.   [111] *Ibid.* p. 678.

2. Our Ladye of Pity; and,

3. Our Ladye of the Assumption. Lights were kept constantly burning before them.[112]

XVI. St. Leonard's Priory.

Here there was a celebrated image of our Blessed Ladye in the Priory of St. Leonard's on Mousehold, called St. Leonard's Without, to which great offerings were made, and many pilgrimages.[113]

Mrs. Paston, after hearing of her husband's illness, wrote to him on the 28th September, 1443:

"I have behested to go on pilgrimage to Walsingham, and to St. Leonard's for you."[114]

XVII. The Leper-house in the parish of St. Clement's.

Here was an image of our Ladye with a light before it.[115]

XVIII. St. Martin in Coslany.

1. An image of Our Ladye of Pity, with a light, either a lamp or a wax taper, constantly burning before it.

2. The chapel of our Ladye, with her altar, was at the east end of the south aisle, together with an image of the Blessed Virgin and a light.[116]

3. Our Ladye of the Oak.

This church was commonly called St Martin's at the Oak, from a large oak which stood in the churchyard, and which contained the celebrated image of our Ladye of the Oak.

Blomefield says:

"It seems that this oak and statue began to be of remark about the time of Edward II., for then I find it first called *atte the oke*. What particular virtue this good Ladye had, I don't know, but certain it was she was very much visited by the populace, who left many gifts in their wills to dress, paint, and repair her. This was a

---

[112] Blomefield, p. 673. [113] *Ibid.* p. 797; and *Ind. Mon. Diæc. Norv.* p. 66.
[114] Paston Letters, vol. iii. p. 21. Edit. Fenn. Lond. 1787.
[115] Blomefield, p. 822. [116] *Ibid.* p. 837.

famous image of the Blessed Virgin Marye placed in the oak which grew in the churchyard, so that it was seen by all that passed in the street, from whence the church took the name of St. Martin at the Oak, it being always before called St. Martin in Coste Lane (near the side of the river) or Coselany, the whole part of the city from Black-friars' Bridge, or New Bridge to St. Martin at the oak gates being called so because it lies on the *coste* of the river.

"At the coming of Edward VI. to the Crown, our Ladye was dismounted, and I am apt to believe the poor oak cut down also, least that should be visited for our Ladyship's sake; for the present oak which now grows in the place hath not been planted a hundred years, as appears by the Parish Register in these words: 'I, John Tabor, constable and overseer, did bring the oak from Ranner Hall near Horningferry, before me on my horse, and set it in the churchyard of St. Martin of Coselany. I set it March 9, 1656.'

"Then also the rich vestments and plate were sold, and the money employed to mend and fye the river." [117]

In 1513, John Buxton, worsted-weaver, was buried in the churchyard before the image of our Ladye in the Oke, and gave to our Ladye in the Oke, 6d. [118]

XIX. St. Martin formerly called at the Palace Gate.

In this church there was an image of our Ladye with a light. [119]

XX. St. Marye in Coslany.

1. In this church the principal image of our Blessed Ladye stood in its usual place on the north side of the high altar.

2. In our Ladye's chapel on the south side was her altar and image.

3. In this chapel there was also an image of our Ladye of Pity.

All the images had lights before them.

---

[117] Blomefield, p. 836.   [118] *Ibid.*   [119] *Ibid.* p. 748.

In 1464, Robert Wood was buried before our Ladye of Pity.

In 1465, Henry Toke founded a candle before our Ladye of Pity, and another one before the principal image of our Ladye.[120]

The Marye bell was inscribed:

Uirginis egregie bocor campana Marie.[121]

XXI. College of St. Marye in the Fields.
1. Our Ladye of Pity.
Her image stood in the south side.
2. Our Ladye at St. James's altar.
The Marye-Mass was daily celebrated before her image at this altar by the first prebend, who was commonly called the Prebend of the Morning Mass of the Blessed Virgin Marye.[122]

In 1475, John Spendlove, a chaplain, was buried before St. James's altar, where the Morning Mass is said before the image of our Blessed Ladye there painted.[123]

XXII. St. Marye the Less.
In 1464, Mabel, wife of Richard Apulton, was buried in the chancel before the principal image of our Blessed Ladye there.[124]

XXIII. St. Michael in Coslany.
The chapel of our Blessed Ladye, commonly called Thorpe's Chantry, was founded and endowed by Robert Thorpe in the reign of Henry VII., and there was a constant light before her image.[125]

XXIV. St. Michael at Pleas.
The chapel in the south transept was dedicated to our Blessed Ladye, and a light kept burning before her image.

In 1405, Thomas Porter, after the death of his wife and his niece, leaves his messuage in this parish to find a wax candle burning on the Roodloft before our Ladye there, daily, at Matins, Mass, and Vespers, and to find a weekly Mass on Mondays.[126]

[120] Blomefield, p. 840.   [121] *Ibid.* p. 842.   [122] *Ibid.* p. 608.
[123] *Ibid.* p. 614.   [124] *Ibid.* p. 572.   [125] *Ibid.* pp. 843–846.   [126] *Ibid.* p. 718.

XXV. St. Michael at Thorn.

Here was an image of our Lady on the north side of the church.[127]

XXVI. St. Peter, Mancroft.

1. On the south side of the south aisle opposite to the chapel of St. Nicholas is the chapel of our Blessed Ladye, which in former days was a place of great repute.[128]

In 1320, Cecily, wife of John de Wroxham, was buried by him in the chapel of our Ladye, and gave a legacy to St. Mary's Mass; and in 1458, Marion Mason, widow, gave a white silk vestment to serve on holidays of our Ladye.[129]

In 1497, ten marks were given to paint our Lady's image and tabernacle in this chapel, and to keep a continual light before it.[130]

In 1500, Florence Johnson gave seven wax candles to burn before the image of our Ladye in her chapel for four years, viz., the middle candle to burn at all times of divine service, and the other six only while the *Salve* is sung.[131]

This image of the Blessed Virgin was called our Ladye of Millain, and it stood in a tabernacle.

This may have been a copy of some celebrated image of our Ladye in Milan. In the church of Notre Dame de la Chapelle at Brussels, there existed a confraternity of our Ladye of Milan, which was suppressed with the approval of the bishop in 1483.[132]

2. Our Ladye of Pity.

3. Our Ladye in the nave of the church on the perke, or bracket, to which in 1493, Thomas London, mercer, who was buried before it, gave 40s. for the gilding.[133]

XXVII. St. Peter, Mountergate.

At the east end of the chancel is a chapel of our Ladye, and on the outside of the wall exactly

---

[127] *Gen. Hist. of Norfolk*, p. 1077.
[128] Blomefield, v. xi. p. 632.
[129] *Ibid.* p. 638.
[130] *Ibid.* p. 633.
[131] *Ibid.* p. 639.
[132] *Hist. de la ville de Bruxelles.* Par A. Henne, et A. Wauters archiviste de la ville. Brux. 1845, v. iii. p. 456.
[133] *Ibid.* v. ii. p. 639.

opposite to the altar within was an image of the
Blessed Virgin, and under it, two statues of the
founders, and a brass plate with an inscription
which is lost.[134]

XXVIII. St. Paul.

At the east end of the aisle is a chapel now
used as a vestry, which was dedicated to our
Ladye, before whose image at her altar there hung
a lamp which was always kept burning in service-
time.[135]

XXIX. St. Simon and St. Jude.

An image of our Ladye stood in the alley in
the churchyard.[186]   One of the bells bore the
inscription :

Uirginis egregie vocor campana Marie.

XXX. St. Stephen.

In the Eighth of Edward II., 1314-1315,
Richard Priour settled 4*s.* a year out of John
Sparwe's tenement in this parish to keep a wax
candle lighted before the image of our Blessed
Ladye.   In 1509, Beatrix Krikemer was buried
in this church.   In her will she says : "*Item.* I
bequeath to our Ladye in the same church my
best beads to hang about her neck on good days."
In 1523, Alice Carre gave her coral beads to the
beautifying the image of our Ladye on the festefull
days in this church.

The east window in the Ladye chapel was
very fine.   It contained the whole history of our
Ladye's life, with the inscription,

Salve Regina Mater misericordiae ;
and

Ave Regina coelorum, ave domina, &c. [137]

2. Our Ladye of Pity.

There was a light kept burning before this
image.[196]

XXXI. Carrow, outside the city.

The Saddlers and Spurriers' Gild of Norwich,
established in 1385, was held here.

[134] Blomefield, p. 553.   [185] *Ibid.*
[186] *Ibid.* p. 739.   [137] *Ibid.* p. 596.   [138] *Ibid.* p. 602.

"To ye honor of oure lady seynt Marie, and of alle halwen, yese ordenaunce of fraternyte of Sadeleres and Sporyeres, in ye cite of Norwyche wern be-gunnen in ye yer of oure lordis birthe ihesu crist, a thowsande three hundred four skore and ffiue, and perpetuelli schal ben holden a-forn ye ymage of our lady at ye heye auter in ye chirche of nunnes in ye nunrye of Carrowe be-syden Norwyche." [139]

ORMESBY, IN CLEVELAND. Sir John Conyers of Ormesby, by his will dated July 2, 1438, desires that his executors shall cause the altar and windows in our Ladye's chapel to be repaired, and that the image of the Blessed Virgin which stands over the high altar shall be placed over the altar aforesaid. [140]

OTTERY ST. MARY. From Domesday Book it is clear that the Chapter of St. Marye at Rouen, in Normandy, held the manor of Otrei of William the Norman. It was the gift of St. Eadward the Confessor to them in 1061. His grant of the vil or manor of Otregia to the church of St. Marye of Rouen is recited in a Patent of the fourth year of Richard the Second. [141]

The College of St. Marye was founded by Bishop Grandison. He also built the Ladye Chapel ; and by his will, dated September 8, 1368, amongst other legacies, he bequeathed to the college an image of silver, gilt, of our Blessed Ladye.

In the constitutions he made several dispositions about the Marye Mass and Office of the Blessed Virgin ; and by statute No. 17 he ordained that the bell which was rung for the Marye Mass shall also peal for the *ignitegium*, or evening Ave. [142]

Statute 19 is to this effect :

"We ordain that every day, at least one canon who desires to have the blessing of Blessed Virgin Marye shall assist at her Mass, that he may always see if it be celebrated with decorum and devotion. Equally let the other canons and vicars

---

[139] *English Gilds*, &c. Early English Text Soc. 1870, vol. xl. p. 42.
[140] Test. Ebor. vol. ii. p. 64.
[141] P. 1, m. 3 ; Oliver, *Mon. Dicec. Exon.* p. 259.   [142] *Ibid.* p. 268.

who are not engaged, for some good reason, at the time, unless they are saying their own Masses, go to the Mass of the Blessed Virgin, if they love her more than their own vain pleasures, so that they may obtain more copiously in their necessities the blessings of the Mother of Christ, and the grace of her Son. To those who shall thus be present we grant a daily pardon of twenty days."

Statute 20. "We also command the cantor, equally as the sacristan, and the chaplain of the Blessed Virgin, to see who come late to the Marye Mass, or behave themselves ill during it, and cause them to be punished as bad and ungrateful servants of the Blessed Virgin by the custos and seneschals, if they desire to obtain the assistance of the same Blessed Virgin at the hour of their death."

Statute 53. "We also ordain that each year, on the festival of the Assumption of the Glorious Virgin, . . . the whole college shall eat together, and in token of the spotless virginity of the Dear Dove of Paradise, they shall all wear surplices during dinner, without which absolutely no one, unless he be a religious man, shall be permitted to eat."[143]

Then follow long regulations in regard of the candles and lights of our Blessed Ladye.

". . . Therefore, let not the lights which we have ordained in honour of God and the Mother of Eternal Light, at any time, *quod absit*, be withdrawn by the negligence, or malice, or for the convenience of those who, as sons of darkness, seek more after their own affairs than those of God. But if some, inspired by God, and prevented by His grace, may augment the lights, may God grant them light here and for eternity, and may perpetual light shine upon them. But may those who shall withdraw them incur exterior darkness where there is weeping and gnashing of teeth, unless they speedily repent."

These constitutions are dated Exeter, 3 kal. Octob. (29 September) 1339.[144]

---

[143] Oliver, *Mon. Diœc. Exon.* p. 261.   [144] *Ibid.* p. 273.

The seal represents the coronation of our Blessed Ladye, with the inscription :

+ ✿. 𝕮𝔬𝔩𝔩𝔢𝔤𝔦𝔦 𝔅𝔢𝔞𝔱𝔢 𝔐𝔞𝔯𝔦𝔢 𝔡𝔢 𝔒𝔱𝔢𝔯𝔦.

OXENEY.

In the year 1192, the Abbot Akarius erected a *tabula*, or reredos, with an image of the Blessed Virgin Marye above the altar at Oxeney, near Dover.[145]

OXFORD.

I. All Saints.

Our Ladye's chapel, on the south side of the nave, was erected by the gild of the cordwainers in Oxford. There were many benefactors to this gild ; amongst others may be named I. Peggy, a burgess and cordwainer, who describes himself as a brother of the gild, and makes a bequest to this chapel in 1349.[146]

II. Priory of St. Frideswithe.

The Barbers of Oxford, at their first incorporation, on the order of Dr. Northwade, then Vice Chancellor of the University, agreed that they would yearly keep and maintain a light before our Ladye, in our Ladye's chapel in this church ; for the sure continuance of which every man or woman of the same profession, that kept a shop, should pay twopence every quarter, two journeymen one penny, and to keep it always burning under the pain of 6*s.* 8*d.* This continued till the Reformation.[147]

Close by the grange of St. Frideswithe's Priory was a cell or hermitage called that of our Ladye, from her image affixed in the wall, and a little oratory adjoining.[148]

III. The Grey Friars.

Our Ladye of Pyle.

Probably this is a misprint for Our Ladye of Pyte. The only notice I have is, that Agnes, the wife of Michael Norton, was buried in the Grey Friars, before the image of Our Ladye of Pyle.[149]

[145] *Glos. of Architecture.* Oxford, 1850, p. 456.
[146] *City of Oxford.* By Anthony à Wood. With additions by the Rev. Sir J. Peshall, Bart. London, 1773, p. 39.
[147] *Ibid.* p. 123.
[148] *Ibid.* p. 294.
[149] *Ibid.* p. 162.

IV. St. Marye's.

In the latter part of the reign of Henry the Third, Dyonisius, son of Simon Geldynsmith, gave a tenement in School Street towards the light of the church of the Blessed Virgin Marye.[150] And in 1270, Reginald de la Legh, a beadle of the University, gave his house in Gropeland, and its annual rent of half a mark, towards the maintenance of the chapel, and the celebration of the Mass of our Ladye for his soul, and those of his parents.[151]

The porch immediately facing Oriel Street was erected, in 1637, by Dr. Morgan Owen, chaplain to Archbishop Laud. Over it is a statue of the Blessed Virgin, with her Divine Son in her arms, holding a small crucifix, which, at the time of its erection, gave such offence to the Puritans, that it was included in the articles of impeachment against the archbishop.[152] A. à Wood describes it as a capital statue of the Blessed Virgin, with her infant Christ in her arms, which much attracts the observation of the curious and foreigners.[153]

Not far from the Church was St. Marye's Entry, which belonged to St. Marye's. It was sometimes called St. Marye's House, and paid to the church for the use of our Ladye's image, altar, lights, &c., 8s. a year.[154]

V. St. Michael's.

In the reign of Henry the Third, a yearly rent of two shillings was given by one of the old halls, called, in those days, Stapled, or Stapel-Ledyne-Hall, to the maintenance of the lights in St. Marye's chapel in this church.[155] Several lands and tenements were allotted for the maintenance of ornaments, lights, and other trinkets, that did always attend the images of the Blessed Virgin Marye, St. Catherine, St. George, and others, as they formerly stood on pedestals in this church.[156]

VI. St. Nicholas.   The Black Friars.

At the end of the reign of Henry the Third, R. Mulner gave them lands in the parish of

---

[150] *City of Oxford*, p. 60.   [151] *Ibid.* p. 61.   [152] Parker, *Guide to Oxford.* Ed. 1873, p. 27.   [153] *City of Oxford*, p. 54.   [154] *Ibid.* p. 73.   [155] *Ibid.* p. 31.   [156] *Ibid.* p. 22.

St. Aldgate; and when he gave his nephew, H. Wycombe, a part of the neighbouring messuage, he did so on the condition that he and his successors should pay yearly four shillings to maintain a light at the altar of the Blessed Virgin Marye in the church of St. Nicholas, where the Friars Preachers live.[157]

St. Edmund was one of the very few great saints whom the Anglo-Norman Church has produced; and he died in exile at Portigny, in France.

In his early youth his pious mother Mabel sent him to Paris to pursue his studies; and the outfit which she gave him consisted of a copy of the Sacred Scriptures and a hair-shirt. She herself constantly ' were herde heyre for oure Ladie's loue." Her death recalled him from France, and he then went to continue his studies at Oxford. Here, whilst he was studying grammar, by the advice of a priest he made a vow of perpetual virginity; and he espoused himself to our Blessed Ladye in the following manner. He had two gold rings made, on which was engraved the Angelical Salutation.[158] One of them he put on the finger of an image of the Blessed Virgin, and the other on his own. The chronicler of Lanercrost says that "when he was a boy at Oxford, studying grammar, he secretly espoused an image of the glorious Virgin, which we, as well as the whole University, have often seen, by placing on the finger of the Blessed Virgin a ring of gold, which many have since beheld with their own eyes."[159]

Peter de Natalibus gives a different version. He mentions only one ring, that one which St. Edmund placed on the finger of our Ladye's image, and says that it was miraculously found on his finger at his death.[160] But from a letter which I have had the honour of receiving from Père Boyer, of the Abbey of Pontigny, I regret to

[157] *City of Oxford*, p. 263.
[158] Capgrave, *Legenda Anglie*. Wynkyn de Worde, 1516, f. cv.
[159] Ad ann. 1227. *Bannatyne Club*. Edited by J. Stephenson, Esq. Edinburgh, 1839.
[160] *Catalogus Sanctorum*. Lugduni, 1508, f. cclxxxi.

learn that nothing is known there of St. Edmund's ring, except what history has recorded of it.

None of the chroniclers or biographers of St. Edmund make any mention, so far as I have been able to ascertain, of the locality where this venerated image of our Ladye stood. My esteemed friend, Mr. Charles Aloysius Buckler, who is well acquainted with every stone and corner of Oxford, informs me that it was probably in the church of the Blackfriars. In this there is no anachronism, because the church of St. Nicholas had already existed for some time previously to the arrival of the Dominicans in Oxford. And it is worthy of notice, that the seal of the Black Friars of Oxford represents our Blessed Ladye with her Divine Son in her arms, and at her feet a little personage on his knees, whom Mr. Buckler—who saw an impression of this seal attached to a document now at Pontigny—presumes to be intended for the young St. Edmund. Under the lower arcade of the seal is a supplicant religious. The legend is ✠ SIGILL : CAPITVLI : FRAT : PREDICATORV : OXON.

The statue of our Ladye which bore the ring of St. Edmund was an object of especial veneration for the whole of the University. St. Edmund died on the 16th of November, 1242, and was canonized by Pope Innocent the Fourth in 1247. Hence it is by no means improbable that the Dominicans of Oxford should have perpetuated, in their common seal, this celebrated act of St. Edmund.

VII. Osney Abbey.

An image of our Ladye stood over the great north gate, with the shield of St. George on one side, and the arms of Doiley, which were those of the abbey, on the other.[101]

VIII. St. Peter's.

In the beginning of the reign of Henry the Third, St. Edmund Rich, or, as he is generally styled, of Abingdon, founded a chantry in this church, together with a chapel dedicated to the Blessed Virgin Marye.[102]

---

[101] *City of Oxford*, p. 303.   [102] *Ibid.* p. 79.

In the parish archives for the year 1490, there is an entry of 8s. paid to William Hangfre, carver, for a tabernacle made for the image of the Blessed Virgin Marye.[163]

IX. Smith Gate.

On the north of Smith Gate, opposite to Cat Street, stood a chapel of our Ladye. It was round, and was said to have been an ancient synagogue of the Jews. A fair wrought niche on the east side of this round chapel contained the image of our Ladye, with other figures, very neatly carved in stone, which remained there until destroyed by the Rump Parliament. Over the chapel door was the Salutation of the Blessed Virgin by the angel.[164]

Merton College.

In 1268, the chancellor, masters, and scholars of the University, attended with all the parochial clergy, going in a solemn procession on Ascension Day to visit the relics of St. Frideswithe, with the cross borne before them, a certain Jew of the most consummate impudence, violently snatched it from the bearer, and trod it under his feet, in his contempt of Christ. To punish which impious affront, as soon as it was made known to the King (by his son Prince Edward, who happened to be then at Oxford), he caused strict search to be made after the criminal, and upon not finding him, commanded all the Jews of the town to be imprisoned; and that they should erect at their own proper cost and charges, in the place where the crime was committed, a stately marble cross of the most perfect workmanship, having, on one side, the figure of Christ crucified, and on the other, the image of the Blessed Virgin Marye, with our Saviour in her arms; all which was to be gilt with fine gold, and at the top of the cross was to be an inscription containing the cause of erecting it. They were likewise ordered to present another portable cross of silver, gilt, to the two proctors, to be used by them in all future processions of the University, the size of which was to

---

[163] *City of Oxford*, p. 82.   [164] *Ibid.* p. 201.

be such as was usually borne before archbishops; and as the sheriff of the county was to see all this done before the vigil of next Epiphany, he was commanded out of hand to levy the expenses of it, and to suffer no Jew to dispose of any of his effects, till he had either paid his proportion or given security for it. But (as they had timely notice given by their friends in London of what was coming against them) before the writ could be delivered to the sheriff, they had privily made over their goods to several of the townspeople, so that the work could not possibly go forward for want of money. To remedy which fraud, the King by a writ,[165] in which he recited all that had passed, commanded the sheriff to take to his assistance the mayor of the city, and seize upon the Jews' effects wherever they could find them, and then to carry on the work with the utmost expedition. A sufficient sum was then raised, but the work was stopped by an objection that the cross could not be erected in the place appointed without damage to some of the neighbouring inhabitants; whereupon the citizens desired that it might be placed on a void piece of ground near the synagogue. But the King and his Council, disliking that place more than the other, ordered it to be set up in the area of Merton College, and the portable cross to be delivered to the scholars of the said house, for the use of the University, as appears from a second document.[166] Finally, however, the King desired the silver cross to be placed in the Monastery of St. Frideswithe.

The marble cross fell to the ground in the time of Henry the Sixth. John Ross copied the inscription on it, which was as follows :

Quis meus author erat ? Judæi. Quomodo ? Sumptu.
Quis jussit ? Regnans. Quo procurante ? Magistris.
Cur ? Cruce pro fracta ligni. Quo tempore ? Festo.
Ascensus Domini. Quis erat locus ? Hic ubi sisto.[167]

St. Marye's College of Winchester, in Oxford, commonly called New College.

[165] Rot. Claus. 53 Hen. III. m. 12.
[166] *Ibid.* m. 18.
[167] *Anglia Judaica.* By D'Blossiers Tovey, LL.D. Oxford, 1738, pp. 168—175.

Founded by William of Wykeham in 1379. The gateway is of that year; over it, as well as over the hall, there are still three niches, filled with elegant images of our Blessed Ladye in the centre, and on either side an angel,[168] and the founder, in a kneeling attitude. The charter of foundation is dated November 25, 1379.[169]

PETERBOROUGH, formerly MEDESHAMSTEDE.

It was burnt by the Danes, and its name then changed into Burch, or Burg. It was called Peterborough after its restoration by Æthelwold, Bishop of Winchester, in 970.

This is another of the great foundations of our Anglo-Saxon forefathers, and under Abbot Leofric it attained a high degree of splendour. He was a worthy member of the noble family to which he belonged; and the zeal for the house of God, and His greater glory, which animated the pious Leofric and the peerless Godgifu, Earl and Countess of Mercia, did not burn less brightly in the bosom of their nephew Leofric, Abbot of Peterborough. He was a religious of great merit, and an ornament to the Order of St. Benedict. Whilst Abbot of Peterborough, he held four other abbacies as well, Burton, Coventry, Croyland, and Thorney. I have not ascertained who was his father, but from his name, I am inclined to believe that he was a son of the Duke Northman, son of Earl Leofwin, and elder brother of Earl Leofric, the founder of Coventry.[170]

Under the year 1052, the Saxon Chronicle says:

"Archbishop Stigand succeeded to the archbishopric of Canterbury, and at the same time Arnwi, Abbot of Peterborough, left the abbacy in sound health, and gave it to Leofric, a monk, by leave of the King and of the monks; and Abbot Arnwi lived afterwards eight winters. And the Abbot Leofric then so enriched the monastery, that it was called the Golden-borough; it then waxed greatly in land, in gold, and in silver."[171]

[168] *Oxford Guide Book*, p. 63.
[169] Louth, *Life of W. of Wykeham*. Oxford, 1777, p. 166.
[170] Vide ante pp. 20, 36.
[171] Rolls Edit. p. 157.

It is by no means improbable that the Abbot of Peterborough shared considerably in the munificent generosity of his uncle and aunt, Leofric and Godgifu.

Under the year 1066 the Saxon chronicle continues—

"And then was Leofric, Abbot of Peterborough, with the same force (*i.e.*, with his cousin Harold at the battle of Hastings), and sickened there and came home, and died soon after, on All Hallows Mass-night. God be merciful to his soul! In his day there was all good and all bliss at Peterborough; and he was dear to all the people, so that the King gave to St. Peter and to him, the abbacy of Burton and that of Coventry, which Leofric, who was his uncle, had before founded, and that of Croyland, and that of Thorney. And he did much for its good to the monastery of Peterborough, in gold, and in silver, and in clothing, and in land, as never any other did before him, or any after him. Then Golden Borough became Wretched Borough."[172]

The Lady chapel was begun in the year 1272, in the time of Abbot Richard de London. The foundation stone was laid by the prior, William Parys.

This chapel was built of stone and wood, and roofed with lead, and fairly adorned with windows of glass, and the Abbot caused to be made in a handsome manner an image of the glorious Virgin, with her genealogy around her, which is called a Jesse. He also had painted on the walls the series of the Kings of England, from the first to the last, with a brief summary of their lives written beneath them. This prior, William, purchased an annual rental of five pounds of silver and more for the lights of the said chapel. He died in 1826, and lies buried in the church before the Blessed Virgin Mary, with her Son seated on a pillar,[173] before the west end of the church. This chapel was destroyed for the value of its materials after 1651.[174]

---

[172] Rolls Edit. p. 170. [173] W. de Whytleseye, *Hist.* pp. 149, 150.
[174] *Associated Architectural Societies,* vol. iii. pt. i. p. 212.

In the inventory of treasures taken on November 30, 1539, in the Lady chapel, is enumerated— *Imprimis* an image of our Ladye with reddis rissey, set in a tabernacle, well gilt upon wood, with twelve great images and four-and-thirty small images of the same work about the chapel.

Item, . . . one tabernacle of the Trinity, and one other of our Ladye.[175]

In the body of the church was the altar of Our Lady of Pity, described as the Altar of Our Ladye's Lamentation, gilt. ·

PLYMBRIDGE, CO. DEVON.

The Chapel of our Ladye of Plymbridge had the indulgences of Portiuncula, and the Roman Stations. Boniface the Ninth, 1389—1404, granted that all who said three *Paters* and *Aves* before the images of our Blessed Ladye, and St. Peter and St. Paul, on the Nativity, Circumcision, and Epiphany, Good Friday, Easter Sunday, the Ascension, Pentecost, and the Nativity, Annunciation, and Assumption of the Blessed Virgin, should gain these indulgences.[176]

PLYMPTON PRIORY.

At page 17 of the rental of Plympton Priory, September 30, 1481, it appears that William Strode held of the Convent two tenements, with gardens adjoining, in Boryngdon Manor, by the payment of wax to the amount of 4s. and 6d., to be burnt before the statue of our Blessed Ladye in the conventual church.[177]

PLYMPTON.

The seal of the Priory is curious and interesting. It represents the Divine Infant, Jesus Christ, seated on the lap of His Immaculate Mother, our Blessed Ladye, who bears on her wrist a hawk, with its hood and bell.

POLESWORTH.

In the time of Henry the Fourth, Robert de Herthall gave a rent rising out of lands in Freseley to the lights of the chapel of our Blessed Ladye in the monastery of Polesworth.[178]

---

[175] *Mon. Angl.* vol. i. p. 366.
[176] Polwhele, *History of Devonshire,* 1797, vol. i. p. 299.
[177] *Mon. Diæc. Exon.* p. 130.
[178] Dugdale, *Antiquities of Warwickshire,* London, 1656, p. 150.

PONTEFRACT.

William Hoghwyk of Pontefract, esquire, by will dated October 8, 1414, left to the image of the Blessed Virgin Marye, which stood in the ladye chapel in the church of All Hallows, a chain of gold, with a relic of our Lord's cross enclosed.[179]

Dugdale gives an abstract of the will of Antony Widvile, Earl Rivers, dated June 23, 1483,[180] which is reproduced in the *Testamenta Vetusta;*[181] the whole will is given by Bentley. He says—

"I will that my heart be carried to our Ladye of Pue, adjoining to St. Stephen's College at Westminster, there to be buried by the advice of the Dean and his brethren; and in case I die south of the Trent, then I will that my body be also buried before our Ladye of Pue."

Subsequently, and after the testing of his will, he adds—

"My will is now to be buried before an image of our Blessed Ladye Marye, with my Lord Richard, in Pomfrete, and Jhu have mercy of my soul."[182]

He was succeeded by his brother, Sir Richard Widvile, a knight hospitaller, who had been received into the Order of St. John of Jerusalem in 1469, a fact not generally known.

PYLALE.

Not far from this spot, which I have hitherto failed to identify, there was an image of our Blessed Lady which was held in great veneration. It is mentioned in the life of Richard the Second, by a Monk of Evesham,[183] who, relating the capture of Sir Edmund Mortimer, Earl of March, by Owen Glendower, on the feast of St. Alban's in 1401, says, that whilst Mortimer was at Ludlow, news was brought to him that Owen Glendower had come over from the Welsh mountains, and was on one of the hills by Pylale, where there was an image of the Blessed Virgin Marye, which was greatly venerated, and not far from Ludlow.

[179] Test Ebor. vol. i. p. 375.   [180] Baronagium, t ii. p. 233.   [181] P. 379.
[182] Bentley, *Exerpt. Hist.* p. 248.   [183] Edit. Hearne, p. 178.

QUARRYWELL.
In Oldham's Register, says Dr. Oliver, there is a petition of David Waryn heremyte of the chapel of Our Ladye of Grace at Quarrywell, within the boundaries of Plymouth, dated April 10, 1518.[184]

REEPHAM, NORFOLK.
Here was a celebrated image of our Blessed Ladye, to which many pilgrimages were made. They are mentioned in 1428.[185]

RIEVAULX.
Henry le Scrope, by will dated August 6, 1515, orders his body to be buried before the altar of Our Ladye of Pity, in the Abbey of Rievaulx.[186]

ROCHE ABBEY.
Matilda, wife of Richard Plantagenet, commonly known as Richard of Coningsborough, Earl of Cambridge, by will, dated August 15, 1446, desires her body to be buried in Roche Abbey, in the chapel of the Blessed Virgin Marye, before her image which stands in the south part of the abbey church.[187]

ROTHERAM, YORKS.
John Lister, of Rotheram, by will dated October 10, 1453, leaves to our Ladye's light iijs. iiijd.[188]

ROTHLEY, Co. LEICESTER.
Bartholomew Kingston, Esq., by his will, executed in 1486, leaves a candle to burn before the image of our Ladye.[189] This curious will is engraved on a tombstone in Rothley Church, and is given in full in the History of Leicester by Nichols.[190]

ROYDON, Co. NORFOLK.
In 1488 lights were given to burn before the tabernacle of the Blessed Virgin Marye.[191]

RUDBY IN CLEVELAND.
Christopher Conyers, Rector of Rudby, by will, dated June 22, 1483, leaves two candles to be burnt before the image of our Ladye in the choir on the day of his burial; also six torches

---

[184] *Mon. Diæc. Exon.* p. 131.
[185] *General History of Norfolk*, p. 229; Index, *Mon. Diæc. Norv.* p. 66.
[186] Mon. Ebor. p. 336.
[187] Test Ebor. vol. ii. p. 118.   [188] *Ibid.* p. 169.   [189] Test. Vet. p. 387.
[190] Vol. iii. pt. ii. p. 960.   [191] Blomefield, vol. i. p. 27.

J

to burn before his body during the elevation, two of which he bequeathed to the image of our Ladye in the aforesaid basilica, to be burnt whilst the Masses are being celebrated in it.[192]

RUSTON.

Jane Lady Wombwell, widow, by will, dated July 10, 1454, leaves to the service of our Blessed Ladye in Ruston, xiijs. iiijd.[193]

RYTON.

William de Menville was High Sheriff of the Palatinate in 1363 and again in 1370. By his will, dated June 20, 1471, he left to the light of our Ladye's altar, xiijs. iiijd.[194]

ST. ALBAN'S ABBEY.

Every week there was a procession in honour of the Blessed Virgin, the monks wearing surplices ; Badulf, seventeenth abbot, 1146—1151, ordained that it should be made to the altar of our Ladye.[195]

Robert, eighteenth abbot, 1151—1166, on his return from Rome, offered costly gifts at the high altar of St. Alban's, and caused to be made a beautiful image of our Blessed Ladye (*pulchram Mariolam*) with its appurtenances.[196]

The shrine of St. Alban, made by Simon, nineteenth abbot, 1166—1185, was the most magnificent one which Walsingham had seen in his day ; on the side which faced the west there was an image of our Blessed Ladye, in high relief, representing her seated on a throne, holding her Divine Son in her lap, and adorned with gems and precious ornaments of gold.[197]

William, twenty-second abbot, 1214—1235, seeing that in all the principal churches in England a Mass of the Blessed Virgin Marye was sung each day to note, ordained that a daily Mass of our Ladye should be sung by six monks in rotation ; a monk was also appointed to be the guardian and attendant of our Lady's altar.

[192] Test Ebor. vol. iii. p. 287.
[193] *Ibid.* vol. ii. p. 177.
[194] *Wills and Inventories*, &c. pt. i. p. 32.
[195] Gesta Abbatum Monast. S. Albani, a Thoma Walsingham, v. i. p. 107. Rolls Edit.
[196] *Ibid.* p. 179.
[197] *Ibid.* p. 189.

"We believe," adds Walsingham, "that these arrangements were very pleasing to God and the Blessed Virgin His Mother, since, from thenceforth the altar received a happy and unexpected increase of various ornaments, gold and silver plate, silk vestments, and lights." The altar was dedicated by John, Bishop of Ardfert; Abbot William said the first Mass and presented a handsome Missal to it, in commemoration of his celebration of the Divine Mysteries. He also gave a most harmonious bell, which was consecrated by Bishop John, and named "Saint Marye," to be rung daily, three times, to summon the ministers appointed for altar duty, to wit, the six monks, together with the custos of the altar, and others of the faithful of Christ and devout humble clients of the Blessed Virgin, who were about to serve, and to pray, for the prosperity of the Church and their own.[198]

"Furthermore it redounds to the praises of the same Abbot William," continues Walsingham, "that he presented to our church a most lovely image of the Blessed Virgin Marye, which the oft-mentioned Master Walter of Colchester had sculptured with the most consummate skill, and had it hallowed by Bishop John aforenamed; and the image, which stood previously where he so handsomely placed the new one, he set up in a conspicuous place over the altar, where the Mass of the Blessed Virgin Marye is daily sung to note; and the wax candles, which we have been accustomed to wreathe with flowers, he appointed to be lighted before the celebrated image of the Blessed Virgin, on the days and nights of her principal festivals, and in the procession which is made in commemoration of the same."

"Abbot William also beautified the church in a wonderful manner with a ceiling of that kind which we call *labrescura* or *celatura*,[199] with which

---

[198] Gesta Abbatum Monast. S. Albani, pp. 284, 285.

[199] *Labrescura.* This word is incorrect; the scribe has omitted to put a stroke over the first *a*, or the copyist has neglected to mark it in his transcript. It should be *lambrescura*, or *lambruscura*, whence the French *lambris*. Coupled with *celatura*, it means, most probably, an embossed ceiling. Thus, in the Council of Exeter, A.D

he concealed the row of timbers above the famous image of the Blessed Virgin, lest the old age of the rafters or beams should offend the eyes of the beholders; and for a similar reason, he also whitened the walls of a greater portion of the church. . . . Moreover, as he had removed the ancient image of the Blessed Virgin, Abbot William substituted a new one, and set it up in another place; and the displaced old beam which formerly was over the high altar, and which Adam the Cellarer had erected, he put up in the south part of the church near the famous image, to the great adornment of this edifice. On this beam were figures of twelve Patriarchs and the twelve Apostles, and in the midst the Majesty, with the Church and Synagogue. In like manner he erected a new rood in the middle of the church, and a new image of the Blessed Virgin over the altar of St. Blaise; and he transferred the old rood and the image of our Ladye, which he had previously put up, to the north part of the church, for the edification of the laity and all who came thither, and for the comfort of seculars, lest he might seem to mar in any degree the good works which he had done." [200]

Hugh de Eversdone, twenty-seventh abbot, 1308—1326, had an especial veneration for the Blessed Mother of God above all His saints. Amongst his acts, which were always on a magnificent scale, he completed, in a praiseworthy manner, the ladye chapel at the east of the church, which had been commenced many years previously by John de Hertford. This he was enabled to accomplish by the help of his friends, Walter de Langley and Alice his wife, and Master Reginald of St. Alban's, a friend resident at Rome, who left him two hundred marcs. [201]

Thomas, thirtieth abbot, 1349—1396, pre-

1287 : "Can. XII.   Onera omnium ornamentorum prædictorum parochiani, sicut hactenus, ita de cetero supportabunt, libris matutinalibus, unico scilicet psalterio, fenestris vitreis in cancello, et *celatura* supra majus altare dumtaxat exceptis, quæ rectores vel vicarii supportabunt, prout in nostra diœcesi hucusque fieri consuevit."— Labbé. *Concilia,* t. xi. col. 1278.

[200] *Ibid.* p. 287.

[201] *Ibid.* v. ii. p. 114.

sented some magnificent vestments in honour of our Ladye. He also gave the picture over the high altar, which had been painted in Lombardy, and cost, including carriage from London and all other expenses, 40*l.* 10*s.* 8*d.* Moreover, he gave to the altar of the Four Candles five pictures valued at five marcs, which were afterwards put into wooden frames by Stephen Sothere the sacristan.[202] The habitual ejaculations of this good abbot were *Jhesu miserere, Sancta Maria adjuva!* "Jesus, mercy! Holy Marye, help!"[203]

Therefore at St. Alban's there were—

1. The beautiful image of our Ladye presented by Abbot Robert, 1151—1166, which was removed by Abbot William, 1214—1235, and set up over the altar where the Marye Mass was daily sung.

2. The image of our Lady given by Abbot William, and which he subsequently transferred to the north aisle.

3. The image of our Ladye, the work of the sculptor Master Walter of Colchester, called *Sancta Maria Pulchra*—"Our Ladye the Beautiful," which stood in the south transept near the chapter-house.[204]

4. Our Ladye over the altar of St. Blaise.

5. The altar of our Ladye called of the Four Candles, or *Quatuor Cereorum.* It was so called because four candles offered by four officials of the abbey were daily lighted. And at this altar, in addition to other Masses, two Masses were usually celebrated every day for the Church and for the Dead.[205]

6. An image of our Lady stood in the nave, before which brother William Wyntershalle, the almoner of the abbey, erected an altar.[206]

ST. EDMUND'S BURY, FORMERLY BEO-DERIC-WEORTH.

I. The abbey-church, erected by Cnut, was consecrated on St. Luke's day in 1032 by Ægelnoth, Archbishop of Canterbury, in honour

---

[202] Gesta Abbatum Monast. S. Albani, v. iii. p. 381.

[203] *Ibid.* p. 421.

[204] *Ibid.* p. 448. The south transept is also called the south cross aisle (ala).

[205] Annales Monast. S. Albani a J. Amundesham monacho, ut videtur, conscripti, 1421—1440, v. i. p. 436. Rolls Edit.

[206] *Ibid.* v. i. p. 448.

of Christ, His Virgin Mother, and St. Edmund the King and Martyr.[207]

In this church were —

1. Our Ladye's altar to the north of the choir;

2. Our Ladye's altar and chapel behind the high altar;

3. The crypt of our Ladye under the shrine of St. Edmund.[208]

Amongst the distinguished monks of this celebrated abbey was Dom Galfrid Waterton, by some called *Bedericius*, or of Bury. He was brother to William Waterton of Waterton, or Watretone, as it is given in Domesday. He is described by Bale and Pits as profoundly versed in sacred and profane philosophy. and constantly at his studies, except when called off by the obedience of his rule, psalmody in choir, or contemplation and meditation. He had made his studies, especially in polite literature and theology, with such fruit, that, as soon as he had taken his Doctor's degree, he applied himself to writing, in which he made happy progress on account of the ease and purity of his style, as well as the continual meditation which he had long practised in sacred literature. He flourished about the year 1350. He wrote five works, one of which was a book on the Angelical Salutation, and another a *Mariale*, or a treatise in praise of our Blessed Ladye.[209]

II. St. Marye's.

Prior to the great apostacy this church was distinguished for its numerous altars, images, and pictures.

1. The image of Our Ladye of Pity stood in the south aisle.

2. Our Ladye's altar.[210]

Here her image stood in a tabernacle or "housyng" over the altar. John Baret, by his will executed in 1463, says:

---

[207] Gillingwater, *Historical and Descriptive Account of St. Edmund's Bury.* St. Edmund's Bury, 1804. P. 50.

[208] *Index Mon. Diœc. Norv.* p. 78.

[209] Joh. Pitsii, *De illustr. Britannia scriptoribus.* Paris, 1619, p. 473. Bale, *Scriptor. illustr. nationis Brytan.* Basle, 1557, *sub. nom.*

[210] Gillingwater, p. 171.

"*Item*, I wille there be made a goodly newe crowne of metal gylte, or ellys wel dō in tymbyr for the ymage of oure Lady in the housyng of ye rerdoos of Seynt Marie auter." [211]

He also desired that the reredos should be painted with the story of the *Magnificat.*

"*Item*, I geve and be quwethe x marks to the peyntyng rerdoos and table at Seynt Marye avter of the story of the *Magnificat.*" [212]

The altar of St. Marye had chimes; there were also chimes in the steeple.

John Baret says in his will:

"*Item*, I wille yt John Elys serche sewrly and owyr se the chymes at Saynt Marie awter and the chymes in yᵉ stepyl . . . And I wil that the berere of the paxbrede longyng to Seynt Marie awter have yeerly viijd. so he take hede to kepe my grave clene, the chymes, and Seynt Marie awter, to wynde vp the plomme of led as ofte as nedith and to do the chymes goo at yᵉ sacry of the Messe of Ihv, at the sacry of Seynt Marie Messe on the Sunday . . ." [213]

3. Our Ladye at the Pillar.

John Baret says:

"*Item*, I wil that the ymage of oure Lady that Robert Pygot peynted be set vp ageyne the peleer next yᵉ pcloos of Seynt Marie awter with the baas redy therto, and a hovel with pleyn sydes comyng down to the baas, and in the myddes of the baas, my candylstykke of laten with a pyke to be set afore a tapir I have assygned unto ye v taperes longgyng to the natyvite gylde wiche stant alofte before the aungelys, with chymes to be sette abowte our Lady at the peler." [214]

ST. NEOTS.

Roger, prior of St. Neots, and the whole Convent grant to John Nevill, clark, the five shillings every year which Allan Gery owes us for his land in Deuelho to be paid to our sacristy for the maintenance of a lamp in perpetuity to

---

[211] Tymms. *Bury Wills and Inventories,* &c., Camden Society, 1850, p. 20.
[212] *Ibid.* p. 19. Table here signifies the frontal of the Altar.
[213] *Ibid.*
[214] *Ibid.*

burn night and day, in the time of service, before the image of the glorious Virgin Marye, Mother of God, in our church of St. Neot. . . . We also wish the sacristan to procure a candle as well, to burn for ever on festal days at High Mass and Matins and Vespers, and every day during the Mass of our Blessed Ladye.[215]

SALISBURY.

In the list given in the *Witten bouc*[216] the pilgrimage from Ghent to our Ladye of Salisbury —*t'ons Vrauwe te Sallebry*—is put down at five *livres.*[217]

Bishop Poore or Poure died on April 15, 1237, at Farrant-Crawford, in Dorset, the place of his birth, in a monastery of his own foundation, and there his heart was buried, but his body was carried to Salisbury, and Leland gives the inscription from his tomb in the ladye chapel. *Orate pro anima Ric. Poure quondam Sarum Episcopi, qui Ecclesiam hanc inchoari fecit in quondam fundo ubi nunc fundata est, ex antiquo nomine Miryffeld, in honore Beatæ Virginis Mariæ.*[218]

On the greater festivals of the year two wax tapers were kept burning during service time before the image of our Blessed Ladye.

In August, 1644, Colonel Middleton sent up to the Parliament, from Sarum, many copes, surplices, tippets, hoods, plate, and the picture of the Blessed Virgin Mary taken in the minster there; the other relics being divided amongst the soldiers.[219]

SALLE, NORFOLK.

Thomas Brygges, Esq., by his will, executed in 1494, founded a chantry priest to sing for his soul, for ten years after his decease, at the altar by the image of our Blessed Ladye in the chapel of St. James on the south side of the Church of St. Peter and St. Paul in Salle.[220]

[215] *History and Antiquities of St. Neots*, by George Cornelius Gorham, M.A. London, 1820, p. 312.
[216] Vide ante, p. 65.
[217] Cannaert, p. 354.
[218] Itin. v. iii. p. 77.
[219] Whitlock, *Memorials of the English Affairs*, &c., 1732, p. 98.
[220] Blomefield, v. ii. p. 641.

SANDAL,
YORKSHIRE.

Jane Lady Wombwell, widow, by will dated July 10, 1454, leaves to the service of our Blessed Ladye in Sandall church, xiii *s.* iv *d.*[221]

SANDWICH.

In 1473, amongst the "jewills that longith unto oure Ladye cherche withyn the town of Sandewich 'there was a crown of sylver and gylt for our Lady yn the hygh autre.'"[222]

SCARBOROUGH.

Margaret, widow of Richard Aske of Aughton, by will dated August 7, 1465, leaves a cross of gold set with pearls to the image of the Blessed Virgin Marye of Scarborough.[223]

In the castle green are the remains of an old chapel. Here, in 1817, was found a piece of sculpture which is thus described: "It is two feet high, one foot three inches broad, and one foot thick. It has a perforation in the centre, apparently to attach it to a pillar. On one side is sculptured, under an ornamental canopy, the crucifixion, with figures on either side of the cross representing our Ladye and St. John; on the opposite side, also under a canopy, are our Blessed Ladye with her Divine Son, and at each end a figure in a pontifical habit, with a mitre and a crozier. It is now in the Scarborough Museum."[224]

Our Ladye of Scarborough is one of the sanctuaries named by William Escopp, rector of Heslerton, in his will dated September 6, 1472, and to which he desires that a pilgrimage shall be made for him, immediately after his death.[225]

Under an arched vault in the castle yard, and near the ruins of the ancient chapel, there is a reservoir of water called the Ladye's Well, supposed to be the spring mentioned by the old historians, and to have been consecrated "in the

---

[221] Test. Ebor. vol. ii. p. 177. I presume this to be Sandal-Magna, near Wakefield.

[222] Boys, *Hist. of Sandwich.* Canterbury, 1792, p. 374.

[223] Test. Ebor. vol. ii. p. 276.

[224] Theakston's *Guide to Scarborough*, 1865, p. 9.

[225] Vide ante sub Gisbro', p. 42.

days of superstition" to the Blessed Virgin Marye.[226]

SEGEFIELD.

Thomas Trollop of Thornley, Esq., by will dated April 10, 1552, bequeaths to o[r] Ladye of Pety of Sedgfeld, vi *s.* 8 *d.*[227]

SELLYING.

In 1485, Richard Tilley of Sellying bequeaths to the making of a new image of our Blessed Ladye in the same church, lxvi *s.* viii *d.*[228]

SETERINGTON.

In 1422, Sir John Bygod, Knight, Lord of Seterington, desires to be buried in his parish church before the image of the Blessed Virgin Mary. Will dated Monday before the feast of St. Lawrence, martyr.[229]

SHEFFIELD.

In 1485, a bridge of three arches was erected across the river Don; it was called St. Marye's bridge from a convent dedicated to our Blessed Ladye which was near it.[230]

Here was a chapel of our Blessed Ladye of the bridge.

George, Earl of Shrewsbury, K.G., Lord Steward of the King's Household, in his will, dated August 21, 1537, says:

" I will that three priests, for the space of twenty years next after my decease, shall sing for my soul; whereof two in the parish church of Sheffield, at the altar where Lady Ann, late my wife, lieth, and the other in the chapel of our Blessed Ladye of the Bridge in Sheffield, and that every one of them have xiii marks yearly."[231]

SHAPP,
WESTMORELAND.

The abbey of Shapp, formerly Hepp, of the Premonstratensian canons. Here, on every Sunday, there was an alms of a loaf of bread, of the value of two pence, called "Saynte Mary loffe," *i.e.,* Saint Marye's loaf.[232]

SHIRBURN IN ELMET,
YORKSHIRE.

Eufemia Lady Langton, widow of Sir John Langton, by her will dated August 26, 1463, leaves to the altar of the Blessed Virgin Marye,

---

[226] Hinderwell, *Hist. and Antiq. of Scarborough and its vicinity.* York, 1811, p. 96.
[227] *Wills and Inventories,* p. 105.   [228] Test. Vet. p. 384.
[229] Test. Ebor. vol. i. p. 411.   [230] Lewis, Typogr. Dict. *sub nomine.*
[231] Test. Vet. p. 681.   [232] Valor Ecclesiasticus, t. v. p. 294.

below the cemetery of the parish Church of Sherburn in Elmett, an image of the Blessed Virgin, in alabaster, with a collar of SS gilt, part of silver, and part of gold, also a chain of gold with three pearls and one ruby set in it, and two fillets of pearls, which are never to be taken away from the said image, but to remain with it for ever.[233]

SIGGESTON.

At the burial of John Scroby of Siggeston : "To ye lyght of our Ladye, ii *d*."[234]

SILVERTON, DEVON.

June 18, 1478 : " I, John Suyffnore, Person of Silferton, hale of minde, . . . make my testament and will as folowith ; ffirst I bequethe my sowle to God, my body to be beryed in the chancell of Silferton afore our Ladye."[235]

Here was the fraternity of our Ladye, founded by Sir Nicholas Waddame, Knight, and Lawrence Dobell, priest, to find a priest to pray for them and the benefactors of the fraternity. The yearly value of the lands and possessions was vi *l.* ii *s.* x *d.*[236]

SCUTTERSKELF.

Richard Lyndelay, or Lindley, by will dated January 18, 1480–1, leaves a wax taper to burn before the image of the Blessed Virgin Marye in the porch.[237]

SLAPTON.

Collegiate chantry of.
1. Our Ladye of Pity.
2. Our Ladye on the left side of the altar.
To each Sir Nicholas Morton leaves iii *s.* iiii *d.*, will dated August 26, 1524.[238]

SOMERSBY, Co. LINCOLN.

Is a village about six miles from Horncastle. In the churchyard, in 1800, there was standing an ancient cross, the height of which was fourteen feet, including the base. The shaft is octagonal ; on one side of the cross is our Lord crucified, and on the other side, or the reverse, an image of our Blessed Ladye and her Divine Son. It is engraved in the Archæologia.[239]

[233] Test. Ebor, vol. ii. p. 258.   [234] *Wills and Inventories,* p. 99.
[235] Oliver, *Ecclesiastical Antiq. of Devon,* vol. i. p. 89, quoting from Bishop Courtenay's Register, f. 126.
[236] Mon. Diœc. Exon, p. 474.   [237] Test. Ebor. vol. iii. p. 260.
[238] Mon. Diœc. Exon. p. 333.   [239] Vol. xiv. p. 276, plate 50.

SOUTHAMPTON.

Leland says:

"About two miles (from the mouth of Hamel-rise Creeke) upward brekith in a great creke out of the main haven, and goith into the land by north.

"On the left hand of this creke by west, a little from the shore stondith a chapelle of Our Ladye of Grace, some time hauntid with pilgrimes.[240]

Offerings of Henry the Eighth to this sanctuary are recorded in his Majesty's Privy Expenses:

"August 4, 2nd Henry the Eighth, 1510—

"Offerings at Our Ladye of Grace at Southampton, 6 s. 8 d.[241]

"August, 8th Henry the Eighth, 1516:

"Offering at Our Ladye of Grace at Southampton, 10 s. [242]

SOUTHWARK.

I. St. Margaret.

John Barkley, parish clerk of St. Margaret, by his will leaves four tapers of the light in the same church to burn against his body there during his dirge.[243]

II. St. Marye Overies, Overy, over the Rie, that is, across the river, now St. Saviour's.

The original foundation appears to have been due to an Anglo-Saxon maiden of the name of Marye, who possessed a ferry-boat, or a Cross-ferry, or a Traverse-ferry, as Stow calls it, where London Bridge now stands. The ferryman and his wife, at their death, left the ferry to their only daughter, a maiden named Marye. "Which," continues Stow, "with the goods left by her parents, as also with the profits rising out of the said ferry, builded a house of sisters, in place whereof now standeth the east part of St. Marye Overies Church, above the choir where she was buried: unto which house she gave the oversight and profits of the ferry."[244]

---

[240] Itin. vol. iii. p. 94.

[241] Letters and Papers Henry VIII. pt. ii. p. 1447.

[242] *Ibid.* p. 1472.

[243] Manning, *Hist. of Surrey*, vol. iii. p. 580.

[244] Vol. i. p. 53; and vol. iv. p. 8. Stow makes his statement on the report of Bartholomew Linsted, *alias* Fowle, last prior of St. Marye Overies.

Subsequently it became a college for priests; aud in 1106 for canons regular. "In this yeare (1540)," says Wriothesley, "after Christmas the priore of Sainct Marie Overis in Sothwarke was made a parish church."[845]

On the 8th of November, 1428, forty men were drowned in the Thames, owing to the arrogance of the Earl Marshall, John Mowbray, Duke of Norfolk, who would sail to Greenwich. It was with difficulty any were rescued from the waves, but, owing to the outcry raised by persons in the neighbourhood, some were drawn upon land; but scarcely ten lives were saved. One of those thus rescued was by birth a gentleman, Stapleton by name, who when sinking to the bottom of the Thames after the barge had broken asunder, beheld the whole of London beneath the water, and a countless multitude of demons there; and then, thinking of the Blessed Virgin, he suddenly came up again, and was dragged out by the head at St. Katherine's, near the Tower, and being thus saved, he declared this to all persons in London, to the praise of his Ladye, the Mother of our Lord.[846]

Fabian gives the above date, but does not mention Stapleton.[847]

Joan de Cobham, daughter of Sir Thomas de Berkeley, and widow of Reginald, Lord Cobham—who died 35th Edward the Third—died on October 2, 1369. In her will she says:

"My body to be buried in the churchyard of St. Marye Overhere, in Southwark, before the church door, where the image of the Blessed Virgin sitteth on high over that door; and I will that a plain marble stone be laid over my body, and thereon these words:

Œus qui per ici passiety
Pur lalme Joane de Cobham priety.

She left seven thousand Masses to be said for her soul.[848]

[845] *Chron. of England*, vol. i. p. 113. Camden Soc. 1875.
[846] Annales Mon. S. Albani, vol. i. p. 31.
[847] *New Chronicles*. Edit. Ellis. London, 1811, p. 599.
[848] Test. Vet. p. 81.

III. St. Olave's.

In 1738, John Mockyng, of Southwark, leaves to the light of St. Marye, in St. Olave's Church, 3s. 4d. Will dated Tuesday after the feast of St. Edmund, King and Martyr.[249]

SOUTHWELL, NOTTS.

John Baddesworth, Rector of Laxton, by will dated December 1, 1472, leaves to the high altar of St. Marye of Southwell his best silver cup with its cover to be made into an image of the Blessed Virgin Marye.[250]

SOUTHWICK, CO. SOUTHAMPTON.

Leland says :

" Southwic is a good bigge thorough fare, but no celebrate market. The fame of it stoode by the Priory of the Blake Chanons there, and a pilgrimage to our Ladye." [251]

Among the privy expenses of Henry the Eighth in September, 1510, occurs an

" Offering of the King to Our Ladye of Southwick, 6s. 8d.[252]

SOUTHWOLD.

The image of our Ladye of Pity was in a very rich tabernacle, painted and gilt.[253]

SOWERBY, YORKSHIRE.

Richard Lassell's, of Sowerby, leaves xiiis. iiiid. to the support of the light of our Ladye. Will dated April 5, 1472.[254]

At Sowerby, there was a house called Ladye Well, near which was a remarkable fine spring, which in former times seems to have been appropriated to "superstitious uses," and to have been dedicated to the Virgin Marye, honoured at that time with the title of our Ladye : if, indeed, the country hereabouts was not the property of some religious house, for a considerable part of it went by the name of Ladyland, as appears from an entry in MS. Harl. 797, of the 44th of Edward the Third.[255]

[249] Manning, vol. iii. p. 607.
[250] Test. Ebor. vol. iii. p. 202.
[251] Itin. vol. iii. p. 98.
[252] Letters and Papers, &c. Henry VIII. vol. ii. pt. ii. p. 1446.
[253] Nichols, *Illustrations of Manners and Expenses of ancient times in England.* London, 1797, p. 186.
[254] Test. Ebor. vol. viii. p. 198.
[255] *Hist. and Antiquities of the Parish of Halifax.* By the Rev. John Watson, M.A., F.S.A. London, 1775, p. 303.

STANWELL, MIDDLESEX.

Thomas Windesor, Esq., of the parish of Stanwell, in the county of Middlesex, by will dated August 13, 1479, desires :

" My body to be buried on the north side of the quire of the church of Our Ladye of Stanwell . . . before the image of our Ladye. . . Item, I will that there be one hundred children, each within the age of sixteen, at my month's mind, to say our Ladye's Psalter for my soul in the church of Stanwell, each of them having four pence for his labour ; and that at my month's mind the candles burnt before the rood in the said church, with all the other lights before our Blessed Ladye, the Trinity, or any other saints in the said church be renewed and made at my expense."

He was the father of the first Lord Windsor, who died in 1489.[256]

STAMFORD.

In the procession of the gild of the Blessed Virgin Marye, five torches were carried in her honour.[257]

Our Ladye of Stamford is mentioned in the will of Sir William Bruges, Garter-King-at-Arms, dated February 26, 1449.[258]

STANFORD, NORFOLK.

Thomas Fekys, of Sturston, was buried in the church of Stanford, in 1529, and ordered a light to be found for ever before our Blessed Ladye in her chapel of Stanford, which was the gift of Richard Fekys.[259]

STOKE BY CLARE.

At first it was an alien priory of Austin Friars ; in 1415, it was converted into a collegiate church by Sir Edmund Mortimer, Earl of March. The chapel of our Ladye attached to this church is named in the College Statutes as *Capella Beate Marie de Stoke*, and appears to have been a distinct foundation.

In 1490, Margaret, Duchess of Norfolk, devises :

" My body to be buried in the choir of the

[256] Collins's *Peerage.* Edit. 1768, vol. iv. pp. 59—62.
[257] *Norwich volume of the Royal Archæological Institute,* p. 143, note.
[258] Test. Vet. p. 266 ; and Nichols' *Illustrations,* &c. p. 132.
[259] Blomefield, vol. i. p. 543.

church of our Ladye in Stoke before the image on the right side of the high altar.[260]

In the household accounts of Elizabeth of York, March 24, 1502 :

"Offering to our Ladye of Stoke clare, xx d."[261]

STOWMARKET.   The south aisle was called St. Marye's aisle, because the chapel of our Ladye was at the east end of it.

This chapel was furnished with a candle-beam, and an image of our Ladye, which stood in a niche of tabernacle work, to the making of which Margaret Wetherard, in 1457, bequeathed the sum of 40s.; and to the mending of the candle-beam, which was not, however, completed in 1491, Edward Dilhoo left 3s. 4d. He also directed a set of vestments to be prepared for the priest who officiated at our Ladye's altar. Another vestment for our Ladye's altar was provided, in 1521, out of a bequest for that purpose by Margaret Goddard. In 1491, Jone Ry left 33s. 4d. towards the upholding of the Mass of our Ladye at this altar. The wills of the parishioners contain many bequests for providing candles for the candle-beam of this chapel.[262]

Here, before the Holy Sepulchre, stood the "Common Light;" and there was also another known as the "Bachelor's Light," being maintained at the cost of the single men of the parish. To this light, in 1533, Thomas Coyne bequeathed eight coombs of malt.[263]

STRATFORD-ON-AVON.   In 1367, William Whittlesey, Bishop of Worcester, granted forty days of pardon to those who, for the sake of pilgrimage, oblation, or devotion, should visit the image of the glorious Virgin Marye in the parish church of Stratford-on-Avon ; or so often as, before that image, they should devoutly recite, five times, the Angelical Salutation, in honour of the five chief Joys of our

---

[260] Test. Vet. p. 404.
[261] Privy Expenses, p. 3.
[262] *Proceedings of the Suffolk Archæological Institute,* v. ii. p. 254.
[263] *Ibid.* p. 252.

Blessed Ladye, kneeling, or with devout inclination of the body, or head.[264]

STRATTON, NORFOLK.   In 1471 Edmund Cross, rector of this church, was buried before the image of our Ladye.[265]

SUDBURY, SUFFOLK.   In the household expenses of Elizabeth of York :

"March 24, 1502.

"Offering to our Lady of Sudbury, ii *s.* vi *d.*"[266]

SWAINSTHORP.   The Church of St. Mary was demolished at the Reformation. In 1503 it was called the old church, and the principal image of our Ladye was almost decayed.[267]

SWANLAND.   By will, dated September 5, 1405, Sir Gerard Usflete leaves one acre of arable land, at the east end of the village of Swanland, for the support of a light before our Ladye in the chapel of Swanland for ever.[268]

TANWORTH.   Robert Fulwode, Esq., bequeathed a year's rent of v *s.* in this form, viz., viii *d.* to find a lamp before the image of our Ladye in his chancel there, and the remainder for the reparation of the church, and other purposes.[269]

TEWKESBURY.   William of Malmesbury derives the name of Tewkesbury, or as he writes it, Theokesberia, from *Theotokos-beria*—Θεοτόκος-*beria*—and signifying "the town of the Mother of God."[270] I am afraid, however, that this derivation will not hold good.

On the other hand, Leland derives it from a hermit of the name of Theocus, whose cell was near the river, whence Theokesbyria. "Sum say that Theocus' chapelle was aboute the place

---

[264] *Pilgrimages to St. Mary of Walsingham,* &c. By Erasmus. Translated by J. Gough Nichols, F.S.A.. Note, p. 99.

[265] *Gen. Hist. of Norfolk,* p. 110.

[266] P. 3.

[267] Blomefield, Parkin's continuation, vol. iii. p. 41.

[268] Test. Ebor. vol. i. p. 340.

[269] *Notices of the Churches of Warwickshire.* Warwick, 1847. Vol. i. p. 4.

[270] *De Gest. Pontificum Anglorum,* lib. iv. p. 294. Rolls Edit.

K

wher syns the Jues' synagogue was."[271] This derivation seems more probable.

Here two Mercian dukes, Oddo and Doddo, built a small monastery on their land near the Severn, in honour of the Assumption of our Blessed Ladye, in the year 715,[272] where they placed a prior and four or five monks. Oddo and Doddo died, according to Leland, in 725. Their brother, Almaric, was buried at Deorhurste in the little chapel opposite the gate of the priory there. Formerly this chapel had been a royal palace. His tomb is shown there to this day, says Leland, and on the wall above the door is written:

HANC AULAM DODO DUX CONSECRARI FECIT IN ECCLESIAM, AD HONOREM BEATÆ MARIÆ VIRGINIS OB AMOREM FRATRIS SUI ALMARACI.[273]

Our Ladye of Tewkesbury was held in great veneration; but I have no particulars of her shrine.

Isabella Beauchamp, Countess of Warwick, by her will, dated December 1, 1439, desires to be buried in the Abbey of Tewkesbury. After giving directions how her statue on her tomb is to be made, she desires that on the sides thereof there be "the statues of poor men and women in their poor array, with their beads in their hands. I desire that a chalice be made of my great sharpe,[274] and offered to our Ladye in the Lady Chapel at Tewkesbury." She also gave her wedding gown and all her clothes of gold and silk, one only excepted.[275]

The following account of an image of our Ladye at Tewkesbury was communicated to Guppenberg for the Atlas Marianus. His correspondent in England was F. Francis Forster, S.J.:

[271] *Itin.* vol. vi. p. 72.
[272] *Mon. Ang.* t. ii. p. 53.
[273] *Ut supra, loc. cit.*
[274] "Sharpe." Johnson gives the word as a noun, expressing, by ellipsis, something to which the adjective applies, *e. g.*, a poniard or dagger. Halliwell gives the fifth meaning of the noun "a sword," and quotes this very sentence.
[275] Test. Vet. p. 240; and Dugdale, *Baron.* t. i. p. 247.

"At Tewkesbury an image of our Ladye survived all the fury of the heretics. For several years a heretic had endeavoured to obtain it of the Magistrates. At last, after long asking for it, he received it as a present. Forthwith he threw it on the ground, and kicked it with his feet; he then scooped it out for a trough, and often filled it with dirty water; nay, more, he frequently caused his pigs to drink out of it. But this sacrilege did not remain long unpunished. All the pigs that drank out it died; and his children were equally affected, for there was not one who was not either blind or lame, or afflicted by some disease too horrible to mention. The wicked man himself was reserved for a greater punishment, so that posterity might know that the impious are often punished by means of the object by which they sin. There had been a stone trough in which the pigs were fed, before the statue of our Ladye was desecrated for this purpose. It was removed and placed close to the mouth of a well which was unprotected. The unhappy man one day, in a state of frenzy, jumped across the stone trough and threw himself headlong into the well. This horrible occurrence took place about the year 1625."[276]

THETFORD.

This sanctuary of our Ladye was much frequented by pilgrims. The following account is from Blomefield:

"While the bishopric was at Thetford, and the see placed in the parish church of St. Marye, the image of the Holy Virgin was set at the high altar of that church; and when the monks left it, it was carried and fixed at the high altar of their new church. But afterwards, a finer image being made, it was taken down and set in an obscure place. At that time there was a poor workman in the town, who incessantly called upon the Blessed Virgin for relief from an incurable disease that he laboured under. To him the Virgin appeared in the night, telling him that if he would be cured he must hasten to the prior of her monastery, and in her name command him

[276] *Atlas Marianus,* n. dlxviii. p. 656.

to build her a chapel on the north side of the choir, which he had newly repaired. But upon neglecting the message she appeared to him thrice, upon which he acquainted the prior with it, who, being much astonished, resolved to obey the command, and build a chapel of wood. But after this, the sick man returns, and tells him that she ordered it to be built with stone, and shews him the very place where she would have it done. Not long after the prior went out of town, and the man, going to talk with him and not finding him at home, went to a religious old man who had lived a long time in the monastery, and gave him a token where the foundation-stone of the chapel should be placed, by showing him and everybody else that would see it, for two hours together, the shape of a cross upon it, wonderfully adorned with gold and jewels, which afterwards disappeared. After this, the prior returning, and not hastening the building, the Virgin appeared in like manner to a certain woman in the town, and commanded her to desire the prior to build the chapel immediately, which the woman neglecting to do, the Virgin came to her in the night and much blamed her for contemning her command, and with that touched her arm, and she immediately lost the use of it. The woman, when she awoke, perceiving it, and much grieving for her negligence, ran to the monk, and with many tears told him her misfortune, who advised her to offer an arm made of wax to the Holy Virgin; which being done, her own arm was restored.

"As soon as the chapel was built, the prior, desiring to increase the people's devotion to the Blessed Virgin, causes the image which stood by a door near the chapel to be taken down and new painted; and as the painter was cleaning it, he found a silver plate well nailed on to the top of its head, and shew it to the prior, who called the monks, and ordered it to be taken off in their presence, and then they found the relics of many saints wrapt in lead with their names upon them, all which were first sent to Stephen of Provence, prior of this house, by William, prior

of Merlesham, at the request of Hugh Bygod,
and Sir Ralf, monk of Thetford, and most of
them, first of all, came from the Holy Sepulchre at
Jerusalem, there being pieces of the Purple Robe
of our Lord, of the Girdle of the Virgin Marye,
of the Holy Sepulchre, of the Rock of Calvary,
of the Sepulchre of the Blessed Virgin, of our
Lord's Manger, of the earth found in St. John
the Evangelist's Sepulchre, of St. George's Body,
with other reliques of St. Vincent the Martyr, and
of St. Leodegar or Leiger, St. Barbara, St. Gregory,
St. Leonard, St. Jerome, with some of St. Agnes'
hair, and of the wooden coffin miraculously kept
from decay, in which King Edmund the Martyr,
many years after his passion, was found whole,
and looked as if he had been alive, with pieces
of St. Ethelred's coffin, in which she was found
eleven years after her death, whole, and as if she
had been asleep. Pieces also of St. Lazarus'
cloaths and sepulchre, besides divers others whose
names are not known, all of which were placed
in the head of the image which the aforesaid
Sir Ralf, monk here, who was born and brought
up in this town, caused to be made at his own
expense, with a tabernacle adorned with small
images, painting, gold, and precious stones. And
besides this, he, with the assistance of Ralf de
Coam, clerk, who was a great friend to the monastery, persuaded the Lady Maud de Samundeham,
a lay-sister, and great friend of the house, to
purchase the famous picture of the Blessed Virgin
in the refectory. All which things he performed
with much labour and great difficulty, and therefore, for these services, his anniversary was for
ever to be held on the ides of October (15
October).

"All these reliques were kept in the chapel
till its dissolution, by means whereof it was
richly adorned, such as visited it by way of
devotion usually offering there, it being famous
for the many miracles performed by this image,
which were noised about in the country, two or
three of which the aforesaid monk tells us of;
as first, that a woman in Thetford overlaid her
child, and finding it dead in the morning, takes

it up, and runs to the image with it naked, and at the Virgin's intercession, it came to life again. Another is of a woman in Thetford who became dumb by a disease in her throat, upon which account many gave her money to go and make her offering to our Ladye at Wulpit, in Suffolk, and pray for her recovery; but the woman made signs that she would go to the image in the new chapel of the monks, which being consented to, she was restored, the woman affirming that the Blessed Virgin appeared to her, and pulled her tongue up from her throat, which cured her, wherefore she vowed to keep a candle burning before the image during her life. Another is of one William Heddrich the younger, a carpenter, and Isabel his wife, who lived in Hokham, and in harvest-time, according to custom, carried their boy, about three years old, with them into the field, and whilst the mother was mowing, towards evening, the child laid down and fell asleep, and soon after a cart ran over the head and killed it, which the father, who followed the cart, perceiving, took him up, and being much vexed for his death, runs to a physician in the town with the child, who assured him he was dead; but upon their vowing to go a pilgrimage, stark naked, to the image of the Blessed Virgin in her chapel at Thetford, the child came to life again about midnight, and its parents performed their vows and made large offerings to the Holy Virgin."[377]

These details are given in a MS., *De ædificatione Capellæ Virginis Mariæ in Thetford, et de Imagine Virginis Beatæ in illa*, by John Brame, a monk of Thetford, and which is now at Cambridge, in the Library of Corpus Christi College.

NOTE.—This may appear strange according to our present ideas, but it was by no means unusual, in those days, for pilgrims to undertake a pilgrimage partially, if not more undressed. In the representations of the principal miracles wrought by our Blessed Ladye of the Potterie at Bruges, the oldest sanctuary of our Ladye in Belgium, which are depicted on ancient tapestry, there is

[377] Vol. i. pp. 449, 450.

represented the cure of Victor Carr, of Ypres, who had vowed a pilgrimage in his shirt—*in syn lynen cleet*—to our Ladye of the Potterie.[278]

Another instance is mentioned in the Annals of St. Alban's. On the Sunday within the octave of the Nativity of the Blessed Virgin Marye, in 1430, John Turke, preaching to the people, mentioned the miraculous recovery from apparent death of a boy who had been run over by a cart. He was carried home, seemingly dead, to his father's house, where by the prayers of his neighbours and parents, and the bending of a piece of money, and the intervention of the holy martyr, St. Alban, he was restored to his former health (*vitam*); and on that day, in the presence of the abbot and community, the boy, clad only in his shirt, carrying a candle in his hand, and accompanied by his father, mother, and the neighbours, went in solemn procession to return thanks to God. The abbot intoned the *Te Deum*, which the community took up in plain chant, and all the bells were rung.[279]

THIRKLEBY.	Thomas Fulthorpe, Esq., of Thirkilbe, leaves a velvet doublet to the support of our Ladye's light in the church. Will dated June 29, 1471.[280]
THIRSK.	To the light of our Ladye in the choir of St. Marye's Church John Barker of Thresk, leaves iii*s.* iiii*d.* Will dated the Friday after St. Martin, 1395.[281]
THRULEGHT, SURREY.	In 1473, William Sondes, Esq., leaves a sum of money to the light of our Ladye in the church here.[282]
THURLTON, NORFOLK.	The image of our Ladye stood on the north side of the church.[283]

[278] *N. Dame de la Potterie.* Bruges, 1845, plate vi. p. 24.
[279] *Annales Mon. S. Albani,* vol. i. p. 54. Rolls Edit.
[280] Test. Ebor. vol. iii. p. 241.
[281] *Ibid.* vol. i. p. 206.
[282] Test. Vet. p. 332.
[283] *Gen. Hist. of Norfolk,* p. 95.

THOMPSON, or
THOMESTONE,
NORFOLK.

There was a light kept burning before the image of our Blessed Ladye where her gild was held.[284]

TOTTINGTON,
NORFOLK.

A Gild of the Nativity of our Blessed Ladye was kept at her altar in this church, and a light was continually burning before her image in service time.[285]

TRURO.

Our Ladye Portall.

Thomas Tretherffe, Esq., in his will dated 1529, says :

"Item, I will to the image of our Ladye, called our Ladye Portall at Truro, to the use and intent thereof, and for the reparations of the said chapel, and of and for part of the priest's wages there singing, and of and for the name of the said Thomas to be put upon the beadroll of the said chapel xx*s*. sterling.[286]

TUNSTEAD.

In this chapel were the tabernacles and images of our Ladye of Pity and of the Holy Trinity, the "Plough light" of Upgate and Hungate, and several gilds.[287]

WAKEFIELD.

1. The parish church.

Richard Bate of Wakefield, tanner, by will dated Tuesday after the feast of St. Mark, 1401, leaves to the high altar ii*s*. Also to the Blessed Virgin Marye of the same church ii*s*. ; and to her light vi*d*.[288]

Our Ladye's chapel was on the south side of the church.[289]

"Wakefield upon Calder," says Leland, "ys a very quik market towne, and meately large ; well served of flesch and fische ; both from the se and by rivers, whereof divers be thereabout at hande. So that al vitaile is very good and chepe there. A right honest man shal fare wel for 2 pens a meale. In this town is but one chefe church. There is a chapel beside."

---

[284] Blomefield, vol. i. p. 625.   [285] *Ibid.* p. 618

[286] Test. Vet. p. 644.   [287] *Gen. Hist. of Norfolk*, p. 961.

[288] Test. Ebor. vol. i. 286.   [289] Whitaker, *Loidis and Elmete*, 1816, t. i. p. 281.

2. Our Ladye on the Bridge.

"There is also a chapel of our Ladye on Calder Bridge, wont to be celebrated a *peregrinis*. The faire bridge of stone, of nine arches, under the which renneth the river of Calder; and on the east side of this bridge is a right goodly chapel of our Ladye, and two cantuarie priestes founded in it, of the foundation of the townesmen as sum say; but the Dukes of York were taken as founders for obteyning the mortmayne: I herd one saye that a servant of King Edwarde's (the Fourth) father, or else of the Earl of Rutheland, brother to King Edward the Fourth was a gret doer of it."[290]

By many this chapel is believed to have been erected by Edward the Fourth, the brother of young Edmund of Rutland—who was so ruthlessly murdered by the Earl of Clifford, who, says Leland, "for killing of men at this batail was called the 'boucher'"—for the repose of the soul of his unfortunate brother, and those who fell in the battle of Wakefield.

Although this little gem is called the chapel of Edward the Fourth, it existed long previously to his time. By charter dated Wakefield, 31st Edward the Third, 1357, it appears that the said King vested a rent charge of 10*l.* yearly on William Kay and William Bull, chaplains, and their successors for ever, to celebrate divine service in the chapel of our Blessed Ladye, then newly erected on Wakefield bridge. In 1391, William de Bayley, of the parish of Mitton, leaves —"C. sol. ad confirmacionem cantarie in capella Sce. Marie sup Pont. de Wakefield.[291]

In 1398, there were two chantries ordained in the chapel on Wakefield bridge, which were founded by William, the son of John Terry of Wakefield, and Robert de Heth, or Heath, who obtained licenses of the King—Richard the Second—to give and assign to the chaplains celebrating divine service in the chapel of St. Marye on Wakefield bridge, lately built, 10*l.* rent in Wakefield, Stanley, Ossett, Pontefract, Horbury,

---

[290] *Itin.* vol. vii. p. 41.

[291] Tyas, *Battles of Wakefield.* London and Wakefield, 1854, p. 67.

Heckmondwike, Shapton, Darfield, Purston, Jackling, and Fryston by the water. Thus there is evidence that the chantry on Wakefield bridge was erected long prior to the battle of Wakefield, and the connection of Edward the Fourth with it appears to have been confined to its re-endowment. However, there was an estate at Wakefield charged with the payment of 3s. annually, dated 27 September, 32nd Henry the Sixth, 1453.[292] The payments were to be made on the festival of St. Michael, the Purification of the Blessed Virgin Marye, and Pentecost.

A Protestant historian writes: "Since that time, *i.e.*, 1460, when its cresset-light acted as a guide to the wayfarer, and to the navigator of the Calder, it has no doubt frequently been visited by travellers, whose first step upon entering a town was to call at some chapel dedicated to the Virgin, and return thanks for preservation from danger by flood and field. The chantry has undergone many strange metamorphoses. It has been degraded into an old clothes shop, a warehouse, a shop for flax-dressers, a news-room, a cheese-cake house, and a tailor's shop. It has been rebuilt in perfect accordance with its original design, and is, perhaps, as pretty a specimen of the style of architecture of the time of Edward the Third as will be found within the compass of the three kingdoms."[293]

When the restorations were effected in 1848, the original front being much delapidated by age, was taken down, and sold to the late Honourable George Norton, who erected it by the side of the small lake in the picturesque grounds of Kettlethorpe Hall, with the object of serving for a summer-house.

WALBERSWICK.

In the churchwarden's accounts there is an item in 1453 of 5s. for "peynting the image of our Ladye." In 1491 another similar entry occurs: "Peyd for peynting of our Ladye, 13s. 4d."[294]

In 1474, the tabernacle of our Ladye of Pity here was ordered to be painted and gilded

[292] *Gentlemen's Magazine*, 1801, p. 723.
[293] Tyas, *ut sup.* p. 73.   [294] Nichols, *Illustrations, &c.* p. 186.

according to the form of the image of our Ladye of Pity at Southwold.[295]

In 1500, John Almyngham by his will dated October 7, gave to the church 20*l.*, of which 10*l.* were for an organ.

"Item, with the residue of the said sume I will a canope over the hygh awter welle done with oure Ladye and 4 anngelys, and the Holy Ghost goyng upp and down with a cheyme."[296]

WALSINGHAM, formerly GALSINGAHAM.

This was the most celebrated of all the English sanctuaries of our Blessed Ladye ; and so great was the veneration in which it was held, that it was called the Holy Land of Walsingham. An old ballad says—

> As ye came from the holy land
> Of Walsingham :

and other instances occur.[297] How applicable to this sanctuary were those words of Tobias : "Nations from afar shall come to thee, shall bring gifts, and shall adore the Lord in thee, and shall esteem thy land as holy."[298]

Walsingham, or more correctly, Little Walsingham, is a parish, formerly a market town, in the northern division of the hundred of Greenhoe, in the county of Norfolk, twenty-eight miles north-west of Norwich, and one hundred and fourteen from London. It is about eight miles from the sea, and seven from Wells, the nearest port ; but it is probable that most of the pilgrims who came by sea would land at Lynn Episcopi, now Lynn Regis, which is twenty-seven miles distant. Ships belonging to Lynn Episcopi are often mentioned amongst the pilgrim-transports.

Two hundred feet due east from the east end of the priory church are two wells, commonly called the "Wishing-wells," but this appears to be a comparatively late designation, and to which is attached a modern superstition, that

[295] *Vide ante sub* Southwold, p. 142.
[296] Nichols, p. 187.
[297] Bishop Percy's folio Manuscript, *Ballads and Romances.* Ed. Hales and Furnevall. Lond. 1868. V. iii. p. 471. *Vide* also p. 465.
[298] Tobias, c. xiii. v. 14.

whoever drank of these waters might obtain what they wished for while they drank.

In or about the year 1061, a little chapel, similar to the Holy House at Nazareth, and dedicated to the Annunciation, was built here by Richeldis or Recholdis,[299] a widow, in consequence, as the tradition says, of an injunction received in a vision from the Blessed Virgin Marye.[300]

In the Pepysian Library there is an unique copy of an anonymous ballad, printed by Robert Pynson, and which bears internal evidence of having been composed about the year 1460. Its title runs thus—

> Of thys chappel see here the foundatyon,
> Builded the yere of Christ's incarnatyon
> A thousande complete sixty and one,
> The tyme of Saint Edwarde, Kinge of this region.

It relates how "the noble wedowe," some time Lady of the town of Walsingham, Rychold de Faverches by name, was favoured by the Virgin Mother of God with a view of the Holy House at Nazareth, and commissioned to build its counterpart at Walsingham, upon a site thereafter to be indicated. It relates very circumstantially the widow's perplexity—

> When it was al formed, then had she great doubte
> Where it should be sette, and in what manner place,
> Inasmuch as tweyne places were foune out,
> Tokened with meracles of our Laydie's grace.
>
> · · · · · ·
>
> The Wedowe thought it moste lykely of congruence
> This house on the first soyle to build and arrere:
> Of thys who lyste to have experience;
> A chappel of Saynt Lawrence standyth now there,
> Faste by tweyne wellys, experience do thus lere:
> There she thought to have sette this chappel,
> Which was begone by our Ladie's counsel.
> All night the Wedowe permayneing in this prayer,
> Our Blessed Laydie with blessed minystrys,
> Herself being here chief Artificer,

---

[299] Richeld is an old Norfolk name. In 1233, Bartholomew de Creke makes a grant to Richeld, widow of Robert de Creke. Blomefield, Parkins' continuation, v. iii. p. 37.

[300] *Index. Mon. Dioc. Norv.* p. 26. Leland Collect. v. iii. p. 26.

Arrered thys sayde house with angells handys,
And not only rered it, but sette it there it is,
That is tweyne hundrede foot and more in distaunce
From the first place fokes make remembraunce.[1]

The tradition, therefore, is, that Richeld, being
in a state of doubt as to the exact spot on which
to erect the little chapel, but inclining to the
site by the two wells—"there she thought to
have sette this chappel"—spent the night in
prayer, and that our Blessed Ladye, "herself
being here chief artificer," reared it with the
assistance of angels, and then "sette it there it
is." This tradition fully explains the extraordinary veneration in which the sanctuary of
our Lady of Walsingham was held. "Whatever
uncertainty," says Harrod, "may still exist about
the precise date of the chapel, there can be no
doubt as to its having been the great source of
attraction which drew pilgrims from all parts,
and made the priory one of the richest in the
world. Almost from the foundation of the priory
up to the dissolution there was one unceasing
movement of pilgrims to and from Walsingham.
. . . The image of the Blessed Virgin in the
small chapel, 'in all respects like to the Santa
Casa at Nazareth, where the Virgin was saluted
by the Angel Gabriel,' was the original, and continued to the dissolution the primary object of
the pilgrims' visit."[2]

Soon after the norman invasion, Geoffrey de
Faveraches, as he is named, the son of Richeldis,
founded and endowed a priory of Austin Canons,
to whom he gave the above-named chapel. The
charter of foundation is to this effect:

"To all, &c. Geoffrey de Faveraches, &c.

"Be it known to you that I have given and
granted to Edwin, my clerk, for the institution
of a religious order which he will provide, and
for the health of my soul and the souls of my
parents and friends, in perpetual alms, the chapel
which my mother founded in Walsingham, in

[1] *Journal of Royal Arch. Instit.* v. xiii. pp. 115, 116.
[2] Harrod, *Gleanings among the Castles and Convents of Norfolk.* Norwich, 1857.
P. 157.

honour of the Ever Virgin Mary, together with the possession of the Church of All Hallows, in the same vill, with all its appurtenances, &c."[3]

Geoffrey went on pilgrimage to Jerusalem, but the date of his journey is not given.

Subsequently Gilbert, Earl of Clare, confirms to his clerics of Walsingham, Ralph and Geoffrey, for the health of his soul and the souls of his parents, in perpetual alms, the chapel which Richeldis, the mother of Geoffrey de Faveraches, had founded in Walsingham, with all its appurtenances.[4] And a charter, of a later date, of Robert de Brucurt, addressed to William, Bishop of Norwich, dated A.D. 1146—1174, makes known that he gives and grants to God and St. Marye, and the canons of Walsingham, for the health of his soul, &c., all the possessions which that church held on the day when Geoffrey de Faveraches set out on his journey to Jerusalem.[5] This is the correct early history of Walsingham, and which some writers have strangely confused; and there appears no reason to doubt that Richeld, the mother of Geoffrey de Faveraches, was the original founder of the celebrated chapel of our Ladye, and at the period usually assigned, A.D. 1061. The chain of evidence is satisfactory.

The chapel of our Blessed Lady stood lengthways, east and west, on the north side of the church, which was built up to it, and communicated with it by a door. This church was two hundred and forty-four feet in length by seventy-eight in width, interior measurement. The priory adjoined the church on the south side. About two hundred and thirty feet due north, on a line drawn from the east end of the church, stood the " Knight's Gate," leading into what is now called " Knight's Street."

This renowned sanctuary is generally spoken of as having been the counterpart of the Holy House at Nazareth. Fortunately the dimensions of the Walsingham chapel have been preserved by William of Worcester, and thus a comparison

---

[3] *Mon. Ang.* vi. p. 71, MS. Cott. Nero. E. vii. f. 7.
[4] *Ibid.* [5] *Ibid.* p. 73.

becomes possible. I propose, therefore, briefly to give such details of the Holy House of Nazareth, now of Loreto, as bear upon the question, using for my principal authority a most interesting work, entitled *Loreto and Nazareth*, drawn up from the researches of many writers, and from his own most careful investigations in both places, by the late lamented Father of the Oratory of St. Philip, William Antony Hutchison.[6] It is to be regretted that this instructive book is not more known. It has lately been translated into German.

The Holy House was miraculously translated by the angels from Nazareth, and placed by them on the summit of a hill at Tersatto, a small town near Fiume, about sixty miles south of Trieste, on the eastern side of the Adriatic gulf, on the 6th of May, A.D. 1291.[7] Three years later, on the 10th of September, it was again translated across the Adriatic, and placed in a wood, about a mile from the sea-shore, and four miles from Recanati.[8] In August, 1295, it was transferred to the hill of the two brothers; finally, in December of the same year, it was translated to its present position.[9] The wood where the Holy House rested was in a district called *Lauretum*,[10] either from the laurels that grew in abundance there, or because it belonged to a rich lady of Recanati, called Laureta; and hence the appellation of *Domus Lauretana*, or "House of Loreto," which has ever since remained attached to it.[11]

"Although," says Father Hutchison, "the House now at Loreto is identically the same as

[6] *Loreto and Nazareth*. London: E. Dillon, 2, Alexander Place, Brompton, 1863.

[7] *Ibid.* p. 4.

[8] *Ibid.* p. 17.

[9] *Ibid.*

[10] I have found instances of both these names elsewhere in the thirteenth century. Thus the Chartulary of Notre Dame of Paris contains a charter, dated November, 1264, of Peter, called Tonniaus de Lorreto in Boscagio, and Anne his wife (vol. ii. f. 224, n. xix.). In February, 1256, there is a precept of Henry, Archbishop of Sens, given at Loretum in Boscagio (*ibid.* n. i, f. 290); and in a charter of June, 1258, some lands are described as lying contiguous to the vineyard of Philip de Loreto (*ibid.* f. 468, n. cvi.). This place was Lorrez-le-Bocage, in the department of Seine et Marne, in the arrondissement of Fontainebleau. And a lady of the name of Laureta was an early benefactor to the Knights Hospitallers of St. John of Jerusalem in England.

[11] *Ibid.* pp. 25, 26.

when it arrived there nearly six centuries ago, yet some alterations have been made in it, of which we now proceed to give an account. Soon after the House was finally settled in its present site, the people of Recanati, seeing that it stood on the bare earth without foundation, feared to allow its ancient walls to be exposed to the violence of the wind and the rain. They determined, therefore, to surround the Holy House with a thick brick wall, which should serve as a support and protection to the ancient walls; but when it was finished, it was found that the new wall had separated from the old walls in such a manner, that a boy with a lighted candle in his hand could easily pass between the two. This separation was commonly thought to be miraculous, and it was believed that our Lady wished to show that she had no need of human assistance to support the walls of her Holy House. Had the separation only taken place here and there, there would be nothing astonishing, as it might be thought to be merely the effect of a settlement of a new wall; but from the account given, something more than this seems to have taken place, as the new walls all round the building seem to have separated from the old walls, and to a considerable distance. But whatever may have been the reason, there was no doubt of the fact, for Riera, who died anno 1582, says that in his day there were living many who had beheld this prodigy with their own eyes; and amongst the rest, Rainerius Nerucci, the architect of the Holy House."[12]

In the course of time the magnificent church, which contains the Holy House under its dome, was erected. It seems to have been begun about the year 1468 by Pope Paul the Second, and was greatly added to and beautified by Clement the Seventh. This Pontiff determined to complete the incrustation of the Holy House with marble, according to the plan decided on by Leo the Tenth. Whilst the sculptors were preparing their work, Nerucci, the architect, removed the brick wall, which, as has been said, was built around the House. He then erected

[12] *Loreto and Nazareth,* p. 14.

in its place a new wall, which was afterwards clothed with marble. On this wall the present roof of the Holy House is supported; for the Pope fearing lest the ancient roof, which was of wood, might take fire some day through the quantity of lamps that were always burning in the House, ordered a new roof of stone to be put in its place.[13]

It has been ascertained on several occasions that the walls of the Holy House have no foundations whatever.[14]

The successive renewals of the pavement from time to time were rendered necessary by the crowds of worshippers who frequented the Holy House. Originally a pavement of tiles seems to have been laid down, either at Tersatto or Loreto; but in the time of Sixtus the Fourth, this was replaced by a pavement of marble, the pilgrims having carried off most of the tiles of the ancient pavement as relics.[15]

May not the bequest of William Haute, in 1462, of "one piece of that stone on which the Archangel Gabriel descended when he saluted the Blessed Virgin Marye" have been in reality, a bit of this ancient pavement? It will be observed that this piece of stone is not spoken of as being considered a relic, and, as such, exposed for public veneration, but the testator merely bequeaths it to be placed under the foot of the image of our Ladye at Bourne.[16]

The great alteration, however, which was made in the Holy House at this time, was one which, though very convenient for the faithful, was such a bold step, that only one possessed of the authority of Supreme Pontiff could have ventured to order it. Up to the time of Clement the Seventh, the Holy House had but one door, the ancient door, namely, on the north side. This was found to be very inconvenient, and to cause much confusion among the crowds who were striving to enter or to leave the House. Besides this, the doorway in question existed in

Loreto and Nazareth, p. 28.   [14] *Ibid.* p. 29.   [15] *Ibid.* p. 31.
    [16] See *ante,* p. 4, *sub* Bourne.

L

the times of the Holy Family. It was, therefore, manifestly unseemly that so sacred a spot should be the scene of those undignified struggles on the part of the people. The Pope, therefore, determined to close up the ancient door, and to break three new doorways in the walls of the House—two of them being respectively in the north and south walls, towards the western extremities, and giving to the people ample means of entry and egress; the third doorway is in the south wall, and opens into the Sanctuary of the Holy House, behind the altar. His Holiness accordingly gave orders that these doorways should be made.[17]

During the progress of these works, the small window in the west wall was enlarged and brought nearly into the centre of the wall, instead of being, as theretofore, nearer to the north than to the south wall. The materials of the new doorways were used partly to block up the ancient doorway, partly to enlarge the *Sagro Cammino*, and the remainder were buried underneath the pavement. At the same time the altar, which formerly stood against the middle of the south wall, was removed to its present position, *i.e.*, about twelve feet from the east end, it is about four feet six inches long, with the top stone projecting, which is a dark black-looking slab, apparently of marble. It is all enclosed within the present altar. Behind the altar the *Sagro Cammino*, or Sacred Hearth, was considerably added to and brought into its present form. Above this, the image of our Lady of Loreto was placed, which had come in the Holy House when it arrived at Tersatto. These works were commenced on the 10th November, 1531, and were not finished till the 5th July, 1538.[18]

Summing up, therefore, the following data are obtained :

1. The Holy House of Nazareth had but one door, which was nearly in the centre of the north wall, and one window which was in the west wall, and nearer to the north than to the south wall.

[17] *Loreto and Nazareth*, p. 32.   [18] Pp. 35, 36.

Father Hutchison is inclined to believe that formerly there was a second doorway where the *Sagro Cammino* now stands.[19]

2. The altar stood against the south wall. It is not stated where the image of our Ladye was placed.

3. These arrangements were all changed, the alterations made by order of Clement the Seventh, when the altar was placed about twelve feet from the east end, and the image of our Ladye in the enlarged niche called the *Sagro Cammino.*

The dimensions of the Holy House, internal measurement, are, length 31 ft. 3⅝ in., breadth 13 ft. 4½ in.

Now to return to the Walsingham sanctuary, the little chapel of the Annunciation "arrerd with angells handys," which formed the glory of Walsingham in its most palmy days, and which is described as being similar to the Holy House of Nazareth. It is certainly curious and interesting to notice how a miraculous translation is also associated with its early history, nearly two hundred and thirty years before the actual translation of the Holy House itself from Nazareth to Tersatto in 1291.

The earliest details extant about this renowned sanctuary are those given by William Botoner, generally known as William of Worcester. He was born at Bristol, c. 1415, and was educated at Oxford, mainly at the expense of Sir John Fastolf, of Caistor in Norfolk, whose squire he afterwards became. His Itinerary is preserved in the library of Corpus Christi College, Cambridge, and was published by Nasymth in 1778. He was at Walsingham, probably, in 1479.

It appears that, like the Holy House of Loreto, the chapel of the Annunciation at Walsingham—which I shall call, in the words of William of Worcester, the *Capella Beata Maria*—was covered in by an outer building, but I have found no record of the date when this outer covering was erected. William of Worcester calls

[19] Pp. 67—88.

it the *novum opus*, or new work; but this term is applied both to new buildings, and to buildings pulled down and rebuilt, therefore his words only prove that at the time of his visit, a new building, which enclosed the *Capella*, had recently been erected. These are the measurements which he has recorded: *Longitudo* novi operis *de Walsingham continet in toto* 16 *virgas; latitudo continet infra aream* 10 *virgas*, or 48 by 30 feet. *Longitudo* capelle Beate Marie *continet* 7 *virgas* 30 *pollices; latitudo continet* 4 *virgas* 10 *pollices*,[20] or 23 ft. 6 in. by 12 ft. 10 in. Thus there was ample space for pilgrims to circulate between the walls of the *capella* and those of the *novum opus.*

Erasmus, who was at Walsingham in May, 1511, describes the Ladye chapel by *templum*, and as not completed, within which was the sanctuary of our Ladye, which he variously calls the *intimum sacellum, sacellum angustum*, and *conclave divæ Virginis*.[21] Therefore the *templum inabsolutum angustum*, and the *conclave divæ Virginis* or *sacellum angustum* of Erasmus are, respectively, the *novum opus* and the *Capella Beatæ Mariæ* of William of Worcester.

The description of the position of the Ladye chapel which Erasmus gives, is confirmed by some excavations made at Walsingham not many years ago. It adjoined the priory church on the north side. Erasmus, speaking of the *templum inabsolutum*, says: "Our Ladye does not dwell here for the building is not yet finished;" and then, like a Dutchman, he feelingly adds: "the place is very draughty on all sides; the windows are open, and the doors are open, and not far off is the ocean, the father of winds"—*Locus est undique perflabilis patentibus portis, patentibus fenestris, et in propinquo est oceanus, ventorum pater.* "'Tis

---

[20] *Itineraria Symonis Simeonis et Will. de Worcester*, ed. Nasmyth, 1778, p. 335. In Browne Willis' *Mitred Abbeys*, Addenda, vol. ii. p. 330, this passage of William of Worcester is thus given: "*Latitudo continet* infra aream 10 *virgas.*" The Rev. James Lee Warner has most obligingly sent me a tracing of the original MS., which gives *aream* beyond all doubt whatever.

[21] *Peregrinatio religionis ergo. Inter Colloquia Erasmi, Opp. Lug. Batav.* 1703, t. i. col. 774, et seq.

a hard case," says Menedemus,[22] "where then does our Ladye dwell?" Ogygius, *i.e.* Erasmus, replies: "Within that building, which I have said was unfinished, there is a small chapel *ligneo tabulatu confectum*, which admits by a narrow little door, on either side, those who come to salute our Ladye; the light is feeble, in fact, scarcely any, excepting from the wax-candles. A most delightful fragrance gladdens one's nose"—*in eo templo quod inabsolutum dixi, est sacellum angustum, ligneo tabulatu constructum, ad utrumque latus per angustum ostiolum admittens salutatores. Lumen est exigum; nec fere nisi ex cereis; fragrat odor naribus gratissimus.* It is, indeed, an agreeable surprise to learn that anything was pleasing to this jesting and conceited ex-Augustinian canon.

I accept his statements for the simple reason that he had no object to gain, no whim to gratify, by being otherwise than correct in them. In regard of the *patentes portæ*, it is most probable that the *capella* had no doors, a measure, which the convenience for the constant influx of pilgrims into the little chapel, would suggest; and it is extremely likely that the doors in the north wall of the *novum opus* and in the twelve foot passage from the church though the south wall were also kept open during the day for the same reason. Erasmus had announced his intended visit to Walsingham in a letter to Andrew Ammonio, dated Cambridge, 8th May, 1511.[23] Now it so happens, that just about this time, the windows of the *novum opus* were being glazed at the expense of the king. In the royal payments of the third and fourth years of Henry the Eighth, there are two entries as follows:

1—8 June, 1511, part payment for glazing our Ladye's chapel at Walsingham, 20*l*.[24]

November (no date), 1512, Bernard Flour, for glazing our Ladye's chapel at Walsingham, 23*l*. 11*s*. 4*d*.[25]

[22] One of the two characters of the dialogue.
[23] Ep. cxiv. Opp. t. iii. pt. i. col. 106.
[24] Letters and Papers, &c. Henry the Eighth, vol. ii. pt. ii. p. 1451.
[25] *Ibid.* p. 1458.

These fully explain how the windows happened to be open when Erasmus was at Walsingham, and confirm his account.

Several years ago the Rev. James Lee Warner, cousin to the present proprietor of Walsingham, made some excavations, and laid bare the foundations of the ladye chapel. He has given a very interesting account of his discoveries, accompanied by plans, in the *Journal of the Royal Archæological Institute.*[26] I have read and studied it with great pleasure, and it has afforded me valuable assistance. To use his words: "The measurements of this building coincide so exactly with the dimensions of the *novum opus*, as already quoted from William of Worcester, that not a shadow of a doubt can exist as to their identity."[27] From the plans which Mr. Lee Warner has prepared, the walls of the *novum opus* were of considerable thickness. There were three doors, one in the north, and one in the south wall, opposite to each other, and no doubt facing the two doors of the *sacellum angustum*, which Erasmus mentions: they were nearly in the centre of the two walls. The third door, and apparently of smaller dimensions, was in the west end, and not in the centre, but nearer to the south wall. The pavement of the *novum opus* was about 2 ft. 6 in. above the level of that of the church, from which the entrance was up three steps. In the plan of the ruins of Walsingham made by Mr. Lee Warner, the east wall of the *novum opus* is represented as of an extraordinary thickness, it being almost twice that of the other walls, and consequently about 24 feet wide.

And now two questions arise: 1. William of Worcester describes the width of the *novum opus* as being ten yards: *latitudo continet infra aream 10 virgas.* What is to be understood by *infra aream ?*

Mr. Lee Warner, in the interesting article, to which I have already alluded, says: "The *area* (whatever it was) seems to have been identical with the platform of solid masonry which forms

26 Vol. xiii. pp. 115—125.   27 *Ibid.* p. 123.

the eastern end of the *opus novum*. The expression *infra aream* may imply that it was elevated, but why William of Worcester excluded it from his internal measurement of the chapel, of which it formed the most honourable part, is not quite so apparent.[28] But, in a letter to me on this subject," he says : "Upon subsequent reflexion, I believe that the great thickness of the east wall was apparent, not real ; and that it was in fact only a portion of wall lying flat, having been partially undermined, and so fallen : but roots of trees presented a difficulty in exploration. Are you cognizant of a remark of Matt. Paris ? who, describing the solemnity, A.D. 1247, in the confessor's chapel, says : "Rex advocavit eum, et præcepit residere in gradu, qui erat medius inter sedile suum et aream. P. 980, 4to ed. 1551."

This exploration has removed one difficulty, for I had been at a loss to account for the extraordinary apparent thickness of the east wall of the *novum opus*, viz. about 24 ft. There can be no doubt that *area*, as used by William of Worcester, refers to the floor of the *capella*, which must have been above the level of the pavement of the *opus novum*. Moreover, in all probability, a step ran round the outside of the *capella*, whether level or not, with its floor, as is the case at Loreto and Einsiedeln ; and this step and floor, together, formed the *area* of William of Worcester. I think that *infra aream* is to be taken as applying equally to *longitudo* and *latitudo*. Unfortunately, the ruins afford no assistance. If the pavement of the *novum opus* had been spared, it would have supplied valuable evidence for a solution of the question ; but Mr. Lee Warner informs me that "the pavement of the *capella* was so thoroughly upturned by Thomas Cromwell and his agents, that not only wood, but stone, had for the most part vanished." And this leads to the second question.

2. Was the *area* of William of Worcester the *ligneus tabulatus* of Erasmus ?

In eo templo, says he, *quod inabsolutum dixi,*

[28] Vol. xiii. pp. 123, 124.

est sacellum angustum, ligneo tabulato constructum, &c. How is the expression *ligneo tabulatu constructum* to be construed? Weever renders it, "a small chapell, but all of wood;"[29] Gough Nichols, "a small chapel made of boards;"[30] and Mr. Lee Warner speaks of it as the "wooden sacellum," but the reading which he quotes is, *ligneo tabulato constructum.*[31] The text which I have used is that of Vander Aa's edition of 1703; and I have examined five other editions of the *Colloquia,* all of which give *ligneo tabulatu.*[32] Facciolati does not mention the word;[33] Ducange gives only one meaning, *pavimentum*—"a floor."[34]

It seems to be the general impression that the *capella* of Walsingham was built of wood, but I have found no authority for it, unless these words of Erasmus have given rise to it. The real solution of the difficulty lies in the sense in which Erasmus used them. But what is to be understood by these lines of the anonymous ballad of the year 1460, which I have already quoted?

> When it was al formed, then had she great doute
> Where it should be sette.

Do they refer to the completion of the building materials, and as being ready for the builders; or will they warrant the inference that the little chapel was built of wood, and fitted together, and put up, prior to its being finally erected?

The sanctuary of our Ladye, the *Capella Beatæ Mariæ* of William of Worcester, the *Conclave Divæ Virginis* of Erasmus, is very briefly described by him. "When you look in you would

---

[29] *Anc. Funeral Monum.* p. 860.

[30] *Pilgrimages to St. Mary of Walsingham,* &c. Newly translated by John Gough Nichols, F.S.A. Lond. 1875, p. 13.

[31] *Journ. Roy. Ant. Inst.* vol. xiii, p. 124.

[32] 1. Amsterdami, 1638, p. 271. 2. Lugd. Bat. 1664, p. 416. 3. *Ibid.* 1665, p. 368. 4. Paris, 1674, p. 358. 5. Lugd. Bat. 1729, p. 416. I have not been able to see the Basle edition by Frober of 1540.

[33] Ed. Patavii, 1805.

[34] Ducange says: "Tabulatus, *pavimentum.* Andreas Floriac. in Vita MS. S. Gauzlini Archiep. Brituric. lib. i. *Novumvicum etiam lapideo Tabulatu fabricavit ecclesiam.* Hinc: Tabulatus pro *pavimento stratus.* Chronicon Romualdi ii. Archiep. Salern t. 7. Muratori col. 194. *Panormi palatium satis pulchrum jussit ædificari, in quo fecit capellam miro lapide tabulatam.*

say that it is the abode of the saints, so brilliantly does it shine on all sides with gems, gold, and silver." What light there was was afforded by the numerous wax candles, therefore the inference is that it had no windows. But where did the altar stand, and where was the celebrated image of our Blessed Ladye placed? All that is known on this point is from Erasmus, who laconically remarks that "our Ladye stood in the dark at the right side of the altar"—*illa stabat in tenebris ad dextram altaris;* and one of the canons was in constant attendance—*adstat altari canonicus quidam*—to receive and take care of the offerings of the pilgrims. As to the actual situation of the altar nothing is known. Judging from the position of the doors of the *opus novum*, which must have corresponded with those of the *capella*, it is most probable that the altar stood at the east end, and the image of our Ladye in the south-east angle.

The celebrated image of our Ladye was of wood. Erasmus describes it as "a little image, remarkable neither for size, material, or execution"—*imaguncula, nec magnitudine nec materia nec opere præcellens;* and this is the only description extant, so far as I can ascertain, of Our Ladye of Walsingham. Whether it was a standing or a seated image is a question which must remain unanswered. The seal of Walsingham represents our Ladye as seated, but I do not think that it can be received as evidence of the image of our Ladye. I may add, that the image of our Ladye of Loreto is standing, and about three feet in height.

On comparing the measurements of the *capella* of Walsingham with those of the Holy House of Loreto, it will be seen that they do not correspond. The dimensions of Loreto are—length, 31 ft. 3¼ in.; breadth, 13 ft. 4½ in. Of Walsingham—length, 23 ft. 6 in.; breadth, 12 ft. 10 in.[35] Loreto is built of the limestone of Nazareth; there is no record of what material the *capella* of Walsingham was built, for *ligneo tabulatu constructum* cannot be

[35] *Loreto and Nazareth,* p. 82.

construed as "built of wood." [86] Both were enclosed by an outer building. Presuming the door in the north wall of the *novum opus* to have been opposite to the door of the *capella*, the position of this latter one would have corresponded with that of Loreto before the alterations commenced by Clement the Seventh in 1531. The altar at Loreto formerly stood against the north wall : nothing is known of the position of the altar of the *capella* except that the image of our Ladye was on its right. And was the image itself of English workmanship, or was it a copy of our Ladye of Nazareth, and brought from the Holy Land by Geoffrey de Faveraches, the son of the founder ?

The anonymous ballad, written about the year 1460, records that a chapel dedicated to St. Lawrence stood by the two wells, on the spot where Richeld originally intended to have erected the chapel of our Ladye. Erasmus describes this chapel as being "full of wonders ;" and adds, that the wells were covered by a wooden shed, which, as the guide informed him, was brought thither suddenly, in the winter season, from a long distance. Evidently he was indistinct in his recollections, and confounded the tradition of the chapel of our Ladye with the shed. He ridicules its pretended antiquity, and remarks that it bore no signs of old age ; moreover, that when he expressed his doubts on this point, his guide, while seeming to assent to what he said, pointed out an old bear's skin attached to the rafters of the shed, and seemed amazed that he had not noticed this evident proof of antiquity ! Erasmus gives a very plausible account of what passed in conversation between himself and his guide, yet he himself did not understand a word of English, for he mentions, in another part of the Dialogue, that he had to avail himself of the services of young Robert Aldrich as an interpreter. No doubt the lively Cantab and the East Anglian guide must have been poking fun at the Dutchman ; indeed Erasmus seems to hint as much in another

[86] See Parker's *Architectural Glossary* for details.

part, when he says that he was afraid to place entire confidence in Aldrich. It does not matter how this bear's skin came thither; it may have been hung up by a pilgrim as a curiosity and an offering, just as Erasmus hung up his Greek ode in the Ladye chapel.

The latest account of the wells is by John Henry Parker, C.B., D.C.L., in 1847: "The holy wells are quite plain, round, and uncovered, and on one side of them is a square bath; on the other side a small early English doorway."[37]

The story of the Knight, and of the Knight's Gate, which opened into Knight Street, is given by Blomefield on the authority of an old MS.; but it is to be regretted that he did not add where this MS. was preserved. This is what he relates:

"Near the entrance into the close of the priory, on the north, was a very low and narrow wicket door 'not past an elne hye,' and three quarters in breadth; and a certain Norfolk knight, Sir Raaf Boutebourt, armed cap-a-pié, and on horseback, being in days of old (1314) pursued by a cruel enemy, and in the utmost danger of being taken, made full spede for this gate, and invoking this Lady for his deliverance, he immediately found himself and his horse within the close and sanctuary of the priory, in a safe asylum, and so fooled his enemy."[38] Erasmus says that a brass plate representing Sir Ralph was nailed to the gate. The name of the "Knight Street" is the sole local evidence now remaining of Sir Ralph Boutebourt's escape.

The principal road by which pilgrims arrived at Walsingham passed by Newmarket, Brandon, and Fakenham; it is still known by the names of the Palmers' Way, and Walsingham Green Way, and it may be traced pretty accurately along the principal part of its course for nearly sixty miles through the diocese. The pilgrims who came from the north crossed the Wash near Long Sutton, and went through Lynn, most probably taking the way which passed by

[37] Norwich vol. of the Royal Arch. Institute, p. 188.   [38] Vol. ix. p. 280.

the priories of Flitcham, Rudham or Roodham, and Cokesford. Another great road used by passengers on pilgrimage to Our Ladye of Walsingham led from the east, through Norwich and Attlebridge, by Bec Hospital, where gratuitous accommodation for thirteen poor pilgrims was provided every night; this was also sometimes called the Walsingham Way. At Hilburgh, Southacre, Westacre, Lynn, Priors—Thorns, Stanhoe, Caston, and many other places, were chapels in which the pilgrims offered up their prayers as they passed on to Our Ladye of Walsingham.[39] The Galaxy, or Milky Way, was also called the "Walsingham Way," as pointing to that angle, and it retained this name to the days of Blomefield, who mentions that he had heard old people use it.[40]

The prosperity of the little town of Walsingham was dependant upon the crowds of pilgrims, who flocked thither from all parts, and consequently inns and hostelries predominated. This feature will have been noticed by those who have been at Einsiedeln, and other celebrated places of pilgrimage, where the sanctuary alone is the object of attraction.

On entering Walsingham from the south, close to the walls of the priory stood "le Beere," formerly "le Dowe." Then in the Friday marketplace were the "White Horse," and "Crownyd Lyon;" in the adjoining street the "Mone and Sterr," the "Cokk," the "Sarassyns Hede," the "Swan and the Bull," which had appropriated part of the buildings of the "Angel now wasted;" and then the "Ram" offers hospitality. In Stonegate, there were the "Chekker," and the "Bolt and Toun." In North Town-end there were the "White Hart" and the "Madynhede;" by the Prior's water-mill the "Gryffon" and the "Bell;" in Church Street the "Crane," and by the churchyard, the "George." And there were, no doubt, many more.[41]

[39] *Index. Mon. Diœc. Norv.* Introd. p. xix.
Vol. i. p. 486.
[41] Augmentation Office Papers, D. 9. This contains a survey of the Prior's possessions in the town. See Harrod. p. 175.

Some of the inn-holders of Walsingham seem to have considered the pilgrims as fair objects to be "fleeced," and fleeced them accordingly. It is surmised that this extortion led to the conflagration of four of the hostelries in 1431. John Amundesham relates that "in this year, after Easter, there was a great fire in Walsingham Parva, which consumed four of the inns in that town; by whom, or through what cause, this misfortune happened, no mortal knew, except that it might be from revenge for the excessive and unjust extortionate charges, which the persons living in those inns had exacted from the pilgrims for their victuals."[42]

The Kings of England, and their subjects of every class, loved to go on pilgrimage to this sanctuary.

> Heremytes on an heape with hoked staves
> Wenten to Walsyngham:

so wrote John Longland, in his Vision of Piers Plouhman, A.D. 1362. And many foreigners came from abroad. In the *Witten Bouc*, a pilgrimage from Ghent "T'ons Vrauwe te Walsinghe," is put down at four *livres*.[43]

Henry the Third is the first English King who is recorded as a pilgrim to Walsingham. This was in the twenty-sixth year of his reign— 1248.[44]

Edward the First was twice there. " It was known," says Walsingham, " 'that he did abide under the protection of the God of heaven.' For once, while he was a young man, he chanced to be playing at chess with a knight in a vaulted chamber, when suddenly, and without any occasion, he rose, and went away; when, lo! an immense stone, which would have crushed him if he had remained, fell on the very spot where he had been sitting. On account of this miracle, he very heartily honoured Our Blessed Ladye of Walsingham, to whose favour he attributed his escape from this danger."[45] In 1296, at Candle-

[42] *Annales Mon. S. Albani*, vol. i. p. 62. Rolls Edit. [43] Cannaert. p. 354.
[44] *Mon. Angl.* vol. vi. p. 71. [45] *Hist. Anglicana*, vol. i. p. 9. Rolls Edit.

mas, he again went on pilgrimage to his Protectress in dangers and adversity, Our Ladye of Walsingham, where his procurators, Hugh le Dispenser, and Walter de Beauchamp, steward of his household, at his command, and in his presence (it not being the usage for him anyways to swear in his own person) did swear *en la chapelle de Notre Dame à Walsingham*, for him and his heirs, Kings of England, and in his name, according to the power given them (which he acknowledged) that they should perform and fulfil all matters and things contained in the instrument of alliance between him and the Earl of Flanders. *Nous que de usage avoms, qui nous en propre Persone ne jurromy, reconissoms que le dit Monsieur Hue et Monsieur Wautier nous Procurers et lour donans poer e mandement, &c. par le tesmoign de cestes presentes Lettres.* Dated at Walsingham, *le jour de la Chandeleur*, in the year of grace, 1296, and of our reign the twenty-fifth.[46]

Edward the Second was a pilgrim to Walsingham in 1315;[47] and in 1332, Isabella of France, whilst residing at Castle Rising, made a pilgrimage to Walsingham; and in the municipal records of Lynn there is an entry of 20s. for bread sent to Isabella, Queen Dowager, when she came from Walsingham.[48]

In 1361, Edward the Third went to Walsingham;[49] and in this year he granted out of his treasury the sum of 9l., as a gift, to John, Duke of Brittany, for his expenses in going on pilgrimage to Walsingham.[50]   In the same year he also gave leave of absence from London, for a month, on account of his health, to his nephew, the Duke of Anjou, to visit Our Ladye of Walsingham and St. Thomas of Canterbury.[51] And three years later, Edward the Third sent Letters, dated the 20th of February, to the Warders of the Marches towards Scotland, directing them to

[46] Brady, vol. ii. p. 44.   [47] Mon. Angl. vol. vi. p. 71.
[48] Agnes Strickland, *Life of Isabella, Queen of Edward the Second*, p. 243.
[49] *Mon. Angl.* vol. vi. p. 71.   [50] Fœdera. Edit. 1740, vol. iii. pt. ii. p. 40.
[51] *Ibid.* p. 43.

give safe conduct to David de Bruys, King of Scotland, who was to be accompanied by twenty knights, then intending pilgrimage to Walsingham.[52] Was he the King of Scotland to whom Norden alludes as being cured by the water of the well of Our Ladye of Muswell?[53]

In 1427, on the morrow of Saints Gervase and Protase, Queen Johanna, widow of Henry the Fourth, visited St. Alban's, on her way from Walsingham, Norwich, and St. Edmund's Bury, to Langley, and was received in solemn procession by the monks, arrayed in white copes.[54]

Writing from Oxnead, on Saturday, the 28th of September, 1443, to John Paston, Mrs. Margaret Paston says :

"I have behested to go on pilgrimage to Walsingham and to St. Leonard's for you ;[55] by my troth, I had never so heavy a season as I had it from the time that I wist of your sickness, till I wist of your amending."[56]

Sometime in 1457—1458, the Duke of Norfolk was on pilgrimage at Walsingham ; for Sir John Fastolfe, in a letter to John Paston, his cousin, dated Caistor, the 18th of November, year not given, but before 1459, says: "My Lord of Norfolk, is removed from Framlingham on foot to go to Walsingham, and daily I wait that he would come hither."[57]

In 1469 Edward the Fourth and his Queen were at Walsingham. James Hawte, writing to Sir John Paston on Whitsun Monday, the 22nd May, 1469, says: . . . "and as for the King, as I understand, he departyt to Walsingham upon Friday come seven-night, and the Queen also, if God send her hele."[58] Two years later, the Duke of Norfolk was again on pilgrimage at Walsingham. On the 13th or 14th of September, 1471, Sir John Paston writes to Mrs. Margaret Paston, or her son, Sir John Paston, in haste, and says: "I

[52] Fœdera, p. 86.   [53] See ante, p. 103.
[54] *Annales Mon. S. Albani*, p. 16.   Rolls Ed.   [55] In Norwich.   See ante, p. 112.
[56] *Paston Letters*.   Edit. Fenn, 1787, vol. iii. p. 21.
[57] *Ibid*, vol. i. p. 167.   [58] *Ibid*. vol. ii. p. 17.

heard yesterday that a Worsted[59] man of Norfolk that sold worsteds at Winchester said that my Lord of Norfolk and my Lady were on pilgrimage at our Ladye on foot; and so they went to Caistor."[60]

In the same year William Ponte bequeaths "to any of those who will pilgrimage for me to Blessed Marye of Walsingham" vi *s.* viii *d.*[61] And in 1472 our Ladye of Walsingham is one of the sanctuaries to which William Ecopp, Rector of Heslerton, desires that a pilgrim or pilgrims shall be sent immediately after his burial, and to offer there iv *d.*[62]

In 1478 the Duke of Buckingham was on pilgrimage at Walsingham.[63]

On the insurrection of the nobles in favour of Lambert Simnel, in 1487, Henry the Seventh made a pilgrimage to our Ladye of Walsingham, and there offering up his vows and prayers, implored her assistance in delivering him from his enemies. After the battle of Stoke, when the rebels were overthrown, in gratitude for the success which had attended his arms, that monarch sent his banner to be offered at the shrine of our Ladye of Walsingham, as a monument of the victory which he had gained by her assistance.[64] The last royal pilgrims to our Ladye of Walsingham were Henry the Eighth and Queen Catherine.

In the Privy Purse expenses of Henry the Eighth, 19—26 January, 1511, there is an entry of an offering at our Ladye of Walsingham of 1 *l.* 3 *s.* 4 *d.*[65] In all probability this offering was made by the King in person, as he was then on a visit to Sir Robert Cotton.[66] The King started from East Barsham Hall[67] on his pilgrimage to

---

[59] Worsted in Norfolk, a town celebrated for the spinning of fine thread with which the yarn called worsted is made.

[60] *Paston Letters*, vol. ii. p. 37.

[61] *Test. Vet.* p. 326.

[62] See *ante sub Gisbro*,' p. 42.

[63] *Paston Letters*, 23 or 25 August, 1478.

[64] Harpsfeld, sæc. xv. c. 18, p. 640. Cf. also Bacon, *History of Henry VII.*

[65] Letters and Papers, &c. Henry VIII. v. ii. pt. ii. p. 1449.

[66] Add. MSS. 7100

[67] Norwich volume of the Royal Arch. Inst. Introd. f. ix.

Walsingham, and Spelman says that he walked barefoot, and offered a valuable necklace to our Ladye.

After the victory of Flodden Field, Queen Katherine went on pilgrimage to our Ladye of Walsingham in fulfilment of her vow, and on the 16th September she announced her intention of doing so to the King:

". . . And with this I make an ende, prayng God to send you home shortly, for without this noo joye here can be accomplisshed ; and for the same I pray, and now goo to our Ladye at Walsingham that I promised soo long agoo to see.

At Woborne the xvj. day of Septembre.[68]

In her will Katherine of Aragon says :

" I supplicate, &c.

" Itm, that some personage go to our Ladye of Walsingham in pilgrimage, and in going by the way, dole xx. nobles.[69]

Three years previously Erasmus had been to Walsingham, and he describes his visit in the colloquy entitled, *Peregrinatio religionis ergo*,[70] a name it by no means deserves.

There was an old saying in regard of Philo the Jew: *aut Philo Platonizat, aut Plato Philonizat*, and of Erasmus it has been said : *aut Erasmus Lutherizat, aut Luther Erasmizat*.[71] As a writer he is well described as *damnatus in plerisque, suspectus in multis, caute legendus in omnibus*.[72]

It is notorious that Erasmus loved to exaggerate the vices of his age, and to cast all possible ridicule upon the practices of that Holy Faith, of which, nevertheless, he was only too glad to continue an unworthy member. His pen is never more fruitful of sarcasm than when treating of

---

[68] MS. Cott. Vesp. F. iii. f. 15.

[69] *Test. Vet.* p. 37.

[70] It is needless to give the references to the *Peregrinatio religionis ergo*, which is contained in his Colloquies. It gives an account of Walsingham, and of the shrine of St. Thomas at Canterbury. The text which I have used is that of Vander Aa's edition, 1703. Opp. t. i. Walsingham extends from col. 774 to col. 783.

[71] Lyræus, *Trisagion Marianum*, p. 437 ; also Weiss, *Bib. Biograph.* Edit. 1841, sub nom.

[72] *Vide* Feller. Edit. 1848, sub nom.

M

ecclesiastics and religious men. Did he judge of them by himself? He has drawn his own character with the hand of an artist. *Ut ingenue, quod verum est, fatear,* says he, *sum naturâ propensior ad jocos quam fortasse deceat, et linguæ liberioris quam nonnunquam expediat.*[73]

Sir Thomas More discovered the venom latent in Erasmus before they had been together an hour. Christopher Cresacre More, third in descent from Sir Thomas, our mutual great ancestor, writes as follows:

"But of all strangers *Erasmus* challenged vnto himself his love most especially, which had long continued by mutuall letters expressing great affection, and increased so much that he tooke a iournie of purpose into *England* to see and enioy his personall acquaintance and more intire familiaritie; at which time it is reported how that he, who conducted him in his passage, procured that Sir Thomas More and he should first meete togeather in *London* at the Lo: Mayor's table, neither of them knowing each other. And in the dinner time, they chanced to fall into argument, *Erasmus* still endeauouring to defende the worser parte; but he was so sharpely sett vpon and opposed by Sir Thomas More, that perceauing that he was now to argue with a readier witt then euer he had before mett withall, he broke forth into these wordes not without some choler: *Aut tu es Morus aut nullus;* whereto Sir Thomas readily replied: *Aut tu es Erasmus, aut diabolus;* because at that time he was strangely disguised, and had sought to defende impious propositions; for although he was a singular Humanist, and one that could vtter his minde in a most eloquent phrase, yet had he alwaies a delight to scoffe at religious matters, and finde fault with all sortes of clergie men. He tooke a felicitie to sett out sundrie Commentaries vpon the Father's workes, censuring them at his pleasure, for which cause he is tearmed *Errans mus,* because he wandreth here and there in other men's haruests; yea, in his writings he is sayd

[73] Feller, who gives the reference lib. i. ep. ii.

to haue hatched manie of those eggs of heresie,
which the apostate fryar *Luther* had before layde;
not that he is to be accounted an heretike, for he
would neuer be obstinate in anie of his opinions,
yet would he irreligiously glaunce at all antiquitie
and finde manie faultes with the present state
of the Church. When he was in *England* Sir
THOMAS MORE vsed him most courteously, doing
manie offices of a dear friend for him, as well
by his word as his purse; whereby he bound
Erasmus so straytely vnto him, that he euer
spoke and wrote vpon all occasions most highly
in his praise; but Sir THOMAS in successe of
time grew lesse affectionate vnto him, by reason
he saw him still fraught with much vanitie and
vnconstancie in respect of religion; as when
Tindall obiecteth vnto Sir THOMAS that his
darling·*Erasmus* had translated the word *Church*
into *Congregation*, and *Priest* into *Elder*, even as
himself had donne, Sir THOMAS answered thereto,
yf my darling Erasmus *hath translated those places
with the like wicked intent that* Tindall *hath donne,
he shall be no more my darling, but the Divell's
darling.* Finally, long after, having found in
Erasmus's workes manie thinges necessarily to be
amĕded, he counselled him as his friend in some
latter booke to imitate the example of *S. Augustin*,
who did sett out a booke of Retractations, to
correct in his writing what he had vnaduisedly
written in the heat of youth; but he that was
farre different from *S. Augustin* in humilitie, would
neuer follow his counsell; and therefore he is
censured by the Church for a busie fellow: manie
of his bookes are condemned, and his opinions
accounted erroneous, though he alwaies lived a
Catholike Priest; and hath written most sharpely
against all those new Gospellers who then beganne
to appeare in the world; and in a letter to *John
Fabius*, Bishopp of *Vienna*, he sayth that he
hateth these seditious opinions, with the which
at this day the world is miserably shaken; neither
doth he dissemble, saith he, being so addicted
to pietie, that if he incline to any parte of the
ballance, he will bende rather to superstition than

to impietie; by which speach he seemeth in doubtfull words to taxe the Church with superstition and the new Apostolicall bretheren with impietie."[74] Such was the man who went on pilgrimage *religionis ergo* to Walsingham.

In 1509 Erasmus came to reside at Cambridge. It should be borne in mind, that every one who was able made a pilgrimage in person to our Ladye of Walsingham, and many sent their yearly offerings; indeed, Camden says that those who were able and did not go thither were considered as impious, and Erasmus mentions the annual offerings. A pilgrimage, therefore, to Walsingham was the τὸ πρέπον—the "correct thing;" and Erasmus was nothing loath; he, as a time-server, would do as others did. They went in a spirit of devotion. He saw that a visit to Walsingham would enable him to gratify his inordinate pride, to perpetrate an unseemly joke in the hallowed sanctuary itself of our Ladye, and to make a display of his fancied superior acquirements in letters, at the expense of many distinguished University men and the excellent Augustinian Canons of Walsingham, who bore a very high reputation for culture. Moreover, it would give him a character for piety and a consequent better position at Cambridge. Otherwise, one is at a loss to understand why this ex-Augustinian Canon, who so much disapproved of pilgrimages, or, as he endeavours to explain it, the abuse of pilgrimages, should, in accordance with a practice, which he lost no opportunity of condemning, have gone himself on a pilgrimage to Walsingham. No doubt Erasmus felt that a pilgrimage, undertaken by Erasmus, could under no circumstances be considered as an abuse, but rather, that it ought to be regarded as a model of what a pilgrimage *religionis ergo* should be. To judge, however, from his own description, it is about the greatest abuse of a pilgrimage on record.

[74] *The Life and Death of Sir Thomas More.* Written by M. T. M., s.l.v.s., pp. 109—113.

Those who go on pilgrimage usually prepare themselves by some extra act of piety, or mortification, and by approaching the Holy Sacraments and receiving the blessing of Holy Church. Erasmus did not do in like manner. He composed an ode, in Greek Iambics, to our Ladye, in which there is more than one allusion to himself, but no mention of, nor prayer for, the success of the Church, which was the ostensible motive of his visit to Walsingham. Having incubated these verses, he wished their appearance to be noised abroad, and so cackled accordingly. The *Times* was as yet in the womb of time; consequently, he could not advertise his movements, or announce that, on such a day, Erasmus would go to Walsingham for the purpose of hanging up a Greek ode, so that his friends and the public might attend to witness the performance; but he did the next best thing, which was, to write from Cambridge on the 8th of May, 1511, to his friend Andrew Ammonio,[75] telling him "that he has made a vow for the success of the Church; will go to see our Lady of Walsingham, and hang up a votive Greek ode there: and enjoins him, if he should go thither, to enquire for it." *Ego, mi Andrea, pro felici rerum ecclesiasticarum statu votum suscepi. Jam scio religionem probas. Visam Virginem Walsagamicam, atque illic Græcum carmen votivum suspendam. Id si quando te illo contuleris, require.*[76]

Provided that the Greek ode was hung up, and that some one of position, like Ammonio, would enquire for it, and so draw attention to it, the success of the Church, might, for all that Erasmus cared, have gone to the four winds.

[75] Ammonio, born at Lucca, c. 1470, went to Rome, then came to England, where Sir T. More was his protector. About 1513 he became Secretary of Latin Letters to Henry VIII., whom he attended on his campaign in France, and celebrated his victories in a Latin poem, which is lost. Leo X. named him Nuncio in England, which office he fulfilled, still keeping his post of Latin Secretary, till his death in 1517.

[76] Opp. t. iii. pt. i. col. 106. ep. cxiv. In the Catalogue of Letters and Papers, &c., Henry VIII. vol. i. p. 244, where I first found this letter, the date given is the 9th of May, and the reference, Ep. Eras. vii. 17.

This is the ode, with its title; and from what Erasmus says, it is evident that the lines were written together, and without a break. I reproduce them strictly in accordance with his own words, viz., in capitals or uncial letters. "The title," says he, *descriptus erat verbis ac literis Romanis, sed majusculis. Græci versus erant descripti Græcis majusculis, quæ prima specie videntur referre majusculas Latinas.* This was the pith of the joke.

DESIDERII ERASMI ROTERODAMI CARMEN
IAMBICVM EX VOTO DICATVM VIRGINI
WALSINGAMICAE APVD BRITANNOS
Ω ΧΑΙΡ' ΙΗΣΟΥ ΜΗΤΕΡ ΕΥΛΟΓΗΜΕΝΗ,
ΜΟΝΗ ΓΥΝΑΙΚΩΝ ΘΕΟΤΟΚΟΣ ΚΑΙ ΠΑΡΘΕΝΟΣ.
ΑΛΛΟΙ ΜΕΝ ΑΛΛΑΣ ΣΟΙ ΔΙΔΟΑΣΙ ΔΩΡΕΑΣ,
Ο ΜΕΝ ΓΕ ΧΡΥΣΟΝ, Ο ΔΕ ΠΑΛΙΝ ΤΟΝ ΑΡΓΥΡΟΝ,
Ο ΔΕ ΤΙΜΙΟΥΣ ΦΕΡΩΝ ΧΑΡΙΖΕΤΑΙ ΛΙΘΟΥΣ.
ΑΝΘ' ΩΝ ΑΠΑΙΤΟΥΣ' ΟΙ ΜΕΝ ΥΓΙΑΙΝΕΙΝ ΔΕΜΑΣ,
ΑΛΛΟΙ ΔΕ ΠΛΟΥΤΕΙΝ, ΚΑΙ ΤΙΝΕΣ ΓΥΝΑΙΚΙΟΥ
ΚΥΩΝΤΟΣ ΕΡΑΤΟΝ ΟΥΝΟΜ' ΕΛΠΙΖΕΙΝ ΠΑΤΡΟΣ,
ΠΤΛΙΟΥ ΤΙΝΕΣ ΓΕΡΟΝΤΟΣ ΑΙΩΝΑΣ ΛΑΧΕΙΝ.
ΑΥΤΟΣ Δ' ΑΟΙΔΟΣ ΕΥΜΕΝΗΣ, ΠΕΝΗΣ Γ'ΟΜΩΣ,
ΣΤΙΧΟΥΣ ΕΝΕΓΚΑΣ, ΟΥ ΓΑΡ ΕΞΕΣΤ' ΑΛΛΟ ΤΙ,
ΔΟΣΕΩΣ ΑΜΟΙΒΗΝ ΕΥΤΕΛΕΣΤΑΤΗΣ, ΓΕΡΑΣ
ΜΕΓΙΣΤΟΝ ΑΙΤΩ, ΘΕΟΣΕΒΗ ΤΗΝ ΚΑΡΔΙΑΝ,
ΠΑΣΩΝ Θ' ΑΠΑΞ ΑΜΑΡΤΙΩΝ ΕΛΕΥΘΕΡΑΝ.
ΕΥΧΗ ΤΟΥ ΕΡΑΣΜΟΥ.[77]

Hail ! Jesu's Virgin Mother ever blest !
Alone of Women Mother eke and Maid !
Others to thee their several offerings make :
This one brings gold, That silver, while a third
Bears to thy shrine his gift of costly gems
For these each craves his boon—one strength of limb ;
One wealth ; one, through his spouse's fruitfulness
The hope a father's pleasing name to bear :
One Nestor's eld would equal. I, poor bard,
Rich in goodwill, but poor in all beside,
Bring thee my verse—nought have I else to bring—
And beg, in quital of this worthless gift,
That greatest meed—a heart that feareth God,
And free for aye from sin's foul tyranny
       Erasmus his vow.

[77] Opp. t. v. col. 1325.

This ἰυχή is characteristic of the writer. Neither a Greek ode, nor a Latin ode, nor a Dutch ode was required; a sincere devotion to our Blessed Ladye would have suggested, that whatever he wrote, should have been in the vernacular, for the edification of the majority of the pilgrims; and any of his Cambridge friends would gladly have put his words into elegant English for him. But no! This would not have suited his purpose. His ideas were not those of our Ladye's liegemen. Erasmus wished it to be known that he, Erasmus, the great Greek scholar, as he fancied himself, from down among the Dutchmen, had been to see Walsingham, and suspended a Greek ode there.

Erasmus wrote much against the Catholic practice of making rich offerings at the different sanctuaries of our Ladye, and consequently in his ode he says to her that "others present valuable gifts, and expect favours in return from her, such as to attain the age of Nestor,"—a curious petition to make in a prayer—"but that he, a poor poet τίνης γ'ὅμως—penniless—and rich in good will alone, can only offer her some verses." But, then, they were Greek lines, and by Erasmus! and therefore, in his own estimation, priceless beyond gold and silver and precious stones. I imagine that, in τίνης γ'ὅμως, there is an allusion to his hackneyed grievance about the vigilance of the English custom-house officers. By the laws of the realm, no one was allowed to carry out of the kingdom more than six angels in coin; all above that sum was seized; and consequently, as he was leaving Dover, in 1499, after his first visit to England, the officers took from him all the money he possessed beyond that amount, 20*l.* more or less. It is gratifying to learn from him that our custom-house officers were so vigilant, and, that as loyal Englishmen, they did their duty with their usual impartiality, even although Erasmus was the victim, and heedless of the risk they ran of being denounced by him to posterity in a Greek ode.

Erasmus gives, also, the prayer which he

recited in the sanctuary of our Ladye, and which bears the marks of having been carefully prepared for the occasion. Pilgrims, as a rule, do not publish the prayers which they make at various sanctuaries.

"O alone of all women, Mother and Virgin, Mother most happy, Virgin most pure, now we, impure as we are, come to see thee (*visimus*) who art all pure; we salute thee; we worship thee as how we may with our humble offerings; may thy Son grant us, that, imitating thy most holy manners, we also, by the grace of the Holy Ghost, may deserve spiritually to conceive the Lord Jesus in our inmost soul (*intimis animi visceribus*), and once conceived, never to lose Him.   Amen."

In the colloquy Erasmus says he made two journeys to Walsingham, which seems very improbable; and there is a strong presumption that what he relates of the second visit is the fruit of his own imagination.   The colloquy is divided into two parts, dinner intervening.

A good morning's work had now been done; -
the hammer and nails and ladder had been procured, the Greek ode hung up, and the prayer to our Ladye repeated.   Erasmus, exhausted with acting the part of a pilgrim *religionis ergo*, and with his labours, went off to dinner, doubtless at the principal hostelry, for although *audax omnia perpeti*, he would scarcely have had the impudence to intrude himself upon the hospitality of the Canons his former brethren, when he had secretly resolved, in his mind, to make them the subject of his own coarse sarcasm.   It is to be hoped that the landlord had not degenerated from the reputation which his predecessors enjoyed during the previous century, as John Amundesham has related; and that he received the conceited Dutchman as an illustrious stranger, and fashioned his little bill accordingly.

What follows, Erasmus professes to relate as having occurred on his second visit to Walsingham.   After dinner he returned to the priory-church; the ostensible motive was to enquire for the history of an object which, he says, was shown there as a relic of our Blessed Ladye's milk. After indulging in his usual language, he casually remarks that he was just about to leave the church, when "up come some of the *mystagogi*,[78] who cast side looks at us, point at us with their fingers, run up to us, retire, come back again, nod to us, and seem as if they would like to say ' How d'ye do?' to us, if they had the courage." Erasmus, according to his own account, was pleasant, and looked benignantly on them and smiled—soberly, of course ; he had enjoyed his little dinner, and was not suffering from a surfeit of Norfolk pippins. He was in a high good humour. "At length one comes up and asks me my name. I give it. Am I, then, he, who two years previously had nailed up a votive inscription written in Hebrew ? The very man, said I," thus telling a lie, of which he convicts himself in the next lines. "Do you, then, write Hebrew?" enquires Menedemus. "Oh, dear, no !" replies Ogygius, *i.e.* Erasmus, "but these 'muffs' call everything Hebrew which they don't understand." [79]

Presently the Sub-Prior appears ; and, like a true English gentleman, he courteously greets the visitor to Walsingham. "He told me," says the vulgar Dutchman, "how many persons have laboriously exerted themselves, *quantopere sudatum est a multis*, to read those verses; how many spectacles had been wiped to no purpose. Whenever any aged doctor in theology or in the law had arrived, he was taken to the tablet; one said the letters were Arabic, another that they were no letters at all ; finally one was found who could read the title ! This was written in Roman words and letters, but in uncials. The verses were

---

[78] I give the word which Erasmus uses. *Mystagogus* is employed by Cicero, and means one who shows the rarities of a temple to strangers. I am unable to say whether the *Mystagogi* of Walsingham were lay-brothers of the Priory, or externs, corresponding to the modern vergers. Erasmus says that the Canons themselves did not act as showmen, perhaps, in reality to let it be inferred that he was considered a person of consequence since the Sub-Prior came to him.

[79] *Sed isti quidquid non intelligunt Hebraicum vocant.* As the word "muff" is now given in Bellow's most excellent *Bona-fide Pocket Dictionary of the French and English Languages* (London : Trübner & Co.),—I presume its use is so far warranted as to be placed in the mouth of Erasmus.

written in Greek uncials, which, at first sight, appear to resemble Roman ones. On being requested, I gave the meaning of the verses in Latin, construing them word for word."

This is the key to the real purport of the *carmen votivum*, and the main, if not the sole, motive of his visit to Walsingham, under the cloak of a pilgrim *religionis ergo*. As Achilles said to Ulysses—

ἐχθρὸς γάρ μοι κεῖνος ὁμῶς Αΐδαο πύλῃσιν,
ὅς χ᾽ ἕτερον μὲν κεύθει ἐνὶ φρεσίν, ἄλλο δὲ βάζει.[90]

It was intended as a display of his fancied superior learning, and Walsingham was selected as being the most frequented spot in all England, as indeed Erasmus mentions, and often visited by foreign pilgrims. On this hitherto unchallenged evidence of his, many writers have not hesitated to hold up the worthy Augustinian Canons of Walsingham to scorn for their excessive ignorance, and to base upon it a wholesale conclusion that the other religious houses of England were in no better condition; a conclusion which it is impossible to draw from what Erasmus has written. I will admit that Greek was not so generally taught then as it now is; but no one will venture to affirm that Greek was absolutely unknown at Oxford and at Cambridge. Therefore, what amount of belief is to be given to Erasmus's sweeping charge against the aged doctors in theology and in the law, many of whom were University men? for the charge is quite as heavy against them as against the Canons of Walsingham. Certain it is that the Augustinians understood Latin, if the evidence of Erasmus is received, for he says: "On being requested, I gave the meaning of the verses in Latin, construing them word for word." But it may be suggested that young Robert Aldrich was at hand, and may have acted as interpreter of the Latin. Possibly; but all that Erasmus says of his capabilities is, that he was well skilled in German. Another most essential point has been overlooked, because the real bearing of the

[90] *Iliad*, ix. 312, 313.

Roman uncial letters is not understood. At the time when Erasmus hung up his ode, Roman letters were scarcely, if at all, known in England. They would have been a novelty at Walsingham, as elsewhere, for all the printing in the land was in black letter, and therefore it would be no proof of ignorance to be unacquainted with Roman uncials. Not very long ago, in the sale of Mr. Bragge's splendid collection of illuminated manuscripts, a breviary which had belonged to the last Prior of Walsingham, Richard Vowell, and contained a fair amount of pretty flower pattern, was sold for 126*l.* The ode of Erasmus would not have fetched as many farthings. In all likelihood this breviary had been written and illuminated in the scriptorium of the Priory. Yet there are now many educated men who would be utterly unable to read one line of it, and to whom a column of black letter, printed with contractions, would be so much "Hebrew." It would be very unfair for palæographists and antiquaries to charge them with ignorance on that account ; nevertheless, this is the reasoning of Erasmus. And this being said, I gladly take leave of Erasmus and of Erasmus his ode.

The following letter from the Lord High Admiral of England to his sovereign would have rather astonished my Lords of the Admiralty of the present day. A captain of the fleet, being in great danger of losing his ship, invoked our Ladye of Walsingham, and made a vow, if she would preserve him, never to eat flesh nor fish until he had been on pilgrimage to her. The Lord High Admiral gives him leave of absence to fulfil his vow; and this is the letter from Sir Edward Howard to his sovereign, dated April 17, 1513 :

"Sir,—(I have) taken all Master Arthur's folks and bestowe them in the arme, wher (I am deficient by) reson of deth, by casualte and otherways. And, Sir, (I have given him liber)te to go hoome ; for, Sir, when he was in extreme danger . . . from hym he called upon Our Ladye of Walsingham for help and com(fort, and made) a vow that, an' it pleased God and her to deliver him out of the pe(ril, he wde vol)ner eet fleshe nor fyche tyl he had seen heer. Sir, I a(ssure you) he was in mervelous danger, for it was merveil that the shipp bey(ng with) al her sayls strikyns full but a rok with her starn that she br(ake) not in peces at the furst stroke." And adds, his absence will be a great loss to them. Recommends him highly to the King. Hopes he will give him comfortable words for his bravery.[81]

The last pilgrimage to Walsingham which I shall notice is that of Cardinal Wolsey, in August, 1517. Writing in that month to Henry the Eighth he says that he is anxious to see his Grace and know of his good estate, but has been so vexed with the sweat, he dare not yet come to his presence. Proposes to start for Walsingham on Monday next, and from thence to Our Ladye of Grace, in fulfilment of his vow, which may correct the weakness of his stomach.[82]

On the 30th of August the Venetian Ambassador, Sebastian Giustiniani, writes to the Council of Ten saying that he had sent his secretary to Wolsey several times for an audience: could never get one: so at last, as Wolsey is going on a pilgrimage to fulfil a vow at a shrine some hundred miles hence, resolved at any rate to speak to him. Found him with a troubled countenance and bent brow. Told him of the Turkish news, which he said he had heard already. Perceiving that he said nothing at all to me on this or any other topic, I then offered to accompany his right reverend lordship on his journey with an honourable train, at my own cost; but without appearing flattered even by this proposal, he said he had no need of any additional company beyond his own retinue, which was both honourable and numerous. He has been ill of late; and really his appearance, in addition to his mental perturbation, indicates this, although the profuse perspiration endured by him has not quite carried off his wrath.[83]

[81] Letters and Papers, &c. Henry VIII. vol. i. n. 3903, p. 538. MS. Cott. Calig. E ii. 141.
[82] Letters and Papers, &c. Henry VIII. vol. ii. p. 1538, n. 38, Appendix.
[83] *Ibid.* p. 1154.

Thirteen days later—*i.e.*, September 12—
Guistiniani writes to the Doge that a French
ambassador has arrived from the Emperor, a man
of no account, apparently only to borrow money.
He has not yet had an audience of the King, who
keeps aloof at Windsor to avoid the sickness, or of
Wolsey, who has gone to Walsingham.[84]

On his return from his pilgrimage, Wolsey
writes to Sir R. Wingfield, saying he has been so
vexed with fever since his return from Walsingham, that he has been obliged to detain
Wingfeld's servant Bysshop, &c. This letter has
no date.[85]

A document in the Public Record Office
contains a declaration of the expenses of the
household of Thomas, Cardinal of York, for three
years, ending December 4, tenth Henry the
Eighth. The expenses for the ninth year, including the journey to Walsingham, come to
2,616*l.* 5*s.* 2¾*d.*[86]

Offerings, bequests, &c., to Our Ladye of Walsingham.

It is greatly to be regretted that the "Annals
of the chapel of Walsingham," from which
Capgrave quotes, have perished. They appear to
have been a register of the principal offerings and
donations to our Ladye. Roger Ascham, who
visited Cologne in 1550, makes this observation:
"The three Kings be not so rich, I believe, as
was the Ladye of Walsingham. Erasmus speaks
of the votive statues of gold, and of silver gilt,
which were shown to him; and says that a day
would not suffice to describe the world of admirable
things which he saw there, and which were kept
under the altar of our Ladye, from whence they
were brought out for him to see."[87] Consequently,
some idea may be formed of the riches of the
sanctuary of Our Ladye of Walsingham.

By an entry in the Wardrobe book of the
28th of Edward the First, it appears that

---

[84] *Ibid.* p. 1160, n. 3675.
[85] *Ibid.* p. 1540, n. 40, Appendix. [86] *Ibid.* p. 1412, n. 4623.
[87] *Depromit* (mystagogus) *ex ipso altari mundum rerum admirabilium.*

the King was accustomed to make a yearly offering to our Ladye: "On the 15th of May of this year, *i.e.* 1300, he offered to the image of our Ladye in the chapel of Walsingham a clasp of gold of the value of eight marcs; and on the same day the Queen offered to our Ladye, by the hands of John de But, a clasp of the value of six and a half marcs."[88]

Of Henry, Duke of Lancaster, who died at Leicester, on the 13th of May, 1361, Capgrave says:

"In the annals of the chapel at Walsingham it is mentioned that this Henry gave to our Blessed Ladye a vase with handles,[89] on which he expended almost four hundred marcs. In the same annals it is also written that the father of this Henry, who was Earl of Lancaster, and not Duke, offered to our Ladye an Angelical Salutation with precious stones—*salutationem angelicam cum lapidibus pretiosis*—the value of which several persons esteemed at four hundred marcs."[90]

This is one of the many instances of the difficulty which the archæologist has to determine what is to be understood by *Salutatio Angelica*. It has been suggested that this offering consisted of a valuable pair of beads; but I have never found any instance of a pair of beads being described by *Salutatio Angelica;* moreover, it is *cum lapidibus*, and not *de lapidibus*. Hence it is most probable that this was a tablet with a representation of the Annunciation, and adorned with precious stones. Six years later, in 1367, Sir Thomas de Uvedale left to the chapel of Our Ladye of Walsingham a tablet of silver, gilt, with the Salutation of the Blessed Virgin, together with a painted image.[91]

Sums of money for offerings and candles are frequently recorded.

Thus in the accounts of Elizabeth of York:

---

[88] Lib. Garderobæ, p. 334.

[89] The manuscripts differ here: one has *urnam illam cum libis ;* another, *urnam illam cum aliis.*

[90] *De illustr. Henricis*, p. 164. Rolls Edit.

[91] *Surrey Archæol. Collect.* vol. iii. p. 151.

" March 26, 1502 :

" Offering to Our Ladye of Walsingham, vi *s.* viii *d.*" [92]

In many cases these were not casual, but annual, offerings; and frequently made more than once during the year. Thus in the Northumberland Household Book of 1512 :

" Item. My Lorde usith to send afor Michaelmas for his Lordschips offerynge to Our Lady of Walsyngeham iiij *d.*" [93]

" Item. My Lorde usith and accustumyth to send yerely for the Upholdynge of the Light of Wax which his Lordschip fyndith birnynge yerly befor Our Lady of Walsyngham, contenynge xi. lb. of Wax in it after vii. ob. for the fyndynge of every lb. redy wrought. By a Covenaunt maid with the Channon by great for the hole yere for the fyndinge of the said Light byrnning, vi *s.* viii *d.*" [94]

The Earl also remunerated the services of the canon for keeping his light burning during service time throughout the year.

" Item. My Lord usith and accustomith to syende yerely to the Channon that kepith the Light before Our Ladye of Walsingham for his reward for the hole yere for kepynge of the said Light, Lightynge of it at all service-tymes daily throwout the yere, xii *d.*" [95]

In the accounts of the Duke of Buckingham on the 18th of May, 1519, the following entry occurs :

" To Russell, for my offering to Our Ladye of Walsingham, 6 *s.* 8 *d.*" [96]

Another contemplated offering to Our Ladye of Walsingham is now recorded, unique of its kind, and which was even more curious than the donation to Our Ladye of Loreto made by a a king—I think of Saxony—and which I saw displayed in one of the cases in the Treasury of Loreto, when I was on pilgrimage there in 1857, in the suite of the Sovereign Pontiff Pius the

[92] *Surrey Archæol. Collect.* vol. iii. p. 3. [93] *Ibid.* p. 337.
[94] *Ibid.* p. 338. [95] *Ibid.* p. 342.
[96] Letters and Papers, &c. Henry VIII. vol. iii. pt. 1, p. 499, no. 1285.

Ninth. It consisted of his Majesty's wedding suit, coat, vest, and nether garments.

On the 15th of May, 1515, Sir R. Wingfeld, English Ambassador to the Emperor, writes to Henry the Eighth for some place, the name of which is decayed in the original, and describes a great dance of fresh and fair bourgeoises maydens ordered by the Emperor to be held at . . . (Malines?) on Sunday the 13th of May, at which the ambassadors were also present, excepting the Pope's nuncio.

"Some of the women," says he, "were marvellous fair, well fed, and clean washen, in such wise that, an I were young as my beard is white, your Grace might think by the manner of my writing that the sight of them touched me nearer than it did, and the rather because I deem that fair bodies, gentlewomen and others, take but small pleasure to see white hairs, which I have gotten in the cold snowy mountains, which have the power to make all hares and partridges that abide amongst them white, where my beard (which I have promised to bear to Our Ladye of Walsingham, an God give me life) is wax so white, that whilst I shall wear it I need none other mean to cause women rejoice little in my company."[97]

Two years later Sir Robert writes to the King for permission to resign his functions in order that he might go to Walsingham to make an offering of his beard to our Ladye. The letter is dated Malines, May 3, 1517. In it Sir Robert says, that on the 16th of this month he will have served seven years as ambassador to the Emperor, having the pilgrim's fortune to change many lodgings, and find few friends. Begs the King will have his poverty in remembrance, and give him licence to lay down his office, that he may visit Our Ladye of Walsingham, "where by the leave of God I would gladly leave my beard, which is now of so strange a color that I need none other arms or herald to show what favour I

[97] Letters and Papers, &c. Henry VIII. vol. ii. pt. 1, p. 130, n. 463. Vitellius, B. xviii. 150.

am worthy, or am like to have from henceforth amongst ladies and gentlewomen."[96]

Whether Sir R. Wingfeld ever carried his wish into execution I know not. He appears to have returned to England shortly after the date of this last letter.

In the Privy Expenses of Henry the Eighth an entry occurs on the 14th of May, 1532:

"Paied to Maister Garneys for the King's offering to Oure Ladye of Walsingham, vii *s.* vi *d.*"[99]

This is the last offering which I have found of Henry the Eighth.

Many bequests are contained in the wills of our forefathers.

In 1347, John, eighth and last Earl of Surrey, by his will dated June 24, devised to the chapel of Our Ladye of Walsingham a jewel which he describes as his family eagle, and the rings arranged in the form of a constellation about it;[100] at least, so I read the bequest: *Mon Egle des saune les anels qe scount mys par constellation.*"[101]

In 1381, William de Ufford, Earl of Sussex, says in his will:

"I will that a picture of a horse and a man, armed with my arms, be made in silver, and offered to the altar of Our Ladye of Walsingham."[102] This "picture" was evidently an image.

Isabel, Countess of Warwick, in her will dated December 1, 1439, says:

"I will that my tablet, with the image of our Ladye having a glass for[103] it, be offered unto our Ladye of Walsingham; as also my gown of green alyz cloth of gold with wide sleeves; and a tabernacle of silver, like in the timber to that over

---

[96] Letters and Papers, &c. p. 1029, n. 3199. Galba B. v. 203.

[99] *Ibid.* p. 214.

[100] Test. Ebor. vol. i. p. 41.

[101] I suspect that *saune* is intended for *saune,* which is also given *saunch, saung, saunk,* and explained as signifying *sang, parenté, lignée, race,* &c. See the *Glossaire de la Langue Romane.* By J. B. Roquefort. Paris, 1808.

[102] Test. Vet. p. 115.

[103] Afore, before.

our Ladye of Caversham."[104] She had made a valuable bequest to Our Ladye of Caversham.[105]

In 1453, John, Lord Scrope of Masham, by his testament dated March 18, wills: "Yat ye house of Walsingham have x. marcs for forgeten avowes and beheestes by me made to our Ladye yer."[106]

In 1474, Dame Elizabeth Andrews wills that one of her two rings with the diamonds should be sent to our Ladye of Walsingham.[107]

Antony Widvile, Earl Rivers, whose will, dated June 23, evinces great devotion to our Ladye, says in it :

"My trapper of blakk[108] of gold I geve to Our Ladye of Walsingham."[109]

Henry the Seventh offered a figure of himself, kneeling, made of silver and gilt, to Our Ladye of Walsingham,[110] to whom on the 25th of February, 1505-6, Katherine, widow of Sir John Hastings, bequeathed her velvet gown.[111]

Pilgrims to Walsingham generally made an offering or donation of a small piece of money at the shrine of our Ladye, a practice which stirred up the choler of Erasmus, who, nevertheless, took care to record that he, too, made his offering of a few pence.

In the chapel of our Lady was a chauntry priest for the souls of King Edward the First and King Edward the Second, and of Sir John Ovidale, Knight ; and an annual distribution of 12s. 6d. to twenty-five poor persons in Bedingham for their souls. There was another chaplain to pray for the souls of John Marshall and Alice his wife. The stipends of these priests were 5l. 6s. 8d. each in 1534.

In the King's book of payments, 1—10th Henry the Eighth, there is an entry on the 1st of July for—

"William Halys, King's priest, singing before

---

[104] Test. Vet. p. 240.
[105] See ante, p. 10.   [106] Test. Ebor. vol. ii. p. 192.   [107] Test. Vet. p. 329.
[108] This would seem to be a misprint for cloth.   [109] Bentley, *Excerpt. Hist.* p. 248.
[110] See his will, printed in full by Thomas Astle, F.R.S. &c. London, 1775.
[111] Test. Vet. p. 329.

Our Ladye at Walsingham, half a year's wages , 100*s*."

Same for the King's candle there, 46*s*. 8*d*.[112]

Again in November, 1515 :

Sir Richard Warde, singing before our Ladye at Walsingham, half a year's wages, 100*s*.

The King's candle, 46*s*. 8*d*.'[113]

Hence it would appear that the King kept a candle constantly burning at Walsingham.

Sir Bartholomew Burghersh, K.G., and one of the original knights of the order, who died on the 5th of April, 1369, by his will dated on the previous day, desired to be buried in our Ladye's chapel. " I desire," says he, " my body to be buried in the chapel at Walsingham before the image of the Blessed Virgin, and thither to be carried with all speed, having one taper at the head, and another at the feet, where it rests the first night. And also I will that a dirige shall be there said, and in the morning a Mass, whereat a noble shall be offered for my soul : that two torches be carried along, one on one side and the other on the other side, which are to be lighted at passing through every town, and then given to that church wherein it shall rest at night."[114]

Erasmus mentions an object which he says was shown at Walsingham as a relic of the Milk of our Blessed Ladye, but most of his comments are too impious to quote. It was enclosed in crystal, and stood on the right side of the high altar of the Priory church, and he describes it as "dried up, looking like pulverized chalk mixed with the white of an egg"—*concretum est: dicas cretam tritam, alboque ovi temperatum*. On the occasion of his visit it was brought down from the altar by one of the canons to Erasmus, who, kneeling, recited the following prayer, which he mentions that he had already prepared beforehand :

---

[112] Letters and Papers, &c. Henry VIII. vol. ii. pt. 11, p. 1442.
[113] *Ibid*. pt. 11, p. 1469.
[114] Test. Vet. p. 77 ; also Dugdale, *Baronage*, vol. ii. p. 36.

"O Virgin Mother, who with thy maiden breasts has deserved to give milk to the Lord of heaven and earth, thy Son Jesus; we wish that being purified by His Blood, we also may advance to that happy infancy of dovelike simplicity, which knowing nought of malice, fraud, or deceit, eagerly desires the milk of the precepts of the Gospel, until it attains the perfect man, to the stature of the fulness of Christ, Whose happy company thou enjoyest for ever, with the Father and the Holy Ghost. Amen."

After his dinner, as I have already said, he revisited the church, his avowed object being to examine the history or authentication of this relic. Young Aldrich was with him; a circumstance which is adverse to his alleged second visit, for it does not appear that Aldrich accompanied Erasmus on what he describes as his first visit to Walsingham, since he speaks of meeting the young Cantab on that occasion as if by chance.

"Dinner over," says Erasmus, "we returned to the church, . . . an eagerness to see the tablet" —*i.e.*, the history of the relic—"to which the *mystagogus* had referred me attracted me. After some considerable search we found it, but fixed so high that not every one's eyes could read it. Mine eyes are such that I cannot be called lynx-eyed, nor altogether dim-sighted. Wherefore, whilst Aldrich read it, I casually followed him with my eyes, not sufficiently trusting him in a matter of such weight."

This is, in a few words, the history which Erasmus relates as purporting to be contained in the tablet:

"One William, born in Paris, had a great love of collecting relics; and after visiting many churches and monasteries and countries in quest of them, he at last arrived at Constantinople, where his brother was bishop—*hujus Gulielmi frater illic tunc agebat episcopum.* Being about to return home, his brother told him of a certain virgin consecrated to God who possessed some of the milk of our Blessed Ladye, and he succeeded in obtaining half of what she had. On his journey homewards, he was taken ill, and feeling his end approaching, he summoned his most intimate companion of his travels, a Frenchman, and told him to convey the relic to the altar of our Ladye in the Church of Notre Dame in Paris. Shortly afterwards the friend was seized with a mortal illness, and confided the relic to an English comrade, desiring him to fulfil the commission which he himself had been unable to execute. The Englishman did as he was requested, and delivered the relic to the canons of Notre Dame in Paris, from whom he obtained the half of it, which he brought to England, and finally conveyed to Walsingham, 'being,' as Erasmus adds, 'called thither by the inspiration of the Holy Ghost.'"

Says Menedemus: "Certainly this account is charmingly consistent." Ogygius, *i.e.*, Erasmus: "Yes; lest any doubt might remain, there were appended to it the names of the suffragan bishops, who to those who visit this milk, and make some little offering, grant as much pardon as their faculties admit of. Another proof of pious sincerity was added; the milk of the Blessed Virgin which was shown in many places was sufficiently to be venerated, but this relic was far more venerable than the others, because whilst they had been scraped from stones, this one had flowed from the very breasts of our Ladye."

Menedemus: "How is this proved?"

Ogygius: "Oh, the maiden of Constantinople, who had given the milk, mentioned it."

Menedemus: "And she, perhaps, had been informed by St. Bernard!"

Ogygius: "Most probably."

Menedemus: "Whose good fortune it was to taste the milk from the same breast which was sucked by the Infant Jesus. . . . But how can that be called the milk of the Blessed Virgin which did not flow from her breasts?"

"Ogygius: "It flowed as the other did, *but being received by a stone on which she chanced to sit, it dried up, and then, by the will of God, it was thus multiplied.*"

Menedemus: "Exactly so."

Now here Erasmus contradicts the statement which he has just previously made—viz., "that the other relics of the milk had been scraped from stones, but that this one flowed from the very breast of our Ladye;" yet here he says that this one fell on a stone as well." Stripped, however, of its specious and Erasmian clothing, the real nature of the relic is quite apparent from what Erasmus says in the person of Ogygius. It is most improbable that the tale, which Erasmus relates, was ever written on the tablet on the wall at Walsingham; and the historical assertions are utterly incorrect.

1. The maiden of Constantinople heard the history of the relic from St. Bernard. He lived from A.D. 1091 to 1159, and was never at Constantinople. Anyhow this gives a date.

2. William was a Frenchman. Paris was his birthplace, and he was on his way homewards to Paris when he died. The date of his death is not recorded; but as he received the relic from the maiden of Constantinople who had seen St. Bernard, it must, at the latest, have occurred before A.D. 1200.

Now the brother of William, equally a Frenchman, was Bishop—*i.e.*, Patriarch of Constantinople; but the Patriarchs of Constantinople were all Greeks. Consequently the brother of William is a myth, and therefore William himself and the maiden of Constantinople are nowhere. The Latin Patriarchs of Constantinople only commenced in the year 1204; and they were six in number, and not one of them was a Frenchman! (1) Thomas Morosini, a Venetian; (2) 1215, Gervase, also called Eberard, a Tuscan; (3) 1221, Matthew, Bishop of Jessol, in the Duchy of Venice; (4) 1227, Simon, Archbishop of Tyre, whose nationality is unknown[116]; (5) 1234,

---

[115] *Acta SS.* t. i. Aug. pp. 150, 151, nn. 906, 907. Le Quien, *Oriens Christianus,* vol. iii. col. 805. I have only examined the list of the Greek Patriarchs from Sergius the Second, A.D. 999, to John the Twelfth, A.D. 1294. *Art de vérifier les Dates,* vol. i. pp. 290—314; and Le Quien, t. i. coll. 257—291.

Nicholas of Piacenza, Bishop of Spoleto; and
(6) 1253, Pantaleo Giustiniani, a Venetian, who
returned to Italy after the taking of Constantinople
by the Greeks in 1261.[110]

Moreover, in the lists of the relics belonging
to the Church of Notre Dame which are given in
the Chartulary, no mention is made of the milk
of our Ladye.[117] But Ferreol Locri says that there
was a relic of our Ladye's milk both in the
cathedral and in the royal chapel.[118]

The allusion of St. Bernard refers to an old
legend, that on one occasion our Blessed Ladye,
with her Divine Son in her arms, appeared to him,
and fed him with some drops of her milk. I have
several engravings of the seventeenth century
which represent the apparition. The Bollandists
discuss the various accounts of it, and the opinions
given by different writers, and sum up in favour
of those who treat it as a legend.[119]

The relic at Walsingham must have been
brought from the East, possibly from Constantinople, by some English pilgrim.

Robert Du Mont, describing the battle of
Ascalon, in the year 1124, and the advance of the
little Christian army, says that the princes marched
at the head, the patriarch bore the Cross of
Christ[120] as a standard, Pontius, Abbot of Cluny,
carried the Lance which had pierced the side of
of our Lord, and the Bishop of Bethlehem bore
the milk of the Blessed Virgin Marye in a pyx.[121]
And in the year 1248, St. Louis of France sent to

---

[110] *Art de vérifier les Dates.* Paris, 1783, vol. i. p. 308, et seq.

[117] *Cartulaire de l' Eglise Notre Dame de Paris.* Edit. Guérard. Paris, 1850,
vol. iii. p. 375 ; vol. iv. pp. 39, 110, 125, 126, 203, 207, 208.

[118] *Maria Augusta.* Arras, 1608, p. 525.

[119] *Acta SS.* t. iv. Aug. pp. 206, 208.

[120] After the death of Heraclius in 636, the Church of the Holy Sepulchre was
burnt by the infidels, and the faithful determined to divide the Holy Cross into
nineteen portions, which were distributed thus : Constantinople received three, the
island of Cyprus two, Crete one, Antioch three, Edessa one, Alexandria one, Ascalon
one, Damascus one, Jerusalem four, and two were distributed in Georgia (*Mémoire
sur les Instruments de la Passion de N. S. J. C.* par Ch. Rohault de Fleury. Paris,
1870, p. 56).

[121] *Continuation de la Chronique de Sigisbert.* *Bib. des Croisades,* pt. iii. p. 92.
Also Baronius, ad ann. 1124, t. xii. p. 158. Antw. 1609.

the Chapter of Toledo, by the hands, and at the request of the Archbishop of that city, some precious particles of the relics which he had received from the imperial treasury at Constantinople—viz., of the wood of the Cross of our Lord, of the milk of the glorious Virgin Marye, &c. Mariana gives the letter of St. Louis to the Chapter of Toledo; it is dated Estampes, in the month of May of the year above named.[122]

Guibert, who was Abbot of Saint Marye of Nogent-sur-Seine for twenty years, and died A.D. 1124, mentions that some of our Ladye's milk was preserved in a dove made of crystal at Laon; but he maintains that our Ladye never forced any of her milk from her breast to be kept for future veneration, since that would have been quite inconsistent with her humility.[123] D'Achery, who published the works of Guibert in 1651, commenting on this passage, says he hears and reads that other relics of our Ladye's milk are venerated in France and elsewhere; and therefore he is in perplexity of mind which side to take.[124] The Bollandists noticed the perplexity of D'Achery, and Father Cuperus admits that he is similarly perplexed, because if he adopts the opinion of Guibert, he is at variance with Italians, Spaniards, French, and Belgians,[125] who in different churches claim this as one of their most precious relics. He then refers to the letter of St. Louis given by Mariana, and remarks:

"If I at once believe evidences of this kind, so remote from the days of our Ladye, I shall appear over credulous to severe critics of history, and as multiplying continual miracles without necessity. But I had rather appear over credulous than over censorious. Although I dare not pass a certain judgment as to the veracity of such like

---

[122] *De rebus Hispaniæ.* Mogunt, 1619, lib. xiii. c. viii. p. 554.

[123] *De pignoribus Sanctorum,* lib. iii. c. iii, § 3, inter opp. Guiberti, *Patrol. Lat.* t. clvi, col. 659. Edit. Migne.

[124] *Ibid.* col. 1044.

[125] Cf. Locri, *Maria Augusta,* pp. 524, 525; also Morlot, *Metropolis Remensis Historia,* t. ii.; Remis, 1679, pp. 474, 475, for a relic of our Ladye's milk sent by Pope Adrian, c. 1276.

relics, still I am far away, and I wish to be far
away, from the impious Calvin and the supercilious
Erasmus of Rotterdam, who wantonly reject the
tradition of all those churches; and whom, on
that account, John Ferrand of our Society deservedly censures in his dissertation on Relics.
Indeed, I freely admit with Ferrand, that Almighty
God could have preserved that milk from corruption for so many centuries, but I am anxious to
learn from evidence, most ancient and trustworthy,
whether He ever really did so, and wished this
continual miracle to exist in so many places. For
it is necessary that this evidence should be pro-
portioned to the prodigy, so that undoubted
historical faith may be given to it. Therefore I form
no positive opinion on the truth of this matter;
and here I derive great satisfaction from the
opinion of Pope Innocent the Third—A.D. 1198
—1216, who, speaking of certain relics of our
Lord, concludes as follows: '. . . Nevertheless,
it is better to commit all to God rather than to
define anything rashly.' This opinion of the
Pope, which I have given in capital letters, I
desire to apply to the present subject. In the
meantime, let other churches rejoice in so
precious a treasure of the milk of the Blessed
Virgin if each of them can confirm what they
possess by solid documents proportionate to so
great antiquity."[126]

The significance of this well-expressed opinion
of the Bollandists is manifest, and solves the
difficulty. But now two very important questions
arise: (1) Was the object called the milk of our
Blessed Ladye shown in good faith *as such;* or
(2) was the term "milk of our Ladye" a conventional one, and applied to an object, the real
nature of which was well known and understood?

1. Considering the careful supervision exercised
by the bishops, and that no relic can be exposed
publicly for veneration unless sealed with an
authorized seal, and duly authenticated, it seems
in the highest degree improbable that "our
Ladye's Milk" was ever shown as being *really*

[126] *Acta SS.* t. iv. Aug. pp. 20, 21.

such. The suppression of the devotion to the Holy Blood of Windesnack in Brandenburg, to which there was a great pilgrimage for many years, proves the vigilance of the Church in regard of relics not wholly satisfactory.[127] No one in his senses would ever dream of exhibiting a flask of white Rhine wine as "milk," and much less as "our Ladye's milk;" or a bottle of red wine as the "tears" of Christ our Lord; yet the well-known *Liebefraumilch*, which is commonly called "Maiden's milk," means literally "our dear Ladye's milk;" and every visitor to Vesuvius remembers the *Lachryma Christi* wine. In both these instances the names are purely conventional, and known to be such.

2. There can be no doubt that the term "Milk of our Ladye" as applied to objects shown as such is a purely conventional name.

Between two and three hundred paces south-east from the Basilica on the eastern side of the hill on which Bethlehem stands, there is a grotto venerated alike by Christians and Mussulmans and commonly called the *Crypta Lactea* and *Grotte du Lait.* The Arabs call it *Meharet es-Sitti*, the Grotto of our Ladye.[128] It belongs to the Franciscans, who go there every Saturday to celebrate Mass, and to sing the Litanies of our Blessed Ladye.

There are many traditions as to the origin of its name; indeed Mislin says that every one has his own version; but they are all unanimous on one and the main point, which is that our Ladye spilt some drops of her milk in this grotto.[129] Hence its name : and this is the reason why the earth brought from it is called the *Milk of our Blessed Ladye.*

[127] For its history see J. P. de Ludewig, *Reliquiæ Manuscriptorum omnis Ævi Diplomatum ac Monumentorum.* Francofurti et Lipsiæ, 1731, vol. viii. pp. 438—468. For the suppression see Riedel, *Cod. Dipl. Brandenburg.* t. ii. p. 121 et seq.

[128] *Description Géographique, Historique et Archéologique de la Palestine.* Par M. V. Guérin Imprimée, par autorisation de l' Empereur à l' Imprimerie Imperiale. Paris, 1868, t. 1, p. 186.

[129] *Les Saints Pieux. Pélerinage à Jerusalem,* &c. Par Mgr. Mislin, Abbé Mitré de Sainte Marie de Deg. en Hongrie. Paris, 1858, t. iii. pp. 31—33.

Some say that our Ladye often retired to this grotto ; others that she reposed one night in it on her way to Egypt; others, again, that being alarmed by the threats of Herod, her milk suddenly dried up, and that she retired to this cave, believing she would be in greater security there than elsewhere. Finding herself unable to nourish her Divine Son, she made her prayer to the Almighty, and forthwith her milk returned in such abundance that a few drops fell upon the ground. Hence why the rock is said to derive its peculiar property, when pulverized and mixed in water, and then imbibed, of preventing those who nurse from suffering of a diminution of their milk.

This is no modern belief; on the contrary, it appears to be very ancient. In 1598, John Cotwyck, of Utrecht, a *Doctor Utriusque Juris*, embarked at Venice on his way to Syria and the Holy Land. He evidently brought back some of the earth called our Ladye's Milk from the Grotto of the Milk, because he says that he had seen the effects of it amongst his own people, and thus learned that the opinion of the Orientals was not without foundation.[180] Then there is the evidence of the Commissary Apostolic and Guardian of the Holy Sepulchre, Father Francis Quaresma or Quaresmi,[181] who bears witness to similar results ; so does a Canon of St. Paul's at Saint Denis, in 1652 ;[182] and also Surius, a few years later ;[183] while Father Michael Nau, of the Society of Jesus, says—

"*Je n' assure pas que cette terre sert beaucoup dans les autres maladies, mais pour ce qui est de rendre le lait aux femmes qui l'ont perdu, et d'en faire venir à celles qui en ont peu c'est une chose si certaine et si infallible que les infidèles mêmes en ont fait mille fois l'expérience.*"[184]

[180] Cottovicus, *Itinerarium Hierosolymitanum et Syriacum.* Antv. 1619, p. 238.

[181] Quaresmius, *Historica, Theologica et Moralis Terræ Sanctæ elucidatio.* Antv. 1639, t. ii. p. 678.

[182] *Le Voyage de la Terre Sainte,* &c. Fait l'an 1652. Par M. J. D. P. Chanoine. de l' Eglise Royale et Collegiale de Saint Paul à Saint-Denis en France. Paris, 1657, cap. xix. pp. 164, 165.

[183] *Le Pieux Pèlerin ou Voyage à Jerusalem.* Bruxelles, 1666, p. 148.

[184] *Voyage nouveau à la Terre Sainte,* p. 426.

Mislin and Guérin, who are the latest writers, and Quaresma, Father Nau, and the Canon of Saint Paul's, all mention that there is a continual resort to this grotto by the women of the neighbourhood, Christians, Arabs, Mussulmans, and Jewesses, who pray in it. According to Mislin the earth is like chalk, very white, and easily reducible to powder, and it is then made into little cakes which are sent all over the country, and which pilgrims carry away with them as objects of devotion or curiosity. This is a custom which dates very far back, and so great is the demand for "our Ladye's Milk," that the grotto, which originally was small, has now become greatly enlarged; a fact which Quaresma mentions as well.[135]

There is a slight discrepancy in the description of the earth excavated from the grotto. Quaresma says it is reddish, but that when powdered in a mortar and reduced to powder and then well washed and sifted and exposed to the sun it becomes as white as milk—*lacti simillima evadit.* The Canon of St. Paul's observes that by this process it is made *blanche comme le laict.* Mislin describes the earth as chalky, very friable, and easily reduced to powder. Guérin says that it consists of a sort of calcareous tufa, like chalk, and very friable, and easily scraped from the grotto. Like all the other writers, he bears testimony to the great antiquity of the custom of carrying away portions of this earth known as our Ladye's Milk.

Mislin also notices a circumstance which I have not seen mentioned by others. He says that sometimes in damp weather a liquid substance exudes from the sides of the cave, which is called the Milk of our Ladye, instead of the milk of the grotto of our Ladye.[136]

The precise manner in which the Milk of our Ladye at Walsingham, as described by Erasmus, coincides with the account which these writers give of what is called our Ladye's Milk in Palestine leaves no doubt that it was a portion of the

[135] *Ut sup. l. c.*   [136] *Ut sup.* p. 33.

scrapings from the *Crypta Lactea* of Bethlehem. In 1854 Canon Bourassée, of Tours, the learned editor of the *Summa Aurea*, was commissioned by the Cardinal Archbishop of that city to open a silver shrine, and identify the relics which it contained. Amongst the contents he found a fragment of stone, resembling marble, and of the colour of snow; it was folded up in a piece of vellum, on which was written *De lacte Beate Virginis.*[137]

This seems to be the real history and signification of what is called "Our Ladye's Milk;" hence it is easy to account for the quantity of it, which has been brought at various times into Europe. Indeed, considering the veneration which is attached to pieces of earth, or stone, or wood brought away from any of the holy places connected with the Life, Passion, and Death of Christ our Lord, it is most natural that the *Crypta Lactea*, so intimately associated by tradition with the Infancy of our Lord and His Blessed Mother, should have come in for a share of that veneration. Relics of this description are mentioned at an early period; thus St. Augustine speaks of earth brought from the Holy Sepulchre and of the veneration in which it was held.[138] Neither Venerable Bede,[139] nor St. Adamnan, Abbot of Hy,[140] mention the *Crypta Lactea;* but Hardouin, Bishop of Le Mans in the time of Clovis the Second, received some of the "Milk of our Ladye" from a pilgrim who had returned from the Holy Land.[141]

Several of these relics from the Holy Land were found enclosed in lead, in the head of the ancient image of our Ladye of Thetford.[142]

[137] *Summa Aurea*, t. xi. col. 710, note. Cf. Colvener. *Kalendarium Marianum* ad diem 4 Febr. § 11. 3.

[138] *De Civitate Dei*, lib. xxii. cap. viii.

[139] *De locis Sanctis*, opp. t. iv. cap. xv. p. 434. Edit. Giles.

[140] *De locis Sanctis*, lib. ii. cap. ii. Patrol. Lat. t. lxxxviii. col. 795. Edit. Migne.

[141] Quoted by Darras. *La Legende de Notre Dame*, Paris, 1852, p. 113.

[142] See *ante*, p. 149.

Erasmus puts into the mouth of Menedemus some expressions about the quantity of our Ladye's Milk which was said to exist, and which I will not quote; but they seem to have been introduced in order to give himself, in the character of Ogygius, the opportunity of saying as follows:

"So they say of the Cross of our Lord which is shown publicly and privately in so many places, that, if all the fragments were collected together, they would appear to form a fair cargo for a merchant ship, and yet our Lord bore His whole Cross." This latter assertion is quite at variance with the Gospels, for our Lord never carried His Cross, in the sense of balanced on His shoulder and wholly raised from the ground. The third part of the Homily against the Peril of Idolatry says that, "if all the pieces thereof were gathered together, the greatest ship in England would scarcely bear them."

Calvin, I believe, generally has the credit of being the originator of this stupendous lie which has been so sedulously propagated by his followers and by heretics of all persuasions, and to which implicit faith is given by very many in these days. Now this colloquy of the *Peregrinatio*, in its present form, appears to have been printed, at the latest, in 1524, at which time Calvin was only fifteen years of age, he having been inflicted upon the world at Noyon, in Picardy, on the 10th July, 1509. Consequently, he would seem only to have adopted the fable, which, in common fairness, must be attributed to the fertile and mischievous brain of Erasmus.

I have so often met with references to this fable, and moreover, I have so often heard it asserted in reply, and often in perfect good faith, that the multiplication of the wood of the True Cross was miraculous,[143] that I feel I shall do a good service to the cause of truth if I give a brief statement of the real facts. Indeed, as Erasmus commences his attack on the True

[143] Cf. e.g. Morlot, *Hist. de la Ville de Reims.* Reims, 1843, v. iii. p. 533.

Cross in his *Peregrinatio* to Walsingham, it is fitting that he should receive his refutation under the protection of our Ladye of Walsingham, the Blissful Queen of Heaven, whose Dower it is England's glory still to be; a title which, by the way, England has never lost, notwithstanding that recently, and for the first time, an attempt has been made to rob her of it.[144]

A few years ago a learned French gentleman, M. Rohault de Fleury, applied himself to a careful study and critical examination of the relics of the various Instruments of the Passion of our Lord, but more especially of the Holy Cross and the Crown of Thorns. He received every facility for carrying out his object. He commenced his investigations by submitting portions of four well authenticated pieces—those of the Holy Cross of Jerusalem in Rome, of the Cathedral of Pisa, of the Cathedral of Florence, and of Notre Dame in Paris—to a microscopical examination, in his presence, by two learned men of undoubted reputation, M. Decaisne, Member of the Institute, and Signor Peter Savi, Professor in the University of Pisa. The result of this examination proved that the wood of the True Cross was of the genus fir. The specific gravity of the various conifers differs: Scotch fir, 0·56; pinus abies, 0·46; pinus epicea, 0·52; yellow pine, 0·66. M. de Fleury has selected 0·56 as the mean, and for his standard, and on these figures he has based his calculations.[145]

Now it has been established by Paucton, that a porter can carry a weight of 90 kilogrammes, or 198 lbs., a distance of 5 kilometres, or 3½ miles, in one hour; and a carrier of coals, who often rests, can bear 115 kilogrammes, or 253 lbs.;[146] but Laisne[147] and Charles Duffin give lesser weights.

---

[144] In the Introduction, cap. ii. which was written several years ago, I have given the full history of how England became the *Dos Maria*, and how she still preserves the title.

[145] *Mémoire sur les Instruments de la Passion de N. S. J. C.* par Ch. Rohault de Fleury, ancien élève de l'Ecole polytechnique. Paris : Lesort, 1870, p. 71.

[146] *Métrologie*. 1780, p. 94.

[147] *Aide-mémoire des Officiers du génie*, 1853, p. 69.

The late M. Duprez, who was an able practitioner, considered that a strong carpenter can carry a *décistère*[148] of wood—equal to about 100 kilogrammes, or 222 lbs.—a distance of 40 to 50 metres at most; that is to say, by walking for two minutes, and then resting for three; and that he could continue in this way for an hour. Under these conditions, it would have taken an hour to pass along the Via Dolorosa. Now the weight of the Cross was such that our Lord was unable to support it all the while, and required the assistance of Simon the Cyrenean.

If, therefore, the weight of 100 kilogrammes be taken as a maximum, it should be considered that our Lord was terribly weakened by His sufferings, and that His executioners were rapidly exhausting His remaining strength; consequently, the weight of the Cross might be estimated at three-fourths, or 75 kilogrammes. As the Cross was not balanced on the shoulder, but trailed on the ground, the diminution of weight may, in consequence, be taken at 25 kilogrammes; therefore, on this calculation, the full weight of the Cross may be estimated at 100 kilogrammes, or 222 lbs.

Now, from these figures it is easy to calculate the bulk of the Cross, by dividing the weight by the density of the fir, 0·56, which gives 178,000,000 of cube *millimetres*.[149]

Having obtained these results, M. Rohault de Fleury began to examine the size and bulk of all the known authentic relics of the Holy Cross; and in nearly every instance he has given plans of the various pieces; and in his calculations he leaves a margin, so that he is invariably, if anything, over the mark. He wrote for plans and details on all sides; and after this exhaustive inquiry, his investigations have succeeded in making up the volume of all the known relics of the Holy Cross only to 3,941,975 cube *millimetres*—say, in round numbers, 4,000,000. Now, allowing a very large margin for relics of the

---

[148] Or 3½ cubic feet.   [149] A *millimetre* is 0·39337 of an inch.

Holy Cross which may be in private hands, or may not have come to the notice of M. Rohault de Fleury—say, multiply the quantity known by 10—this quantity, which must convince the most sceptical only amounts to 40,000,000, or less than one-fourth of the bulk; and there is a deficit of 138,000,000 *millimetres* still to be accounted for!

I am aware that the Commissioners, who were employed in the suppression of the Monasteries in England, reported that at Bury St. Edmunds there were "peeces of the Holie Crosse able to make a hole crosse of;"[150] but this is one of the usual official lies of the period, and does not deserve even a contemptuous notice. To this particular one I have merely referred, because some writers, either from malice or ignorance, seem to consider it valuable evidence.

Sometimes small pieces of the Holy Cross were mounted in a wooden cross of larger size, into which a small cavity had been scooped out to receive the relic. A cross of this description, and presented by the Prince of Bosnia, is now preserved in the Treasury of St. Mark's at Venice, and is figured by M. Rohault de Fleury.[151] These outer crosses in reality served as reliquaries.

In 1534 the Canons of Walsingham acknowledged the Royal Supremacy. I have not ascertained whether the whole of the Community signed the deed, but the names of twenty-two, including the Prior and Sub-Prior, are affixed to it. The document is in Latin, and commences thus:

Quum ea sit non solum Christiane religionis et pietatis ratio, sed nostre etiam obediencie regula, Domino Regi nostro Henrico ejus nominis octavo, cui uni et soli post Christum Jesum servatorem nostrum debemus universa, non modo omnimodam in Christo et eandem sinceram, integram, perpetuamque animi devotionem, fidem et observanciam, honorem, cultum, reverenciam prestemus, sed etiam

---

[150] *Letters relating to the Suppression of the Monasteries,* p. 85.

[151] Plate viii. n. 2, p. 103. It is greatly to be desired that this most valuable work were translated into English.

*de eadem fide et observancia nostra rationem quo-
tiescunque postulabitur reddamus et palam omnibus
(si res postulat) libentissime testemur;*

Let all to whom the present writing may
come know that we, the Prior and Community
of the Priory of Walsingham, in the diocese of
Norwich, with one mouth and voice, and with
the unanimous consent and assent of all, by this
deed, given under our common seal in our
chapter-house, do, for ourselves and our successors, all and each, for ever, declare, attest,
and faithfully promise and undertake, that we,
the said Prior and Community and our successors,
all and each, will ever render an entire, inviolate,
sincere, and perpetual fidelity, submission, and
reverence to the lord our King, Henry the
Eighth, and to Queen Anne, his Consort, and
to the issue of him by the said Anne lawfully
begotten, as well as to be begot; and that we
will make known, preach, and counsel the same
to the people whenever an opportunity or an
occasion shall be given.

Item, that we hold as confirmed and ratified,
and will always and for ever hold, that the aforesaid Henry our King is the Head of the Anglican
Church.

Item, that the Bishop of Rome, who in his
Bulls usurps the name of Pope and arrogates
to himself the sovereignty of Chief Bishop, has
not any greater jurisdiction conferred on him
by God than any other extern Bishop.

Item, that none of us, in any holy discourse
to be held in private or in public, shall call the
said Bishop of Rome by the name of Pope or
Chief Bishop, but by the name of the Bishop
of Rome, or of the Roman Church; and that
none of us shall pray for him as Pope, but as
Bishop of Rome.

Item, that we will adhere to the said lord
the King alone, and to his successors, and will
maintain his laws and decrees, renouncing for
ever the laws, decrees, and canons of the Bishop
of Rome which shall be contrary to the Divine
Law and Holy Scripture.

Item, that not one of all of us shall, in any sermon, public or private, attempt to misconstrue any passage taken from Holy Scripture into a foreign sense; but each shall preach, in a catholic and orthodox manner, Christ and His words and actions, simply, openly, sincerely, and to the form (*normam*) and rule of the Holy Scriptures, and of the truly catholic and orthodox doctors.

Item, that each of us, in his accustomed prayers and supplications, shall recommend to God and the prayers of the people, first of all the King as Supreme Head of the Anglican Church, then Queen Anne with her offspring, and then, lastly, the Archbishops of Canterbury and of York, with the other orders of clergy as shall seem fit.

Item, that we all and each aforesaid, Prior, Community, and our successors, firmly bind ourselves by the pledge of our conscience and our oath; and that we will faithfully and for ever observe all and each of the promises aforesaid. In testimony whereof we have affixed our common seal to this our writing, and, each with his own hand, have subscribed our names. Given in our chapter-house, the 18th day of the month of September, the year of the Lord one thousand five hundred and thirty-four.[152]

> *per me* RICARD VOWEL, Priorem.
> *per me* WILLELMUM RASE.
> *per me* EDMUNDUM WARHAM, Subpriorem.
> *per me* JOHANNEM CLENCHWARDTON.
> *per me* NICHOLAUM MYLEHAM.
> *per me* ROBERTUM SALL'.
> *per me* ROBERTUM WYLSEY.
> *per me* WILLELMUM CASTELLACRE.
> *per me* SIMONEM OVY.
> *per me* JOHANNEM HARLOW.
> *per me* JOHANNEM LAWINXLEY.
> *per me* RICARDUM GARNETT.
> *per me* JOHANNEM CLARK.

[152] Original preserved in the late Treasury of the Exchequer, in the Chapter-house, Westminster. Acknowledgments of Supremacy, n. 112. *Journal of Royal Archæological Institute*, v. xiii. p. 128.

per me JOHANNEM AWSTYNE.
per me JOHANNEM MATHYE.
per me THOMAM PAWLUM.
per me EDWARDUM MARSTONE.
· *per me* JOHANNEM BYRCHAM.
per me JOHANNEM HADLAY.
per me THOMAM HOLTE.
per me THOMAM WALSYNGHAM.
per me UMFREDUM LONDON.

(*L.S.*)

Amongst the Harleian MSS. are preserved some Articles of Enquiry which were to guide the Commissioners in their unholy proceedings. The three first have an especial eye to the plunder.

1. In primis, whether there be any inventarie allweys permanent in the house betwene the priour and the brethern of this house, as welle of alle the juelles, reliques, and ornamentes of the churche and chapel, as of alle the plate and other moveable goodes of this house? *Et si sic exhibeatur.*

2. *Item*, yf there be no suche inventarie, whether there be any boke made therof, and of the guyſte of the juelles that have bene geven to our Ladye? *Et si sic producatur.*

3. *Item*, whether any of the said juelles, ornamentes, plate, or goodes hathe bene alienated, solde, or pledged at any tyme heretofore? And yf there were, what they were, to whome they were solde, for how moche, whan, and for what cause?

4. *Item*, what reliques be in this house that be or hath bene most in th' estimacion of the people, and what vertue was estemed of the people to be in theym?

5. *Item*, what probacion or argument have they to shewe that the same are trewe reliques?

6. *Item*, in howe many places of this house were the said reliques shewed, and whiche were in which; and whether the kepers of the same did not bring about tables to men for their offering, as though they would exacte money of

theym or make theym ashamed except they did offer?

7. *Item,* for what cause were the said reliques shewed in divers [and] sundrye places more than alltogether in one place?

8. *Item,* what hathe th' offring made to our Ladye and to the said reliques bene worth a yere whan it hathe bene most? what commonly? and what the laste yere?

9. *Item,* yf the said reliques be nowe layde aside, howe long ago, and for what cause they were so?

10. *Item,* what is the greatest miracle and moste undoubted whiche is said to have bene doon by our Ladye here, or by any of the said reliques? and what prouffe they have of the facte or of the narracion thereof?

11. *Item,* whether thane (yf the facte be welle proued) the case might not happene by some naturalle meane not contrarie to reasone or possibilitie of nature?

12. *Item,* yf that be proved also, whether the same mighte not procede of the immediate helpe of God? and why the successe of that case shulde be imputed to our Ladye and yet that to the image of our Ladye in this house more than another?

13. *Item,* whether the miracle were wonte to be declared in pulpite heretofore, and for what cause they were soe?   a Whitesonne Monday the faire tyme they were wonte to be opened?

14. *Item,* what is the sayng of the buylding of our Lady Chappelle, and the firste invencion of thimage of our Lady there? what of the house where the bere skynne is, and of the knyght; and what of the other wonders that be here, and what proves be therof?

15. *Item,* whether they knowe not that mene shulde not be lighte of credite to miracles, unlesse they be manifestly and invinciblie proved?

16. *Item,* whether our Lady hathe doone so many miracles nowe of late as it was said she did whane there was more offring made unto her?

17. *Item*, what prouffe were they wonte to take of the miracles that the pilgremes did reporte shulde be made by our Lady? and whether they bileved the parties owne reporte therin, or toke witnes, and howe they toke the deposicions of the same?

18. *Item*, whether our Ladye's milke be liquide or no? and yf it be *interrogetur ut infra*.

19. *Item*, who was Sextene upon a X. yeres agoo or therabout, and lett hym be exactely examined whether he hath not renewed that they calle our Lady's milke whane it was like to be dried up; and whether ever he hymself invented any relique for thaugmentacion of his prouffit; and whether the house over the welles were not made within tyme of remembrance, or at the leste wise renewed? [153]

Erasmus had taken good care not to publish the account of his visit to Walsingham until he had left England, and crossed the Ocean, the Father of Winds, never to return. Copies of it, however, must have found their way to England, and it is impossible not to come to the conclusion that many of the articles for this enquiry must have been suggested by it.

I have been unable to ascertain whether the Commissioners made any report in detail, in reply to these queries; but a letter from Southwell to Cromwell has been preserved.

On the 25th of July, 1536, Southwell writes to Cromwell—

It may please your good lordshipe to be advertised that Sir Thomas Lestrange and Mr. Hoges, accordinge unto the sequestratyon delegate unto them, have bene at Walsingham, and ther sequestred all suche monney, plate, juelles, and stuff, as ther wasse inventyd and founde. Emoung other thinges the same Sir Thomas Lestrange and Mr. Hoges dyd there fynd a secrete prevye place within the howse, where no channon nor onnye other of the howse dyd ever enter, as they saye, in wiche there were instrewmentes,

153 MS, Harl. 791, f. 27.

pottes, belowes, flyes of suche strange colers as the lick non of us had seene with poysies [154] and other thinges to sorte and denyd [155] gould and sylver, nothing there wantinge that should belonge to the arte of moultyplyeng. Off all wiche they desyred me by lettres to advertyse you, and alsoo that frome the Satredaye at nigh tyll the Sondaye next folowinge was offred at their now beinge xxxiijs. iiijd. over and besyd waxe.

Of this moulteplyenge it maye please you to cawse hem to be examyned, and so to advertyse unto them your further pleasuer. Thus I praye god send your good lordshipe hartye helthe.

Frome my pore howse this xxv. of Julii a° xxviii.

Humblye yours to commande

RIC. SOUTHWELL. [156]

To the right honerable and my syngular good lord my lord prevye ceale.

This description and "arte of moulteplyeng" evidently refer to the laboratory where the badges and pilgrims' signs were made. Such a privy furnace, very probably destined for a similar purpose, may still be seen in an upper chamber in Canterbury Cathedral. [157] The only multiplier in the case is Southwell, who possessed, in common with many others, the "arte of moulteplyeng" lies for the satisfaction of Cromwell.

I have never met with a Walsingham badge; but a cast of one is described in the *Journal of the Royal Archæological Institute.* It is a small rectangular ornament of lead, on which appears the Annunciation, with the vase containing the lily between our Blessed Ladye and the Archangel Gabriel, and underneath is 𝕮𝖆𝖑𝖘𝖞𝖌𝖍𝖆𝖒. [158]

In 1537, an insurrection broke out at Walsingham. The cause was this. The inhabitants found

---

[154] *i.e.* weights.

[155] Probably foreign money.

[156] MS. Cott. *Cleop.* E. iv. f. 231 ; *Letters relating to the Suppression of the Monasteries,* p. 138.

[157] *Journal of Royal Arch. Inst.* v. xiii. p. 133.

[158] *Ibid.* v. xiii. p. 133.

out that the dissolution of religious houses, and the suppression of pilgrimages to the ancient and venerated sanctuary of our Ladye would, in a great measure, prove their ruin.[159]   This little disturbance was quelled with a savage and bloody hand; and in the same year "two of the rebelles" who had taken part in the insurrection, were hanged at Great Yarmouth, and drawn and quartered.[160]

On the 20th of January, 1538, Roger Townsend writes to Cromwell, the Lord Privy Seal.[161]

Please itt your good lordshipp to be avertysed that ther was a pore woman of Wellys besyde Walsyngham, that imagyned a falce tale of a myracle to be doon by the image of our Ladye that was at Walsyngham syth the same was brought from thens to London; and upon the tryall thereof, by my examinacōn from one person to another, to the nomber of vi. persons, and at last came to her that she was the reporter thereof, and to be the very auctour of the same, as ferforth as my consciens and perceyvying cowd lede me; I commytted her therfor to the warde of the constables of Walsyngham.   The next day after, beyng markett day ther, I caused her to be sett in stokkes in the mornyng, and about ix. of the clok when the seyd markett was fullest of people, with a papir sett aboute her hede, wreten wyth thes wordes upon the same, *A reporter of falce tales*, was sett in a carte and so carryed about the markett-stede, and other stretes in the town, steying in dyvers places wher most people assembled, yong people and boyes of the town castyng snowe balles att her.   Thys doon and executed, was brought to the stokkes ageyn and ther sett till the markett was ended.   This was her penans; for I knewe no lawe otherwyse to ponyshe her butt by discrecōn; trustyng itt shall be a warnying to other lyght persons in such wyse to order them self.   Howe be itt I cannot

---

[159] *General History of Norfolk*, pp. 607, 608,

[160] Manship. *Palmer's Notes*, v. I. p. 413.

[161] He was made Lord Privy Seal, 2nd of July, 1536.

perceyve, but the seyd Image is not yett out of sum of ther heddes . . . Wreten the xxth of January.

Humbly at your comande,

ROGER TOUNESHEND.[162]

At the suppression, fifteen of the Canons of Walsingham were condemned for high treason, of whom five were executed.

The deed of the surrender of Walsingham and all its property to the King was executed in the chapter-house on the 4th of August, in the thirtieth year of Henry the Eighth. No names are appended to it, it is merely stated that the Prior and Convent caused their common seal to be put to it. The following memorandum is attached to it. *Et memorandum quod die et anno predictis venerunt predicti Prior et Conventus in domo sua Capitulari apud Walsyngham coram Willielmo Petre, pretextu Commissionis dicti Domini Regis ei in hac parte directe, et recognoverunt scriptum predictum ac omnia et singula in eodem contenta in forma predicta.*[163]

This Sir William Petre was a great favourite of Cromwell's, and one of the Commissioners employed by him to visit monasteries, of which Henry the Eighth had nominated Cromwell General Visitor. Sir William was afterwards Secretary of State, and held posts of high trust in four successive reigns. He had large grants out of the spoils of the monasteries as enumerated in the *Biographia Britannica;*[164] and in the reign of Queen Mary he obtained from Pope Paul the Fourth, a Bull permitting him to retain them.

The venerated Image of our Ladye of Walsingham was burnt at Chelsea, but there is a discrepancy as to the date of the perpetration of this sacrilegious act.

"Allso this yeare, 1538," says Wriothesley, "in the moneth of July, the images of our Ladye of Walsingham and Ipswich were brought up to

---

[162] State Paper Office, Second Series, xliii. p. 193.
[163] Given in full in the *Journal of Royal Arch. Inst.* v. xiii. pp. 129—131.
[164] *Life of Petre.*

London with all the jewelles that honge about them, at the King's commaundement, and divers other images both in England and Wales, that were used for common pilgrimages, because the people should use noe more idolatrye unto them, and they were burnt at Chelsey by my Lord Privie Seale." [165]

Hall says it was in the month of September. "In September, by the speciall mocion of the Lorde Crumwel al the notable images vnto the which were made any speciall pilgrimages and offerynges were vtterly taken awaye, as the images of Walsyngham, Ypswirche, Worceter, the Lady of Wilsdon, with many other." [166] And according to Speede, they were burnt in the presence of Cromwell. [167]

The following elegy is preserved in a volume lettered "Earl of Arundell MS.," amongst the Rawlinson MSS. in the Bodleian library, Oxon.

> In the wrackes of Walsingam
> Whom should I chuse
> But the Queene of Walsingam
> to be guide to my muse?
> Then thou Prince of Walsingam,
> graunt me to frame
> Bitter plaintes to rewe thy wronge,
> bitter wo for thy name.
>
> Bitter was it, oh to see
> the seely sheepe
> Murdred by the raueninge wolues,
> while the sheephardes did sleep.
> Bitter was it, oh to vewe
> the sacred vyne,
> Whiles the gardiners plaied all close,
> rooted vp by the swine.
>
> Bitter, bitter, oh to behould
> the grasse to growe
> Where the walles of Walsingam
> so statly did sheue.
> Such were the workes of Walsingam
> while shee did stande
> Such are the wrackes as now do shewe
> Of that holy land !
> Levell, Levell with the ground
> the towres do lye,

[165] V. i. p. 83.   [166] *Chronicles,* Lond. 1809, p. 826.
[167] *Hist. of England,* p. 1026.

Which with their golden glitteringe tops
pearsed once to the skye.
Where weare gates, no gates are nowe ;
the waies vnknowen
Wher the presse of peares did passe
while her fame far was blowen.
Oules do scrike wher the sweetest himnes
lately weer songe ;
Toades and serpentes hold ther dennes
wher the Palmers did thronge.

Weepe, weepe, O Walsingam
whose dayes are nightes,
Blessinges turned to blasphemies,
holy deedes to dispites.
Sinne is wher our Ladie sate,
heauen turned is to hell,
Sathan sittes wher our Lord did swaye,
Walsingam, oh farewell.[146]

An impression of the seal of Walsingham Priory, in white wax, is appended to the acknowledgment of Supremacy. It is about three inches in diameter, and circular. On the obverse is represented a cruciform church of Norman character, and the inscription SIGILLVM ECCL'IE BEATE MARIE DE WALSINGHAM. The reverse represents our Blessed Ladye seated on a peculiar high-backed throne ; she holds her Divine Son on her left knee, His right hand is extended in the attitude of blessing, and in His left hand He holds the Book of the Gospels. On her head is a low crown, an elegantly floriated sceptre is in her right hand ; the draperies are poor and in low relief, and above the figures is a sort of canopy with curtains looped back at either side, and falling in ungraceful folds. The Angelical Salutation is engraved around the margin. ✠ AVE : MARIA : GRACIA : PLENA : DOMIVUS : TECUM. In addition to the less archaic effect of the workmanship, suggesting the notion that this side may be the reproduction of an earlier seal, it may be noticed that the word PLENA is blundered, a D being found in the place of N, an error which might easily occur from the similarity of the two letters in the particular character here used.

[146] Rawl. MSS. Poet. 242, given also in Percy's Folio Manuscript: *Ballads and Romances.* Edit. Hales and Furnivall. Lond. 1868, v. iii. pp. 470, 471.

From the general execution, however, of the seals, their date may probably be assigned to the later part of the twelfth or commencement of the thirteenth century. This impression supplies an example of the rare practice of impressing an inscription upon the edge or thickness of the seal, as on that of Norwich Cathedral, the city of Canterbury, and a few others.[169] In the present instance, the following words of a Leonine verse may be decyphered—VIRGO : PIA : GENITRIX : SIT : NOBIS : (MEDIATRIX ?).[170]

At Bodmin there was a Gild of Our Ladye of Walsingham.[171]

After passing to different proprietors, Wal: singham was purchased in 1766 by Dr. Warner, Bishop of Rochester; and it still continues in the family of Lee-Warner. The site of the renowned Sanctuary of our Ladye has recently been deeply buried beneath a terraced parterre. May it be hoped that the Lily and the Marygold, and the Forget-me-not—*les yeux de Notre Dame,* as it was called—are amongst the flowers which blossom on that once hallowed soil.

And now, for the present, Walsingham, oh ! farewell !

Felix et sancta fuisti;
Sis modo qualis eras, sic pia vota petunt !

WARWICK.

Richard Beauchamp, Earl of Warwick, who died at Rouen on the 30th April, 1439, by his will, dated Caversham, 9th August, 1435, leaves directions that he is to be buried within the Collegiate Church of Our Ladye of Warwick :

"Where I will that in such place as I have already devised (which is well known), there be made a chapell of our Ladye, well, faire, and goodly built, within the middle of which chapell I will that my tombe be made.

"Allsoe I will that in the name of Herryott to

---

[169] See remarks on this peculiarity by the late Sir F. Madden.   *Archæologia,* v. xx.

[170] *Journal of Royal Arch. Inst.* v. xiii. pp. 126, 127.

[171] Lysons, *Magna Britannia, Cornwall,* p. 35.

our Ladye there be given myne image of gold, and of our Ladye there to abide for evermore.[172]

This is the description of the image of our Ladye from the inventory taken on the last day of March, 1468.

"A feire ymage of gold of oure ladi goddes moder crouned with gold beryng hir sone in the right arme holdyng in his hande a braunche made of a ruby and iiij. perles and in the middes of thoo iiij. perles is pight a litel grene stone. This ymage stant on a tablement of gold, whuche tablement and the forseide crowne are richly garnished wᵗ perles balices and safiers completly as it was furst made save onely in the said tablemēt ther failleth in ii places. This ymage my seide lord late Erl of Warrewik bequath for his heriet to his chirche colleg' aforeseide therein to abide for evermore. And this ymage weieth in al p'cious stones and gold as it is now $\frac{xx}{iiij}$ and xv unc and di unc.[173] And it bereth in heighte fro the lower side of the tablement to the over part of the crowne xx unches large."[174]

WELLS.

There was a foundation for the support of a lamp to burn before the image of our Ladye in the cathedral.[175]

In 1311, by his will, Richard de Chepmanslade, vicar of Wells, leaves 40 *d.* for the light of our Ladye where the *Salve Sancta Parens* is sung, behind the high altar.[176]

WENSLEYDALE.

Our Ladye of Wynsladale, mentioned under Coverham.[177] I have not ascertained which particular sanctuary of our Ladye in Wensleydale in the North Riding of Yorkshire was known by that name.

WESTMINSTER.

I. The Abbey.

Henry the Third pulled down the abbey built by St. Eadward, and laid the first stone of the

[172] *Notices of the Churches in Warwickshire.* Warwick, 1847, vol. i. p. 54.
[173] *i.e.* 95½ oz.   [174] *Notices, ut sup.* p. 56.   [175] *Valor Eccl.* vol. i. p. 139.
[176] *Third Report of the Royal Commission on Historical MSS.* p. 361.
[177] See *ante*, p. 27.

new one in the fifth year of his reign, 1220. The erection occupied fifty years.

The Queen set up the celebrated silver image of our Blessed Ladye in the feretory of St. Eadward; and in the twenty-eighth year of his reign, Henry the Third caused Edward Fitz-Odo, keeper of his works at Westminster, to place upon the forehead of that image of our Ladye an emerald and a ruby taken out of two rings which the Bishop of of Chichester had left to the said King for a legacy.[178]

On the opposite side was an ivory image of our Ladye which had been highly prized by St. Thomas of Canterbury, and offered by him to the shrine of St. Eadward.

In the same year, 1220, Henry the Third laid also the foundation of our Ladye's chapel, called the New Work, to which he gave his coronation spurs, as is proved by one of the Close Rolls.

"The King, &c. Deliver from our treasure to the Prior of Westminster our gold spurs, which were made for our first coronation at Westminster, which we have given to the New Work of the chapel of Blessed Marye at Westminster. Tested at Westminster, 19 November."[179]

This chapel of our Ladye was taken down by Henry the Seventh, who replaced it by the one generally now called by his name. It had the indulgence of the *Scala Cœli*, which Pope Alexander the Sixth had given to the chapel of St. George at Windsor. Henry the Seventh had originally determined to be buried at Windsor, and consequently obtained this Pardon from the Sovereign Pontiff; but having changed his mind and resolved to build the chapel of our Ladye at Westminster, in which his body should be laid, he had this indulgence transferred to it by Pope Julius the Second, in whose Bull, dated 20th May, 1504, these details are set forth. The indulgence, however, was not general; it was confined to three of the monks and one secular priest.[180]

---

[178] Stow, bk. vi. p. 8.   [179] Close Rolls. 5 Hen. III. vol. i. p. 440.
[180] *Mon. Angl.* vol. i. p. 320.

2. Our Ladye at the North Door.

The inventory of Westminster Abbey, taken at the dissolution, mentions

"Oon cote of clothe of golde for Oᵣ Ladye at yᵉ North Dore."[181]

NOTE.—In this series more than one notice has occurred of images of our Ladye at the north door of churches. Thus the celebrated image of Our Ladye of Chatham[182] is believed to have stood in a niche over the entrance-arch to the north porch ; and one of the most venerated images in London was that of Our Ladye of Grace at the north dore of Polles, *i.e.* St. Pauls.[183] Here also stood the celebrated "Rood of North Dore," as it is so often called, which, according to the legend, was believed to have been carved by St. Joseph of Arimathea.[184] It was taken down on St. Bartholomew's eve (August 24), 1538, by Richard Sampson, Dean of St. Paul's and Bishop of Chichester.[185]

Such a remarkable episode in regard of an image of our Blessed Ladye "at the North Door," occurs in the *fasti* of the Church of England as by law established, for this present year, 1876, that I feel I am justified in making a brief mention of it.

During the months of April and May, some curious correspondence relating to the restoration of Bristol Cathedral appeared in the *Times.* In the north porch the Restoration Committee had erected statues or images of the four Doctors, St. Ambrose, St. Augustine, St. Gregory, and St. Jerom ; and over the archway, in a niche or tabernacle, they had, most correctly and properly, placed an image of our Blessed Ladye, the Glorious Virgin Marye, Mother of God.

The presence of this image of the Blessed Mother of God over the north door had a marvellous effect upon the Dean. Evidently he feared

---

[181] *Transactions of the London and Middlesex Arch. Inst.* vol. iv. p. 342.

[182] See *ante*, p. 11.   [183] See *ante*, p. 70.

[184] *Life of St. Joseph of Arimathea.* Early English Text Society, vol. xliv. p. 44.

[185] Wriothesley, *Chron. of England*, vol. i. p. 84.

its influence upon others, and he caused it to be destroyed.

Forthwith a correspondence ensued between the Dean and the architect, Mr. Street, which was published. Mr. Street, after replying to certain inquiries of the Dean, asks: "Is it impossible to arrive at a peaceful solution of this difficulty even now? I should be only too glad to do anything to facilitate such an end." Four days later, Dean Elliot answers Mr. Street's question in a letter, in which he says: "I desire very ardently a 'peaceful solution' of the question, but it must be founded, as a *sine qua non*, on the substitution of Scripture characters for those which have been taken away." To this Mr. Street replies as follows: "Dear Mr. Dean,—I will send your letter received this morning on to the Nave Restoration Committee. They will probably be better able than I am to understand your concluding paragraph. I understood that you objected to the substitution of a Scriptural subject for a passage from a story of St. Augustine, in the niche over the archway, in which I now suppose I was mistaken, and I am informed that your agents have destroyed the figure of the Blessed Virgin, *than which it is difficult to conceive a more Scriptural character.*[186] I suppose they must have done this by mistake, in which case its restoration will be a very pleasant task for me." The Dean, in forwarding the correspondence for publication, expresses his fear "that we are yet far from a 'peaceful solution' of the matter."[187]

Under the date of the 25th April, Dean Elliot sends to the *Times* portions of a letter addressed by him to the chairman of the Restoration Committee, "explaining the course taken by the Dean and Chapter." This document is dated Saturday, 15th April, 1876. It is only necessary to quote an extract.

"Leaving the correspondence to tell its own tale, I must now ask your attention to what I am about to say as to the motives or reasons on which I founded my objection to the employment

[186] The italics are mine.   [187] *Times*, April 19, 1876.

or retention of these figures, as also of that of the Virgin Mary, in or about the porch, and why I deprecate any attempt to replace them there.

" First of the Virgin Mary.

" I object, because I accept the spirit of the Act of Edward the Sixth, commanding the removal of certain images as essentially wise.

" I think that at the time of the Reformation they were wisely removed. I think that at this time there is afloat far too much of the spirit of the idolatry against which that Act was directed, to allow its suggestions, if not its positive directions, to be disregarded.

" I object, then, to any separate statue or effigy of the Virgin Mary being erected in any part of the cathedral, because I believe its presence there would be illegal, and if not illegal, its presence there would in some sort or degree be supposed to countenance a feeling towards the Blessed Virgin, growing up in our Church, which for my part I cannot distinguish from Mariolatry, and if not from Mariolatry, then not from infidelity and ingratitude towards that God most merciful, Who hath given us in His Son, the mediator and the intercessor, on Whose name only those who call shall be saved.

" Next as to the four images which have been removed.

" I object to them certainly not on any motive derived from the Act of Edward the Sixth.

" I do not know—indeed, I do not believe—that these images are idolatrous, or could be supposed to lead to idolatry, and are therefore illegal.

.   .   .   .   .   .

" That porch is illustrated richly, perhaps beautifully, by figures of all the hierarchy of the Holy Scriptures of the later Testament. I should have thought it incongruous that figures of men, albeit of purest, highest character, should have been mingled with these."

It certainly is an astounding opinion that the Blessed Virgin Marye Mother of God is an " unscriptural character ;" and it is utterly incom-

P

prehensible how any one professing to be a Christian could venture to express it. Nevertheless, it is most gratifying to learn from such an authority as the Dean of Bristol, that a feeling of devotion to our Blessed Ladye is beginning to grow up in the Anglican Church.

Happily all Anglicans are not of the Bristol iconoclastic school. On the 31st of May, 1855, a distinguished archæologist, Mr. J. R. Walbran, F.S.A., London, Newcastle, and Edinburgh, read a paper before the Yorkshire Architectural Society assembled at Skipton, on some excavations at Fountains Abbey. "There was also found," said Mr. Walbran, "a large image of the Blessed Virgin, 'with her Almighty Infant in her arms,' that had been thrown down from the niche that it occupied above the great western window, bearing the date of 1494. Both figures are headless, and there is little in the composition to attract admiration, yet these might be, even now, not inaptly restored to a position whence for three centuries they had been ignominiously deposed; that emblem of the great patroness of the house, to which generations of faith have directed their eyes with feelings of piety or veneration."[188]

But to return to the North Door.

In the ages of faith the north doors of churches were generally dedicated to our Blessed Ladye; and the reason is given by the celebrated French archæologists, Father Cahier and Father Martin.

"*Le Nord est la region des frimas et des orages, c'est à dire des passions et de l'endurcissement dans le peché; c'est ainsi que Saint Augustin voit revenir du septentrion l'enfant prodigue quand il reprend la route du toit paternel. Les commentateurs d'Ezechiel ne parlent pas autrement; et c'est aussi pourquoi les vieux architectes consacraient le portail septentrional à celle qui est la Mere de Misericorde. C'est le fanal du retour signalant les plages funestes ou le navigateur imprudent court se briser, c'est un cri de*

[188] *Report of the Associated Architectural Societies*, vol. iii. p. 67.

rappel qu'on lui addresse et une invitation à se jeter dans le fort."[180]

All honour, therefore, to Mr. Street for having revived one of the most interesting and beautiful features of Catholic architecture. It is a most hopeful sign for the future.

3. The chapel of our Ladye called "the Olde Ladye of Pewe."

This chapel stood in the north side of the abbey church, but I have failed to identify it. The only chapels on the north side of a line drawn from East to West through the centre of the church, are those (1) of St. Paul, (2) St. John the Baptist, (3) St. Erasmus, (4) St. John the Evangelist at the corner of the north transept, (5) St. Michael, and (6) St. Andrew, on the east side of the same transept.

The image of Our Ladye of Pewe or Pue was one of Our Ladye of Pity, that is, of our Ladye seated, bearing the dead Body of her Son on her knees; and it is very probable that a celebrated image of Our Ladye of Pity stood in one of these chapels, which, in consequence, may have been called the chapel of Our Ladye of Pue, but which must not be confounded with the renowned chapel of Our Ladye of Pue on the south side of St. Stephen's. This would not be a solitary instance of giving a second name to a chapel. So great was the reputation for sanctity which Mabel, the mother of St. Edmund of Canterbury, bore, that after her burial in the abbey of Abingdon, the chapel in which she was interred was called the chapel of St. Edmund's mother.

The only mention I have found of the Old Ladye of Pue is in the indenture of the foundation of the chapel called of Henry the Seventh, which commences thus—

This Indenture, made the seconde day of Marche, the xxi th yere of the reigne of the moost Cristen and moost excellent kyng henry the vii th, by the grace of god," &c.

---

[180] *Melanges d'Archéologie.* Par les RR. PP. Cahier et Martin, t. i. pp. 82, 83.

It is provided—

"that euery of the said ye monkes shall from the date of thees presentes daily while the world shall endure, except the daies only called Chereth-mas-day, Goode fryday, the Uigill of Estre, and the daies of coronations of kinges and quenes of Englond, dououtlie say their masses in the churche of the said monasterie at the auter in the chapell of oure ladie in the Northside of the same churche called the olde lady of Pewe, unto the tyme of the chapell of our lady in the same monastie which the said king our souerayn lorde hath nowe be-gonne be edified and bilded at the costes and charges of the same king our soverayne lord or his executors, and a Tombe made in the same chapell at the costes and charges of the said princes or her executors for the interement of her body.[190]

II. St. Margaret's.

The following entry occurs in the church-warden's accounts for the year 1545:

"Paid to Mr. Barnard for the table of the Concepcion now standing on the high altar, 16 *l.* 10 *s.* 0 *d.*"[191]

In this instance "table" is used to express a reredos.

The usual form under which the Conception of our Blessed Ladye was represented in the West is designed from the account of the birth of our Ladye which is supplied by the apocryphal gospel of the Nativity of the Blessed Virgin,[192] and the proto-gospel of Jacob.[193] It describes St. Anne in her garden at prayer, receiving, by the mouth of an angel, the promise of the birth of the Blessed Virgin Marye her daughter, and St. Joachim receiving the same promise in the mountains, whither he had retired.

The *Guide of Painting* of Mount Athos follows this ancient narration almost word for word.

[190] Book of Indentures, &c. Lansdowne MS. 441.
[191] Nichols, *Illustrations*, &c. p. 12.
[192] *Evangelia Apocrypha.* Edit. C. Tischendorf. Lipsiæ, 1853, p. 106.
[193] *Ibid.* p. 1.

"The Conception of the Mother of God;—
houses;—a garden with various trees;—in the
centre, St. Anne at prayer;—an angel above
blesses her;—outside the garden a mountain,
where St. Joachim is at prayer;—an angel blesses
him."[194]

And a similar description is also given in the
poem of the Nun of Gandersheim, Hrotsuitha,
who flourished about the year 999.[195]

III. Chapel of St. Stephen.

In the inventory of the plate belonging to this
chapel at the dissolution, a pendant pix is thus
described :

" *Item*, a trinitie of sylver and gilt, iiii angelles
of sylv. and gilt, and an image of Or Ladye and
the holy-gost beryng the Sacrament of sylver and
gylt hangyng ovr the hie aulter of iiicxvi oz. di."
i.e. 316½ oz.[196]

IV. Chapel of Our Ladye of Pewe.

I find this celebrated chapel described in a
variety of ways from the year 1369 to 1525. Our
Ladye de Pewa ; Capella Beate Marie de la Pew ;
Capella de la Pewe; St. Marye in Puwa; Le Pewe;
Our Lady of Piew; St. Marye de Pewa; St. Marye
de la Pewe ; Our Lady of Pue ; Our Ladye of
Pewe, or Scala; Our Ladye of the Pewe; Our
Ladye of Piewe ; Our Ladye of Pyewe; Our
Ladye of Pew ; and Our Lady of Pwe.

The image was one of Our Ladye of Pity,[197]
that is, which represents our Blessed Lady seated,
and bearing our Saviour on her knees, dead, as
He was taken down from the cross.[198] She is
compassionating Him, and at the same time she
is the object of our pity or compassion; and under
this type or representation—and this one only—

---

[194] Didron, *Manual d'Iconographie Chrétienne*, p. 279.

[195] Historia Nativitatis laudabilisque conversationis Intactæ Dei Genetricis, inter poemata Hrotsuithæ monialis Gandersheimensis. Migne, *Patrol. Lat.* t. cxxxvii. coll. 1067, 1068.

[196] *Transactions of London and Middlesex Arch. Inst.* vol. iv. p. 373. See also *ante*, sub Ludlow, p. 99.

[197] *Transactions of London and Middlesex Arch. Inst*, vol iv. p. 373.

[198] See *ante*, p. 29, under the heading of Durham.

is the Blessed Virgin described as Our Ladye of Pity.[199]

Many conjectures have been made as to the meaning or origin of the name. Some say it was so called from the four wells or *puits* which were near it; viz., one in the Speaker's courtyard, another at the eastern extremity of New Palace Yard, a third in Cotton Garden, and the fourth in the south cloister of St. Stephen's chapel, close to the entrance of the room now (1807) used as the Speaker's state dining-room, but which was anciently the Chapel of St. Marye in the vaults, directly under the House of Commons.[200] Others suggest that it may have had some connection with the gild of Our Ladye of Puy, in London.

Neither of these explanations or derivations seem well founded. Any one who is acquainted with old English historical documents knows how common it is to meet with a combination of English, French, and Latin, in one sentence. Thus, *e.g.*, William of Worcester, describing the length of the chapter-house of St. Edmund's Bury, gives it as *longitudo de le chapter-house;* and in the gild-book of the Gild of Our Ladye of Walsingham, there is an entry *pro novi factioni de le new peyr of orgeyns.*[201] Hence *de Pewa* and *de la Pewe* are only common variations for Pue. What, then, is the derivation of Pewe or *Pue?* Three explanations suggest themselves to me, and I offer them without venturing to express any definite opinion myself.

1. In some of the images of Our Ladye of Pity, the Blessed Virgin is sitting upright; in others she is represented as leaning over and embracing her dead Son—almost as if leaning on His Body. Our Ladye, therefore, *qui s'appuye sur son Fils* would soon become Our Ladye *qui s'appuye*, Our Ladye *qui 'puye*, Our Ladye of *Puye* or Pue. Or, again, it may have had reference to the seated attitude of Our Ladye. The Latin

---

[199] For full details see Introduction, chapter on Iconography.

[200] Smith, *Antiquities of Westminster*, London, 1807, p. 123, seq.

[201] *Norwich vol. of Royal Arch. Inst.* p. 145.

word *podium*,[202] whence the Dutch *puyd*, *puye*,[203] the old French *puy*,[204] and the English *pue* or *pew*, are derived, originally meant in the Latin of the middle ages *anything on which we lean.* The meaning is derived from the *podium* [205] of the circus, a word which is used by classical authors. The general signification is retained in the derivative *appodiare*, in modern French *s'appuyer*,[206] to support oneself. By an easy transition it denotes a staff, &c., but this sense of the word is not retained in English. Another derived signification is a heap of stones; hence it came to signify a hill or mountain. *Le Puy Lawrens* and *Le Puy Morin* are, in Latin, *Podium Laurentii, Podium Marini.* A third sense of *podium* was the desk in the stall of a choir, and from signifying the desk it came to mean the seat generally, and thence, in process of time, an enclosed seat or *pue* or *pew*.[207] The word occurs in *Piers Plouhman.*[208]

2. It is by no means improbable that the image of Our Lady of Pue was a copy of the old Lady of Pue in Westminster Abbey. From the

[202] *Podium*, a place made without a wall for men to stand and beholde thynges, an open galerie, also a stage, whereon is set candles or bookes (*Bibliotheca Eliotæ*, or. *Eliotes Dict.* Lond. 1552).

[203] *Puye*, Lieu esleué au marché ou deuant la maison de la ville pour publier quelque chose (Sasbout, *Dictionaire Flameng-Francoys*. 1576).

[204] *Pieu*, a stake (Furetière. *Dict. universel des mots François.* La Haye, 1690).

[205] *Podium*, projectura in summo muro arenam circi vel amphitheatri proxime cingente. Quia vero podium arenæ proximum erat, ideo dignissimus is orchestræ gradus (nam plurium orchestra graduum erat) qui proximus podio; fuitque is latior, cum in eo suggestus fuerit Imperatoris; ac consules, prætores, aliique, quibus id jus, sederint in eo, sellis curulibus cum lictoribus, apparitoribus, et magistratus sui pompa. Sed et in eodem fuit tribunal editoris, et Virginum Vestalium sedes. Dicitur etiam de quolibet loco porrecto extra domus parietem, instar pulpiti qui aliter dicitur *Mænianum* (Facciolati).

Podium, baston pour apoier, ou appoieur (Du Cange).

[206] *Appodiare*, appuyer, s'appuyer. In the Roman *de Floire.* MS.—

"L'en li amoine un vaïron
Tos fut coverts d'un siglaton
Li Seneschaux i est puié."

Appodiamentum, appuy (*ibid.*).

[207] In 1458, Will. Wintringham wills his body to be buried, . . . and an inscription to be fixed in the wall near his wife's pew—*Ad sedile vocas' Anglice* pewe (Gough, *Sepulch. Monum.* vol. ii. p. 171).

[208] Among wives and wodewes ich am ywoned sate yparroked in pewes. *Passus* vii. p. 95, ed. Whitaker, Lond. 1813.

foregoing evidence, it seems very likely that the image in the Abbey was placed on a large bracket or stand, like the image of Our Ladye of Pity in the church in Farm Street, or perhaps on a platform approached by steps, like an altar. This would account for the name.

3. Pity or Pitie, contracted, in old English becomes *ptie*, and those who are acquainted with the manner of writing in those days well know that it only required a careless scribe, or the omission of the cross stroke of the t, to make *ptie* into *pue*.

I have found no record of the date of the building of this chapel, or by whom it was founded. That of St. Stephen's was built by King Stephen, and rebuilt by Edward the Third. The exact position of Our Ladye of Pue has not been ascertained, but it was not far from the chapel of St. Stephen's, if indeed it did not join it.

During the reign of Richard the Second, a dispute as to jurisdiction arose between the Abbot of Westminster and the Dean of St. Stephen's, and an appeal on the subject was made to Rome. A composition was entered into between them by which it was agreed, *in primis*, that the chapel of St. Stephen, and the chapel of the Blessed Virgin Marye *sub volta*, and their respective vestibules, above and below, and the little chapel contiguous to the said chapel of St. Stephen on the south side, and the chapter-house, and the *chapel de la Pewe*, and the houses or places occupied by thirty-eight persons who serve God in the said chapel of St. Stephen's, &c., be exempt from the jurisdiction of the said Abbot.[200]

Smith quotes from the ceremonial for creating the Duke of York a Knight of the Bath in 1394, in which it is said of the knights then to be created, that they took their way secretly by our Ladye of Pieu through St. Stephen's Chapel on to the "steyr-foote of the ster chamber end." From this it would certainly appear that the chapel of Our Lady of Pue was on the south side of St. Stephen's Chapel.

[200] Westminster Muniments, at Westminster, parcel. 23, pt. 3.

On the night of the 7th February, 1393, some enemies of God, members of the devil and thieves, broke into the chapel of Blessed Mary de la Pew at Westminster, and carried off many jewels and treasures from it. Shortly afterwards some of them were taken at Oxford, and the plunder was recovered.[210] Smith cites a Patent of the 6 March, 16 Richard the Second, *i.e.*, the same year, by which the King grants to the Dean and Canons of his free chapel at Westminster the restitution of the jewels, ornaments, and other ecclesiastical goods, which had lately been stolen out of the *King's closet of St. Marye de la Pewe*, near the aforesaid chapel, and for that reason forfeited to the King.[211] I give this Patent on the authority of Smith, for I have had a search made for it among the Patent Rolls in the Public Record Office, and it cannot be found. This I much regret, because, if Smith quotes it correctly, the term "King's closet" being applied to the chapel of Our Ladye of Pue, would warrant the belief that it adjoined St. Stephen's, and formed what would now be called the Royal Tribune or Pew, and opening or communicating with the Royal Chapel of St. Stephen's, and thus the image would be called Our Ladye of the King's Pue, Our Ladye of the Pue. It is impossible, however, to form a decided opinion without seeing the exact words of the Patent, and Smith does not say whether he saw the original himself, or took it on the authority of some other writer.[212]

Newcourt mentions that, on the 29th September, 1369, King Edward the Third gave to John Bulwick out of his exchequer ten marks yearly, to celebrate Mass every day before the image of Our Ladye the Blessed Virgin Marye, in this chapel of

---

[210] *Life of Richard II.* By a Monk of Evesham. Ed. Hearne. Lond. 1729, p. 125.
[211] *Antiquities of Westminster.* London, 1807, pp. 123, seq.
[212] Cf. Ward.

> "Kirks thus prepar'd for Common Pray'r,
> In new-erected closets there
> They sit 'em down ; I mean in Pews,
> As close as Hawks are penn'd in Mews "
>   (*England's Reformation.* Lond. 1719. Canto I. p. 98).

Our Ladye, near to the King's chapel of
St. Stephen, Westminster.[213]

In 1381 Richard the Second went to pray in
this chapel before setting out to meet the rebels
under Wat Tyler at Smithfield. Froissart con-
founds the chapel of Our Ladye of Pue with one
in Westminster Abbey, unless he was alluding to
the chapel of the old Ladye of Pue in the north
side of the Abbey church; but anyhow, Lord
Berners changes the text in his translation, and
construes *en celle eglise*, "besyde the churche"—
i.e., near to, or hard by.

"The Saturday (after Corpus Christi, 15 June),
the Kynge departed fro the Warderobe in the
Royall, and went to Westmynster and harde
masse in the churche there and all his lordes
with hym; and besyde the churche there was a
lytel chapell, with an image of our lady, which
did great miracles, and in whom the Kynges of
Englande had ever great truste and confydence.
The Kynge made his orisons before this image
and dyd there his offeryng; and then he lepte on
his horse and all his lordes, and so the Kyng rode
towarde London."[214]

Smith mentions a foundation of five shillings
yearly, which was made in 1411 for an anniversary
for John Ware, late a Canon of St. Stephen's, and
directed to be applied for the maintenance of a
silver lamp before the image of St. Marye in Pewa
every day in the year, from the first opening of

---

[213] *Repertorium*, v. i. p. 722, giving the ref. "Rot. Pat. 43 Edw. III. p. 2," but
this ref. cannot be found. It is rather vague, but the roll has been well searched.

[214] *Chronicles*. Lord Berner's translation, reprint. London, 1812, v. i. cap. 384,
p. 649. "Le Samedi au matin se départyt le Roy d'Angleterre de la Garderobbe la
Royne (qui sied en la Riolle) et s'en vint a Westmontier & ouyt Messe en l'Eglise &
tous les Seigneurs avec luy. En celle église a vn image de Nostre Dame en vne petite
chapelle : qui fait de grans miracles & de grans vertus, et a laquelle [another version
has en laquelle] les Roys d'Angleterre ont tousiours eu grand 'confiance et creance.
Là fit le Roy ses oraisons deuant ceste image : & s'offrit à elle et puis monta à cheval
et aussi tous les Barons qui la estoyent delez luy, et pouuoit estre enuiron heure de
tierce" (*Histoire et Cronique de Messire Jehan Froissart. Reueus & corrigé sus diuers
Exemplaires & suyuant les bons Auteurs par Denis Sauvage de Fontenailles en Brie.
Historiographe du Trescrestien Roy Henri IIe. de ce nom.* A. Lyon par Ian de Tovmes.
Imprimevr du Roy, 1559, tom. ii. p. 141). Buchon's edition gives the same almost
word for word, liv. ii. c. 135, t. 8, p. 49. Paris, 1824.

the chapel in the morning to its closing late in the evening.[215]

In 1452 this chapel and the celebrated image of our Blessed Ladye were consumed by fire. Stow says—"Amongst other things of this chapel I have read that, on the 17 February, 1452, by negligence of a scholar appointed by his schoolmaster to put forth the lights of this chapel, the image of Our Ladye, richly decked with jewels, precious stones, pearls, and rings—more than any jeweller could judge the price for—was, with all this apparel, ornaments, and the chapel itself, burnt, but since re-edified by Anthonie, Earl Rivers, and Lord Scales."[216]

Some years, however, must have elapsed before the chapel of Our Ladye of Pue was rebuilt, for at this time Antony Widvile was only ten years old, he having been born in 1442. And whilst the chapel remained in ruins, that of Our Ladye *sub volta* seems to have been used, because, on the 19th July, 1453, Bishop Lyndwoode made a foundation for a chauntry in the chapel of St. Marye *de Pewa*, the chauntry being described as *infra bassam capelle S. Stephani Westm.*[217]

It is also said that Earl Rivers obtained for this chapel the Pardon of the *Scala Cæli* at Rome, and in 1480 the chapel is described as Our Ladye of Pewe or Scala.

In the description of the reception of Louis de Gruthuyse in England in 1472, it is mentioned that "the said Lord went into a chamber by Our Ladye of Pue, and put upon him the habiliments of an Erle.[218]

The unfortunate Antony Widvile, Earl Rivers, when a prisoner in Pontefract Castle, and expecting his untimely death, bequeathed his heart to Our Ladye of Pue, as I have already mentioned.[219]

In 1498, Anne Lady Scrope, widow of John Lord Scrope of Bolton, by her will, dated

[215] *Antiq. of Westminster,* l.c.
[216] Bk. vi. p. 2, ed. Strype.
[217] Rot. Pat. 32, Hen. VI. m. 4. This patent has been found.
[218] *Archæologia,* v. xxvi. p. 281.
[219] See ante, p. 128.

28th August, 1498, left one decade of her great beads of gold to Our Ladye of Pue.[220]

Our Ladye of Pue was a most favourite chapel for the celebration of Masses of Requiem. Smith quotes a deed of foundation for an anniversary for Richard Green and his parents and relations, dated the 28th July, 1480, in which it is stated, as a reason for choosing that sanctuary, that it was a spot of great devotion, by the frequent attestation of miracles, abounding in indulgences, as well for the benefit of the living as for the relief of the departed, and particularly the indulgence *de Scala Dei,* otherwise *de Scala Cæli.*

The church of S. Maria *de Scala,* at Rome was one of the three at the Three Fountains, or *Aquæ Salviæ,* beyond St. Paul's without the Walls. It was so called because it is said that one day, when St. Bernard was celebrating Mass in it, he beheld a ladder reaching from earth to heaven, by which were ascending to eternal glory the souls of those for whom he was offering the Holy Sacrifice.[221]

Antóny Widvile, Earl Rivers, by his will, desires that they who succeed to the lands of his first wife shall devote five hundred marks for sundry purposes, one of which was to find a priest for one year at Our Lady of Pue, to pray for the souls of his brothers and all Christian souls.[222]

The will of Elizabeth Uvedale, dated 14th October, 1487, contains the following legacy.

"*Item.* To a devoute prieste x*l.* to sing Seint Gregories trentalle at Our Ladye of Pewe, or Scala, which if it not be doone by my life, then I carge you my said Ex°ⁿ that it be doone as soon as I am deceased, as ye will answer afore God."[223]

On the 9th of May, 1494, Henry the Seventh offered £2 at Our Ladye of the Pewe,[224] and on the 14th July there occurs this entry—

[220] Test. Ebor. v. iv. p. 153.

[221] Migne, *Dict. des Pélérinages religieux,* t. ii. col. 811.

[222] *Test. Vet.* p. 379.

[223] *Surrey Archæol. Collections,* v. iii. pp. 169, 170.

[224] Privy Purse Expenses. *Excerpt. Historica,* p. 98.

"To my lady the Kinge's Moder for the wages of Sir John Bracy singing before Our Ladye of the pewe, for a quarter's wages, £2."[225]

Several offerings of Elizabeth of York are recorded.

"1502. March 24.

"Offering to Our Lady of Piewe, iis. viid.[226]

"June 14.

"*Itm.*, to John Hamerton for money by him delivered to the Quene for his offring at hire departing from West^m to Our Ladye of Piewe and to Bowe, vis. ixd.[227]

"*Itm.*, (same day), to Thomas Spurley, for money by him delivered for thoffring of the Quene to Oure Lady of Piewe, viid.[228]

"December 8.

"*Itm.*, for thoffering of the Quene to Oure Lady of Pyewe upon thevyn of the Concepcōn of Our Lady, vis. viiid.

"*Itm.*, for thoffering of the Quene upon the day of the Concepcōn of Oure Lady, vs.[229]

"December 13.

"*Itm.*, for thoffering of the Quene to Oure Lady of Pyewe at hure departing from West-minstre to the Towre, vis. viiid.

"*Itm.*, to a monk that brought Our Lady gyrdelle to the Quene in rewarde, vis. viiid.[230]

There are many records of Masses being celebrated at our Ladye of Pewe.

In the household accounts of Elizabeth of York :

"February 26, 1503.

"*Item*, to Sir Robert Byrche singing at our Ladye of Piewe, vil. xiiis. iiijd."[231]

In the King's book of payments there are many such items.

1511. January (no date) apparently the 1st

[225] *Excerpt. Historica*, p. 99.
[226] Privy Purse Expenses, p. 3.
[227] *Ibid.* p. 21.
[228] *Ibid.* p. 23.
[229] *Ibid.* p. 77.
[230] *Ibid.* p. 78.
[231] P. 102.

"To Dr. Rawson, for 42 priests singing at our Ladye of Piewe on All Souls Day, 8 *d.* each.[232]

"1512. January.

"Dr. Rawson. Masses at our Ladye of Pewe on All Souls Day, 32 *s.*[233]

"——. December 5—12.

"To Dr. Rawson, for Masses at our Ladye of Pewe on All Souls Day, 43 *s.*[234]

"1515. February. The King at Greenwich.

"Dr. Rawson, for 25 priests singing 25 Masses before our Ladye of Pewe on All Souls Day, 16 *s.* 8 *d.*[235]

"1516. January. The King at Greenwich.

"Dr. Rawson, for 49 priests at our Ladye of Pewe, 8 *d.* each.[236]

"1519. January.

"To Dr. Rawson, for Masses said at our Ladye of Pewe, 15 *l.* 14 *s.* 3 *d.*[237]

"——. December.

".To Dr. Rawson, for 54 priests singing for the King at our Ladye of Piew on All Souls Day, each 8 *d.*"[238]

Such was the early piety of King Henry the Eighth.

On the 5th July, 1508, the Duke of Buckingham offered 3 *s.* 4 *d.* to our Ladye of Pewe;[239] in June, 1514, on the morrow after Ascension Day, Henry the Eighth offered 10 *s.*;[240] on the 31st January, 1519, Henry Courtenay, Earl of Devon offered 4 *d.*;[241] and in the expenses of the journey of the Earl of Cumberland, newly created, from Skipton to London, amongst the almonses and offerands is mentioned one of 1 *s.* viii *d.* to our Ladye of Pewe.[242]

A visit to our Ladye of Pewe was included in the ceremonies attendant on the creation of serjeants-at-law, which occupied several days; thus

[232] Letters and Papers, &c., Henry VIII. v. ii. pt. ii. p. 1449.
[233] *Ibid.* p. 1454.   [234] *Ibid.* p. 1458.   [235] *Ibid.* p. 1466.
[236] *Ibid.* p. 1469.   [237] *Ibid.* p. 1533.   [238] *Ibid.* p. 1538.
[239] Letters and Papers, &c., Henry VIII. v. iii. pt. i. p. 497.
[240] *Ibid.* v. ii. p. ii. p. 1464.   [241] *Ibid.* v. iii. pt. i. p. 51.
[242] Whitaker, *Hist. and Antiq. of the Deanery of Craven.* London, 1805: p. 232.

in Trinity Term in the thirteenth of Henry VIII.
—1521—Dugdale says that—

"Vpon Tewesday the said new serjeants goo ageyn in sober maner to Westminster with the said Warden of the Flete and the Marchall, and odyr offycers affore them, and their servaunts after them in their lyveries; and goo thorough Westminster-Hall onto ower Lady of Pewe."[243]

WESTON, SUFFOLK. This church formerly possessed a celebrated image of our Blessed Ladye. Here in the tower is a Gabriel bell inscribed—

"MISSUS VERO PIE GABRIEL FERT LETA MARIE."[244]

WHITBY ABBEY. In 1461 Dame Catherine Pease, of Whitby, by her will, proved the 24th February, ordered her sepulture at the place where our Ladye's Mass was daily sung.[245]

WILLESDEN. A very ancient pilgrimage; and our Ladye of Willesden is often mentioned.

In the expenses of Elizabeth of York:

"March 24, 1502.

"Offering to oure Ladye of Willesdone ij *s.* vi *d.*

"February 26, 1503.[246]

"*Item*, to a man that went on pilgremage to our Ladye of Willesden by the Quene's command-ment, iij *s.* iiij *d.*[247]

"In 1517 William Lychefelde, clerk, desires to be buried in the parish church at Willesden before the image of the Blessed Virgine.[248]

WINCHESTER. Our Ladye of Winchester is described by Guppenberg as *Speciosa*, and he relates a story on the authority of Gonon—reference not given —who says he had read it in an ancient MS.; but it is needless to give it, since it has no his-torical interest.[249]

The celebrated image of our Ladye of Win-chester stood against the fifth pillar on the south

---

[243] *Origines Juridicales.* London, 1671. Cap. xliv. p. 114.
[244] Suckling. v. i. 99.　　[245] Burton, *Monasticon Eboracense*, p. 82.
[246] P. 3.　　[247] *Ibid.* p. 96.　　[248] Test. Vet. p. 564.
[249] Atlas Marianus, n. dclxxxiii. p. 744.

side of the nave of the church, and an altar was erected before it. Great was the popular devotion to it; and many votive offerings adorned the pillars. Conspicuous amongst the numerous clients of our Lady was William of Wykeham, who constantly came to pray before this image; and before which he was buried. Speaking of the beautiful Wykeham chantry, his Protestant biographer, Dr. Louth, says that it was not well chosen in in regard of the building, "but Wykeham was determined to the choice of this peculiar place by a consideration of a very different kind—by an early prejudice and a strong religious impression which had been stamped on his mind from his childhood. In this part of the old church there had been an altar dedicated to the Blessed Virgin with the image standing above it. At this altar a Mass used to be celebrated every morning, which seems to have been a favourite one and much frequented when Wykeham was a boy and at School at Winchester; for it had gotten a peculiar name among the people, and was called the Pekis-Masse, from the name of a monk of the convent who usually officiated in it. Young Wykeham was constant in his daily attendance and fervent in his devotions at this Mass. He seems even then to have chosen the Blessed Virgin as his peculiar Patroness, to have placed himself under her protection, and in a manner to have dedicated himself to her service; and probably he might ever after imagine himself indebted to her especial favour for the various successes which he was blessed with through his life. This seems to have been the reason of his dedicating to her his two colleges, and calling them by her name, over all the principal gates of which he has been careful to have himself represented as her votary in the act of adoration to the Blessed Virgin as his and their common guardian; and this it was that determined this situation of his chantry. He erected his chapel in the very place where he had been used to perform his daily devotions in his younger days—between the two pillars against one of which stood the altar above-mentioned.

He dedicated the chapel to the Blessed Virgin. The altar was continued in the same place as before, and probably the very same image was erected above it, which, with the other ornaments of the same kind, both within the chapel and without, was destroyed in the last century by the zeal of modern enthusiasm, exerting itself with a blind and indiscreet rage against all the venerable and beautiful ornaments, whether of ancient piety or superstition !"[250]

In consideration of the benefactions made by the Bishop, of about twenty marks, and for having rebuilt their and his cathedral, the Prior and Convent engaged, by deed dated 16th August, 1404, to have sundry services for the health of his soul and the souls of his parents and benefactors, *inter alia*, three Masses daily in the chapel where he was buried, the first being the Marye Mass. They also engage that the charity boys of the Prior shall, every night for ever, sing at the said chapel, in honour of the Blessed Virgin Marye, the anthem *Salve Regina*, or *Ave Regina*, and the *De profundis*.[251]

The Ladye Chapel at Winchester contains some interesting mural paintings illustrative of miracles of our Blessed Ladye, the procession at Rome, and St. Gregory carrying the picture of our Ladye ascribed to St. Luke, the painter saved from a fall, and many others. They were painted in the time of Prior Silkstede, A.D. 1498—1524.

II. The College.

William of Wykeham built the College here, which he dedicated to our Blessed Ladye, whose statue yet stands in a niche over the principal gate, and on one side he is represented on his knees, as at Oxford, over the gate of New College.[252]

Until recently the old Catholic custom was observed by the scholars, who used to take off their caps as they passed our Ladye.[253]

[250] Louth, *Life of William of Wykeham.* Oxford, 1777, p. 255.
[251] *Ibid.* p. 259.
[252] See *ante*, p. 125.
[253] Kindly communicated to me by an old Wintonian.

Q

An antiphon of our Ladye was sung in the evening, until the time of Edward the Sixth, whose commissioners forbade it, saying, " Let the scholars and children henceforth omit to sing or say *Stella Cæli*, or *Salve Regina*, or any such like untrue or superstitious anthem."[254]

Henry the Sixth founded his public school at Eton and his college at Cambridge entirely upon Wykeham's plan, whose statutes he transcribed without any material alteration.[255] Those which bear upon devotion to our Blessed Ladye I have given in the Introduction.

III. THE CASTLE.

The Liberate Rolls contain several mandates of Henry the Third.

In 1238 the King orders the Sheriff of South-ampton to make a Mariola, *i.e.* an image of our Ladye, with a great tabernacle for the chapel of our aforesaid Queen, and a certain painted tablet to be placed before the altar of the same chapel. Writ tested at Woodstock, 14th November.[256]

In 1247 the sheriff of Southampton is ordered to cause to be painted in the King's chapel over the altar, the image of St. Marye; and towards the south in the same chapel the image of God and His Mother. Writ tested at Winchester, 28th December.[257]

In 1252 the sheriff of Southampton is ordered to cause an image of the Blessed Virgin Marye with her Child to be made on the front of the chapel of St. Thomas in Winchester Castle. Writ tested at Winchester, 28th December.[258]

And in 1266 the constable of Winchester Castle is ordered . . . to paint all the doors and windows of the King's hall and chamber with his arms; to make a certain window of white glass, and to cause the Nativity of the Blessed Virgin Marye to be painted in it. Writ tested at Westminster, 11th February.[259]

[254] Walcott, *Hist. of W. of Wykeham and his Colleges*, p. 152.   [255] Louth, p. 180.
[256] Lib. Roll. 23 Henry III.
[257] *Ibid.* 32 Hen. III.   [258] *Ibid.* 37 Henry III.
[259] *Ibid.* 50 Hen. III.

IV. THE CARMELITES.

The church and convent of the Carmelites stood in a close called College Mead, opposite the Church of St. Michael. It was dedicated to the Blessed Virgin, and founded by Peter, who is called the parish priest of St. Helen's, Winchester.[260]

I now resume the narrative of Father Swanyngton, which broke off under the heading of Newenham.[261]

"On the 17th of the kalends of August (*i.e.*, July 16), as the aforesaid blessed Simon, with myself as his companion, was journeying to Winchester to obtain letters commendatory[262] for our Lord Pope Innocent the Fourth from the Bishop of Winchester, who was favourable to our Order, the Dean of the Church of St. Helen's of Winchester, Peter de Lynton, driving at full speed, met us, and implored the blessed Father that he would hasten to assist his brother who was dying in a state of despair. His name was Walter. He had no shame in committing dishonest actions; he was quarrelsome, and addicted to ungodly magic; he despised the sacraments, and harassed his neighbours. One day, quarrelling with another man of noble birth, he was mortally wounded by him, and seeing himself already cited before the Divine Judgment, and the devil putting all the crimes which he had committed before his eyes, he refused to hear either God or the sacraments spoken of; but blaspheming, as long as he had utterance, he yelled out— 'O devil, avenge me on my slayer.' On entering the house we found the man foaming at the mouth, gnashing his teeth and rolling his eyes like a mad dog. Blessed Father Simon, making the sign of the Cross, and throwing the Scapular (*habitus*) over the sick man, raised his eyes and prayed for a token from God that what Christ had ransomed should not become the prey of the

[260] Milner, *History of Winchester*, vol. ii. p. 139; *Mon. Angl.* t. vi. p. 1570.
[261] See *ante*, p. 106.
[262] *Ad impetrandum formatas.* See Ducange for all details about this word.

devil; and all of a sudden the sick man, who was dying, recovered his strength and reason and speech, and signing himself with the sign of salvation, rebuked the demons, and with moans and tears cried out: 'Alas! wretch that I am! how I shake at my eternal damnation! my iniquities have grown above the sands of the sea; have mercy on me, O God, Whose mercy exceeds Thy justice! O Father! help me; I wish to make my confession.' When I had withdrawn into a corner of the house, the aforesaid Dean Peter told me that, seeing the impenitent heart of his brother, he prayed alone in his room, and forthwith this voice reached him: 'Arise, Peter, seek my beloved servant Simon, who is on his way coming to this place.' And looking around to see whence these words proceeded, the voice sounded a second and a third time. Wherefore prudently believing that this was a voice from heaven, he hurried off for his horse, so that he might intercept the venerable Father on his journey; and returned thanks for finding him so opportunely. After his confession Walter publicly renounced the devil, and received the sacraments of the Church, evincing signs of great repentance. He made his will, and having received his brother's assurance on oath that he would carry out his intentions, he desired that the ill-gotten goods should be restored, and that reparation for the injuries he had committed should be made. About the eighth hour of night he peacefully breathed forth his soul, which appeared to his brother, who was in doubts of his salvation, signifying that all was well with him, and that through the most powerful Queen of Angels, by the scapular (*habitus*) of the blessed man as if by a shield, he had escaped the snares of the demons.

"The fame of this event flew through the whole city. Forthwith the said Peter de Lynton went to the venerable Bishop of Winchester, and committing every detail in due order to writing, desired to know his opinion in such an extraordinary circumstance. The Lord Bishop was amazed, and having consulted thereon with his

Chapter, it was determined that the Blessed Simon should be interrogated as to the virtue of the scapular (*habitus*). He appeared before the Lord Bishop, and in obedience to his orders, concealed nothing, and the Lord Bishop desired that everything should be committed to writing under an authentic seal.

" The aforesaid Peter the dean, in thanksgiving for the miracle wrought by the glorious Virgin Marye on his brother, made a foundation for our Brothers in Winchester, giving them ground, and building a very commodious and spacious convent for the Order. The account of this event was spread throughout England and abroad; and many cities offered us dwelling-places; and many of high rank begged to be affiliated to this holy Order, desiring in order to participate in its graces to die with the scapular (*habitus*), so that by the merits of the glorious Virgin Marye they might have a happy departure out of this life. Thus by degrees did the Order of the Blessed Virgin Marye of Mount Carmel, under the favour of our Lord Jesus Christ, and Marye His Blessed Mother, begin, in the West, to be multiplied into many provinces, and the provinces to have many houses, and these convents to have communities which bore great fruit to the augmentation of the Catholic faith."[203]

NOTE.—This narrative of Father Swanyngton will raise an objection, which I will therefore anticipate. He is very precise in his dates: the vision occurred at Newenham before daybreak on the morrow of the Division of the Apostles, *i.e.*, the 16th July,[204] and according to the narrative St. Simon Stock and Father Swanyngton arrived at Winchester on the evening of the 17th of the kalends of August, *i.e.*, the 16th of July, or the same day. Now St. Simon was in his ninety-first year, and Winchester is one hundred and thirteen miles distant from Newenham, or Cambridge, as the bird flies, and in the time of Wykeham the road between London and Winchester was not

[203] *Speculum Carmelitanum*, t. i. p. 519, nn. 2078, 2079.   [204] See *ant.*, p. 106.

in a good condition,[265] consequently it is very unlikely that it was in a more satisfactory state two centuries previously. In the narration there is no allusion to any supernatural manifestation, *i.e.*, as of bi-location, and it would have been a physical impossibility in the thirteenth century for two White Friars to have ridden one hundred and thirteen miles in their habits, within sixteen, or at most eighteen hours, presuming, of course, that they did ride, for it seems by the narration that they must have journeyed on foot. Hence it appears most probable that there is a mistake in the date assigned for the arrival of St. Simon Stock at Winchester.

The learned author of the *Speculum Carmelitanum* suggests another solution of the difficulty, saying:

"It should be noticed that from the context of the narration this miracle appears to have been wrought upon the man Walter, not at Winchester, but in some place between Cambridge and Winchester, as the distance between the two cities would suggest."[266]

WINDHAM, WYNDHAM, or WYMUNDHAM. Here was a gild of our Ladye at her altar, which gild kept a light, called Our Ladye's Light, before her image in her chapel.[267]

Here was also a Light of Jesus. Harpsfeld mentions some miracles wrought at this sanctuary.[268]

William, twenty-second abbot of St. Albans, A.D. 1214—1235, sent a beautifully-illuminated psalter of great price to the Church of St. Marye's, Wymondham, to be chained to a desk which was placed before the high altar and the image of our Ladye which stood over it, so that it might remind the monks who used it to remember the donor in their prayers.[269]

WINDSOR. Although the chapel at Windsor is called that of St. George, it was in reality dedicated to the

---

[265] Louth, *ut supra*, p. 272.
[266] Vol. i. p. 520.   [267] Blomefield, vol. i. p. 735.   [268] Sæc. xv. c. 18.
[269] Gest. Abb. Mon. S. Albani, vol. i. p. 294. Rolls Edit.

honour of our Blessed Ladye, St. George, and St. Edward, King and Confessor. The foundation deed of Edward the Third, dated the 6th of August in the twenty-second year of his reign, evinces great devotion to the Blessed Virgin Marye.[270]

In this chapel there were several images of our Blessed Ladye.

1. The Little Image of our Ladye.

In the inventory of the Treasury taken in the eighth year of Richard the Second, 1384—1385, Sir Walter Almaly being then the custos, there are enumerated four lilies which are wanting in the crown of the little image of the Blessed Virgin Marye. There were also three crowns of silver gilt, adorned with divers precious stones, one of which was for our Ladye, another for her Divine Son, and the third for St. Edward. Five stones were wanting in the crown of our Ladye, and a flower of delicate workmanship in that of our Lord.[271]

2. The image given by Henry the Fourth.

This is described as being made of silver and gilt: in her right arm our Ladye bears her Divine Son, Who is playing with a bird.[272]

The following entry occurs in the Issue Rolls of the Exchequer, Michaelmas, the sixth of Henry the Sixth, November 11, 1427:

"To our lord the King in his chamber. In money paid to the same chamber by the hands of Conus Melver, goldsmith, for the value of 20 lbs. 3½ oz. of silver in mass, purchased for repairing an image of the Blessed Marye for the King's Chapel of St. George in Windsor Castle, price the pound, 30*s.*, 30*l.* 8*s.* 4*d.*"[273]

3. The silver image given by Henry the Sixth.

Issue Rolls of the Exchequer, March 11, 1428.

"To our lord the King in his chamber. In money paid to the same chamber by the hands of Conus Melver, goldsmith, for making a certain

---

[270] Rot. Pat. 22 Edward III., p. 2. m. 6; *Mon. Angl.* v. vi. pp. 1351—1356.
[271] *Mon. Angl.* vol. vi. p. 1367. [272] *Ibid.* p. 1364.
[273] Issue Rolls of Exchequer, p. 357.

image of the Blessed Virgin Marye for St. George's within the King's Castle of Windsor, 30 *l.* o *s.* o *d.*"[274]

4. Our Ladye behind the high altar.

This is mentioned by Foxe. Speaking of one Robert Testwood, a chorister in the Royal Chapel at Windsor, he says :

"It chanced Testwood one day to walk in the church, at afternoon, and to behold the pilgrims, especially of Devonshire and Cornwall, how they came by plumps, with candles and images of wax in their hands, to offer to good King Henry of Windsor."[275]

Testwood spoke to a group of them against pilgrimage, &c.

"Then he went further and found another sort licking and kissing a White Lady made of alabaster, which image was mortised in a wall behind the high altar, and bordered about with a pretty border, which was made like branches, with hanging apples and flowers. And when he saw them so superstitiously use the image as to wipe their hands upon it, and then to stroke them over their eyes and faces, as though there had been great virtue in touching the picture, he up with his hand, in which he had a key, and smote down a piece of the border about the image, and with the glance of the stroke chanced to break off the image's nose. 'Lo, good people !' quoth he, 'you see what it is—nothing but earth and dust, and cannot help itself; and how then will it help you? For God's sake, brethren, be no more deceived.' And so he gat him home to his house, for the rumour was so great, that many came to see the image how it was defaced."[276]

This sacrilegious wretch lost his life under Henry the Eighth, for denying the Real Presence. Our Ladye of Windsor is mentioned in the household book of Elizabeth of York.

March 24, 1502.

Itm., delivered to Sir William Barton preest for thofferinges of the Quene to our Ladye and

---

[274] Issue Rolls of Exchequer, p. 358.

[275] *i.e.*, Henry VI.

[276] *Book of Martyrs.* Edit. Cattley, vol. v. p. 467. London, 1838.

St. George at Wyndesoure and to the holy crosse there. ii *s.* vi *d.*[277]

WINFARTHING, NORFOLK.

Nathaniel Hallyet was a benefactor, who, at the same time, founded a light before Our Ladye of Peace, to the value of 2 *s.*, for which he tied a close called Cokkys close.[278]

WOOLPIT.

Is mentioned in the Atlas Marianus.

The church is described as one of the most interesting in Suffolk. One of the choir seats in the chancel has an elegant figure of our Ladye with the pot of lilies by her side.

1. Our Ladye of Woolpit appears to have been an image of repute in the county and much frequented by pilgrims. It was situated in the chapel of our Ladye at the end of the south aisle, and stood under a rich canopy or tabernacle, which appears, from the will of John Stevynesson, to have been newly made in 1451. In 1469, Geoffrey Coley bequeathed one wax candle, of a pound and a half weight, to burn during Divine Service. In the will of Robert Agas, of Thurston, our Ladye of Woolpit is enumerated as one of the seven local pilgrimages which he directed his son to "go or do gon." In 1507, John Calabour bequeathed to oure Ladye of Wolpitte a gold rynge.[279]

In 1474, Dame Elizabeth Andrews leaves one of her two diamond rings to our Ladye of Woolpit.[280]

2. Our Ladye of Pity.

In this church was also an image of Our Ladye of Pity. In 1477, Amy Fen bequeathed to the painting of Our Ladye of Pyte in this church, 20 *s.* and 20 *d.*, and two bushels of malt. It is not known where this image was situated.[281]

In connection with our Ladye of Woolpit, it may be mentioned that in a meadow near the church is a far-famed well, called Ladye's well,

[277] P. 3. [278] Blomefield, vol. i. p. 120.
[279] *Proceedings of Suffolk Archæological Institute,* vol. ii. p. 196.
[280] *Test. Vet.* 329.
[281] *Proceedings of Suffolk Archæological Institute,* vol. ii. p. 199.

which was the continued resort of pilgrims in former ages. A chapel is said to have formerly existed near this spring, but no vestiges of it remain.[292]

In the household book of Elizabeth of York, on the 24th March, 1502, there is an offering to Our Ladye of Wolpitte of xx*d*.[283]

WOODBRIDGE, SUFFOLK.

There was an image of our Blessed Ladye in the wall of the Priory churchyard, much frequented for the miraculous powers it possessed. The Priory was dedicated to our Blessed Ladye.[284]

WOODSTOCK.

"The King to Walter de Tywe, keeper of the Manor of Woodstock. We command you . . . to make a certain cross with Marye and John, and a certain image of Saint Marye to be placed in the aforesaid new chapel."

Writ tested at Woodstock, 10th September, 1239.[285]

In 1251, John de Haneburg is commanded to crenelate the Queen's chapel at Woodstock . . . and to make a seat in the Queen's chapel for her use; and to cause the image of the Blessed Virgin near the same seat to be better painted.

Writ tested at Woodstock, 3rd February.[286]

In the following year the King commands the wardens of his works at Woodstock to make a glass window with an image of the Blessed Virgin Marye in the new chapel.

Writ tested at Woodstock, 1st February.[287]

And in the month of August of the same year the keepers of the King's manor at Woodstock are ordered to put a tablet painted with the figure of the Blessed Virgin Marye in the chapel of St. Edward.

Writ tested at Woodstock, 29th August.[288]

In 1256 orders are given to repair the chimney of the Queen's inner wardrobe at Woodstock;

[292] *Proceedings of the Suffolk Archæological Institute,* vol. ii. p. 199.   [283] P. 3.
[284] *Ind. Mon. Diœc. Norv.* p. 117; *Mon. Angl.* vol. vi. p. 600.
[285] Lib. Rolls, 23 Hen. III.   [286] *Ibid.* 35 Hen. III.   [287] *Ibid.* 36 Hen. III.
[288] *Ibid.*

and to buy a certain image of the Blessed Virgin Marye for the chapel of the King's chamber there. Writ tested at Woodstock, 20th February.[289]

WORCESTER.

Originally founded in 678 or 680, and dedicated to St. Peter; it was served by a chapter of secular clerks, and was soon called St. Marye's.[290]

The first mention of the church as St. Marye's Minster is in a charter of the year 743.[291]

In 983, Oswald completed the new Minster, which he dedicated to our Blessed Ladye, and in which he erected twenty-eight altars.[292]

Pre-eminent amongst the benefactors to this church are Leofric and Godgifu, Earl and Countess of Mercia, although there is evidence in connection with Worcester, that, in his younger days, the Earl was not such a devoted son of Holy Church as his subsequent acts proved him to have become, and to which I have alluded under the heading of Coventry.[293] Heming says, that about the year 1007, many lands were taken from the Church. Heamton belonged to the monastery, because Wlstan or Wulstan recovered it by law from Earngate, the son of Grim, but could not obtain possession of it because Earl Leofric, who greatly favoured Earngate, prevented it, and kept it by force. Earngate besought the Bishop to make his son a monk, but Wlstan refused, insisting that he should do right to the Church, and restore all the land, or, at least, give that portion of it, called *Thiccan Apel Treo*, to it, together with his son. But Earngate refused, saying that his son should have it after him; they came to no agreement, and in little time he had not one son of his family left to inherit it.[294]

In Oxfordshire, one Simund, a Dane, a soldier of Earl Leofric's, endeavoured to dispossess the monks of what they had in Crowl, for he so plagued them with suits and trespasses, that he drove away the farmers, and so they were forced

[289] Lib. Rolls, 40 Hen. III. [290] *Angl. Sacra.* vol. i. p. 469.
[291] *Mon. Angl.* vol. i. p. 567. [293] *Ibid.* p. 568.
[292] See *ante.* p. 19. [294] *Chartular. Eccl. Wigorn.* pp. 260, 261.

to grant the lands to him for his life, on condition that he should serve for them in the wars by sea and land, and should acknowledge the prior for his lord, by paying, yearly, a horse, or money in lieu thereof.[205] But to make some amends for their losses, Earl Leofric, on the death of his father, Leofwine, restored to them Wulfardlea and Blackwell, which had for a long time been withheld from them. And he also promised to restore to them at his death Chadesley, Beolne, Broctun, and Forfeld.[206]

On the death of Earl Leofric in 1057, Godgifu, who is described as a lady of great praise, came to the monks and gave them for the health of his and her soul three cloaks, two curtains, two coverings for benches, two candlesticks finely wrought, and a library, desiring that she might hold these lands during her life, paying yearly a certain sum of money, and that at her death they should return to the abbey, to which the monks readily assented.[207]

Earl Leofric was represented in two of the windows of the monastery, with the inscription, *Leofricus Comes dedit Blackwell.*[208] The real donation, however, was on the part of Leofric and Godgifu, of five hides at Wolverley and two at Blackwell, for the use of the refectory.[209] The charter in Anglo-Saxon together with a translation into Latin is given in the Codex.[300]

1. The celebrated image of Our Ladye of Worcester stood over the high altar. There was a huge image of our Ladye at Worcester, says Burnet, that was had in great reverence, which when it was stripped of some veils that covered it, was found to be the statue of a bishop.[1]

This evidence of Burnet's has been eagerly seized and commented upon by more than one writer, as a proof of the deceit practised by the excellent monks. A more groundless charge was never trumped up; it convicts itself, and is one of the sensational lies of the period.

---

[205] *Chartular. Eccl. Wigorn*, p. 265. [206] *Ibid.* p. 261. [207] *Ibid.* pp. 261, 262.
[208] Thomas, pp. 18—32. [209] Heming, p. 408.
[300] Vol. iv. pp. 72, 73. Chart. DCCLXV. [1] *Hist. of Reformation*, 1681, vol. i. p. 243.

In the first place there was nothing unusual if the image had been a colossal one. It was a principal object in the church, and therefore had to be seen from a distance. But an image of our Ladye would have had her Divine Son in her arms, for an image of our Ladye alone would have been most unusual at that period, and therefore our Lord would have been missed at once if the bishop had been substituted for our Blessed Ladye. Nevertheless the reformers were quite capable of making such a substitution. And as far as regards the size of the statue, an image of our Ladye called "the long," *dite la Longue; die lange Moeder Godts*, was venerated in the Church of Notre Dame at Bruges.[2]

The commissioners in their report to Cromwell are silent as to the discovery of the bishop, but Latimer calls the image of our Ladye the "grett Sibyll." "I trust your lordshype wyll," says he, "bestow our grett Sibyll to some good purpose, *ut pereat memoria cum Sonita (sic)*. She hath byn the Devyll's instrument to bryng many (I feere) to eternall fyre : now she heresylff with her old syster of Wolsyngham, her young syster of Ipswych, with ther other too systurs of Dongcaster and Penryesse, wold make a jooly mustere in Smythfeld. They wold nott be all day in burnynge."[3]

Froude believes this silly story;[4] but the latest historian of Worcester, Noakes, who has had access to all the municipal and other documents has found no trace of this legend. Its absurdity is patent to all who have any knowledge of the iconography of our Blessed Ladye.

In 1439, Isabel, Countess of Warwich, bequeathed to our Ladye of Worcester her great image of wax, then in London.[5]

In the Privy Purse expenses of Elizabeth of York, there is an entry on the 24th March, 1502, of 5s. for an offering to our Ladye of Worcester.[6]

---

[2] Beaucourt, *Description de l'Église de N. Dame, Bruges.*
[3] *Latimer's Letter to Cromwell. Ellis's Original Letters:* Third Series, vol. iii. p. 205.
[4] *Hist. of England,* iii. p. 288.   [5] *Test. Vet.* p. 240.   [6] *Ibid.* p. 3.

Thomas Bouchier, Cardinal Archbishop of Canterbury, bequeathed to the church of Worcester an image of our Ladye of silver, gilt, of the value of £69.[7]

Thomas de Cobham, Bishop of Worcester, bequeathed to the altar, before which he should be buried, an image of our Blessed Ladye, which he had received as a present from the Abbot of St. Augustine's, Bristol.[8]

WORKSOP PRIORY.

Several distinguished personages were buried before the image of our Blessed Ladye.

Sir Thomas Nevill, Treasurer of England,

aboven the quere is tumulate :

. . . . .

And his doghter Molde of right hye degree
In Saynt Mary chappel tumulate lyeth shee,
Afore our Blessed Ladye, next the Stall side
There may she be seene, she is not to hyde.

And Sir William Talbot

was beried even tho
Which forsaid Sir William was greatly enduid with grace:
For five Candells perpetuall in that chappell
He ordeyned to brynne afore our Ladye.[9]

WOTTON.

Eustace Grenville, ancestor to the present Duke of Buckingham and Chandos, by his will dated on the feast of St. Clement, 1479, bequeaths to the light of the Blessed Virgin Marye in the said church of Wotton three pounds of wax in candles and two torches ; and to the altar of the Blessed Marye in the said church one bushel of wheat, and as much barley.[10]

WROXHALL.

A convent for Benedictine nuns was founded here, at an early period, by Sir Hugh, son of Richard, lord of Hatton ; and among the first nuns were the two daughters of the founder, Edith and Cleopatra.

A MS., ascribed to the time of Edward the Fourth, gives the following narrative respecting the foundation of the Ladye Chapel.

"Dame Alice Craft, sometime nunne and lady of this place, poor of worldly goods, but

[7] *Angl. Sacra.* vol. i. p. 795   [8] *Mon. Angl.* vol. i. p. 575.
[9] *Mon. Angl.* vol. vi. p. 123.   [10] *Test. Vet.* p. 351.

riche of vertues, desired heartily of God and our Ladye, that she in her dayes might see here a a chapell of our Ladye. To that intent she prayed oft time: and on a night time there cam a voice to her, and bad her, in the name of God and our Ladye, beginn and performe a chapell of our Ladye. She remembred her therof, and thought it but a dreme, and toke no heede thereof. But not long to, another night following, came the same voice to her againe, and gave her the same charge more sharplye." Still delaying to execute the work, she is visited by our Ladye who reprimands her for her neglect; on which she, going to the prioress and stating that she had only the sum of fifteen pence to commence with, is yet encouraged to undertake the work in the trust that our Ladye would increase her store. "Then this Dame Alice Croft gave her to prayers, and besought our Ladye to give her knowledge wher she should build it, and how much she should make it. Then she had by revelation to make it on the north side of her churche, and she should find markyd the quantity. This was in harvest, between the two feasts of our Ladye, and on the morrow earlye she went unto the place assigned her, and there she found a certeyne ground covered with snow, and all the churchyard else bare without snow. She, glad of this, had masons ready and marked out the ground, and built the chapell, and performed it up. And every Satturday whilst it was in building she would say her prayers in the allyes of the churchyard, and in the playne pathe she should and did finde weekely sylver suficient to pay her workmen, and all that behoofull to her worke and no more. This good lady Dame Alice Croft died on vii. calends of Feverell, on the morrow after the Conversion of Saint Paul, and she is buried under a stone in the same chapell afore the dore entering into the quire." [11]

[11] *Mon. Angi.* t. iv. pp. 90—92. Cf. *Notices of the Churches in Warwickshire,* voL i. p. 47.

WYKE.

The chapel of Wyke, near Winchester, was formerly dependent upon our Ladye of the Valley, or Valleys. The Ecclesiastical Taxation of Pope Nicholas the Fourth in 1290, records the church of our Ladye of the Valley, with the chapel of Wyke taxed at 10*l.* In the time of Cardinal Beaufort, 1405—1447, this church and chapel were united to the parish church of St. Anastasius. Previously to the dissolution, with other statues there was one of our Ladye, and to her light Agnes Complyn, widow of William Complyn, by will dated 30th September, 1503, bequeathed three ewe sheep—*tres oves matrices.*[12]

YARMOUTH, or GREAT YARMOUTH, NORFOLK.

I. ST. NICHOLAS.

1. Our Ladye in St. Nicholas' Church was a great object of popular devotion, and in a long series of Yarmouth wills there are constant legacies to her light. Sometimes they are left to her light, sometimes to her light in St. Nicholas' Church, and sometimes again to her light in Yarmouth; but they all relate to one and the same object, for the Ladye-light in St. Nicholas' Church was pre-eminently our Ladye's light in Yarmouth.

In 1280, Beatrice, late wife of Thomas Mount, gave to the light of the Blessed Virgin 2*s.* of an annual rent to be paid at the feast of St. Martin, out of a messuage in Great Yarmouth for ever.

On the 14th April, 1349, Simon de Halle leaves 6*s.* 8*d.* to St. Marye's light in St. Nicholas: in May, William Fleming leaves 5*s.*: on the 4th June, John de Brouneswelle 12*d.*, and Jeffrey de Stalham, burgess, 13*s.* 4*d.*: on the 30th July, John Yue half a mark of silver, all to the same light: and in this year also, Roger Wolvyne left 1*d.*, John de Norton 6*d.*, to St. Marye's light; and William Motte 2*s.* for the light; and to the image of our Ladye there two clasps of gold. In 1355, William Oxney, burgess, leaves 40*s.* to St. Marye's light in St. Nicholas' Church: in 1356, Richard Fastolfe 20*s.*, and also an annual rent of 6*s.*, to be received out of a tenement for ever:

12 *Journal of British Archæol. Association,* 1863, pp. 185, 200.

in 1362, Stephen de Stalham, burgess 20s. to the light of St. Marye in Yarmouth church : in 1374, John de Stalham 20s. : in 1379, William de Stalham 20s., and Simon atte Gappe 6s. 8d. : in 1381, Peter Bennett leaves to the bailiffs and commonalty of Great Yarmouth, for an aid and support of St. Marye's light in the Church of St. Nicholas, 5s. of an annual rent to be received yearly for ever : and in 1385, Nicholas Wildegoose leaves to our Ladye's light 10s. These extracts are sufficient. I have cited them because they are of earlier dates than the majority of the legacies which I have quoted in this Series ; but the list which Swinden gives occupies many pages.[13]

In the *compotus* of Yarmouth Priory in 1484, they received for herrings offered to our Blessed Ladye 16s. 4d.[14]

2. Our Lady of Arneborg, Arneburgh, Arnesberg, Arnesburgh, Ernesburgh.

Thus variously is the name given in various documents ; but the correct form is our Ladye of Ardenberg, or, as is written in the Low Countries, Aardenberg.

Froissart relates, that after the great victory which Edward the Third gained at sea, off Sluys, in 1340, "on the next day, y* whyche was Mydsomer-day, the King and all his toke land, and the King on fote went a pylgrimage to our Ladye of Ardēbourge, and there herd masse and dyned, and thañe take his horse and rode to Gaunt wher the Quene receyved hym with great ioye."[15]

Now, of the two hundred and sixty ships . which composed the English fleet, sixty, at least, were from Yarmouth, and manned by stalwart East-Anglians.[16] It is very probable that many of these brave men of Yarmouth accompanied their sovereign to Ardenberg, and, that on their return home, they founded an altar to our Ladye

[13] *History and Antiquities of Great Yarmouth*, pp. 804—820. Norwich, 1772.
[14] Palmer, *Perlustration of Great Yarmouth*, vol. iii. p. 52, note. 1875.
[15] Vol. i. c. 50, p. 73. Ed. cit.
[16] Barnes, *Life of Edward III*. p. 180.

R

of Ardenberg, in the church of Nicholas, in thanksgiving for the victory.

It is shortly after this date that mentions of our Lady of Ardenberg occur. On the 14th April, 1349, Simon de Halle bequeaths 12d. to the altar of St. Marye de Arnesberg.[17]

About the year 1370, the prior of St. Olave, Roger de Haddisco, built a chapel at the east end of the chancel of the church of St. Nicholas, and dedicated it to our Ladye of Arneburgh.[18]

In 1508, Walter Schaue, of Great Yarmouth, desires "his wretched body to be buryed w'ought the north door of the chapel of or Ladye of Arneburgh, in the churchyard of St. Nicholas, in the foreseed Yarmouth."[19]

There was a gild of St. Marye of Arnesburgh.[20]

In 1452, Ardenberg, described as once a chief town of Flanders, was burnt by the men of Ghent, and the magnificent church of our Ladye—one of the finest in the world—was destroyed.[21] The celebrated image of our Blessed Ladye was saved from the fire and transported to Bruges, where it was placed in a niche in the façade of the Hotel de Ville.[22]

3. Our Ladye of the Porey's chapel.

This chapel was in the church of St. Nicholas. Mr. Charles J. Palmer, F.S.A., the learned continuator of Manship and Historian of Great Yarmouth, informs me that Porey is not the name of any known Yarmouth family.

Many old chapels of our Ladye bear names, the signification of which has perished, and which cannot now be explained.

Amongst the nineteen gilds in Yarmouth, one was the gild of St. Marye *de le Pere*, or *de la Pere*.[23] Swinden adds in a note, that Pere is a town in France. There are several villages called Pere, Perey, le Perey, in France. · There was also a celebrated priory of our Ladye *du Perrey*, founded by Robert the Fourth, called le Gros, lord of

---

[17] Swinden, p. 807.   [18] *Ibid.*
Palmer, *History of Great Yarmouth.*   [20] Swinden, p. 812.
[21] Barnes, p. 184.   [22] Weale, *Guide to Belgium*, &c., p. 168. London, 1859.
[23] Palmer, vol. i. p. 244 : Swinden, p. 811.

Bétheune, outside the walls of Bétheune in 1110, which was pillaged by the English in 1406.[24]

Or is Porey a corruption of *Dorée?* Several images of our Ladye in France were thus named. Under the ramparts of Orleans there was *La Dorade,* or *Notre Dame la Dorée,* otherwise *Notre Dame de la Regle,* called in a Bull of Eugenius the Third, in 1152, *Beata Maria inter murum et fossatum;*[25] whilst at Ghent there existed from time out of mind, in that part of the city called Overschelde, a gild of our Lady *du Mont D'Or.*[26]

II. St. Mary *ultra Pontem.*

This church, so called from its position connecting Yarmouth with South-Town, was the ancient church for West-Town and South-Town before these benefices were consolidated with the living of Gorleston, in 1511. It was demolished in 1548, and its ruins were used in constructing and repairing the haven and piers.[27]

Here was a gild of St. Mary de West-Town *ultra Pontem,* to which, in 1479, Robert Atkins bequeathed 12 d.[28]

YORK.

I. The Minster.

1. Our Ladye in the Crypt.

This altar was coeval with the Minster, and the Marye-Mass was daily sung at it.[29]

The master of the choristers "was to keep the Lady-Masse at all tymes accustomed with the said queresters or children within the chapell of our Ladye (in the crypt) in the same church, and also keep and play of the organes within the said chapell during the said Masse."[30]

It seems that there was a Ladye-Mass in the Minster as well. Sir John Gisburgh, by his will,

---

[24] A. de Cardovaque, *Notice sur le Prieuré de N. D. du Perroy,* p. 6. Arras, 1859.

[25] Hamon, *Notre Dame de France,* p. 332.

[26] Diericx, *Mémoires sur la Ville de Gand,* p. 430.

[27] Manship, pp. 91, 92.

[28] Palmer, vol. i. p. 244.

[29] York vols. of the Royal Archæological Institute, vol. ii. p. 58.

[30] Register, Ga. a. f. 51. Browne, *History of the Metropolitan Church of St. Peter, York,* p. 297. London, 1847.

dated April 21, 1479, desires to be buried before the image of our Ladye in the north aisle, and wills that if it in any manner can be done, the Mass of the Blessed Virgin Marye be celebrated at the altar of St. Stephen at the day of his burial.[31] And by his will, dated November 6, 1487, John Carr of York says:

"I bewit my gold ryng with the diamond to hyng about the nek of the ymage oure Ladye y[t] standes abowne oure Ladye altar in the Mynster where they sing oure Ladye Messe. Also I bewit another ryng w[t] a ruby and one torcos to hyng aboute oure Lord's nek that is in the armis of the same ymage of oure Ladye."[32]

2. Our Ladye at the High Altar.

The high altar, says Browne, was generally considered the altar of our Ladye; and to enhance its dignity, an image of our Ladye, gilt, and splendidly adorned, was placed near the south end of the altar, and no Mass was expected to be said at that altar without two large wax candles burning before the image, in addition to the wax candles on the altar.[33]

By will, dated April 10, 1493, Master Robert Este left twenty marks, English money, to gild the image of the Blessed Virgin Marye at the end of the great altar in the Metropolitan Church at York, on the south side of the said altar.[34]

It was the rubric in this Cathedral that the Hebdomary, *i.e.*, the canon of the week, who sang the daily High Mass, should carry every day, as he went from the sacristy to the high altar, an image of our Ladye of silver gilt, which he then placed upon the altar. This image represented our Ladye with her Divine Son in her arms, Who held a sapphire in His hand. It weighed 5 lb. 11 oz.[35]

3. Our Ladye's Altar behind the High Altar.

Thomas Karr, who had been one of the sheriffs of the city of York in 1428, by his will,

---

[31] Register By. f. 350 b. Browne, p. 263.
[32] Test. Ebor. vol. iv. p. 27. [33] P. 175.
[34] Register By. f. 380 b. as. f. 356, By. f. 381. Browne, p. 263.
[35] *Mon. Angl.* vol. vi. p. 1204.

dated April 24, 1444, left 100 shillings to buy two chains of gold, one to be placed around the neck of the image of the Blessed Virgin Marye, at her altar behind the high altar of the cathedral church of St. Peter's, York, and the other to be placed around the neck of her Son, Who is in her arms. He also bequeathed a gold ring, of the price of 13*s*. iv*d*., to be placed and chained around the neck of the image of our Blessed Ladye.[36]

4. Our Ladye at the door of the north aisle of the choir.

The Fabric Rolls for the year 1518 contains this entry:

Paid to two painters, for painting two images of the Blessed Marye, with their tabernacles and histories, one at the red chest, the other at the door of the north aisle of the choir, they finding the gold, bice, and other colours in gross, 10*l*. 0*s*. 0*d*.

5. Our Ladye on the north side of the church.

The same entry continues:

"And 20*s*. given by the hands of Thomas Water, Registrar of the Lords, the Dean and Chapter of the Church of York, for a painting of the Blessed Virgin Marye, on the north side of the same church.[37]

6. Our Ladye at St. Stephen's altar.

This celebrated image is sometimes described as our Ladye *in the north aisle.* It was erected in 1419, in which year the sum of 23*s*. and 4*d*. were assigned "for the purchase of an image of Blessed Marye, with the making of its tabernacle and the painting of the same, standing above the 'parclose' before the altar of St. Stephen."[38]

In 1479, Sir John Gisburgh desired to be buried before this image, and wished the Marye Mass to be sung at this altar,[39] as I have just mentioned. And in 1493, by his will, dated April 10 of that year, Master Thomas Este gave his body to be buried in the north aisle of the

---

[36] Test. Ebor. vol. ii. p. 92.
[37] Browne, p. 271. [38] Fab. Rolls, *sub anno*.
[39] Register By. f. 350.

cathedral, near the tomb of Sir John Gisburgh, late Canon Residentiary of the Minster, and before the image or figure of the most exalted Virgin Marye.[40] · Many other similar instances are recorded.

7. Our Ladye in the south side of the Minster.

Nicholas Blackburn, senior, citizen and merchant of York, by his will, dated February 20, 1431—2, desires to be buried in the cathedral, in the south side, before the image of our Blessed Ladye there, under the marble slab already prepared for that purpose in that spot.[41]

And two years later, his widow, Margaret, desires to be buried by his side, before the same image of our Ladye.[42]

8. Our Lady at the altar of the Most Holy Trinity over the treasury.

In 1348, by will, dated Tuesday after the feast of the Holy Trinity, Sir Thomas Sampson, Canon of the Cathedral of York, bequeaths, with other objects, an image of our Ladye, of alabaster, to the altar of the Blessed Trinity newly constructed over the treasury in the cathedral.[43]

9. Our Ladye over the Red Ark.

The *Rubea Arca*, or red ark, or chest, was placed against the south side of the south-east pier of the large tower, about the year 1441, and above it stood an image of our Ladye.[44]

The red ark was placed here to receive offerings and donations towards the fabric of the cathedral, as appears from the will of Robert Esyngwald, a proctor at York, dated August 1, 1443, by which he desires to be buried in St. Peter's, York, before the image of our Ladye placed where the people make their offerings to the fabric of the church.[45] Five months previously, Master William Otterbourn, the sacristan, had desired to be buried before this image.[46]

The red ark was painted periodically: thus, in the Fabric Roll of 1515, there is an entry,

---

[40] Register By. f. 380 b. Browne, p. 218.
[41] Test. Ebor. vol. ii. p. 47.   [43] *Ibid.* p. 46.
[43] Zouch's Register, f. 335. Browne, p. 127.   [44] *Ibid.* p. 236.
[45] Test. Ebor. vol. ii. p. 90.   [46] Register By. f. 256.

"for painting the red chest under the image of the Blessed Virgin Marye for receiving the alms to be offered and kept for the use of the fabric, 21*d.* And for three quarters (?) of gold for gilding one star above the image of the Blessed Virgin Marye, 5*s.* And to the painter for painting and gilding the same star, 20*d.* And in 1516, Ursyn Milner, for the binding of books and the painting of the red ark beneath the image of our Ladye, received the sum of 49*s.* 4*d.*[47] This same Ursyn Milner had printed the Office of our Blessed Ladye *ad usum Eboracensem,* of which only one copy was known to exist.[48]

Several of the carved bosses in the minster represent our Blessed Ladye.[49]

One boss in the centre of the archway, in the screen which separates the chancel from the rest of the church, deserves mention. It represents our Ladye standing, her hands placed together, palm to palm, before her, but not clasped ; her hair is flowing, and she has neither veil nor crown. She is figured within a pointed oval moulding, which is supported by four angels. I have often heard this particular sculpture mentioned as being intended for the Immaculate Conception, but as none of the attributes of that mystery are given, it must be considered as the Assumption, which, in English art, is usually thus represented.

II. St. Clement's, in the suburbs.

Isabella Bruce, widow of Robert Bruce, esquire, desires to be buried in the Convent of nuns, at St. Clement's, in the suburbs of York, by the grave of her sister Joan, under the images of our Ladye and St. William. Will dated 30th July, 1477.[50]

III. St. Helen's.

In 1392, Matilda, widow of William Marshall,

[47] Fab. Rolls, p. 97.
[48] Ames. *Typographical Antiquities,* vol. iii. p. 1438. Edit. Herbert. Cf. Davies, *A Memoir of the York Press,* p. 20. Westminster, 1868.
[49] See Browne, plates, 96, 101, 106, 126.
[50] Test. Ebor. vol. iii. p. 231.

left to the high altar of the Church of St. Helen by the walls of the city of York, an image of our Blessed Ladye of alabaster.[51]

IV. St. John the Baptist in Hundgate.

William Riche left xx*s.* for the painting of the image of our Ladye below the choir of St. John's.[52]

V. St. John's by Ouse-bridge.

John Baxter, citizen of York, leaves vi*s.* viii*d.* to the making of two tabernacles, one of which is for the image of our Ladye in the north chancel. Will dated 28th January, 1478.[53]

VI. St. Marye's Abbey.

This was founded by the good old Saxon Earl of Northumberland, Sigweard, commonly now called Siward, the friend of Leofric and Godgifu, in 1054. Hither he came to die, under the protection of our Ladye.

In 1401, Isabella, wife of William Belgrafe, leaves a pair of amber beads with a ring of silver and gold to hang before the image of our Blessed Ladye in the Abbey of St. Mary's, York.[54] In 1402, Isabella, wife of John Catclough Barbour, leaves a gold ring to this image of our Ladye.[55]

VII.

Near this abbey there was a chapel of our Ladye, and to the image which was in it, in 1442, Richard Cotingham, citizen of York, bequeathed a red belt well adorned with silver.[56] And in 1464, Eufemia, widow of Sir John Langton, left to the same a necklace of pearls with a balas-ruby.[57]

VIII. St. Sampson.

In 1392, Nicholas de Scherburn of York, chaplain, left iii*s.* and iiii*d.* for a tabernacle of alabaster for the image of our Ladye in the choir of this church.[58]

---

[51] Test. Ebor. vol. i. p. 183.   [52] *Ibid.* vol. ii. p. 270.   [53] *Ibid.* vol. iii. p. 243.
[54] Test. Ebor. vol. i. p. 280.
[55] *Ibid.* p. 291.   [56] *Ibid.* vol. ii. p. 84.   [57] *Ibid.* p. 258.
[58] *Ibid.* vol. i. p. 172.

IX. THE HOLY TRINITY IN GOTHEROMGATE.

In 1402, John Couper, of York, leaves xii*d.* to the lights of the Holy Cross and our Ladye.[59] And in 1463, Henry Salvane or Salvin, esquire, leaves four pounds of wax to be made into four tapers to be burnt before the image of the Blessed Virgin Marye in the choir of this church.[60]

The following were omitted in their proper order; but it has since been thought advisable to insert them.

ACKLAM IN CLEVELAND.

In 1402, Sir Thomas Boynton, knight, leaves to the light of our Ladye in the church of Acclom, xiii*s.* iiii*d.*[61] And in 1453, Thomas Lynehouse, of Seventhorpe, leaves to the lights of the Holy Rood and our Blessed Ladye, in the same church, xvi*d.*[62]

ARLINGHAM, GLOUCESTERSHIRE.

Bigland quotes as follows from an old MS. at Berkeley Castle:

"In this parish also were divers lands and tenements dedicated to the service of the Blessed Virgin Marye, to whom, also, I think the parish church was dedicated; which lands in the time of King Henry the Fourth were under the disposinge and lettinge of the *Procuratores Servitie beate Marie Virginis de Arlingham;* the house the preist then before dwelt in, and after, was, and yet is, called our Ladies preist's house."[63]

ARUNDEL.

Thomas, Earl of Arundel, K.G., by his will dated October 10, 1415, wills that his executors cause to be built at the gate called Marye Gate in Arundel a certain chapel in honour of the Blessed Virgin Marye. This chapel stood at a short distance from the Marygate, and within the town.[64]

[59] Test. Ebor. p. 289.
[60] *Ibid.* vol. ii. p. 264.
[61] *Ibid.* vol. i. p. 287.
[62] *Ibid.* vol. ii. p. 171.
[63] *Historical, Monumental, and Genealogical Collections relative to the County of Gloucester,* p. 66. Lond. 1791.
[64] Test. Vet. p. 186.

Another chapel of our Ladye stood over the Marygate, which was erected at the close of the thirteenth century, but the first and only mention of it occurs in the statutes of the College in 1387. In that document the chapel over the gate is described as already existing, one of the brethren of the College is specially appointed to its service, and a daily Mass is ordered to be celebrated within it.[65]

BERKELEY CASTLE. The following extract from Smyth's MS. History of the Hundred of Berkeley, preserved in the Castle, as quoted by Bigland, will show that the chapel had fallen into disuse before 1364, and that it was then restored:

"In this Castle were of late years (not yet wholly ruined or deformed) two beautiful chapels or oratories, endowed with divers privileges from the Bishops of Rome. The one of them in the keep, with a goodly well of water under (now destroyed); the other at the upper end of the great hall stairs leading to the dyning chamber: and for the devout keeping of the ornaments thereunto belonging, divers allowances were by the lords yearly made, as from divers accompts and deeds in the evidence house in this Castle appears. Maurice, Lord Berkeley (fourth of the name), 38 Edward the Third (1364) obtained of Pope Urban the Second,[66] by his Papal Bull and power, to the end his two chapels, the one of our Ladye the Blessed Virgin, the other of St. John the Baptist, founded in the Castle of Berkeley, might be renewed and frequented with due honours: forty days of pardon and release of the penance enjoyned to every one who should, in the said chapels on the festival days of the year, heare Masses, or say kneeling three *Ave Marias*, or give any vestments or chalices, or any other aids of charity to the said chappels. And whosoever shall there pray for them that obtained these presents, and for the

<hr />

[65] Tierney, *Hist. and Antiq. of the Town and Castle of Arundel*, p. 675. Lond. 1834.

[66] This is evidently a misprint or a mistake for Urban V. 1362—70.

life and good estate of the noble Lord Maurice de Berkeley, and the Lady Elizabeth his wife, and for their children, and for the soul of Lord Thomas, his father, being in Purgatory, shall bee also released of forty days of the penance enjoyed them. And this faculty, grace, or instrument of infallibleness is alsoe under the seales of eleven of the Pope's Cardinals; perhaps alsoe somewhat the rather procured by that lord's wisdom through the great schisme of three Popes at once that then raigned in the Church." [67]

GREAT BERKHAMP-STED.

Nicholas Talbot, in his will, dated June 8, 1501, says:

" . . . my body, if it happyt me to depart within vii myle of. Gret Berkehamstede to be buryed ther within .the chapell of oure Ladye betwyx the ymage of oure Ladye of Pyte and the image of oure Ladye of Grace within the parysche chyrche of the seyd town." [68]

BEVERLEY.

I. COLLEGIATE CHURCH OF ST. JOHN OF BEVERLEY.

Our Ladye above the Red Ark.

It would almost seem as if the Chapter of York had taken the idea of the Red Ark from Beverley. I have not as yet ascertained when it was first put up, but in 1398, William Bird of Beverley, by his will, dated the feast of St. Lambert, martyr (September 17), bequeaths to the image of the Blessed Virgin Marye above the Red Ark in the collegiate church of St. John at Beverley, one piece of his best silk velvet. [69]

II. CHURCH OF ST. MARYE.

Our Ladye in the middle of the nave.

Dionisia Holme,. of Beverley, widow, by her will, dated January 3, 1470—1, bequeathes a silk belt, adorned with silver and gold, to the image

---

[67] *Domestic Architecture of the Middle Ages:* XV. century, pt. ii. pp. 255, 256; Bigland, vol. i. p. 154.

[68] Bury Wills and Inventories, p. 85.

[69] Test. Ebor. vol. i. p. 240.

of the Blessed Virgin Marye, in the nave of the church.[70]

In 1471, Henry Holme, of Beverley, leaves, to adorn the image of the Blessed Virgin Marye in the church of our Ladye at Beverley, in the middle of the nave of the said church, a pair of beads of six tens of gold—*preces lx. ex auro.* Will dated August 31.[71] And in 1479, Thomas Dicson, of Beverley, weaver, desires to be buried in St. Marye's Church, and leaves to the image of the most sweet Virgin Marye his belt of red silk, embroidered with silver, and one good napkin.[72]

It is most probable that the following bequest refers to this image:

By will dated February 25, 1497—8, Agnes Hilyard bequeathes one old noble to be offered for the image of the Blessed Virgin Marye at Beverley, to hang round the neck.[73]

BISHOP'S CANNING, WILTS.

In the church here there is a chantry dedicated to "Our Ladye of the Bower."[74]

Bower, in Anglo-Saxon, Bur, Bure, means a conclave, an inner chamber, a parlour, a bower—from the German Bawen, or Anglo-Saxon Byan, to inhabit, to indwell.

Hence the title of this chapel has evidently reference to the Divine Maternity of our Blessed Ladye, who is called the *domus Dei,* because she bore in her womb for nine months the Son of God; or as the words of Ecclesiasticus applied to our Ladye in the Liturgy of the Church express it, *Qui creavit me requievit in tabernaculo meo*—"and He that made me rested in my tabernacle."[75]

In an old English poem, entitled *Veni coronaberis,* or a "Song of sweetness from Christ to His Daintiest Dam," our Lord says:

Macula, moder, was neuer in thee,
Filia Syon, thou art the flour,
Ful sweteli schalt thou sitte bi me,
And bere a crowne with me in tour,
And alle my seintis to thin honour

---

[70] Test. Ebor., vol. iii. p. 182.
[71] *Ibid.* p. 192.   [72] *Ibid.* note.   [73] *Ibid.* vol. iv. p. 133.
[74] *Notes and Queries,* Second Series, vol. vii. p. 376.   [75] Ecclus. xxiv. 12.

> Schal honoure thee, moder, in my bliss,
> That *blessid bodi that bare me in bowur*,
> *Veni, coronaberis*.[76]

Bower corresponds to the French *celle*. Thus, in a poem composed by Philip de Vitry, 1350—1357:

> A Toi, Glorieuse Pucelle,
> Qui du Fils Dieu fus chambre et *celle*.
> Et Qui seule fus vièrge et mère,
> Et qui seule enfantas ton père,
> A toi soit loenge et honnour,
> Sur tous, après le Seignour.[77]

BLYTHE, or BLYDE. In 1347, Alice, wife of John Henriot, of Blyda, bequeaths to the light of our Ladye on the Bridge of Blye her green tunic with its hood.[78]

BOULOGNE-SUR-MER. Our Ladye of Boulogne was a very favourite pilgrimage of our English forefathers, and from historical associations, deserves to be mentioned in this list.

The legend of the image of our Ladye is briefly this—

About the year 633, a boat arrived at the shore in which there was an image of our Ladye, a copy of the Bible, and two relics. Attracted by this unusual occurrence, some of the townspeople went towards the boat, when our Blessed Ladye appeared visibly to them and told them that she wished a church to be built in her honour, and the image and relics, which had just arrived, to be placed in it. They alleged their poverty, whereupon she commanded them to dig in a certain spot which she indicated, saying they they would find the money that was necessary for the buildings, and then disappeared. Such is the tradition, and nothing more is mentioned for several centuries. The image of our Ladye is described as being carved of oak, about three feet high, standing, and with her Divine Son in her left arm.

Geofrey de Bouillon offered to our Ladye the crown which he refused to wear as King of

---

[76] *Hymns to Christ and our Blessed Lady.* Early Eng. Text Soc. vol. xxiv. p. 1.
[77] Hamon, *Notre Dame de France*, p. 250.
[78] Test. Ebor. vol. i. p. 46.

Jerusalem, and it is mentioned in an inventory as late as the year 1791.[79]

From the year 1212 there was a constant succession of pilgrims to the sanctuary of our Ladye of Boulogne, and of miracles wrought through her all-powerful intercession.

Amongst the English kings who came hither on pilgrimage to our Ladye may be named Henry the Third in 1254; Edward the Second was married there; Edward the Third came several times; on one occasion he went on foot from Calais to Boulogne, accompanied by the Dukes of Clarence and York; and the names of many distinguished Englishmen are also recorded, as well as the offerings which they made. The Earl of Shrewsbury presented a magnificent robe of cloth of gold with his coat of arms embroidered on it; the Earl of Warwick, Governor of Calais, gave an image of our Ladye in silver gilt, with the demon under her feet; and an English merchant offered a turquoise of extraordinary size, which was set in a cross, already so richly ornamented with jewels that it was called *La Belle Croix.*

One remarkable custom at Boulogne was that the civil authorities used to offer the *vin d' honneur* to distinguished pilgrims; and in the municipal accounts for one year, 1415 to 1416, there are entries thirteen times of the *vin d' honneur* being offered to thirteen different bodies of pilgrims, it being stated in each case that they had come on pilgrimage to our Ladye of Boulogne.[80] And from the year 1273 there are innumerable records of persons who were condemned by judicial authority to make the pilgrimage to our Ladye of Boulogne in expiation of their crimes. This practice formed a part of the penal law of France for the lay tribunals as well as for ecclesiastical justice. This is also proved by the Registers of the Inquisition of Carcassonne, which were copied in the seventeeth century by order of the Commissary, Doat;

[79] Haigneré, *Hist. de N. Dame de Boulogne,* p. 26. 1864.
[80] *Ibid.* p. 120.

and these volumes form one of the most curious collections in the Bibliothéque Nationale. In one of these Registers there is a list of the chief sanctuaries in Europe, classified according to their importance, and the four greater ones are Rome, Compostella, St. Thomas of Canterbury, and Cologne. Our Ladye of Boulogne, together with Puy, Vauvert, Chartres, Roc-Amadour, and many other sanctuaries of the Blessed Virgin are given among the lesser ones.[81] In all these cases the pilgrims had to bring back a certificate of having fulfilled their sentence.

In 1478 Louis the Eleventh solemnly invested our Ladye of Boulogne with the sovereignty of the *Comté* of Boulogne, by Letters Patent, given at Hesdin in the month of April of that year, in which he declared himself and his successors to be the vassals of our Ladye, and acknowledges her as his sovereign. In these Letters Patent he bears testimony to the great and constant miracles which are daily wrought by the intercesion of our Ladye of Boulogne in her sanctuary, and furthermore binds himself and his successors to offer a heart of gold as their feudal tribute : . . . *Et outre, pour l' honneur et révérence de ladite Dame. Nous et nosdits successeurs seront tenus, en faisant ledit hommage, d'offrir et présenter devant ladite Dame notre cœur en espèce et figure de métail d'or fin, de la pesanteur de treize marcs d'or, qui sera employé au bien et entretènement de la dite église.*

This was no mere consecration, but a real investiture of our Ladye with sovereign rights, she, in virtue thereof, being entitled to the homage of the King as her vassal. To her were also paid all the fines and other sums to which the kings had heretofore been entitled.

In 1532 Henry the Eighth and Francis the First of France spent some days at Boulogne, and they daily assisted at Mass in our Ladye's chapel, and made their offerings to her.[82] Subsequently, in 1544, on the 18th July, Henry came to lay siege to the city. It surrendered on the 14th

[81] Reg. Doat. t. xxxvii. f. iii.   [82] Hall, p. 791 ; see *ante*, p. 4.

September.   The English monarch seems to have
acted the part of another Alaric.   What else
could be expected from the spoiler of the
monasteries and convents of his own kingdom,
and whose hands were stained with the innocent
blood of Sir Thomas More, Cardinal Fisher, and
many other glorious martyrs.   The church was
robbed of all its riches, and turned into an
arsenal ; the chapel of our Ladye was destroyed ;
the venerated image of our Ladye was subjected
to all sorts of insults, her face was injured, her
nose cut off, and finally it was carried off to
England.   The English did not confine themselves to the pillage of the churches : the
inhabitants had to quit the city, and the brutal
soldiery stripped even the ladies of their dresses,
leaving them to depart barefoot and clad only
in their chemises.[83]

In 1550, Louis de la Trimouille, Prince of
Talmond, and subsequently first Duke of Thouars,
who had been one of the French hostages sent
to England, was instructed by his King to demand
the restoration of the image of our Ladye ; a
request with which Edward the Sixth at once
complied.   Its return to Boulogne was the cause
of universal rejoicing ; and within five or six
years from this date, the new riches in the treasury,
consisting of votive offerings, were valued at two
hundred thousand *livres*.

In 1567, when the Huguenots had begun to
infest France, on the morning of Sunday, the 12th
October, it was discovered that the miraculous

---

[83]   "Le roy d'Angleterre estant demouré maitre de la Haulte et Basse-Boulongne,
donna congé aux habitans de pouvoir s'en aller avec leurs biens et ce qu' ilz pouvoient
emporter, lesquelz, se confians en ce sauf-conduit, et se retirans à la file sans aucune
doute, estoient desvalisez et mis en chemises par les Anglois qui les attendoient aux
passages, en quoy receurent les povres Boulonnois dommages inestimables tant en
leurs biens qu'en leurs personnes : car ceux qui vouloient ou fai faisoient semblant de
résister estoient taillez en pièces.   C'estoit grand pitié de voir les povres dames et
damoiselles eschappées de ces cruelz chiens, se sauver nuds pieds et despouillez de
leurs habits et aornemens, trainant leurs petis enfans.   Et ne fault pas dire si les
povres filles à marier eurent à souffrir en ce tumultuaire département, ès personnes
desquelles furent commis plusieurs cruelz exemples et excès de tyrannie intollérable."
(*Histoire de nostre temps faite en latin.* Par M. Guillaume Paradin, et par luy mise en
françois, p. 137.   Lyon, 1550).

image of our Ladye had been carried off. It was sought for on all sides but with no result. On the horrible scenes which followed I need not dwell. After the Huguenots had taken their departure in April, 1568, the city officials were employed in searching for the image everywhere, in the houses, gardens, cellars, wells and tanks, but their efforts were unsuccessful.

In 1588, a labourer of Bellebrune, James de Wismes, who had gone to the wars, heard from a sergeant named Bertrand Brillart, a Protestant, the fate of the venerated image of our Ladye. Speaking of the pillage and massacres of the priests at Boulogne, Brillart admitted that he and some others had carried it off from where it stood; they endeavoured to burn it, but it would not take fire, although surrounded by fifteen faggots of wood; they tried to split it into pieces but without success; finally they buried it in a dung-heap, where they left it for three years; and then going to see if it had become rotten and spoiled, they found it wholly untouched, whereupon they threw it into a well.

Not far from Boulogne, and in the parish of Wimille, is the Chateau of Honvault. In the year 1607 an old gentleman, John de Frohart, who had taken an active part in the religious wars, was still living in it. He had been accused of having shed the blood of some of the priests in 1567. For some time past, however, he had rarely left his chateau, where, having abjured the errors of his earlier years, he was calmly preparing himself for his death. Occasionally he would receive a visit from a relative, a man of noble birth, Vespasian de Fonteynes by name, who led the life of a hermit in the forest of Desvres, a few miles from Boulogne, where he devoted himself to prayer and mortification. One day de Frohart said to him : " Wouldst thou be very happy, brother Vespasian, if I were to give thee for thy little wooden chapel, a precious treasure which I possess ? The ancient image of our Ladye of Boulogne, which was carried off from her altar by some of my former comrades in arms, was

S

thrown into the well of my chateau, where it was found by my wife. We have not ventured to speak of it to any one, lest we should be charged with having stolen the treasure of the church, but I cannot die without placing this precious deposit in the hands of some pious and religious man." Vespasian accepted the offer with joy, and took into his council a priest of Boulogne, by name Anthony Gillot, and they resolved to transport the image to the city, so that our Ladye might be restored to her ancient honours.

Before, however, the image could be exposed for veneration it had to be identified, and the process of its verification occupied some years. Moreover, the Ladye chapel had to be rebuilt; and it was not until Holy Saturday, the 30th March, 1630, that the image of our Ladye was placed over the altar in her chapel by the Bishop of Boulogne, Victor Bouthillier, and his Chapter; and from this time many miraculous cures were wrought at this sanctuary, and pilgrims flocked to it from all parts as heretofore. Hither, too, in December, 1688, came James the Second of England and his Queen, Maria d' Este, who vowed their son to our Ladye of Boulogne.

At four o'clock in the afternoon of the 24th January, 1791, the Cathedral was closed, and the canons were forbidden henceforth to exercise the ministry of their sacred office, on pain of being prosecuted as disturbers of the public order. An inventory of all the objects of value was made, and the image is described as "a representation of the Virgin, in wood, very ancient, holding the Infant Jesus in her arms, and being the object of the veneration of the people." Amongst the *ex-votos* are named, a herring in silver offered by the master-fishermen of Boulogne in 1788, and a silver cow presented by the inhabitants of Ambleteuse in 1776, when the cattle plague was raging there.

On the 10th November, 1793, the Feast of Reason was first celebrated, with hideous orgies in the Church of St. Nicholas; and on the same

day, to make away with the "ancient super-
stitions," a bonfire was made of "statues of wood,
heretofore known under the denomination of
saints." The image of our Ladye was spared.
When it was removed from the Cathedral it was
taken into the *salle du district*, now the *sous-
préfecture*, and placed against the chimney-piece,
where it remained for a while. Finally, on the
29th December, 1793, it was burnt in the public
square in the midst of satanic exultations and
shouting and dancing. A sans-culotte placed a
red cap on the head of the sacred image, and it
was then thrown into the bonfire. The represen-
tative of the city, Andrew Dumont, presided at
this disgraceful scene; and he thus related it to
the Convention—

"*A Boulogne, la très-sainte et la très-incompré-
hensible, la très-sainte Vierge noire que les Anglais
n'avaient pu brûler, fut, dans la plus belle fête qui
se peut célébrer, jetée dans le bûcher et réduite en
cendres sans miracles. Tout Boulogne, hors les
détenus, hommes, femmes et enfants, tous crièrent*
Vive la Montagne! *et se jurèrent union eternelle.
L' allégresse fut telle que la nuit se passa en bals,
où se trouvèrent tous les citoyens . . . Jamais le
républicanisme ne se prononça mieux.*" [84]

But was the venerated image really burnt?
The Abbé Haigneré relates that he has often
heard old people at Boulogne say, that our Ladye
would be found again. Moreover they relate
that the patriots kept the bonfire alive on the
place d'armes, until nine or ten o'clock at night,
and although they procured more wood and
grease and oil, *the statue would not burn.* [85] What
then has become of it?

Great is the present devotion to our Ladye of
Boulogne, and many an *Ave* is breathed in the
new sanctuary that her venerated image may be
discovered. From the Assumption till the end
of the month of August there is one continued
succession of pilgrimages from all the country
around, sometimes twenty in a day. At other

[84] *Moniteur* of the 4th January, 1794.
[85] Haigneré, *ubi. sup.* p. 319.

times of the year the *matelottes* come by hundreds to pray for their husbands, who are fishing in the North Sea; and these brave fellows never set sail until they have made their pilgrimage to our Ladye's sanctuary. And on the occasion of one of their great pilgrimages, they are not content with a Low Mass; they will have a *Messe à trois mâts*, as they express it, *i.e.* a High Mass celebrated for their welfare and success.

Images of our Ladye stood in niches over the Porte de Calais and Porte des Dunes. The former one seems to have been put up by the Mayor and Corporation in 1659, probably to replace an older one. Our Ladye is represented in a boat, and holding a heart in her right hand. The image was solemnly blessed by the Dean of the Cathedral, on returning from the procession of the Gang-days; and our Ladye was then solemnly invoked by all the clergy, three times, as *Patrona nostra singularis.* This is an invocation peculiar to Boulogne, and by permission of the Sacred Congregation of Rites, it is inserted in the Litany of Loreto when recited or sung in Boulogne.[86]

The two statues over the gates of the city were taken down after the Revolution, but they escaped destruction. In the year 1851, they were recovered by a lady, whose name is associated with every good work in Boulogne, Madame Lipsin, who on the 29th of June, ere the break of day, caused them to be replaced where they formerly stood. Great was the surprise and delight in Boulogne when it was discovered that our Ladye had come back again to watch over the gates of her ancient city.[87]

BRACEWELL. By his will, dated August 26, 1427, Sir Richard Tempest of Bracewell desires to be

---

[86] Haigneré, *ubi. sup.* p. 261.

[87] For authorities Cf. Montfort, *Hist. de l'ancienne Image de Nostre Dame de Boulogne-sur-mer* (Paris, 1634); Le Roy, *Hist. de N. D. de Boulogne* (Paris, 1682); Haigneré, *Hist. de N. D. de Boulogne* (Boulogne-sur-mer, 1864); *Ibid. Etude sur la Légende de N. D. de Boulogne* (Boulogne-sur-mer, 1863). This contains the legend of our Ladye of Boulogne, printed from a MS. of the fifteenth century in the Library of the Arsenal, and giving six miniatures which are highly interesting.

buried in the parish church, and leaves to the light of our Ladye of Braswell vi *s.* viii *d.*[88]

BRIDLINGTON.

The reredos at the high altar of S. Mary's Priory must have been a glorious composition. It is thus described:

"The reredos at the high altar representing Christ at the Assumption of our Ladye, and the twelve Apostles, with divers other great images, is excellent well wrought and as well gilted: and between the same and the east window is St. John of Bridlington Shrine in a fair chapel on high, having on either side a stair of stone for to go and come by."[89]

CARLISLE.

Our Ladye of Carlell is mentioned under the head of Gisbro'.[90]

CHEVINGTON, SUFFOLK.

Here was a light of our Ladye. In 1450 Roger Nycole left 6 *s.* 8 *d.* to the new painting of the image of the Salutation over our Ladye's altar, and bequeathed a cow to the light before the same image. In 1524 Robert Parnan left 20 *s.* to make a tabernacle in which to set an image of our Blessed Ladye on the south side of the high altar.[91]

CHRISTCHURCH, HANTS.

The Priory.

The ladye chapel here is of great beauty, and the stone screen of rich tabernacle work is of an elaborately minute design, and when in a perfect state, with all its gorgeous display of painted and gilt statuary, must have produced a striking effect on every spectator.

It has been restored from existing fragments, and some pieces of the statue of our Ladye which probably stood in the centre niche were found during the late repairs.[92]

[88] Test. Ebor. v. i. p. 413.
[89] *Associated Architectural Societies' Reports and Papers*, 1854, v. i. pt. i. p. 51.
[90] See *ante*, p. 42.
[91] *Proceedings of the Suffolk Archaeological Institute*, v. iii. p. 437.
[92] *Antiquities of the Priory of Christchurch, Hampshire*, by B. Ferrey, and E. W. Brayley, F.S.A.; revised by John Britton, F.S.A.; p. 47. London, 1841.

CLARENDON.

The King to the Sheriff of Wiltshire:

"We command you to make . . . in the chapel of All Saints at our manor of Clarendon . . . a crucifix, with two images on each side, of wood, and an image of Blessed Marye with her child. . . . In the chamber of the Friars Minor let there be made images of the Holy Trinity and of Blessed Marye, with a certain glass window, and repair it when necessary."[93]

Writ tested at Gillingham, July 30, 1250.

In December the King writes to the Sheriff of Wiltshire:

"We command you to put a glass window in the chamber of our Queen (at Clarendon), and in the same window cause to be made a *Mariola* with her Child, and a queen at the feet of the same Marye, with clasped hands, holding in her hand *Aue Maria*."

Writ tested at Clarendon, December 7.[94]

In 1251, the King to the Sheriff of Wiltshire:

"We command you to make images of the Blessed Marye, St. Edward, and Cherubim, and place them in our chapel" (at Clarendon).

Writ tested at Marlborough, July 2.[95]

CONISBOROUGH, CO. YORK.

In 1476-7, by will dated 6 March, Katherine Fitz-William, widow, the second wife of Edmund Fitz-William, Esquire, desires to be buried in the church of Connesburgh, before a certain image of Our Ladye of Pity.[96]

COUGHTON.

Sir Robert Throckmorton, in 1518, by his will devised that the image of our Ladye should be set on the north side at the end of the altar in the south aisle, and the image of the angel Gabriel on the same side of the altar, at the pillar between the aisle and the chancel (at Coughton), with a roll in his hand of greeting, looking towards our Ladye. This roll means, of course, a scroll with the salutation, *Ave gratia plena*. These images were to be richly painted and gilded.[97]

[93] Lib. Roll, 34 Hen. III.   [94] *Ibid.*   [95] *Ibid.* 35 Henry III.
[96] Test. Ebor. v. iii. p. 227.   [97] Dugdale, *Warwickshire*, v. ii. p. 751.

DARFIELD.

In 1452, Thomas Wombwell of Wombwell, Esquire, leaves to the service of our Lady in the church of Darfield, iii *l.*
Will dated February 14.[98]
Two years later, by will dated July 10, Jane Lady Wombwell, widow, leaves to the same service of our Ladye, xiii *s.* iiij *d.*[99]

EASINGTON.

William de Menville, by his will, dated January 20, 1371, leaves ten marcs to support for ever five wax candles before the altar of our Blessed Ladye, in the chapel of Esyngton church.[100]

ECCLES.

Eccles, about four miles from Manchester, takes its name from the old church of St. Marye's mentioned in Domesday, where it is called *Ecclesia.*
Leaving College Croft, and proceeding along Regent Road in the direction of Manchester, is to be seen, on descending a flight of thirty-six steps, our Ladye's Well, which is dedicated to her. A statue of our Ladye under a canopy once stood over the well, but it has been removed. Not far distant is another well called our Lord's well.[101]

ELLERTON.

In 1497, Sir John Aske, of Aughton, knight, desired, by his will, dated April 8, to be buried in the chancel of the Monastery of Ellerton, before the image of the Blessed Virgin, where the Gospel is wont to be read by the Deacon.[102]

FELSHAM.

In 1467, Baldwin Coksedge leaves a cow to provide two pounds of wax to burn before the image of the Blessed Virgin in the chancel of St. Peter of Felsham for ever.[103]

FETHERSTON.

Walter Frost, by his will dated in March, 1528, leaves to the altar of our Ladye at Fetherston, 20 *s.*[104]

[98] Test. Ebor. v. ii. p. 163.   [99] *Ibid.* p. 177.
[100] *Wills and Inventories,* pt. i. p. 32 ; see also *sub* Ryton, p. 130.
[101] *The Lamp,* v. viii. pt. xlvi. pp. 235, 236.
[102] Test. Ebor. v. ii. p. 275.   [103] *Bury Wills,* p. 273.
[104] *Yorkshire Archæological Journal,* v. i. p. 147.

FEVERSHAM.

In 1535, Henry Hatche desires to be buried in the church of our Ladye there, before the Bachelor's light.[105]

FOUNTAINS ABBEY.

In the inventory of the church is mentioned one ymage of o^r Ladye, silver and gilt, weighing 104 oz.[106]

GLASTONBURY.

The legendary history of the celebrated image of Our Ladye of Glastonbury is that it was carved by St. Joseph of Arimathea. In the old life of this Saint printed by Pynson in 1520 it is stated that—

> There Joseph lyued with other hermyttes twelfe,
>   That were the chyfe of all the company,
> But Joseph was the chefe hym-selfe ;
>   There led they an holy lyfe and gostely.
> Tyll, at the last, Jhesu the mighty,
>   He sent to Joseph thaungell gabryell,
> Which bad hym, as the writyng doth specify,
>   Of our Ladye's Assumpcyon to bylde a chapell.
>
> So Joseph dyd as the aungell hym bad,
>   And wrought there an ymage of our Lady ;
> For to serue her gret devocion he had,
>   And that same ymage is yet at Glastonbury,
> In the same churche ; there ye may it se.
>   For it was the fyrst, as I vnderstande
> That ever was sene in this countre ;
>   For Joseph it made wyth his owne hande.[107]

The Abbot Henry of Blois, who was nephew to Henry the First, assigned, in the year 1126, a pension of 50s. for the support of a wax candle which should burn continually before the image of our Ladye in the old church.[108] It was this Abbot Henry, and not Henry Swansey, as I inadvertently stated under the heading of Glastonbury,[109] who discovered the great sapphire.

HAVERING.

In 1251, the Bailiff of Havering is commanded . . . to cause a Marye with her Child, and the

---

[105] Test. Vet. p. 661.

[106] Burton, Mon. Ebor. p. 144 ; see *ante*, p. 235.

[107] *Life of Joseph of Arimathia.* Early Eng. Text Soc. vol. xliv. p. 43, lines 201—216.

[108] John of Glastonbury, *Hist. de Reb. Glast.* p. 166.

[109] See *ante*, p. 44.

Annunciation of the Blessed Marye to be painted in the Queen's chapel.

Writ tested at Waltham, August 26.[110]

In 1253, the King commands the Bailiff of Havering to wainscote his Majesty's upper chapel at Havering, and to place an image of the Blessed Virgin Marye in the lower chapel.[111]

Writ tested at Havering, April 8.

HOUNSLOW.

Under the picture of the Blessed Virgin here, says Weever, these following verses were depainted, now almost quite worne out—

Virginis intactæ cum veneris ante figuram
Prætereundo cave ne sileatur Ave.[112]

IRTHLINGBOROUGH, CO. NORTHAMPTON.

In the belfry of the church there still exists an old image of our Blessed Ladye.[113]

LONDON.

Our Ladye of Newgate.

Our Ladye of the New Gate is intimately associated with the memories of three of our glorious English martyrs, Father Campion, Father Briant, and Father Sherwine of the Society of Jesus.

" In the splash and mud of a rainy December morning, Campion was brought forth from his cell. . . . There were two hurdles in waiting, each tied to the tails of two horses. On one Sherwine and Briant were laid and bound ; Campion on the other. . . . The procession took the usual route by Cheapside and Holborn. . . . A little further, and the hurdles were dragged under the arch of Newgate, which crossed the street where the prison now stands. In a niche over the gate stood an image of the Blessed Virgin that was yet untouched with the axes and hammers of the iconoclasts. Campion, as he passed beneath, with a great effort raised himself and saluted the Queen of Heaven, whom he hoped so soon to see. Christian Issam, a priest, who saw the martyrs on their way, always declared

[110] Liberate Roll 35 Henry III. [111] *Ibid.* 37 Henry III.
[112] Anc. Fun. Mon. p. 530.
[113] *Churches of the Archdeanery of Northampton,* p. 118.

that they had a smile on their faces, and as they drew near Tyburn, actually laughed. There was a cry raised among the people, 'But they laugh; they do not care for death.'"[114]

SOUTH ELMHAM.

In 1473, John Tasburgh, by his will desires to be buried in the chapel of our Blessed Ladye St. Marye, on the north side of St. Peter's Church, before her image.[115]

WADDINGTON, near CLITHEROE.

In one of the old painted windows here there is a representation of the Eternal Father blessing a nude female infant. Other similar examples are to be found out of England, and although the design is by no means a pleasing one, it is intended nevertheless for the Immaculate Conception of our Blessed Ladye.

WALES.

In Wales there are one hundred and forty-three churches dedicated to our Blessed Ladye, fifty-three to St. David, and ninety-three to St. Michael.[116]

ABERGAVENNY.

There is an image of our Ladye in the Herbert chapel in the Priory church, which is particularly interesting from an iconographical point of view. It is now fixed in the south wall at the back of the sepulchral recess which contains the tomb and effigy of Richard Herbert of Ewyas, Esquire, but it has evidently been taken down from some other place. It is of alabaster, and is described as "a tall female figure in the costume of a lady of the time, (*i.e., temp.* Henry the Seventh), wearing a close-fitting gown, and over it a mantle fastened across the chest with a cord, the ends of which hang down. On her head she wears a veil, which falls down behind. Her arms are broken off, but

---

[114] *Edmund Campion.* A Biography by Richard Simpson. London, 1867, p. 318.

[115] Suckling, vol. I. p. 231.

[116] Rees, *Essay on the Welsh Saints*, &c. Lond. 1836, p. 40.

there is no appearance of having held a child in them. Her feet are supported by an angel, and at her right side kneels a man in armour, and at her left a lady; above these on either side are two angels, one above the other, as if supporting her. There is neither nimbus nor glory apparent about the head, but above it there seems to be an object like a triple crown held by a figure above, whilst on either side of it above her shoulders are two larger figures, having very large glories or nimbi behind their heads, which are, however, broken off. . . . It seems that the group can only represent the crowning of the Virgin, and so Symonds, who saw them uninjured, describes it, and gives a rude sketch of it as it then was; in this it is quite clear that the object over the Virgin's head is a triple crown which has been greatly injured, and that the three figures represent the three Persons of the Holy Trinity, Who are jointly placing the crown on her head. Each figure himself wears a crown, and the right hands are raised in the act of benediction; the centre figure represents the Father, having on His right hand the Son, Who bore a cross, the stem of which may still be seen, and on His left the Holy Spirit.[117]

The three crowns are of rare occurrence. I have two old prints which represent Our Ladye of Loreto with a triple crown. They evidently designate the coronation of our Blessed Ladye as Queen of the Church Triumphant, the Church Militant, and the Church Suffering—Heaven, Earth, and Purgatory; or, as she is described in an Anglo-Saxon poem of the tenth century contained in the *Codex Exoniensis*, "Lady of the Glory-host, of the world, and of hell,"[118] *i.e.*, in the sense of Purgatory.

CARDIGAN.

Burnet says that that which drew most pilgrims and presents in those parts was an image of our Ladye with a taper in her hand, which

---

[117] *Account of the Ancient Monuments in the Priory Church, Abergavenny.* By Octavius Morgan, Esq. M.P. F.R.S. F.S.A. Newport, 1872, p. 65.
[118] Lond. 1842, p. 17.

was believed to have burnt nine years, till one foreswearing himself upon it, it went out, and was then much reverenced and worshipped.[119] Its history is given by Froude as follows: "The story of our Ladye's Taper at Cardigan has a picturesque wildness, of which later ages may admire the picturesque beauty, being relieved by three centuries of incredulity from the necessity of raising harsh alternatives of truth or falsehood. An image of the (Blessed) Virgin had been found, it was said, standing at the mouth of the Tivy river, with an Infant Christ in her lap, and the taper in her hand burning. She was carried to Christchurch in Cardigan, but 'would not tarry there.' She returned again and again to the spot where she was first found; and a chapel was at last built there to receive and shelter her. In this chapel she remained for nine years, the taper burning, yet not consuming, till some rash Welshman swore an oath by her, and broke it; and the taper at once went out, and could never be kindled again. The visitors had no leisure for sentiment. The image was torn from its shrine. The taper was found to be a piece of painted wood, and on experiment was proved submissive to a last conflagration."[120]

Barlow, the then Bishop of St. David's, writing from Carmarthen on the last day of March to Cromwell, says: ". . . Concerning your lordship's lettres addressed for the taper of Haverforde West, yer the receyte of them I had done refourmacion and openly detected the abuse therof, all parties which before tyme repugned penitently reconcyled. But sythen I chaunced upon another taper of moch greater credyte and of more shameful detestacion, called our Ladye's Taper of Cardigan, which I have sente here to your lordship with convenyent instructyons of that develish delusion."[121]

---

[119] *Hist. of the Reformation*, bk. iii. pt. i. p. 243.
[120] *Hist. of England.* Lond. 1858, vol. iii. p. 287.
[121] *Letters relating to the Suppression of the Monasteries*, p. 183.

Inclosed within this letter was the following document :

"Thexaminacion of Thomas Hore, Prior of Cardigan, donatyve of the late monasterye of Chersey,[123] concernynge the pretensed taper of our Lady there.

"*Inprimis*, the said pryour, sayeth that he hath been prior there for the space of five yeres.

"*Item*, that he never saw the taper of our Lady within, but at the neder ende, where it appered wood unto his judgemente.

"*Item*, that he estemed the same to be a holy relyque to his judgemente, accordinge to the fame of the cuntrey, unto the tyme that he saw it opened. And then he confesseth hym selfe to have been deceaved therin.

"*Item*, that the image now situate in the church of Cardigan, which ys used for a greate pilgremage to this presente daye, was founde standinge upon the ryver of Tyve, beinge an arme of the see, and her Sonne apon her lappe, and the same taper bernynge in her hande.

"*Item*, that the said ymage was caryed from thens unto Christes church of Cardigan, and the sayd ymage wold not tarry there, but was founde thre or fowre tymes in the place where now ys buylded the Church of our Lady, and the taper brunnynge in her hande, which contynued still burnynge the space of nyne yeres without wastinge, untill the time that one forsware hymselfe theron, and then it extincted, and never burned after.

"*Item*, that sence the ceasinge of burnynge of the sayd taper, it was enclosed and taken for a greate relyque, and so worshipped and kyssed of pylgremes, and used of men to sweare by in difficill and harde matters, whereof the advauntage admounted to greate sommes of money in tymes passed, payenge yerely of the same xx ti nobles for a pencion unto thabbot of Chersey."

---

[123] There was at Cardigan a small priory of Benedictine monks dependent on the abbey of Chertsey in Surrey, founded before the year 1291.

"Thexaminacion of Syr Morgan Meredeth, vicar of our Lady Church there.

"*Inprimis*, he sayeth that he hath be vicar there xxi ti yeres.

"*Item*, that prior Johan Frodsam tolde hym that because the people toke the wax awaye, he had put the tree beneth, that the people shuld not dyminesh the substance of the taper, otherwise he assenteth and agreeth in all thinges with the priour.

"*Injunctiones dictis priori et vicario facte et injuncte, decimosexto die mensis Mercij, auctoritate regia mediante.*

"*Inprimis*, that the sayd priour and vicare, *alternis vicibus*, shall preach and declare the Gospell or the Epistle reade apon that daye in the mother tongue, exponynge the same syncerly as farre as their lernynge will extende, openynge to the people the abhominable idolatri and disceatfull jugglinge of their predicessours there in worshippinge and causinge to be worshipped a pece of old rotten tymber, puttinge the people in belefe the same to be a holy relique, and a taper which had burned without consumynge or wast, &c.

"*Item*, the sayd priour and vicar shall so preach every Sondaye and holyday betwixte this and *dominica in albis*.

"*Item*, the sayd pryour and vicare shall do awaye or cause to be done awaye all maner of clothes, fygured wax, delusyons of myracles, shrowdes, and other entysementes of the ignorante people to pilgremage and ydolatry.

"*Item*, that they shall take an ynventory of all and every soch clothes, wax, shrowdes, and other entysements, and the same shall converte into the use of pore people, or otherwise to some good use, makynge thereof a recknynge in writinge, declaringe the trewe bestowynge and usinge of the same.

"*Item*, that all and synguler these injunctyons shall be inviolablye observed in payne of contempte."

From this document .it appears that Prior

Frodsham had placed a small bit of wood at the end of the candle to prevent the wax from being taken away by pilgrims, and therefore the false story invented by Barlow, and propagated on his authority by others, is convicted and refuted. There is no credible evidence that the candle was found to consist of a piece of painted wood.

PENRICE.

Our Ladye of Penrice was a celebrated image.

By his will, dated June 11, 1511, Thomas Cadogan, *valettus corone*, leaves to the church of Blessed Marye of Penrice his best tunic.[123]

ST. DAVID'S.

Bishop Nicholls, who died in 1433, directed his body to be buried in the chapel of our Ladye and before her image.[124]

SCOTLAND.

ABERDEEN.

The armorial bearings are a pot of lilies, which by their whiteness are an emblem of chastity, and of the town being under the patronage of the Blessed Virgin Marye.[125]

1. Our Ladye *at* the Bridge of Dee, described as Our Ladye at the Brig.[126]

Mention is made of the building of a bridge over the Dee in 1459. On the 2nd of December there is an entry in the Council Register that "the vicar of Inverugg, Maister John of Levington, be maister of works at building a bridge over the Dee for ten years, and the alderman and council to give 20*l.* a year of their common purse;" but it was not completed.[127]

In the next century, Bishop Gavin Dunbar completed another bridge over the Dee, which had been begun by his predecessor, Bishop

---

[123] Test. Vet. p. 515.

[124] *Hist. and Antiq. of St. David's.* Lond. 1856, p. 122.

[125] *Collections for a history of the Shires of Aberdeen and Banff.* Spalding Club, 1843, p. 152.

[126] *Ibid.* p. 243. *Atlas Marianus*, p. 777, n. dccxxiv.

[127] Spalding Club, 1844, p. 22.

Elphinstone, and which he presented to the town, as well as an endowment to keep it in repair. On the 1st of April, 1527, there is an entry in the Council Register that "the haill tovne in ane voce, thankit gretly thar lord and bischop of Aberden for the gret plesour and proffeit done to thame in the biging of the brig of Dee, and of the gret offeris promittit to tham be his lordschip for the vphald of the samyn," &c. And they promised to deliberate upon the said offers, and to give a finell ansuir to the said lord after Pasche.[128]

On the 3rd of June the reply was given to the bishop; and the cautious terms in which it is couched are very characteristic of the worthy provost and baillies of Aberdeen. After referring to his lordship's "guid mynd . . . tuching of your l(ordschipis) brig of Dee, fundit . . . for the perpetuall commond weill of the cuntra and of ws; of the quhilkis guid deid and mynd God eternall revard you for we ma nocht," they observe that his lordship requires them and their successors to keep the bridge in repair "in the maist souer wise cane be divisit be wismen and men of craft in all thingis necessaris; and at your lordschip will infeft ws and our successouris in your landis of Ardlar, to be haldin of yow and your successouris in few, we are hartlie contentit of the same, makand ws souer thairof be the pape, the prince, your chartour, and all wther handis necesser, for we desyir na inconvenient, bot to be maid souer; quhilk we vnderstand in your l(ordschipis) guid mynd."[129]

All was arranged satisfactorily, and on the 8th of November the townsfolk were informed by a proclamation that the provost and baillies and council had taken upon them the responsibility of "keeping and ouphalding the brig of Dee, salang as thai and thar successouris bruikis, or may bruik, peciabilly the landis of Ardlar, gevin and assignit to thame be his l(ordschip) for the ouphald of the said brig; and gif the sadis landis beis ouptenit fra thame be the law, that this band

128 Spalding Club, 1844, p. 116.   129 *Ibid.* p. 122.

salbe of nayn availl frathinfurth and thai sall nocht be indettit langar to uphold the same."[130]

Hitherto no mention occurs of the Ladye chapel : but on the 9th of January, 1530, Sir William Ray, "vmquhile chaplane to our lady chappell of the brig of Dee, deliuerit in iugment[131] to the bailzies and counsaill ane chaleis of siluer ane ymage of siluer of our lady, baicht ouir gilt . . . togidder with the key of the offerand stok, to be kepit to the vtilitie and proffite of the said chappell."[132] This chapel was at the north end of the bridge.

The explanation of this proceeding would appear to be that the chapel was temporarily closed whilst some works were being carried out ; for on the last day of February, 1530, James Cheyne, "procuratour to the laird of Abirgeldie, requirit Dauid Andersoun and Master Androwe Tulydef, bailzies, sittand in iugment, to mak ane esy gait and passage betuix the brig of Dee and chappell of the samyn."[133] This distinctly proves that the chapel was not on the bridge.

A few days later the laird of Abergeldie and his accomplices were to be prosecuted for hewing of the bulwark of the brig of Dee ; . . . and on the 16th of March James Cheyne informed the provost and baillies that he was included in the indictment as "assistar and pairt takkar with the laird of Abirgelde in the cutting of the bulwark of the brig of Dee, maid far sawite of the cheppale of the samyn."[134]

On the 17th of May, 1530, the provost and town council appoint our "louit familiar seruitour, Alexander Monypeny, mason at a yearly stipend of five marks, for the quhilkis the said Alexander sall daylye intend and aduert to oure brig of Dee, bulwarkis and chappell of the samyn."[135]

---

[130] *Ibid.* p. 119.
[131] This term, which often occurs, appears to be equivalent to "in council assembled."
[132] *Ibid.* p. 129.
[133] *Ibid.* p. 126.
[134] *Ibid.* p. 130.
[135] *Ibid.* p. 141.

T

Hence there appear to have been two chapels here, one on the bridge of Dee of which I have no particulars, and one of our Ladye near the bridge, called Our Ladye of the Brig of Dee.

On the 7th of July, 1559, Bishop Gordon, the last Catholic bishop of Aberdeen, gave over the silver work of the cathedral to the keeping of the canons, and these articles were intrusted to the care of three of the burgesses of Aberdeen, by command of the provost and council, who gave an acknowledgment; amongst them was our Ladye chalice of the Brig chapel, weighing 20 oz.[186]

Nigh to this chapel at the brig of Dee was a well dedicated to our Ladye; of which Guppenberg, quoting from Wichmans, relates as follows :

"*Sacello fons propinquus est, etiam Deiparæ sacer. Catholicorum non interrupta pietas satis probavit Deiparam hic miraculose beneficam olim fuisse, quod, ut facilius fidem inveniret, nostro sæculo expertus est hæreticus, magno fidei nostræ bono, sed malo suæ, quin et suo : is cum templo et Virgini nocere non posset, ad fontem consedit, et alvum exoneravit : pauca sed gravia fatus in Virginis ludibrium ; non tamen inultus. Fames canina hominem torsit ita, ut vix uni prandio satis esset quod alias suffecerat duobus, vel etiam plurimis ; ventre tamen semper obstructo ac sensim intumescente : dum tandem horrenda morte animam evomeret. Fassus est se ultionis divinæ exemplum esse, monuitque adstantes frequenter Matrem Dei ne contemnerent. Quia tamen fidem veram amplexus non est, sine spe salutis e vita migravit.*"[187]

A chapel also stood near the old bridge of Don, which spans the river Don near old Aberdeen. In 1443, the magistrates of Aberdeen voted the admission fees of a burgess of gild to be paid to Sir William Ettles, the chaplain, for defraying the expense of repairing the bridge.[188]

---

[186] Keith's *Scottish Bishops.* Edinburgh, 1824, p. 129.

[187] *Atlas Marianus*, p. 777. Cf. also *Brabantia Mariana.* Antv. 1632, tom. i. l. 2, c. ii. p. 297.

[188] Cf. Kennedy, *Annals of Aberdeen*, 1818, *sub. ann.*

II. St. Nicholas.

This church had thirty-one altars ; the curate was chaplain of our Ladye's altar.[139]

Our Ladye of Pity in the vault.

The choir of this church has underneath it a chapel dedicated to Our Ladye of Pity, where a bursar of the canon law in the King's College was always chaplain. It is now called the Pitty vault, and the plumbers are allowed to melt their lead in it.[140]

III. The Cathedral.

Four images of our Ladye are recorded.

1. Our Ladye of Pity, which stood on the south side of the altar of the Blessed Virgin in the nave of the church—*in navi ecclesia.*[141] Before this image stood a large candelabrum on which to burn candles, presented by one of the canons of Aberdeen, Master John Clatt.[142]

2. The silver image of our Ladye of Pity. It weighed 120 oz., and was presented to the high altar by the treasurer, Master Andrew Lyell, on the feast of the Visitation, 1499. And the Bishop of Aberdeen desired that it should be solemnly carried round the cathedral on all the festivals of the glorious Virgin Marye, and to all who should go before, or follow it, in the procession, he granted an indulgence of forty days.[143]

3. The inventory of 1436 says that the dean of Aberdeen, Master Richard Forbes, amongst other donations, had given two images, one of our Blessed Ladye, and the other of St. Maurice, to the high altar.[144]

4. The fourth escaped destruction until the 5th of August, 1640. Its history is thus given by Spalding :

"On Wednisday, 5th August, the Erll of Seafort, collonell, maister of Forbes," and others,

[139] *Coll. for a Hist. of Aberdeen and Banff,* p. 206.
[140] *Ibid.* p. 209.
[141] *Registrum Episcopatus Aberdonensis.* Edinb. 1845. Spalding Club, vol. ii. p. 169.
[142] *Ibid.* p. 148.
[143] *Ibid.* pp. 169, 170.
[144] *Ibid.* p. 137.

" cam all ryding wp the get, cam to Maucher kirk, ordanit our blissit Lord Jesus Christ his armes to be hewen out of the foirfroont of the pulpit thairof, and to tak doun the portrait of our Blessid Virgyn Marie and her deir Sone Babie Jesus in hir armes, that had stand since the vpputting thairof, in curious wark wnder the sylring at the wastend of the pend, quhairon the gryte stepill standis, on movit quhill now; and gave ordour to collonell, maister of Forbes, to sie this done, quhilk he with all diligence obeyit: and besydis, whair there wes ony crucifixis set in glassin windois, this he causit pull out in honest menis houssis. He causit ane mesoun strik out Christis armes in hewin wark, on ilk end of bischop Gawin Dumbaris tomb; and siclike chissel out the name of Jesus, drawin ciphar wayis IHS, out of the tymber wall on the foirsyd of Maucher Iyll, anent the consistorie dur. The crucifix on the Oldtoun cross dung doun; the crucifix on the Newtoun cross cloissit wp, being loth to brak the stane; the crucifix on the wast end of Sanct Nicholas kirk in New Abirdene dung down, quhilk wes neuer troublit before. Bot this diligent collonell, maister of Forbes, keipit not place long tyme thairèafter, bot wes schortlie casseirit, as ye may sie, folio 288; and efter diverss fortouns at last he, with his lady, went to Holland to serve."[146]

When the English were carrying fire and sword into Scotland in 1544, the bishop of Aberdeen, William Stuart, ordered all the jewels, ornaments, and treasures of the cathedral to be taken into the country for safety by some of his friends and retainers. Scarcely had they crossed the Don, when they were treacherously attacked by James Forbes of Corssinday, attended by some satellites " sons of Satan," who not having God before their eyes, by instinct of the devil, as it is presumed, carried off all the jewels and plate, with the exception of six chalices, which were spared for the use of the cathedral; and the

objects so plundered were only restored to the
bishop on the payment of six hundred marks. It
seems, however, that a portion only was given
back, the remainder was carried off by Forbes.
Several articles were applied to profane uses, and
never restored.[146]

The first notice of the Reformation at Aberdeen occurs on the 4th of January, 1559, when
the baillies explained that certain strangers and
some of the townsmen "hes enterit to the blakfreris and quhyt freiris of this toun, and spulzeit
thair placis, and takin away the gere and gudis of
samen with the tymmar wark and insicht, togiddir
with the leid of the kirkis, and now are enterit
apoun the ruiffis of the kirkis and biggingis, and
takand away the sklayttis, tymmer, and stanis
thairof applyand the samen to thair awin particular
uses."[147] How invariably the so-called "Reformation" begins everywhere with plunder! The
baillies therefore requested to know whether the
town thought it expedient to preserve these for
the "commond weill of the toune and specially
for the furthesettin of Goddis glory, and his trew
word and prechours tharof ; and that the toune
may be the moir habill to concur and assist for the
defence of the libertie of the realme, expelling or
strangeris, and suppressing of idolatrye."[148] The
assembled townsmen, with one exception, authorized the treasurer of the burgh to intromit with
the friars' places and property, for the purposes
above specified. . . . In a few days the treasurer
explained that he could not watch so closely as
was requisite for the preservation of the friars'
property "quhairthrow thair wald inlayk mekill
thair of without diligent attendance war takin
thairto," and four persons were elected to "awayt
on the doun taking and keping of the samen."[149]
These persons were also ordered to "resayf in
thair keeping the chalices, silvar wark, and ornaments of thair paroche kirk, quhill the toune
consultit quhat were expedient to be done thairwitht."

146 *Reg. Epis. Aberd.* p. 195.   147 *Council Register*, p. 315.
148 *Ibid.*   149 *Ibid.* p. 316.

On the 12th of January, the provost, Thomas Menzies of Petfodellis,[150] who had been absent from the previous meetings, when these proceedings were sanctioned, protested against them ; and his protest was adhered to by fifteen of the inhabitants, but nothing followed of it.[151]

"Amongst the siluar wark and ornamentis were :

"*Imprimis*, the eucharyst[152] of four pound and two unce of silver.

"*Item*, ane chalice of our Lady of Pity in the wowlt, nyntene unce.

"*Item*, our Lady chalice of the sowth yill, nyntene unce and ane quart unce.

"*Item*, our Lady chalice of brig cheppell twenty unce.

"Which on the 15th of January, 1559, four burgesses of Aberdeen acknowledged to haf resawit."[153]

On the 11th of March it was resolved to support "the Congregatioun," and a tax of £400 was levied to defray the expense of forty men of war, who were to be sent to its assistance.[154]

On the 16th of June following, the chaplains of St. Nicholas' church presented a supplication to the council, making mention :

"That quhair thai ar suirly aduertist and it is notowrly knawin that certane persones in to the southt partis of Scotland hes interpryssit at thair awin hands, without ony ordor or consent of the authorite to distroy kirks, religious places, and the ornaments and polacie of the same, thairfor desyrand the provost, baillies, and counsell to provyd the esiast way of remeid as thai sell think guid, for defending and mentening of thair said proche kirk, and preserving of the chalices, siluar wark, kaippis, and ornaments of the same, and to

---

[150] The family of Menzies of Pitfodels continued to adhere to the Catholic Church until the family became extinct at the death of the late John Menzies of Pitfodels without issue in 1843.

[151] *Council Register*, p. 318.

[152] *i.e.* the ciborium.

[153] *Council Register*, p. 320.

[154] *Ibid.* p. 322.

put the same in suir firmance and keiping quhill
the said uproir and tumilt war put to tranquilite
be the antient and wyse counsell of the realme.
Quhilk bill being red, and the contents thairof
understand and considderit, the hail counsell
thocht expedient to transport the townis euidents
furth of the kirk, and siclyk the gret occryst,
chalices, siluer wark, and the maist coistly ornaments of the kirk, and to put the same in suir
firmance and keeping, and ane invitor to be maid
thairupoune, and to intromett, preserve, and keip
the tounis euidentis, nemit and chesit Thomas
Menzies, prouest, Dauid Mar, Maister Patrick
Ruyerford, and Walter Cullane, quhilkis accepit
the said cuir and charge upoun thame." [155]

On the 7th of July, 1559, Bishop Gordon
delivered over the silver work of the cathedral to
the keeping of the canons. To Mr. John Leslie,
parson of Oyne, the image of our Ladye, weighing
114 oz. And subsequently to the Earl of Huntly.
two crowns with precious stones, in custody, upon
his bond of custody and restitution, given Nov.
13, 1559. [156]

On the 6th January, 1561, the haill toun beand
lauchfully warnit to this day to heir and se the
siluar work, keppis, and ornaments of thair
parroche kirk ropit, and the same to be sauld and
disponit to thame that vil offer maist for the same;
and the money gotten for the samyn to be
applawdit to the commond weill and necessar
adois of this guid toun . . . the grytest sovme
offerit for the same wes ane hundredth fourtie tua
pound, be Patrick Menzies for the keppis, xx*s.*
for ilk vnce of silver, xvi*s.* for ilk stone of brass
extending in the haill to the sovme of fyw
hundredth xl lib. money of Scotland. . . . The
said day Gilbert Menzies and Gilbert Collysone
dissentit to the said roiping, selling, and dispo-
sicioun for thame selffis and their adherans, lyk
as thai haue discernit and protestit in sic caices
ewer obefoir, as thai alleigit, and tuk act of court
tharwpoun. [157]

[155] *Council Register*, p. 323.
[156] Keith, pp. 125, 126.   [157] *Ibid.* p. 329.

Our Ladye of Good Success.

In a chapel built on the north side of the church of Finisterre in Brussels, there stands over the altar an image of our Blessed Ladye called "of Good Success." This image is stated to have been formerly in the Cathedral at Aberdeen. Much has been written about it; one writer seems to have copied the other, omitting or adding details, and as these writers are principally foreigners, much confusion has arisen. Wichmans is the principal author on the subject; he gives the substance of what was communicated to him by the Prior of the Augustinians at Brussels, in 1628, in whose church the image was originally placed; but his account contains some strange anachronisms, and Guppenberg has followed him.

A Scottish priest, Father Blackall, gives a somewhat different account, and I will begin with him. He says:

" I was very scant of money. I had non but what I gotte for saying the first Messe, every morning, at Notre-Dame, *de bone successe,* a chapelle of great devotion, so called from a statu of our Ladye, which was brought from Aberdein, in the north of Scotland, to Ostend by a merchant of Ostend, to whom it was given in Aberdein. And that same day that the shippe in which it was did arrive at Ostend, the Infanta did winne a battaile against the Hollanders, the people thinking that our Ladye, for the civil reception of her statu, did obteane that victorye to the princesse, who did send for the statu to be brought to Brusselle, wher the princesse, with a solemne procession, did receave it at the porte of the toune, and place it in this chappel, wher it is much honored, and the chapelle dedicated to our Ladye of *bonne successe,* which befor was pouer and desolat, now is riche and wel frequented. The common beleiff of the vulgar people ther is, that this statu was throwen into the sea at Aberdein, and carried upon the waves of the sea miraculously to Ostend. So easie a thing it is for fables to find good harbour,

wher verities would be beaten out with cud-
gelles."[138]

Wichmans, writing in 1632, relates that this
image is said to have been venerated in the
Cathedral of Aberdeen for six hundred years, *si
fidæ traditioni credimus.* Bishop Gavin Dunbar
had a great devotion for it, and daily he would
repair from his palace, through a private door, to
the Cathedral to say his prayers before it. It is
also said that on one occasion whilst he was in
prayer before it, he heard a voice saying, "Well
fare thee, Gavin! thou wilt be the last bishop
here who will obtain eternal salvation!" This
tale seems highly improbable, for Bishop Dunbar,
who died on the 19th of March, 1532, was
succeeded by two other Catholic bishops; and,
moreover, so far as I am able to ascertain, it is
not mentioned by any contemporary writer, nor,
in fact, earlier than a hundred years after his
death. This excellent bishop enjoyed a high and
widely-spread reputation for holiness of life, and
his body was found incorrupt when disinterred by
the Reformers. Wichmans, who, as I have just
said, wrote in 1632, places the death of Bishop
Dunbar as having occurred two centuries
previously !

In the month of April, 1863, spending a few
days in Brussels, I was most anxious, on archæological grounds, to see the image of our Ladye of
Good Success, for which an antiquity of nine
hundred years was claimed, and being introduced
to the curé, M. Van Genechten, I requested to be
permitted to inspect the statue divested of the
stiff robes with which it was disfigured. My
request was refused on the plea that it would be
irreverent to *déshabiller Notre Dame.*

Subsequently the curé seems to have changed
his ideas in regard to the custom of dressing our
Ladye, for her image now appears divested of its
silk and velvet robes, and it has been repainted.
He has done a good service, for no doubt can

---

[138] *A Breiffe Narration of the Services done to three noble Ladyes.* By Gilbert
Blakhall, Preist of the Scots Mission in France, in the Low Countries, and in
Scotland, 1631—1649. Spalding Club, 1844, p. 43.

exist as to the date of the image, unless possibly it may have been recarved after it was brought to Brussels, which is by no means likely. It is a standing image with our Lord on the left arm of His Mother, and the earliest date which can be assigned to it is late in the fifteenth century; and in this opinion I am confirmed by a learned English architect, who never fails to say an *Ave* in this chapel when he chances to be in Brussels. Therefore all that can be said of this image, with any degree of certainty, is that it was one of several which were in the Cathedral of Aberdeen, and that it escaped destruction.

For a while it was preserved by some Catholics, after it had been removed from the Cathedral. It then fell into the hands of the Reformers, who although often resolved to destroy it, were providentially moved never to carry their impious scheme into effect. At last, as if impelled by some irresistible power, they handed it over to a man, who hid it in his house, and from whom it came into the possession of William Laing, who is described as the Procurator of the King of Spain. He determined to send it as a present to the Infanta, Isabella, and therefore placed it on board of a Spanish ship which was then lying in the harbour of Aberdeen. The captain made sail for Dunkirk, and escaped the Dutch pirates who were infesting the channel by being convoyed by two English men-of-war. He delivered the image into the hands of Father de los Rios, an Augustinian in the suite of the Archduchess, who was then at Dunkirk. She destined it for the chapel of the palace at Brussels, but Father de los Rios begged that it might be given to the newly-built Augustinian church, to which, on the 3rd of May, 1626, it was solemnly conveyed. On this occasion the image of our Ladye was arrayed in a magnificent robe, and adorned with the jewels of the Archduchess, who followed the procession on foot, and for whose "Good Success" High Mass was celebrated in the church. This is the origin of the title.[159]

[159] *Brabantia Mariana*, t. i. lib. ii. pp. 299—303; *Atlas Marianus*, p. 776, n. dccxxvii.

At the French Revolution the image of our Ladye of Good Success was saved by Mr. Morris, an English Catholic, who kept it till 1805, when it was restored to the Augustinians; and finally in 1814 it was removed to the church of Finisterre, and placed in a tabernacle by the side of St. Joseph's altar. In 1852, M. Van Ghenechten built the side chapel where it now stands over the altar.

It seems highly probable that the history which is told of this image belongs, in reality, to one of the other statues in the Cathedral of Aberdeen, which did not escape destruction. If it had been of the age assigned to it, it would have been a seated image, and of the type of the seal of the monastery of St. Marye's, Kelso, which is the finest and earliest British seal representing our Ladye and her Divine Son that has come under my notice.[160]

AYR.

The monastery of the Observantines was founded here in 1474; and Wadding mentions an image of our Blessed Ladye, which was greatly venerated there, and brilliant for its miracles.[161]

DESKFORD.

There was a chapel of our Ladye of Pity at Skieth, whose image in wood was preserved there.[162]

EDINBURGH.

Our Ladye of Holyrood.

In the Church of the Sacred Heart of Jesus, Lauriston Street, there is an image of our Ladye holding her Divine Son in her arms, which formerly was in Holyrood. For many years it was in the possession of the family of the Earls of Aberdeen; and at a sale which took place in London after the death of George, fourth Earl of Aberdeen, in 1860, it was purchased by a dealer in old furniture, of Peterborough, by name Waterhead, who placed it over the door of his shop. One day in 1865, as the writer was passing through Peterborough, the image attracted his

---

[160] Laing, *Catalogue of Scottish Seals.* Edinburgh, 1850, p. 189, n. 1057.

[161] *Annales Romæ* 1735, t. xiv. p. 117, n. xxxviii.

[162] *Collections, &c. ut sup.* p. 664.

attention, and on learning its history he purchased it. It was in a delapidated condition, and after causing it to be repaired, the writer sent it to the Church of the Sacred Heart, with the condition, that if the Fathers of the Society of Jesus should at any time leave Edinburgh, this image of our Ladye should revert to the Sodality chapel at Stonyhurst College.

HADDINGTON.

Hector Boece, writing under the approximate date of 1355, says:

"Nocht lang efter, King Edward came to Hadingtoun, to the gret dammage of all pepill lyand thairabout. Ane part of his nevy spulyeit the Kirk of our Lady, callit the Quhit Kirk, and returnit with the spulye thairof to thair schippis. Bot thair sacralege was not lang unpunist; for suddunly rais ane north wind, and raschit all thair schippis sa violently on the see bankis, and sandis, that few of thaim eschapit, saif only sa mony as swame to land. King Edward, in contemptioun of God, becaus his navy was trubillit in this maner, persewit all abbayis and religius placis quhare he come, with gret cruelte. Treuth is, ane Inglisman spulyeit all the ornamentis that was on the image of our Lady, in the Quhite Kirk; and in continent the crucifix fel doun on his heid, and dang out his harnis." [163]

Our Ladye of Haddington is mentioned in the Atlas Marianus. [164]

LEITH.

The seal of the borough represents our Blessed Ladye with her Divine Son, seated under a tabernacle, in a boat. This representation has a great resemblance to the ancient type of our Ladye of Boulogne-sur-Mer, but our Ladye of Boulogne bore our Lord in her left arm; in the seal of Leith He is in His Mother's right arm; this variation, however, may be due to the engraver of the seal.

[163] *Hist. and Chron. of Scotland*, reprint of orig. ed. c. 1536. Edinb. 1821, vol. ii. Buke xv. c. xiv. p. 446.
[164] P. 798, n. dccxlix. and described as Sancta Maria Alba.

It would be interesting if the circumstances under which the town of Leith adopted our Ladye of Boulogne for its seal, could be brought to light. In the middle ages devotion to our Ladye of Boulogne was widely spread, and confraternities and chapels in her honour were often established. Thus early in the fourteenth century, the inhabitants of Paris erected a church of our Ladye of Boulogne at Menus, a village near Saint-Cloud, which became a favourite pilgrimage for those who were unable to make the longer one to Boulogne-sur-Mer. Menus soon became called Boulogne-sur-Seine, and the forest in its neighbourhood the *Bois* de Boulogne. Boulogne-lez-Chambord, Boulogne-la-Grasse, and Boulogne-sur-Gesse are believed to owe their names to similar foundations, but in these latter-named places the memory of our Ladye of Boulogne has perished.[168] Was any such foundation ever made at Leith?

MUSSELBURGH. Our Ladye of Loreto.

" I find by approved authors," says Father Tursellino, "that manie yeares agone, two churches were erected to our B. Ladie of *Loreto* in the Kingdome of *Scotland ;* the one in the towne *Perth*, otherwise called *S. Johns*, the other by the high way that goeth to *Missilburrow*, not far from *Edinburrow*, the chief citie of *Scotland*. In both places, the B. Virgin of *Loreto* was most religiouslie reuerenced ; and that in the suburbs of *Missilburrow* was most famous for the resort and concourse of pilgrims, and the miracles of our B. Ladie, as long as the Catholic religion remayned in *Scotland*. But after *Caluins* pestiferous doctrine began to rage and raigne in that kingdome (heretofore most religious) those furies destroied that sacred house of our B. Ladie, but so notwithstäding, that the ruines therof might remaine, both as tokens of their madnes, and also as manifest signes of the ancient religion of the Scottish people. And this (as we vnderstand) was the beginning of the Chappell of *Missilburrow*. Manie yeares agone, in the attire and habit of a

[168] Haigneré, *Hist. de N. Dame de Boulogne*, pp. 77, 110, 111, 401.

Pilgrime, a Scottish Eremite came to *Loreto* to salute the B. Virgin, who at his departure carried with him into his countrey, a small part of the sacred roofe, and begging monie of godlie men, not far from the towne of *Missilburrow,* erected a little church some thing like to the Sacred House of *Loreto;* which was verie famous, as well for reuerence of the sacred reliques, which were placed there, as also for the deuotion of the people to the B. Virgin herself (whose name was illustrious among them) vntill, as we said before, the mad furie of Heretick's threw it downe."[166]

This chapel stood at the east end of the town, with the hermit's cell adjoining; during the ravages of the Earl of Hertford in May, 1544, he destroyed this famous chapel, with a part of the town: it was soon repaired, but it was finally abolished at the Reformation, and in 1590 the materials of the chapel, which had once so many votaries, were converted to building the Tolbooth of Musselburgh.[167]

NEWHAVEN.

On the festival of the Annunciation, 1507, James IV. offered 14s. in our Ladye chapell of the New Havin.[168]

The seal of Newhaven represents a demi-figure of our Ladye and her Divine Son surrounded by a flamboyant aureola. It appears appended to a charter given by Robert Leslie, principal baillie of our Ladye's Port of Grace, *alias* Newhaven, A.D. 1520.[169]

PAISLEY.

George Schaw, abbot of the Cluniac monastery, enlarged and beautified it, and enclosed the gardens and orchards with a wall of stone, a mile in circuit, in 1484. In one of the corners of this wall on the outer side was a niche in

---

[166] *Hist. of our Blessed Ladye of Loreto,* bk. 3, c. 5. p. 236. Douay, 1608.
[167] Carlisle, *Topographical Dict. of Scotland.* Lond. 1812, *sub voce.*
[168] *Letters of Ric. III. and Hen. VII.* vol. ii. p. lxviii. Rolls Edit.
[169] Laing, *Cal. of Scottish Seals,* p. 216, n. 1195.

which stood an image of our Blessed Ladye, with these lines under her feet :

𝕳𝖆𝖈 𝖓𝖊 𝖛𝖆𝖛𝖊 𝖛𝖎𝖆 𝖓𝖎𝖘𝖎 𝖛𝖎𝖗𝖊𝖗𝖎𝖘 𝕬𝖛𝖊 𝕸𝖆𝖗𝖎𝖆.
𝕾𝖎𝖙 𝖘𝖊𝖒𝖕𝖊𝖗 𝖘𝖎𝖓𝖊 𝖛𝖆𝖊 𝖖𝖚𝖎 𝖙𝖎𝖇𝖎 𝖛𝖎𝖈𝖎𝖙 𝕬𝖛𝖊.[170]

PERTH.

The church of St. John the Baptist had forty altars, all endowed; amongst which were five dedicated to our Blessed Ladye, and one to St. Joseph :

1. Our Ladye's altar.

2. Altar of Our Ladye's Presentation, richly endowed.

3. Altar of Our Ladye of Consolation.

4. Altar of the Salutation of our Ladye and St. Gabriel.

5. Altar of the Visitation, or Our Ladye of Grace.[171]

II. Chapel of Our Ladye of Loreto.

This chapel, vulgarly designated *Allareit*, stood on the north side of the head of South Street. The circumstances connected with its foundation are unknown. Mr. Lawson adds in a note that unlike similar chapels of our Ladye of Loreto in other places, the one at Perth seems to have had no miraculous influence.[172]

III. Our Ladye's chapel at the Bridge.

This chapel was situated at the foot of the High Street or North Street, near the old bridge. No traveller, however wearied, omitted to put up his *Ave.*[173] It is described as an old building as anciently as A.D. 1210, when it was considerably injured by a fearful inundation of the Tay. It was afterwards rebuilt farther from the river, and a portion of it is known as the Old Prison, having been so appropriated after the Reformation. With the exception of part of St. John's

---

[170] Keith, *ubi supra.* p. 413.

[171] *Book of Perth*, pp. 61—64. By John Parker Lawson, M.A. Edinb. 1847. In the list these altars are numbered respectively, 8, 17, 22, 29, 30; and that of St. Joseph, 36.

[172] *Ibid.* p. 79.

[173] *Ibid.* p. 99.

Church, this is the only remaining ecclesiastical memorial of the ancient hierarchy in Perth.[174]

STOWE, formerly WEDALE.

Across the Tweed, six miles to the west of that heretofore noble and eminent monastery of Mailros, stood Gwaedol, or Wedale, in English Woe-dale, in Latin *Vallis Doloris.* It is now called Stowe.[175] Here was the Church of St. Marye, where were once preserved, in great veneration, the fragments of that image which King Arthur on his return from Jerusalem[176] bore upon his shoulders, and through the power of our Lord Jesus Christ and the Holy Marye, put the Saxons to flight, and pursued them the whole day with great slaughter. Nennius says that Arthur *portavit imaginem crucis Christi et Sanctæ Mariæ semper Virginis super humeros suos ;*[177] Matthew of Westminster, that the image of our Ladye was painted on his shield; and Henry of Huntingdon the same.[178] Now, as in Welsh *ysguyd* is a shoulder, and *ysguydd* a shield, a Welsh original must have been differently translated by them.[179]

This is the image of our Ladye which Guppenberg gives as two different ones in the Atlas Marianus, viz., *Miraculosa Regia de Monte Badonico,* and *de Clypeo.*[180]

A little above the church is a very fine perennial spring known by the name of the Ladye's well; and a huge stone, recently removed in forming the new road, but now broken to pieces, used to be pointed out as impressed with the (Blessed) Virgin Marye's foot.[181]

It is unnecessary for me to notice here the

[174] *Book of Perth,* p. 76.

[175] *Sculptured Stones of Scotland,* append. to pref. f. lxvii. By J. Stuart, Spalding Club. 1866.

[176] Pilgrims from Britain are mentioned by St. Jerome. There is therefore no historical improbability in the legends of Arthur's pilgrimage to the Holy Sepulchre. Merlin, pt. iii. p. lxxvi.

[177] *Monumenta Historica Britanniæ,* p. 73. 1848.

[178] See *ante,* pp. 102, 103.

[179] *Arthurian Localities,* Merlin, pt. iii. p. lxxvi. Early English Text Society.

[180] See *ante,* pp. 86, 102.

[181] Skene, *Four Ancient Books,* vol. ii. p. 412, quoted in *Arthurian Localities,* p. lxxvi. *ut supra.*

arguments about King Arthur, and the theories in regard of the Arthurian localities.

TARBAT.

Near Tarbat, in the Synod of Ross, there is a plentiful spring of water which continues to bear the name of *Tobair Mhuir*, or Marye's well.[182]

IRELAND.

DUBLIN.

I. Our Ladye at the Dame's Gate.

Before the first arrival of the Anglo-Normans in Ireland in the twelfth century, the eastern gate of the city of Dublin, styled *La Porte de Sainte Marie del Dam*, stood at the western extremity of the line of street at present known as Dame Street, contiguous to the Church of our Ladye. The Northmen, who landed in 1171, endeavouring to regain the city from which they had been driven by the Anglo-Normans, directed their main efforts against this gate, which was built with towers, and armed with a portcullis. Until the Reformation, a statue of our Ladye stood in a niche above it.[183]

II. Our Ladye of St. Marye's Abbey.

This image is mentioned by Ware in connection with Lambert Simnel, A.D. 1487. "They say that the crown wherewith he was crowned was borrowed from the statue of the Blessed Virgin Marye kept in a church called by her name, situate near the gate called the Dame's Gate."[184]

This is the legend of the origin of the abbey.

"About the time that the O'Tooles swayed, an honest goodman, called Gilmohollmot, lived between the plane called Clonlife, where it now standeth, and Clontarf, by the river. It pleased God to trye the patience of the man, and his wife Rosina, by visiting them with blindness, which affliction they bore with greate submission and patience, never repining at the said affliction, but

[182] *Statistical Account of Scotland*, vol. vi. p. 431.
[183] Gilbert, *Hist. of the City of Dublin*, vol. ii. p. 256. 1861.
[184] *Annals, ad. ann.* 1487.

U

giving thanks to God, knowing that they deserved greater punishment for their iniquities. In this state they lived a greate while, disposing very charitably of what God sent them, distributing it unto the poore. One day as he sat on a greate logge of wood before his doore, after distributing to the needy what he had, of a sudden he smelled a very sweet savour, with which he was so much surprised, that he groped about him, feeling the block of wood that he sat on, trying whether he could find that which smelled so sweet; at last he wondered very much to feel a branch that sprung out of the block of wood, yet feeling again, his hand lighted upon an apple though it was in winter time; the man took the apple and eat of it; immediately he received his sight, and calling his wife Rosina, he feeling another apple on the same branch, he gave it to her, by which she received her sight also; and another being left he bethought with himself of Malaghlin, the King of Meath, who afterwards was called Malachias the Great, being Monarch of all Ireland, who was at that time blind in the monastery of *Timonshall Tharagh*, and did believe that this apple might be designed for him, wherefore he and his wife began their journey towards him, and being come where he was he gave him the apple, and upon eating the same, the sayd King received his sight and blessed God. Hearing a whole relation of this miracle from Gilmohollmot, he desired him to hand him that place called Clonlife, and in exchange of it, he would give him twice as much ground, more beneficial, elsewhere, to which offer Gilmohollmot agreed, and consented thereunto. King Malachias dedicated the ground to the honour of our Blessed Ladye for a monastery of fryars, who were bound to praise God and honour her name.

"It is remarkable that this ancient statue, representing our Ladye with her Divine Son in her arms, is carved out of the trunk of a tree, and that our Lord holds an apple in His hand."

In the year 1541 this abbey was seized, and

its property sequestrated. . . . "The statue of the Blessed Virgin, already mentioned, was condemned by the modern iconoclasts, and as it was supposed, consigned to the flames. One half of it was actually burnt, but it was that part which, when placed in a niche, is not much missed.[185] The other part was carried by a devout Catholic to a neighbouring inn-yard, where with its face buried in the ground, and the hollow trunk appearing upwards, it was for years concealed, until it was restored to its original use in the old chapel of St. Micham, Marye's Lane, grown up from the ruins of the abbey to which it had belonged."[186]

This image is now venerated in the Carmelite Church in Dublin, for which it was secured by the Very Rev. Dr. Spratt. Within the last few years, says a writer whom I have quoted, the ancient silver crown with which it was adorned, was taken from our Ladye's head, sold for its intrinsic value as old plate, and melted down. He also adds: "The crown itself we have often seen exposed for sale in the window of the jeweller to whom it was sold. It was a double arched crown, such as appears on the coins of Henry the Seventh, and his only."[187] But the double arched crown was not confined to the coins of Henry the Seventh. Even the groat of Perkin Warbeck bears it.

III. *S. Maria Alba*: I presume Our Ladye *ad Nives*.

The Book of Obits records the death, on the 10th of the Kalends of August, of John White, formerly Mayor of Dublin, and "a brother of our congregation," who bequeathed a girdle of the price of 20s. to the image of Our Ladye "the White."[188] John White occurs as Mayor of

---

[185] This partial burning is noticed by another writer (*Dublin Penny Magazine*, pp. 308, 309, vol. I. no. 39, 1833). The flames in fact, under providential guidance, had left the statue for its original purpose very nearly as serviceable as ever.

[186] Battersby, *The Jesuits in Dublin*, pp. 18—20. Dublin, 1854.

[187] *Dublin Penny Magazine, ubi. sup.*

[188] P. 33.

DROGHEDA.

Dublin in 1424, 1431, and 1432, and is the only one of that name on the roll.[189]

In 1345, Richard Fitzwilliam, Mayor of Drogheda had licence to assign four acres of land adjoining the same, for increasing and maintaining lights before the image of our Blessed Ladye.[190]

KILCORBAIN.

In the Dominican priory here, there was an image of our Ladye called "of the Rosary," celebrated for miracles.[191]

LIMERICK.

A commission before the King's Commissioners was held here on the 13th of February, 33 Henry the Eighth, when it was deposed that :

"Wee doe find that in the 30th yeare of King Henry the Eighth, Edmond, Archbishop of Cassel, and Walter Cowley, the King's solicitor, taking uppon them to be the King's Commissioners, did take of the image of the holly roods, shoes of silver, wheing twentie-seaven unces troy weight. Wherein weare divers stones of the value whereof wee cannot tell. And alsoe did take the image of our Ladye of the said church showes of silver weighing six unces with divers stones, and fifteene buthons of silver valued at three shillings, 9 d. str." [192]

MUCKROSS FORMERLY IRRELAGH.

A misprint in Wadding has led many astray. The image is described as *Imago B.M.V. Irialacensis*, instead of Irialacensis, and Dr. Northcote gives it as Our Ladye of Tralee.[193] It is the only Irish sanctuary of our Ladye mentioned in the Atlas Marianus by Gupperberg, who quotes from Wadding.[194]

The monastery of Oirbhealach (anglicised Irrelagh by Ware) at Carraig-an-chinil, at the eastern end of Lochlein in the diocese of Ardfert in Munster was founded for Franciscan Friars by MacCarthy More, Prince of Desmond (Donnell, the son of Teige) ; and the chiefs of the country

---

[189] Walsh, *Hist. of Dublin*, append. ix. p. lxiv. Dublin, 1818.
[190] D'Alton, *Hist. of Drogheda*, vol. i. pp. 42, 43.
[191] De Burgh, *Hibernia Dominicana*, Col. Agripp. p. 344. 1762.
[192] Lanihan, p. 90.
[193] See Sanctuaries of the Madonna, *sub. nom.*
[194] No. dlxxxix. p. 748, *ed. cit.*

selected burial places for themselves in this monastery. Amongst these were O'Sullivan More, and the two O'Donohues.[195] The abbey was situated within the demesne of Muckross, from whence it has taken its modern appellation.

Wadding also notices how fond people were of being buried in this abbey out of love of our Ladye.[196]

The image of our Ladye was greatly venerated. When the English were devastating the abbey, and had torn down and trampled on the figure of our Lord on the Rood, some of the friars carried off the image of our Ladye, and placed it at the foot of a dead tree which had lost all its bark. Lo! immediately the dead tree revived, and budded forth leaves and shoots which formed such a thick shelter that the rain never penetrated for a year and concealed the statue. It is also related that on one occasion a woman perjured herself before it, and with signal discomfiture.[197]

NAVAN.

On the 19th of July, 1539, the image of our Blessed Ladye, so long held in veneration here, was torn from her altar and indignantly destroyed.

In the abbey church of Navan there was an image of the Blessed Virgin Marye held in great repute, to which people from all parts of Ireland, princes and peasants, rich and poor, were in the habit of making their pilgrimages. In the Parliament of Dublin in the year 1454, it was ordered "That letters patent of the King be made, in the form laid down, for taking into protection all people, whether rebels or others, who shall go in pilgrimage to the Convent of the Blessed Virgin of Navan."[198]

In a Parliament held at Drogheda, A.D. 1460 —38 Henry the Sixth—under Richard, Duke of York, an Act was passed summoning Thomas Bathe, Knight, "pretending to be Lord of Louth,

---

[195] *Four Masters, ad ann.* 1340. A note says that it should be Donnell, son of Cormac, instead of the son of Teige ; most probably a mere error of transcription. See note, vol. iii. p. 566.

[196] *Ad ann.* 1340, n. xxvi.

[197] Wadding, vol. vii. p. 241.

[198] Hardiman, *Statute of Kilkenny*, p. 51.

wherein he hath no title or inheritance," to appear before the prince on the Tuesday before the next St. Patrick's Day, under penalty of forfeiture of all his property, and of being excluded from the King's protection, to answer the charges of which he was accused. In the preamble of this Act it is stated that Bathe, for the purpose of obtaining the King's favour, suborned one of his servants to falsely accuse Dr. John Stackbolle, doctor of each degree, and one of the dignitaries of the abbey of Navan, of high treason, for which he was imprisoned in Dublin Castle, sent to England, and was there vindicated and set free; that Bathe next robbed Dr. Stackbolle, and refused to make restitution; that Dr. Stackbolle "being in despair of any remedy against the extortion, violence, and oppression" of the said Bathe, wrote to the Pope and obtained an order for Dr. Ouldhall, Bishop of Meath, to threaten him with excommunication, unless within a limited time he made reparation; that restitution being refused, and Bathe continuing in his contumacy, the Bishop of Meath, in accordance with the Pope's order, went in solemn procession to the market-place of Navan (where the old cross of Navan stood) on a market day, and there excommunicated Thomas Bathe; that after this, Bathe sent some ruffians to the abbey of Navan, who forcibly carried off Dr. Stackbolle to Wilkinston, and there cut off his tongue and put out his eyes; that Dr. Stackbolle was carried back to the abbey, and cast before the image of the Blessed Virgin, and "*by her grace, mediation, and miraculous power, he was restored to his sight and speech.*" [199]

TRIM or
ATH TRUIM.

This was the most celebrated sanctuary of our Ladye in Ireland, and stood in the abbey of the Canons Regular of St. Augustine, for whom this house, originally founded by St. Patrick, was rebuilt sometime in the thirteenth century by the DeLacy family. [200]

[199] Hardiman, *ut sup.* p. 25. Cogan, Dioc. of Meath, ancient and modern, Dublin, 1867, vol. i. p. 225.
[200] Cogan, vol. i. p. 299.

There is a confirmation, dated at Avignon, the 3rd of the Ides of July, in the fifth year of his Pontificate, by Gregory, of a grant of privileges to the abbot of Trim by Celestine III. 1191—1198.[201]

To this sanctuary, says Cogan, pilgrimages were made from all parts of the country; the Irish and Anglo-Irish vied in reverencing and enriching it with their votive offerings.

In 1472, an Act was passed in Parliament held at Naas, which confirmed Letters Patent granting to this abbey two water mills, with the entire manor of Mathreene, in the parish of Trim, and all the timber and underwood lying thereon, for building the said mills; also the custom and services of the villeins in the manor of Trim, for the purpose of erecting and supplying a perpetual wax light before the image of the Blessed Virgin in the church of the said house, and for supporting four other wax lights before the said image, on the Mass of St. Marye; also for confirming other Letters Patent, granting the sum of 10*l.* to find a perpetual Mass in the said house, &c.[202]

There were many miracles wrought here.

In 1397, Hugh MacMahon recovered his eyesight by fasting in honour of the Holy Cross at Raphoe, and of the Blessed Virgin Marye at Ath Trim.[203]

1412. The image of the Blessed Virgin Marye wrought many miracles.[204]

In 1444 a great miraculous cure was wrought by the image of the Blessed Virgin Marye at Trim; namely, it restored sight to a blind man, speech to a dumb man, and the use of his feet to a cripple, and stretched out the hand of a person which had been fastened to his side.[205]

In 1464 great miracles were wrought by the image of our Blessed Ladye of Trim.[206]

[201] Theiner, *Vet. Mon. Hibernorum et Scotorum histor. illustr.* p. 354, Docum. 712. Romæ, 1864.
[202] Cogan. vol. i. p. 300.
[203] *Annals of the Four Masters,* ad ann.
[204] *Ibid.* ad ann.
[205] *Ibid.* ad ann.
[206] Cogan, vol. i. p. 300.

The image of our Ladye of Trim shared the fate of our Ladye of Walsingham. In 1537, say the *Four Masters*, "they (the 'Saxons') afterwards burned the images, shrines, and relics of the saints of Ireland and England; they likewise burned the celebrated image of the Blessed Virgin at Trim, which used to perform wonders and miracles, which used to heal the blind, the deaf, and the crippled, and persons affected with all kinds of diseases." [207]

"And . . . there was not," continues another chronicler, "in Erinn a holy cross or a figure of Marye, or an illustrious image over which their power reached, that was not burned." [208] Ware adds that the gifts of the pilgrims were taken away from thence. [209]

George Browne, Archbishop of Dublin, and the great promoter of the Reformation, wrote thus from Tallagh, June 20, 1538, to Cromwell:

"These shalbe to advertise you that I endevor my selff, and also cause others of my clergie to preache the Gospell of Christe, and to sett forthe the King's causes. There goethe a comen brewte amonges the yrish men that I entende to ploke downe our Ladye of Tryme with other places of pilgramages as the holy Crosse and souche like, which in deade I never attempted, although my conscience wolde right well serve me to appresse souche ydolles." [210]

Up to the month of October in that year, the image of Our Ladye of Trim had not been burnt, for Thomas Allen, writing from Dublin on the 20th of that month to Cromwell, says:

"They thre (Archbishop Browne, Mr. Treasurer, and the Master of the Rolls) wold not come into the chapel where the Idoll of Trym stode, to th' extent they wold not occasion the people; notwithstanding my Lord Deputie veray devoutely kneeling before Hir, herd thre or fower Masses." [211]

Dextram Scriptoris benedicat Pater Amelis.

[207] Vol. v. p. 1447.   [208] *Book of Obits*, pp. 16, 17.   [209] *Ann.* p. 99.
[210] Irish State Papers, Henry VIII. vol. vii. n. 7.   Public Record Office.
[211] *Ibid.* n. 50.   A note in the *Four Masters, ad ann.* 1397, gives the date of this letter as the 10th of August.   I have examined the original, and the printed catalogue gives the correct date, October 20.

ALPHABETICAL LIST OF PRINCIPAL PLACES
MENTIONED IN BOOK THE SECOND.

ADDENDA ET CORRIGENDA.

BOOK THE FIRST.

P. 4, ref. 4, *for* " pp. 143 seq." *read* " pp. 143 et seq."

P. 61, line 16, *for* " yzt " *read* " zyt."

P. 62, ref. 104, *for* " amd " *read* " and."

P. 67, note 6, *for* " *quam* . . . *ædificatum, et* . . . *dedicatum*," *read* " *ædificatam dedicatam.*"

P. 69, line 5, *for* " ; " *read* "."

P. 73. The Gabriell Bell. At Northampton the large town bell is called " Old Gabriel " (*Times*, July 18, 1878).

P. 76, line 31, *for* " implore the help," *read* " implore her help."

P. 86. Relics. Relics cannot be bought or sold ; and when it is said that Archbishop Ægelnoth bought the arm of St. Augustine at Pavia (see S, pp. 21, 22), it is probably to be understood as having reference to the valuable case in which it was enshrined.

P. 91, line 29, *for* " La Puy " *read* " Le Puy."

P. 93, line 21, *for* " Caverthan " *read* " Caversham."

P. 113, line 4. *Vous veuilliés (estre presente)* &c., leave out parenthesis.

P. 124, line 3, from the " Boke of Curtesay," " With felowe," &c., *should be* " with your felowe," &c.

P. 134. This English priest, John Wilson, was secretary to Father Parsons, S.J., at Rome. In 1604 he was placed at the head of a printing establishment at St. Omer's, by the English Fathers S.J. He brought out the English Martyrologe, which bears his initials, J. W., in 1608. (*Recherches sur les Calendriers Ecclésiastiques, Dissertation posthume du R. P. Victor de Buck, S.J. Bollandiste.* Bruxelles, 1877, p. 24.)

P. 144, line 11, *for* " hyghe moost " *read* " moost hyghe."

P. 153, line 20. *A Maria Mater pia*, so given by More.

P. 156, note 21, *for* " *dignitorum* " *read* " *digitorum*."

P. 158, line 21, *for* " beads " *read* " bead."

P. 166, line 1, *for* " *plenas* " *read* " *plenus*."

P. 174, ref. 224, *for* " Camden Holten," *read* " Camden Hotten."

P. 202, ref. 122, *dele* vol. ii.

P. 231, line 7, *for* " tale," *read* " seal."

P. 256, line 7, *for* " Lambeth," *read* " Lambert."

P. 261, references (in margin) 183, 184 inverted. Should be thus : " 183. 3. pp. 128, 235. 184. Opus. Edit. cit.," &c.

BOOK THE SECOND.

P. 5, line 14, *for* "coming from " *read* "coming from Guysnes."

P. 5, ref. 33, *for* "p. 154" *read* "1549."

P. 10, ref. 51, *for* "Test. Vestut." *read* "Test. Vetust."

P. 17, ref. 79, *for* "p. 2334" *read* "col. 2334."

P. 20, ref. 91, *for* "xi." *read* "ii."

P. 21, ref. 94, *for* "xi." *read* "ii."

P. 25, line 21, *read* "foundations."

P. 26, ref. 113, *add* "vol. i."

P. 27, line 21, *read* "Henry Courtenay."

P. 42, line 15, *add ref.* "Wilkins, *Concilia*, t. ii. p. 423."

P. 46, lines 8, 10, *read* "mancuses or *mancusæ*."

P. 54, *for* "Howe on Hoo" *read* "Howe or Hoo."

P. 54, ref. 201, *for* "South Meols" *read* "Ancient Meols, &c., London, 1869."

P. 57, ref. 209. "This miracle was represented in a mural painting, now defaced, in Thaxted Church, Essex; but a fragment of the inscription yet remains" (Neale, *Views of Collegiate and Parochial Churches*. London, 1824, vol. i. sub. nom.).

P. 82.   For more about Sabedin and Argon, see Rohrbacher, *Hist. Universelle de l'Eglise Catholique*.   Paris, 1858, t. xix., pp. 116—122.

P. 83, ref. 293, *for* "c. vii." *read* "vol. vii."

P. 91, ref. 20, *for* "1942" *read* "1642."

P. 98, line 28, *for* "April 12" *read* "April 28."

P. 101, *for* "MIDDLEBOROUGH" *read* "MIDDLESBOROUGH."

P. 102, "MOLSA," *add* "or MEAUX."

P. 102, line 17, *velorum de sipirs*, *i.e.*, cloth from Cyprus. Eleanor Bohun, Duchess of Gloucester, in her will, dated August 9, 1399, mentions *un vestement, le champ de baukyn blue diapres des autres colours ove cerfs dor de Cipre* (Nichols, *Royal Wills*, p. 179). Also, *un lit de drap d'or de Cipre (Ibid.* p. 183).   Ducange mentions, *Aurifrigia opere Ciprensi nobilissimo.*

P. 103, line 34, *for* "name of the hall" *read* "name of the well of the hill."

P. 104, line 10, *for* "stopped there" *read* "stepped thereinto."

P. 104, ref. 73, *add* "Newcourt, *Repertorium*."

P. 107, line 5, *for* "Rood of the wall" *read* "Rood in the wall."

P. 111, line 17, *for* "aisle" *read* "south aisle.'

P. 111, ref. 104, *add* "vol. ii."

P. 112, ref. 112, 115, *add* "vol. ii."

P. 113, ref. 117, *add* "vol. ii."

P. 115, ref. 128, *for* "v. xi." *read* "vol. ii."

P. 115. ref. 133, *for* " Ibid." *read* " Blomefield."

P. 116, line 30, *for* " Regina " *read* " Regina."

P. 116, ref. 135, *add* " p. 853."

P. 121, line 10, *for* " Portigny " *read* " Pontigny."

P. 124, ref. 167, *for* " D'Blossiers " *read* " D. Blossiers."

P. 126, line 38, *for* " 1826 " *read* " 1286."

P. 129, *for* " ROTHERAM " *read* " ROTHERHAM."

P. 131, ref. 198, *add* " vol. i."

P. 142, line 22, *for* " Lassell's " *read* " Lassells."

P. 145, ref. 270, *for* " p. 294 " *read* " p. 296."

P. 161, ref. 16.   "Another bit of this pavement was preserved at St. Alban's. In the list of the Relics is enumerated: *De loco ubi Christus annunciatus est Virgini gloriosæ* (*Mon. Angl.* t. ii. p. 234).

P. 166, line 4, and wherever it occurs, *for* "Rev. James Lee Warner" *read* " Lee-Warner."

P. 168, ref. 32, *for* " Frober " *read* " Froben."

Pp. 170, 171.   The bear's skin at Walsingham.   There is nothing improbable in the story of the bear's skin.   It only proves that Erasmus was no archæologist.   Bishop Leofric bequeathed, together with other ornaments, to his Cathedral at Exeter ij. tæppedu and iij. *berascin* or bear skins (*Cod. Dipl. Aevi Sax.* v. iv. p. 275, n. dccccxl.).   And Ingulph records that, A.D. 1050, Brichtmer, eleventh Abbot of Croyland, gave twelve *ursinas pelles quarum coram diversis altaribus quædam usque ad nostra tempora perdurarunt* (*Hist. Ingulphi, inter rer. Angl. scriptores.* Francofurti, 1601, p. 894).   Here, then, is early evidence that bear-skins were used for altar carpets, and the bear skin which Erasmus saw at Walsingham had no doubt been used for that purpose.   Moreover, the fact of its being hung up at the wells suggests the natural conclusion that it had been conveyed thither for the purpose of being washed.

P. 176, ref. 64, *to* " Life of Henry VII." *add* " pp. 20, 23."

P. 177, ref. 72, *for* " Feller " *read* " De Feller."

P. 178, line 10, *for* " mutual great ancestor " *read* " common great ancestor."

P. 185, note 79.   " Muff " in the same sense which it now has is used in Thomas Skelton's translation of *Don Quixote*, pt. ii. ch. x. (*Notes and Queries*, 5 Ser. ix. p. 396).

P. 188, line 1, *for* " out of the pe(ril, he wde vol)ner eet " *read* " out of the pe(ril he wold ne)ver eet."

P. 188, ref. 83.   The history of this distemper is given in Dr. Friend's *History of Phisick*, v. ii. p. 335.

P. 189, line 2, *for* " Guistiniani " *read* " Giustiniani."

P. 194, ref. 110, *add* " p. 37."

P. 202, ref. 127, *for* " pp. 438, 468 " *read* " 338, 368."

P. 207. "The wood of the True Cross of the genus fir." Venerable Bede, speaking of the three portions at Constantinople, says that the Relics are exposed for veneration on Maundy Thursday, Good Friday, and Holy Saturday, when the chest, in which they are contained, is set on a golden altar. "As long as it remains open on the altar, a wonderful odour spreads through the whole church. For an odoriferous liquor like oil flows from the knots of the holy wood, the least drop of which cures every complaint with which a man may be afflicted." *Cujus etiam si aliquis infirmus modicam particulam contingat, omnem ægritudinem sanat* (*De Locis Sanctis*, Opp. v. iv. p. 440. Edit. Giles).

P. 218, line 13, *for* "Ypswirche" *read* "Ypswitche."

P. 219, line 37, *for* "DOMIVUS" *read* "DOMINUS."

P. 234, ref. 214, *for* "Histoire et Chroniqre" *read* "Histoire et Chroniqve."

P. 260, line 30, *for* "Hebdomary" *read* "Hebdomadary."

P. 283, line 37. John Hobersal, Notary and Stationer, by his will dated January 30, 1492, bequeathes "My soulle unto Almighty God, my Creator, Savyour and Redeemer, to his most Blessed Moder Saint Marye Virgin, Quene of Heven, Ladye of al the world, and Empresse of Helle" (Howe. Edit. Strype, bk. iii. p. 144).

P. 308, line 20, *for* "did take the image" *read* "did take off the image."